A History of Economic Theory

JÜRG NIEHANS

A History of Economic Theory

Classic Contributions, 1720–1980

The Johns Hopkins University Press
Baltimore and London

Published with assistance from the Karl and Edith Pribram Endowment

Softshell Books edition, 1994
03 02 01 00 99 98 97 96 95 94   5 4 3 2 1

The Johns Hopkins University Press, 2715 North Charles Street,
Baltimore, Maryland 21218-4319
The Johns Hopkins Press Ltd., London

Library of Congress Cataloging-in-Publication Data
Niehans, Jürg.
   A history of economic theory: classic contributions, 1720–1980 /
   Jürg Niehans.
        p.   cm.
   Bibliography: p.
   Includes index.
   ISBN 0-8018-3834-7 (alk. paper)   ISBN 0-8018-4976-4 (pbk.)
   1. Economics—History.   I. Title.
HB75.N54   1990   330´.09—dc20   89-45489

A catalog record for this book is available from the British Library.

Contents

Contents

II
The Marginalist Era (ca. 1830–1930)

III
The Era of Economic Models (since about 1930)

Contents

Preface and Acknowledgments

If I could not go to heaven but with a party, I would not go there at all.
—Thomas Jefferson to Francis Hopkinson

ECONOMISTS have sometimes turned to the history of their science out of despair. Unable to discover new truths, perhaps even unable to discriminate between good and bad science, they found solace in contemplating past efforts. This book is not written from this agnostic perspective. It is rather based on the conviction that understanding of the historical dynamics of research can make present research more productive. If the past is forgotten, research may lose its direction. The book, therefore, is not about the frustrating struggles between obsolete half-truths and the irrelevant opinions of long-defunct men and women but about the progressive evolution of modern economic theory. I hope it will show living science in a clearer light.

The forgotten librettist of a forgotten opera left us the saying that we always return to our first loves. My first love in economics was the history of economic doctrines. For kindling this love I am indebted to my teacher at the University of Zurich, Manüel Saitzew. A brilliant skeptic, he would have been more at home in the salons of the eighteenth century than he was in modern theory, and he had lovingly accumulated a superb collection of first editions. In his seminar I gave my first student paper on Karl Marx, and under his guidance I wrote my dissertation on mercantilism and its (fortunately shortlived) revival in the twentieth century. One of the first courses I taught was on the history of economics, and in my inaugural lecture at the University of Zurich I developed the idea that economic laws tend to be born as empirical propositions and to die as logical tautologies. One of my earliest literary projects was a handbook on the history of economics, but it never progressed beyond my dreams. I first needed to learn contemporary theory, which, as it turned out, consumed all of my energy for thirty years. When I returned to my first love, my interest had shifted from the biographical and bibliographical facts to the substantive contributions to economic theory.

A debt of a different nature I owe to my students at the University of Bern. Their radical wing, supported by some members of the law faculty, complained that the economics program was lacking what they called a historical dimension. The thrust of this criticism was clearly ideological and political, but I took it as a challenge to provide a history of economics that would help to make better economists out of students of any political orientation. I am happy to acknowledge that students with radical leanings were among the most active and constructive participants in my classes.

The transformation of notes into a book largely took place during extended stays at the University of California, Berkeley. Both its School of Business Administration and its Department of Economics made some of their scarce office space available to me, and the latter also gave me the opportunity to teach a graduate course in the history of economics. This interest and support is gratefully acknowledged.

For *The New Palgrave* I wrote biographical essays on Thünen, Gossen, Launhardt, Auspitz, and Lieben.[1] I thank the publisher for permission to use this material in the present book.

I owe a special debt to Carola Duff. She was not only my secretary, who did all the word processing with diligence and expertise, but also my editorial assistant and draftsperson. Her mastery of the English language helped me to improve the style of the book, and she was untiring in checking references and resourceful in locating material.

In the last phase of my work, I also had the help of three outstanding economics students at the University of Bern, Stefan Felder, Daniel Heller, and Anton Hofmann. They checked my draft chapter by chapter, hunting for errors and acting as devil's advocate on as many points as possible. Their critical zeal led to innumerable corrections and improvements. An anonymous reader, clearly of great erudition and editorial expertise, made suggestions that not only saved me from error but also resulted in important additions. At the copy-editing stage, Irma Garlick was expert in preparing the manuscript for the typesetter and in the process corrected many deficiencies in my references and style. For all this help I express my thanks.

I know that, despite all efforts, the present work is imperfect. The history of economic theory is an immense field, and for each aspect there are specialists, past and present, who know (or have known) more than I shall ever know. If this book has merit, it arises not from completeness but from selectiveness. It raises the question of what contributions to the history of economics deserve to be regarded as classic, and the answer is given not in an abstract discourse but by naming and describing these contributions. Most readers will inevitably disagree with some of my choices, decisions, and judgments, but I hope they will nevertheless put the book away with a deeper understanding of the science we call economics.

1. *The New Palgrave: A Dictionary of Economics*, ed. John Eatwell, Murray Milgate, and Peter Newman (London: Macmillan Press; New York: Stockton Press, 1987).

A History of Economic Theory

1

Prologue: Populating the Pantheon

Subject Matter

ECONOMICS, as the term is commonly understood, includes a vast area of intellectual endeavor. Its object is human life and history, particularly economic life and history, in all their uniqueness and complexity. Its content includes all the manifold ideas, views, opinions, and doctrines that were expressed about this subject. It also includes those mental constructs that are called economic theories. Still another part of economics is the art of choosing those theories in such a way that they are helpful in the understanding of economic life and their practical application to real-life problems.

From these diverse and equally important elements, the present book selects only one, namely economic theory. The assorted views and doctrines of defunct economists on all sorts of things, social, economic, philosophical, or political, will be considered only inasmuch as they shed light on the dynamics of science and human motivation. As a matter of fact, there is no particular reason why a modern economist should be more interested in them than in the opinions of anybody else.

Perspective

Economic theory may be regarded as a perpetual inventory of analytical tools. New tools are continuously added to the inventory by innovative research. Old tools simultaneously drop out. In most cases they drop out simply because they have not been used for a long time and thus fall into oblivion. In other cases they turned out to be faultily constructed.

Whatever is in the inventory at a given time may be called the mainstream economics of that period. Opinions about the content of mainstream economics will inevitably differ. There is no dogmatic authority watching over the purity of the faith and unity of doctrine. The basic test of mainstream economics is whether a particular piece of analysis is being found useful in practical application or promising for further research. At any given time, mainstream economics includes theories that were added to it in different earlier periods. Some of them may be of recent origin, others may have been in the toolbox for centuries.

This book does not undertake to investigate what was regarded as mainstream economics in different periods of the past. There will be no synthetic interpretations of "classical," "Marshallian," or "Keynesian" economics and the like. Nor will there be readers' guides summarizing "what the readers got" from Adam Smith, Karl Marx, Alfred Marshall,

1

or Paul Samuelson. These aspects are extensively treated in the literature, and the present author does not feel he could do better. To find out what the reader gets from a book, there is no substitute, after all, for reading it.

The scope of this book is more modest. Modern mainstream economics, in all its vagueness and imperfection, is taken as a standard of reference. The economic literature of the last three centuries is then scanned for pieces of innovative analysis that have become part of modern mainstream economics. These are the classic contributions mentioned in the subtitle. Whatever in the past literature, however brilliant or famous it may be, has not become part of modern mainstream economics will at most be mentioned in passing and more likely remain in the dark. Sometimes failed efforts shed light on the dynamics of science.

To change the metaphor, present-day mainstream economics may be likened to a building. In old cities one often finds buildings whose parts date from various ages. While some steel and glass may just have been added, one annex is perhaps Bauhaus, one facade is Victorian, the bulk is Renaissance and some foundations may be medieval. Such buildings are unlikely to have the symmetry, purity, and perfection of some Gothic cathedrals or Greek temples. They are more likely to be rambling structures with an odd plan. This seems to be about the character of present-day mainstream economics. This book undertakes to identify the builders who made major contributions to the edifice as it stands today and also the building blocks they contributed. Building plans that were never executed or, if executed, were later followed by demolition, will not appear in this account.

History, thus conceived, will have to be rewritten by each generation. Just to write additional chapters will not be enough, because every generation has its own mainstream economics whose ancestry it wishes to trace. Past writings that look irrelevant today may become important contributions tomorrow; other writings that look important today may look insignificant tomorrow.

It is inherent in this approach that it does not involve much explicit criticism of past efforts. The important part of criticism is implied, consisting in the decision whether or not a piece of analysis meets the just discussed mainstream test. If the test is met, further criticism would require a standard of science that is ahead of its time. If the test is not met, that piece of analysis does not deserve to appear onstage in the first place. The essential criticism is thus performed not by the historiographer but by the history of economics itself. In a biological selection process the fitness of a species is judged not by the observing biologist but by its survival.

The history of science, in this view, appears necessarily as a tale of cumulative progress. The emphasis is on the word *necessarily*. No meta-

2

physical belief in human progress and no optimism about the blessings of science is involved. Whatever is regarded as mainstream science today has inevitably accumulated over time. If valuable knowledge fell into oblivion, this very fact would prevent the historian from recording it. Some omniscient being may perhaps perceive that today's mainstream economics is inferior to that of, say, the turn of the century and that the standards of modern mainstream economics are faulty. The author of this book is modest enough not to claim such superior insight. Modern mainstream economics, in all its imperfection, is the best he knows, and he does not even know all of it. He can thus do no better than to take it as his standard.

Populating the Pantheon

The history of science can be organized either around persons or around subjects. Both principles are equally legitimate. The present book is organized primarily around persons. The emphasis is on a concise characterization of their principal contributions, but this is preceded by a biographical sketch and a brief characterization of their main works. This approach results from the conviction that history is interesting not so much because of the interaction of anonymous forces and abstract concepts as for what it teaches about human beings. They are the only force in history that can really be understood. It should be added, however, that hardly any of the biographical material in this book is based on original research. The original work all went into the interpretation of economic writings, based on the primary sources, and the critical separation of the wheat from the chaff.

To change the metaphor again, what this book tries to achieve may be compared to a pantheon of economic theory. The basic decision is how to populate the pantheon. The table of contents reveals the result. In the nondogmatic and polytheistic culture of science, opinions on such a choice will often differ. Also, the pantheon will usually contain different monuments or niches for major and lesser deities. Again this is a matter of judgment about which the book will try to give a reasoned opinion.

One way to avoid such decisions is to rely on fame. The famous thus get ornate monuments while the less famous get hardly a small niche. This criterion is closely related to that of popular success. Those whose works were widely successful are venerated as heroes or founders; those who failed to attract attention are the precursors. By still another criterion, authors are judged by the amount of commotion they managed to stir up in the world. The movers and shakers are regarded as greater than the quiet researchers. Historiographers who rely on these criteria, in effect just running with the crowd, evade their obligation. They are clearly called upon to reevaluate the judgments of past historiographers and critics and to make up their own minds. The present book results from an effort to do just this. Many of the resulting judgments confirm the conventional wisdom. Others may look unconventional. It is hoped that in all cases they will look balanced and well reasoned.

Periodization

The book, as its title indicates, covers the period from 1720 to 1980. No precision is claimed for the two limits. The contributions of the early classical period were a natural outgrowth of the scholastic and mercantilist traditions, and these antecedents are briefly surveyed in chapter 3. At the end of the period, the developments of the 1980s were a natural outgrowth of the contributions described in this book. They will eventually become history, too, but at the present time it seems difficult, and perhaps impossible, to survey them in the same perspective as Richard Cantillon and Adam Smith.

A play is usually divided into acts, separated by curtains. History is no stage play. It evolves in a continuous flow without curtains or intermissions. This is also true for the history of economics. It consists of a seemingly chaotic flow of contributions blending imperceptibly into one another.

Historians have usually regarded it as necessary to transform the chaotic flow into a stage play, divided into acts and scenes. In fact, they are virtually forced to do this if they want to make history intelligible to their readers or listeners. Some labels, however conventional, are useful for communication. Thus the present book will be organized around such labels, too. In particular, the history of economics since about 1680 is divided into a classical era, a marginalist era, and a model-building era. (Whereas *classic* will be taken to mean exemplary, *classical* thus refers to an historical period.)

In what sense such labels are arbitrary and in what sense they have meaning can be explained in a mathematical metaphor. History may be compared to the sequence of digits in a number. Some may argue that this sequence is essentially random. Einstein erred: God plays dice. Though this may perhaps be true, it is not a fruitful hypothesis because it precludes any search for deterministic elements, however fragmentary.

Others may argue that history, metaphorically speaking, is a rational number whose digits exhibit periodic fluctuations. Thus the Hegelians believe that history evolves in cycles of breakthrough, stagnation, and crisis. This was the notion of Karl Marx, which Joseph Schumpeter transferred to the history of economics. Though this may be a fruitful hypothesis, it seems to reflect more the aesthetic needs for an intellectually pleasing architecture than the true dynamics of science.

Still others might liken history to an irrational number whose digits follow each other in a sequence that is, in principle, perfectly determinate but nevertheless lacks periodicity and cannot statistically be distinguished from a random sequence. It may be argued that this is the most promising way to look at history. God does not play dice, but he makes it difficult for us to detect that he does not. For the history of economics, this view implies that it does not break into natural periods.

It is nevertheless true that each impulse of scientific progress, even though it may appear as random, is small relative to the large stock of inherited economic theory. This stock, therefore, often retains certain common characteristics for extended periods. To the untrained eye, looking at the accumulated stock of knowledge, it may appear as if economics were progressing in some sort of cycles. These, though irregular, can then be used to describe the broad stages of the history of science. In this sense the history of economics is here presented as divided into different eras. Though this facilitates the exposition, it should be borne in mind that the dividing lines between successive eras are mostly in the eye of the beholder.

In particular, the successive eras cannot be identified with specific schools, doctrines, or models. They are, rather, meant to be characterized by a common spirit or leitmotiv that pervades the economics of a given era across all controversies. A page of Paul Samuelson looks very different from a page of Léon Walras, which in turn looks very different from a page of Adam Smith. This is the sort of difference that is intended to be epitomized by the distinction between successive eras. The specific nature of these differences is described in the introductions to the different parts of the book.

Organization

The chapters of this book are of two types. About two thirds of them are name chapters, treating of an individual author. The others are subject chapters, treating, loosely speaking, of a field of economics. With the sections within each chapter it is the other way around. The subtitles of the name chapters refer to the subject matter of specific contributions. The subtitles of the subject chapters, on the other hand, refer to the individual contributors. Basically, the whole book, as was explained above, is primarily organized from a name point of view. It is about the heroes and not about their deeds (but only deeds make heroes). It will thus be found that within each subject chapter the sections are again like little name chapters. The only substantive difference is that the authors treated in name chapters have made classic contributions in a number of diverse fields, perhaps in a wide area, whereas subject chapters include a number of authors with more narrowly circumscribed contributions. This does not necessarily express a judgment about the relative importance of authors or contributions. With this organization of chapters, even readers interested primarily in a certain subject matter should find it reasonably easy to find their way. All they have to do is add to the respective subject chapters the relevant sections from name chapters.

5

I
The Classical Era
(ca. 1680-1830)

2
The Leitmotiv of Classical Economics

THE ADJECTIVE *classical*, if it does not refer to antiquity, generally means first-class, exemplary, worthy of emulation. In this general sense it was applied to economics as early as 1804 by Pietro Custodi in the title of his collection of Italian writings on political economy, many of them from the preclassical era. In the same laudatory sense, Adam Smith's *Wealth of Nations* was called classical within a year of its publication in a review in the *Göttinger Gelehrte Anzeigen* (*Göttingen Scholarly Review*) (Roscher 1874, 599). In these contexts *classical* does not denote an era or school of economics in contrast to other eras or schools but simply describes outstanding achievements in contrast to less successful efforts. This, clearly, is not what the adjective is supposed to mean in the present context.

For three-quarters of a century after the publication of the *Wealth of Nations*, the term *classical economics* had no other meaning. Followers of Adam Smith were called Smithians, and his economics was sometimes called the industrial system. The concept of a classical economics was created by Karl Marx. In *The Misery of Philosophy* of 1847 he distinguished between classical economics and romantic economics as the two branches of a fatalistic school of economics. Both are fatalistic in the sense of being impervious to the evil consequences of the bourgeois economic system. Classical economics, in particular, represents the rising bourgeoisie, still supported by the proletariat, in the offense against the feudal order. Romantic economics, on the other hand, represents the defense of the bourgeoisie, after its victory over feudalism, against the rising proletariat.

The fact that Marx used those shopworn literary labels suggests that he had something else in the back of his mind. Almost a century earlier, the great archeologist Winckelmann had defined the spirit of classical art as "noble simplicity, calm grandeur." Whereas the classicist would abstract from the ephemeral in search of the general, the romantic would lose himself in the peculiarities of the individual case. For Marx classical economics, despite the shortcomings he criticized, was indeed classic, exemplary economics. It was the mainstream that he undertook to extend, whereas the romantics were mere epigones.

Later, in *Theories of Surplus-Value* (Marx 1905–10, 3: 570f), the antithesis to classical economics became vulgar economics, and so it remained in *Capital* (1957–62, vol. 1, ch. 1, sec. 4, fn. 32). From this salient, classical economics conquered the historiography of economics. The change from *romantic* to *vulgar* was not so great for Marx as it looks today. *Romantic* had, in fact, the connotation of "vulgar" from the beginning. The adjective was used to describe the literature in one of the Romance languages, which were vulgar in contrast to classical Latin. To be vulgar in the sense of "close to the people" was part of the original program of the Romantic movement (Schlegel 1967, liif., 189). In Marx's time this movement had long been dead, and Marx meant both terms in a derogatory sense.

The question is what classical economics is supposed to embrace. Marx was quite specific on this point (1939–41, 843; 1957–62, vol. 1, ch. 1, sec. 4, fn.32, and pref. to 2d ed.). Classical economics, for him, began with William Petty and Pierre de Boisguilbert, it reached a climax with Adam Smith, and it ended with David Ricardo and Simonde de Sismondi. What followed was vulgarization. Later historiography tended to shift the beginning forward to Adam Smith and the end to John Stuart Mill and John Elliott Cairnes. This periodization has been so widely accepted that the original Marxian terminology is all but forgotten.[1] Joseph Schumpeter went one step farther by letting classical economics begin around 1790, thus dropping Adam Smith. John Maynard Keynes, on the other hand, extended it far beyond 1870 by including even Arthur Pigou. The historiography of political economy thus exhibits a remarkable tendency to use the adjective *classical* for the mainstream economics of yesteryear, whatever it may be. This is clearly not helpful. Labels are inherently arbitrary, but they should be kept on the same bottle.

In fact, Marx's original definition makes perfectly good sense, though not for the reason Marx had in mind. The economics from about 1680 to about 1830 did indeed have common features that distinguished it from other eras. Richard Cantillon, François Quesnay, and David Hume were much more than minor predecessors of Adam Smith. They made path-breaking contributions in their own right, and some of the fundamental accomplishments of classical economics were clearly established before the *Wealth of Nations*. At the other end, Johann Heinrich von Thünen, Antoine Augustin Cournot, and Hermann Heinrich Gossen, writing between 1820 and 1860, were not merely the predecessors of the heroes of the 1870s. They were marginalist heroes in their own right, overshadowing, as creative theorists, classical epigones like John Stuart Mill. The new horizons were not opened in 1776 and 1871, but rather in the 1720s and the 1830s. The acceptance of Marx's periodization implies, by the way, that classical economics was less British than according to the conventional terminology. In this context it should be remembered that it was William Stanley Jevons (1905, 155f.) who emphasized the fundamental French contribution.

Though the demarcation of classical economics in this book essentially follows Karl Marx, it goes beyond him in one important respect, namely

---

1. Ironically, Blaug (1987, 1: 434) actually calls Marx's definition tendentious, apparently forgetting that Marx, as the creator of the concept, was free to give it any meaning he wanted.

by also including Marx himself. Marx would probably have objected. He admired classical economics much as he admired capitalism. He believed, however, that classical economics, like capitalism, had worked itself into an impasse. Just as socialism, in his view, was opening a new era of history, so he regarded his own theory as opening a new era of economics. As a matter of fact, if Marxian economics is reduced to its analytical skeleton, it is seen to be very much in the Ricardian tradition. On the other hand, the fundamental characteristics of the marginalist era are missing. The problems Marx tried to solve were still those of Ricardo; the problems of Cournot, Thünen, and Gossen did not interest him. *Capital* was a classical anachronism in the marginalist era.

Which characteristics did classical economics, thus defined, have in common? It has been found very difficult, and probably impossible, to identify a coherent body of economic doctrines or propositions that were shared by all classical economists but not by others.[2] Marx found the common element, to nobody's surprise, in the labor theory of value. Classical economists used it, in his view, to analyze the conflicts of interest between the social classes. They were prevented, however, from discovering the whole truth by the misconception that the labor theory is valid only in a mythical golden age whereas capitalist reality requires a cost theory of value. This interpretation was indeed tendentious because none of the important classical economists actually held a labor theory of market value (nor did Marx, for that matter) except under very artificial assumptions.

A common characteristic of classical political economy, from the beginning to Marx, was the emphasis on economic growth and capital accumulation. Unfortunately, this does not distinguish classical economists from other eras, both earlier and later. Mercantilists were no less growth-minded. Walras, often regarded as the incarnation of stationary equilibrium, actually developed his theory for the temporary equilibrium of a growing economy with positive saving and investment; ironically, his solution fails precisely for the stationary case. Alfred Marshall and Joseph Schumpeter could hardly have been more evolutionary, and modern economics has made growth and accumulation one of its main preoccupations.

Still another feature that has often been held to distinguish classical economics is its "deductive," "abstract," or even "mathematical" method (an example is Oncken 1902, 4f.). It is true that the leading economists of the classical era differed from their nontheoretical (or even antitheoretical) contemporaries inasmuch as they produced quantitative theory, which is inevitably akin to mathematics and logic. However, the same was true in other eras. Even Aristotle tried his hand, unsuccessfully, at constructing

2. Recent interpretations of classical economics (from Smith to Mill and Marx) were brilliantly reviewed by Blaug (1987).

an exchange model, and in the marginalist era the method became progressively more mathematical. In fact, in most classical writings mathematics was well disguised, and Adam Smith hardly strikes a modern reader as a mathematical economist.

Though the economics of the classical era was not united by a distinctive doctrine or method, it nevertheless had a common leitmotiv. This was the conception of a circular flow of income, of the economy as an interdependent system. It is true that the seeds of this conception can be found in preclassical literature and that it bore most of its fruits in postclassical times. In the classical era, however, this conception reached full bloom. Using hindsight, one is tempted to interpret it as the classical "research program."

In the microeconomic analysis of individual prices and markets, classical economists hardly went beyond the scholastics and mercantilists. They went far beyond them, however, in their macroeconomic analysis of the economy as a whole. Around 1680, Petty began to look at the economy with the eyes of a national income statistician, and Boisguilbert expressed crude, but sound, notions about competitive resource allocation. This set the stage for the first input-output accounts, constructed half a century later by Cantillon and Quesnay. Under the impact of monetary disorders, mercantilist notions about the stimulating effects of money developed into an explicit monetary macrodynamics with the quantity theory of money as its static counterpart. For Hume gold was distributed by a self-regulating feedback control mechanism. Smith extended this idea to the economic system as a whole, governed by the "invisible hand" of competition. Malthus applied feedback control to population and Ricardo to capital accumulation. Ricardo's fundamental concern became the eventual self-braking of the growth process by the shifts in distribution caused by diminishing returns. In the classical era economics became a (crude) form of macroeconomic systems analysis.

With the rise of marginalism, the macroeconomic insights of the classical era did not disappear. They were revealed not as false but merely as incomplete. What was missing was an explicit analysis of the microeconomic calculus by which households and firms optimize their decisions. This analysis was the collective achievement of the marginalist era. To the extent that the microeconomic problems were solved, the results were gradually incorporated into the circular flow system inherited from the classical era. There emerged the general equilibrium synthesis of the Walrasian era.

It would be wrong, however, to visualize the classical economists as pure scientists. Economics was not yet professionalized, and economic writings were mostly policy-oriented. Political economy was indeed taught at many universities, often combined with law, administration, and political science. The leading classical economists, however, were not professors. Law was a gambler and projector of schemes. Cantillon was a hard-nosed banker. Hume earned a hard living as an essayist and librarian. Quesnay was a court physician. Turgot excelled as an administrator. When Malthus became famous, he was a parson. Ricardo went from investment banking to Parliament. Marx was a journalist and conspirator. The great exception was Adam Smith, who was a well-trained scholar, an experienced lecturer and a brilliant expositor. His unsurpassed effectiveness may well be due to the combination of an inquisitive mind with academic professionalism.

As a consequence of its nonprofessional character, economic theory was more directly influenced by political, social, and economic developments than in later periods. In the course of the nineteenth century, the progress of economic theory managed to emancipate itself largely, though with notable exceptions, from historical events, seemingly following its own immanent dynamics. In the classical era this emancipation had not yet taken place. The historical background, therefore, was more important than later.

The classical era was an age of revolutions, spanning roughly the period between the Glorious Revolution in Britain and the July Revolution in France, with the French Revolution in between. It was also an age of great wars, including the wars of Louis XIV, the Seven Years' War, the American Revolution and the Revolutionary and Napoleonic wars. The fiscal needs of governments were correspondingly insatiable and led to monetary disorders and oppressive taxation. Absolutism was in decline, monarchy was becoming constitutional. The replacement of small professional armies by large people's armies gave power to the masses, thus preparing the ground for democracy. But general suffrage was still far away. Society continued to be stratified into classes, dominated by landed aristocracies. The bourgeoisie was in the ascendancy, in both wealth and power. At the same time workers began to be aware of being a separate class; one offspring of the French Revolution was socialism.

Economically, this was the time of the Industrial Revolution. Rapid declines in mortality, particularly infant mortality, made population growth accelerate, though the full effect was felt only later. Manufacturers and merchants were increasingly dissatisfied with mercantilist regulation, exemplified in Britain by the Navigation Act and the Corn Laws. "Laissez faire" and "Better government is less government" became slogans of the liberals.

Intellectually, this was the period of the Enlightenment. Newton had demonstrated that the universe was a system of interdependent heavenly bodies, whose laws of motion could be mathematically formulated. Natural law, a legacy of scholastic philosophy, postulated that human society is also an interdependent system, governed by laws whose nature could be discovered by the rational mind.

The writings of the classical economists were mostly responses to these challenges. Boisguilbert reacted (often intemperately) to oppressive taxes.

13

John Law proposed miraculous remedies to the fiscal crises. The quantity theory was a by-product of inconvertible paper money. Hume and Smith attacked mercantilism. Malthus exposed the Poor Laws as a bottomless pit. Ricardo was drawn into economics by inflationary finance. The three-factor theory of distribution was meant to apply to the classes of society. For many contemporaries, political economy became identified with free trade and laissez faire (except perhaps with respect to money), but there was also a utilitarian streak that led to government intervention and perhaps even to socialism.

Given these circumstances, it is hardly surprising that the purely theoretical achievements of classical economics, by modern standards, were not overwhelming. Economists were relatively few, and most of them did not devote a large part of their lifetime to research. As a consequence the progress of economic science, though much faster than before, was still rather slow. This explains why in this book the classical era spans about 150 years whereas the marginalist era includes about a century and the model-building era only half as much. The remarkable thing is that classical economists accomplished as much as they did. From Boisguilbert to Ricardo is a long way. At the end of the classical era, economics had reached, at least in Britain, a first plateau of public acceptance and prestige. Jane Marcet and Harriet Martineau popularized it for schoolchildren and the working classes. On the Continent the economic literacy of the British people was regarded as a powerful factor behind their industrial supremacy. Political economy had arrived.

3

Antecedents: Supply and Demand

THOUGH PRECLASSICAL economic thought was concerned with numerous aspects of economic life, its main focus was on supply and demand in particular markets. What distinguishes it from classical economics is the lack of an analytical framework for what was later called the circular flow of income, the national accounts for the economy as a whole.

Political economy, as it became established in the eighteenth century, was historically nourished from three principal sources, namely from everyday experience, from scholastic moral philosophy, and from mercantilist literature. While the main narrative of this book begins around 1720, the present chapter, sketchy as it is, is intended to provide historical background and perspective. Nothing is born from nothing.

Commonplace Economics

In a sense, economic thought is as old as mankind. Since the expulsion from paradise man has been confronted with the same basic problems of scarcity, resource allocation, and exchange. As a result he must have been familiar from time immemorial with many of the fundamental insights that are expounded in a modern course of economic principles.Though economic science learned to express these insights in a progressively more precise form and took them as a basis for extensive analytical developments, the insights themselves must have been commonplace at the time of Hammurabi.

The nature of this commonplace economics may be illustrated by the following seven propositions:

1. Successive units of a commodity are less and less urgently needed. (This was the source of Midas's predicament. In the Book of Kings, Solomon is said to have made silver so abundant that it was not considered as anything. When horses became scarce enough, Richard III was willing to give a kingdom for one.)
2. Abundance makes prices fall and scarcity makes them rise (an insight profitably applied by Joseph in Egypt).
3. A decline in price stimulates demand but reduces supply (a proposition regarded as self-evident by Xenophon).
4. Higher fertility and better location result in higher land rent.
5. An increase in the money supply raises prices.
6. Voluntary exchange is advantageous to both parties.
7. Trade occurs because different regions have different natural endowments (*non omnis fert omnia tellus,* "the earth does not bear everything everywhere," said Vergil).

In the case of such commonplace notions, it makes no sense to search for their historical origins. As the French moralist La Bruyère expressed it at the beginning of his *Caractères,* everything has been said, and one is too late, because human beings have been thinking for more than seven thousand years. Commonplace economics, though valuable, gives no claim to fame, because it requires nothing beyond everyday experience. For the history of economic science, the concept of commonplace economics is useful mainly as a benchmark from which analytical achievement can be measured. It marks the zero point of scientific progress.

This zero point was not clearly exceeded before the thirteenth century. It is true that the literature of classical antiquity often touched upon economic subjects, but it is also true that it failed to progress beyond trite commonplaces.[1] This is most clearly exemplified by Aristotle.

The inequality of human talents, Aristotle explains, results in a division

---

1. A collection of excerpts can be found in Laistner 1923.

of labor, which in turn requires association and thus holds society together (*Politica* 1.2. 1252–53; *Ethics* 5.5. 155–56). Exchange arises because some have too little of a good, others too much, which applies both to individuals and to states (*Politica* 1.9. 1257). Exchange leads to the use of money, both as a medium of exchange to save transactions costs and as a unit of account (*Politica* 1.9. 1257; *Ethics* 5.5. 155). Common property tends to result in waste and quarrels (*Politica* 2.5. 1263)—Marshall's external economies. When Thales the Milesian foresaw an abundant olive crop, he is reported to have cornered the market for oil presses, thus creating what Aristotle, apparently for the first time, called a monopoly (1.11). Too much of a useful thing will do harm or at least no good, which suggests diminishing marginal utility (7.1. 1323). In deciding which of two things is more desirable, one should judge which would do more harm if it were lost (*Topica* 3.1. 117–19)—Carl Menger's loss principle.

The important point is that Aristotle did not go beyond such ruminations. Even the description of a simple market exchange was too much for his analytical powers and led his interpreters into interminable confusion (*Ethics* 5.5. 154–55). Aristotle thus reminds us how difficult it often is to advance beyond commonplace notions. Nobody before Hermann Heinrich Gossen in 1854 could make diminishing marginal utility analytically useful, differential rent still gave Adam Smith a hard time, and the fundamental significance of transactions costs for exchange remains imperfectly understood to the present day.

The Scholastics

The first steps beyond commonplace economics were due to the scholastics of the Middle Ages. Though deeply influenced by Aristotle, they soon went beyond him, thus making the earliest identifiable contributions to modern mainstream economics. In many respects their teaching has survived to the present day.[2]

The scholastics or "schoolmen" were essentially the professors of the medieval universities, most of them of course clerics, who formed a cosmopolitan community of scholars. Some of the greatest names were those of Thomas Aquinas, Albertus Magnus, and Duns Scotus in the thirteenth century, Nicolas Oresme in the fourteenth century, and in early modern times that of the Spanish Jesuit Luis Molina.

These theologians were originally motivated to study economic problems not by scientific curiosity, by a passion for knowledge for its own sake, but by a practical need. They were supposed to be the authorities

---

2. Detailed surveys of scholastic economics can be found in Schreiber 1913, Schumpeter 1954, De Roover 1955 and 1971, Gordon 1975, Spiegel 1983, and Pribram 1983. Special topics are discussed by Höffner (1941), Dempsey (1943), De Roover (1951, 1958) and Grice-Hutchinson (1952, 1978).

on what was good and evil, they had to interpret canon law, and they had to teach ethics from the pulpit and in the confession box. They looked at economics from the point of view of legalistic business ethics.

Fortunately, however, these moral philosophers were not content to derive their ethical norms from revelation, from received dogma, or from their imagination but rather tried to derive them from what they called the nature of things. They were thus led to inquire about the nature of things, which basically is not an ethical problem. Divine law became natural law. With increasing clarity, moral philosophers declared as "just" whatever serves the general interest. Scholastic economics thus became an early form of welfare economics.

But things reveal their nature only to those who know them. The scholastics thus found it necessary to descend from theology into the everyday world of economic reality, of early capitalism, foreign trade, monopoly, banking, foreign exchange, and public finance. What one knew about these things in the School of Salamanca was hardly less than Adam Smith knew two hundred years later, and more than most students know today.

In particular, the search after the criteria of a just price gradually led to a theory of price that was not significantly surpassed before the nineteenth century. Its central concept was the notion of a natural price, which results from the interplay of supply and demand under free competition. Molina expressed this in the following words: "If in a certain region or locality the custom has emerged to trade a commodity at a certain price, without fraud, monopoly, or other manipulations, then this price should be taken as the measure and rule of the just price for those commodities in that region or locality, as long as there is no change in the circumstances through which the price may legitimately rise or fall" (Höffner 1941, 135). The ethical norm was provided by the competitive market; monopoly was generally condemned. This implies that for most scholastics (Duns Scotus is a notable dissenter) the just price does not necessarily reflect the cost of production, because a simple cost rule would allow the producer to charge the consumer for any waste of resources due to inefficient production.[3] In fact, the scholastic tradition explained value essentially by subjective utility and scarcity. Juan de Luga, for example, explained in 1642 that prices of commodities fluctuate "on account of their utility in respect of human need" and "communal estimation, even when foolish, raises the natural price of goods" (Grice-Hutchinson 1978, 101f.). Compared to the scholastic teachings on value, commonplace as they are, the classical emphasis on labor cost was a step backward.

The scholastic notions about interest developed in the same direction. True, the prohibition of interest, long forgotten, was reaffirmed in the

---

3. The same argument was still used by Friedrich Wieser at the end of the nineteenth century.

thirteenth century. The scholastics clearly perceived, however, that interest could not be eradicated from economic life. They gradually achieved a reconciliation of church doctrine and reality on the basis of two considerations. First, interest is permissible inasmuch as it compensates the lender for his cost, consisting either of risk or, more controversially, of the profit forgone by not investing the money somewhere else. Second, interest is permissible, it was argued, inasmuch as it represents the creditor's share in the profit obtained by the debtor with the borrowed money. It does not take much imagination to perceive, as through a haze, the notions of opportunity cost and of the marginal product of capital in a competitive loan market.

A third area of notable achievement was money. Molina, having observed the consequences of American gold first hand, understood perfectly well that scarcity of money lowers prices and that plentiful money produces inflation. He also understood that a flow of gold from the Indies to Spain and farther on to Flanders must be associated with commodity prices that were highest in America and lowest in Flanders (Höffner 1941, 119f.; Grice-Hutchinson 1952, 112f.). From here to David Hume is but a short step.

Beyond such specific contributions, the scholastics made a general contribution of great scientific significance. From the concept of law as an ethical and legal norm they progressed to the idea of law as a scientific proposition, to the idea that social life was governed by scientific laws, so that the events of tomorrow, at least in part, are determined by those of today and thus may sometimes even be predicted. With this idea economic thought was well on its way to becoming economic science. Though scholasticism declined, its legacy lived on in the philosophical and mercantilist literature of the seventeenth and eighteenth centuries.

Mercantilism

The third source of political economy was mercantilism. The notion that the economic ideas and policies prevalent from the sixteenth to the eighteenth century constitute a "system" is due to the physiocrats, and the Marquis de Mirabeau, in his *Rural Philosophy* of 1763 (3:91), already designated this system as mercantile. It was Adam Smith, however, who brought the concept of a mercantile system into general use. The concept was thus created for polemic purposes, as a straw man to knock over. Like other isms, including capitalism, Marxism, Keynesianism, and monetarism, it belongs to the realm of ideologies and not of science.

The word *mercantilism* denotes both an epoch of economic history and a body of economic writings. The literature on all aspects of mercantilist economic policy is vast, but from the point of view of this book it is not relevant. The literature on mercantilist writings, however, is surprisingly small, highly scattered, and much of it dated. Since Heckscher's massive, though analytically disappointing, treatise (1955), originally published in

1931, there has been no comprehensive survey. Chapters on mercantilism are found in most histories of economic doctrines, and a masterly overview was provided by Jacob Viner in his article "Mercantilist Thought" in the *International Encyclopedia of the Social Sciences* (1968). Consistent with the introductory character of this chapter, the following pages offer no more than a broad outline.

Adam Smith described mercantilism as an economic policy whose specific objective was the accumulation of gold and silver through an active trade balance. Readers of mercantilist tracts can easily satisfy themselves that there is much truth in this description. Thus Thomas Mun, already quoted by Adam Smith, wrote in 1664 that "the ordinary means therefore to encrease our wealth and treasure is by *Forraign Trade,* wherein wee must ever observe this rule; to sell more to strangers yearly than wee consume of theirs in value" (McCulloch 1954, 125).

Nevertheless, Adam Smith's description of mercantilists as confusing wealth with gold was a distorting simplification—just like Keynes's description of classical economics. In reality, the economic literature of the seventeenth and early eighteenth centuries was much richer, more varied and more interesting. Above all, mercantilism was no system but rather an unsystematic assortment of arguments, measures, and ideas with wide differences from one country to another. Rather than by the presence of certain unifying principles, it was characterized by their absence.

The general historical conditions of the period still left their imprint on the mercantilist literature. This was the age of the emerging nation-states, of rising capitalism, and of absolutism. The economic literature, in all its diversity, thus shares certain common characteristics. This common philosophy may perhaps be summarized in the following propositions.

The ultimate objective of economic policy is the political power of the state, both internal and external. The Austrian Philipp Wilhelm von Hornigk epitomized this clearly in the title of his tract of 1684: "Austria above all if she only will." It is consistent with this down-to-earth objective that the typical mercantilist author was not a speculative philosopher but a cabinet minister, administrator, government adviser, merchant, lobbyist, or adventurer.

Power, however, is inherently relative. It is never absolutely great or small but only relative to rivaling powers. The power one gains is inevitably lost by another. As Montaigne expressed it, "the profit of one is the loss of another." As a consequence, nations were seen to be engaged in a perpetual conflict of interest. This is in sharp contrast to a philosophy that regards as the basic objective something like per capita real income. In the latter case, everybody may gain at the same time.

For the mercantilists, power consisted of men and money. Men were needed as workers and soldiers; money (in the treasury) was needed to pay for armies and navies, to finance the government, and to pay for extravagant courts. Mercantilists, therefore, were typically populationists and fiscalists.

Population growth and high fiscal revenues, in turn, were seen to require prosperity of industry and trade. Economic welfare, therefore, emerged as one of the central concerns of mercantilist writers. The German cameralist Wilhelm von Schroeder expressed this in particularly colorful words: "The farmer must put manure on his acre if he wants to harvest, he must fatten his cattle before they are slaughtered, and he must well feed his cows if he expects them to give good milk. Thus the prince must first provide his subjects with a good livelihood if he wants to take something from them."

But economic prosperity, mercantilists argued, depends on a high quantity and rapid circulation of money. "Money matters," mercantilists affirmed. Their emphasis on what later would be called effective demand led John Maynard Keynes to claim them as his predecessors. However, even Keynes's harshest critics will concede that the mercantilist commonplace arguments come nowhere near the macroeconomic model that made Keynes famous.

In the absence of domestic gold and silver mines, so the mercantilist argument continues, an increase in the quantity of money can be obtained only through a trade surplus. (For countries, such as Spain, with their own mines, the trade balance would determine how much of the precious metals they could retain.) Foreign trade, therefore, is the "gold mine of Peru." It follows, as François de Forbonnais expressed it, that "the balance of trade is really the balance of power."

One's own balance of payments surplus and the deficit of one's rivals thus became the primary objectives of economic policy, to be achieved by all sorts of import restrictions, duties, bounties, subsidies, and regulation. Jean-Baptiste Colbert expressed the consequences succinctly: "Trade causes a perpetual battle, both in peace and in war, between the nations of Europe." It also caused a perpetual battle within each country among the various interest groups.

An intellectual environment dominated by these ideas is hardly conducive to rapid progress of economic science. It is true that the volume of economic writings increased rapidly, that the quantity of factual information multiplied, and that the economic debate became general and active. However, this rapid quantitative progress was associated with rather slow progress in the quality of economic reasoning. For two centuries one finds the same weak or loose arguments repeated over and over. Valuable contributions often remained unexploited. Mercantilism was predominantly still commonplace economics.

At the same time the insights that became available during this period should not be underestimated. Even without deep analysis, commonsense had produced some useful results. Some illustrative examples, though fragmentary, may help to provide background for the following chapters.

1. It seems the term *political economy* was first used by Antoyne Montchrétien in the title of his book *Traicté de l'oeconomie politique*, published in 1615 (Montchrétien 1889). It was meant to distinguish the subject from the household economics ancient authors usually had in mind.

2. Jean Bodin, like scholastic writers before him, argued in 1568, that the principal, and practically the only, cause for the continuous rise in prices was the abundance of gold and silver (Bodin 1946). For the mercantilists this insight was indeed commonplace. Thomas Mun, for example, loved to contemplate how trade surpluses lead to a rise in land prices.

3. Mercantilists were also clear about the stimulating effect of an increasing money supply on output and employment, while monetary contraction was seen to result in recession. They were far from clear, however, about the temporary nature of these real effects. It took the catastrophe of John Law, to be described in chapter 6, to demonstrate this point. The emphasis on the short run was indeed something that mercantilism, like most commonplace economics, had in common with Keynes.

4. In the sixteenth century, Thomas Gresham, financial agent, expert, and wizard of Queen Elizabeth, was well familiar with the proposition that "bad money drives out good money." If one gold coin can be obtained in exchange for fifteen silver coins, while the metal in the gold coin is worth the metal in twenty silver coins, then silver money will drive gold money out of circulation (De Roover 1949). An admirable analysis of competing commodity moneys and debased currencies had been provided by Nicolas Copernicus, famous as an astronomer, as early as 1517 (Sommerfeld 1978).

5. To Gerrard de Malynes it was clear in 1601 (as it was to scholastic doctors in Salamanca even earlier) that the abundance of money results not only in rising domestic prices but also in rising prices of foreign exchange (Officer 1982a). This was not the genuine purchasing power parity proposition, though, as was sometimes alleged, but only the law of one price applied to gold. Full-fledged purchasing power parity had to wait for inconvertible paper money.

6. In 1696 Gregory King wrote down (but did not publish) his empirical estimate of the price elasticity of the demand for wheat. If a harvest failure reduces domestic wheat production to one-fourth its former level, price will rise fourfold. This will result in large imports, but a tripling of price will still be associated with a reduction in consumption by about one-fifth, which implies a price elasticity of demand of about (minus) one-fifth (Evans 1967; most references in the literature actually relate to King's friend Charles Davenant).

7. In 1588, Giovanni Botero published a theory of population, to which Malthus had little to add. Human fertility, he argued, would allow pop-

ulation to grow beyond any limits. The means of subsistence, however, are limited. This imposes a limit also on population growth that takes effect either through celibacy or through war, famine, and pestilence (Botero 1956, *Greatness of Cities*, bk.3).

8. The merchant and man of letters Bernardo Davanzati, in 1588, formulated the principle of utility maximization by saying that all men work in order to be happy, and they hope to find happiness by satisfying all their wants and desires. The purpose of trade he found, as did the scholastics before him, in the exchange of the relatively superfluous against the relatively necessary. He also resolved the water/diamond paradox before it had even been perceived by pointing out that the value of water depends on its scarcity, on the degree of thirst (Davanzati 1965, 32f.).

9. In a debate with Colbert, probably in Lyons around 1680, merchants seem to have demanded, "Laissez-nous faire." Vincent de Gournay later expanded the phrase to the maxim "Laissez faire, laissez passer" (Oncken 1886).

10. Starting from the ancient truth that not all countries can grow everything, mercantilists eventually developed a theory of international trade that even included the principle of comparative advantage. Samuel Fortrey expressed this principle in 1663 in the following terms: "Our care should . . . be to increase chiefly those things which are of least charge at home, and greatest value abroad . . . wherefore, could we employ our lands to anything of more worth, we could not want plenty of corn, though we had none of our own; for what we should increase in the room of it, of greater value by exportation, would not onley bring us home as much corn as that land would have yeelded, but plenty of money to boot" (McCulloch 1954, 226). In the anonymous "Considerations on the East-India Trade" of 1701, the principle, now applied to resource inputs instead of money, is illustrated by numerical examples of almost Ricardian character (549f.).

11. With respect to scientific method, William Petty, in a book published posthumously in 1690, developed the program of a "political arithmetic," which became the mercantilist form of econometrics. In the preface the program is set out in the following words: "The Method I take to do this, is not yet very usual; for instead of using only comparative and superlative Words, and intellectual Arguments, I have taken the course . . . to express my self in Terms of *Number, Weight,* or *Measure*; to use only Arguments of Sense, and to consider only such Causes, as have visible Foundations in Nature; leaving those that depend upon the mutable Minds, Opinions, Appetites, and Passions of particular Men, to the Consideration of others" (Petty 1963–64).

12. The transition from mercantilism to classical economics, finally, is marked by Pierre le Pesant, Seigneur de Boisguilbert (1646–1714). He was

a Norman nobleman who, after dabbling in literature (he published a life of Mary Stuart), became a provincial judge and magistrate. A restless, cantankerous, and bellicose man, he spent his life in conflict with his environment. His main work is "Le détail de la France" (1695), but the definitive expression of his ideas is the "Dissertation de la nature des richesses, de l'argent et des tributs" (1707), which has been conjectured to have served Adam Smith as an unnamed source (Roberts 1935). The "Factum de la France" (1706) is a strident diatribe against the French tax system with little lasting value.

Though Boisguilbert presents his ideas as if they were the panacea of a crank, they are fundamentally sound economics. The root cause of the rotten state of the French economy is found to be the confusion between money and wealth, "that pernicious idolatry of money, the source of all evil" (Boisguilbert 1966, 2:981). To maintain his armies, the king does not need money as such, which is an insignificant thing, but command over goods and services. The real burden of taxes depends not simply on their amount, but largely on the more or less distorting way in which they are levied, taxes on individual commodities being the most detrimental. Boisguilbert was the supply sider of the reign of Louis XIV who argued that, by reducing the deadweight burden of taxation and thus making the economy more efficient, the king could both increase his real fiscal revenues and raise his subjects' after-tax incomes.

Efficiency, in Boisguilbert's view, requires appropriate "proportions" between the various sectors of the economy (1966, 2:890f.); wealth depends on relative prices and distortions lead to misery (997). "Equilibrium, . . . the only protector of public wealth" (995), is reached when resources are allocated in such proportions that prices cover costs and factors earn competitive incomes (1007f.). Whereas policy would find it impossible to impose this equilibrium by force of arms against the conflicting interests of profit-seeking individuals, providence would establish it automatically if only nature were left to itself (*pourvu qu'on la laisse faire*) (891f.).

Boisguilbert was sometimes celebrated as the founder of political economy. Being no theorist, he was very far from it. However, he had a clear, if sketchy, vision of the competitive allocation of resources in competitive equilibrium. The analytical implementation of this vision would fill the following two centuries in the history of economics.

AT THE BEGINNING of the eighteenth century, as this brief introduction has shown, most of the elements of a viable theory of supply and demand were available in the literature. It is true that scholastic and mercantilist economics, to the modern reader, consists of some grains of valuable analysis in a large heap of chaff, but if somebody had collected those grains, he could almost have constructed, one feels, the economic theory of Alfred Marshall two centuries before his *Principles*. One crucial ingredient of such a construction was still missing, though, namely the concept of a circular flow of income in general economic equilibrium. This decisive advance was the contribution of early classical economists such as Richard Cantillon and François Quesnay.

Intellectually, Adam Smith pushed mercantilism into the background. However, in the discussion about current affairs, in political oratory, parliamentary debates, pronouncements of trade associations, and economic journalism, mercantilism lives on. For a vivid picture of mercantilism one has only to follow current discussions about trade deficits, international competitiveness, and capital flows. Commonplace economics is immortal.

4
Richard Cantillon

THE DISCOVERY of the circular flow of income, the construction of the first system of national accounts, took place in the first half of the eighteenth century. It initiated the era of classical economics.

Many economic writers claimed to have laid the basis of a new science, some (like Hermann Heinrich Gossen and Léon Walras) coming reasonably close, while others even failed to advance existing science. Adam Smith made no such claims. In the course of time, however, the light of his *Wealth of Nations* (1776) tended to outshine the existing literature to such an extent that earlier contributions dropped into the darkness of oblivion. One of them was the *Essay on the nature of commerce in general* by Richard Cantillon.

In conventional terminology classical economics begins with Adam Smith. Cantillon, accordingly, is classified as a preclassical economist. This terminology, at least from an analytical point of view, is misleading. Marx, when he contrasted classical to vulgar economics, saw things in a different, and historically more revealing, light. For him, as was mentioned in chapter 2, classical economics began with William Petty and Pierre de Boisguilbert around 1680 and ended with David Ricardo and Simonde de Sismondi around 1820. As a matter of fact, from the point of view of analytical concepts, Cantillon is closer to Smith than Smith is to, say, John Stuart Mill. As a theorist he is indeed one of the shining stars of the classical galaxy.

Life

Knowledge about Cantillon's life is still fragmentary. The most up-to-date account, with many new facts, is provided by Antoin E. Murphy's (1986) exhaustive monograph. Important earlier sources are the papers by

Joseph Hone (1944), Friedrich Hayek (1931b), Henry Higgs (in Cantillon 1931) and Anita Fage (1952).

Richard Cantillon was born probably between 1680 and 1690 (Murphy 1986, 10), the second son of an Irish nobleman, Richard Cantillon of Ballyheigue, in the county of Kerry. His ancestors were traced back to a Norman knight who had followed William the Conqueror to England; they had moved to Ireland in the twelfth century. The grandmother of the economist's grandfather is said to have been a Stuart, and most of the family were staunch Jacobites, who lost their land in the Cromwellian revolution. Richard's older brother seems to have been a Jacobite army captain and later a farmer in Ireland; the younger brother, like Richard, became a "Mississippian," making an unsuccessful effort to found an Irish settlement in Louisiana.

Little is known about Cantillon's youth, but after extensive travels as a merchant and financial agent, he arrived in Paris in 1714 to join the banking firm of an older relative, Sir Richard Cantillon. Sir Richard had fought for James II at the Battle of the Boyne and later became the trusted banker of the Jacobite exiles surrounding James's son, the Old Pretender. Sir Richard died in 1717, leaving large debts, which his nephew, himself a creditor, later paid to clear the family name. From then on, Richard Cantillon, who had become a French citizen as early as 1708, was on his own in the world of high finance.

As a matter of fact, he seems to have been a financial genius, rapidly amassing a huge fortune. How this was possible can be understood only in the context of those hectic years. Soon after Cantillon came to Paris, John Law, son of an Edinburgh banker, having gained the ear of the regent, Philip of Orléans, founded his Banque Générale. By 1719 this had become a huge colonial conglomerate, commonly called the Mississippi Company. Mississippi shares started to rise rapidly. Not only all of Paris, but all of France and, indeed, of Europe, began to speculate in the rue Quincampoix. As an associate of John Law, Cantillon made huge capital gains on his Mississippi shares. He sold out, however, before the market had reached its peak, temporarily withdrawing to the sidelines.

In the speculative fever of 1719–20, Cantillon must have been one of the few who kept a cool head. In fact, his critical remarks caused Law to threaten him with the Bastille, whereupon Cantillon thought it wise to stay away from Paris for a while. Preferring to remain in the background, he became the silent partner of an English banker in Paris, John Hughes, whom he used as a front.

When other speculators lost their shirts, Cantillon made another fortune in the foreign exchange markets. Law had predicted that the French *livre* would rise against sterling, and the market tended to believe him. Speculators, many of them British aristocrats in Paris, both men and women, thus borrowed from Cantillon large amounts of sterling (at interest rates sometimes exceeding 60 percent)[1] to buy French *livres*, depositing their Mississippi shares as collateral. Cantillon, on the other hand, had perceived that, given Law's expansion of the French money supply, the French *livre* was bound to depreciate. He therefore moved large sums from *livres* into sterling. In the end, his debtors lost and he gained, and he was reported to have made millions in a few days. He also became entangled in numerous acrimonious and colorful lawsuits with debtors. He seems to have won most of them, but some cases were settled only long after his death.

After 1720, Cantillon traveled all over Europe. He is said to have owned houses in seven cities and spent most of his time in London, Amsterdam, and later again in Paris. On 16 February 1722, in London, he married Mary Ann Mahony, the attractive young daughter of a wealthy Irish officer in Paris. A son seems to have died early, but a daughter survived him. After Hughes's death in 1723 the banking firm was liquidated, which led to another lawsuit, this time with Hughes's widow for her share of the profits. (It was said that Cantillon had credited the successful operations to his personal account while charging the unsuccessful ones to the partnership.)

In 1734, Cantillon rented a house in Albemarle Street, London. One evening he retired early with a candle to read in bed, as was his habit. Later in the night there was a big fire, and Cantillon was found dead in his bed. It was first thought that he had fallen asleep with the candle burning, but it was later determined that a former cook had broken into the house with several accomplices to burglarize it and that they had murdered Cantillon and set fire to the house to cover their crime. The main culprit was never apprehended. A large part of Cantillon's papers seems to have perished in the flames, but some documents turned up in the Dutch colony of Surinam, where the murderer, if such he was, may have fled.[2]

Richard Cantillon must have been above all an astute businessman who knew how to drive a hard bargain, a speculator with iron nerves and cold judgment, a financial wizard who, by the age of twenty, had mastered the intricacies of trade and banking, which most mortals fail to learn about in a lifetime. He had a keen power of observation and incessantly collected evidence and statistical data. He was also widely read, both in classical and contemporary literature, and familiar with many of the economic writings of the period. Ideologies, religious beliefs, and moral philosophy were not important to him, though. His scientific mind wanted to solve analytical

---

1. Cantillon later justified these rates with the modern-sounding argument that they included an allowance for the expected change in the exchange rate (Murphy 1986, 144).
2. Murphy (1986, 293f.) speculates that Cantillon may actually have faked a murder, using a corpse, to cover his own escape to Surinam.

problems of practical importance. The combination of early financial success with analytical superiority makes him the Ricardo of eighteenth-century economics.

The *Essai*

The circumstances surrounding the publication of the *Essai sur la nature du commerce en général,* Cantillon's only published work, are still unclear. The title page shows 1755 as the year of publication, which is generally accepted. That the book appeared fully twenty-one years after the author's death may be plausibly explained by the pending lawsuits. Though the publication was anonymous, the identity of the author was widely known at the time (but later he was often confused with his nephew Philip Cantillon). The book is described as a translation from English. Though an English original has never been discovered, this may well be correct since long passages were found by Friedrich Hayek to be incorporated in a prospectus of a dictionary by Malachy Postlethwayt that appeared in 1749. The Marquis de Mirabeau reported that he possessed a copy of the French version for sixteen years and that the translation was prepared by Cantillon himself for the benefit of a friend.

It is not known whether the 1755 edition is based on Mirabeau's copy (perhaps reclaimed by the author's heirs) or whether the heirs had another copy. Nor is it known where the book was published. On the title page it is said to be printed by Fletcher Gyles in London, probably for reasons of censorship, but Murphy (1986) makes a convincing argument for Guillyn in Paris. In any case, the 1755 edition was the basis of all further editions and translations. The statistical supplement, which is often referred to in the text, has never been found. If Cantillon, as Mirabeau reported, had written other works, they are lost.

A Land Theory of Value

The basis of Cantillon's economics is his theory of value. As such it is not original, following in the broad stream flowing from the scholastics to Adam Smith. The market price of a commodity fluctuates perpetually around its intrinsic value given by its cost of production (Cantillon 1931, part 1, ch. 10). Cost consists of land, labor, capital goods, and raw materials. However, as Petty had shown, capital goods and raw materials can, in turn, be resolved into land and labor. As a consequence, the intrinsic value of a commodity is measured by the land and labor that, directly and indirectly, enter into its production. In the first stage, Cantillon thus arrives at a land-and-labor theory of value. He recognized, of course, that wages differ depending on the skills of the worker and the attractiveness of the job. His discussion of these differentials was not improved upon for a century.

A land-and-labor theory of value is ultimately not satisfactory, though.

Cantillon, like Petty before him, was thus looking for a par value for labor in terms of land. Petty had thought that this could be derived from the relationship between the annual land rent and the purchase price of land, which corresponds to the rate of interest. Cantillon, recognizing that this would not do, took a different tack by regarding human reproduction itself as an "industry" transforming commodity inputs into labor. This led him to population theory (which is more fully discussed in Spengler 1965).

This theory, too, though it inspired Mirabeau, was not, in itself, original, going hardly beyond Giovanni Botero more than a century earlier. The novel element was the use of population theory as one of the main components of the theory of value. This remained one of the basic features of economic theory for a century. More than any other single feature, it gave that theory its classical character.

Cantillon's population theory is based on the proposition that men, if they have unlimited means of subsistence, "multiply like mice in a barn" (Cantillon 1931, part 1, ch. 15). In substance, though not in words, this is the famous "geometric progression." In the world we live in, however, the means of subsistence are limited by the quantity of land. As a consequence, the growth of population, through reproduction or migration, in a given area will gradually slow down until, sooner or later, it comes to an end; population becomes stationary. The stationary state is characterized by a certain subsistence wage that just suffices to keep population from either growing or declining. For Cantillon this subsistence wage is not a physical constant but dependent on conventional living standards and social conditions and thus variable. His estimate that a worker, to support his family in the stationary state, needs a wage of about twice the amount required for his personal subsistence, was the point Adam Smith thought worthy of a reference (1776, bk. 1, ch. 8).

Cantillon conjectured that between 1.5 and 6 acres of land (of average fertility) per head would be required in the stationary state, depending largely on the composition of household demand. He supported these estimates by numerous observations (Cantillon 1931, part 1, ch. 11), but most of his data were lost with the supplement.

Once this par value is known, the intrinsic values of all commodities can be reduced to land only. "The real value of everything used by man is proportionable to the quantity of land used for its production and for the upkeep of those who have fashioned it" (Cantillon 1931, part 2, ch. 1). On his assumption of constant returns to scale, he thus ends up with a land theory of value. A mathematical representation of this theory is provided below in the appendix to this chapter. For a world with endogenous labor and exogenous land, this theory was analytically superior to a labor theory of value along the lines of David Ricardo's or Karl Marx's (Brems 1978). However, the Ricardian problems of unequal capital intensities remained unsolved. Of course, from the point of view of modern theory, both a labor theory and a land theory of value can be valid only in highly special cases.

Intrinsic values relate to a stationary economy in competitive equilibrium. Since market prices fluctate around theses equilibrium values, their future course is uncertain (Cantillon 1931, part 2, ch.2). To bear the risk inherent in this uncertainty is, in Cantillon's view, the economic function of the entrepreneur (part 1, ch. 13). The entrepreneur thus emerges in a role hardly less important than, seventy years later, in the economics of Jean-Baptiste Say (*Traité d'économie politique*, 1803). With respect to the theory of price, Léon Walras might well have based his mathematical formulation of general economic equilibrium (*Eléments d'économie politique pure,* 1874–77) directly on Cantillon.

The "Three Rents"

Cantillon uses his theory of value as the analytical basis for a model of the flows of goods and money between different sectors of an economy. In a closed economy he distinguishes two productive sectors, namely agriculture, scattered over the countryside, and manufactures, concentrated in the cities. His model of a spatial equilibrium between city and country (Cantillon 1931, part 2, ch. 5), rudimentary as it is, was not improved upon until Thünen's famous *Isolated State* (1826).

There are three social classes, namely the landowners, the entrepreneurs, and the hired workers. The landowners consume but do not produce; they lease their land to farmers, who are agricultural entrepreneurs, against the payment of rent. The farmers, besides paying rent, hire their laborers and buy manufactures in the cities. They sell foodstuffs and raw materials to landlords and in the cities, using the difference between revenue and cost for their own upkeep. The artisans and merchants in the cities, urban entrepreneurs, use the proceeds from selling their manufactures to landlords and farmers to buy raw materials from agriculture, to pay their workers, and for their own subsistence. What emerges is the tripolar *Tableau Economique* of François Quesnay described in words (the similarities are traced in Foley 1973).

Cantillon's efforts to estimate the annual magnitudes in this circular flow model make him a precursor of national income accounting and input-output analysis. The food consumption of landlords is regarded as negligible. One-half of the population is assumed to live in cities and the other half in the countryside. Food consumption is divided accordingly.

The landlords are estimated to receive about one-third of the annual product of land, which is all used to pay for the manufactures and services from the cities. One-third of agricultural output is retained by farmers as their entrepreneurial income. The remaining one-third is used partly to feed agricultural workers and partly in exchange for manufactures in the city. These are Cantillon's famous "three rents" (1931, part 2, ch. 3).

How is the last one-third divided between food and manufactures? This can be calculated from the population structure. Since the city contains one-half of the population, it needs one-half of the foodstuffs. One-third of the foodstuffs can be bought from agriculture with the proceeds from the manufactures sold to the landlords. The remaining one-sixth has to be bought from agriculture in exchange for manufactures. The only final demand is that of the landlords, the remaining population being at subsistence levels, and the only ultimate input is land.

In terms of a numerical example, this model of the economy can be summarized in an open input-output system for two sectors as described in table 4.1.

TABLE 4.1

	Sector Input			
			Final Demand	Total
Sector Output	Agriculture	Manufactures	(Landlords)	Output
Agriculture	150	150		300
Manufactures	50	150	100	300
Rent (land)	100			
Total cost	300	300		600

The numbers are based on an (arbitrary) agricultural output of 300. The first line says that one-half of this amount is used up within agriculture while the remainder is consumed in the manufacturing cities. Of the total manufacturing output, one-third is consumed by the landlords, one-half is used up within the cities, and the remaining one-sixth flows to agriculture. All rent income of landlords is transformed into final demand.

The circular flow aspects of this model can perhaps be visualized more easily in the arrow graph of figure 4.1. The arrows represent commodity or (in the case of land) service flows. With each arrow there is associated a money flow in the opposite direction, whose amount is indicated by the number in parenthesis.

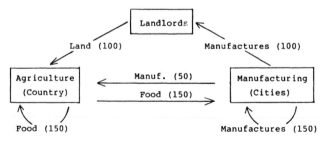

FIGURE 4.1

Cantillon explained that his model can be interpreted in two ways (1931, part 1, ch. 14). In one case the whole economy is treated as if it were a single estate, centrally administered by one landlord. In the other case the land is divided among numerous landlords, and production, both agricultural and manufacturing, is managed by risk-bearing entrepreneurs who hire the wage-earning workers. Cantillon's point was that both interpretations would lead to the same allocation of resources. About 180 years before Enrico Barone, he thus put forth the proposition that perfect competition and perfect central planning are, in some sense, equivalent. It would take economic theory more than two centuries to provide a proof of this conjecture, and then only for highly simplified cases. (From a practical point of view, however, it is probably more important to know under what system highly imperfect reality is farther away from the theoretical optimum.) Competition, in Cantillon's thinking, appeared as the circumspect planner fifty years before Adam Smith's "invisible hand."

With his simple linear model, Cantillon provided virtually all the purely analytical content of Quesnay's *Tableau Economique*. Beyond this he built the prototype for a long sequence of linear general equilibrium models down to Wassily Leontief.

Classical Monetary Theory

Cantillon's third major contribution concerned money, a subject he understood particularly well (for a more detailed account see Bordo 1983). By money he meant commodity money, consisting, in view of relative transaction and storage costs, mostly of gold and silver coins. As a consequence, the value of money, like the value of commodities, can ultimately be expressed in terms of the quantity of direct and indirect land going into its production (Cantillon 1931, part 1, ch. 17). In Cantillon's time this cost-of-production approach, exemplified by Jean Bodin and William Petty, was the mainstream approach, and it was, of course, entirely valid. It implies that money, since it consists of pieces of metal dug out of the ground and processed, cannot be expected to be "neutral." The quantity theory of prices, whereby a doubling of the quantity of money leads to a doubling of all prices (compared to what they would have been otherwise), is not strictly applicable.

The demand for money, for Cantillon, depends on what he calls *la vitesse des paiements* or *la vitesse de la circulation* (1931, part 2, chs. 3, 4). He thereby introduced the concept of velocity of money. He did not create it out of thin air, though. Petty had analyzed the significance of payment habits and the frequency of payments for the demand for currency, and John Locke, in discussing these factors, had even mentioned the "quickness of circulation." Nevertheless, the definitive contribution was Cantillon's. Switching back and forth between the demand for currency per unit of payment and the number of payments performed by a unit of currency, he made it clear from the beginning that there was no basis for a doctrinal split between a cash balance approach and a velocity approach. On the basis of the three rents, the demand for currency is conjectured to be about one-third of the annual rents paid to landlords (ch. 3).

Cantillon's most fundamental contribution to monetary theory was the analysis of the dynamic effects of money on the economy (1931, part 2, ch. 6). In particular, he provided an analysis of the "real" effects of money on relative prices, expenditures, and interest rates that, though rudimentary in technique, turned out to be virtually definitive in economic substance.

Some of these effects would be permanent, but no general statement can be made concerning their exact nature. A reduction in the production cost of gold (for example, through a newly discovered mine) would, in the long run, tend to push up prices, both nationally and internationally, but not necessarily in exact proportion to the increase in the money supply (Cantillon 1931, part 2, ch. 7). For Cantillon's case of commodity money, not much more could be said today.

Most of the real effects of money, however, would be temporary. In a first round of effects, those who work in the gold mines have more money to spend; this "real balance effect" raises their demand for goods and services. This results in a secondary expansion of output and employment in other industries; there is what two hundred years later might have been called a multiplier effect. The rising demand cannot fail to raise prices. Price increases induce farmers to cultivate more land and to increase their own expenditures. People with fixed incomes, such as landlords with rigid rents and workers with rigid wages, suffer a loss of real income, which perhaps forces them to emigrate.

Gradually prosperity turns into "stagflation." The rising prices reduce the competitiveness of the domestic economy in international markets; export industries suffer while imports increase, and thus a trade deficit results. To the extent production costs rise, the initial incentive for increased production vanishes. The additional gold is now needed to finance the import surplus. In due course the abundance of gold disappears; rising prices are now accompanied by stagnating trade and employment. Gold mining and foreign countries remain the only beneficiaries of the gold discovery.

Cantillon had a particularly keen perception of the international aspects of monetary expansion. In substance his analysis of the specie flow mechanism, though less effectively presented, is superior to David Hume's inasmuch as it assigns to income (or real balance) effects their proper role without misleading the reader into overestimating the role of price effects. This is entirely consistent with Cantillon's thoroughly mercantilist emphasis on the importance of a large gold stock, which, in his view, determines the comparative greatness of kingdoms and states (1931, part 1, ch. 14).

In fact Cantillon is careful to point out that a large amount of gold can be retained in a country only by a large demand for it (part 2, ch. 8). It is true for gold, according to both Hume and Cantillon, that demand creates its own supply.

Once and for all, Cantillon dispels the notion that an increase in the quantity of money is necessarily accompanied by a decline in interest rates (1931, part 2, ch. 10). Whether or not this is true, he points out, depends on the nature of the forces behind the monetary expansion. If this expansion is due to an increase in the supply of money, the common notion is valid. If, however, the increase in the quantity of money is due to an increased demand for it, perhaps because of improved business expectations, the rate of interest will be high. The real effects of an increase in money thus depend crucially on the way the increase was brought about (chs. 8, 10). In part 3, Cantillon shows himself as a lucid expositor of the intricacies of foreign exchange markets, bimetallism, and banking, but without adding fundamental insights.

Overall, Cantillon, though no more creating economic science than any other single person, must be regarded as the founder of the classical tradition in monetary theory, of which Thornton's *Paper Credit of Great Britain* of 1802 (1939) was the peak achievement.

Place in the History of Economics

The *Essai*, written almost half a century before the *Wealth of Nations*, is the work of a mercantilist who believed that the relative greatness of a nation depends on its reserves of gold and silver. Nevertheless, the *Essai* opens with a piece of brilliant rhetoric that pointed far into the future. "The land is the source or matter from whence all wealth is produced. The labor of man is the form which produces it: and wealth in itself is nothing but the maintenance, conveniences, and superfluities of life." The physiocrats and Adam Smith could hardly have said it better.

Despite the opening flourish, the *Essai*, by the standards of the time, was an austere book, too demanding for elegant salon conversation. Compared to Mirabeau's easy-flowing rhetoric, its style is terse and unadorned. As a consequence, it was more widely acclaimed than read. It was nevertheless influential. Mirabeau wrote to Jean-Jacques Rousseau in 1767 that he got his views on population from Cantillon. In fact his *L'ami des hommes*, dated 1756 but published in 1757, had first been planned as a free commentary on Cantillon's manuscript, then in Mirabeau's possession. Friedrich Hayek provides evidence for intended plagiarism. The publication of the *Essai* forced Mirabeau to write his own book, but his population theory, if it can be called a theory, was still substantially borrowed from Cantillon (Fox-Genovese 1976, 145f.). Mirabeau, in his orgy of prolixity, seemed to understand neither the three rents nor the circular flow, though.

François Quesnay also knew the *Essai*, for he referred to Cantillon already in his article "Grains," which appeared in the *Encyclopédie* in 1757, in connection with the formation of cities. It is not known to what extent the *Tableau Economique*, emerging from his discussions with Mirabeau, was directly inspired by Cantillon's three rents, but it must have been considerable. Though Quesnay purported to eradicate Cantillon's fallacies from Mirabeau's mind, it almost looks as if, in fact, he had tried to explain to his friend what Cantillon had really meant. The particular form of the "zigzag," which represents an effort to find a static equilibrium by a dynamic period analysis, is, of course, Quesnay's. The underlying static content, however, looks like an adaptation of Cantillon's scheme. Fox-Genovese (1976, 273) felt justified in saying that "Quesnay took over Cantillon's formal analysis in its entirety." It should be noted in this context that the *Tableau Economique* was first presented to the public in the 1759 edition of *L'ami des hommes*, which, as was mentioned above, had originally been planned as a commentary on the *Essai*.

To what extent Adam Smith had learned from Cantillon is unknown. The only reference to him in the *Wealth of Nations* probably does not indicate the true amount of the influence. In any case, thanks to the references in Mirabeau, Quesnay, and Smith, Cantillon's name never quite disappeared from the pages of the history of economic thought (extensive references are given in Hayek 1931b). It nevertheless amounted almost to a rediscovery when in 1881 William Stanley Jevons (1905, 155f.) proclaimed the *Essai* to be the first treatise on economics and "more emphatically than any other single work 'the Cradle of Political Economy.' "

From this judgment there was, of course, dissent. Thus August Oncken (1902, 279) denied Cantillon the title of founder of a science because, as he said, he was lacking a background of moral philosophy. Oncken's criterion reflects his own weakness as an economic theorist, but in refusing to regard the *Essai* as the fountainhead of a new science, historians of economic thought have generally sided with Oncken rather than with Jevons.

Aside from futile claims to the title of founding father, however, Jevons's high opinion of Cantillon's contribution prevailed. Arthur Monroe (1951, 246) ranked the *Essai* as the most important work on economics before the *Wealth of Nations*. Joseph Schumpeter (1954, 217, 223) called it a "great work," a "brilliant performance, which in most respects stood unsurpassed for about a century" (which century, be it noted, included both Smith and Ricardo). For Joseph Spengler (1954), Cantillon was the "first of the moderns." More recently, Mark Blaug (1978, 21) described the *Essai* as "the most systematic, the most lucid, and at the same time the most original of all the statements of economic principles before the 'Wealth of Nations.' "

Appendix: A Mathematical Restatement of the Land Theory of Value

Cantillon's model of resource allocation can be mathematically formulated in the following way: Denote the number of workers by W, land by B, food output by X_1 and manufacturing output by X_2, while R_2 stands for the landlord's consumption of manufactures. The demand for labor depends on outputs according to

$$W = a_{01}X_1 + a_{02}X_2, \tag{4.1}$$

where a_{0i} is the (fixed) input of labor per unit of the respective output. Agricultural output is partly consumed by the workers according to their subsistence needs while the remainder is used as input in both agriculture and manufacturing, depending on their production levels:

$$X_1 = c_1W + a_{11}X_1 + a_{12}X_2. \tag{4.2}$$

The same is true for manufacturing output except that it is partly consumed by landlords:

$$X_2 = c_2W + a_{21}X_1 + a_{22}X_2 + R_2. \tag{4.3}$$

Since manufacturing uses no land, land requirements just depend on agricultural output,

$$B = bX_1. \tag{4.4}$$

This system of linear equations can be solved for W, X_1, X_2, and R_2 in terms of B; land is the only exogenous factor. The structure of the economy, for given land, depends on the technical coefficients. Cantillon paid particular attention to the influence of consumption habits as expressed by c_1 and c_2; the influence of landlord consumption could be formalized in an analogous way.

This allocation model has a counterpart in a price model. Competition sees to it that the wage rate, w, equals subsistence consumption evaluated at market prices, p_1 and p_2,

$$w = c_1p_1 + c_2p_2. \tag{4.5}$$

The price of agricultural output equals its cost in terms of wages, raw materials, and rent,

$$p_1 = a_{01}w + a_{11}p_1 + a_{21}p_2 + br. \tag{4.6}$$

The same is true for manufactures except that their cost includes no rent,

$$p_2 = a_{02}w + a_{12}p_1 + a_{22}p_2. \tag{4.7}$$

This is a linear-homogeneous system in all prices. It can be solved by standard techniques for the relative price

$$\frac{p_2}{p_1} = \frac{c_1 a_{02} + a_{12}}{1 - c_2 a_{02} - a_{22}}, \tag{4.8}$$

where the viability of the system requires a positive denominator. One observes that relative prices depend only on technical coefficients. Wage and rental rates have no influence.

According to Cantillon's proposition, relative prices reflect land requirements, both direct and indirect. The correctness of this proposition can be checked on the basis of the allocation model.[3] The aggregate land cost of manufactures can be determined by assuming that landlord consumption is raised by dR_2 and calculating the increment in land requirements, dB. By differentiating equations 4.1–4.4 one obtains

$$\frac{dB}{dR_2} = b \, \frac{c_1 a_{02} + a_{12}}{\Delta}, \tag{4.9}$$

where Δ is a determinant.

The corresponding land cost of agricultural output is obtained by assuming that, instead of manufactures, the landlords consume only food, R_1. Equation 4.2 then reads

$$X_1 = c_1 W_1 + a_{11} X_1 + a_{12} X_2 + R_1, \tag{4.10}$$

while $R_2 = 0$. The result is

$$\frac{dB}{dR_1} = b \, \frac{1 - c_2 a_{02} - a_{22}}{\Delta}. \tag{4.11}$$

The relative land cost of manufactures, therefore, is

$$\frac{\dfrac{dB}{dR_2}}{\dfrac{dB}{dR_1}} = \frac{c_1 a_{02} + a_{12}}{1 - c_2 a_{02} - a_{22}} = \frac{p_2}{p_1}, \tag{4.12}$$

which is indeed equal to the relative price in equation 4.8. If, as in the present case, manufacturing uses no land, the direct land requirements have no influence on the price ratio; the indirect requirements are all that matters. Equation 4.12 can also be interpreted as the marginal rate of commodity substitution.

---

3. Brems 1978 offers an argument based on dimensionality.

5
François Quesnay

WITHIN ten years after the publication of Richard Cantillon's *Essai*, the circular flow of income, national accounting, and input-output became the talk of the fashionable salons. In the declining reign of Louis XV there was in Paris a group of reformist intellectuals who called themselves the "Economists." One of them, the Abbé Baudeau, said that the true economists are easily recognized, because they acknowledge one master, namely Dr. Quesnay, and one doctrine, namely that of the *Philosophie Rurale* and the *Analyse Economique*, they acknowledge classical treatises, namely *La Physiocratie*, and one formula, namely the *Tableau Economique*, and they have their jargon, just like the scholars of ancient China. After the classical treatise their contemporaries called this group the physiocrats. All of its fundamental ideas came from its master François Quesnay, one of the most original spirits in the history of economics.

Life

François Quesnay was born in 1694 in the village of Méré, about fifteen miles west of Versailles, where his father was a peasant and shopkeeper.[1] His ancestors, like those of John Maynard Keynes, had come from Normandy, and the similarity of their names gave rise to speculation about a genealogical link, but it seems to be unfounded. François, the eighth of thirteen children, received only the most elementary schooling but was a voracious reader.

At age seventeen, Quesnay decided to learn the trade of a surgeon. However, by the time he had progressed to bleeding, the instruction he got left him dissatisfied. He went to Paris and began an apprenticeship as an engraver. As part of his training he visited medical courses and clinics, and at the same time he studied anatomy, natural sciences, and philosophy. By 1716 he had completed his training not only as an engraver but also as a surgeon.

In 1717, Quesnay married the daughter of a Paris spice merchant. In the same year he passed the examinations as a master surgeon and opened a practice in Mantes, on the Seine below Paris. His wife died ten years later, and Quesnay did not remarry.

Gradually, Quesnay's reputation grew, and in 1735 he was called to Paris as physician to the Duke of Villeroy. At that time surgeons were not allowed to practice medicine, and their status was much inferior. Quesnay,

---

1. This section is mostly based on the biographical essay by Jacqueline Hecht in Sauvy 1958.

now secretary of the French Association of Surgeons, fought vehemently against this discrimination. In the end, however, he applied for a doctorate in medicine, which he obtained in 1744. He became a member of the French Academy of Sciences and a fellow of the Royal Society in London.

In 1749, Quesnay was appointed personal physician to Mme. de Pompadour, the intelligent and powerful mistress of Louis XV; he thenceforth lived in the palace of Versailles in a little suite not far from the marquise. Held in high esteem, he became one of the four consultant physicians to the king, and at one time he is said to have saved the life of the dauphin.

Quesnay also developed broad intellectual interests. He was close to the group around the *Encyclopédie*, which brought him in contact with men like d'Alembert, Buffon, Diderot, Helvétius, and Condillac, and he wrote several articles for the *Encyclopédie*, including one entitled "Farmers" and another, "Corn." He also became acquainted with the economic literature, including Cantillon's *Essai*, published in 1755, which had a decisive influence on his thinking.

Quesnay's ideas began to attract a group of disciples. With the characteristics so aptly described by Baudeau, the physiocrats were the first "school" of economics. Their adversaries, of which there were many, went farther and called them a sect; today they would call Quesnay a guru. Few, if any, other schools later achieved the same doctrinal unity, the early Marxists perhaps coming closest. From the point of view of scientific discovery, this is fortunate; good economists do not run in schools.

The first and foremost of the disciples was Victor de Riqueti, Marquis de Mirabeau (1715–89), celebrated author of *L'ami des hommes* and father of the revolutionary orator. Paul Pierre le Mercier de la Rivière, author of *L'ordre naturel et essentiel des sociétiés politiques* (1767), was important enough to be parodied as one of the "economystifiers" by Ferdinando Galiani (Kaplan 1979, 71) and to be satirized by Voltaire in *L'homme aux quarante écus*. Pierre Samuel Dupont, later called de Nemours after the district he represented in the Constituent Assembly, edited the two volumes of collected essays that became the classical treatise and also the party organ of the group, the *Ephémérides du Citoyen*.[2]

Closely associated with the group, though not belonging to it, were Vincent de Gournay and Anne Robert Jacques Turgot. One of the visitors in Versailles was Adam Smith. The physiocrats maintained a fervent missionary agitation, but in substance they added little to Quesnay's ideas, and after the productive years of the 1760s, the movement declined.

In the midst of the hectic crosscurrents, intrigues, and follies at the court of Louis XV, Quesnay must have been a pole of calm, honesty, and

---

2. A friend of Jefferson's, he emigrated under Napoleon to the United States, where his son established the powder mill that became the firm that still bears his name.

sagacity. Mostly through gifts from the Pompadour, he became quite wealthy and bought an estate. In his old age his interest drifted from economics to mathematics; he claimed to have solved the problems of the trisection of the angle and the squaring of the circle, which even his followers found embarrassing. After the accession of Louis XVI, he fell into disgrace and had to leave the palace. He died shortly after, in 1774.

Works

Quesnay's early writings were, naturally, on medical subjects like bleeding, suppuration, fevers, and gangrene. His first economic essay, the article "Farmers" in the *Encyclopédie*, appeared in 1756, when he was 62. His economic and philosophical contributions, as far as they were known at the time, were collected in 1888 by August Oncken; this edition is still the basic source. Additional writings are found in Sauvy 1958. English translations of important pieces were published by Ronald Meek (1962), who also provided an authoritative commentary.

The central piece of physiocratic analysis is the *Tableau Economique*, the most celebrated single page in the history of economics. Of all the celebrated pages it is also the most obscure, and it is precisely its obscurity that accounts for much of its fame. Growing out of Quesnay's efforts to convert Mirabeau, the table was probably first sketched in 1757.

It seems Quesnay also tried to use the *Tableau* to gain the king for his reformist ideas. The time was indeed ripe for reforms. French armies had been badly defeated by Frederick II, foreign trade suffered from naval warfare, manufactures stagnated, agriculture had long been in a desolate state, and the government was, once again, nearly bankrupt. It is reported that Quesnay, supported by the Pompadour, devised a plan to attract the king's interest through his boredom. To entertain him, they had a little *de luxe* printing shop installed in the palace where the king could amuse himself with typesetting. As manuscript, so the story goes, they gave him the *Tableau*, of which the king is said to have set about one-half before getting bored again.

The available facts about the early editions of the *Tableau* are set out in Kuczynski and Meek 1972. The earliest extant version is a three-page manuscript in Quesnay's handwriting, probably from 1758. The second edition was part of the material published in Quesnay 1894. A copy of the third edition, probably published in 1759, was rediscovered by Marguerite Kuczynski in the 1960s in a U.S. library founded by the Du Pont family. The general public was first acquainted with the *Tableau* through the 1759 edition of Mirabeau's *L'ami des hommes*, and in successive publications it underwent many modifications. Quesnay supplemented it with a set of explanatory notes and a number of policy maxims. The table, the notes, and the maxims constitute Quesnay's claim to fame.

The *Tableau Economique* as a Circular Flow

The *Tableau Economique*, most certainly derived from Cantillon, is an input-output model of the French economy as it would look with an efficient allocation of resources. It is intended to serve as a frame of reference for policy analysis inasmuch as the consequences of various measures and changes in data can be described as deviations from the basic table. Quesnay explained it thus in a letter to Mirabeau: "I have tried to construct a fundamental *Tableau* of the economic order for the purpose of displaying expenditure and products in a way which is easy to grasp, and for the purpose of forming a clear opinion about the organization and disorganization which the government can bring about" (Meek 1962, 108).

The outline of this model is most easily understood if it is represented as a circular flow diagram, which is identical to the exposition Quesnay called the formula except that the arrows are arranged in a triangle. There are three classes, namely the productive class, the sterile class, and the proprietary class or the landlords, including the government, the army, and the church. There are two industries, namely agriculture, in which the productive class is employed, and manufacturing, which gives employment to the sterile class. The landlords own the land, which they rent to the farmers as agricultural entrepreneurs. The rent income is spent partly for agricultural goods and partly for manufactures.

The productive class, consisting of farmer entrepreneurs and hired workers, produces food and raw materials, which are partly used inside agriculture, while the remainder is sold to the landlords and to the manufacturing sector. On the other hand, agriculture buys manufactures and pays rent to landlords.

The manufacturing sector, finally, buys food and raw material from agriculture and sells manufactures to both agriculture and landlords. The table does not show how the manufacturers obtain their own manufacturing products; it seems they get them from abroad in exchange for excess food.

The payment flows in this system are graphically represented in figure 5.1, where each arrow stands for 1,000 monetary units. The model is in equilibrium in the sense that receipts equal payments for each sector.

FIGURE 5.1

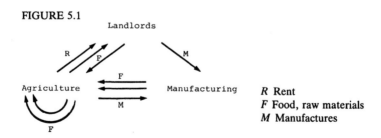

R Rent
F Food, raw materials
M Manufactures

Not at all content with an abstract specification of his model, Quesnay also tried to estimate the relevant magnitudes and relationships, thus extending the tradition of William Petty's "Political Arithmetick." This makes him, as Joseph Schumpeter rightly put it (1954, 209f.), an eighteenth-century econometrician.

The *Tableau Economique* as an Input-Output Table

For the modern economist it is natural to transform the circular flow diagram into an input-output table. Such an arrangement was proposed by Phillips (1955), but Meek (1960) and Maital (1972) pointed out that a closed input-output model, as used by Phillips, does not do justice to Quesnay's thinking; what is needed is an open model with land as the exogenous resource and landlord consumption as final demand.

Such a model would look like table 5.1. The physiocrats, like Cantillon, treated workers as reproducible at the subsistence wage. In a more explicit model, population could thus be exhibited as an "industry" like agriculture and manufacturing; an example was provided in the appendix to the chapter on Cantillon. In table 5.1, as in figure 5.1, workers are consolidated with the sector in which they are employed.

The first line of table 5.1 shows how the total agricultural output of 5,000 units is allocated to agriculture itself, to the manufacturing sector, and to landlord consumption. The second line provides the same information for manufacturing output (the zero was explained in the preceding section). The third line states that the landlords receive rent payments from agriculture in the amount of 2,000. Land thus appears in this table as the only ultimate resource. Its income, namely rent, is correspondingly the only "net product" in the sense that it exceeds reproduction costs (which are zero). All other factors earn just enough to reproduce themselves; their earnings represent gross income, not net income. For the economic philosophy of the physiocrats this doctrine of the *produit net* was of crucial importance.

Quesnay's aims went far beyond a mere statistical description. He wanted to *explain* the entries in the table, and thus the structure of the

TABLE 5.1

Output	Input		Final Demand	Receipts
	Agriculture	Manufacturing		
Agriculture	2,000	2,000	1,000	5,000
Manufacturing	1,000	0	1,000	2,000
Land (rent)	2,000	0		2,000
Cost	5,000	2,000	2,000	

economy, from the underlying technical and behavioral coefficients. Today this could be achieved by rewriting the three lines as

$$x_1 = a_{01}x_1 + (a_{02} + a_{12})x_2 + k_1 R \tag{5.1}$$

$$x_2 = a_{21}x_1 + k_2 R \tag{5.2}$$

$$B = b \, x_1 \tag{5.3}$$

where the coefficients have the following meanings and values:
a_{01} = 0.4   workers' food per unit of agricultural output;
a_{02} = 0.5   workers' food per unit of manufacturing output;
a_{12} = 0.5   raw material input per unit of manufacturing output;
a_{21} = 0.2   input of manufactures per unit of food output;
k_1 = 0.5   landlords' food consumption per unit of rent;
k_2 = 0.5   landlords' manufactures consumption per unit of rent; and
b = 1   land needed per unit of agricultural output.

This model can easily be solved to determine the structure of the economy for given land. If land is B = 5,000, the result is

$$x_1 = 5,000 \qquad x_2 = 2,000 \qquad R = 2,000,$$

just as in the circular flow diagram. By changing the appropriate parameters of the model, one can further determine the consequences of different changes in data or policies. This is the sort of application Quesnay had in mind.

The *Tableau Economique* as a Zigzag

Unfortunately, Quesnay did not possess the mathematical means to solve such problems directly. He was thus forced to grope for a roundabout approach. He believed he had found it in the zigzag. Like so many tortuous arguments in Karl Marx, Quesnay's zigzag graph must thus be interpreted (and excused) as an obsessive effort by an original and idiosyncratic mind to cope with problems for whose solution his fragmentary training had not equipped him. Technique without vision leads to tedium (and perhaps Ph.D. dissertations), but vision without technique leads to frustration.

The zigzag as used in Mirabeau is set out in figure 5.2. It describes what happens in a given year. At the beginning of the year, the landlords are in possession of last year's rent of 2,000, which they spend on food and manufactures in equal parts. For every unit of their sales, farmers pay one unit of rent, so that in the first period a rent arrow of 1,000 leads horizontally to the landlord column. For every unit of sales, agriculture also buys half a unit's worth of manufactures, but only in the following period; this results in the declining arrow from agriculture to manufacturing. On the other hand, the manufacturing sector needs half a unit of food for every unit of its output, again with a lag; this is expressed by the arrow declining from right to left. In this way the zigzag proceeds, the amounts

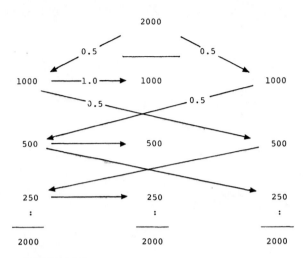

Agriculture   Landlords   Manufacturing

FIGURE 5.2

becoming progressively smaller. For each column, one thus obtains annual income or expenditure as the sum of a geometric series.

This representation suffers from evident defects, though. Above all, it is not clear what happens to the other half of manufacturing receipts; they seem to be "lost." Agriculture, on the other hand, seems to spend more than it earns, and its total output is only 2,000. This deficiency can be remedied by adding a horizontal arrow from manufacturing to agriculture representing payments for raw materials, as shown in figure 5.3. At the same time, rent payments are now two-thirds of total receipts of agriculture for both food and raw materials. The demand of agriculture for manufactured goods is similarly based on total output in the proportion of one-third. As a consequence of these modifications, the result of the zigzag corresponds to the input-output table and the circular flow diagram (but again own-consumption of agriculture is not shown).

The idea of the zigzag, therefore, is fairly clear. It consists in solving comparative-static multiplier problems by a dynamic period analysis, describing events in successive "rounds." In elementary Keynesian multiplier analysis this was a fairly workable device. In Quesnay's more complicated model the expedient did not (and, as Paul Samuelson [1966–86, vol. 5, ch. 343] has emphasized, could not) succeed. Nevertheless, the apparatus was used by Quesnay to analyze the comparative statics of policy changes such as the liberalization of corn exports and excise taxes, but, contrary to Quesnay's promise, it turned out to be extremely difficult to handle. No

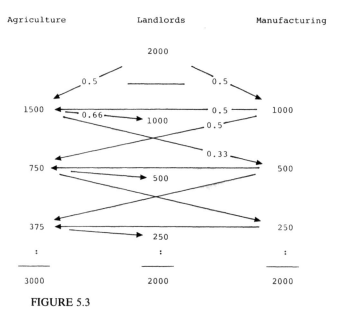

FIGURE 5.3

convincing theory of economic policy emerged, and after the appearance of the *Wealth of Nations*, no economist ever tried to use and perfect Quesnay's apparatus.

Capital

The preceding summary of the *Tableau Economique* abstracts from capital. In fact, capital played a crucial role in Quesnay's thinking. On the one hand, this marked a clear advance over Cantillon; on the other hand, it prepared the way for Turgot and Smith. The productivity of agriculture, for Quesnay, was largely a question of its being equipped with sufficient capital, which had to be accumulated by saving. His ideal farmer was an entrepreneur who uses capital-intensive methods, their paradigm being the horse-drawn plough (Quesnay 1888, 159–92).

Capital consists of "original advances" corresponding roughly to fixed capital, and "annual advances," consisting mostly of inventories. In the *Tableau*, agriculture needs annual advances of 2,000 and manufacturing needs 1,000; these advances are replaced from current production. The original advances of agriculture amount to 10,000, of which one-tenth has to be replaced each year. In modern technical language, Quesnay thus conceived his *Tableau* as a dynamic input-output system that includes capital coefficients. However, the problems of interest, waiting, and differences in capital intensities were far from being satisfactorily solved. By the

44

introduction of another primary factor of production besides land, these phenomena would have been incompatible with the underlying land theory of value. It remained for Quesnay's friend Turgot to abandon the assumption of fixed capital coefficients and thus to open the way for an explicit analysis of capital accumulation.

Policy Maxims

Quesnay supplemented his *Tableau* with thirty "General Maxims for the Economic Government of an Agricultural Kingdom." From the point of view of the history of economic science, the following four are of particular importance.

MAXIM III. "That the sovereign and the nation should never lose sight of the fact that the land is the unique source of wealth, and that it is agriculture which causes wealth to increase" (Meek 1962, 232). The same principle is also expressed in the explanatory notes to the *Tableau*: "Everything which is disadvantageous to agriculture is detrimental to the nation and the state, and everything which favours agriculture is profitable to the state and the nation" (160). More precisely, the general interest is identified with the interest of agricultural entrepreneurs, particularly in large-scale farming, which Quesnay regards as much more efficient than small peasants.

This notion seems to have different roots. First, we note that Quesnay came from a peasant family and that he later became a landowner himself. Second, Colbert's mercantilist policies had favored manufacturing at the expense of agriculture, which had long suffered from neglect. In the second half of the eighteenth century, a reaction in favor of agriculture was generally in the air. This was the time of Rousseau, of the "back to nature" movement and pastoral fashions, when duchesses dressed up as dairy maids. Third, the *Tableau Economique* exhibits land as the only ultimate factor of production, all other inputs being reducible to land. Land appears as the only productive factor in the sense that its return exceeds its cost (which is zero), while all other factors are sterile inasmuch as they earn only what they cost. This was one of the cases in which theoretical analysis seemed to give strong support to clear-cut policy rules.

In fact, of course, it did not. From the fact that land appeared in the *Tableau* as the only ultimate resource, it does not follow that agriculture is more significant for national wealth than manufacturing or anything else. Specifically, a technical improvement in manufacturing has, in the context of the *Tableau*, the same sort of effect on real output as an improvement in agriculture. The *Tableau*, as an analytical device, therefore lends no support to the physiocratic predilection for agriculture, no matter how necessary agricultural reform may have been for other reasons.

MAXIM V. "That taxes . . . should be laid directly on the net product of landed property, and not on men's wages, or on produce, where they would increase the costs of collection, operate to the detriment of trade, and destroy every year a portion of the nations's wealth" (Meek 1962, 232). In other words: All the innumerable taxes of that time should be consolidated into a single tax on *rents*.

With this postulate, Quesnay revived the idea of Pierre de Boisguilbert and Sébastien de Vauban, Marshal of France, but, instead of being based on sound intuition only, it was now brilliantly derived from economic analysis. The *Tableau* clearly showed that, regardless of how a given amount of taxes was levied, it would ultimately be borne by the landlords. Clearly, if workers and entrepreneurs, under the pressure of competition, always end up by just covering their subsistence needs, there is no effective way to tax them.

It may be objected that if, within the framework of the *Tableau*, other taxes can be no better than a single rent tax, by the same token they are no worse. At this point, Quesnay clearly appealed to considerations outside the scope of the *Tableau*, namely primarily collection costs and also deadweight losses through price distortions. The idea that land taxes minimize distortions remained alive throughout the nineteenth century.

MAXIM VII. "That the whole of the sum of revenue should come back into the annual circulation, and run through it to the full extent of its course; and that it should never be formed into monetary fortunes, or at least that those which are formed should be counterbalanced by those which come back into circulation" (Meek 1962, 233). Otherwise production, profits, employment, consumption, and fiscal revenues would decline.

Here we hear the echo of mercantilism, but the maxim also foreshadows the classical insights into the potentially serious (though temporary) effects of hoarding, the Malthusian concern about effective demand and the notions of John Maynard Keynes.

MAXIM XXV. "That complete freedom of trade should be maintained; for the policy for internal and external trade which is the most secure, the most correct, and the most profitable for the nation and the state, consists in full freedom of competition" (Meek 1962, 237). This was summarized in the slogan "Laissez faire, laissez passer." Its first part, according to Oncken, was coined by the Marquis René Louis d'Argenson, and the second part was added by Vincent de Gournay, both precursors of the physiocrats, but similar expressions are already found in Boisguilbert. With this maxim the physiocrats made themselves vehement protagonists of economic liberalism.

Place in the History of Economics

Assessments of Quesnay's contribution to economics vary from nearly infinity to hardly more than zero. For the physiocrats their master's words were gospel. Mirabeau, man of big words, counted the *Tableau Economique* among the three greatest inventions of mankind, the others being writing and money. For adversaries such as Voltaire and Galiani, Quesnay was a target of ridicule.

While these adversaries made fun of Quesnay's idiosyncrasy, they made no effort to understand his message. What is worse, even the disciples had trouble understanding the *Tableau*. Its direct influence, therefore, was negligible. It must have had a certain influence on Adam Smith, who knew and respected the physiocrats, but in the *Wealth of Nations* he only criticizes their doctrine of the exclusive productivity of agriculture without making use of their analytical apparatus. The only nineteenth-century economist who took the *Tableau* seriously was Karl Marx. For him, who got embroiled in similar two-sector problems, it was an inspiration, and in *Theories of Surplus-Value* (Marx 1905–10; 1963, part 1, 334) he called it "an extremely brilliant conception, incontestably the most brilliant for which political economy had up to then been responsible."

If the physiocrats were influential, it was not through their economic theory but through their fervent championship of laissez faire and the key role of agriculture. In France they contributed to the temporary liberalization of the corn trade from 1764 to 1770 and briefly again under Turgot. The physiocrats also maintained an extensive network of international contacts. Mercier de la Rivière was called to the court of Saint Petersburg by Catherine II. Margrave Carl Friedrich of Baden and others spread physiocracy in Germany, Isaac Iselin was active in Basel, and in Bern an Economic Society pioneered agricultural innovations and sponsored an essay contest in which Mirabeau won an honorable mention.

Among modern economists opinions about Quesnay's *Tableau* diverge hardly less than among the contemporaries. Alexander Gray (1963, 93) and Paul A. Samuelson (1966–86, 5:653) agree that it is only a footnote in the history of economic thought, and Gray calls it a "vast mystification." Schumpeter, on the other hand, regarded Quesnay as a giant "to whom all economists look up as one of the greatest figures of their science," and he even added that he knew no dissenters (1954, 223). Wassily Leontief presented his input-output model as an attempt to provide an empirical implementation of the *Tableau Economique* (1951, 9).

The divergence of views may be largely explained by the fact that Quesnay tried to move economic science along a different track than was actually taken by mainstream economics. Already in Cantillon the theory of value provides the core of economic analysis, and Adam Smith fixed it in this place for (at least) two centuries. Quesnay, on the other hand, developed Cantillon's multisectoral model without using value theory as its core. As a consequence, the *Tableau* was left in a dead-end street in the history of science. Marx's efforts to combine the two approaches were not successful.

It remained for Léon Walras to reunite an explicit model of the circular flow with value theory, and it remained for national income statistics to provide an accounting framework. Quesnay was more than a century ahead of his time. In one sense, this meant scientific failure; this is what Samuelson expressed. In another sense, to have constructed the first explicit structural model of a multisector economy with empirical estimates of the relevant parameters was a brilliant achievement.

6
Money: The Emergence of the Classical Tradition

RICHARD CANTILLON, the founder of the classical tradition of monetary theory, confined his attention to commodity money. Even before Cantillon wrote his *Essai*, John Law had already begun to spread the gospel of paper money. His catastrophe left a lasting imprint on subsequent monetary theory. Around the middle of the eighteenth century, David Hume added important building blocks by analyzing the long-run neutrality of money, its short-run nonneutrality, and its automatic international distribution. Shortly afterward, the Swedish experience with paper money led Pehr Niclas Christiernin to what seems to be the first statement of a full-fledged quantity theory of prices and of the purchasing power parity proposition.

At the time when Adam Smith was writing his *Wealth of Nations*, therefore, the basic propositions of the classical monetary tradition had been articulated, both for commodity money and for fiat money. The sequence of events from a monetary disturbance to the final equilibrium had become visible at least in outline, and for fiat money the final equilibrium was seen to imply the quantity theory of prices and purchasing power parity.

John Law

John Law of Lauriston (1671–1729), though a mercantilist, became influential for classical monetary theory in two respects, namely (1) by being the first to assign paper money an important economic role, and (2) by providing a dramatic example for the disasters that may result from the failure to have a correct understanding of this role.

Law was the son of a reputable banker in Edinburgh with aristocratic connections. He studied economic and financial affairs, but without going to a university. In 1694 he had the misfortune to be sentenced to death for having killed his adversary in a duel. He was thus forced to live abroad, traveling widely (he was pardoned in 1717). He lived with another man's wife, whom he introduced as Mrs. Law and who bore his children. He was well read in economic affairs, a colorful man of the world with the gift of persuasion.

Law composed numerous bank projects with which he tried to gain the ear of princes and governments in Scotland, France, and Savoy. Their common basis was the thoroughly mercantilist notion that the wealth, prosperity, and power of a country depend on its money supply; he was a genuine monetarist (whereas modern "monetarists" are quite the opposite). Law's specific point was that money might just as well be made of paper as of gold or silver. He represents "paper mercantilism." His principal work, published in 1705, is *Money and Trade Considered, with a Proposal for Supplying the Nation with Money*. His collected writings were edited by Harsin and published in three volumes in 1934.

Law's main argument may be summarized as follows. The point of departure is a quantity theory for real output: "Domestick trade depends on the money. A greater quantity employs more people than a lesser quantity. A limited sum can only set a number of people to work proportioned to it" (Law 1750, 20). In this crude formulation, this presupposes that prices and the velocity of circulation are constant, which does not do full justice to Law's thinking, but the inaccuracy is minor.[1] The economy gains from the added employment even though the employer may suffer losses (23), which is the familiar argument for pyramid building.

The money supply can be increased by devaluation, debasement, prohibition of gold exports, or regulation of foreign trade, but "the use of banks has been the best method yet practised for the increase of money" (Law 1750, 64). Bank notes should not be based on silver or gold, because (1) the precious metals are subject to the risk of devaluation, and (2) their value fluctuates with supply and demand (114f.). Law, the prophet of a managed currency, thus argues that paper money, if properly managed, may be given a more constant value than commodity money; this has remained the basic argument for fiat money to the present day. Law adds that bank notes also have an advantage from the point of view of transactions and storage costs.

It is clear, however, that a mismanaged paper currency will be much less stable than commodity money. What sort of management does Law thus propose? His solution is a paper money backed by land (Law 1750, 157f.). It should be issued by a banking commission by making mortgage loans at the current rate of interest with land serving as collateral and also by buying land outright. Within four months any other money should cease

1. According to Viner (1937, 37f.), William Potter argued in 1650 that output grows even more rapidly than money because the velocity of circulation increases.

to serve as means of payment. Law assured his readers that this paper money, since land has the most stable value, would have all the advantages of silver money and none of its disadvantages. In particular, the quantity in circulation would automatically adjust to the demand for it, and its value would therefore be stable (166f.).

This is where Law committed his fundamental error. Under a gold standard, the money supply is linked to a physical quantity, inasmuch as thirty-five dollars, say, can be obtained for one ounce of gold. Under Law's scheme, on the other hand, the money supply is linked to a nominal value, inasmuch as one thousand dollars, say, can be obtained for one thousand dollars' worth of land at the going land prices. This means that there is no effective limit to the money supply. Whenever land prices rise, the potential money supply rises in proportion, which results in a further increase in land prices, and so on. The decisive factor in such a fiat money system is the interest rate at which the banking commission is willing to lend. If this rate is low, the money supply and prices will rise without limit. If the rate is high, there will be deflation. The land backing of money does not provide a brake at all.[2]

Law's early projects came to naught, but the fundamental flaw in his monetary theory was not identified. France finally gave him the opportunity for an experiment on the grandest scale. When Louis XIV died in 1715, the country was in a desperate state; the government was bankrupt and the economy depressed. In this situation the regent, Philippe d'Orléans, governing for Louis XV, turned to Law. It was like the parents of a sick child, after legitimate doctors have left no hope, finally putting their faith in a quack.

In 1716, Law began by establishing the Banque Générale.[3] Though the regent was a shareholder, it was at first a private bank, which engaged in traditional banking business. In the following year, Law also organized a colonial enterprise, the Company of Louisiana and the Occident, commonly called the Mississippi Company. It owned more than half of the territory that is now the continental United States excluding Alaska, it also owned lucrative domestic monopolies, and it soon expanded to Africa and the East. In 1719 the bank, now nationalized as the Banque Royale, was practically merged with the Mississippi Company, and the conglomerate acquired the general tax farming privilege and most of the government mints. The economy began to prosper. In 1720, Law became Catholic, at least officially, and minister of finance. He later described himself as the

---

2. The same fundamental error reemerged later in the form of the "real bills doctrine," according to which (at least in its crude form) money is self-regulating if it is issued in discounting bills based on real commodities.

3. Authoritative accounts of subsequent events can be found in Hamilton 1936 and Lüthy 1961.

most powerful uncrowned person Europe had ever seen. In the same year, Law's "system" collapsed, and in December he had to leave France. He lived out his days as an impoverished gambler in Venice, forever justifying his system. What had gone wrong?

From the beginning, and in accordance with Law's conception, the bank had been aggressive in issuing notes, but there was an economic need for them, and initially they were fully convertible into silver. The Mississippi Company then engaged in a grandiose conversion of government debt by buying back obligations with its own bank notes, thus monetizing the public debt. At the same time there developed a speculative boom in Mississippi shares, which engulfed all of Europe (its British counterpart was the South Sea Bubble). The bank helped to inflate the bubble by giving margin loans to speculators with its own shares as collateral. Share prices rose about fiftyfold in two years. People even speculated in tickets for the stagecoach that took speculators to Paris.

All seemed to go well until, in the spring of 1720, the bank declared a dividend that disappointed the speculators. Share prices peaked. To prevent a further decline, Law now offered to buy the bank's own shares at a price of 9,000 *livres*. This amounted to a gigantic monetization of shares. Commodity prices began to rise, doubling in about a year. Monetary expansion resulted in inflation. Efforts to stop the monetization process led to panic. By October the bank notes were worthless. This was the first financial crisis that drew all of Europe into its vortex.

John Law was neither a swindler, as was often said, nor a genius, as Schumpeter maintained. He was an adventurer who had grasped the potential advantage of fiat money without having the economic understanding to make this insight useful. His disastrous experiment nevertheless had a lasting influence on economic science. In particular, it taught two important lessons. First, it became clear that the stimulating effect of monetary expansion on output and employment, so dear to the mercantilists, is only temporary. What is left in the end is inflation. Classical and neoclassical economics never forgot this lesson. It briefly seemed to fade into oblivion in the post-Keynesian period, when respected economists believed that "a little inflation always helps." Those who remembered John Law did not need "monetarism" to remind them of the fallacy involved.

Second, Law's experiment demonstrated that securities and bank notes are not perfect substitutes. Law had assumed that an exchange of securities for bank notes, since it leaves total financial assets unchanged, would make no essential difference except in reducing the government's tax burden. On this assumption he engaged in open-market operations on a grand scale. The result showed that money is essentially different from debt and that open-market operations thus can produce inflation. Overall, John Law is the paradigm of an economist who provided important building blocks for his science precisely by his errors.

David Hume

David Hume belongs to the history of philosophy more than of economics. Perhaps his most influential, though unspecific, contribution to economics was his vision of moral philosophy as an empirical science of man in his social, political, and economic environment, based on historical experience. His more specific contributions to economic analysis were of a relatively minor order. Hume knew less about economic matters than many contemporaries and predecessors, he was not widely read in economics, and his mind was better at analyzing problems of a qualitative than of a quantitiative nature. Nevertheless, he started an analytical line of thought that became an important part of mainstream economics.

David Hume was born in Edinburgh on 26 April 1711, the third child of a country gentleman and advocate in comfortable circumstances (for a biography see Mossner 1954). His father died early, and his mother had to raise her children on the limited income of the family estate. First educated at home, David, at age twelve, went to the University of Edinburgh for two or three years of classics without obtaining a degree. It was decided that he should become a lawyer, but after about three years of halfhearted efforts, Hume decided to seek fame as a writer, scholar, and philosopher. The intense creative struggle that followed was accompanied by nervous crises. After a brief and frustrating experience in a merchant's office in Bristol, Hume went to France, where *A Treatise of Human Nature* (published in 1739–40) was finally written. Though his first book was later judged also to be his greatest, the reception was disappointing. His *Essays Moral and Political* (published in 1741–42), better suited to the popular taste, were more successful but still did not provide Hume with enough income for his life as a scholar. His effort to obtain a professorship at Edinburgh having failed, Hume improved his finances (and widened his experience) by acting as companion and tutor to the mad Marquess of Annandale and by serving as secretary to General James Sinclair during a ridiculous invasion of the French coast and on missions to Vienna and Turin. He subsequently tried, also without success, for a professorship at the University of Glasgow. Hume's works now poured forth in rapid succession. The *Political Discourses* (published in 1752) were an immediate success, the *History of England* (published 1754–62) established his fame as a historian, and in 1762 Boswell could describe him as the "greatest writer in Britain." Hume had achieved his ambition.

In 1752 the Faculty of Advocates of Edinburgh appointed Hume as its librarian, which gained him not much income but access to a large library. In 1763, as a secretary of the British embassy in Paris, he became a great success in the salons, not only with the philosophers but also with the ladies. Returning to London in 1766, he brought with him Jean-Jacques Rousseau, but his efforts to find a refuge for his paranoid friend only provoked bitter accusations. In 1769, after two years as undersecretary at the Foreign Office, Hume finally settled in Edinburgh, where he died, after a long illness from an intestinal disorder, in 1776. His friend Adam Smith considered him "as approaching as nearly to the idea of a perfectly wise and virtuous man, as perhaps the nature of human frailty will permit."

Hume's specific contributions to the history of economics are found in the *Political Discourses* (1875), in which the important essays are those on money, interest, and the balance of trade. They may be described under the headings of the long-run neutrality of money, its short-run nonneutrality, and the specie flow mechanism. The economic writings were collected in Hume 1955.

THE LONG-RUN NEUTRALITY OF MONEY. At the time of David Hume, economists had a fairly good understanding of the dual nature of gold coins, on the one hand as costly pieces of metal, on the other as a means of payment. They had known for centuries that the value of such coins was, in the last analysis, determined by production costs and that their quantity was endogenously determined by demand and supply. They also understood that gold discoveries, by lowering the production costs of gold, would result in higher prices. They realized, furthermore, that an increase in the quantity of money would thus be associated with inflation, but not necessarily in exact proportion.

Hume did not add to this body of accumulated knowledge; in a way, he rather subtracted from it. His knowledge of financial affairs was quite limited compared to experts such as Cantillon, and the power of his intellect was more effective in stripping arguments to what he regarded as their bare essentials than in developing new lines of analysis. In monetary theory he was influential mainly as a simplifier.

The main simplification was that the commodity aspects of money were dropped into the background. Supply was treated as if it were exogenously given; demand was left in possession of the field. The only function of money was to serve as a means of payment. "Money is not," Hume wrote, "properly speaking, one of the subjects of commerce; but only the instrument which men have agreed upon to facilitate the exchange of one commodity for another" (1875, 1:309). Money has "chiefly a fictitious value," which arises "from the agreement and convention of men" and not from the cost of production (321).

As a consequence, money became neutral in the sense that a change in its quantity could affect nothing but the price level, and this effect was proportional. For a closed economy "it is evident, that the greater or less plenty of money is of no consequence; since the prices of commodities are always proportioned to the plenty of money" (Hume 1875, 1:309). "Where coin is in greater plenty . . . it can have no effect, either good or bad . . . any more than it would make an alteration on a merchant's books, if, instead of the ARABIAN method of notation, which requires few characters, he should make use of the ROMAN, which requires a great many" (312).

This immediately raised one of the conundrums of monetary theory. If money was really neutral, it could not contribute to the wealth of an economy, and yet it was generally accepted that monetary exchange was, as a rule, vastly superior to barter. Hume already disposed of this problem by the expedient used later by John Stuart Mill and a long chain of more modern writers, namely, by metaphor. Money, he said, "is none of the wheels of trade: It is the oil which renders the motion of the wheels more smooth and easy" (Hume 1875, 1:309). The further discussion of this lubricating function leads to suggestive hints about transactions costs (315f.).

In an open economy gold coins could also be useful as a store of value to pay for mercenaries, foreign wars, and subsidies to allies; with this any mercantilist could have agreed. Hume even expresses doubts about the usefulness of paper money because it diminishes the amount of gold a nation would attract. The damage could be reduced, Hume thought, if the banks kept 100 percent gold reserves against their bank notes.

If Hume had envisaged a pure paper currency costlessly supplied by the government, his analysis would have been a clear advance, supplementing the traditional case of commodity money by the polar case of fiat money. Hume did not do this. Instead he treated commodity money *as if* if were fiat money. His contribution, therefore, was ambivalent. On the positive side, he provided some of the basic building blocks of what became the theory of fiat money. On the negative side, he obscured the difference between commodity money and fiat money, thus initiating a long history of misunderstandings that plagued monetary theory and policy far into the twentieth century.

THE SHORT-RUN NONNEUTRALITY OF MONEY. It was commonly accepted in Hume's time that the real effects of money are much stronger in the short run than in the long run. In Hume's analysis this valid insight was sharpened into the proposition that money has powerful effects on output and employment in the short run but none in the long run. In the long run, the whole effect would exhaust itself in neutral price increases (Hume 1875, 1:312–15, 320–22). With this proposition, Hume provided one of the cornerstones of mainstream macroeconomics.

The short-run effects of money, Hume argued, are due to the inertia of prices. Alterations in the quantity of money "are not immediately attended with proportionable alterations in the price of commodities. There is always an interval before matters be adjusted to their new situation; and this interval is as pernicious to industry, when gold and silver are diminishing, as it is advantageous when these metals are encreasing" (Hume 1875, 1:315). Hume thought that this interval was actually quite long, apparently lasting several years (314). Classical economists were far from believing that monetary policy was ineffective also in the short run.

Hume even provided some "micro foundations" for the short-run output effects (1875, 1:313f.). The basic element is a distribution effect inasmuch as additional money is concentrated at first in the hands of a few merchants. It is the process of its gradual dispersion that stimulates industry. Another element is the notion that increases in prices have to be triggered by declines in inventories and that increases in wages are called forth by increases in employment. These hints are not clearly worked out, of course, and they do not go beyond Cantillon. They suggest, however, that it was inventories, both of commodities and of unemployed labor, that were supposed to provide the essential transmission mechanism from money to prices.

THE SPECIE FLOW MECHANISM. Hume's best-known contribution to monetary theory is his articulate description of the self-regulation of gold stocks through the specie flow mechanism (1875, 1:330–36). Suppose four-fifths of a nation's stock of gold coins were miraculously annihilated overnight. In a closed economy, Hume argues, prices would fall to one-fifth. In open economies, however, domestic prices cannot differ significantly from foreign prices because of commodity arbitrage. As a consequence, it is the gold stocks that have to adjust through an inflow of gold from abroad in payment for temporary export surpluses. The international distribution of precious metals, therefore, appears as entirely demand determined. Whichever nation has a higher demand for real cash balances, be it for trading or for hoarding, will obtain a higher share of world gold. This must have been one of the first explicit descriptions of an automatic feedback control mechanism in the history of science. Cantillon had described the same mechanism, to be sure, years before Hume, but his *Essai* was only published three years after Hume's *Political Discourses*.

Hume's model is usually called the price–specie flow mechanism. This reflects the notion that it assigns a crucial role to differences between domestic and foreign prices. This interpretation was open to the well-known objection that, in reality, the mechanism would work even if perfect commodity arbitrage prevented any international price differential from emerging. The stage was thus set for the two-centuries-long scientific controversy about the nature of the relevant price differential and possible "forgotten factors." Adam Smith, in explaining the specie flow mechanism in the *Wealth of Nations*, made no reference to his friend Hume, though he had earlier mentioned him in his *Lectures on Jurisprudence* of 1766 (Smith 1976–83, 5:507). Viner called this one of the mysteries of the history of economic thought (1937, 87). It may be conjectured that one reason was precisely the realization that Hume's exposition was misleading in that it directed too much attention to international price differentials. (Another possible reason may have been the knowledge that others had described the mechanism before Hume.)

At the level of economic substance, Hume did not assign to such differentials a crucial role. His example of a parallel reduction of the gold stock and prices was intended as a *reductio ad absurdum* of the notion that significant price differentials for internationally traded goods could persist for any length of time. It was precisely this impossibility that made specie flows inevitable. Hume (1875, 1:334) realized, of course, that trade impediments and transport costs could insert a wedge between national prices.

Gold was, for Hume, like water in two communicating vessels that rapidly finds the same level. If the connections are wide enough, the transitory differences will be infinitesimal. Hume's expression of money everywhere maintaining its proper level clearly means that the ratio between the stock of money and the demand for real cash balances must everywhere be the same; but that ratio is simply the price level (if prices are expressed in coins with the same gold content). The economic substance of Hume's argument, therefore, though not innovative, was more solid than was often supposed. His exposition, however, though effective, was more misleading than Cantillon's or Smith's.

Overall, Hume pulled a switch that led from the track of commodity money to the parallel track of inconvertible paper money. However, he still expressed his argument in terms of commodity money and convertible notes, thus confusing the basic differences between the two sets of problems.

Pehr Niclas Christiernin

The Swedish economist Pehr Niclas Christiernin (1725–99) was discovered for English-speaking readers by Robert V. Eagly (1963) in the early 1960s. Eagly also published a partial translation of Christiernin's work (1971). These selections show convincingly that Christiernin made contributions to the theory of money that are not inferior to those of Hume, Smith, and Ricardo. Though they left no trace in the subsequent literature, they may be the first clear expression of ideas that became important building blocks of economic analysis.

The son of a Protestant clergyman, Christiernin registered at the University of Uppsala at the age of eight.[4] After studies in philosophy, theology, mathematics, and physics, he obtained a master of arts degree. In the first part of his academic career he was a professor of law and political economy at Uppsala. The *Lectures on the High Price of Foreign Exchange in Sweden*, published in 1761, are his claim to a place in the history of

---

4. A detailed biographical essay by B. Boëthius can be found in the *Svenskt Biografiskt Lexikon* (Stockholm: Albert Bonniers, 1929), 8:474–90.

economics. Despite the controversy surrounding his views, he was awarded a doctorate of jurisprudence in 1763.

Christiernin did not regard economics as his true calling, however. In 1771 he switched faculties to become a professor of philosophy. As a matter of fact, he became at least as much a theologian as a philosopher. In particular, he made himself a vocal opponent of Kant. Eventually he was ordained and became a church dignitary.

Christiernin was strong-willed, opinionated, and pugnacious in everything he did. As an economist he battled his colleagues and the government. As a philosopher and rector he battled unruly students. At the same time, he was a man of talent, dedication, and learning, widely read in the literature of his time, and endowed with the gift of clear thinking and writing. That his career did not quite match his gifts was due to his provocative temper.

The historical context of Christiernin's contribution to economics is well described by Eagly. At the time Christiernin gave his lectures, Sweden had an inconvertible currency and floating exchange rates. An expansionary monetary policy had driven up domestic prices, and the exchange rate stood far above the gold parity. In the Riksdag there were two parties, the Hats and the Caps. The Hats, who then were the ruling party, were in favor of vigorous promotion of industry through an expansionary credit policy. Their program was paper money mercantilism along the lines of John Law. Inflation, in their view, was a consequence of the trade deficit. The Caps were, by and large, the laissez-faire party. They attributed inflation and exchange depreciation to the excessive issue of paper money and were in favor of deflation back to the old gold parity. The issues, therefore, were essentially the same as later in the English bullionist controversy.

In this debate, Christiernin, though coming from the side of the Hats, accepted the diagnosis of the Caps, but he warned against their proposed therapy, which, he argued, would lead to depression. Instead he advocated the stabilization of prices at close to their current level by a gradual return to a noninflationary monetary policy. This is essentially the position later taken by Henry Thornton. In support of these views, Christiernin developed the first clear theory of monetary policy and foreign exchange for a fiat currency.

For the first time, monetary theory is presented for the polar cases of a gold standard with endogenous money supplies and a fiat currency with floating exchange rates. On commodity money, Christiernin did not go beyond predecessors such as Cantillon, whom he knew, but he seems to have been the first to develop essentially the modern theory of paper money. Elements of this theory could already be found in the writings of John Law, but Law, as a good mercantilist, did not look beyond the short run whereas Christiernin embedded the transitory phenomena in a long-run analysis. Elements of Christiernin's theory can also be found in Hume, whom he also knew, but they are misleadingly derived from mental experiments for a commodity money.

Christiernin's main propositions, familiar as they are today, can be briefly summarized as follows: For an inconvertible paper currency the quantity theory of money is valid in the long run. "The price of all goods is in proportion to the circulating money supply and its faster or slower velocity" (Eagly 1971, 95), and "general high prices that affect all products . . . cannot be caused by other than the increase in the money supply" (65). If, through a reduction in interest rates, the supply of bank notes is doubled, "the effect must be the same as if the face value of each bank note was doubled" (76). Some people may confuse an increase in nominal wealth with an increase in real wealth, but no misconception could be more unfounded than this (in modern terminology) money illusion (53). In the long run fiat money is neutral.

The quantity theory of money also applies to the price of foreign exchange (Eagly 1971, 65, 75). In the long run, therefore, exchange rates reflect the effects of money on commodity prices (76). This is the principle of purchasing power parity. In the trivial form of the law of one price for costlessly traded goods (such as, approximately, gold), this had long been commonplace; its validity could be directly experienced by any merchant or banker regardless of his analytical acumen. In the more interesting form of a comparative-static proposition for fiat money, Christiernin seems to have no known forerunners. His formulation is actually superior to many modern ones inasmuch as the causal chain runs not from prices to exchange rates but from money to both prices and exchange rates.

Marjorie Grice-Hutchinson (1952, 1978) claimed that the purchasing power parity principle was formulated already in the sixteenth century by the scholars of Salamanca. This claim was strongly endorsed by Lawrence Officer (1982b). However, the texts on which these claims are based have, in fact, nothing to do with purchasing power parity. Relating to metallic currencies, they explain international deviations from the law of one price in terms of transport and transactions costs. Their high point is the insight, more or less clearly perceived, that the sign of these deviations depends on the direction of the gold and commodity flows. If there are net gold flows from Spain to Flanders in exchange for goods, the Spanish exchanges on Flanders tend to be at a discount while the Flemish exchanges on Spain are at a premium. At the same time, goods will be more expensive in Spain. This is sound economics, but it is a far cry from the proposition that changes in the exchange rate between inconvertible currencies correspond to the relative changes in price levels. The latter insight had to wait for inconvertibility as experienced in Sweden at the time of Christiernin.

Though changes in the money supply are neutral in the long run, they cause serious disturbances in the short run. Inflation produces temporary prosperity. Real estate prices are the first to rise (Eagly 1971, 73). Since wages are sticky, manufacturers profit. However, "continuous inflation gives rise to uncertainty in commerce and causes disturbances which hinder trade and industry" (96). Debtors gain at the expense of creditors (88). Receivers of fixed incomes see their real income decline. (Taxes, so Christiernin suggests, could be indexed by expressing them in wage units [97].) The future course of prices becomes more uncertain. For these reasons, further inflation should be prevented.

Deflation, on the other hand, would be even more disruptive. It would, at one blow, destroy the current prosperity (Eagly 1971, 89f.). Since different prices are unequally flexible, the structure of relative prices would be disturbed. Inventories would accumulate, money would be hoarded, investments would be postponed, and many workers would be unemployed. Since prices are even more rigid downward than upward, the losses of employment would exceed the earlier gains.[5] The situation of debtors, including the government, would become critical. A financial panic would shock the economy like an electric jolt.

Christiernin's policy prescription is "to prevent further changes in the value content of the monetary unit" (Eagly 1971, 96), in other words, a policy of price stability. If, in view of the lag in price adjustments, recent additions to the money supply are not yet reflected in prices, they should be neutralized by open-market sales of government securities by the central bank.

In the acrimonious controversy that these arguments provoked, Christiernin defended himself quite effectively. Sweden's policy makers, however, did not follow his wise advice. When the Caps came to power in 1765, they undertook to restore the pre-1745 gold parity, which implied cutting prices roughly in half. Four years later, the consequent depression brought the Hats to power again. After a period of political seesaw, a coup d'état replaced parliamentary government by an absolute monarchy. Convertibility was restored at existing prices in 1777. These events, as described by Eagly, are mentioned here because they suggest parallels in the following two centuries. Christiernin would clearly have been a leading figure in the bullionist debates of 1810 and again in the controversies of the interwar period when Keynes wrote, in vain, his *Essays in Persuasion*.

5. Eagly calls Christiernin "uniquely Keynesian" in this respect (1963, 629). It would be historically more accurate to call Keynes classical, because the classical tradition, of which Christiernin provides one example, was precisely to explain unemployment by price and wage rigidities.

7

Adam Smith

AROUND the middle of the eighteenth century, despite a voluminous literature of tracts and treatises, there was no discipline called political economy. The expression had been used in French by Antoyne de Mont-chrétien, as was noted in chapter 3, but the first to write a systematic treatise on the "Principles of Political Economy" was James Steuart in 1767. Though he thus created the new discipline in name, he did not create it in fact. Despite occasional praise, his book was soon forgotten, and with good reason.[1] Political economy was established as a discipline nine years later, in the same year, 1776, in which James Watt built the first steam engine and the American colonies declared their independence from the British crown. This was the work of Adam Smith.

Life

Smith was born 1723 in Kirkcaldy, a small town with a seaport about seven miles from Edinburgh.[2] His father was a solicitor, who became clerk of the Court Martial in Scotland and comptroller of customs, but he died before his first child was born. Adam Smith was thus raised by his mother, who also came from a respected and wealthy family, and to whom he remained closely attached for the rest of her long life. He seems to have been a sickly child, possessed by a passion for books, but well beloved by his schoolmates for his friendly and generous personality. It is reported that he used to speak to himself, and his absent-mindedness was the subject of many anecdotes throughout his life.

At the age of fourteen, in 1737, Adam Smith moved from the local grammar school to the University of Glasgow, at that time one of the leading British universities. He studied moral philosophy, ethics, mathematics, natural law, and political economy. A particularly strong influence on him was that of Francis Hutcheson, professor of moral philosophy, a social rationalist who originated the phrase *greatest happiness of the greatest number*.

Scholastic excellence earned Adam Smith a scholarship to Oxford, where he went in 1740. In contrast to Glasgow, Oxford was then a place of intellectual stagnation. The unhappy experience later supplied Smith

---

1. Schumpeter managed, characteristically, to call it a book of first-rate importance and simultaneously to doubt (except with respect to population) whether it contained any wheat among the chaff (1954, 176).
2. The classical biography is by John Rae (1965), not to be confused with the capital theorist. For recent studies see West 1976, Recktenwald 1976, and Campbell and Skinner 1982.

with vivid examples of the corrupting influence of faulty incentives and lack of competition. He read the Greek and Latin classics, learned foreign languages, and acquired an extensive knowledge of literature and philosophy. Abandoning the plan to enter the ministry, he left Oxford after six years and before the expiration of his scholarship.

Returning to Kirkcaldy in 1746, Smith hoped to obtain a post as a tutor but could not find one. A turn in his fortunes came two years later when he was invited to give a series of lectures in Edinburgh. He turned out to be a successful lecturer and also earned a good income. Within a few years, his renown was such that in 1751 he was elected to a professorship at Glasgow, first in logic and later in moral philosophy, where his duties included lectures on rhetoric, literature, ethics, jurisprudence, and political economy. The publication of *The Theory of Moral Sentiments* made him one of the luminaries of his university. He also became a close friend of David Hume. This was a happy and productive period in his life.

In 1764, Smith resigned his professorship to accompany the young Duke of Buccleuch as tutor on a trip to France. By so doing, he earned, besides his travel expenses, about the income of a professor for life. The first eighteen months were spent in Toulouse, where Smith (whose spoken French was bad) was bored and began to work on the *Wealth of Nations*. A stay in Geneva gave him the opportunity to visit Voltaire in Ferney. During the final nine months in Paris, where Hume was chargé d'affaires, Smith frequented all the famous literary salons, attended the meetings of the physiocrats, whose master was Quesnay, and was the constant companion of Turgot. After the duke's brother had died in Paris (even Quesnay, whom Smith had consulted, could not help), the party returned to London in 1766.

Smith, with his life pension, now retreated to Kirkcaldy, where he lived with his mother, writing the *Wealth of Nations*. Six years later he emerged from isolation with a largely finished manuscript. He moved to London, where he led an active social life, was admitted to the Royal Society, and became a member of prestigious clubs. The *Wealth of Nations* made him a celebrity, one of the leading minds of his time.

In 1778, Smith accepted an appointment as one of the five commissioners of customs in Scotland, which trebled his income, making him quite well off. He settled in Edinburgh, where he was joined by his mother, who seems to have been the only important woman in his life. In 1787 he was elected rector of the University of Glasgow. He maintained an open house—including an extensive library—where he entertained many guests and visitors, and he was active in many clubs. Gradually Smith's health declined. He died in 1790, and his simple grave can be seen in Edinburgh.

Works

Adam Smith published two books. The fruit of his Glasgow years was *The Theory of Moral Sentiments*, published in 1759. It would be enough to assure its author a respected place among the Scottish moral philosophers, and Smith himself ranked it above the *Wealth of Nations*. It completely dispels the notion that Adam Smith was an apologist of materialistic self-interest. Its central idea is the concept, closely related to conscience, of the impartial spectator who helps man to distinguish right from wrong. For the same purpose, Immanuel Kant invented the categorical imperative and Sigmund Freud the superego.

It was sometimes argued that between 1759 and 1776, Smith changed his mind, moving from "moral sentiments" to crude self-interest. In fact, from Smith's point of view there was no inconsistency; acknowledging the force of self-interest implies no denial of ethical imperatives. Consequently, he prepared new editions of the *Moral Sentiments* long after the *Wealth of Nations* was published.

An Inquiry into the Nature and Causes of the Wealth of Nations, after more than twelve years of preparation, finally came out in 1776. Though always controversial, it was an instant and complete success. The first edition was sold out in six months, and four additional editions came out during Smith's lifetime. It is the work of an experienced expositor, written in precisely the right style for the intelligent lay person of its time, with telling and colorful anecdotes from everyday life and from history, and displaying an encyclopedic erudition. By modern standards it is also verbose; intuitive plausibility often takes the place of analysis; and the main argument is encumbered by many historical digressions. The tone of irreverent skepticism with which it describes the motives of men and governments has influenced the style of economic discourse to the present day. One of the most characteristic examples is the famous discussion of the corrupting influence of faulty incentives on academic teaching (Smith 1776, bk. 5, ch. 1, part 3, art. 2). It shows Adam Smith as a shrewd judge of institutional arrangements.

Besides the two books, Smith published only a few literary essays during his lifetime. A volume of essays on philosophical subjects came out posthumously (in 1795); they testify to an amazing range of intellectual activity. In particular, the essay on "the principles which lead and direct philosophical enquiries, illustrated by the history of astronomy" shows brilliant insight into the logic of scientific discovery.[3]

Shortly before his death, Smith asked two friends to help him burn sixteen volumes of manuscripts. The notes of his lectures on jurisprudence

3. Schumpeter, in one of his capriccios, actually ranked it far above the *Wealth of Nations*, but this sheds more light on Schumpeter than on Smith (1954, 182).

were discovered only in 1895 and those on rhetoric and belles lettres in 1958. To celebrate the bicentenary of the *Wealth of Nations*, the University of Glasgow published a complete edition of the works and correspondence of Adam Smith in six volumes (1976–83).

Price

In modern terms, the subject matter of the *Wealth of Nations* is the competitive allocation of resources in a growing economy. Its main determinants are described in this and the following sections.[4] An efficient allocation of resources requires a division of labor. This, in turn, leads to exchange. The ratio at which one good is exchanged against another, its value in exchange, thus assumes a strategic role. As in Cantillon, the theory of allocation is essentially a theory of price. The centerpiece of the analysis is the distinction between the market price of a commodity and its natural price. The natural price is defined as being "neither more nor less than what is sufficient to pay the rent of the land, the wages of the labour, and the profits of the stock employed in raising, preparing, and bringing it to market, according to their natural rates" (Smith 1976–83, 2:72). The market price is regulated by the proportion between the quantity actually supplied and what Smith calls effectual demand, which is the quantity that would be demanded at the natural price. If supply exceeds effectual demand, the market price stands below the normal price, and vice versa, the extent of the difference depending on the characteristics of demand.

The difference between market price and natural price in turn controls the dynamic adjustment in factor allocation. If the market price falls short of the natural price, some factors earn less than their natural rate and will be withdrawn. The consequent reduction in output will help to eliminate the price discrepancies. In the opposite case some factors will earn more than their natural rate, and the price discrepancy will be eliminated by an expansion of output. Market prices are thus made to gravitate toward natural prices by an automatic feedback mechanism.

This mechanism has remained the centerpiece of value theory to the present day. It is all the more important to realize that Smith did not discover it. In fact, it was accepted doctrine for centuries, transmitted from the scholastics to the mercantilists and fully described by early classical economists such as Richard Cantillon.

Land, labor, and capital enter symmetrically into Smith's natural price. Cantillon's land theory of value was thereby discarded for good. It had never been explained how the waiting embodied in capital goods (as distinct from mere depreciation) could be resolved into land, and with respect to

4. Recent interpretations of Smith's economics can be found in Hollander 1973, Skinner and Wilson 1975, and O'Driscoll 1979.

labor Smith was evidently not content to resolve it into the land required to sustain it.

On the other hand, Smith did not propose a labor theory of value either. In the "early and rude" state of society before the appropriation of land and the accumulation of capital goods, a beaver and a deer would indeed exchange in proportion to the labor they would, on average, cost to the hunter, but in the actual state of society, this would not be so. In fact, no classical economist explained natural prices in terms of labor only, and even Marx made it clear that relative prices generally deviate from relative labor inputs.

Smith did assign labor a special role, though, namely as a constant-utility deflator. In comparing different prices at the same moment, he explains, one commodity can serve as a *numéraire* as well as another. In comparing prices over time, however, one would like to have a *numéraire* of constant utility. In long-term contracts, for example, the real value of rents could be protected over centuries by stipulating them in terms of such a *numéraire*. For this purpose, Smith proposes labor as the most suitable standard (followed by corn), because, as he argues, one day of toil and trouble always represents the same disutility. Though this argument begs the question why the disutility of labor should be less variable in the long run than, say, the utility of a glass of wine, it might have initiated a fruitful discussion of index number problems.

However, only in competitive markets will market prices gravitate toward natural prices. "The monopolists, by keeping the market constantly under-stocked, by never fully supplying the effectual demand, sell their commodities much above the natural price, and raise their emoluments, whether they consist in wages or profit, greatly above their natural rate" (Smith 1976–83, 2:78). Smith did not provide an analysis of monopoly price. That it is "the highest which can be got" is all he had to say about the subject. His main point was that monopoly would distort the factor allocation.

Being an advocate of free competition did not make Adam Smith an advocate of business interests. In his view businessmen were the principal enemies of competition, the perennial seekers of monopoly and privilege. "People of the same trade," he wrote, "seldom meet together, even for merriment and diversion, but the conversation ends in a conspiracy against the publick, or in some contrivance to raise prices" (Smith 1976–83, 2:145). Smith did not believe that such meetings could be prevented, but they should not be facilitated or encouraged.

In his rejection of monopoly, too, Smith had nothing to add to received doctrine. In identifying the just price with the competitive price and condemning monopoly as evil, the scholastics had used the same reasoning centuries before.

The Social Accounts

The aggregate national product "of all the inhabitants of a great country, comprehends the whole annual produce of their land and labour" (Smith 1976–83, 2:286). Smith is careful to distinguish between gross and net product. Net product is defined as what the inhabitants have left after deducting from gross product "the expence of maintaining; first, their fixed; and, secondly, their circulating capital; or what, without encroaching upon their capital, they can place in their stock reserved for immediate consumption" (286f.).

The important point in Smith's definition of net product is the absence of a deduction for maintaining the labor force. The physiocrats had defined the social product net of the subsistence of labor. On their assumption of subsistence wages, this excluded wages from net product. Since they failed to account for interest income (as distinct from capital consumption), net product was reduced to rent. Smith, in contrast, included workers' consumption and thus their wages, and he also allowed for capital income. Economic science followed his lead. The physiocratic accounts became obsolete.

In part, the difference between Smith and Quesnay is merely a matter of terminological convention. In part, however, it reflects substantive differences. First, the physiocrats were deluded by their accounting system into believing that the wealth of nations depends only on agriculture. Smith, though still believing that the help of nature made agricultural labor somehow more productive than manufacturing labor, saw clearly that manufacturing, too, contributes to wealth. This is true even for the physiocratic net product, but Smith's more inclusive definition makes it less easy to forget it.

Second, rent makes good sense as the proper maximand for economic policy if (1) interest is irrelevant, and (2) labor, since it can be freely reproduced at the subsistence wage, is not a scarce factor. Smith, unlike Quesnay in the *Tableau Economique*, was unwilling to make these assumptions. As a consequence, he needed a more inclusive maximand.

Though this certainly marked an advance over the physiocrats, it also created an asymmetry that plagues social accounting to this day. Capital income is defined net of what is needed to maintain capital intact. Labor income, however, is defined gross of what is needed to maintain the labor force intact. Whereas capital income is a net surplus, labor income is in large part merely a replacement cost of human capital. Adam Smith's definition of net product thus obscured a fundamental difference between property income and labor income that the physiocratic accounts made clear.

The price of any commodity, Adam Smith explains, resolves itself into wages, rents, profits, and the replacement of used-up raw materials. But such replacement can again be resolved into wages, rents, and profits. It follows that each price can be resolved, directly or indirectly, into wages, rent, and profit. Since these prices add up to aggregate product, it further follows that aggregate product, too, is the sum of wages, rent, and profits (Smith 1976–83,2:68f.).

Each of these shares goes to a different class of people. "These are the three great, original and constituent orders of every civilized society, from whose revenue that of every other order is ultimately derived" (Smith 1976–83, 2:265). The structure of the social accounts is thus taken to reflect the structure of society. This notion became one of the hallmarks of classical economics. Clearly expressed already in Cantillon, it survived far into the nineteenth and even into the twentieth century.

Labor and Wages

Annual output depends largely on the productivity of labor, which, in turn, depends largely, but not exclusively, on the division of labor. Smith illustrates this with his famous pin-making example (apparently borrowed from the *Encyclopédie*): While one unskilled worker can hardly make 20 pins a day (if any), ten workers, dividing the process into about 18 different operations, can make up to 48,000 pins, thus increasing labor productivity in a proportion of more than 240.

This requires, obviously, that there be a market for 48,000 pins per day. Smith concludes that "the division of labor is limited by the extent of the market" (1976–83, 2:30f.). Restrictions on market size, through craft guilds, trade associations, monopolies, customs duties, and the like, thus lower labor productivity. In addition, a more extensive division of labor usually requires a higher stock of capital.

The advantages to be gained from the division of labor imply increasing returns to scale. To the extent that these are internal to the firm (as they are in the pin example), the limitation of the market must appear in the form of a falling demand curve for the firm's output. It seems, therefore, that Smith does not assume pure competition in the sense of a parametrically given market price. Before his eyes he rather has the Chamberlin-Robinson case of monopolistic competition, preferably with free entry. The analytical problems that were thereby raised still troubled Alfred Marshall a hundred years later.

While a higher productivity of labor benefits the economy as a whole, it does not generally benefit the individual worker. There are two reasons for this. First, mobility of labor between locations and industries sees to it that productivity gains at any one point are eventually spread out over the whole economy. Ultimately, wage differentials depend on the risks, dangers, toil, and trouble in different occupations, regardless of differences in productivity gains.

Second, in a stationary economy the overall wage level gravitates toward a subsistence wage, which is just high enough to raise, on average, a family of a size to keep population constant. This is the "natural" rate of wages. In this context Smith quotes Cantillon to the effect that the wage of one worker has to provide subsistence for about two persons. One also hears the echo of Cantillon (and many predecessors) in the sentence "Every species of animals naturally multiplies in proportion to the means of their subsistence" (Smith 1976–83, 2:97). In a growing economy, however, wages can be permanently above the subsistence wage. It follows that "it is not the actual greatness of national wealth, but its continual increase, which occasions a rise in the wages of labour" (87). These are the general tendencies. For specific cases and labor markets, Smith is perfectly willing, of course, to allow for all sorts of modifying circumstances.

Land and Rent

Rent tends to be equal to the excess of the product over the natural wage and the natural profit of the tenant; it is the excess of the product over what is needed to keep the factors employed. It has nothing to do with the cost of improvements and is due merely to the scarcity of land (which Smith, misleadingly, confounded with monopoly).

Though "resolving" price into wages, profits, and rents, Smith emphasized that rent is not a cause of high market price but an effect of it: "High or low wages and profit, are the causes of high or low price; high or low rent is the effect of it" (1976–83, 2:162). Rent is paid because market price exceeds the cost of wages and profit. Smith was unable, however, to give a precise explanation of this doctrine. How can rent fail to affect price if, together with wages and profits, it is a component of price? Smith was perfectly clear about differences in rent due to differences in fertility and location; he also understood how farmers plan crops to maximize rents. He nevertheless could not elucidate the relationship between rent and price.

The analytical gap was partially filled, as an immediate reaction to the *Wealth of Nations*, by James Anderson's rent theory, which later became the theory of Edward West, Robert Malthus, and David Ricardo. In part, however, the gap remained unfilled far into the twentieth century. In fact, once economic theory had abandoned Cantillon's land theory of value, Adam Smith's proposition was no longer generally true. (The reasons are given in chapter 9.)

Smith argues correctly that economic progress "tends either directly or indirectly to raise the real rent of land" (1976–83, 2:264). He wrongly concludes that rents must rise not only per acre of land but also in proportion to total output. In any case, landlords, like workers, have a clear interest in economic progress. Smith, though descended from landowners, does not show particular sympathy for them as a class; like other men, he says, they "love to reap where they never sowed" (67). However, their self-interest, like that of workers, is in harmony with the general interest, while that of profit earners is not.

Capital and Profit

The social product is largely (though not exclusively) determined by the accumulated stock of capital goods. On the one hand, capital goods are needed as a wage fund (to use a later expression) to sustain the workers during the period of production. Thus "the demand for those who live by wages . . . cannot increase but in proportion to the increase of the funds which are destined for the payment of wages" (Smith 1976–83, 2:86), and "the number of those that can be continually employed . . . must bear a certain proportion to the whole capital of that society, and never can exceed that proportion" (453). On the other hand, capital goods raise the productivity of labor and thus "enable the same number of labourers to perform a much greater quantity of work" (287). "The quantity of industry, therefore, not only increases in every country with the increase of the stock which employs it, but, in consequence of that increase, the same quantity of industry produces a much greater quantity of work" (277).

Capital is accumulated by saving. "Capitals are increased by parsimony and diminished by prodigality and misconduct" (Smith 1976–83, 2:337). Saving is equivalent to investment. "Whatever a person saves from his revenue he adds to his capital, and either employs it himself in maintaining an additional number of productive hands, or enables some other person to do so, by lending it to him for an interest, that is, for a share of the profits" (337). It follows that "every prodigal appears to be a publick enemy, and every frugal man a publick benefactor" (340).

As in the case of labor, the mobility of capital under the pressure of competition continually sees to it that profit rates are equalized between industries. If, in the course of economic growth, capital is accumulated, profit rates tend to fall. "When profit diminishes, merchants are very apt to complain that trade decays; though the diminution of profit is the natural effect of its prosperity, or of a greater stock being employed in it than before" (Smith 1976–83, 2:108). In a rich and mature economy, therefore, "both the wages of labour and the profits of stock would probably be very low" (111). Competition would have pushed "ordinary profit as low as possible," "but perhaps no country has ever yet arrived at this degree of opulence" (111).

It follows that profit earners, unlike rent earners and wage earners, have little interest in general economic progress. Though they have more economic understanding than the landowners, they tend to use it not in the general interest but in their particular interests (Smith 1976–83, 2:266f.). Businessmen, therefore, are bad advisers on general welfare.

The Invisible Hand

The preceding sections relate to individual product and factor markets. Taken together, these components suggest a model of a growing economy. With fixed land, the wage rate depends positively on the growth rate of the economy. The profit rate depends negatively on the progress of capital accumulation. Eventually, the economy will reach a stationary state of maturity with subsistence wages, low profit rates, and high rents. (This is elaborated in Samuelson 1966–86, vol. 5, ch. 342.) Much remained for coming generations in the progressive articulation of this model, but Adam Smith had outlined the framework.

Though, in this growth process, the allocation of capital to individual industries is governed by the self-interest of each investor, it will turn out to be optimal for society. "Every individual is continually exerting himself to find out the most advantageous employment for whatever capital he can command. It is his own advantage, indeed, and not that of the society, which he has in view. But the study of his own advantage naturally, or rather necessarily leads him to prefer that employment which is most advantageous to the society" (Smith 1976–83, 2:454).

What is true for investment is true for economic activities in general, for "every individual necessarily labours to render the annual revenue of the society as great as he can. He generally, indeed, neither intends to promote the publick interest, nor knows how much he is promoting it," but "by pursuing his own interest he frequently promotes that of the society more effectually than when he really intends to promote it" (Smith 1976–83, 2:456). In short, "it is not from the benevolence of the butcher, the brewer, or the baker, that we expect our dinner, but from their regard to their own interest" (26f.).

The force that causes the individual to promote the general interest is Adam Smith's famous "invisible hand." The individual, he says, is "led by an invisible hand to promote an end which was no part of his intention" (Smith 1976–83, 2:456). This invisible hand is, of course, competition. Competition is thus visualized, as before by Cantillon, in the role of a central planner, guiding the economy to the social optimum.

Adam Smith had little respect for those who believe that the invisible hand needs to be assisted by "social responsibility." He declared he had "never known much good done by those who affected to trade for the publick good. It is an affectation, indeed, not very common among merchants, and very few words need be employed in dissuading them from it" (Smith 1976–83, 2:456).

Liberalism and Mercantilism

The principle of the invisible hand led Adam Smith to free trade. His argument for free international exchange is derived from interpersonal trade. "It is the maxim of every prudent master of a family, never to attempt to make at home what it will cost him more to make than to buy" (Smith 1976–83, 2:456). "What is prudence in the conduct of every private family, can scarce be folly in that of a great kingdom. If a foreign country can supply us with a commodity cheaper than we ourselves can make it, better buy it of them with some part of the produce of our own industry, employed in a way in which we have some advantage" (457).

The relevant consideration is whether a commodity can be purchased abroad with exports that cost only a part of the factor inputs that the domestic production of that commodity would have cost (Smith 1976–83, 2:457). This is clearly the principle of comparative advantage. It had been stated at least as clearly in the earlier literature, and a full analysis had to wait for Ricardo.

Adam Smith, while contributing little to international trade theory, gave a strong impulse to the free trade idea that was then gaining strength. He was not a dogmatic freetrader, though, for he recognized valid reasons for protection for the sake of defense (with the Navigation Act as the prime example), for the equalization of domestic taxes, and possibly for retaliation, and he advocated a gradual lowering and not a sudden abolition of protection.

As his ideological opponent, he created the "system of political economy" that he called mercantile and that was later called mercantilism. He created it for much the same dialectic purpose for which Marx created "capitalism," as the embodiment of what he opposed. In caricaturing mercantilists as confusing wealth with gold, he did many of them a serious injustice, but no reader of mercantilist tracts can fail to be struck by the central importance they attach to the balance of trade. And no reader of present-day tracts can fail to notice the continued relevance of Smith's polemics.

Adam Smith stands in history as the most effective protagonist of economic liberalism the world has ever known. "Smithianism" became synonymous with liberalism. He was all the more effective because he did not use ringing rhetoric but rather made a sober critical argument. He was far from advocating free enterprise for the sake of business. Businessmen, in his view, were rather the villains against whose resistance free competition had to be established. To borrow a term from the "new political economy," society was pictured as rent seeking, each special interest group using its influence on political decisions to extract rents at the expense of other groups. In this respect, too, Smith was more effective than original. The maxim "Laissez faire" had been coined already in Colbert's time, and among the physiocrats it was commonplace that "better government is less government."

Nor was Smith doctrinaire in his liberalism. In particular, he attributed to the government three duties that might require expenditure and regulation. The first duty is defense, which, he said, "is of much more importance than opulence" (Smith 1976–83, 2:464f.). The second duty is "an exact administration of justice" to protect every member of society against injustice and oppression by other members (708). If this had been all, the later charge that the state is conceived to be no more than a night watchman might have had some substance. Smith added, however, the duty of "erecting and maintaining those publick institutions and those publick works, which, though they may be in the highest degree advantageous to a great society, are, however, of such a nature, that the profit could never repay the expence to any individual or small number of individuals" (723). Transportation facilities and educational institutions are discussed in this context. It is evident that in view of externalities, public goods, and scale economies, this duty may serve to justify extensive government activities.

Place in the History of Economics

If greatness of an economic work is measured by the mere power of its influence on the history of mankind, the *Wealth of Nations* is rivaled only by Karl Marx's *Capital*. But surely the nature of the influence must also be considered. Whereas the negative spirit of Karl Marx was obsessed with the revolutionary destruction of the existing order, the positive spirit of Adam Smith was concerned with the peaceful construction of a new and better order of society. If this is taken into account, the historical importance of the *Wealth of Nations* is surpassed by no other economic book.

Liberal Victorians expressed its historical role in glowing terms. Henry Thomas Buckle, in his *History of Civilization in England*, expressed the opinion that, "looking at its ultimate results," the *Wealth of Nations* "is probably the most important book that has ever been written, and is certainly the most valuable contribution ever made by a single man towards establishing the principles on which government should be based" (1873, 1:214). Of Adam Smith he said "that this solitary Scotsman has, by the publication of one single work, contributed more towards the happiness of man, than has been effected by the united abilities of all the statesmen and legislators of whom history has preserved an authentic account" (216). These are big words, but Walter Bagehot also said about the *Wealth of Nations* that "the life of almost everyone in England—perhaps of everyone—is different and better in consequence of it" and that "no other form of political philosophy has ever had one thousandth part of the influence on us" (1880, 1).

This historical influence required generations, of course. It began almost imperceptibly soon after the book was out, but even in Britain the transition from mercantilism to liberalism took seventy years, and in most other countries victory was never complete.

In the history of science, however, influence on human affairs is not the appropriate criterion of greatness. A person or a book may produce violent historical commotion without being great in science, and vice versa. A more appropriate criterion might be scientific discovery. By this standard, Adam Smith is not in the first rank. He was not a forger of new tools but found virtually all the analytical components he needed in the existing literature. In fact, he often made no use of recent and promising contributions, perhaps because he felt they were not ready for the intelligent lay reader. Ferdinando Galiani's and Etienne Bonnot de Condillac's utility theories, Turgot's diminishing returns, and the *Tableau Economique* of Cantillon and Quesnay are cases in point.

For the talented theorist, therefore, the *Wealth of Nations* is not an exciting book to read. It is consistent with this observation that the twenty years following its publication were a period not of vigorous analytical advances but rather of stagnation. Great teachers of "intelligent laymen" do not necessarily attract and stimulate scientific talent. In the nineteenth century, Adam Smith was often celebrated as the founder of the new science of political economy. Such claims are doubtful in any case, but in Adam Smith's case they are quite untenable, because no major part of the science he expounded was his original discovery.

The pertinent question in the present context concerns Adam Smith's contribution to mainstream economics. As was just said, no individual part can be attributed to him. His contribution was of a different nature. It was mainstream economics itself. Smith, for the first time, put together the body of economic knowledge that can still be recognized as an early form of what today may be called mainstream economics. Adam Smith was a genius not of discovery but of synthesis. He reorganized the valuable insights of scholastics, mercantilists, and philosophers into a comprehensive theory of economic policy, showing convincingly that, in the framework of appropriate institutions, competitive self-interest could be a powerful motor of economic growth. As yet this theory was very imperfectly articulated, but it nevertheless provided a standard of reference for a century of economic research. Indeed, there is little in Jean-Baptiste Say, Robert Malthus, David Ricardo, and John Stuart Mill that is not, more or less, directly, an elaboration of Adam Smith. At the same time, precisely because it provided this standard of reference, the *Wealth of Nations* caused earlier contributions, perhaps of greater originality, to fade into oblivion.

8
Production and Factor Supply

AT THE BEGINNING of the classical era, Cantillon's model of the circular flow was based on a production theory with fixed input coefficients. The same simplifying assumption was used by the physiocrats. Johann Heinrich von Thünen, at the beginning of the next era, used an almost complete marginal productivity theory based on cost minimization. Between these two signposts production theory during the classical era evolved around the law of diminishing returns. First clearly articulated by Jacques Turgot, it became the most famous and most durable proposition of classical economics. Associated with it was a theory of rent, to which James Anderson made an important contribution. Whereas rent was the income of the fixed factor of production, namely land, the other factors, namely labor and capital, were regarded as variable. Robert Malthus supplied the classical explanation of the supply of labor, which David Ricardo also applied to capital. It was left to John Rae, at the end of the classical era, to provide a theory of capital that contained all the basic ingredients later worked out, more than half a century later, by Eugen von Böhm-Bawerk, Knut Wicksell, and Irving Fisher.

Jacques Turgot

By introducing variable input proportions and diminishing returns, Anne Robert Jacques Turgot (1727–81) made the single most important contribution to the theory of production between Richard Cantillon and Johann Heinrich von Thünen. This cannot mean that up to that time peasants believed returns to be constant. That beyond a certain point it would be wasteful to apply more labor to a given piece of land must have been known from time immemorial. Turgot's achievement was to forge this commonplace insight into an analytical proposition.

Turgot was the son of a Paris merchant from the lower nobility. He first planned to enter the clergy and acquired an extensive education, but then became disenchanted with the church. He had a highly successful government career in which he combined intellectual brilliance with practical sense and reformist ideas. Under Louis XV he was chief administrator of the district of Limoges. In 1774, Louis XVI made him minister of the navy, and only a few weeks later we find him as general comptroller of finances, which means minister of finance. The state of government finances was once again desperate, and Turgot, the liberal friend of the physiocrats, was greeted as a Messiah. However, his audacious reforms failed, not because they were economically unsound, but politically. In 1776 Turgot was dismissed in disgrace; the financial disaster took its fateful course toward the revolution.

Turgot's collected works, and voluminous other material concerning him, have been edited by Schelle in 5 volumes (Turgot 1913–23). His contributions to economics were recently translated and edited by Peter Groenewegen (1977), who also wrote an authoritative assessment (Groenewegen 1983).

Most of Turgot's economic writings, in one way or another, grew out of his administrative duties. In fact, there is only one tract that can be regarded as an independent monograph, namely the *Reflections on the Formation and Distribution of Wealth* (1766), written originally as an outline of economic principles for Mr. Ko and Mr. Yong, two Chinese visitors to the Jesuits. It is not known whether the two travelers were as much impressed by physiocratic economics as the physiocrats were by the alleged virtues of the government of China. The little booklet is justly famous as the most concise and lucid introduction into economics up to the end of the eighteenth century. Written at the time when Adam Smith was in close contact with Turgot in Paris, it clearly had considerable influence on the *Wealth of Nations*, but whereas the latter is verbose, the *Reflections* are terse.

Turgot is best known as the physiocrat who came to power and as a protagonist of laissez faire. At the analytical level, however, his principal contribution was the explicit analysis of capital accumulation. Whereas in Quesnay's *Tableau Economique* the "advances" were assumed to bear a fixed proportion to land, Turgot now considered the capital/land ratio as variable through saving or dissaving. The saver thus became the public benefactor, because "the spirit of thrift in a nation continually tends to increase the amount of the capitals," while "the habit of luxury has precisely the opposite effect" (Groenewegen 1977, 84). The stationary *Tableau Economique* was thus transformed into the vision of a model of an economy in (unbalanced) growth. It is worth noting that, in Turgot's view, all classes contribute to capital accumulation (94).

As the capital stock grows, interest rates decline; the tendency of profits to fall moves into the foreground. At any moment, the rate of interest depends on the relationship between accumulated savings and investment opportunities. From the whole inventory of capital projects, those that are executed are those whose expected profit exceeds the market rate of interest. With a declining interest rate, the number of these projects increases. Turgot uses the apt metaphor of land rising out of the sea: As the water level falls, more and more mountains emerge from the sea. The interest rate, to use Turgot's other metaphor, is the thermometer of capital scarcity (Groenewegen 1977, 87).

A court case gave Turgot an opportunity to elaborate his views on interest. These views, though defending interest against the scholastic injunctions, went hardly beyond the reasoning that permitted the scholastics to reconcile theology with economic reality. In particular, interest is justified by the productivity of capital to the borrower and the risk and opportunity cost to the lender. Turgot states it as a general axiom that present money is worth more than future money (Groenewegen 1977, 157), which naturally endeared him to Böhm-Bawerk.

In this context, Turgot made his only contribution to the theory of value. Interest is like a price. If an isolated seller trades with an isolated buyer, the resulting price is indeterminate. However, if there are several traders on each side, competition will see to it that a unique price is established, satisfying the condition that aggregate supply must equal aggregate demand. In this case, each individual trader regards price as an "independent phenomenon" on which he has only negligible influence (Groenewegen 1977, 156f.). Parametric prices can hardly be described more precisely.[1]

Capital accumulation on given land means variable proportions. They led Turgot to his most important contribution to economic theory, namely the laws of returns. Though he used different terms, he thus became the father of marginal productivity. The decisive paragraphs in Turgot's "Observations on a Paper by Saint-Péravy" (1767) are worth quoting in full.

The marginal product curve begins with a segment of increasing returns. "Seed thrown on a soil which is naturally fertile, but has not been prepared at all, would be virtually a waste of expenditure. If the soil were tilled once, the produce would be greater; tilling it a second or a third time would not just double or triple, but quadruple or decuple the produce, which will thus increase in a much larger proportion than the expenditure, and this would be the case up to a certain point, at which the produce would be as large as possible relative to the advances" (Groenewegen 1977, 112).

Sooner or later, however, marginal returns begin to diminish, finally reaching zero. "Past this point, if the advances are still further increased, the product will still increase, but less so, and continuously less and less until an addition to the advances would add nothing further to the produce, because the fertility of the soil is exhausted and art cannot increase the product any further" (Groenewegen 1977, 112).

Once the marginal-product curve is established, it is used to determine

1. Turgot also considers exchange in an unfinished essay, "Value and Money," of 1769 (Groenewegen 1977, 133–48). He begins with isolated barter between a freezing owner of corn and a hungry owner of firewood. Each trader is supposed to decide on the least favorable exchange ratio at which he is willing to trade, and the actual exchange ratio is said to be the average of the two. Turgot, disappointingly, failed to point out that here, too, the presence of several traders (on at least one side) is necessary for a determinate outcome, and he left it for John Stuart Mill to explore the relationship between the exchange ratio and the aggregate quantities demanded and supplied. The fruit seems to have been within reach, but it was not plucked.

the optimal amount of investment at a given rate of interest. It would be wrong, Turgot points out, to maximize the marginal product. "I will mention that it would be a mistake to imagine that the point at which the advances yield the most is the most advantageous one which the cultivator can attain." The correct maximand is rather the net product after deduction of interest, and investment must thus be extended as long as the increment in this net product is positive, which means as long as the marginal product exceeds the interest rate. "Although further increments in advances do not yield as much as the preceding increments, if they yield enough to increase the *net product* of the soil, there is an advantage in making them, and it will still be a good investment" (Groenewegen 1977, 112). Thünen expanded this analysis, generalized to several factors, to a theory of production. As a description of the law of variable proportions, however, Turgot's analysis was not surpassed before the advent of production functions. Explicitly intended as a criticism of the assumption of fixed input coefficients, it eventually transformed the constant returns model of Richard Cantillon and François Quesnay into the diminishing returns model of Robert Malthus and David Ricardo.

Aside from production theory, Turgot was not a great analytical innovator. A busy man, he could not spare the time and energy that are necessary for extensive original work. His talent, like that of Adam Smith, seems to have been more for synthesis than for innovation. His *Reflections* show how respectable a level of general economic understanding had been reached by the time Adam Smith finished the manuscript of the *Wealth of Nations*.

James Anderson

Another step forward was achieved by James Anderson (1739–1808), a Scottish agronomist and editor who wrote extensively on agriculture, fisheries, and manufactures. In 1775 he wrote a book, *Observations on the Means of Exciting a Spirit of National Industry* (1777), dedicated to the Duke of Buccleuch (from whom Adam Smith received a pension), on the promotion of the Scottish economy. Before the book was out, the appearance of Adam Smith's *Wealth of Nations* caused Anderson to add a *postscriptum* of eighty pages in defense of the stabilizing effect of export bounties on corn. Toward its end is found a fairly comprehensive statement of the theory of rent. This passage, too, is worth quoting.

> In every country there are various soils, which are endued with different degrees of fertility; and hence it must happen, that the farmer who cultivates the most fertile of these, can afford to bring his corn to market at a much lower price than others who cultivate poorer fields. But if the corn that grows on these fertile spots is not sufficient fully to supply the market alone, the price will naturally be raised in that market to such a height, as to indemnify others for the expence of cultivating poorer soils. The farmer, however, who

cultivates the rich spots, will be able to sell his corn at the same rate in the market with those who occupy poorer fields; he will, therefore, receive much more than the *intrinsic* value for the corn he rears. Many persons will, therefore, be desirous of obtaining possession of these fertile fields, and will be content to give a certain premium for an exclusive privilege to cultivate them; which will be greater or smaller according to the more or less fertility of the soil. It is this premium which constitutes what we now call *rent*; a medium by means of which the expence of cultivating soils of very different degrees of fertility may be reduced to a perfect equality. (Anderson 1777, 376)

In the same year, Anderson presented substantially the same explanation of rent in his *Inquiry into the Nature of the Corn Laws with a View to the New Corn-Bill Proposed for Scotland* (1859). He imagines land to be subdivided into different fertility classes—A, B, C, and so on—which will be cultivated in sequence until the price of corn ceases to cover production costs. The marginal class will remain rentless and the intramarginal classes will pay rent according to their cost advantage (322f.).

What, if anything, did Anderson discover? A highly developed theory of absolute rent for scarce land of uniform quality, available at least since Cantillon, had been widely used and popularized by the physiocrats. The notion that land of better quality or location commands higher rent must have been commonplace (at least) since the times of the Pharaohs. Economic relationships that are evident from everyday experience cannot give rise to discoveries. In any case, Adam Smith had already described the microeconomics of differential rent in loving detail. He also coined the phrase that high rent is the effect of a high price of corn and not its cause. Nevertheless, Smith's treatment remained unsatisfactory, mainly because it confused rent with monopoly prices and did not make clear why rent, though it is said to be a component of price, does not influence it. To have clarified these points is Anderson's contribution. He thereby brought the microeconomic theory of rent into a form to which Edward West, Robert Malthus, and David Ricardo had nothing to add. What remained to be done was to incorporate rent into a macroeconomic model of distribution and growth.

Thomas Robert Malthus

For Cantillon, Quesnay, and Smith, land was the only primary factor of production, whereas labor and capital goods were secondary factors endogenously supplied by the economy. For labor, they relied on population theory to provide an explanation. It was Malthus who forged their suggestions, making implicit use of diminishing returns, into a dynamic theory of factor supply. That this theory became as famous and notorious as it did was largely due to the population explosion that accompanied the Industrial Revolution. During the century ending with Malthus's death, the excess of births over deaths in England increased about tenfold. Declines in infant mortality put a brake on the improvement in living standards. This was a case where social conditions had an undeniable influence on the history of economic theory.

Thomas Robert Malthus was born in 1766, the sixth of seven children, in the country house his father had built in Wotton, Surrey.[2] His father had abandoned law to lead the life of a country gentleman with literary interests. He knew and adored Rousseau, whom he invited, unsuccessfully, to stay at his house just around the time when Robert was born. He was also an eccentric and restless man who never stayed long in the same place. Robert was born with a harelip and cleft palate and thus suffered from a lifelong speech defect.

Young Malthus was educated by tutors and in private schools until, in 1784, he was sent to Jesus College, Cambridge. He acquired a broad knowledge of natural philosophy (that is, the sciences) and mathematics, but he also read Gibbon and used Newton's *Principia Mathematica*, in Latin. He finished the mathematical science program as ninth in his class. He must have been exposed to good mathematics, but his works make it hard to believe that he had mathematical talent. His father had wanted his son to become a surveyor, but Malthus, despite his handicap, decided to enter the church. He was ordained in 1788 and so became the Reverend Robert Malthus.

Little is known about the next ten years except that in 1793, Malthus was made a fellow of Jesus College, which provided him with a small income as long as he remained unmarried, and was appointed curate of a little chapel in Wotton. The baptisms, weddings, and burials of his parishioners may have given him some firsthand insights into positive and preventive checks, moral restraint, vice, and misery.

The *Essay on the Principle of Population*, by making sexual behavior the key to social improvements, made Malthus instantly famous. Together with men like Darwin and Marx, he became one of the great vortexes of controversy of the nineteenth century. Long trips to Scandinavia and to the Continent gave him an opportunity to collect extensive material on population. In 1803, Malthus became rector of Walesby (in Lincolnshire), which gave him an income for life with no other obligation than to pay a curate. In the following year, at age thirty-eight, he married a distant cousin, with whom he had three children.

In 1805, Malthus was appointed professor of general history, politics, commerce, and finance at the newly founded East India College near London. He thus became the first British professor of political economy. For the remaining twenty-nine years the uneventful history of Malthus's life was the history of the successive editions of the *Essay*, his other publications, and his controversies. His main duty was the instruction of the

---

2. This biographical note is based on the exhaustive study of Patricia James (1979).

(sometimes recalcitrant) future employees of the East India Company. The college was clearly not a temple of learning; it left Malthus enough energy to join numerous clubs, to maintain an extensive correspondence, and to go to London to see his many friends, the closest of whom was Ricardo. He died at the end of 1834, apparently from a heart attack.

On population, Malthus convinced many, but as an economist he always stood alone, in opposition to Ricardo and the Ricardians. Politically he was a Tory who defended the Corn Laws against the free traders. He had a great capacity to provoke, he was argumentative and ambitious, but he was also kind and amiable in his personal relations. He and Ricardo provide the history of economics with a shining example of scientific opponents who were friends.[3]

Malthus's fame rests on his first book, *An Essay on the Principle of Population, as it Affects the Future Improvement of Society*, first published in 1798 (Malthus 1926). Stimulated by discussions with his father, he undertakes to show that, contrary to the utopian speculations of the Marquis de Condorcet and William Godwin, technical and social progress, be it ever so large, cannot improve the human lot as long as population behavior remains what it is. In particular, the Poor Laws do not make the poor better off but only make them more numerous. What is important for the modern economist can all be found in the first chapter. The second edition of 1803 was essentially a new book. The brilliant first essay had now become a ponderous treatise, which would probably not have made its author famous if he had not already been so. In later editions the book grew to three volumes.

The Poor Laws led Malthus into economics proper. In the pamphlet *An Investigation of the Cause of the Present High Price of Provisions* (in Malthus 1970) he argued that welfare payments, if they are escalated to the price of corn, contribute to the increase in the cost of living. Fifteen years passed, however, before he made a substantial contribution to general economics in the pamphlet *An Inquiry into the Nature and Progress of Rent and the Principles by which it is Regulated* (1815). The rent theory it propounded was not new; it had been suggested by Adam Smith and clarified by James Anderson. Malthus's restatement, together with the simultaneous essay by Edward West (West 1903),[4] is nevertheless historically significant because it attracted Ricardo from money into general economics and supplied him with an important building block.

Malthus's second major work, the *Principles of Political Economy, Considered with a View to their Practical Application* (1820), was an ambitious attempt to gain ascendancy over Ricardo, who, with his *Principles*

---

3. The best study of Malthus's personality is Grampp 1974.
4. Sir Edward West (1782–1828) was a distinguished lawyer who became chief justice of Bombay.

of 1817, had become the leading political economist. In particular, Malthus undertook to show that economic growth could suffer from the insufficiency of "effectual demand." He agreed with Adam Smith (against Lord Lauderdale) that there is never "too much" capital and that all savings are invested; the problem he saw did not arise from hoarding. He nevertheless believed that excessive saving, because of insufficient consumption demand, could weaken the incentive to invest. In modern terminology, he seemed to be groping for some golden rule of capital accumulation, but he was never able to make his meaning clear. His attempt, therefore, was a failure, and the second edition (published in 1836), which found a publisher only after Malthus's death, did not correct the deficiencies. It was natural that John Maynard Keynes, in the *General Theory*, claimed Malthus as his predecessor, but, in fact, the two iconoclasts had very different things in mind. Malthus's last book, *Definitions in Political Economy* (1827) is a collection of a loser's quibbles about words.

Malthus summarized his population theory in three propositions:[5]

1. "Population, when unchecked, increases in a geometrical ratio."
2. "Subsistence increases only in an arithmetical ratio."
3. "This implies a strong and constantly operating check on population from the difficulty of subsistence" (1926, 14).

The precise meaning of these propositions would have been less consistently misunderstood if they had been formulated approximately as follows:

1. Population, when subsistence is abundant, increases in a geometrical ratio, which may be called the biological ratio.
2. Subsistence, when population increases in the biological ratio, increases only in an arithmetical ratio.
3. When subsistence becomes less abundant, population growth is gradually diminished below the biological ratio and eventually turns into progressive decline.

The dynamic model contained in these propositions is represented in figure 8.1, the substance of which is found in Boulding 1955. The vertical scale measures the real wage, w. In the right-hand panel, the horizontal scale measures population growth rates, $g = \dot{P}/P$. If wages are at the abundance level, w^*, population grows at the biological rate, g^*. For lower wages, the growth rate is positively related to the wage rate by a growth curve that declines to the left. At wage $\bar{w}$ population becomes stationary; this wage is called the minimum of subsistence. At even lower levels of w, population growth is negative. This is the analytical content of propositions 1 and 3.

The forces that push population growth below the biological rate are Malthus's checks. The positive checks force a movement along a given growth curve under the pressure of declining real income or, in Malthus's

---

5. On the historical origins of the ratios see the illuminating paper by Hartwick (1988).

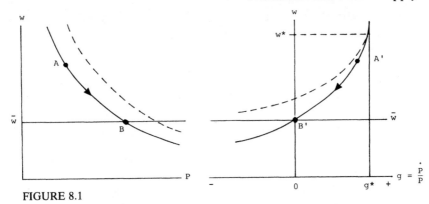

FIGURE 8.1

terms, "misery and vice." The preventive checks originate from "foresight of the difficulties attending the rearing of a family" (Malthus 1926, 62) and thus shift the whole curve to the left, as indicated by the broken variant. The stronger they are, the higher the living standards for any given growth rate and the higher the minimum of subsistence (89f.). The main change in the second edition is the emphasis on "moral restraint" as a preventive check that might gradually alleviate misery and vice.

Proposition 2 was Malthus's way of expressing the law of diminishing returns in terms of his ratios. If labor input, as the proposition implies, is an exponential function of food output, then food output is a logarithmic function of labor input.[6] For such a function, marginal (and average) product declines.[7] If workers receive their marginal product (an assumption Malthus did not state), the wage rate declines as population increases. This is depicted in the left-hand panel of figure 8.1.

Joseph Schumpeter has said that the law of diminishing returns is entirely absent from Malthus's *Essay* (Schumpeter 1954, 581). The long footnote on pages 106–7 and the explanations on pages 187–88 show clearly that this is not even true for the first edition. In the 1807 edition, Malthus was even more explicit: "The improvements of the barren parts would be a work of time and labor; and it must be evident to those who have the slightest acquaintance with agricultural subjects, that in proportion as cultivation extended, the additions that could yearly be made to the former average produce must be gradually and regularly diminishing" (1807, 11; similarly 9). When Malthus wrote, diminishing returns had indeed become commonplace. Through the arithmetic ratio they were incorporated into

6. If $P = e\,(Q/c)$, then $Q = c\ln P$. That Malthus's population theory implies a logarithmic production function was noted by Stigler (1965, 163).

7. The derivative of the function in note 6 is $dQ/dP = c/P$, which declines with rising P.

Malthus's model. It should be noted that Malthus regarded the arithmetic ratio not as a precise rule but only as an upper limit of likely reactions of output to labor input. The arithmetic ratio has often been ridiculed. Once its meaning is understood, it appears, in fact, as a quite ingenious (though unnecessarily roundabout) way of formalizing diminishing returns.

Population dynamics are determined by the interaction of the two panels of figure 8.1. If the economy is initially at *A*, growth is high, as indicated by *A'*. This will move population to the right, inevitably lowering the wage level along the left-hand curve. At first, *g* will still be positive, though declining. The stationary state will be reached at *B*, where the wage is at the subsistence level.

If, thanks to technical progress or social reforms, the efficiency of the economy is raised, the marginal product curve on the left side shifts upward, as indicated by the broken variant. Nevertheless, real income in the stationary state will be no higher than before; the same misery will simply be shared by more people. This was the basic message Malthus opposed to Condorcet and Godwin. The key to happiness, he argued, was to be found in the right-hand panel, namely in moral restraint. This became the battle cry of the Malthusians.

Malthus rejected any claim to originality for his individual propositions; as he said, they were widely available in the literature (Giovanni Botero was mentioned in chapter 3 and Richard Cantillon in chapter 4). His contribution, in his opinion, was the detailed analysis of the various forces that determine the slope and the shifts of the population growth curve (1926, preface). And this is precisely what he became famous for. "What is the brief abstract of his success?" asked his detractor De Quincey, and he supplied his own answer. "It is this: he took an obvious and familiar truth, which until his time had been a barren truism, and showed that it teemed with consequences" (1890b, 134). In addition, the obvious applicability of Malthus's model to plants and animals, noted by Malthus himself, helped to stimulate the thinking of Charles Darwin. From the more narrow point of view of economic theory, Malthus's contribution was the combination of diminishing returns and population growth to a dynamic model of labor supply, which was versatile enough to be applied to other factors such as capital or specific investment goods such as houses. This does not make him a Richard Cantillon or an Adam Smith, but it puts him at the level of, say, David Hume or Jacques Turgot.

John Rae

In explaining capital accumulation, Ricardo was essentially content with applying Malthus's population theory to the other variable factor of production. Only a few years after Ricardo's death, John Rae provided a remarkably original analysis of capital accumulation based on time preference and capital productivity. It was unsurpassed for half a century.

Rae had a most colorful life.[8] He was born in 1796 near Aberdeen. His father was a prosperous businessman, and the seven children received a good education, but there was also much tragedy. Rae's parents' unhappy marriage was dissolved, the father went bankrupt, three brothers died early, and his father and one brother perished together in a shipwreck. The only sister acquired renown as an educator and writer in Canada.

After finishing college with an M.A. degree, Rae went to Edinburgh University as a medical student but did not obtain a medical degree. He was rather attracted to natural philosophy, and he hoped for a life as a scholar, but these hopes were shattered by his father's bankruptcy. At about the same time, he married, it is reported, the daughter of a Scottish shepherd. In 1822 the young couple emigrated to Canada, where Rae's married sister was already living. Rae first became a schoolteacher in the backwoods, fifty miles from Montreal. On the side he practiced medicine, for which he was legitimated by his M.A. degree, and acted as coroner.

In 1834, after an interlude to finish his book on political economy, Rae became headmaster of a grammar school in Hamilton, Ontario. He seems to have been highly regarded as a teacher and beloved by his students. In 1848, however, after a period of bitter religious dissension, the trustees dismissed him; the actual reasons remain obscure. His wife died of cholera soon after. In December 1849, Rae decided to start a new life in California.

Working on the way as a ship's doctor, he became ill in Panama. In California he kept himself from starvation by teaching school and making tools for the gold miners. Gradually his health recovered, and in 1851 he sailed for Hawaii. He settled in Hana, on Maui, where he operated a farm, acted as a pharmacist and doctor, and became a judge. He also undertook extensive studies of the geology and language of Hawaii. When his health later declined, he went to live with a friend on Staten Island, New York, where he died a year later, in 1872.

Rae was a man of wide erudition, both in the classics and in the sciences. He was a lucid expositor and had a colorful writing style abundant in telling examples. He was a restless spirit who had never learned to compromise. Above all, he was an ever hopeful inventor, who constantly produced innovative ideas in the most diverse fields, including mechanical inventions, economics, geography, geology, and philology. None of them was ultimately successful, however. In every case, it seems, there was lacking the final degree of technical equipment and professional competence. Thus Rae remained a brilliant amateur.

Rae's fame rests on the *Statement of Some New Principles on the Subject of Political Economy*, published in 1834. According to the subtitle, the book purports to expose "the fallacies of the system of free trade and

8. The following biographical note is based on James 1965.

of some other doctrines maintained in the *Wealth of Nations*." Rae thus poses as an anti-Smith protectionist. He indeed put forth a mild infant industry argument, far from new at the time and similar to that of Friedrich List, and he advocated for the Canadian colony close ties with the mother country, but the subtitle is nevertheless completely misleading. The main subject of the book is not trade policy but capital accumulation.

With this ambiguity of purpose, it is not surprising that the initial reception was discouraging; Rae never wrote about economics again and later did not even possess a copy of his book. Actually, the book was less ignored than its author knew at the time. Nassau Senior brought it to the attention of John Stuart Mill, who (though not bringing out the important points) praised it highly in his *Principles*, reproducing entire sections. Through the *Principles*, Rae gradually became known to everybody working in this field. Eugen von Böhm-Bawerk, once made aware of the nature of Rae's contribution, was generous in his acknowledgements, though, true to form, he mixed them with pedantic quibbles. Irving Fisher called the *New Principles* "truly a masterpiece, a book of a generation or a century" (James 1965, 1:183), and he dedicated his *Theory of Interest* to the memory of Rae and Böhm-Bawerk.

What was the nature of Rae's contribution? His main topic is the formation of capital goods. He actually uses the term *instruments*, which are supposed to include stocks of consumer goods and land, but the relevant component is the stock of reproducible means of production (James 1965, 2:171). Additions to the capital stock can be made in two ways, namely by accumulation or by augmentation (264). By accumulation Rae means the addition of capital goods at an unchanged technology through the operation of the "accumulative principle," which we would call saving. The term capital augmentation denotes the virtual increase in the capital stock that, even in the absence of saving, results from the operation of the "principle of invention," which we would call technological progress. This was probably the first time technical progress was described as capital augmenting.

Rae criticized Adam Smith for overemphasizing the relative role of saving, and the *New Principles* were written largely to draw attention to the important role of invention and innovation. Invention, he wrote, "is the great immediate maker of almost all that is the subject of our thoughts, or ministers to our enjoyments, or necessities" (James 1965, 2:208). In particular, technical progress counteracts the decline in profit rates that, in its absence, would result from progressive accumulation (263).

Rae's chapter on "the causes of the progress of invention, and of the effects arising from it" (James 1965, 2:208f.) is a brilliant essay on the sociology of innovation. Most men, Rae argues, are essentially imitative, "transmitters of things already known" (213), "walkers in well-beaten paths" (215). His heroes are the "real inventors" who create something new. The number of these geniuses is small. Though ultimately the great benefactors of mankind, they are usually rejected by their contemporaries, and their rewards are shabby. They are those "who, through hopes disappointed, and errors committed, over the waste of the world, and the ruins of their own hearts, can look confidently and courageously forward, to a brighter, though far distant prospect" (221). This was clearly a self-portrait.

With his vision of innovation, Rae provided the essential elements that were elaborated by Schumpeter eighty years later. While this vision is stimulating, intuitively persuasive, and even moving, it does not amount to economic analysis. Just like Schumpeter, Rae did not have the analytical techniques to implement his vision. His lasting contribution concerned accumulation rather than invention.

Irving Fisher let the rate of interest be determined by the impatience to spend income and the opportunity to invest. This approach is essentially due to John Rae. Investment opportunities, in Rae's theory, are described by people's expectations about the durability and the internal rate of return of each projected capital good. Durability can be extended at the price of a higher initial cost, but this will usually lower the internal rate of return.[9] Rae is far from explicitly using compound interest, though, and the internal rate of return is measured by the time it takes to double the initial cost. By this criterion capital goods are classified in different "orders," descending from doubling in one year to doubling in two years, and so on. He thus ends up with Turgot's pyramid of investment projects. A higher volume of investment projects can be realized only at a lower return.

Rae realized that his concepts presented difficulties once one tried to go beyond simple point-input/point-output cases. He illustrated the difficulties by the example of a horse, whose costs and returns are spread between breeding and the disposal of the carcass. He clearly was not equipped to calculate the internal rate of return in such a case, but he saw that it should, in principle, be possible (James 1965, 2:105f.). It is to his credit that (unlike Böhm-Bawerk) he did not let himself be trapped in the analytical blind alley of the average period of production. In fact, Rae seems to have realized, about 130 years before Robert Solow (1963), that the concept of an aggregate capital stock is redundant.

The other blade of Rae's analytical scissors is what he calls the "effective desire of accumulation." The formation of every capital good, Rae explains, "implies the sacrifice of some smaller present good, for the production of some greater future good" (James 1965, 2:118). The effective desire of accumulation is defined as the "determination to sacrifice a certain

---

9. This discussion later was the basis for Åkerman's analysis (1923–24) of the optimal durability of capital goods.

amount of present good, to obtain another greater amount of good, at some future period" (119). In modern terminology, this is time preference. More specifically, it is net (or pure) time preference, because the time preference resulting from differences in present and expected future income is not taken into account. Time preference is treated as a universal law; it is raised by uncertainty, the finiteness of life, myopia, and improvidence, but is lowered by foresight, love for one's family, altruism, and social stability. It varies greatly between individuals, and those with a high propensity to accumulate will save while others will dissave. Capital goods with a given rate of return tend to move to individuals with a relatively low time preference, because they pay the highest prices.

The actual investment process is determined by confronting the demand for capital, as represented by the schedule of time preferences, with the supply of capital goods, as represented by the schedule of internal rates of return. The market will tend to establish a uniform rate of return. Capital projects are executed, beginning with the highest yields, down to the point at which they cease to find savers who are willing to accept those rates.

Rae's specific contribution to economic theory is the first correct description of the interplay of capital productivity and time preference. He thus anticipated much of what would later be found in Jevons, and he was actually superior to Böhm-Bawerk, who began with an elaborate description of time preference (before he knew Rae) and then failed to use it, replacing it by the assumption of a fixed capital stock. However, whereas Jevons, Böhm-Bawerk, and Fisher sought to determine the rate of interest, Rae was focusing on capital accumulation; interest rates are hardly mentioned (James 1965, 2:195f.).

9
David Ricardo

ARMS SILENCE the muses. During the decades of the French Revolutionary and Napoleonic wars, the progress of political economy stagnated, though monetary theory, under the impact of inflation, rose to new heights and Malthus put forth his population theory. Lord Lauderdale (1804) challenged Adam Smith's proposition that every saver is a public benefactor but in analysis was unequal to the task. Jean-Baptiste Say was silenced by Napoleon. A new impulse came after Waterloo when a London banker decided to shift his mental energies from war finance to political economy. The banker was David Ricardo.

Life and Works

Ricardo was born in London in 1772.[1] His father, Abraham, was a respected commodity and security broker. He came from a family of Sephardic Jews, which, expelled from Spain, had first moved to Livorno, then at the beginning of the eighteenth century to Amsterdam, and finally, a few years before David's birth, to London. Wherever they went, they seem to have been solid and prosperous businessmen.

David spent his childhood in an environment of wealth, orthodoxy, and social isolation. He went to school until he was fourteen, spending two years with an uncle in Holland, where, besides going to school, he learned languages and probably passed through some sort of apprenticeship. In later years his father was quite willing to hire tutors in fields that David found interesting, but for purely intellectual pursuits without practical applicability this merchant's family seems to have had little enthusiasm. Whereas Adam Smith was a professional scholar, Ricardo always remained an audodidact.

At the age of fourteen, David entered his father's brokerage firm, which was now specializing in bills of exchange and securities. Two years later we already find him in charge of two younger family members on a trip to the Continent. Increasingly he found himself in conflict with the orthodox family tradition. In 1793 he married a Quaker, which caused a break with his parents (though not with the rest of the family), and it seems that he became a Unitarian. It was a happy marriage, blessed by three sons and five daughters.

The estrangement from his father forced Ricardo to start his own business as a stockbroker. The beginning was difficult, but soon he was successful. At twenty-six he was wealthy and independent; in his early forties he owned a fortune on the order of magnitude of half a million pounds and was an influential financier. The Napoleonic Wars seem to have been golden times for English bankers (one of Ricardo's colleagues was Nathan Mayer Rothschild).

Financial security allowed Ricardo to resume his studies, particularly in mathematics, chemistry, physics, and, above all, mineralogy and geology. On accompanying his wife to Bath, where Mrs. Ricardo took the waters, he came across the *Wealth of Nations* in a lending library. He borrowed the book, read it, and was thereby won for political economy.

Ricardo became one of a group of friends who used to discuss economic problems, among them James Mill, Robert Malthus, Jeremy Bentham, and Henry Thornton. Out of these debates grew his first publication, an anonymous article, "The Price of Gold" (published in 1809). It made him a

---

1. This life sketch is based on D. Weatherall 1976, J. H. Hollander 1910, and P. Sraffa's editorial notes in Ricardo 1951–55.

protagonist of the bullionist position, according to which the depreciation of the (inconvertible) banknotes was not due to the trade deficit but to the inflationary policy of the Bank of England. In the following year, the article was expanded to a brilliant tract *The High Price of Bullion, a Proof of the Depreciation of Bank Notes*. By the end of 1812, Ricardo was an authority on currency questions, but he had written nothing yet on general economics. In the following years he was increasingly drawn into the debate on the corn trade, which raised more general problems.

Around the time of Waterloo, Ricardo considered himself rich enough. He may also have thought that the golden times for financiers were over. In any case, he bought a beautiful country estate, Gatcomb Park, and withdrew gradually from the stock exchange and from London. This gave him the leisure to expand his *Essay on the Influence of a Low Price of Corn on the Profits of Stock* of 1815 into the *Principles of Political Economy and Taxation* of 1817. For an inexperienced expositor such as Ricardo, this was an arduous task, for which he needed much encouragement from his friends, particularly James Mill. The book, though it sold respectably, was too difficult and arid to be a bestseller, but it made Ricardo the leading political economist. Whereas Adam Smith had sought to explain the size and growth of national income, Ricardo assigned economic science the primary task of determining the distribution of national income between landowners, capitalists, and workers.

In 1819, Ricardo became a member of the House of Commons for the Irish borough of Portarlington. To say simply that he was elected would be misleading, because he had made to the proprietor of the borough an interest-free loan of £20,000 on condition that he would obtain his seat free of expense. He never visited his constituents, but there was nothing objectionable in such arrangements in those times. As a member of Parliament Ricardo was an acknowledged authority on finance. His scientifically productive period, however, had, after only ten years, come to an end. In 1822 we find the Ricardo family, with retinue, on a grand tour through Europe. In Geneva, Ricardo met Simonde de Sismondi, his opponent on "general gluts," and in Zürich the foremost foreign exchange expert was cheated by an innkeeper in a foreign exchange transaction.

Ricardo died unexpectedly in 1823 after a short illness. He seems to have been a sociable man of likeable manners, short but good-looking, a loyal friend and brilliant conversationalist. His works and correspondence, edited by Piero Sraffa, were published for the Royal Economic Society beginning in 1951. Hollander 1979 offers a detailed account of Ricardo's economics, and critical assessments are collected in Wood 1985.

Value

In the *Wealth of Nations*, value makes its first appearance only in chapter 4. In writing the *Principles*, Ricardo was driven to the conclusion that he had to make value the subject of chapter 1, the central concept of economics, which it has remained ever since.

Like Smith, Ricardo had little use for value-in-use. It was for him no more than a necessary condition for value-in-exchange. Another thirty-seven years would elapse before Hermann Heinrich Gossen succeeded in making diminishing marginal utility, in itself long known, a key to the theory of value.

Ricardo also accepted Smith's distinction between the market price of commodities and their natural price, but he had no interest in the market price and focused his attention on the natural price. Ricardo's value theory thus became an equilibrium theory.

A further distinction was between commodities available in fixed quantities, such as rare coins, and those whose supply can be increased by production. On the first, Ricardo did not go beyond saying that their value is determined by scarcity and depends on demand (1951–55, 1:12); the analysis of monopoly price had to wait for Antoine Augustin Cournot. Ricardo's value theory, far from being a general one, was meant to be a special theory for reproducible goods in equilibrium. In addition, it mostly assumes fixed input coefficients, abstracting from factor substitution and economies of scale.

The analysis proceeds in three stages. In the first, commodities are produced with labor only, as in berry picking. In this case "the value of a commodity, or the quantity of any other commodity for which it will exchange, depends on the relative quantity of labour which is necessary for its production" (Ricardo 1951–55, 1:11). "If among a nation of hunters, for example, it usually cost twice the labour to kill a beaver which it does to kill a deer, one beaver should naturally exchange for, or be worth two deer" (13). Relative prices are exclusively determined by the required labor inputs. If a_{01} and a_{02} are, respectively, the quantities of labor necessary to produce a unit of commodities 1 and 2, then their relative price is simply $p_1/p_2 = a_{01}/a_{02}$. The point is that demand has no influence on relative prices; the relative demand for beaver skins and venison indeed determines the quantities produced, but not their values. Ricardo realized, of course, that labor differs in quality and intensity, but he intuitively applied what later came to be called Hicks's composite goods theorem, according to which different types of labor may be reduced to "common labor" as long as relative wages remain unchanged (20f.).

In the second stage, production requires not only labor but also means of production such as implements, tools, and buildings. These are, in turn, produced with labor and means of production. All input coefficients are still fixed and there is no interest. Under these conditions, relative prices are still determined by relative labor costs, but to direct labor one now has to add indirect labor. As William Petty and Richard Cantillon had pointed out, means of production can be resolved into labor.

To illustrate in algebraic terms, suppose each of two goods, x_1 and x_2, is produced with labor, given in quantity A, and some of the same two goods. Whatever is not used up in production is left for consumption. Denoting the input of x_i in the production of a unit of x_j by a_{ij}, and consumption by c_i, one obtains the linear system

$$x_1 = a_{11}x_1 + a_{12}x_2 + c_1 \tag{9.1}$$

$$x_2 = a_{21}x_1 + a_{22}x_2 + c_2 \tag{9.2}$$

$$A = a_{01}x_1 + a_{02}x_2. \tag{9.3}$$

The three equations determine the alternative combinations of consumer goods, c_1 and c_2, that can be produced from given labor. Society's choice among these combinations clearly depends on demand, and so does the structure of industry.

Relative prices, however, still depend on input coefficients only. In competitive equilibrium, prices equal costs. Denoting the wage rate by w, this results in the conditions

$$p_1 = p_1 a_{11} + p_2 a_{21} + w a_{01}, \tag{9.4}$$

$$p_2 = p_1 a_{12} + p_2 a_{22} + w a_{02}, \tag{9.5}$$

or, in terms of relative prices,

$$(1 - a_{11}) \frac{p_1}{p_2} - a_{01} \frac{w}{p_2} = a_{21}, \tag{9.6}$$

$$a_{12} \frac{p_1}{p_2} + a_{02} \frac{w}{p_2} = (1 - a_{22}). \tag{9.7}$$

This system can be solved for the relative price

$$\frac{p_1}{p_2} = \frac{a_{01}(1 - a_{22}) + a_{02}a_{21}}{a_{01}a_{12} + a_{02}(1 - a_{11})}. \tag{9.8}$$

Again the relative price is independent not only of consumption demand but also of the wage rate. The proposition quoted above that value depends on labor thus continues with the statement that it depends "not on the greater or less compensation which is paid for that labour" (Ricardo 1951–55, 1:11). A change in the wage rate affects all prices in the same proportion.

In the third stage, Ricardo introduces time and interest. If all production activities had the same capital intensities, this would not affect relative price. Ricardo emphasizes, however, that capital intensities may differ greatly between industries. The essential element is the time the producer must wait for the services of capital goods to mature: the brewer waits, on average, many years for the services of his brewery, the farmer waits a year for those of his seed corn, and the baker waits a week for those of his flour. As a consequence, the labor theory of value ceases to be exact.

To employ again an algebraic demonstration, this time Samuelson's (1966–86, vol. 1, chs. 31, 32), suppose all labor is used directly as in the first stage (so that $a_{11} = a_{12} = a_{21} = a_{22} = 0$), but now the outputs accrue after delays θ_1 and θ_2. During this time the producer pays interest on his inputs at rate i. The equilibrium prices thus become

$$p_1 = wa_{01} (1+i)^{\theta_1}, \tag{9.9}$$
$$p_2 = wa_{02} (1+i)^{\theta_2}, \tag{9.10}$$

and the relative price, therefore,

$$\frac{p_1}{p_2} = \frac{a_{01}}{a_{02}} (1+i)^{\theta_1 - \theta_2}. \tag{9.11}$$

For equal duration of the processes, $\theta_1 = \theta_2$, we are back in the world of the pure labor theory of value, but in the general case the rate of interest becomes another determinant of relative prices, raising the prices of capital-intensive goods relative to the others.

This had an important corollary. Ricardo's fundamental theorem, to be discussed below, was the inverse movement of the wage rate and the profit (or interest) rate. If it was valid, relative commodity prices became also dependent on the wage rate. A fall in wages, because it raises the rate of interest, would raise the relative prices of capital-intensive goods. In the interwar period, Friedrich von Hayek called this relationship the Ricardo effect and used it to explain the cyclical fluctuations in investment demand. The Ricardian proposition, however, was strictly static in intent.

Analytically, as Stigler (1965, ch. 12) has emphasized, Ricardo thus had, like Adam Smith, a cost of production theory of value and not a labor theory (Ricardo 1951–55, 8:279; 9:178). He pushed the labor theory of value as far as he could and showed that there were insurmountable limits.[2] Empirically, however, he thought that the influence of a shift between profits and wages was rather small. In his further analysis he therefore decided to disregard this influence and to concentrate on the fluctuations in value brought forth by varying quantities of labor (1:36f.).

2. John Ramsay McCulloch purported to surmount these limits by classifying the force that makes wine mature and trees grow as "labor of nature." Despite this ridiculous play on words, he admitted that the exchangeable value of a commodity does not strictly correspond to the quantity of labor required to produce it (1886, 166). McCulloch's subterfuge was also used, in a veiled form, by James Mill (1966, 260f.).

The Invariable Measure of Value

Ricardo's value theory was meant to be valid for any number of goods. His basic propositions on the distribution of national income were originally derived for a one-good economy producing only wheat. This raised the question of how these propositions could be applied to a multicommodity economy. It led Ricardo to the problem of an invariable measure of value.

The problem came up in different contexts. Suppose that in the primitive hunter economy one beaver suddenly becomes worth three deer. Is this caused by an increase in the input coefficient for beaver, a decline in the deer coefficient, or a mixture of the two? The question could be answered if a commodity were found whose input coefficient is not subject to change. This commodity could then serve as an "invariable measure of value" (Ricardo 1951–55, 1:13f.). Ricardo realized that such a commodity can hardly be found, all input coefficients being subject to change. As a stopgap standard he proposed gold.

The other aspect of the problem arose from unequal capital intensities. A rise in the profit rate, as was pointed out in the preceding section, raises the relative prices of capital-intensive goods, while the relative prices of labor-intensive goods decline. Would it not be possible, Ricardo asked himself, to choose a standard of value with an invariant relative price? His answer was yes, provided a commodity can be found whose capital intensity happens to be an appropriately weighted mean of all capital intensitities (Ricardo 1951–55, 1:45f.).

The idea can be made precise in a three-good example by adding to the two commodities of the preceding section a third with price $p_3 = wa_{03}(1+i)^{\theta_3}$ and $\theta_1 < \theta_2 < \theta_3$. The proportionate change in the price index P can then be defined as a value-weighted mean of individual price changes,

$$\frac{dP}{P} = \frac{p_1c_1\left[\dfrac{dp_1}{p_1}\right] + p_2c_2\left[\dfrac{dp_2}{p_2}\right] + p_3c_3\left[\dfrac{dp_3}{p_3}\right]}{p_1c_1 + p_2c_2 + p_3c_3}. \tag{9.12}$$

If i changes, the consequent change in p_i is

$$\frac{dp_i}{di}\frac{1}{p_i} = \frac{\theta}{1+i}. \tag{9.13}$$

The difference between the change in p_2 and the change in P, therefore, is

$$\frac{dp_2}{di}\frac{1}{p_2} - \frac{dP}{di}\frac{1}{P} = \frac{1}{1+i}\left[\theta_2 - \frac{p_1c_1\theta_1 + p_2c_2\theta_2 + p_3c_3\theta_3}{p_1c_1 + p_2c_2 + p_3c_3}\cdot\right] \tag{9.14}$$

This expression is zero if the square bracket is zero, which means that θ_2 is a value-weighted average of θ_1 and θ_3,

$$\theta_2 = \frac{p_1 c_1 \theta_1 + p_3 c_3 \theta_3}{p_1 c_1 + p_3 c_3}. \qquad (9.15)$$

If a commodity with this property can be found, its price, relative to the general price level, will not be affected by a change in the rate of interest. At the same time such a commodity, if used as a national income deflator, would see to it that a change in the rate of interest affects not the size of real national income but only its distribution. Changes in distribution could thus be clearly distinguished from changes in income itself.[3]

It is clear that the second aspect of Ricardo's standard of value problem is quite different from the first. Ricardo, however, intermingled the two, and he suggested that gold may be a tolerable approximation from the second point of view as well. In fact, he was painfully conscious that he had solved neither problem, and his discussion was shedding more darkness than light.

The mirage of an invariable measure of value haunted Ricardo to the end of his life. The reason is difficult to understand because the problem, except for special and artificial cases, is not only insoluble but also abstruse and devoid of substantive economic meaning. It must be admitted, however, that for Sraffa (1960) and the neo-Ricardians it became a source of new analytical inspiration.

Rent

In the preceding exposition of Ricardian value theory, land and rent do not appear. In the value theory of Ricardo's predecessor Cantillon, land turned out to be the all-important factor. The difference highlights the growing, though still incomplete, understanding of diminishing returns. Cantillon visualized land of uniform quality with fixed output per acre. In 1767, Turgot had clearly expressed the principle of diminishing returns, which Ricardo had early become acquainted with. In 1815, West and Malthus had independently used this principle as the basis of a theory of rent that Anderson had presented thirty-eight years before. Two years later, Ricardo made this theory a cornerstone of his analysis of distribution.

The first question concerns the modification in the laws of value that are required by the scarcity of land. Ricardo answered that no modifications are required at all. To Cantillon's land theory of value he thus opposed a nonland theory. Suppose a given population is endowed with land of varying quality, gradually turning into desert. Land will be cultivated down to the margin where a farmer can just barely make a living. In a competitive

---

3. Write nominal income as $Y = p_1 c_1 + p_2 c_2 + p_3 c_3$ and real income in terms of commodity 2 as $Y_2 = Y/p_2$. Substitute for prices in terms of the interest rate and set the derivative of dY_2/di equal to zero. This gives the condition that θ_2 must satisfy in order to make Y_2 invariant under changes in i. The condition turns out to be the same as in the preceding paragraph.

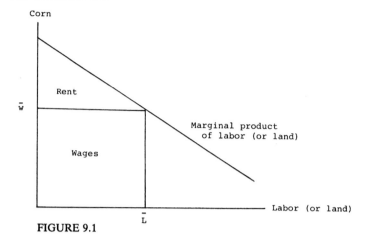

FIGURE 9.1

society, all farmers earn this same subsistence wage. The excess of production over this wage goes to the landlord as rent, which implies that the owners of the marginal land obtain no rent. Factor incomes can thus be analyzed as if rent did not matter by concentrating on this marginal strip of land. As Ricardo put it, "the exchangeable value of all commodities . . . is always regulated . . . by the greater quantity of labour necessarily bestowed on their production . . . by those who continue to produce them under the most unfavorable circumstances" (1951–55, 1:73).

Ricardo recognized three types of rent. Differential rents are due to the different fertility of the soil. Suppose all land is divided into farms of uniform size and the farms are ranked according to the quality of the soil. Farms are operated by families of uniform size with standard equipment. Yields per family (or farm) will then lie along a downward-sloping curve (figure 9.1), representing the marginal product of labor (or land). For a predetermined amount of labor $\bar{L}$, the wage rate will correspond to the marginal product $\bar{w}$. For a predetermined wage $\bar{w}$ (say, the subsistence wage), the number of families supported by the land is $\bar{L}$. Total output is measured by the area under the curve. Of this, the rectangle wL goes to labor as wages, and the residual triangle goes to landlords as rent. The marginal farm, therefore, pays no rent, even though it still yields corn.

Ricardo was well aware that rent would also arise if all land were of uniform quality. To illustrate such intensity rents, suppose that there is a limited area of uniform land. It is being cultivated by a variable number of farmers (each again with his standard equipment), so that the acreage per farm is variable. With an increasing population, total output increases but, in view of diminishing returns, less than in proportion to population. The marginal product, therefore, again declines as described in figure 9.1.

94

The remainder of the argument is the same as before with the "extensive margin" of rentless land now replaced by the "intensive margin" of a rentless "dose" of labor on given land. In the present case, however, there is no rentless land, all acres obtaining the same scarcity rent.

Finally, Ricardo was aware that rent may also be due to locational advantages, but it remained for Thünen, in 1826, to provide a detailed analysis of these spatial aspects.

Ricardo concludes that "rent is not a component part of the price of commodities" (1951–55, 1:78) and "corn is not high because a rent is paid, but a rent is paid because corn is high" (74). Whereas in the *Wealth of Nations* this proposition had appeared as a dogmatic assertion, it was now analytically substantiated. The physiocrats were wrong, therefore, in attributing rent to the fertility of the soil. In fact, rent is due precisely to the limitations in the quantity and quality of land, and the same is true for other natural resources. Though in his general theory of value Ricardo had nothing substantial to say about scarcity, his theory of rent became fundamental for the understanding of the pricing of scarce resources.

Unfortunately, Ricardo's conclusions, as Samuelson (1966–86, vol. 1, chs. 31, 32) has brilliantly shown, though containing much that is true, are neither all true nor the whole truth. In particular, it is not generally correct that rent has no influence on commodity prices. One qualification arises from products with different factor intensities. Suppose there are two crops—say, corn and potatoes. Suppose further that, for quantitites requiring the same amount of labor, corn requires more land. In this case, those quantitites will not have the same exchange value, but the value of corn will be higher.

Another qualification arises from variable proportions between labor and capital for the same product. Suppose corn farmers can choose between different amounts of capital equipment depending on the characteristics of their soil. It is then impossible even to rank the different pieces of land by quality without knowing the prices of corn, labor, and capital equipment. The marginal land cannot be identified without knowing prices, and all prices are determined simultaneously in general equilibrium.

Most fundamentally, once the scarcity of land has obliterated the extensive margin, all land paying some rent, while laborers and capital goods can be reproduced at constant costs, a nonland theory of value becomes completely untenable. Instead of "congealed labor," commodities then become "congealed land." In these circumstances, Cantillon had it right and Ricardo was on the wrong track.

Wages

Once rent was taken care of by the expedient of the rentless margin, there remained Ricardo's central problem, namely the distribution of the product between wages and profits. To the theory of wages Ricardo made

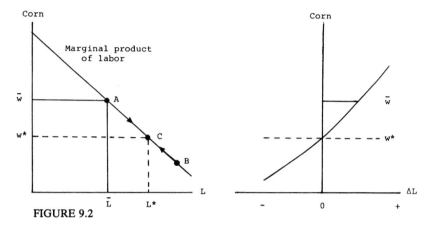

FIGURE 9.2

no original contribution but essentially adopted the theory of Adam Smith as sharpened in the light of Malthus.

On given land, and disregarding capital, the marginal product of labor would decline as described in figure 9.1 and reproduced in the left-hand panel of figure 9.2. Since wages equal the marginal product, the curve also describes the wage rate for any amount of labor. This is the static part of the model. The dynamic part relates the wage rate to the rate of change of the labor force or population growth, as described in the right-hand panel of figure 9.2. There is a subsistence wage, w^*, just high enough to keep the labor force stationary. This is the natural price of labor. It is not a physical or biological constant but highly dependent on social factors and subject to change in the course of historical development. In particular, a prolonged experience of above-subsistence wages may cause the subsistence wage to rise and vice versa. If the market wage is above the subsistence wage (as at $\bar{w}$), the labor force grows; if it is below the subsistence wage, the labor force declines.

In general, a growing labor force is characterized by above-subsistence wages. The steeper the growth curve, the larger is this differential for a given growth rate. In the limiting case of a horizontal growth curve (as represented by the broken line) with an extremely sensitive reaction of population growth to wage rates, even the smallest wage differential would call forth a virtual population explosion. There would be a horizontal supply curve of labor at the subsistence wage. Ricardo did not regard this as a realistic case; he felt that wages could be above subsistence for prolonged periods. However, he often used the horizontal curve as a simplifying assumption.

In the long run, of course, wages are bound to gravitate toward the subsistence level w^* through the interplay of the static and the dynamic part. Both from A and from B the system thus tends to move toward C. This movement can be counteracted, however, by the accumulation of capital, which shifts the marginal product curve upward. Capital accumulation, therefore, helps to keep wages above the subsistence level for extended periods.

This reasoning leads Ricardo to an outline of economic development, though a sketchy one. At the "beginning," with sparsely populated land (as at $\bar{L}$), labor productivity, and thus wages, are high. Population, therefore, is growing. The capital stock may grow still faster, and wages, therefore, may conceivably even increase further. However, this would result in an acceleration of population growth. Sooner or later capital accumulation will become insufficient to prevent wages from falling, which will, in turn, slow down population growth. In the long run there will be stagnation at L^*, though possibly at a comfortable subsistence wage.

Ricardo, again following Malthus, used his wage theory for a trenchant criticism of the Poor Laws. Under the Speenhamland System of 1795, poor workers received from their parish a supplement to their wages amounting to the difference between their market wage and some social minimum standard. Ricardo objected that in the long run this system would only increase the number of the poor but would do nothing to improve their condition.

In terms of figure 9.2, suppose the subsistence wage w^* is considered to be below the social minimum and a supplement is paid in the amount of the difference. This would shift the growth curve downward by the same amount; what is relevant for population growth is clearly the market wage *plus* the supplement. Once the dynamic mechanism has run its course, therefore, the market wage will simply have fallen by the amount of the supplement. An increased supplement will then seem to be required, and so on. To follow the argument to its logical conclusion, market wages would ultimately go to zero and workers would be entirely supported by the government. Ricardo was not socially insensitive, and he was not a pessimist, but, like all Malthusians, he saw the key to improved living conditions in an upward shift of the growth curve, whereas the Poor Laws threatened to shift it down even further.

Profits

For Ricardo, as for Adam Smith, capital consisted of wages advanced to workers, called circulating capital, and more or less durable capital goods, called fixed capital. He also followed Adam Smith in not separating interest from profits, and for his purpose this was entirely adequate.

It had long been clear that profit rates, after allowing for risk, tend to equality in different industries. Mobility has the same equalizing effect on capital as it has on labor. Ricardo's fundamental problem concerned the systematic changes in the profit rate in the course of economic development.

His analysis of this problem is made difficult for a modern reader by the use of labor as a unit of account, whereas we are used to reckoning in terms of commodity units (or bundles). An example may illustrate the difficulty. Suppose the real wage remains constant at the subsistence level of 1 bushel of corn. With a growing population, in view of diminishing returns, 1 bushel of corn costs more and more labor. A modern observer, reckoning in corn units, would say that wages are constant. Ricardo, reckoning in labor units, would say that wages are increasing, because it takes more and more labor to feed a worker. In modern terminology, the inverse movement of profits and wages in Ricardo's fundamental theorem is thus transformed into a parallel movement of profits and marginal returns. The following exposition uses the modern terminology. It thus does not do justice to some aspects that would have been important to Ricardo (and perhaps to Sraffa), but from the point of view of modern mainstream economics, these aspects are not significant.

Ricardo's main contribution is the construction of a theory of capital accumulation and profit in perfect analogy to population growth and wages. It makes Ricardo the Malthus of capital. The main argument can best be explained by using Ricardo's simplifying assumptions that labor and capital are used in fixed proportions[4] and that wages are continually at their subsistence level.

If more and more doses of labor-cum-capital are applied to the same land, the marginal product declines. Of this marginal product, labor receives the subsistence wage, and the residual goes to profits. There is, therefore, an inverse relationship between the capital stock (and population) and the profit rate. In the left-hand panel of figure 9.3, capital K is measured along the horizontal axis. If the capital used by a laborer is called a unit of capital, the horizontal scale also measures labor input. Of the marginal product, measured vertically, the subsistence wage w^* goes to labor. The residual r thus measures the profit rate, and the upper rectangle depicts the amount of profit. As capital increases, the profit rate necessarily declines, just as in Adam Smith.

To this static part Ricardo added a dynamic part. There is a profit rate at which the capitalists have no incentive either to accumulate or to decumulate capital. It is, so to speak, the subsistence level of profits, the natural price of capital. In Ricardo's opinion it is greater than zero; in view of risk and the subsistence needs of capitalists, accumulation ceases long before profits have vanished.

---

4. Inasmuch as capital consists of a wage fund of consumer goods, higher real wages would require a higher capital stock per unit of labor.

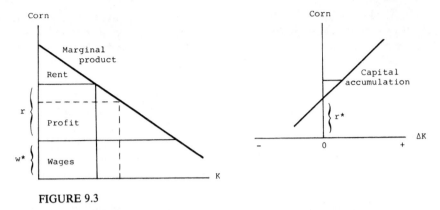

FIGURE 9.3

If profits are above their subsistence level, capital is accumulated through saving; if they are below the subsistence level, capital is used up by dissaving. There is, therefore, an accumulation function for capital analogous to the Malthusian population growth function. It is depicted in the right-hand panel of figure 9.3. The scale of this graph is moved upward to the level of the subsistence wage in the left-hand panel, and the subsistence level of profits is denoted by r^*.

In the situation indicated by the solid lines, profits stand above this subsistence level, and capital accumulation, therefore, is positive. In the next period, the capital stock will thus be larger and the profit rate lower, which reduces capital accumulation. It is clear that the dynamic interplay between the static and the dynamic part of the system will eventually lead to the point indicated by the broken lines, where profits, like wages, are at their subsistence level. All growth will then come to an end. Ricardo believed that, in his time, profits were still far above, and the capital stock thus far below, their subsistence levels. Eventually, however, the tendency of profits to fall must assert itself.

Though Ricardo did not believe that wages, in reality, were always close to their subsistence level, he had no theory about the division of the marginal product between labor and capital for the general case of non-subsistence wages. If there is some mechanism that keeps the capital/labor ratio constant at all times, this gap can readily be filled. In fact, for any given marginal product, there is, with positively sloped growth curves, only one division that provides for equal growth of labor and capital. In the absence of such a mechanism, however, and thus with a variable capital/labor ratio, the dynamics of Ricardian accumulation are not determined.

Taken together, Ricardo's theories of rent, wages, and profit constitute a macroeconomic model of economic growth. Whereas Adam Smith had sketched out the outline of such a model, Ricardo provided the model itself. It should be noted that this was a model of unbalanced growth, eventually ending in stagnation because of the scarcity of natural resources. This theme was later taken up by W. S. Jevons in his book on the coal question, but as a theoretical analysis Ricardo's achievement was not surpassed before the second half of the twentieth century.[5] Paradoxically, Marx's original contribution to growth theory, namely the famous two-sector model, was confined to balanced growth that could go on forever.

Comparative Advantage

One of Ricardo's most brilliant intellectual achievements was the principle of comparative advantage. It says that each of two countries should export those commodities for which its cost advantage is relatively high (or its disadvantage relatively low) and import those commodities for which it has a relatively low cost advantage (or a relatively high disadvantage).

Ricardo's point is that the (relative) international immobility of labor and capital results in a fundamental difference between interregional and international trade. Within the same country, factor mobility equalizes wage and profit rates between regions. Trade, therefore, is simply governed by absolute labor costs. Each region will supply the others with products for which it has the lower costs. Across national borders, however, the (relative) immobility of factors may leave permanent differences in wage and profit rates. Simple labor cost comparisons are not enough, therefore, to determine the efficient allocation of resources. In particular, a commodity may advantageously be exported from a high-cost country to a low-cost country.

The general idea of comparative cost did not originate with Ricardo. It had been clearly expressed by Adam Smith and can be traced back to the anonymous "Considerations on the East-India Trade" of 1701 and to mercantilist writers such as Samuel Fortrey. What mattered, they pointed out, was whether England could obtain more wine by using its labor to produce cloth and then exchanging the cloth for wine than by using it to produce its own wine. England could do so if cloth exchanged for more wine in the international market than in the home market. Robert Torrens observed that foreign trade might thus be advantageous for England even if her production possibilities are superior for both commodities (1815, 263f.). Ricardo's contribution was the development of these rules for profitable foreign trade into a general numerical principle for the efficient allocation of production between two countries and its combination with the theory of specie flows.

Merchants, Ricardo pointed out, are not interested in computations

---

5. A model of this type, based on Solow 1956, is analyzed in Niehans 1963. The present exposition owes much to Samuelson 1966–86, vol. 5, ch. 340.

of comparative advantage; all they care about is money prices. Suppose now we start with an arbitrary situation in which England has a labor cost advantage for both commodities while prices reflect labor costs. England's merchants will then find it profitable to export both wine and cloth. But this situation cannot endure. In the absence of profitable imports, England will be paid in gold. This specie flow will, in turn, raise English prices, while foreign prices decline. The specie flow will come to an end only when international price ratios reflect not absolute labor costs but comparative advantage. With competitive markets, therefore, money prices will guide merchants to an efficient international division of labor.

In formulating his principle, Ricardo, like Hume before him, was not very careful with respect to the Law of One Price for traded goods. He clearly realized, though, that there was no reason why commodity prices should generally be equalized internationally. More importantly, Ricardo, since he limited his analysis to the cost side, could only determine an upper and a lower limit for the international exchange ratio, but not the ratio itself. This gap was filled later by the young John Stuart Mill.

Ricardo did not recognize the general significance of his principle. Today it is easy to see that comparative advantage governs not only the international division of labor but also the division of labor between individuals and firms and the efficient allocation of resources in general. Ludwig von Mises was right, therefore, in calling the principle of comparative advantage Ricardo's "Law of Association" (1949, 158f.). In later marginal analysis its substance was expressed in the postulate that relative prices equal the marginal rate of transformation of commodities in production or their opportunity cost.

In more technical terms, Ricardo had constructed the first linear programming model. Whereas Cantillon had used linear relationships for a descriptive input-output model of the economy, Ricardo had taken the step to optimization. It took economic science about 125 years to advance beyond Ricardo's rudimentary analysis, and even in modern linear programming, the choice between alternative feasible solutions is essentially still guided by comparative advantage.

Monetary Theory

Ricardo, though he was a banker and first acquired a reputation in the bullionist controversy, did not make major original contributions to the theory of money. His historical contribution was the powerful support he gave to the classical tradition that had emerged during the eighteenth century. The main tenets of this tradition, as expressed in Ricardo's writings, can be set forth as follows.[6]

6. The following interpretation is similar to that of Glasner (1985) and Ahiakpor (1985).

There is perceived to be an analytical dichotomy between commodity money, exemplified by the gold standard (with or without convertible bank notes) and inconvertible paper currency. Under the gold standard, monetary authorities determine the price of gold, but they have, ultimately, no power over the money supply (Ricardo 1951–55, 1:104f.; 3:90; 4:64). With an inconvertible currency, the authorities determine the money supply, but they have, ultimately, no power over the price of gold.

The value of money, under the gold standard, depends on the cost of gold production and is, therefore, subject to the same economic laws as the values of other commodities (Ricardo 1951–55, 5:444). A decline in the cost of gold production certainly raises prices, but the quantity theory, despite some misleading formulations (4:56), does not strictly apply. The value of an inconvertible currency, on the other hand, depends on the money supply, on the velocity of circulation (or the cash ratio) and on real output. Velocity and real output are subject to variations, both between countries and in the course of time (3:90; 4:58; 5:417f.). As a result, stable prices require appropriate adjustments in the money supply. However, velocity and real output are not permanently affected by the money supply. Consequently, the quantity theory is valid in the sense that a one-time increase in the money supply results, in the long run, in an equiproportionate increase in prices compared to what they would have been without the increase (5:417f.).

Internationally, the prices of traded goods can exhibit no appreciable differences. Even small differentials are rapidly eliminated by commodity and gold arbitrage (Ricardo 1951–55, 3:90). International specie flows, therefore, cannot be explained by international differentials of price levels. With an inconvertible currency, exchange rates, in the long run, react to monetary disturbances in the same way as domestic prices. Whenever money is the driving force, changes in exchange rates thus correspond to the changes in the relative purchasing power of national currencies (91). Capital, in Ricardo's view, is highly mobile internationally, so that fluctuations in, say, harvests can be accommodated without significant gold flows (103).

Money is supplied by a fractional-reserve banking system in which the central bank holds gold reserves and commercial banks hold central bank money and/or gold. Changes in central bank money thus act on the money supply with, in modern terms, a multiplier (Ricardo 1951–55, 3:86f.). Commercial bank lending is held in check by the loss of reserves (126f.). There is, therefore, no need for quantitative limitations on the issue of bank notes, but there should be liquidity requirements (4:72f.). With a convertible currency, reserve considerations also limit the supply of central bank money. With an inconvertible currency, however, the central bank can expand the money supply indefinitely by maintaining a lending rate below the profit opportunities of borrowers (1:364); this would, of course, create progressive inflation.

For the long run, as is further explained in the section on Jean-Baptiste Say in chapter 10, Ricardo subscribed to Say's law, according to which monetary factors do not cause general under- or overproduction. In the short run, however, even an inconvertible currency would not be neutral, because prices adjust with lags (Ricardo 1951–55, 5:452), because of the existence of old contracts, and also because tax rates may be fixed in nominal terms. This nonneutrality is reflected in short-run variations in interest rates, distribution, and output, but Ricardo, in contrast to others, tended to play down the output effects (3:91, 318f.; 5:445f.; 6:16f.). He had more interest in the long run than in the short run, but precisely because of the potential seriousness of short-run disturbances he advocated a steady course of monetary policy (4:69). If deflation should ever be necessary, it should be gradual to minimize the real disturbances, particularly in distribution (3:94; 5:440).

The guiding principle of monetary policy should be the constancy of the purchasing power of money (Ricardo 1951–55, 4:54; 5:442). However, this objective cannot be attained directly; in fact, in view of the continuous fluctuations of relative prices, the general purchasing power of money cannot even be expressed in a number (4:59f.).[7] In this situation, constancy of the price of gold could serve as a workable, though imperfect, approximation. The most efficient way for the central bank to reach this second-best objective is by standing ready to buy and sell gold (or silver) bullion for paper money at a fixed price, thereby saving the economy the cost of maintaining a large stock of gold coins (66). This would not protect the economy against bank panics, to be sure, but Ricardo thought that such protection could not be secured by any monetary rules (68).

By 1820 the classical tradition, though Ricardo deemphasized the short run, had thus produced a quite elaborate, articulate, and flexible theory of money. Without fundamental revision, this theory could serve as a general framework for the development of business cycle theory, macroeconomics, and international monetary economics to the present day. Though its basic propositions have often been attacked, they turned out to be fairly solid. Modern monetary theory is infinitely richer than Ricardian theory, and (with the exception of the rational expectations approach) it tends to give short-run disturbances more weight, but it is still a continuation of the same classical tradition.

7. Ricardo clearly perceived that changes in purchasing power, if correctly measured, would turn out differently for consumers with different preferences (1951–55, 4:61).

Place in the History of Economics

Ricardo, like most of the great economists, did not create a "school." The true Ricardians number only three, namely, James Mill, John Ramsay McCulloch, and Thomas De Quincey.[8] Marx was, of course, a Ricardian of sorts, for he exaggerated Ricardo's vices without learning from his virtues. Even in the absence of a school, David Ricardo's influence on the history of economics was second only to Adam Smith's and equaled only by Léon Walras. If economics before 1817 was a dialogue with Smith, for the following fifty years it became a dialogue with Ricardo.

It has often been argued that Ricardo's influence was pernicious rather than beneficial. Thus Jevons, in the preface to the second edition of his *Theory of Political Economy,* published in 1879, expressed the opinion that "that able but wrong-headed man, David Ricardo, shunted the car of Economic science on to a wrong line." There is a grain of truth in this assessment. Ricardo went as far as he possibly could in constructing models in which demand has no influence on relative prices but determines only the quantities produced and consumed. In the light of modern linear models, it is clear that this is a much more legitimate endeavor than earlier "subjectivist" critics realized. It is also clear, however, that the endeavor can succeed only under very restrictive and artificial assumptions. Economic science was groping for a general theory of value, and Ricardo's special theory turned out to be an impediment rather than a stepping stone to further progress. The decisive advances in the following decades took place in the direction of microeconomic optimization and not of macroeconomic input-output analysis.

Nevertheless, Ricardo, with the same "strong hand," also lifted economic science to a higher plane. Among his substantive analytical achievements the most significant was probably the completion of what Samuelson (1966–86, vol. 5, ch. 340) has called the "canonical classical model of political economy." It was a vast theoretical structure that provided a suitable framework for most growth theory down to the days of the oil crisis and the "limits to growth." Another signal achievement was the principle of comparative advantage.

Ricardo's most important contribution, however, concerned not specific insights but the techniques of economic analysis. Inferior to Smith in breadth of interests, economic intuition, and judgment on human affairs, he was greatly superior to him in rigor of analysis. For the first time, we

8. De Quincey's "Dialogues of Three Templars" of 1824 (in 1890a) are a dialectic plea for Ricardo's value theory. The "Logic of Political Economy" of 1844 (in 1890a) is intended to clarify the logic of value but drowns it in a deluge of prolixity. About political economy he said that "David Ricardo made the first and the last effort that ever can be made to revolutionize that science" ("Ricardo and Adam Smith," 1842, in De Quincey 1890a).

see a theorist carefully (though often imperfectly) specify his assumptions in such a way that certain macroeconomic propositions could be demonstrated to be true. Whereas Smith presented examples, Ricardo constructed models. Today these models often seem contrived, and they were not faultlessly handled. The recent proliferation of mathematical models "in the spirit of Ricardo" testifies to Ricardo's frequent inability to make his meaning clear. However, he went about as far as an analytical genius could go without scientific training. Further progress was attainable only with the aid of mathematics.

10

Money: The Completion of the Classical Tradition

BY THE END of the classical era, monetary theory had accumulated a body of analysis to which the marginalist era had little to add. This classical tradition was very different from the anemic representations so often found in modern literature. Far from being limited to static equilibrium and the quantity theory of money, it already contained all of the cornerstones of modern monetary macroeconomics. The "neoclassical synthesis" of the 1950s could almost (though not quite) have been achieved around 1830.

The initial building blocks were supplied by Cantillon, Law, Hume, and Christiernin. The tradition was completed in the early decades of the nineteenth century. It received powerful support from David Ricardo, whose contribution is reviewed in the preceding chapter. The suspension of sterling convertibility during the Napoleonic Wars led to the peak achievement of classical monetary theory, namely Henry Thornton's analysis of monetary macrodynamics in a fractional-reserve banking system. Jean-Baptiste Say's law of markets provided the point of departure for a century and a half of macroeconomic debate. Nassau Senior, finally, completed the integration of monetary and value theory for a commodity money system. These key contributions are reviewed in the following sections.

Henry Thornton

Henry Thornton was born in London on 10 March 1760, the third son of a prosperous merchant.[1] His father seems to have regarded piety and charity as more important than knowledge, and Henry thus received but a scant education. Starting as a merchant, Thornton was elected to the House of Commons at the age of twenty-two. Soon afterward he became a partner in a reputable banking firm, which he remained all his life.

---

1. This biographical note is based on Friedrich von Hayek's introduction to Thornton 1939.

Generally supporting Pitt, he became a leading member of the evangelical "party of the Saints," of which William Wilberforce was the driving spirit and the abolition of the slave trade the main achievement.

The banking business was very profitable, although Thornton spent much time on his philanthropic and political activities. Most of his income, six-sevenths as a rule, went to charity, but he could still maintain a large estate, which became a center of the group.

As a member of Parliament, Thornton was highly regarded, though not widely popular. In the course of time he concentrated increasingly on matters of banking and finance, taking a leading part in the work of the Bullion Committee of 1810. He died after a long illness, probably consumption, in 1815.

Most of Thornton's published works are religious tracts and prayer books, which were distributed in large numbers. Except for reports about two speeches in the House of Commons, his only economic publication is *An Enquiry into the Nature and Effects of the Paper Credit of Great Britain*, which came out in 1802. It is the source of his fame as an economist.

Thornton's contribution to economic science was a by-product of his contribution to the debate on current economic problems. In 1797 the Bank of England, after several severe banking crises, had suspended the convertibility of its notes into gold. In the course of time the market price of gold began to exceed the mint price. It was argued that this discrepancy was a clear sign of an excessive issue of bank notes and that it should be corrected by monetary contraction. Thornton wrote his book to show that, in 1802, the premium on gold was due to other causes, that monetary contraction would do more harm than good, and that the suspension of convertibility was preferable to a financial crisis. Adam Smith was wrong, Thornton argued, in attributing every possible discrepancy between the market price of gold and its mint price to monetary policy, for it might, in fact, have "real" causes (Thornton 1939, 200f., 225f.).

This would seem to make Thornton an antibullionist. By the time of the Bullion Report, however, he had become convinced that now the gold premium was indeed due to the excessive issue of bank notes and that contraction, though it should be gradual, was unavoidable. He thus sided with the bullionists, as did Ricardo.

This is not the place for a detailed review of Thornton's policy views. The question is rather what he contributed to mainstream economics. His most fundamental contribution may be said to be the first outline of a model of financial intermediation in an open economy. In James Tobin's terms he was the first to develop a "general-equilibrium approach to monetary theory" (Tobin 1971–75, vol. 1, ch. 18). Gurley and Shaw (1960) might have said that his topic was money in a theory of finance. In this system goods (both foreign and domestic), labor, gold coins, bank notes, bills, trade credit, government securities, and other claims are demanded and supplied depending on market conditions. Market conditions, in turn, are such that (with due regard to inventories) demand and supply are equalized in each market (Thornton 1939, 100f., 170).

Blaming Smith for ignoring the differences between various kinds of liquid assets, Thornton develops the "Radcliffian" view that there is a broad spectrum of means of payment, each with different characteristics (Thornton 1939, 93f.). Coins bear no return and impose, at least in large amounts, significant transactions costs, but they have low risk. Bank notes have negligible transactions costs but also no yield, and they may become risky. Bills bear interest, but this makes transactions costs high. For government securities, the yield has to be weighed against risk and brokerage costs. As a consequence, the average holding period or the velocity of circulation is quite different for different instruments (94). More importantly, velocity fluctuates depending on market conditions; it is high in periods of high confidence, whereas lack of confidence will lead to hoarding (95f.). This analysis of the demand for money was hardly improved upon before John Hicks's "A suggestion for simplifying the theory of money" of 1935 (1981–83, vol. 2).

Thornton's financial sector is a three-tiered banking system consisting of the Bank of England as the central bank, London banks, and country banks. In view of the uncertainty of payments, institutions hold fractional reserves, consisting of gold or central bank notes (Thornton 1939, 171f.). As a consequence, the total amount of liquid assets is a multiple of gold; Thornton is perfectly aware of "banking multipliers." The important point is that reserve ratios are subject to rapid changes. If confidence is undermined, there might thus occur a drastic contraction with widespread distress. The banking system, if left to itself, is inherently unstable.

To stabilize the banking system, in Thornton's view, is the basic function of the central bank, which thus emerges in the role of lender of last resort. The central bank, therefore, should not be guided by profit motives in the same way as commercial banks. Nor should it maintain a constant proportion between its notes and gold reserves (Thornton 1939, 116) but rather let this proportion rise in times of stress and keep it low in times of monetary ease. An effort to attract gold by drastic contraction in time of stress would only make things worse (122, 128, 132, 161f.). The suspension of cash payments would still be better than a financial panic (228). There are no mechanical rules about these short-term measures. In particular, the "real bills" doctrine does not guarantee the required constraint (252f.). The central bank has to use its own judgment in each case (225, 259). In the long run, however, the "great maxim" for credit policy is the requirement of convertibility at a fixed gold parity (111, 220f., 248). We thus see emerge the principle of an iron rule for the long run combined with discretion for the short run.

Thornton the banker was deeply impressed by the evils of abrupt deflation. Scarcity of money results in an immediate decline in the prices of commodities held in stock and of securities (Thornton 1939, 196). In the short run such price declines are far from neutral. They would be neutral if wages were as flexible as prices, but in reality wages tend to be relatively sticky. This is explained, interestingly, by the general expectation that prices, under a gold standard, must soon return to their old level (118f.). On the assumption that prices relate to instantaneous transactions whereas wages relate to an extended period of time, wages would thus be less volatile than prices. As a consequence of wage rigidity, deflation is accompanied by unemployment and a decline in the productivity of labor. At the same time manufacturers' inventories rise (120). The contraction would be aggravated by speculative disturbances and bank failures. In the long run, of course, both prices and output will revert to their equilibrium levels, and deflation will just be reflected in higher gold stocks.

In the case of monetary expansion, the sequence of events is the same but with the opposite sign. A purchase of bills for bank notes by the central bank is expansionary because bank notes have a higher velocity (Thornton 1939, 242). Thornton thus makes it clear that the decisive factor is not a wealth effect, as was sometimes supposed 150 years later, but asset transformation.

For the expansionary process, Thornton provides a microfoundation worthy of the twentieth century (1939, 236f.). The receivers of the new money increase their demand, which depletes inventories and thereby stimulates production. The supply of commodities cannot be instantaneously expanded, though. To induce the nonreceivers of new money to give up some of their own goods and services, the receivers have to bid up prices. This creates inventory valuation gains that add to the output stimulus. Since producers presumably have adaptive expectations, the expectation of further price increases during the production process works in the same direction.

Wages are sticky upward as well as downward, and presumably for the same reason (if perhaps not in the same degree). The workers thus suffer a decline in their "power of purchasing" (the expression appears on p. 256), which forces them to curtail their consumption. The concept of forced saving thus appears on the stage of monetary theory (Thornton 1939, 239). The wage lag provides a further stimulus to output and also results in added capital formation.

However, the expansion of output is constrained by capacity limitations. It cannot possibly keep pace, therefore, with a large increase in the money supply. Though price increases initially lag behind the increase in the money supply, they will gradually catch up, while output recedes (Thornton 1939, 237–9). In modern jargon this would be called stagflation.

A similar process is started if the central bank, instead of discounting a given amount of bills at market rates, discounts any desired amount at a rate below the market rate. Thornton's description of this process is, in substance, identical to the cumulative process reinvented by Wicksell (who did not know Thornton's book at that time) a century later. Suppose expected profits, for some reason, have risen to 6 percent while banks are prevented by usury laws from charging more than 5 percent. Additional investment projects will thus become profitable. At unchanged prices their amount, and thus the additional demand for loans, will be limited, presumably by the declining marginal profitability of investment projects. As a matter of fact, prices cannot fail to rise, and the profitability of investment will thereby be restored. "The temptation to borrow at five per cent will be exactly the same as before" (Thornton 1939, 255f.). The inflationary process continues until the lending rate is finally increased.

One of the essential aspects of Thornton's policy analysis was the distinction between domestic gold losses of the central bank (or internal drains) and gold outflows (or external drains). With respect to foreign exchange, though, he made no original contribution. He is often credited with having invented, or co-invented, the purchasing power parity doctrine. For the most part, however, he just relied on the law of one price, which implies that flows of internationally traded commodities, including gold, are highly sensitive even to infinitesimal changes in relative prices. In this respect he merely followed established tradition, as represented by Adam Smith, and he criticized David Hume for overstating the significance of price differentials (Thornton, 1939, 238). Thornton was, of course, well aware that with an inconvertible paper currency an increase in the money supply would, in due course, be reflected in a proportional increase in both prices and exchange rates (247f.). However, such long-term effects did not interest him much, and they had been more fully analyzed by Christiernin decades earlier.

Thornton represents the peak achievement of classical monetary theory. Hicks has raised the question of whether Thornton was not actually more Keynesian than classical. In so doing, he took the two labels as antithetical in the Keynesian sense (Hicks 1967). In fact, Keynes's interpretation of these labels is bad history. Genuine classical economics embraced both the Keynesian short-run and long-run neutrality. Precisely by including "Keynesian" considerations, Thornton is representative of the classical tradition.

In the field of money, Ricardo hardly went beyond Thornton and was actually satisfied with less. He seems to have differed from Thornton on two minor points of economic substance. First, Ricardo made it a point of principle that overissue was the only possible cause of a gold premium. This doctrine was clearly untenable and, contrary to what Ricardo said, was never accepted by Thornton, though he no longer regarded the "real" reasons as actually relevant around 1809. Second, Thornton had argued that monetary contraction, in view of the decline in output and labor productivity, might worsen the balance of trade rather than improving it (1939, 118f.). This is the point on which Thornton later admitted he had been in error.

The main difference between Thornton and Ricardo was one of emphasis rather than of substance. Whereas Thornton concentrated on dynamic adjustment problems, Ricardo was mainly interested in the steady state. To the extent that Thornton considered the long run at all, his views were perfectly consistent with Ricardo's. In particular, an inconvertible paper money would be neutral, at least approximately, and exchange rates, as was mentioned above, would conform to purchasing power parity (Thornton 1939, 107). On the other hand, Ricardo's short-run views, though not fully articulated, were not in conflict with Thornton's. In particular, Ricardo regarded the velocity of circulation as dependent on market conditions (1951–55, 3:90), he expected monetary expansion to have important, though temporary, real effects (91), and he described the "Wicksell process" in about the same terms as Thornton (1: 364f.). Thornton and Ricardo were united in their advocacy of a stable value of money in terms of gold precisely because they both regarded the short-run disturbances as potentially serious. In the case of a required correction, they were both gradualists. Of the coin of classical monetary theory, Thornton and Ricardo represented, respectively, the short-run and the long-run face.

Thornton was a brilliant and original financial expert, but his *Paper Credit* is dull to read, badly organized, and verbose. Though an authority during his lifetime, he thus fell into near oblivion after his death. However, in his analysis of monetary expansion and contraction in a multistage fractional-reserve system of financial intermediation, there can be found virtually all the important building blocks of monetary macrodynamics for the next 150 years. Thornton, with only a little coaching, would still have been a respected authority in the monetary debates after World War II. His *Paper Credit* is enough to dispel the notion that classical monetary theory had been a sterile exercise in the neutrality of money.

Jean-Baptiste Say

Whereas Thornton's concern was monetary macrodynamics, the static aspects of the classical tradition were made the focus of debate by Jean-Baptiste Say. He was born in 1767, the son of a Protestant merchant in Lyon.[2] He received a good education, which included sojourns in England, and started his business career in an insurance company. The *Wealth of Nations*, which his boss gave him to read, was a revelation to him and made him a follower of Adam Smith. After serving as a volunteer in the 1792 campaign of the revolutionary armies against the so-called First Co-

2. About his life see Teilhac 1927.

alition, he became editor of a literary review, and under the Consulate he was appointed to the Tribunate. The *Traité d'économie politique*, published in 1803, was a great success. Napoleon tried in vain to persuade the author to modify the second edition in favor of his financial policies. As a consequence, Say lost his office and had to postpone the second edition until 1814. For some years he was a successful textile manufacturer in the provinces. After the Restoration he was sent on a mission to England, where Ricardo and his friends received him with enthusiasm. In 1816, Say began to lecture on economics in Paris, but it was 1830 before he was appointed to a regular chair at the Collège de France. His *Catechism of Political Economy* (Say 1815) was a popular success, his lecture notes became the six-volume *Complete Course in Practical Political Economy* (1843), and the successive editions of the *Traité* were widely used, also in the United States, as textbooks. After a succession of strokes Say died in 1832.

Say was more influential as a conceptualizer and verbalizer than as a problem solver. His name is primarily associated with the division of economics into production, distribution, and consumption, with the role of the entrepreneur, and with laissez-faire liberalism. His main theoretical contribution is his so-called law of markets (which would more appropriately be called law of outlets). He compared this doctrine to the fundamental laws of physics and predicted it would change the policy of the world (Say 1803, 6th ed. 1827, LXI).

The law of markets was originally put forth in the first edition of the *Traité* (Say 1803, 152f.). Its principle was explained more fully by James Mill in his *Commerce Defended* (1808, 80f.). Mill did not refer to Say, nor did he claim originality, but a footnote in another context indicates that he knew the *Traité* (76). It is not known whether Say, when expanding the chapter on outlets for the second edition from 3 to 16 pages, was in turn influenced by Mill.

Ricardo, in chapter 21 of his *Principles*, fully accepted Say's argument (Ricardo 1951–55, 1:290f.). Malthus, however, attacked the doctrine as "fundamentally and radically erroneous" (Ricardo 1951–55, 9:112). This led to the great debate within classical economics about the possibility of "general gluts." The debate revealed both Say and Malthus as second-rate theorists. Analytically, Ricardo prevailed, but Malthus, as the second edition of his *Principles* shows, never conceded defeat. The low point in the debate was reached with Say's argument that whatever does not cover its cost does not deserve the designation of product, which gave Malthus ground for the impression that the great principle had now been degraded to a silly tautology.[3]

---

3. This impression, though Say had invited it, was actually in error, because Say's argument related to the limits of production imposed by diminishing returns, which has nothing to do with the law of markets.

Say's law, as it is called today, consists of two propositions, one a premise and the other a conclusion.[4] The premise is that "products are paid with products" (Say 1803, 154). This leads to the conclusion that "it is production which opens outlets to products" (1803, 4th ed. 1819, 1:149). In themselves, these propositions do not represent a great theoretical achievement. Say was never able to make their meaning clear, and they are not, in this form, part of modern economics. However, they became important as the bone of contention in one of the longest debates in the history of economics. As a consequence, Say's law became associated with building blocks of modern economics, the importance of which transcends its own.

Some misinterpreted Say's law as a truism. This can be done in different ways. According to the most trivial interpretation, the law simply states that, in each transaction, the quantity supplied by the seller is necessarily equal to the quantity purchased by the buyer. This is clearly not what Say meant.

According to another interpretation, only slightly less trite, Say's law expresses the fact that in the national accounts aggregate income is necessarily equal to aggregate production. The same fact can be expressed by saying that aggregate saving equals aggregate investment. While sometimes inviting this interpretation, Say made it clear, however, that the meaning of his propositions went beyond accounting identities. He purported to show that it is impossible for all prices to fall simultaneously below the respective costs of production, and this is not a question of double-entry bookkeeping.

Still another misunderstanding limits Say's law to a moneyless barter economy, for which it is trivially true. That Say derived his propositions explicitly from the properties of money is enough to invalidate this interpretation.

It is worth noting, though, that Say's money was a commodity money consisting of coins and possibly convertible bank notes; he described it as a manufacturing product similar to medals and the like. It may thus be argued that he regarded the demand for money essentially as a demand for products of mining and manufacturing. In this case a shift in demand from, say, consumer goods to money would be associated with a shift in factor demand from consumer goods industries to mining and the mint. Though this analytical route would have been perfectly legitimate and consistent with Say's monetary theory, Say, though sometimes describing money as a "merchandise," did not take it. In the exposition of his law of markets, he rather treated the stock of coins as given, so that no current resources are absorbed by coin production. In other words, he treated money as if it were fiat money. Say's law is no truism.

4. I thus follow the interpretation in Würgler 1957.

The intended meaning of Say's law can be paraphrased by the negative proposition that money is not being hoarded, at least not in the aggregate and in significant amounts. This is clearly not a truism, and it may well be false. Abstracting from other financial assets, if a person neither accumulates nor decumulates cash balances, his demand for goods and services, which Say calls products, is equal to his supply. If for one person, because he accumulates cash balances, demand falls short of supply, another person may use up cash balances, so that, in the aggregate, demand still matches supply. In the presence of nonmonetary financial assets, Say would rely on Smith's argument that the interest mechanism transforms any demand for such assets into a demand for capital goods.

The significance of this proposition, if true, was twofold. First, it implied that aggregate production could never be excessive in the sense that it could not be sold at cost. No matter how abundant the factors of production, they could always be productively employed. In more abstract terms, for any volume of aggregate production there is always a composition that assures the sale of all products. Overproduction in some products might easily occur, but it must necessarily have a counterpart in the underproduction of others. The historical significance of this reasoning was that general overproduction ceased to be a respectable explanation of depression.

The second implication was that there could be no oversaving. The main source of additional production for late classical economists was the accumulation of capital, envisaged as an addition to the wage fund to employ more workers. That aggregate production cannot be too large thus implied that capital accumulation cannot be excessive. This was in direct opposition to Lord Lauderdale's underconsumption arguments, and it provided the provocative background for Malthus and Sismondi, who argued that unimpeded growth requires a particular proportion between consumption and saving. By and large, Say carried the day. Neither Malthus nor Sismondi was able to explain the precise nature of those proportions. Underconsumption and oversaving, too, ceased to be respectable explanations of depression.

However, the absence of significant hoarding is only Say's first line of defense. He readily conceded that it might take a long time for changes in revenue to be transformed into changes in expenditures, and in the meantime cash balances would fluctuate. He also explained at length how economic growth would raise the demand for cash balances. Two additional considerations came in at this point. First, if additional cash balances are demanded, Say argued, they could easily be provided by expanding the quantity of money substitutes such as bills, bank notes, or credit lines. He did not, however, specify the mechanism by which this would take place.

The other consideration concerned the price level. In his discussion of the price revolution following the influx of Spanish gold, Say pointed out that this influx, to the extent that it was not absorbed by growth, resulted in increases in the price level. Similarly, if people decide to hold higher real cash balances, these can presumably be supplied without any excess of sales over purchases through a decline in the price level. Say did not actually mention this adjustment mechanism, but his companion-in-arms James Mill did.

The controversy about Say's law was thus essentially reduced to the issue of price rigidity. This is indeed the relevant issue. When Keynes purported to replace the "classical theory" based on Say's law by a more general theory that dispensed with it, he in fact replaced flexible prices by rigid prices. It is price (or wage) rigidity that makes aggregate output an endogenous variable, and it is price (and wage) flexibility that makes Malthus's and Sismondi's "proportions" irrelevant.

To what extent did the proponents of Say's law actually regard prices as flexible? James Mill indeed considered them as fully flexible even in the short run (1821, 121f.). He explicitly criticized David Hume for believing that an expansion in the money supply would temporarily stimulate production and argued that prices would immediately rise in the full proportion of the money supply, thus making money neutral even in the short run. He is the prime example for what some writers in the 1980s began to call classical monetary theory. He also appears to be the only example. No other prominent economist seems to have gone quite that far (though Ricardo sometimes came close), and many explicitly acknowledged that in the short run money had significant real effects. This is precisely why most of them, including Ricardo and Say, advocated a steady monetary policy geared to a fixed price of gold. Short-run neutrality of money is the opposite of the classical tradition. It was John Stuart Mill (1844, 67f.) who gently corrected the extreme position taken by his father, thus leading the discussion back to the tradition of Cantillon, Hume, and Thornton. The clarity of his restatement is still unsurpassed. In his interpretation, Say's law is perfectly compatible with short-term fluctuations in output and employment.

For the classical tradition, Say's law is a proposition about long-run equilibrium. Interpreted in this way, it is valid. Given time, the price system will indeed see to it that resources can be fully employed at any aggregate level. Though the ratio between saving and consumption is important for the course of economic growth, it is not crucial for the ability to sell products without loss.

Besides being a valid long-run proposition, Say's law turned out to be useful as a mental experiment. Suppose some imaginary agency could, as Say vaguely suggested, regulate the nominal amounts of people's cash balances in accordance with demand. It would then be possible to determine equilibrium prices in two stages.

In the first stage the absolute price level would be arbitrarily fixed, and that agency, by handing out or withdrawing cash balances, would see to it that everybody made his purchases equal to his sales, thereby implementing Say's law. Markets could then be left to adjust relative prices in such a way that demand equals supply for each good.

In the second stage, relative prices would be fixed at these equilibrium levels, and individuals would again be equipped with their original cash balances. The absolute price level could then be determined by the requirement that actual real balances equal desired real balances.

By this mental experiment it would be possible to dichotomize the price system into the determination of relative prices and the determination of the absolute price level. The imaginary imposition of Say's law can thus serve as an analytical device to separate value theory from monetary theory. A good example is provided by Knut Wicksell's *Lectures* (1934–35). In the 1940s, Oscar Lange (1942a) and Don Patinkin (1948) initiated a big debate about the validity of this analytical procedure. The outcome was that, as a mental experiment, it is indeed legitimate (Samuelson 1966–86, vol. 4, ch. 265; Niehans 1969).

Nassau Senior

The classical theory of commodity money was completed by Nassau William Senior (1790–1864). He was a prosperous lawyer who became an influential publicist and social reformer and for two five-year terms (seventeen years apart) was professor of political economy at Oxford. Since the incumbent of this chair was required to publish a lecture every year, most of his publications in the field of economic science took this form. His only treatise is the *Outline of the Science of Political Economy*, again compiled from lecture notes and first published 1836 in the *Encyclopaedia Metropolitana*. The magnum opus he had planned was never written. It has often been suggested that a great theoretical talent was squandered on the practical problems of the day, but there is no clear evidence, even in his posthumously published manuscripts (Senior 1928), that the talent was indeed so great.[5]

Senior established himself as a critic of Ricardo, but in substance he hardly went beyond Ricardian economics. To advance the progress of his science, which he regarded as painfully slow, he thought it most useful to concentrate on "discussions as to the most convenient use of a few familiar words" (Senior 1938, 5). For this professorial vice he got his just deserts inasmuch as he is best remembered for his unfortunate proposal to rename capital "abstinence." To the economic substance of capital theory, which

5. An interesting biography is Levy 1970. For an enthusiastic assessment of Senior's economic contribution see Bowley 1937.

was then dominated by the wage fund concept, he made no contribution of lasting signficance, thus offering an instructive contrast to his nonprofessorial contemporary John Rae.

It may also be noted that Senior was one of a large number of economists who recognized that "two articles of the same kind will seldom afford twice the pleasure of one, and still less will ten give five times the pleasure of two" (1938, 12) without finding any analytical use for this principle in the theory of price. To the Ricardian theory of international trade he contributed the observation that relatively high wages in a country reflect a high productivity of labor and, therefore, are not an impediment to profitable international exchange (Senior 1830). With respect to population, he emphasized that the experience of an extended period of above minimum wages can cause the minimum itself to shift upward, to which old Malthus agreed (Senior 1829).

Senior's one significant contribution to economic theory is found in the *Three Lectures on the Value of Money* (1840), delivered in 1828 (similarly in 1928, 2:79f.). It consists in the verbal presentation of a general equilibrium model of the value of commodity money. Suppose an economy produces corn and silver. In view of diminishing returns in silver mining (and possibly also in agriculture), a shift of labor into mining requires a higher relative price of silver, which is equivalent to a lower price of corn in terms of silver. For a given quantity of silver, the required corn price (and thus the value of money) depends on production cost in the marginal mine. In figure 10.1 the supply of silver is measured along the horizontal axis, and the price of corn in terms of silver is measured vertically. Diminishing returns result in a declining supply curve as illustrated by the falling line through A. The question is which point along this curve represents the resulting corn price (and thus the value of money).

To find the answer one has to bring in the demand for silver. One part of the silver supply is used for monetary purposes. Since money is valued for what it can buy, the monetary demand for silver is proportionate to the corn price, as illustrated by the ray through the origin. It must be visualized as a flow demand, resulting either from economic growth or from attrition of the existing money stock. Another part of the silver is used for nonmonetary purposes. This nonmonetary (flow) demand will rise with a declining relative price of silver, which means with a rising corn price. In the graph it is added horizontally to the monetary demand. This results in the total demand curve that goes through A. Equilibrium is reached at point A, where total demand equals supply. The price of corn, the money supply, the production of nonmonetary silver, and (by implication) the production of corn are all simultaneously determined.

Senior put his model through its paces by showing that an increase in the nonmonetary demand for silver would move the equilibrium to a point such as B, with lower commodity prices, a lower demand for silver money,

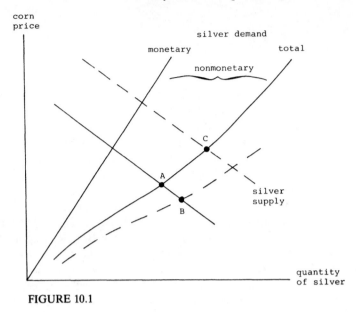

FIGURE 10.1

and a higher production of silver (and thus lower corn production). The monetary circulation would thus tend to cushion fluctuations in the non-monetary demand. The effect would be analogous for a shift in the demand for money. If the discovery of new silver mines shifted the supply curve to the right, the new equilibrium would be at a point such as *C*, with higher commodity prices raising the demand for both monetary and nonmonetary silver. The analysis was also extended to an open economy importing its silver from abroad, to convertible paper money and to bimetallism, where Gresham's law begins to operate.

For a gold or silver standard, Senior achieved a complete integration of monetary theory and value theory. By 1829 he had thus assembled all of the economic substance of the theory of commodity money that was later refined by men like Léon Walras and Irving Fisher. What they could accomplish by systems of simultaneous equations or ingenious graphs, he still had to describe laboriously with the aid of numerical examples. At this point the possibilities for further analytical progress began to be severely limited by the crudeness of the techniques.

11
Utility and Demand

DURING the classical era, with the circular flow absorbing most of the theoretical energies, utility and demand were not among the main topics of analytical efforts. In the field of household demand, the era of individual optimization began late; the first half of the nineteenth century had passed before Gossen's second law of the equalization of weighted marginal utilities signaled its beginning. Nevertheless, important building blocks of the later theory became available during the classical era. In particular, Ferdinando Galiani and William Forster Lloyd, respectively, mark the stage that the theory of marginal utility had reached at the beginning and at the end of the classical era. Daniel Bernoulli and Jeremy Bentham applied diminishing marginal utility to income or wealth. John Stuart Mill showed how demand can be integrated into a cost-of-production theory of value even without using the notion of utility. Jules Dupuit, finally, proceeded from demand to a theory of consumer surplus. These contributions are the subject of this chapter.

Ferdinando Galiani and William Forster Lloyd

By the late nineteenth century economists had persuaded themselves that Stanley Jevons, Carl Menger, and Léon Walras had initiated a revolution of subjective value. Whoever before that time had regarded subjective utility as an increasing function of scarcity was thus celebrated as a precursor. As a matter of fact, diminishing marginal utility never had to be discovered, because it had its roots deeply in commonplace economics.

When the town of Casilinum was besieged by Hannibal, so Pliny reports, mice were sold for two hundred sesterces a piece. In terms of this anecdote, and some similar ones, Italian writers in the scholastic tradition such as Bernardo Davanzati, Geminiano Montanari, and Ferdinando Galiani used to discuss the relationship between utility, scarcity, and value. It was commonplace to them that value, as measured by the exchange ratio between two goods, depends positively on both their usefulness and their scarcity. The so-called water/diamond paradox never presented a serious difficulty, because it was clear that the high utility of water was counteracted by its lack of scarcity, while the reverse was true for diamonds. The remarkable fact is not that they found solutions for the paradox but rather that, in the light of this intellectual tradition, it could ever be presented as a paradox.

Though this train of thought goes back far beyond the period covered by the present account, Galiani may be regarded as representative of the stage it had reached at the time of Cantillon. This was also the stage at which it remained virtually stagnant for another eighty years.

Ferdinando Galiani, born in 1728, was the son of a Neapolitan nobleman. The highly gifted boy received an excellent classical education in the household of his learned uncle, an archbishop who was the royal Neapolitian minister of education. In 1751, at the age of barely twenty-three, Galiani published (anonymously and predated to 1750) the book *Della Moneta* (trans. 1977), that made him famous. That it made him an instant celebrity, with whom even the Pope wanted to converse, reflects the fact that it was more brilliant than innovative. As a reward, Galiani obtained some sinecures, which required him to take (minor) holy orders. The prodigious talents he displayed as a geologist, orator, archeologist, and classical scholar continued to add not only to his fame but also to his income.

In 1759, Galiani was sent as a secretary to the Neapolitan embassy in Paris, where the tiny but vivacious *abbé* dazzled the salons. His polemics against the physiocratic doctrine culminated in 1770 in his other book on economics, the *Dialogues on the Grain Trade* (Galiani 1803). Recalled to Naples in 1769, he held high offices in the king's service, continuing to write on linguistics, literature, and international law, maintaining a far-flung correspondence, and even composing an opera buffa. He died in 1787.

In *Della Moneta*, Galiani conceived value as an exchange ratio between two commodities. Value is seen to depend on utility and scarcity. It is "a ratio which is, in turn, composed of two other ratios expressed by the names *utility* and *scarcity*" (1977, 21). One is thus tempted to express the value of good 2 in terms of good 1 symbolically as

$$v_{21} = -\frac{\Delta Q_1}{\Delta Q_2} = \frac{u_2}{u_1} \cdot \frac{s_2}{s_1}, \tag{11.1}$$

where $\Delta Q_1/\Delta Q_2$ is the ratio in which the individual is willing to exchange the two commodities, u_2/u_1 is the ratio of utilities, and s_2/s_1 the ratio of scarcities. Utility is defined as "the ability a thing has to provide us with happiness" (22), and scarcity is meant to refer "to the proportion between the quantity of a thing and the use which is made of it" (28), but the precise meaning of all these ratios and proportions remains obscure. Taken literally, they do not make sense.

The proposition that utility increases with scarcity is regarded as evident, not requiring detailed analysis: "there is nothing more useless than bread for one who is sated" (Galiani 1977, 26). The mice of Casilinum had demonstrated this two thousand years earlier. It did not occur to Galiani, however, to replace the apparent products $u_1 s_1$ and $u_2 s_2$ by increasing functions $u_1(s_1)$ and $u_2(s_2)$. The law of diminishing marginal utility was clearly implied, but it was not made explicit. As a consequence, it could not be made analytically useful.

Despite this analytical weakness, Galiani, like so many scholastics before him, had reasonable notions on supply and demand. Demand increases as the price declines, and in the case of Neapolitan grain, Galiani believed that demand increases in about the same proportion as the price declines, leaving expenditures unchanged. An increase in supply, on the other hand, must be elicited by higher prices (Galiani 1977, 35f.). Galiani is remarkably clear about the difference between what would today be called a shift in the demand curve and a movement along the demand curve. If supply increases, an increase in quantity is associated with a falling price, and it would be wrong to argue that this, in a vicious circle, again reduces the quantity (35).

Utility and scarcity are only one side of the picture, however. At the same time, value is determined by labor, which "alone gives things value." That a bag of gold is worth more than a bag of sand is thus explained in terms of hours of required work (Galiani 1977, 29).

The word *alone* in the last quotation is not to be taken literally, though. The qualification concerns "the diverse lengths of time it takes different men to begin to enjoy profit from their work." Occupations requiring long training result in higher prices of services, for they "are no different than pine timber and some walnut trees which, because of the length of time they take to grow, are worth more than poplars and elms" (Galiani 1977, 30). That a person (with otherwise constant income), if given the choice, would prefer present goods to the same goods in the future was a notion deeply embedded in the scholastic tradition. Like diminishing marginal utility, time preference needed not to be "discovered" but to be analytically exploited.

In the history of economics, Galiani is often described as a great precursor of the subjective theory of value, whose promising germs were killed by the emerging dominance of the classical labor theory of value. A reading of *Della Moneta* does not bear out this interpretation. In fact, Galiani's analytical framework, inherited from the scholastic tradition, is not significantly different from that of Adam Smith or even David Ricardo. In the background we have utility and scarcity as potentially useful but analytically still unexploited tools, and in the foreground we find supply and demand combined with a labor-cum-time-preference theory of value. Both blades are there, but they do not make functioning scissors yet. That Smith and Ricardo used the words *utility* and *scarcity* less often than Galiani does not necessarily mean that they regarded them as less important. It probably just means that they saw no reason to expand on the elements they did not know how to handle and instead focused on those about which they had something to say.

Galiani had a brilliant, witty, and pragmatic mind, but he did not have the originality, perseverance, and conviction to make important contributions to economic science. He wrote for his time, and thus he failed to be ahead of it. He posed as an innovator, often by unfairly criticizing predecessors such as Davanzati, but in substance he was traditional. Einaudi summed it up fairly when he said of Galiani's contribution to the marginal utility of value that he "came near to the threshold of the discovery" (1952, 76). The threshold was not decisively crossed for another one hundred years.

The first distinct advance beyond the scholastic tradition of the mice of Casilinum is due to the Reverend William Forster Lloyd. Lloyd, born in 1794, was the son of a wealthy Anglican clergyman. He was educated at Westminster School and elected in 1812 to Christ Church, Oxford, then a stronghold of the High Church establishment. He graduated in mathematics and classics and obtained an M.A. in 1818. Ordained in 1822, he stayed on at Christ Church, where his brother, bishop of Oxford, was a most influential professor of divinity. After serving as reader in Greek and lecturer in mathematics, Lloyd in 1832 succeeded Nassau Senior and Richard Whately as Drummond Professor of Political Economy. After the end of his five-year tenure, he retired to his estate in Buckinghamshire, where he lived with his wife in apparent obscurity, possibly in ill health. He succumbed to a stroke in 1852.

Lloyd's only published writings are an historical paper on the prices of corn since the Middle Ages and the lectures he was required to publish each year under the terms of his professorship. Unpublished manuscripts have not been found. All but one of the lectures are on population, the relief of the poor, and rent, and they do not contain contributions to economic theory. One lecture, however, does indeed make such a contribution.[1]

In his *Lecture on the Notion of Value, as Distinguishable not only from Utility but also from Value in Exchange* (1834), Lloyd wanted to show that "it is not true that all value is relative" (37). In modern terminology, he maintained that utility is not only ordinal but cardinal. This, in itself, was clearly a mistaken effort, which could not possibly succeed. As a by-product, however, Lloyd contributed a significant building block to the theory of value, namely the first explicit formulation of the postulate of diminishing marginal utility. What in Galiani had still been a commonplace observation imperfectly understood thereby became a lucid proposition, ready for further analytical use.

Lloyd begins with the first clear distinction between the services derived from the whole amount of a given commodity and the services derived from an incremental unit. The first concept is called utility and the second

---

1. A comprehensive account of Lloyd's economic thinking can be found in Romano 1977.

is called value. The incremental unit itself is defined by its position "at the margin of separation between the satisfied and the unsatisfied wants" (1834, 16). The margin, long familiar with respect to cultivation, thus made its inconspicuous entry into utility theory.

What Lloyd calls value is, in modern terminology, marginal utility. For each commodity there is a marginal utility schedule, beginning at a relatively high level and declining gradually toward zero. This is illustrated by many examples of the usual kind. Marginal utility is gauged by the "loss principle," namely "as the feeling of affection or esteem for the object, arising from a sense of the loss of the gratification contingent on the loss of the object" (1834, 16). Carl Menger, Friedrich von Wieser, and Eugen von Böhm-Bawerk could not have done better.

Lloyd wanted to persuade his readers that marginal utility schedules have meaning even in the absence of markets. Utility, he argued, is more fundamental than exchange. Since he did not have firsthand knowledge of economies without markets, he searched in Defoe's novel for telling experiences of Robinson Crusoe as quasi-empirical evidence (1834, 21f). Lloyd was not quite satisfied with what he found, but Crusoe had thereby obtained his honored place among the paradigms of value theory.

Lloyd failed to define utility as the integral of which marginal utility is the derivative. Though he taught mathematics, he had no use for total utility as a function of quantity. What he calls utility is rather the particular value of that integral at the point of satiation. He thus missed the proposition that total utility is a maximum at the point where marginal utility is zero.

As a physical analogy, Lloyd uses springs. To the decline of marginal utility there corresponds the shortening of the springs resulting from the addition of one unit of weight, which Lloyd describes as their elasticity. Utility is measured by the weight required to compress a spring completely. At this point, Lloyd remarks that springs of different strengths, if the appropriate weights are placed on them, can be made to react to an additional weight unit with the same compression. In economic terms this means that commodities with different satiation utilities, if made available in the appropriate quantitites, may have the same marginal utility. From here it seems only a short step to the equalization of the marginal utilities per unit of resources as a condition for their optimal allocation. As a matter of fact, this step to Gossen's second law took economic theory another twenty years.[2]

Lloyd had stumbled on a principle of great potential significance, which in the edifice of mainstream economics was destined to become the cornerstone of an entire new wing. He did not see it that way, though; all he

---

2. In his lecture on rent, however, Lloyd pointed out that workers balance the diminishing marginal utility of corn against its increasing cost (1837, 94f.).

hoped to accomplish was a minor elaboration of Adam Smith. In particular, he made no use of his principle in the explanation of market prices; there is not even an inkling of a new theory of value. In these circumstances his contemporaries can hardly be blamed for not recognizing the signficance of the principle either. In fact, Lloyd's contribution was entirely ignored until it was discovered (and overpraised) by E. R. A. Seligman in 1903. However, the one original idea of this unobtrusive clergyman was enough to win him a place in the history of economic science.

Daniel Bernoulli and Jeremy Bentham

Long before the principle of diminishing marginal utility for goods and services was analytically articulated, the principle of diminishing marginal utility of income (or wealth) had been formalized by Daniel Bernoulli. Son, brother, nephew, cousin, and uncle of mathematicians, Bernoulli was born in 1700 in Groningen, Holland. He became a mathematician, physicist, physician, and botanist, who, between 1725 and 1757, was awarded ten prizes by the French Academy of Sciences for mathematical contributions and became a member of the academies of Berlin, Paris, and Saint Petersburg and the Royal Academy in London. In 1725 he was called to Saint Petersburg by Catherine I, and in 1733 he became professor of anatomy and botany in Basel, where he died in 1782.

Bernoulli's contribution to economics is contained in a paper entitled, in translation, "Exposition of a New Theory of Risk Evaluation," (Bernoulli 1968) published in Latin in 1738. It puts forth the proposition, novel at the time, that uncertain prospects should be evaluated not at the expected value of the payoffs, but at the expected value of the utility of the payoffs. This makes a difference, he argued, because utility is less than proportional to the payoffs. Equal increases in the payoff provide diminishing increments in utility. More specifically, Bernoulli hypothesized that the "utility resulting from any small increase in wealth will be inversely proportionate to the quantity of goods previously possessed" (17). This hypothesis is shown to imply a logarithmic utility function of the form

$$u = b \log \frac{y}{a}, \tag{11.2}$$

where y is income (or wealth) and a is the value of y at which utility is zero. It is illustrated by Bernoulli in a curve like that in figure 11.1.

This hypothesis is used to analyze different risk problems. It is pointed out that in fair games both players suffer a utility loss. Insurance, however, promises a utility gain provided initial wealth is small enough. In particular, Bernoulli uses his hypothesis to propose a solution to the so-called Saint Petersburg paradox enounced by his cousin Nicholas Bernoulli. Suppose a coin is tossed until "heads" comes up. Paul gets one ducat if this happens in the first throw, two ducats if it happens in the second throw, four ducats

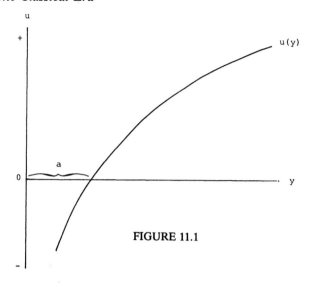

FIGURE 11.1

if in the third, eight ducats if in the fourth, and so on. The paradox is that the expected value of the payoffs is infinite, and yet nobody would advise Paul to pay any amount, however large, for the privilege of playing this game. Daniel Bernoulli solves it by pointing out that, on his hypothesis, the expected value of the utility of the payoffs is finite.

Bernoulli's specific hypothesis about the form of the marginal utility function was at best an expository device. His principle for the evaluation of risky prospects later turned out to be of fundamental importance for the modern theory of decision making under uncertainty. The notion of a diminishing marginal utility of income lay dormant in economics until it was reinvented and applied to political economy by Jeremy Bentham.

Jeremy Bentham, born 1748 in London, was the son of a prosperous businessman.[3] He was a precocious child, studying Latin at four, and morbidly sensitive. He was educated at Westminster School, London, and at the age of twelve he went to Oxford, where standards of scholarship were still as low as described by Adam Smith. In 1767 he obtained a bachelor's degree. His father had hoped for a glorious law career, and Bentham actually studied law at Lincoln's Inn, London, but he detested its practical aspects, for which he had little ability. Instead he returned to Oxford, where he acquired a master's degree.

Sustained by a small income from property settled on him by his understanding father, Bentham then led what he called a miserable life as a private scholar and literary man. He fell in love with a young girl but

3. This life sketch is based on Stephen 1950.

dared to propose to her (in writing) only twenty-five years later, and again when he was almost eighty, but was both times refused. Politically young Bentham was still a Tory, but he speculated upon the reforms those in power should adopt. His guiding light became the "fundamental axiom," attributed by him to Beccaria or Priestley, that "the greatest happiness of the greatest number is the measure of right and wrong." By expounding the implications of this axiom in all its ramifications, he became the father of utilitarianism. Never content with grandiose principles, he specified his schemes in minute detail. His pet project was prison reform, and his naïveté was such that he actually offered himself to the French revolutionaries as a model jailer.

The death of his father in 1792 made Bentham a wealthy man and owner of an estate in Westminster, but he still lived in relative obscurity as a shy and somewhat childlike recluse. He wrote copious notes and essays, and his collected works may eventually fill thirty-six volumes or more, but he published very little; instead he circulated his writings among friends and persons of influence. It was through the translations arranged and edited by his disciple Etienne Dumont that he gradually acquired fame. His attention now shifted to the question why governments do not accept reforms such as he proposed and how governments should be constituted to make such reforms acceptable. The intellectual reformer thus became the ideological leader of political radicalism.

Bentham led a simple life without great passions; he loved gardening, music, and animals, he dressed like a Quaker, and he lived and wrote by a timetable. He died in 1832, and his skeleton was made into a wax figure that is still kept (and shown on certain days) at University College, London. His most important disciple was James Mill, and John Stuart Mill may be described as his spiritual grandson.

Bentham's speculations on law and government could not fail to touch upon economic problems at many points. In particular, he contributed to the classical doctrine of forced saving as a temporary effect of monetary expansion and he emphasized psychological time preference as a determinant of interest (1952–54, 3:447). More importantly, he was one of the many writers who resolved the water/diamond paradox by pointing out that the utility of a good declines as the available quantity rises (87, 446), but he made no further use of this insight as a basis for a theory of value.

Bentham's specific contribution to economic theory was the reinvention of Bernoulli's principle of the diminishing marginal utility of income (or wealth). Like Bernoulli, he thought that equal absolute increments in utility would require equal proportionate increases in income, which implies that utility is a logarithmic function of income (1952–54, 1:113; 2:132f.; 3:437–46). Combined with the assumption of interpersonal comparability of utilities, it is clear that this principle gave Bentham's thinking a strong egalitarian bent. The transfer of a shilling from the wealthy to the poor would generally raise total utility (1:111f.). Though this notion became fundamental for the ideology of income redistribution, it must be noted that it is not a part of modern economic theory with its skepticism about the cardinality and interpersonal comparability of utility. The particular assumption of a logarithmic utility function is completely arbitrary.

Bentham's most important contribution, however, was not at the analytical level. It consisted in conceiving economic decisions as a utility-maximizing calculus of pleasures and pains (which Bentham called mental pathology!), thus moving utility from the wings to center stage. It was left for Hermann Heinrich Gossen, Stanley Jevons, and Léon Walras to make the economic calculus explicit in terms of differential calculus. Three decades later, cardinal utility was purged again from value theory by Vilfredo Pareto. What remained was utility without utilitarianism.

John Stuart Mill

As long as Gossen had not provided the key, the door to a theory of exchange in terms of utility remained closed. However, a theory of exchange can be developed even without the concept of utility, solely in terms of demand and supply. An important contribution to such a theory was made late in the classical era by John Stuart Mill.

He was born in London in 1806, the eldest of nine children of James Mill, who played a dominant role in his life.[4] James Mill, a poor cobbler's son, had through the perseverance of his mother received a good education. Having begun with theology, he became a writer and finally an official of the East India Company, which meant, in fact, of the government of India. He was a close friend of Bentham and Ricardo, a radical utilitarian, but in his economics a Ricardian with little originality.

James Mill was firmly decided to make his son one of the great minds of his age. The methods he used have been described as one of the most extraordinary educational experiments on record. He believed that the human mind at birth is a tabula rasa, and that everything depends on what is written in this blank space. Consequently, he began to teach his son Greek at the age of three, Latin at eight. Then came philosophy, history, and differential calculus. A few years later the prodigy was introduced to Smith and Ricardo, and the latter enjoyed conversing with him on political economy. At the same time, John had to serve as tutor to his younger brothers and sisters.

This hothouse education was finished when young Mill was about fourteen. He then spent some time in France, to which he remained attached for the rest of his life. Naturally, his mind was filled with the loftiest ideals, supported by a firm belief in his own superiority. At the same time

---

4. This biographical note is based on Packe 1954. The basic source is, of course, Mill's *Autobiography*, published shortly after his death.

he was a lonely bookworm with all the burdens of intellectual precocity. When John was seventeen, his father obtained for him a job with the East India Company. A distinguished career eventually led him to one of the top posts, from which he resigned, with a good pension, in 1858 when the administration of India was taken over by the government.

One is not surprised to hear that at the age of twenty Mill suffered a period of nervous depression, which he described as a lack of "feeling." Such spells of depression recurred several times in later years, sometimes impairing his ability to work for months. His health must always have been fragile.

A decisive turn came at the age of twenty-four. Mill fell deeply in love with Harriet Taylor, the wife of a wealthy wholesale druggist. The friendship was, of course, sublimated to the highest platonic level, and Mr. Taylor, who loved his wife, was extremely understanding. Nevertheless the arrangement provoked a scandal, which led to Mill's alienation from his family and to social isolation. After nineteen years of this triangle, John Taylor died in 1849, and two years later Mrs. Taylor became Mrs. Mill. Mill talked about his wife only in the most ecstatic and exalted expressions. It seems she evoked in him the "feelings" that he had confessed to lack. She published hardly anything under her own name, but she had a strong influence on the direction of Mill's work and thinking. She died in 1858 during a trip to Avignon, where Mill not only built a marble mausoleum for her but also bought a house where he and his step-daughter, who looked after him, could be near her grave.

Politically, Mill was a philosophical radical on the Left wing of the Liberals. He saw himself as representing the light of reason against the stupidity of the country squires and parsons. As a young man he was once arrested for distributing shocking Malthusian pamphlets. He was a champion of civil liberties, free trade, women's suffrage, and voting reform. He also supported trade unions, the right to strike, and social legislation, but at the same time he regarded workers as far too uneducated to be given the vote. With his intellectual condescension and arrogance, he was clearly not a born political leader. He was nevertheless elected to the House of Commons in 1865, where his lucidity made an impression, though his oratory was generally ineffective. Only three years later he was ingloriously defeated. Under his wife's influence, he became increasingly more sympathetic to socialism, and if he had lived longer, he might have found himself close to the Fabians.

In his later years, Mill was a figure of national stature, a liberal dispenser of opinions and advice on all sorts of questions, the "saint of rationalism." Much admired, he was also much reviled. He died from an infectious disease in Avignon in 1873.

Mill began to publish when he was sixteen. His duties at the East India Company left him, an efficient administrator, much time for his writing, and his collected works (1963–85), including a voluminous correspondence, fill twenty-one massive volumes. Many of his publications were essays, and their subjects covered almost everything except the sciences; they included literature, philosophy, classics, history, politics, religion, government, ethics, economics, law, education, and women's rights. Writing for magazines with a general readership (including one he owned himself), Mill became an experienced and lucid expositor.

Mill's fame rests, in the main, on three books. He had early identified the "investigation of abstract truths" as his particular ability. The result of this investigation, after twelve years of labor, was *A System of Logic* (published in 1843), his principal philosophical work. Mill wanted to do for induction what Aristotle had done for deduction. The main subject matter of logic, for Mill, was inference and not implication. He asserted that all knowledge consists of generalizations from experience. The treatise established Mill as a leading logician, and it was highly durable as a textbook, but it turned out to be more controversial and less definitive than Mill had hoped. Jevons, who was a more original logician, detested it.

The second of his main books, the *Principles of Political Economy* published in 1848, made Mill the leading teacher of economics. Like the *Wealth of Nations*, it was a successful synthesis, but whereas Adam Smith's synthesis had conquered the world, Mill's synthesis of post-Ricardian economics conquered only the classrooms.

The general tone was set by the infamous statement that, "happily, there is nothing in the laws of value which remains for the present or any future writer to clear up; the theory of the subject is complete" (Mill 1848, bk. 3, ch. 1). Compared to Ricardo's concentration on cost, Mill's theory of value shifted the emphasis to the equilibrium of supply and demand. What Mill might have accomplished in this direction is illustrated by his neat analysis of the prices of joint products (such as coke and coal gas), where the sum of the prices that the consumers are willing to pay for the products must equal their joint costs. A comparison with Cournot's analysis of multiple monopoly also illustrates, however, how much farther the frontier of research had already advanced. That Mill distinguished between demand curves with rising, constant, and falling expenditure is testimony to his competence, but not to his originality.[5]

5. Mill's analysis of interrelated markets was elaborated by the German Hans von Mangoldt (1824–68), professor in Göttingen and Freiburg. His three books show him generally as a competent, well-read, but pedestrian systematizer. He made, however, two brilliant theoretical contributions, both in the same section of his *Grundriss der Volkswirtschaftslehre* (Outline of Economics) of 1863. They reveal a high analytical potential, though their scope is too narrow to put their author at a level comparable to that of Johann Heinrich von Thünen, Hermann Heinrich Gossen, or Wilhelm Launhardt. The first contribution consists in a geometrical, algebraic, and numerical analysis of complements and substitutes in consumption and of jointness and substitution in production. The editor of the second (posthumous) edition thought fit to delete this analysis as being abstruse and indeterminate. In fact, it makes

With respect to labor, Mill affirmed the wage fund theory until mounting criticism induced him to abandon it. Today the reasons for his dramatic recantation hardly seem compelling. Within two decades, Böhm-Bawerk made the wage fund concept, though in different guise, a cornerstone of his theory of interest.

Mill's *Principles*, with its many editions, dominated the teaching of economics for half a century. If the present book were a history of erstwhile mainstream economics, the content of the *Principles* would thus merit detailed attention. However, since the subject matter of this book is the origins of modern mainstream economics, the treatment of the *Principles* can be brief.[6] Though Mill had done no work in economics for more than a decade, he wrote the *Principles* in less than two years. From a research point of view, the book was dated before it came out (Cournot is not mentioned). Mill was a brilliant ecclectic, but for the building of modern economic theory he provided few bricks of his own. The great exception to this statement is his theory of international values, which will be reviewed presently.

The third pillar of Mill's fame is *On Liberty*, popularly the most successful of his books and also the one closest to his heart. It was published in 1859 shortly after the death of his wife, dedicated to her memory, and said by Mill to be coauthored by her. The essay puts forth the proposition that the only legitimate reasons for interfering with the liberty of an individual are self-protection and the prevention of harm to others. In particular, an individual's own good is not sufficient warrant for curtailing his freedom. Characteristically, this proposition is limited to highly civilized societies; in dealing with barbarians despotism is held to be legitimate.

With his theory of international values, Mill indeed provided an important contribution to economic theory, a stepping stone between David Ricardo and Alfred Marshall. In his theory of comparative cost, Ricardo had shown that the international exchange ratio for two commodities establishes itself in the range between the domestic exchange ratios in the two countries concerned. For this demonstration he needed information only on costs. The exact point in the range remained undetermined. This analytical gap was filled by the young John Stuart Mill in a brilliant paper, "Of the Laws of Interchange between Nations; and the Distribution of the Gains of Commerce among the Countries of the Commercial World." The paper was written in 1829 but published only in 1844 as the first of the *Essays on Some Unsettled Questions of Political Economy*. The key to the solution was demand. Demand had long played a role in explaining the

---

perfectly good sense and is determinate, though lacking in lucidity and confined to special cases. An English translation of the relevant section is available in International Economic Papers (Mangoldt 1962). Mangoldt's other contribution will be mentioned presently.
   6. A comprehensive analysis is provided by Hollander 1985.

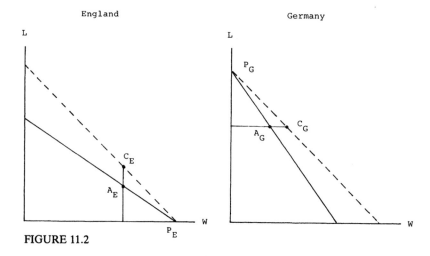

FIGURE 11.2

values of commodities whose supply cannot be increased by production. Mill now began to use it for the products of labor.

Suppose two countries, England and Germany, produce two goods, woolens and linens. Suppose further, in Ricardian fashion, that their production possibilities are linear, as depicted in figure 11.2, with England having a comparative advantage for wool and Germany for linen. In the absence of international trade, both countries would be at their respective autarky points, A_E and A_G. With international trade, England would produce somewhere to the right of A_E and Germany to the left of A_G. In particular, Mill followed Ricardo in concentrating on the case of complete specialization, with England at P_E and Germany at P_G. The two countries' consumption points, C_E and C_G, would then be found along the broken lines through, respectively, P_E and P_G, whose common slope expresses the international exchange ratio. This slope, Mill pointed out, must be such that the English demand for linen just matches the German demand for wool.

Anticipating Alfred Marshall's graphical apparatus, this argument can be expressed in terms of reciprocal demand curves. In figure 11.3, England's exports and Germany's imports of wool are both measured horizontally, whereas England's imports and Germany's exports of linen are measured vertically. If the terms of trade are at the level of England's domestic cost ratio, England is indifferent between the autarky point A_E and complete specialization at her production point P_E and receives through foreign trade just what she could have produced at home. If the terms of trade become gradually more favorable, England's demand for linen against wool increases along her reciprocal demand curve. The reciprocal demand curve for Germany, starting at the production point P_G, is constructed in the same way. International equilibrium is reached where the two reciprocal demand curves intersect.

This apparatus is used to evaluate the gains from trade for the two countries. Mill points out that a technical improvement in one country, by raising the supply of its exports relative to demand, may worsen its terms of trade, but he does not go so far as to suggest that, as a consequence, the improving country may actually be worse off. "Immiserizing growth" was left for later generations to discover. The analysis is also extended to more than two countries and commodities, albeit not in a rigorous fashion.

In his original paper and the early editions of the *Principles*, Mill had explained how the terms of trade depend on the reaction of demand to price. In the third edition he thought it necessary to add that the outcome also depends on the location of the production points P_E and P_G. To explain this he used the special case in which the demand for the imported good has a price elasticity of unity, which implies that the demand, and thus the export supply, of the domestic product is independent of price. In terms of figure 11.2 this means that the English consumption point C_E is vertically above A_E, while C_G is horizontally to the right of A_G. As a result, the reciprocal demand curves are straight lines, as illustrated in figure 11.4.

It is evident that in this case a shift in P_E or P_G is enough to change

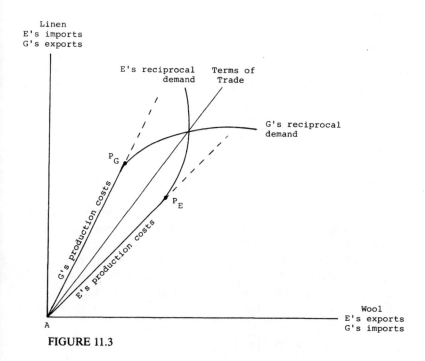

FIGURE 11.3

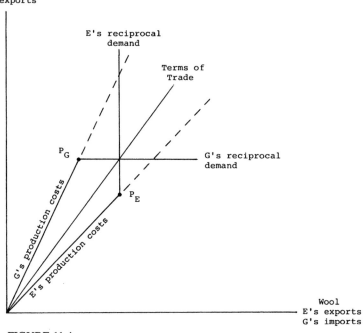

FIGURE 11.4

the terms of trade. If England's export capacity is gradually reduced, the terms of trade will eventually approach the German cost ratio, and vice versa. If England's export capacity is reduced even further, Germany will cease to be fully specialized in linen, but Mill argued, unconvincingly, that in the presence of many goods, this possibility would not materialize.

Though the nature of this second set of circumstances seems straight-forward enough, the way Mill introduced it has misled his readers ever since. He begins with the acute observation, which is itself a minor contribution, that the reciprocal offer curves may intersect at more than one point and might conceivably even coincide over some stretch. The argument concerning the location of P_E and P_G is then introduced to eliminate the resulting indeterminacy. In fact, as Marshall and Edgeworth did not fail to notice, this argument has nothing to do with the possibility of multiple equilibria. On the whole, therefore, the addition in the third edition of the *Principles* represents no significant advance over the early paper.[7]

With his law of international values, Mill provided a bridge from the

7. This evaluation differs from that in Chipman 1965, 1979.

theory of comparative cost to the modern theory of international trade. Hans von Mangoldt, in a piece of ingenious but laborious analysis, extended the argument to more than two goods.[8] Marshall invented the reciprocal demand (or offer) curves and expressed their shape in terms of elasticities. Gottfried Haberler essentially completed the apparatus by replacing Ricardo's linear technology by Irving Fisher's concave production possibility curves. The result, for two countries and two goods, was the "Mill/Marshall/ Meade international trade butterfly."

In fact, the significance of Mill's early paper, though he did not realize it, far transcends the theory of international trade. Mill was right in regarding the paper as an application of the general laws of demand and supply. In turn, the particular piece of analysis he developed became the core of the general theory of exchange between individuals. Edgeworth and Pareto are not separated from Ricardo by a scientific revolution; they are connected to him by an evolution in which Mill's law of international values marks an important link.

Jules Dupuit

The peak achievement of demand theory before the advent of explicit utility maximization was due to Jules Dupuit. He was a Frenchman, born 18 May 1804 in Fossano (Piedmont), where his father was an imperial inspector of finances.[9] He was admitted to the Ecole Polytechnique in Paris in 1822 and two years later entered the service of the Administration of Bridges and Highways as a civil engineer. Working partly in the provinces and partly in Paris, he rose to the rank of chief engineer in charge of municipal services in Paris.

Most of his books and articles are on engineering subjects such as highway maintenance, bridge construction, municipal water supply, and flood control. In the second half of his life, he also became increasingly interested in economic problems. This resulted in several articles in the *Annales des Ponts et Chaussées* and in the *Journal des Economistes*, and also a book on the liberty of commerce. His most important contributions are the essays "On the Measurement of the Utility of Public Works" of 1844 (trans. as Dupuit 1952) and "On Tolls and Transport Charges" of 1849 (trans. as Dupuit 1962), both republished in 1933 under the title *De l'utilité et sa mesure*. A planned treatise on the economics of public works remained unwritten.

In 1857, on the basis of these contributions, Dupuit felt justified in submitting his candidacy for the Academy of Sciences, but, to his disap-

---

8. This is the second of Mangoldt's contributions mentioned above, contained in a long appendix to the section on interrelated markets, which is not included in the translation. It was extensively discussed by Edgeworth (1925, vol. 2), and Chipman (1965, part 1) provided a modern rendition of the argument in terms of linear programming.

9. A biographical note by Mahyer is included in Dupuit 1933.

pointment, he was not elected. After a distinguished civil service career, he died in Paris on 5 October 1866.

Of Dupuit's varied achievements, his contribution to the theory of demand is the only one that shines more brilliantly today than when it was made. His daily work confronted Dupuit with the question of how public investments such as highways, bridges, canals, and railroads should be evaluated. He looked for a measure of the utility of public works. It was clear to him that such a measure, if found, would be applicable to goods in general so that he would end up with a general theory of utility.

However, Dupuit's concept of utility was different from that of Gossen, Jevons, and Walras inasmuch as it was not supposed to express "the quality which things have of being able to satisfy men's needs." The utility of an object was rather measured by "the maximum sacrifice which each consumer would be willing to make in order to acquire the object," which sacrifice can be expressed in terms of money (1952, 89).[10] As a consequence, interpersonal comparability and additivity pose no problem. In modern terminology, Dupuit was concerned with marginal rates of substitution rather than utility.

With respect to the evaluation of a public work—say, a bridge—Dupuit pointed out three common fallacies. First, the utility of the bridge cannot be measured by its cost. In fact, if the bridge was a sound investment its utility is higher than its cost, and if it was a bad investment, its utility is lower. Second, the utility of the bridge cannot be measured by the saving in transportation costs that it allows. A useful bridge may indeed result in such an increase in the quantities transported that aggregate transportation costs increase. Third, utility should not be measured by the increase in the quantity transported evaluated at a uniform value, because the value of a bridge crossing declines with an increase in quantity.

To construct a better measure, Dupuit begins by constructing a schedule indicating which amounts of money a given individual would be willing to give up for successive units of the good. He regards it as evident that these amounts decline with an increase in quantity; diminishing marginal rates of substitution are postulated as a matter of course. From the schedules for each individual, Dupuit constructs a corresponding schedule for all individuals. The result is plotted in a downward-sloping curve, as depicted in figure 11.5 (Dupuit, like Cournot and Walras, actually measured quantity vertically and price horizontally). Since, at any given price, all

10. Mountifort Longfield had already used the same concept in his *Lectures on Political Economy* of 1834. He had proposed to measure the "intensity" of a person's demand by "the amount which he would be willing and able to give for it, rather than remain without it, or forgo the gratification which it is calculated to afford him" (Longfield 1971, 111). Longfield also realized that demand would be satisfied up to the point at which that amount ceases to exceed the price. However, he did not put these insights to productive analytical use.

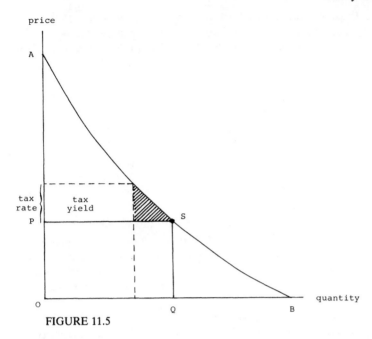

FIGURE 11.5

those units will be demanded whose utility is at least equal to the price, this curve is a demand curve. Complications with the constancy of the marginal utility of money are ignored.

Suppose, in terms of figure 11.5, consumers have to pay price *OP* and the quantity demanded, therefore, is *OQ*. The "absolute utility" of this quantity is then defined by Dupuit as the total amount consumers would be willing to give up for it, as measured by the area under the demand curve, *OASQ*. It is clear that total utility reaches its maximum, *OAB*, when marginal utility (to use the later term), *SQ*, goes to zero. This is perhaps the first clear representation of the relationship between total utility and marginal utility.

The "relative utility" of the product is defined as "the difference between the sacrifice which the purchaser would be willing to make in order to get it, and the purchase price he has to pay in exchange" (1952, 90). It is clear that Dupuit's relative utility, measured by the area of the triangle *PAS*, is the concept Marshall later christened the consumer surplus.

Dupuit uses this conceptual apparatus to analyze the effect of changes in price, say, through a tax (or a toll). The social burden of such a tax, he points out, cannot be measured by the aggregate yield paid to the government; after all, the private burden to the taxpayers is matched by the public benefit to the government. The real social burden rather consists in the lost utility of those quantitites that are no longer consumed because of the tax. It is thus measured by the loss in relative utility as expressed by the shaded triangle. This is the "dead loss" (1962, 12) from taxation. For the first time the old notion, already expressed forcefully by Pierre de Boisguilbert, is made analytically precise.

Since Dupuit assumes typical demand curves to be convex (as drawn), an upper limit for the loss in utility can be obtained by multiplying the change in consumption by half the tax (1952, 103). In the case of a linear demand curve, the utility loss is proportional to the square of the tax. This leads to the important proposition that a given amount of excise taxes imposes a smaller burden if a small tax is levied on many commodities than if a large tax is levied on few commodities. General excise taxes are less onerous than special taxes.

If a tax rate, beginning at zero, is gradually raised, the tax yield first rises to a maximum and then declines, eventually falling to zero as the tax becomes prohibitive. The same yield may thus be obtained with very different tax rates. The consequent loss in utility, however, is not the same. It is important, therefore, to achieve a given yield with the lowest possible rate.

The apparatus was further used by Dupuit to derive pricing rules for natural monopolies. Harold Hotelling claimed Dupuit as an early protagonist of the marginal cost pricing rule (Hotelling 1938, 242), and Ragnar Frisch even called the rule the Dupuit taxation theorem (Frisch 1939, 145). This is a historical error. Though Dupuit's reasoning may easily lead to marginal cost pricing, Dupuit himself did not draw this conclusion. What he envisaged was full-cost coverage at the lowest possible price; he had no sympathy for government subsidies to public enterprises. His thinking went in a different direction.

He realized that the utility loss resulting from the necessity to break even can be reduced by replacing uniform prices by differentiated prices. Ideally, the price for each unit of the commodity should be a given proportion of its utility; by such perfect discrimination, the dead weight loss could be reduced to zero (Dupuit 1962, 16, 29). In reality, of course, this was impossible. With sufficient ingenuity, however, a differentiating monopolist could segment his market in such a way that the welfare losses associated with full-cost coverage would be much reduced (1952, 108f.; 1962). Dupuit provided numerous instructive examples from his practical experience (1962). To mention the most famous illustration, it would not cost a railroad company much to treat everybody like first-class passengers. However, by positively torturing third-class passengers while pampering those in first class, the market can be segmented according to utility, thus enabling the company to practice price discrimination.

This does not make Dupuit a defender of monopolistic exploitation.

He emphasized that natural monopolies operated by private enterprise would not maximize utility, and he was, therefore, in favor of public ownership. His ideal was a public enterprise that covered its cost in a way that maximized social welfare. His contribution to this problem was not surpassed before Frank Ramsey.

Dupuit made no significant contribution to mathematical economics. In his most famous paper (1952) there appears a little piece of calculus, but his reasoning is based on numerical examples and simple graphs. The demand curve was already in Cournot (whose *Researches* Dupuit does not seem to have known) and, in contrast to Cournot, there is no formal optimization.

Dupuit's field was the partial-equilibrium analysis of consumer demand from the point of view of social welfare. His path-breaking contribution in this field was the concept of consumer surplus. Marshall acknowledged that he had learned much of his demand analysis from Dupuit, but he failed to note that with respect to consumer surplus he had added virtually nothing but the name. Dupuit's contribution to the welfare analysis of excise taxes and pricing rules was the most important made before the twentieth century. Unlike the work of Cournot and Gossen, it was never forgotten. Whereas Marshall regarded Dupuit as one of his main teachers, Walras felt compelled to criticize him harshly and unfairly. In Vienna, Rudolf Auspitz and Richard Lieben built directly on his work. In the field of consumer demand, he was the dominant figure before Marshall.

12
Karl Marx

WITH THE EXCEPTION of Buddha, Jesus, and Mohammed, the name of Karl Marx may be more often invoked than that of any other person who ever lived. For those who measure fame by the number of references, he stands at the pinnacle. Clearly, his historical significance far transcends economics. In the present context he matters only as an economist. No effort will be made to do justice to other aspects of his influence.

Chronologically, Marx's economic work belongs to the period whose main program was the incorporation of individual optimization into the circular flow system. Marx did not contribute to this program; he was concerned with the circular flow itself. It is useful to remember that at the time he finished the first volume of *Capital*, Antoine Augustin Cournot, Johann Heinrich von Thünen, and Hermann Heinrich Gossen had long published their pioneering researches and William Stanley Jevons had presented his first paper on a new theory of value. By the time the third volume came out, Alfred Marshall's *Principles* had become the leading textbook. Marx was an analytical anachronism, the rearguard of the Ricardians, an afterthought of classical economics as he had himself defined it.

Life

Karl Marx was born 5 May 1818, in the German town of Trier.[1] His father was a Jewish lawyer who, with his family, became Protestant when Karl was a small boy. He was an educated, kind, and tolerant man. Karl's mother seems to have been the embodiment of what was later called a Jewish mother (or an Italian mama). Theirs was a milieu of the educated bourgeoisie.

Karl's talent was recognized early, though he was weak in mathematics and handwriting. Also recognized was his lack of warm human contacts, his alienation as it might be called in the psychological sense of Marx's favorite term. His verbose declarations of affection combined with coldness and calculation gave his parents early reason for concern.

After a solid high school education, Marx began to study law in Bonn. Soon he moved from Bonn to Berlin and from law to philosophy. Philosophically he associated himself with the Hegelian Left. Working largely as an autodidact, he devoured an enormous mass of literature, but without plan or order and without ever learning the art of communicating his ideas clearly and simply. He conceived many literary projects, but none were completed. An essay on Democritus and Epicurus, also a fragment, finally earned Marx a Ph.D. from Jena, obtained by mail.

Marx left academia with burning ambitions but without marketable skills. Characteristically, his dream became a "humanism" under which everyone could lead the leisurely life of the English upper middle classes without the stresses of scarcity, poverty, and competition. For Marx such a life seemed out of reach. Hopes of an academic career, never very bright, were dashed by the suppression of the Hegelian Left. Marx began to earn a living as an editor of the newly founded *Rheinische Zeitung*, a paper of the Liberal Left. After less than a year the paper was banned by the Prussian censors. It is intriguing to speculate how the course of history might have been changed if Marx had been provided with a professorship. As it was, he became the patron saint of many of those intellectuals whose need for status is not matched by their earning power.

In 1843, after an engagement of seven years, Marx married Jenny von Westphalen. His wife became for him the incarnation of the wealthy and aristocratic establishment to which he so badly wished to belong. The *von* in her maiden name was proudly displayed. Jenny Marx was one of several wives of famous economists who ought to be beatified. She was a loving,

---

1. The classical hagiography is Mehring 1918. Recent biographies are by Raddatz (1975) and Friedenthal (1981).

steadfast, and self-effacing companion who sacrificed everything for her husband and family. Marx, however, though he could be captivating, was generally a petty tyrant with a strong belief in male superiority.

Shortly after their marriage, the young couple, seeing no future in Germany, moved to Paris. Marx began to associate with socialists and communists. The radical liberal became himself a communist. He also met Friedrich Engels, writer and the son of a wealthy textile manufacturer. He was the only friend Marx did not alienate, and he provided not only unwavering loyalty and intellectual collaboration but later also financial support. The years 1845–49 were spent in revolutionary activities in Paris, Brussels, and the Rhineland. To Marx the final collapse of capitalism seemed imminent. The *Communist Manifesto* of 1848, written with Engels, was meant to ring in its demise. What actually collapsed in 1848 were Marx's hopes for an immediate success of revolution. In the following year he emigrated to London, where he spent the rest of his life.

The Marxes had seven children, four of whom died in infancy. To the three daughters who reached adolescence, Marx was a loving and beloved father. The oldest died shortly before her father; the other two later committed suicide. Marx also had an illegitimate son by a maid. To preserve appearances, he was brought up by Engels, who later took the mother as housekeeper. The family lived in straitened circumstances, but with pretensions of bourgeois respectability. Together with Engels' subsidies, Marx earned enough, mainly by writing for American newspapers, to keep the family out of poverty in a statistical sense, but he was a bad householder who could not make ends meet and was often harassed by creditors.

Marx spent much of his time in the British Museum, transforming enormous masses of reading matter into enormous masses of notes. Constantly before his eyes was the great plan of *Capital*. He had led the world to expect a fundamental critique of political economy, and the difficulty of living up to this expectation caused him growing anxiety. He developed boils and various other ailments, particularly of the liver and the eyes, which often forced him, or gave him a pretext, to interrupt his work. Much time and energy was also devoted to communist politics and agitation, with its conspiratorial activities and the innumerable feuds between rivaling factions. In the First International, Marx was the great theoretician in the background. He died, fifteen months after his wife, on 14 March 1883.

Works

The collected works of Marx and Engels fill about forty volumes. Those interested in Marx's "humanism" and philosophy of history tend to concentrate on his early writings up to, and including, the *Communist Manifesto* of 1848 (1932). However, Marx's place in the history of economic science is determined by a single work, namely *Capital* (1911–19; 1957–62).

The history of the writing of *Capital* was essentially the unhappy history of the second half of its author's life. In the *Communist Manifesto*, Marx and Engels had put forth a bold proposition about the inexorable collapse of capitalism. As an ideology, the manifesto was a brilliant creation. As economics, naturally, it fell far short of a scientific analysis. Marx was thus faced with the challenge of providing a scientific proof for what he and Engels had so boldly proclaimed. His response was *Capital*.

Marx found it very difficult, however, to develop his argument in a publishable form. The crisis of 1857 gave him a strong impulse to come to a conclusion because, once more, he thought it might announce the final collapse. A rough draft of 1857–58 was published only in 1939–41, though, as *Outlines of a Critique of Political Economy* (Marx 1939–41). A fragmentary down payment on the grand program appeared in 1859 as *A Contribution to the Critique of Political Economy* (1913). The completion of the first volume of *Capital* took Marx another eight years, until 1867.

The remaining sixteen years of Marx's life were spent in a painful and frustrating effort to complete the work. It was in vain. After Marx's death, Engels was left with cases full of manuscripts, often in a chaotic state, which he eventually shaped into volumes 2 and 3, first published in, respectively, 1885 and 1894. In reading these volumes, one has to keep in mind that some parts were written before volume 1 was published and perhaps even before it was written. Additional manuscripts, mostly containing notes on earlier writers, were edited later by Karl Kautsky under the title (in translation) *Theories of Surplus Value* (Marx 1905–10).

Capital is badly written. It is verbose, opaque, ponderous, and turgid. At times it reads as if a Hegelian journalist had tried to spoof a German professor. The Aristotelian beginning is likely to discourage any reader with a sound sense of logic. The tedious numerical examples may be a challenge to mathematicians, but they spell frustration for the trained economist. The dispassionate scientist is put off by diatribes full of resentment and hate. Flagging interest is constantly rekindled, however, by the promise of fundamental new insights. It is impossible in the present context to describe the content of the roughly 2,100 pages of *Capital*. The following sections concentrate on those analytical elements that ought to be considered as potential contributions to modern economics.[2]

The Dialectic Model of History

At the most general level, Marx proposed a model of history. Often denoted by the term *historical materialism*, it is more accurately described as a dialectic model of history in the sense that history is interpreted as a sequence of economic revolutions. The Hegelian dialectics of thesis, an-

2. An excellent collection of interpretive essays is Nutzinger and Wolfstetter 1974. Samuelson (1966–86, vol. 3, ch. 152) offers a sparkling overview.

tithesis, and synthesis is transformed into the notion that economic progress likewise proceeds in three-four time. Developed in the chapters on Feuerbach in the manuscript "German Ideology" and in the book against Proudhon *The Misery of Philosophy* and summarized in the preface to the *Critique of Political Economy*, it found its most forceful expression in the *Communist Manifesto*. Marx never expounded his philosophy of history in a systematic and lucid fashion. It has thus remained a subject of debate to this day. The following summary clearly fails to do justice to the complexity of Marx's thinking by reducing it to an almost mechanical model. It is hoped that the reader is compensated for the lack of richness in details by a coherent outline of the main skeleton.

The driving forces of economic development, Marx believes, are the efforts of man to preserve his life and, if possible, to improve his condition, to which has to be added population growth. The resulting dynamics is determined by the interplay of three levels of circumstances. The basis is provided by what Marx calls the "productive forces," consisting essentially of natural resources and technology. Examples of the progress of productive forces are discoveries, inventions, conquests, the establishment of colonies, and the like. The second level is formed by the "mode of production," which a modern reader is inclined to call the economic system. It is characterized, in particular, by the class structure of society, the distribution of wealth and income, property rights, the ownership of capital goods, the division of labor, and the assignment of decision-making power. At the third level we find the "ideological superstructure," including the government, law, politics, religion, art, literature, philosophy, and science.

It is essential for Marx's conception that there is a fundamental correspondence between the three levels. To a given state of the productive forces there corresponds a certain mode of production, which in turn requires an appropriate ideological superstructure. In the last analysis the ideological superstructure and the economic system are nothing but reflections of the productive forces. This view is the core of Marx's "materialism."

The fundamental correspondence, however, is subject to serious tensions. The productive forces, Marx assumes, progress relentlessly and inexorably. The ideological superstructure, on the other hand, he seems to regard as relatively rigid. The reason is that it is erected by the ruling class with the express purpose of perpetuating its own dominance. It is essentially an instrument to suppress change in the economic system. Thus held back by the superstructure, the economic system is unable to adjust smoothly to the productive forces. In view of these "internal contradictions," the economic system becomes more and more an impediment to the efficient exploitation of productive forces.

Once the tension has become high enough, it is released in a revolution. This brings a new class into power, establishing a new economic

141

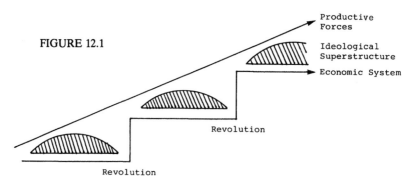

FIGURE 12.1

system, but also with a new ideological superstructure. The stage is set for a repetition of the dialectic cycle. All history, therefore, is interpreted as a history of class struggles.

Figure 12.1 is intended as a schematic representation of this model. The straight arrow stands for the productive forces. The shaded domes symbolize ideological superstructures. As long as a given superstructure is in place, the economic system is prevented from developing. The productive forces thus move away from the economic system. Once the deviation becomes too large, there is a revolution, initiating a steplike adjustment of the economic system, which then is again held in place by a new superstructure.

This scheme raises an identification problem: Where exactly did history stand at the moment Marx was writing? The answer to this question is the main content of *Capital*. It consists of an elaborate effort to demonstrate that the current stage is characterized by the economic mode of capitalism, that capitalism, in view of its internal contradictions, is bound to collapse in a revolution, and that the proletariat will emerge from this revolution as the new ruling class. Marx argued that this would be the last such revolution; from then on, the economic mode would remain perfectly geared to the productive forces without internal contradictions. For the organizational details of this socialist society, he had no interest. He scorned the utopian socialists who tried to devise institutions for a better world. His program was limited to what he regarded as the scientific demonstration of the necessity of collapse. After doomsday, everything would take care of itself. The state, after a temporary dictatorship of the proletariat, would eventually wither away, society would be classless, alienation and exploitation would end, man would be free.

In itself, Marx's dialectic model belongs to the philosophy of history rather than to economics. It nevertheless influenced the progress of economic science by putting economic forces at the center of history, by stressing technological progress as a motor of economic development, by reviving and modifying Adam Smith's concept of alternative economic systems, and by drawing attention to the ideological element in scientific research. In the end, the Marxian argument that economic science is nothing but ideology turned against the Marxists; while they effectively discredited their own motives, others continued to search for disinterested truth.

Marx's model also inspired, directly or indirectly, the interpretation of history in other fields. Joseph Schumpeter (1939) used it to explain business cycles. In his view, the transformation of new ideas into innovations is resisted by a hostile environment. Ideas thus have to accumulate for years before their pressure is high enough to force a breakthrough. Once the breakthrough has emptied the reservoir, resistance again builds up and the cycle is renewed. The same conception was used by Schumpeter to organize his *History of Economic Analysis* (1954). The history of science is thus seen to develop in a sequence of "classical syntheses" interrupted by periods of increasing dissension. Thomas Kuhn (1970), seemingly without being aware of the Marxian heritage, interpreted the progress of science as a sequence of revolutionary "paradigm changes" connected by periods of "normal science." Mancur Olson (1982) has recently revived the notion that revolutions enable nations to rise and that their absence causes them to decline, because resistance to change can be overcome only by revolution. Though all of this may not be very good history, it certainly demonstrates the endurance of Marxian ideas even among non-Marxians and perhaps even anti-Marxians.

Capitalism

The distinctive feature of the economic system of his day, for Marx, is the separation of labor and capital. Whereas medieval artisans owned their tools, his proletarian workers own no capital goods. The heroes of the "bourgeois" economic system are the capitalists, and its central concept is capital. It was natural for Marx's followers to call such a system capitalism, and toward the end of the nineteenth century this term became increasingly common even among non-Marxists.

Today, capitalism is often said to be characterized by the private ownership of capital goods. This is nonsensical terminology, because any society with private ownership of tools or cattle, back to the stone age, would then have to be classified as capitalist. What Marx had in mind was entirely different and much more interesting. He explained it, clumsily, in terms of his two circuits (1957–62, vol. 1, chs. 3, 4).

One circuit concerns the "dual metamorphosis" of commodities. An artisan, say, may initially have a stock of finished commodities, C. He sells these for money, M, in order to buy other goods. This is the famous $C-M-C$ sequence. The other circuit begins with money, which capitalists use to buy commodities in order to sell these for *more* money. This is the $M-$

$C-M'$ sequence.[3] The difference $\triangle M = M' - M$ is the profit or, in Marxian terminology, the surplus value of the capitalist.

The presence of the second circuit is, in Marx's view, the crucial feature of capitalism. It means that there are economic agents whose basic motive is not the satisfaction of human wants but the accumulation of capital. In fact, the allocation of resources is largely controlled by such agents. Capitalism, therefore, is an economic system that is dominated by firms whose behavior is governed not by direct utility but by capital accounts. It was Marx who, in the guise of his two circuits, introduced into economic theory the distinction between utility-maximizing households and profit-maximizing firms.[4]

Marx was convinced that the emergence of capitalist firms permitted an enormous multiplication of the productive powers of the economy. There can be no more ardent admirer of capitalists in their historical role than Karl Marx. At the same time he argued that the dominance of profit-maximizing firms is the source of deep-seated problems. These were the internal contradictions. An economic system in which the satisfaction of human wants is largely supplanted by profit maximization, so he believed, must inevitably collapse. *Capital* was written to substantiate this thesis.

Marx failed to perceive that profit maximization by capital-oriented firms *may* be perfectly consistent with the efficient satisfaction of human wants. This was his basic misunderstanding. There may be all sorts of failures, to be sure, but they are not inherent in profit maximization as such. Two-stage optimization, with firms maximizing profits while households maximize utility, may actually be superior to one-stage optimization.

While economic science, therefore, did not accept Marx's argument of internal inconsistencies, it accepted his concept of capitalism as a distinct economic system. In the wake of *Capital* there developed a vast literature, much of it non-Marxist, on the various forces that were supposed to have contributed to its emergence. The list includes Protestant ethics, the Jews, gold discoveries, piracy, colonialism, double-entry bookkeeping, and much else. At the same time the origins of capitalism tended to recede farther and farther into the mists of early economic history. The eventual collapse, on the other hand, was increasingly replaced by those gradual transformations that are the bread and butter of economic history.

3. It should be noted that this argument has nothing to do with economic growth or with different economic sectors. It relates entirely to the behavior of different economic agents.

4. Profit maximization of firms, as such, had long before been analyzed by Cournot, though.

Value

Like Ricardo's *Principles*, Marx's *Capital* opens with a discussion of value. (A good introduction is Wolfstetter 1973.) It will turn out, however, that the two meanings of *value* are quite different. Like Cantillon, Marx sets up an input-output system, but his accounts are in terms of labor instead of land. He recognizes, of course, that there are different types of labor, but he uses the simplifying assumption that they can all be reduced to "average" labor. He also realizes that some labor may be wasted in inefficient activities. His accounts are meant to be in terms of "socially necessary" labor.

In Marx's accounting system, output is measured in man-hours of labor. Goods produced with the same amount of labor are thus entered with the same number. If a certain commodity, thanks to technical progress, can be produced with less labor, its contribution to total output declines accordingly. Natural resources, including land, which do not absorb labor, do not appear in the accounts at all. Whereas in classical economics the scarcity of natural resources plays a decisive role, in Marx it plays none. The temporal structure of production, sometimes captured by the concepts of "waiting," "abstinence," "impatience," or "time preference," is similarly disregarded.

Besides direct labor, production usually requires intermediate products. These are in turn produced with direct labor and intermediate products, and so on. Once the input-output system is complete, it can be solved to express each output only in terms of labor, both direct and indirect. These are the labor values of the various commodities.

The same principle is applied to labor itself. In the classical tradition, the upkeep and reproduction of the labor force requires a certain subsistence wage, which Marx regards as being determined at least as much by social as by biological considerations. There is much in Malthus that Marx could have given him credit for. This may precisely be one reason why he made him the target of his particular contempt (Meek 1953). The subsistence budget is again expressed in terms of the labor necessary to produce it. Consistent with the nature of these accounts, the reduction of high-grade labor to average labor is not supposed to be based on market wages, as for Adam Smith, but on the higher subsistence requirements of skilled workers due to, say, longer training.

The labor values of commodities can then be compared with the values of labor used in their production. If production is viable, an hour's worth of output costs no more than an hour of labor and usually less. The difference is surplus value. It is appropriated by the capitalists in the form of profit, which expresses the fact that workers, separated from the means of production, receive less than a working day for each working day. Since the wage for average labor, under the pressure of competition, is the same everywhere, surplus value, too, is a uniform fraction of the labor value of output and thus a uniform percentage of wages. It should be noted that all of this is true tautologically, merely by virtue of the accounting definitions. Prices do not appear at all.

The question is why Marx based volume 1 of *Capital* on these labor accounts. His opening chapter gives the distinct impression that the labor values of commodities were intended to explain their exchange values, their relative prices. He also presents an argument to the effect that two commodities exchanged against each other must have a common property, which he said can be nothing but their labor value. While the Aristotelian logic of the argument is ridiculous, it clearly relates to relative price. Generations of readers, both Marxian and non-Marxian, have concluded that Marx was indeed proposing a labor theory of exchange value.

This conclusion is false, though. In the same opening chapter there is a hint that exchange values would later be revealed to be different from labor values (Marx 1911–19, 1:5; the translation—in Marx 1957–62—of this page is unclear). Similar references can be found elsewhere in Marx's writings. In fact, when volume 1 was published, Marx had already written the material that later became volume 2, and in volume 2 it is made very clear that exchange values are generally different from labor values. The difference arises because surplus values in the labor accounts bear a uniform proportion to labor, whereas profits in the price accounts, under competitive pressure, bear a uniform proportion to capital. The difference disappears only in the special case in which the capital/labor ratio, Marx's "organic composition of capital," is the same for all industries.

Indeed, the Marxian theory of price, except for the treatment of rent, is the theory of Adam Smith and David Ricardo. It is a cost of production theory of competitive equilibrium prices with fixed input coefficients. In particular, of two commodities with identical labor inputs, the one with higher capital requirements has the higher price. Marx left no doubt that he did not regard labor values just as empirical approximations to cost prices but emphasized the systematic difference between the two.

Comparing volume 1 and volume 3, Eugen von Böhm-Bawerk (1949), like other economists, criticized Marx for the apparent inconsistency between his two value theories. In view of Marx's own insistence on the difference, this criticism is beside the point. In fact, Marx regarded the juxtaposition of the two sets of values as one of his major contributions. The question is why he put forth the labor accounts in the first place.

The answer is still being debated. It is a plausible conjecture that in volume 1, Marx intended to create a social or ideological theory of value, whereas volume 3 contained the economic theory. The economic theory would always be interpreted by "vulgar" economists as a demonstration that profit is justified as the fruit of capital in the same way that wages are justified as the fruit of labor. In contrast, the social or ideological theory would exhibit surplus value as the fruit of labor alone. It thus reveals the hidden truth Marx claimed to have discovered, while vulgar economists are content with superficial appearances.

There is nothing wrong, in principle, with the Marxian labor accounts. In fact, accounts of the same type could be constructed in terms of land (as exemplified by Cantillon), energy, or peanuts. Landowners, power companies, and peanut growers may have reasons to prefer one type to the others. François Quesnay used the land accounts to attribute net output to land; Karl Marx used the labor accounts to attribute it to labor. Marx might have argued that the labor accounts are particularly significant because they involve human beings and their social relations. For the explanation of economic reality, however, neither type of account would be informative. A modern economist vulgar enough to be interested in observable prices and economic welfare may just as well disregard them.

There is the further question of why Marx misled his readers by pretending in volume 1 to discuss exchange value. Thanks to Baumol (1974, 61), the answer seems fairly clear, though strange. The confusion was created for the express purpose, as Marx wrote, "of continually *setting traps* for these fellows which provoke them to untimely demonstrations of their asininity" (Marx's emphasis). As a matter of fact, the conundrum of the two value theories called forth more brilliance than asininity. Their relationship became known as the transformation problem. Marx had already made an effort to derive prices from labor values. Mikhail Tugan-Baranowsky showed in 1905 that the derivation was incorrect, and at the same time he began to solve the reverse problem of transforming prices into labor values. Two years later, Ladislaus von Bortkiewicz showed the way to a correct solution of Marx's problem (Böhm-Bawerk 1949). Since then, each generation of Marxologists has tried its mathematical skills on the transformation problem.[5] However, since the labor accounts themselves are not operationally meaningful, it is hard to see why the transformation problem should be. From the point of view of modern economics, Marx simply had a conventional cost of production theory of exchange value.

Two-Sector Balanced Growth

For Marx the essence of capitalism is its powerful dynamics. It is consistent with this perspective that he developed a model of economic growth. In the last analysis, faithful to the classical tradition, Marx wanted to demonstrate the impossibility of the perpetual motion of a capitalist system. His model, therefore, should really have been one of unbalanced growth. However, Marx never developed an explicit theory of unbalanced growth leading to eventual stagnation or collapse. What he put on paper

5. The debate is brilliantly reviewed in Samuelson (1966–86, vol. 3, ch. 153) together with the subsequent colloquium in the *Journal of Economic Literature* of 1974.

was a model of balanced growth. His particular analytical contribution to mainstream economics was the first model of balanced growth in an economy with two sectors. This model never reached a publishable form, however. What Marx left behind was a sketch, a fragment, which Engels used to conclude the second volume of *Capital*. An effort will be made in this section to distill from these cumbersome ruminations the simple outlines of the model Marx had in mind.

These outlines are best visualized in three steps. First consider a stationary one-sector economy. In terms of Marxian labor accounts, its gross social product, w, can be written as the sum of capital consumption, αc, variable capital (or wages), v, and surplus value, m (1957–62, vol. 1, ch. 7),

$$w = \alpha c + v + m. \tag{12.1}$$

Whereas c represents constant capital, α is the depreciation rate. The present exposition follows Marx in assuming, for simplicity, that $\alpha = 1$. The ratio of constant capital to total capital, namely

$$\gamma = \frac{c}{c+v} = \frac{c}{k}, \tag{12.2}$$

measures the "organic composition of capital," or, in modern terms, the capital-intensity of production. The ratio of surplus value to variable capital (or the profit/wage ratio),

$$\mu = \frac{m}{v}, \tag{12.3}$$

is called the rate of surplus value or the degree of exploitation.

In a second stage this model is extended to two sectors, but still for a stationary state. This is the case of "simple reproduction" (Marx 1957–62, vol. 2, ch. 20, sec. 1, 2). The first sector produces capital goods, which go into constant capital. The second sector produces consumer goods. An equation similar to equation 12.1 may now be written for each separate sector, namely (for $\alpha = 1$)

$$\begin{aligned} w_1 &= c_1 + v_1 + m_1, \\ w_2 &= c_2 + v_2 + m_2. \end{aligned} \tag{12.4}$$

The rates of surplus value are assumed to be equal, which means

$$\mu = \frac{m_1}{v_1} = \frac{m_2}{v_2}. \tag{12.5}$$

The organic composition of capital, however, may differ between the sectors, so that

$$c_1 = \gamma_1 k_1 \text{ and } c_2 = \gamma_2 k_2. \tag{12.6}$$

Since a stationary economy does not save, equilibrium between the sectors requires that the production of consumer goods equal the sum of all wage and profit incomes:

$$w_2 = v_1 + v_2 + m_1 + m_2. \tag{12.7}$$

If this condition is satisfied, the consumer goods that sector 1 buys from sector 2 are automatically equal in value to the capital goods that sector 2 buys from sector 1. In symbols,

$$c_2 = v_1 + m_1. \tag{12.8}$$

In addition, the output of capital goods in sector 1 corresponds to the capital consumption of both sectors,

$$w_1 = c_1 + c_2. \tag{12.9}$$

Exchange between the sectors can thus proceed period after period in the same way.

The third stage, finally, concerns "reproduction on an extended scale," or balanced growth. Economic growth requires that a certain proportion of income be saved. Marx assumes that all saving comes out of profits whereas all wages are consumed. The average propensities to save, s_1 and s_2, may differ between the two sectors. In balanced growth, total saving per period equals the sum of the increments in constant and variable capital,

$$s_1 m_1 + s_2 m_2 = \Delta c_1 + \Delta c_2 + \Delta v_1 + \Delta v_2. \tag{12.10}$$

In modern terminology this means that saving equals investment.

In addition, the output of consumer goods must equal the aggregate consumption demand. This condition can be written as

$$w_2 = v_1 + v_2 + (1-s_1)m_1 + (1-s_2)m_2 + \Delta v_1 + \Delta v_2. \tag{12.11}$$

The last two terms represent the required increases in the variable capitals or the wage fund. In balanced growth all components of capital must, of course, grow at the same growth rate, g:

$$\frac{\Delta c_1}{c_1} = \frac{\Delta c_2}{c_2} = \frac{\Delta v_1}{v_1} = \frac{\Delta v_2}{v_2} = g. \tag{12.12}$$

The twelve equations 12.4–12.6 and 12.10–12.12 determine the structure and growth rate of the economy (though, of course, not its absolute size) for given rates of surplus value, saving rates, and organic compositions of capital. Different growth rates are associated with different structures of the economy. In general, these relationships are complicated, and Marx's numerical examples, laboriously computed, remain opaque.

A marked simplification is obtained if, as Marx assumes, each sector finances its investments by its own savings, thus obviating the need for intersectoral capital flows. In symbols this requires

$$\Delta v_1 + \Delta c_1 = s_1 m_1 \tag{12.13}$$

which implies $\Delta v_2 + \Delta c_2 = s_2 m_2$. As a consequence,

$$\frac{\Delta v_1}{v_1} + \frac{\Delta c_1}{c_1} \cdot \frac{c_1}{v_1} = s_1 \frac{m_1}{v_1} = s_1 \mu \tag{12.14}$$

which, for balanced growth, can be rewritten as

$$g = \mu s_1 (1 - \gamma_1). \tag{12.15}$$

For sector 2 there is the corresponding condition

$$g = \mu s_2 (1 - \gamma_2). \tag{12.16}$$

To produce this special case, the parameters must thus satisfy the condition

$$s_1 (1 - \gamma_1) = s_2 (1 - \gamma_2). \tag{12.17}$$

Marx assumes that s_2 is adjusted accordingly.

In this special case, the growth rate of the economy is clearly related positively to the profit rate and the savings rates and negatively to the organic compositions of capital. What Marx developed is essentially a Harrod-Domar model of balanced growth for a two-sector economy, but without entering into problems of stability. This model was ahead of mainstream economics by more than half a century. In recent years it has provided mathematical economists such as Morishima (1973) with new inspiration. That the prophet of inescapable doom contributed to modern economics, above all, a model of balanced growth is one of the most poignant ironies in the history of economics.

Falling Profits and the Collapse of Capitalism

That a capitalist economy can grow forever without a change in its structure was just about the last thing Marx really wanted to prove. He wanted to demonstrate the exact opposite, namely the inevitability of collapse. The lever that, in his view, would derail the growth process is the progressive increase in the capital intensity of production and the associated tendency of profit rates to fall (for a detailed interpretation see Wolfstetter 1977). The "law" of the tendency of profits to fall was described by Marx as "a mystery whose solution has been the goal of all political economy since Adam Smith," but which, he claimed, he was the first to solve (1957–62, 3:209).

The tendency of profits to fall in the course of capital accumulation was indeed one of the main themes of classical economics. Ricardo derived this tendency from the law of diminishing returns, and he saw it counteracted by technological progress. Marx refused to have any traffic with

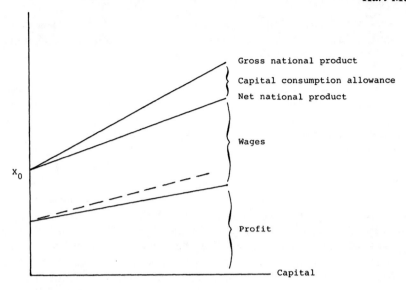

FIGURE 12.2

diminishing returns and thus had to supply another explanation (1957–62, vol. 3, chs. 13–15). It is based on the notion that aggregate profits, since they depend only on labor inputs and wages, are independent of the amount of capital goods, at least in a first approximation. If more capital goods are held, aggregate profits do not therefore rise. It follows tautologically that an increase in capital goods lowers the rate of profits per unit of capital.

Marx presented his argument in terms of his labor accounts. For a modern reader it is more easily understood in national income terms. Some remarks on the translation from output accounts to labor accounts are added in footnotes. Output is produced with labor and capital.[6] Suppose that in the absence of capital the available labor (on the available land) produces a net national product of X_0. Since there is no capital consumption, this is also gross national product. If labor is equipped with increasing amounts of capital, net national product grows. With constant returns, net national product is a linear function of capital as illustrated in figure 12.2.[7] Net national product is divided up between wages and profits in a constant proportion—say, half-and-half.[8]

6. In Marx's terminology these correspond, respectively, to variable capital and constant capital.
7. In terms of labor, net national product is, of course, a constant.
8. Marx notes that an increase in capital raises the productivity of labor. As a consequence, if the wage rate corresponds to the product of a given number of hours, the real wage in terms of commodities rises.

Increasing amounts of capital require increasing capital consumption allowances. With a constant depreciation rate these will be proportional to capital.[9] Gross national product will thus rise even more rapidly than net product.

For Marx, total capital is represented by the sum of wages and capital consumption. This reflects the classical (and physiocratic) notion that the entrepreneur advances wages and capital consumption allowances for one period at a time. The Marxian profit rate, therefore, is the ratio of profits to the sum of wages and capital consumption. It is evident from figure 12.2 that this ratio inevitably declines as capital grows. According to more modern usage, the profit rate would be defined rather as the ratio of profits to the value of capital goods only. It is clear, however, that this ratio declines as well, profits rising less than in proportion to capital.

This argument is based on the assumption of constant profit per unit of wages. Marx explains carefully that the tendency of profits to fall can be counteracted by an increase in the profit share.[10] This is the reason why he insists on talking about a *tendency* for profits to fall. In figure 12.2 the broken line indicates how profits would have to rise to maintain a constant ratio to the sum of wages and capital consumption. It is conceivable that this line never intersects the net national product curve. In this case, the profit rate can remain constant forever without pushing wages to zero. In fact, real wages may not even decline. In other cases the broken line will eventually intersect the net national product line, thus implying negative wages. In such cases the profit rate cannot forever be prevented from falling. Which of these cases materializes depends on the initial profit/wage ratio and on the ratio between the net marginal product of capital and the depreciation allowance per unit of capital.

In Marx, therefore, the tendency for profits to fall is not so much an economic proposition as a logical implication of the way he defines his concepts.[11] However, if the rate of surplus value rises, as it usually will, the implication does not necessarily hold; the falling tendency of profits is not inescapable.

For Ricardo a declining profit rate eventually brings accumulation to

---

9. In the labor accounts, capital consumption will be less than proportional to capital because the national income figure has to be divided by an increasing labor productivity. Capital consumption in terms of labor will actually approach an asymptote.

10. In Marxian terminology this is expressed as an increasing rate of surplus value or, equivalently, as an increasing exploitation rate. In the light of note 8, a rising exploitation rate is perfectly compatible with constant, or even rising, real wages.

11. With s = surplus value, v = variable capital (wages), c = constant capital (capital goods) and δ = depreciation rate, the rate of surplus value is defined in labor units as

$$\rho = \frac{s}{v + \delta c} = \frac{s}{v} \cdot \frac{v}{v + \delta c} = \sigma \frac{v}{v + \delta c}.$$

For a given rate of surplus value, σ, and given variable capital, ρ thus declines with rising c.

a halt. For Marx accumulation is further stimulated because capitalists try to make up for the falling profit rate by holding even more capital. This effort is based on the illusion that more capital will earn more profit, whereas, in fact, with given labor, it just results in a further decline in profit rates. With a given capital/labor ratio, however, the accumulation of capital also results in an increase in the labor force, which indeed raises aggregate profits. The decline of profit rates thus becomes an engine of growth (Marx 1957–62, vol. 1, ch. 28, sec. 1; vol. 3, ch. 13).

In reality, Marx argues, the capital/labor ratio will not remain constant but will tend to rise. This process is accompanied by rising firm sizes and progressive concentration of industries (Marx 1957–62, vol. 1, ch. 23). "One capitalist always kills many" (763). As a consequence, the growth in the demand for labor is retarded. If population growth reflects the demand for labor in an earlier period with more rapid capital growth, this retardation is accompanied by overpopulation and unemployment. There is a growing "industrial reserve army." It actually facilitates the growth process because the capitalists can now expand the labor force without waiting for population growth and without a rise in wages.

Overpopulation and unemployment inevitably lead to deepening poverty; growing wealth is thus accompanied by growing misery. "The relative mass of the industrial reserve army increases therefore with the potential energy of wealth. But the greater this reserve army in proportion to the active labor-army, the greater is the mass of a consolidated surplus-population, whose misery is in inverse ratio to its torment of labor" (Marx 1957–62, 1:644).

The growing misery of a growing working class creates revolt. At the same time, private ownership of capital becomes an impediment to further concentration. "The monopoly of capital becomes a fetter upon the mode of production, which has sprung up and flourished along with and under it. Centralization of the means of production and socialization of labor at last reach a point where they become incompatible with the capitalist integument. This integument is burst asunder. The knell of capitalist private property sounds. The expropriators are expropriated" (Marx 1957–62, 1:763).

These are ringing phrases, to be sure, though only a faint echo of the *Communist Manifesto*. Analytically, however, the Marxian theory of capitalist collapse is weak. Marx was never able to show coherently why a progressive increase in the capital intensity of production is necessarily associated with immiserization, unemployment, and crises. He failed precisely where he so badly wanted to succeed, namely in the scientific demonstration of the inevitability of the collapse of capitalism from its internal contradictions. Just as the early Christians expected the Day of Judgment, he and his followers expected the collapse in the near future. Every little recession was seen as the beginning of the end. By some Marxists it still

is. Most of them, however, have learned to be patient. Evolutionary transformation, in their thinking, has taken the place of revolutionary collapse.

Place in the History of Economics

As an ideologist, Marx was a genius. His power to forge ideas into
weapons for political action and his dream of a human existence freed from
competitive pressure still captivates the minds of innumerable intellectuals
and agitators.

As a prophet, Marx was a failure. It is true that firms became bigger
and more concentrated, but this was not difficult to discern in Marx's time.
It is also true that he understood economic crises as phases in a continuing
cyclical process, but Clément Juglar had published a much superior analysis
of business cycles five years before the first volume of *Capital*. The predictions of the immiserization of the working classes, of the progressive
deepening of economic crises, and of the imminent collapse of capitalism
were patently falsified by events. In the meantime, remnants of feudalism
have been swept away by revolution in many countries, but precisely the
countries with the fullest development of "bourgeois" democracy seemed
immune to revolution. The very notion of social classes turned out to be
a leftover from feudalism. Under democratic capitalism, as in the United
States or Switzerland, there are indeed poor people and rich people, and
perhaps very poor people and very rich people, but at least if race is not
an issue, they are not stratified into distinct classes; transitions are fluid.
What we are wont to call capitalism appears to be capable of virtually
infinite development, transformation, and variation without a revolutionary collapse. The dialectic model of history has failed.

What matters in the present context, however, is Marx's contribution
to economic science. The main points are that he did make a contribution
and that it was mediocre. His most fundamental contribution was the clear
formulation of the question of how political and social institutions interact
with economic processes. For example, how does legislation affect income
distribution, and how do the consequent changes in income distribution,
in turn, affect legislation? This is a profound question, but what Marx
could provide by way of an answer fell far short of a cogent analysis. Marx's
question was deep, but his answer remained shallow. In fact, the program
he outlined still remains largely unfilled. The theory of institutional economics has yet to be written.

A second contribution was the introduction of the concepts of a classical economics and of capitalism. Both were generally adopted by economic science, but they obscured at least as much as they illuminated.
Classical economics, instead of being understood simply as the mainstream
economics of each period, became regarded as a particular school of economics to which there might be any number of alternatives. The use of
capital accounts, instead of being a commonplace concomitant of progress

in business administration, became regarded as the hallmark of a distinctive economic system.

Marx's foremost contribution to economic theory, however, was his model of balanced growth in a two-sector economy. His exposition was clumsy, fragmentary, and almost unintelligible, to be sure, but the basic notions are there, and they are still a source of inspiration for mathematical economists a century later. This was a useful contribution to mainstream economics, but it was not one of the first importance. Moreover, it was devoid of any revolutionary impact.

Marx was an incessant worker, a voracious reader, the writer of innumerable boxfuls of notes, and an untiring collector of facts. The sad truth was that his training had not equipped him for effective scientific research, and he was constantly frustrated by his propensity to pose ambitious problems that he could not solve. In fact, it looks as if, at least after the publication of volume 1 of *Capital*, his work was not so much an effort to complete his program as an effort to escape from it. Whereas Gossen was a tragic figure because, during his lifetime, he won no fame for what he accomplished as a theorist, Marx (like Schumpeter later) was a tragic figure because his accomplishments as a theorist did not measure up to his fame.

II
The Marginalist Era
(ca. 1830-1930)

13
The Leitmotiv of Marginalism

FROM 1830 to 1930 economic theory developed before a background of vast political, social, and economic changes. The stepwise extension of suffrage, punctuated by unrest and revolution, eventually led to representative democracy. The unification of nation-states was fought over in wars, ranging in size from the almost bloodless Swiss War of Secession to the carnage of the American Civil War. Shifts in the balance of power and imperialism resulted in a number of armed conflicts until the balance of power finally collapsed in the cataclysm of World War I.

The first half of the century was largely a period of victorious liberalism fighting for the abolition of mercantilist regulations and for free trade. The second half of the century was a period of rising socialism. The rapid growth in aggregate ouput, initiated by the Industrial Revolution, led to the result that Robert Malthus had so effectively predicted, namely a rapid increase in population without a corresponding improvement (and in some cases even with a deterioration) in living standards. The "social question" troubled the public conscience, and it seemed as insoluble as similar problems at other times. The "system" of society was seen by many to be in need of change. Reformers came forth with all sorts of projects, democratic and elitist, revolutionary and conservative, born of philanthropy and hatred, sensible and bizarre, utopian and pragmatic, individualist and etatist. This was the century of ideologies, with innumerable isms competing for adherents. Beginning with Bismarck's social insurance program, legislatures began to be the spearhead of social reform. The rising welfare state became visible over the horizon.

Rapid economic growth was periodically interrupted by crises, often accentuated by bank panics. They were regarded as another basic flaw in the system. While the classical economists had discussed crises in terms of general gluts, Clément Juglar, and later the National Bureau of Economic Research, made them the subject of intensive empirical research. By the second half of the marginalist era, there had accumulated a large body of facts and hypotheses about business cycles, and the search for countermeasures had led to the emergence of central banks.

As would be expected, the economic literature of the period was largely a reflection of these developments and concerns. Leading economists, as always, were children of their times. However, their views, opinions, and doctrines had little in common. Some were staunch establishmentarians; others were flaming radicals. Some defended property; others proposed the nationalization of land. A few were uncompromising defenders of laissez faire, but most advocated pragmatic government intervention, and some came close to socialism.

And yet, if the literature of the period is scanned for pieces that became lasting contributions to modern mainstream economics, the result is very different. Most such contributions had no clearly discernible association with the political, social, and economic developments of the period. As far as these developments are concerned, they could just as well have been made in the eighteenth or in the twentieth century. It is indeed fairly easy to interpret much of general economic literature in the light of Marxian economic determinism, but for the lasting contributions to economic theory, this interpretation is not convincing.

These contributions had a common leitmotiv, namely the optimization calculus of individuals and firms. Adam Smith, following in the scholastic tradition, had visualized the economy as being governed by the invisible hand of self-interest. Though he illustrated the working of this force with innumerable telling examples, he did not provide a formal analysis. Nor did other classical economists. From Cantillon to Ricardo the spotlight of economic theory was turned toward macroeconomics. What it revealed was the circular flow of income and its distribution among social classes. Microeconomic theory remained rudimentary. Karl Marx, not only the last but also the most intransigent of classical economists, even scorned supply and demand.

After David Ricardo, despite the growing interest in business cycles, the spotlight of economic theory began to shift to microeconomics. The decision making of households, entrepreneurs, and firms became the main subject of innovative research. From the beginning, decision making was interpreted, more or less clearly, as a problem of constrained optimization. Such a problem is solved if no incremental or "marginal" change offers a further improvement. Eventually, after the problem had been clearly perceived, the new approach thus became known as marginalism. When John A. Hobson coined the term (Howey 1972), he gave it a derogatory connotation. In fact, he could hardly have found a more felicitous epithet.

Mathematics had long provided what came to be regarded as the classical tool for the solution of optimization problems, namely differential calculus. Marginalism was thus associated with the penetration of calculus into economic theory. Many of the leading marginalists became protagonists of, and even crusaders for, mathematical economics. This was a slow and laborious process. Augustin Cournot was a professional mathematician, but thirty years after the publication of his pioneering book, it had found hardly any readers. Johann Heinrich von Thünen and Hermann Heinrich Gossen had no more than the most elementary notions of calculus. Léon Walras, the incarnation of mathematical marginalism, had failed to acquire an academic degree because of his deficient background in mathematics, and his analytical progress was blocked until a friendly colleague introduced him to calculus. Nevertheless, by the end of the marginalist era, most productive theorists were well trained in mathematics. This does not mean that they were unhistorical or even antihistorical. In fact, many also shared the historicism and institutionalism of their times and saw no conflict between economic theory and historical or biological evolutionism.

It might look as if the development of a theory of individual optimization had been a conscious research program. This was not so, however. Different economists got hold of different aspects of optimization, apparently without perceiving the unifying theme. Some never even discovered that the economic propositions they so laboriously derived were relatively simple applications of differential calculus. Some actually remained belligerently antimathematical to the end of their lives. Even Walras, who envisaged an all-embracing general equilibrium system, left large analytical gaps and made no concentrated effort to close them after his initial publication. That the marginal productivity theory of distribution was still controversial forty years after Thünen's second volume illustrates the erratic nature of analytical progress more clearly than anything else. Marginalists, like other scientific discoverers, were largely groping in the dark.

Nevertheless, it is hard to avoid the conclusion that the emergence of marginalism was inevitable, the product of an endogenous dynamic process, Blaug's contrary argument notwithstanding (Blaug 1972). The need to provide the invisible hand with an analytical support, thereby making its action more predictable, could not fail to arise and was, in fact, independently felt by a number of people. Characteristically, marginalism was created not in a single stroke of genius but through the work of many, each reacting to the same need in his own way. Marginalism, in its erratic progress, had the inexorability of a tide.

The marginalist era may be loosely divided into two phases. From 1830 to about 1870, the emphasis was on the fundamental partial applications of the optimizing calculus. In particular, Cournot applied it to revenues and costs of profit-maximizing firms, Thünen developed it for cost minimization in production, and Gossen analyzed utility maximization by consumers. These partial aspects continued to absorb analytical efforts far beyond 1870, but the main focus then shifted to the incorporation of optimization into the circular flow. Walras succeeded for the first time in constructing a circular flow model with an arbitrary number of optimizing individuals and firms. Friedrich von Wieser and Alfred Marshall, though less explicit in their analysis, thought along the same lines. Eugen von Böhm-Bawerk determined the rate of interest in a circular flow model with optimization over time. The result was the integration of marginalism into classical economics (or vice versa). Classical economics had not declined or collapsed, but it had acquired new dimensions.

The two phases also differed in another respect. Before 1870 the leading marginalists were not professors of economics. Though no longer policy advisers, from the point of view of the academic establishment they were outsiders and amateurs. As the century advanced, however, political economy was increasingly professionalized. After 1870 most leading economic theorists occupied professorial posts, and the role of amateurs, though still significant, declined rapidly. Professional associations were founded (the American Economic Association in 1885), and specialized journals began to appear (the *Quarterly Journal of Economics* in 1886). In most countries, as is emphasized by Stigler (1972), this resulted in a quickening of the speed with which new theoretical achievements were transmitted and adapted. In Germany, however, it was precisely the entrenched strength of the academic establishment, since it was dominated by the historical school, that impeded the adoption of marginalism.

The progressive professionalization does not mean that economists now felt academically secure. For many of them the struggle for academic recognition was arduous and strewn with personal disappointments. Independent programs in economics were just beginning to be established. On the Continent, in particular, economists usually belonged to the faculty of law and had to satisfy its requirements. The dogmatic and qualitative character of jurisprudence was never a fertile breeding ground for the quantitative analysis of economists, and in some countries this impeded the progress of economics far into the twentieth century. Wherever economics has the image of being narrow-gauge law, it will not attract many talented young minds.

According to conventional historiography, the two phases of the marginalist era were separated by the "Marginal Revolution." This was supposed to have taken place in the 1870s through the path-breaking achievements of William Stanley Jevons, Carl Menger, and Léon Walras, the three "founders." Whoever made contributions before 1870 was classified as a precursor. The historical research of the last two decades has shown convincingly that this interpretation, largely fostered by the Viennese, cannot be maintained (see especially Blaug 1972). In fact, there was no marginal revolution. Cournot, Thünen, Dupuit, and Gossen, far from being merely precursors, had actually made the fundamental contributions. When the books by Jevons, Menger, and Walras appeared, far from igniting a revolution, they produced hardly a stir. The absorption of their work into mainstream economics was a slow, hesitant, and gradual process, taking place over decades. (This is detailed in Howey 1960 and 1972.) In addition, as Jaffé has rightly stressed, the contributions of the alleged founders differed in important respects (Jaffé 1983, ch. 17). Finally, no previous regime was toppled by marginalism, but the inherited economics was gradually extended to accommodate the marginalist insights. [1] Overall,

---

1. If marginalism had a victim, it was Marxian economics, because Marx, resisting the extension, insisted on a circular flow economics *without* individual optimization.

the rise of marginalism may serve as a paradigm of nonrevolutionary change in the history of science.

The result of the marginalist era was sometimes called neoclassical economics. It seems that the term was first used by Thorstein Veblen around the turn of the century (Aspromourgos 1986) to distinguish Marshall (who stressed doctrinal continuity) from authors such as Jevons (who stressed discontinuity). In due course the application of the term was extended to the whole body of marginalism. This was a case of extremely unfortunate terminology for at least two reasons. First, it does an injustice to the originality of marginalism by disparaging it as a mere reedition of classical economics. As has been remarked, it would be equally misleading to call modern physics neo-Newtonian. There is indeed an essential continuity in science, but this does not justify labeling each new phase as *neo-*, *neo-neo-*, and so on. Each generation produces new classic contributions, but it makes no sense to call them neoclassical.

Second, the term *neoclassical* seems to evoke misleading notions about the character of the marginalist contribution. Schumpeter expressed these notions metaphorically by saying that, toward the end of the nineteenth century, the edifice of neoclassical theory created, in the superficial observer, "an impression of finality—the finality of a Greek temple that spreads its perfect lines against a cloudless sky" (1954, 754). Shackle talked about "a Great Theory or Grand System of Economics, in one sense complete and self-sufficient" (1967,4).

In retrospect it is impossible to discover a single work of that period that conveys this impression. It is true that the economists of the second marginalist generation, the Victorians, had a propensity to plan (and promise) comprehensive multivolume treatises. It is no less true, however, that all of these treatises remained unfinished fragments. It was tempting, of course, to attribute the fragmentary character of these works to the pressing burden of other duties, to nervous exhaustion, or to high standards of scholarship. The fundamental reason, however, was more likely to be found at a different level. These were men with burning intellectual ambitions but actually very imperfect analytical tools. The tools were adequate for the solution of some important, but still limited, problems. Many other problems were simply beyond the analytical powers of that generation. The temple of neoclassical economics was perhaps dreamed of, but it was never built. This is meant as a criticism not of marginalist achievements but of the neoclassical mythology. Living science rarely has the finality of a Greek temple but rather resembles those rambling structures to which centuries have constantly added new wings.

14
Johann Heinrich von Thünen

GERMAN PROFESSORS of the nineteenth century loved to criticize Adam Smith for his "rationalism," and they were fond of ridiculing the *homo oeconomicus* he was supposed to have put in the place of real human beings. In the early years of the century, even before David Ricardo had discovered his interest in economics, a young German student of agriculture had a different opinion. He criticized Smith precisely for his lack of an explicit theory, and he undertook to investigate the implications of an explicit optimization calculus for production and factor allocation. His name was Johann Heinrich von Thünen.

Life

Thünen was born on his father's estate, Canarienhausen, near Jever in the German grand duchy of Oldenburg on 24 June 1783.[1] His paternal ancestors were landowners, but despite the *von* they did not belong to the aristocratic Junkers. Thünen lost his father when he was two, and a few years later his mother married a timber merchant. The boy grew up in Hooksiel, a small port town on the northern seaboard, where he obtained a solid high school education.

The prospect of having to take over one of his father's two estates caused him to leave school at sixteen to learn farming. As an apprentice he got to know, and to hate, the hard manual labor on a farm but thought he learned little.

There followed studies on all aspects of agronomy, including natural sciences, mathematics, and economics, at the recently founded agricultural colleges of Gross-Flottbeck (near Hamburg) and Celle. His foremost teacher in Celle was the famous Albrecht Thaer, founder of rational agriculture. Thünen admired his contribution to agronomy, but he was critical of his economics. In particular, he doubted that agricultural techniques that had proved efficient in England could serve as an example for Germany. The optimal choice of techniques, he felt, would generally depend on relative prices. This insight became the leitmotiv of his life.

The desire to learn more economics seems to have caused Thünen soon to move on to the nearby University of Göttingen. Enrolled there for two semesters, he studied the *Wealth of Nations*, and Adam Smith became his great teacher of economics, whose work he wanted to continue. Despite these academic studies, Thünen essentially remained a scientifically

---

1. Schumacher 1868, despite its adulatory tone, is still the basic biographical source. It is updated by W. Braeuer in his introduction to Thünen (1951).

gifted autodidact. He always lacked the balanced education and the facility of exposition that a solid academic training can convey, and his mind was directed more toward practically useful knowledge than abstract principles.

Newly married to the daughter of a respected landowner, Thünen first operated a rented estate. In 1809, with the proceeds from the farm he had inherited from his father, he bought from his brother-in-law the rather rundown estate of Tellow in Mecklenburg, today in the German Democratic Republic, with about 1,200 acres of land. Though his heart was in his intellectual pursuits rather than in practical farming, he succeeded in gradually paying off his initial debt and in raising the value of his property, so that he could leave to his four children a prosperous estate with ample liquid funds.

Like François Quesnay, who came from a similar background, Thünen made the farm his economic paradigm. Together with the physiocrats and Thaer, he belongs to those representatives of the Enlightenment who regarded improvements in agriculture as the key to economic progress. Over the years he kept the most meticulous accounts for all aspects of his operations, down to horse dung and rat catching. He was a model employer with philanthropic, if somewhat paternalistic, ideas on social policy, who even established a profit-sharing plan for his employees.

By 1827, Thünen's writings had made him an internationally known authority on agriculture. Tellow became a mecca for agronomists, attracting visitors from all over Europe. In 1830, Thünen was made a *doctor philosophiae honoris causa* by the University of Rostock. Politically a progressive liberal, he was in 1848 elected to the National Assembly in Frankfurt but could not attend because of his declining health. In the same year the town of Teterow, with flags flying and bands playing, made him an honorary burgher. He died on his estate in 1850, like Quesnay revered as a sage.

Works

In the spring of 1803, before he was even twenty, Thünen conceived the idea that became central to his scientific work. He realized that the net prices obtained by a farmer decline with increasing distance from the market. The influence of relative prices on the optimal choice of crops and techniques could thus be studied by considering farms at different distances from the center. His main conclusion is described in the following sentence: "If it is assumed that a country of 40 miles in diameter has in the center a big city, that this country can sell its products only in this city, and that agriculture in this district has reached the highest degree of development, then one would expect the systems of cultivation around this city to be divided in four classes" (Schumacher 1868, 15). Thünen was a slow but persistent worker. It was to take him twenty-three years to transform this intuitive vision into an analytical model.

The result was his magnum opus, *The Isolated State with Respect to Agriculture and National Economy*. The first part, including the analysis of rent, location, and resource allocation, appeared in 1826. The second part, containing the marginal productivity theory of distribution, appeared only in 1850. Additional papers, including important contributions on forestry, were published in 1863 by Thünen's biographer, H. Schumacher, as part 2, section 2, and part 3. All of this material is united in the third edition of 1875, but Waentig's later edition and also the English translations are limited to part 1 and the first (and more important) section of part 2. Additional material was published by Braeuer in his volume of selected works (Thünen 1951), which also includes a bibliography of Thünen's writings. The literary remains, including unpublished manuscripts, are preserved in the Thünen-Archiv at the University of Rostock.

It has been said that Thünen was a prophet with little honor in any country, and even less in his own. This is inaccurate. It is true that he was at first disappointed about the reception of his book. Nevertheless his fame spread rapidly. The first edition was sold out within seven years and was followed by a second edition in 1842.

Not all of Thünen's scientific contributions were to economics. In agronomy he made extensive and important studies, in the tradition of Thaer, on the "statics" of the soil, which is concerned with the steady state in which fertility, by suitable crop rotation and fertilization, is maintained at an optimal level. The following sections will be limited to economics, however. (Quotations are my translations.)

Rent and Factor Intensities for One Good

Thünen's best-known contribution to economic theory is his theory of rent, location, and resource allocation. It is based on a brilliantly conceived model that Thünen described in his opening paragraph in classic words echoing his early vision: "Imagine a very large city in the center of a fertile plain devoid of any navigable river or canal. The plain itself may throughout consist of the same soil, which is everywhere cultivable. At a large distance from the city, the plain may end in an uncultivated wilderness, completely separating this state from the rest of the world" (1842–63, part 1, §1). This leads to the central question: "What will be the structure of agriculture under these circumstances, and how will the greater or lesser distance from the city affect land use, if the latter is conducted with the utmost consistency" (part 1, §2).

For the case of one good, Thünen's answer may be summarized as follows: Suppose rye is sold in the central city at price P, measured in the northeast quadrant of figure 14.1 along the vertical axis. By deducting from P the costs of transportation, so Thünen explains, one obtains the price received by the farmer, p. Since transportation costs rise with increasing distance, s, the producer price declines. If transportation costs per bushel

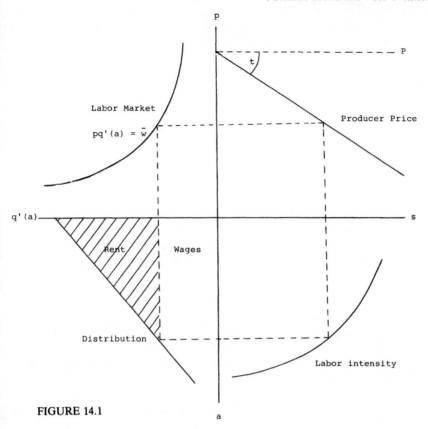

FIGURE 14.1

and mile are constant at t, the producer price as a function of distance is a declining straight line as illustrated in the northeast quadrant. The influence of price can thus be studied by considering distance. As Thünen expressed it, "the increasing distance from the market place thus acts like a decline in the corn price at an unchanged distance" (1842–63, part 2, sec. 1, intro. ii).

Output per acre, q, increases with the labor input per acre, a, according to $q = q(a)$. In view of diminishing returns, the marginal product of labor on given land, $q'(a)$, declines as described in the southwest quadrant.

At each producer price the manager selects his method of production in such a way that the marginal product of labor, evaluated at the producer price, equals the wage rate, w, where the latter may be regarded as given and uniform. In other words, the mathematical product of the producer price and the marginal product of labor must be constant, which relationship is expressed by the hyperbola in the northwest quadrant. The lower the price received by the farmer, the higher must be his marginal product.

167

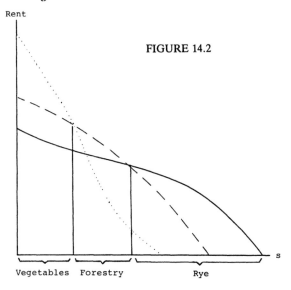

Rent

FIGURE 14.2

S

Vegetables Forestry   Rye

With the aid of these three quadrants, the labor intensity of production can be expressed as a function of the distance from the city. The result is expressed in the southeast quadrant. With increasing distance, the producer price declines, the marginal product of labor rises, and the labor intensity thus declines. The area "below" the marginal product curve in the southwest quadrant is total product. While the rectangle $q'(a)a$ goes to wages, the shaded residual represents land rent. With increasing distance, rent clearly declines.

Resource Allocation and Location for Many Goods

From Thünen's point of view, the one-good case is only a preliminary, however. Unlike Ricardo's corn model, his spatial model is essentially built for many products. By this extension, the isolated state becomes a theory of resource allocation and location based on the maximization of rent.

The basic features of this theory are summarized in figure 14.2. The solid curve, derived from figure 14.1, expresses land rent from rye production as a function of distance. Similar rent-distance functions can be constructed for other products such as vegetables or timber. They are represented by, respectively, the dotted and the broken curves. At each distance the farmer will then concentrate on the product promising the highest rent. In the case of figure 14.2, vegetables will be grown close to the city, followed by a belt of forests, and rye will be produced farther out.

In Thünen's model of a uniform plain, this results in the famous concentric rings, each of which is characterized by specific products. The result is summarized thus:

168

It is generally evident that close to the city there must be cultivated products that weigh a great deal or take up much space relative to their value, and whose transportation costs to the city are so considerable that they cannot be supplied from distant regions. They may also be products that spoil easily and have to be consumed fresh. With increasing distance from the city, the land will be used more and more for the cultivation of products that require lower transportation costs relative to their value.

For this reason alone there will be formed around the city rather sharply delineated concentric circles, in which one or the other product will be the main output.(1842–63, part 1, § 2)

The borderline between two rings can be determined by the condition that "at the margin" the respective products yield the same rent. Allocation thus begins to be governed by marginal equalities. The allocation of land and labor to production is fully determined by the rent-maximizing calculus, and so are the methods of production.

Essentially, Thünen provides a static analysis of spatial equilibrium. In the last analysis, however, he was interested not in mere statics but in comparative statics. He wanted to determine how differences and changes in conditions affect the allocation of resources. To this end he used the classic method of imagining variations in one variable at a time while other conditions remain constant and tracing out the consequences for the rest of the model.

In this way, Thünen was able to show, among other things, that lower transportation costs and more rapidly diminishing returns tend to increase the distance from the city at which a good is produced or a technology is used. It is important to note that Thünen provided not only a theory of location but also of factor intensities. That the relative efficiency of different technologies depends on market conditions is one of the main propositions he wanted to demonstrate. An agricultural technology that is efficient and progressive in England may be inefficient and obsolete in Germany.

The basic model is extended by Thünen in numerous directions. If the required quantities are given, the model determines their market prices. Since the rural workers do not generally pay the given city prices, their money wages will not actually be uniform. Freight costs may not be proportionate to distance. Substitutes and joint products are discussed. To the flows of agricultural products to the market center, Thünen adds the reverse flows of consumer goods and means of production (like manure), and he pays attention to the unequal quality of the soil. The problem of the spatial distribution of several cities is raised, though not solved. It is finally shown that agricultural protection, by reducing the efficiency of land use, makes both parties worse off and that land taxes do not distort allocation. The long-winded discourse is replete with empirical calculations, relating Thünen's analysis to his account books down to the most minute details.

Despite its richness, Thünen's analysis remains partial in the sense that it does not determine a general spatial equilibrium. His notions about the price mechanism are crude. Paul Samuelson (1966–86, vol. 5, ch. 339) has shown brilliantly how a better mathematician might have extended the model to a general equilibrium system, but such an extension was beyond Thünen's powers.

Marginal Productivity

By applying his optimizing approach to several factor inputs, Thünen became one of the originators of the marginal productivity theory of distribution. Using the Ricardian subterfuge of a rentless margin of cultivation, he explains his basic idea as follows:

> Output p is the joint product of labor and capital. How should the share of each factor in the joint product be measured? We measured the effectiveness of capital by the increment in the output per worker due to an increase in the capital he works with. In this context, labor is constant, but capital is a variable magnitude. Suppose now that this procedure is continued, but in the reverse sense of considering capital as constant and labor as growing. In this case, in a large-scale operation, the effectiveness of labor (the contribution of the worker to output) is recognized from the increment in total output due to the augmentation of workers by one. (1842–63, part 2, sec. 1, §19)

For the first time, labor and capital are treated in complete symmetry.

As in Jacques Turgot, the output increments, from both capital and labor, are postulated to decline with an increasing factor input. The profit-maximizing entrepreneur will determine each factor input in such a way that the sales proceeds from the last factor unit are equal to the given factor price. Labor will be increased up to the margin "where the incremental output of the last worker is absorbed by the wage that he receives" (1842–63, part 2, sec. 1, §19). The market return on capital is determined "by the yield of the last particle of capital" (§9), where it must be assumed that yields vary continuously and increments in capital are infinitesimal (§18).

This optimizing calculus clearly implies that, at the point of minimum cost, the ratio of factor prices is equal to the ratio of what today would be called their marginal products. The adjective *marginal* does not occur, but the words *margin* and *limit* are constantly used. In substance, the problem of the optimal allocation of factors in production was solved. What remained was a question of analytical elegance.

For the profits on capital (but not for wages), the marginal productivity principle was also used by Mountifort Longfield. In his lecture 9 of 1834 he explained that "the profits of a single tool will be equal to the difference of the quantities of work which the feeblest labourer could execute with and without its use" (1971, 192). The market rate of profit is accordingly described as "equal to the assistance which is given to labour by that portion of capital which is employed with the least efficiency" (194). In the analytical exploitation of this principle, however, Longfield hardly went beyond Turgot. Whereas Thünen made a classic contribution, Longfield's was minor.

The Natural Wage

From the laws that govern actual distribution, Thünen, deeply concerned with the "social problem," proceeded to the laws that ought to govern it. This led him to the most controversial of his achievements, his famous natural wage formula. In Thünen's economy, per capita output, p (measured in rye), depends on capital per worker, q (measured in terms of the tools a worker can make in a year). Output is divided between the wage, w, and the rental on capital, r, according to $p(q) = w + rq$. In sharp contrast to later notions, savings are supposed to come out of wages while property income is consumed. Specifically, savings are the excess of wages over some subsistence minimum, a. The economy is growing by the construction of new farms at the rentless margin of cultivation.

Since a unit of capital goods costs one man-year, its price is w. The interest rate, therefore, is

$$\frac{r}{w} = \frac{p-w}{wq}. \tag{14.1}$$

By multiplying the interest rate by the annual amount saved, one obtains the return on savings, namely

$$R = \frac{p-w}{wq}(w-a). \tag{14.2}$$

Thünen's natural wage maximizes R on the assumption of fixed q (and thus p). By equating dR/dw to zero, the natural wage is easily determined as the geometric mean of p and a,

$$w^* = \sqrt{pa}. \tag{14.3}$$

Thünen's cumbersome exposition has given rise to many misunderstandings. Some (including Marshall [1975]) argued that the correct interest rate would have been $(p-w)/q$. In this case, the natural wage turns out to be the arithmetic mean $w = \frac{1}{2}(p+a)$ (as already suggested by Knapp [1865]). This criticism would be valid for a one-sector economy in which q is simply a stock of rye. Actually, Thünen (as noted by Samuelson [1983]) considers a (rudimentary) two-sector economy in which capital goods are produced by labor only (at constant cost). Thünen is right, therefore, in valuing q at the wage rate w.

Another objection (raised, among others, by Knut Wicksell and strongly reiterated by Paul Samuelson) concerns the postulated constancy of q. After all, an increase in w presumably leads to an increase in q (and thus in p). Thünen anticipated this objection, for he supplemented his mathematical derivation, both verbally and by numerical examples, with a cogent explanation of how the overall maximum of R is to be found by searching over different q (and thus p). In fact, if output and marginal productivity wages are allowed to adjust to changes in q, the necessary condition for a maximum, as Dorfman (1986) showed, is again Thünen's square root formula.

Many have thought Thünen's natural wage to be inconsistent with his own marginal productivity theory. If wages correspond to the marginal product of labor, how can they at the same time be expected to conform to some particular social ideal? This objection, however, loses its force once it is realized that Thünen (as observed by Dickinson [1969]) determined the capital/labor ratio at which the marginal productivity wage happens to be equal to his natural wage.

The fundamental objection to the natural wage formula is that it makes no sense for workers to be interested in the returns on their savings only. What Thünen seems to have been groping for, more than a century before Edmund Phelps, was a golden rule of capital accumulation leading to some sort of optimal growth path. (In a one-sector model, the arithmetic variant of the natural wage does indeed have such properties; they are analyzed in Samuelson 1986.) Thünen never got it right; in such an optimization problem, the savings parameter, a, can hardly be treated as given. Thünen regarded his formula as important enough to have it engraved on his tombstone in the churchyard of Belitz. It commemorates a brilliant failure.

Capital and Interest

Part 3 of the *Isolated State* is concerned with the efficiency of forest management and thereby extends the incomplete treatment in part 1. The detailed analysis of the optimal spacing of trees is of interest mainly to forest engineers. In analyzing the optimal rotation period, however, Thünen makes another important contribution to economic theory. He had already pointed out in part 1 that the value of a forest should be measured not by the sales value of the timber if the trees were cut today but rather by the present value of the timber if the trees are cut and sold at the end of the optimal rotation period. In an efficient operation, the latter exceeds the former; if not, the trees should be cut at once. Efficient forest management is thus interpreted as a problem of capital and interest which provided economic theory with one of its most fruitful paradigms.

Thünen's optimality criterion, in contrast to those of Wicksell and Fisher, is not the equality of the marginal product of capital and the rate of interest, which, by disregarding the value of land, results in cutting trees too late. As Manz (1986) has shown, Thünen was probably the first to use the correct criterion of maximal land rent, which shortly afterward was so brilliantly developed by Faustmann. The formula derived in part 3 is flawed by incorrect discounting, and the exposition is clumsy. Nevertheless, with respect to substantive content, the capital theory implied in Thünen's forest model is superior to Böhm-Bawerk's, and it was not surpassed in economic science before Wicksell. By 1850 a combination of John Rae and Heinrich von Thünen could have produced an Irving Fisher.

Thünen's Method

Thünen is often celebrated for his scientific method. As a matter of fact, this method is neither particularly innovative nor exceptional, but it is impressive and exemplary not only for its essential correctness but also for the uncompromising persistence and patience with which it was applied.

Like Richard Cantillon, François Quesnay, and David Ricardo, Thünen based his analysis on a theoretical model. Whereas Ricardo derived his model from Smith and Quesnay derived his from Cantillon, Thünen, like Cantillon, constructed his theory from scratch. In the originality of his model building he thus surpasses Ricardo and has no equal in the first half of the nineteenth century.

While Thünen's model encompasses the whole economy, each individual agent is assumed to base his decisions on an optimizing calculus. This idea was forcefully developed by Adam Smith, but in the *Wealth of Nations* the calculus itself remains implicit, and Thünen makes it explicit. The derivation of economic propositions from explicit optimization opened a new era in the history of economic science. It is perhaps Thünen's most fundamental contribution.

Thünen realized early that his program required mathematics, but he also realized that its use would repel some readers. "I am very much afraid that my algebraic computations will have taxed the patience of some of my readers, because I am not unaware how uncomfortable and embarrassing the letter formulas are to many, even some scholars. But the application of mathematics must certainly be admitted wherever the truth cannot be discovered without it. If in other fields of knowledge the distaste for the mathematical calculus had been the same as in agronomy and economics, we would still be in complete ignorance about the laws of the universe" (1842–63, part 2, sec. 1, §18). Amen. The *Isolated State* is indeed replete with algebraic formulas, making Thünen one of the pioneers of mathematical economics.

In particular, optimizing problems led him, almost inevitably, to differential calculus. Braeuer reports that he had used it as early as 1824, which might make him the first to use calculus to solve an economic optimization problem.[2] However, these investigations were published only in

2. In other economic contexts calculus had been used even in the eighteenth century. According to Theocharis (1983, 111f.), the German Georg von Buquoy, in a book published

1850, and what was published in 1826 contains no calculus. By 1850, Augustin Cournot had far surpassed Thünen in this respect. In fact, Thünen's mathematical training, though possibly better than that of young Léon Walras, was rudimentary, and, as with Karl Marx, a good innate ability could not make up for the deficiency.

Thünen was not content with general algebraic expressions. He wanted to replace symbols by numbers. The data were supplied by his account books, a storehouse of information on all aspects of farming. He used them to compute optimal solutions to management problems, which in turn were used to determine the sequence and width of his rings. Business management and political economy are fully integrated. By thus combining economic theory with mathematics and statistical data he was, like Quesnay, a precursor of econometrics.

While marginal productivity aroused the admiration of theorists, the use of vast masses of facts endeared Thünen to the adherents of the historical school. Did he not illustrate Gustav Schmoller's proposition that theory has to be distilled from facts? Thünen never committed such blunders but used his data just as any applied economist would today. It has also been argued that his insistence on the dependence of optimal solutions on market conditions is an expression of historical relativism in opposition to Adam Smith's alleged claims of eternal truths. As a matter of fact, Thünen's insight is of the same sort as Adam Smith's famous proposition that the division of labor is limited by the extent of the market. That different conditions may require different solutions is hardly an exciting discovery.

Place in the History of Economics

Thünen is one of those rare economists who are universally acclaimed. There is a consensus that he was a great economist, perhaps even a genius, though he had nonsensical dreams about an ideal wage formula. This consensus is partly due to Thünen's lack of aggressiveness, his benevolent personality, and civic virtues. In part it is also because he could be acclaimed for different things by different people, including mathematical theorists, empiricists, accountants, agronomists, social philosophers, historicists, liberals, and German nationalists.[3] The main reason is, of course, that Thünen was indeed an economist of outstanding originality and theoretical talent, second to none in this respect in the first half of the nineteenth century, not even Ricardo.

---

in 1815, used calculus to determine the optimal depth to which the soil should be plowed. In an article in the *Westminster Review* of 1824, Thomas Perronet Thompson calculated the optimal inflation tax with the aid of rudimentary calculus.

3. Edgar Salin (1926), with his pompous erudition, even made him a prime exhibit for what translates into English, approximately, as "visualizable theory" in opposition to "rational theory."

Nevertheless, the immediate effect of Thünen's work was slight. Much of the contemporary acclaim was for the wrong reasons, and until about 1870 nobody tried to follow in his footsteps. This was often attributed to his being ahead of his time. It is not clear, however, that this commonplace explanation is valid in his case. As a matter of fact, if Thünen had presented his analysis in a different way and in English, it might have become mainstream economics within ten years, just as marginal utility did after 1871. There was nothing in it that a Ricardian could not have easily followed and appreciated. Thünen, however, presented his analysis in a highly idiosyncratic garb. Never having had the benefit of a rigorous academic education and never having been a teacher except to his apprentices, he encumbered the main line of his argument with tedious numerical examples, repetitions, and digressions. In view of his farmyard examples, one is tempted to say that he cast his pearls before swine. Whittled down and rewritten by Jevons, the *Isolated State* could have been instantly effective.

It is not true, on the other hand, that Thünen had virtually no influence at all, as Joseph Schumpeter (1914, 55) wrote. Alfred Marshall read the *Isolated State* around 1869. He did not recall later whether he had discovered the marginal productivity principle independently, but he wrote to John Bates Clark in 1900 that he had gotten the term *marginal* from Thünen's *Grenze*. He said that he loved Thünen above all his masters (Marshall 1925, 359f.) and that the *Isolated State* was the book that really guided him (1975, 1: 38). Marshall credits Cournot with teaching him analytical techniques, but he credits Thünen with teaching him economics. Through Marshall, Thünen is, of course, linked to the final victory of marginal productivity in the last quarter of the nineteenth century.

In addition to marginal productivity theory, Thünen laid the groundwork of location theory. Cantillon's suggestions about the emergence of cities were now developed into a fully grown theory of the spatial allocation of resources. For about a century this was to remain a Germain domain with Wilhelm Launhardt, Alfred Weber, and August Lösch, though of unequal importance, as the great names.

In summary, Thünen constructed one of the three analytical pillars on which the theory of individual optimization was built in the course of the following half-century. Whereas Cournot provided the theory of the firm and Gossen provided the theory of utility, Thünen contributed the theory of production and distribution. Though the credit for the "marginal revolution" is conventionally attributed to Jevons, Menger, and Walras, the real innovators were Thünen, Cournot, and Gossen. The first triumvirate deserves at least as much glory as the second, and Thünen no less than its other members.

15

Antoine Augustin Cournot

JOHANN HEINRICH VON THÜNEN's economic prototype was the farm. The counterpart analysis for the profit-seeking capitalist firm was provided by Antoine Augustin Cournot. He was the first to express the behavior of an individual firm as a solution to an explicit problem of constrained optimization and to determine the characteristics of this solution by differential calculus. He thereby developed an analytical technique that turned out to be fundamental for a century of economic theory and has retained its usefulness to this day.

Life

Cournot was born in Gray, a small French town east of Dijon in Haute-Saône, in 1801. His ancestors had been peasants in the Franche-Comté for centuries. He grew up in the strongly Royalist family of his paternal grandfather, a notary, where an uncle who had been educated by the Jesuits had a strong influence on him. He became a disciplined, responsible, and judicious middle-of-the-roader in whatever he did and wrote. With less emphasis on self-denial in his education, he might perhaps have become a Newton—or a nobody.[1]

Young Cournot went to the local high school until he was fifteen. The following four years were devoted to independent studies, particularly in law (which is said to have enabled him to win a lawsuit for his family at seventeen) and also in mathematics. In 1821, Cournot was admitted to the Ecole Normale Supérieure in Paris, but the school was closed shortly after for political reasons. Cournot had to transfer to the Sorbonne, where he obtained his license degree in mathematics in 1823. Among his teachers and fellow students were some of the most eminent mathematicians of his time and, for that matter, of any time; Dirichlet became his particular friend.

From 1823 to 1833, Cournot earned his living as the private secretary of a French marshal, whom he helped in writing his memoirs of the campaigns of 1812–13, and as a tutor to the marshal's son. This left him time to write a doctoral dissertation in mechanics and a secondary thesis in astronomy, to publish numerous articles, and also to obtain a law degree. Two translations of works on mechanics and astronomy that he undertook at the end of this period turned out to be his best publishing successes.

Cournot's publications attracted the attention of the great mathematician Poisson, who became his protector and, in 1834, obtained for him

---

1. The most important biographical source on Cournot is his *Souvenirs* (1913). Up to 1860 this is the main source for both Moore 1905 and La Harpe 1936.

a professorship in analysis and mechanics at the University of Lyon. However, before Cournot had finished his first course, he was appointed rector of the Academy of Grenoble. This initiated a long and distinguished career as a university administrator, in the course of which Cournot became inspector general of education in Paris, commander of the Legion of Honor, and rector of the University of Dijon. In 1862 he resigned all his public functions and retired to Paris to devote his time to his scholarly work, in which he was increasingly handicapped by his failing eyesight.[2] He died in 1877 from a stomach ailment; he is buried with his wife and his son.

Cournot seems to have been an unassuming, reserved, and somewhat melancholic introvert. Despite the lack of success of his books, he was not, like Hermann Heinrich Gossen, a tragic figure, for overall he had a successful career and was recognized as an eminent scholar. Efforts were under way at the time of his death to make him a member of the Academy of Moral and Political Sciences.

Works

Cournot's collected works fill many volumes. In the first half of his life, he was mainly a mathematician. Besides his many articles, he published books on differential calculus, on the relationship between algebra and geometry, and on probability. To the extent to which a nonmathematician is able to judge, he was a highly competent, but not a brilliantly creative, mathematician. He may have been right in feeling that he did not quite live up to Poisson's high expectations.

From mathematics Cournot moved gradually toward philosophy. A treatise on the logic of knowledge was followed by three voluminous works on the philosophy of history and the history of ideas. None of these books, published by his friend Hachette, was highly successful, and only the one on calculus saw a second edition during his lifetime. Cournot was an eclectic who presented his material in a balanced, forceful, and orderly way, but without high originality. He said of himself that he was "lacking the special gift of invention."

The great exception to this statement is the *Researches into the Mathematical Principles of the Theory of Wealth*, published in 1838. This slender book opened a new chapter in the history of economics, namely the systematic analysis of profit maximization by firms based on differential calculus. The contemporary economists, however, did not recognize the pioneering quality of this contribution; it was not even reviewed. In part, this may have been because the underlying economics as such was again eclectic. The main reason, however, was that economists did not understand calculus.

---

2. His bad eyesight may have been a cause of the large number of mathematical slips in his *Recherches* noted by the translator, N. T. Bacon.

Cournot felt dejected. Twenty-five years elapsed before he again dared to present his economic theory, but now stripped of all mathematics (1863). The success was no better than before. From a modern point of view, this is perfectly understandable, for his one original contribution was precisely the use of calculus to solve problems of constrained optimization. By rewriting *Hamlet* without the prince of Denmark, Cournot showed that he did not quite understand the true nature of his own contribution. He was rightly convinced that he was an innovator, but partly at least for the wrong reasons.

In fact, he even tried a third time by writing a "summary" of economic doctrines (1877). He was dead before it became clear that, by his standards, he had failed again. His complete works, edited by André Robinet and planned to comprise fourteen volumes, began to appear in 1973 (1973–). His claim to immortality, however, rests on the *Researches*. Papers on Cournot are collected in Brun and Robinet (1978).

The Law of Demand

Cournot was not the first to perceive that differential calculus can be used to solve economic optimization problems. Robert Malthus, in his pamphlet *Observations on the Effects of the Corn Laws* of 1814 (in Malthus 1970), had suggested that "many of the questions both in morals and in politics seem to be of the nature of the problems *de maximis et minimis* in fluxions; in which there is always a point where a certain effect is the greatest, while on either side of this point it gradually diminishes." Whereas Malthus was content with a suggestion, Theocharis (1983) records two or three instances of pre-Cournot use of calculus, but the problems it was supposed to solve were economically meaningless. It was pointed out in the preceding chapter that Thünen may have privately used calculus to solve optimum problems before Cournot. Cournot himself refers to Nicolas-François Canard, but Canard's mathematics did not include calculus, and Cournot mentions him mainly as a warning example of incompetence. Cournot's great contribution was the development of a theory of the firm.

Unlike Hermann Heinrich Gossen, William Stanley Jevons, Carl Menger, or Léon Walras, Cournot was not concerned with the utility of consumers. Like Gustav Cassel seventy years later, he began directly with market demand. His law of demand was the quantity demanded as a function of market price (the notation is not necessarily Cournot's),

$$q = F(p), \qquad (15.1)$$

to be determined by empirical observation. He represented this function in a diagram that differed from Alfred Marshall's later graph by having price on the horizontal axis (figure 15.1). This seems to have been the first time in the history of economics that a general demand function was written and a demand curve drawn. Cournot postulated that the demand curve is

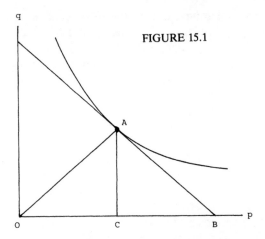

FIGURE 15.1

monotonically declining, continuous, and twice differentiable (1838, sec. 22).

The demand curve is used to derive the consumers' expenditure as a function of price:

$$R = pF(p). \tag{15.2}$$

This represents the revenue of the seller. It has an extreme point at the price for which

$$\frac{dR}{dp} = F(p) + pF'(p) = 0, \tag{15.3}$$

which can be written as

$$\frac{F(p)}{p} = -F'(p). \tag{15.4}$$

For any point A on the demand curve, the left side of this condition is graphically expressed by the slope of OA, and the right side is expressed by the slope of the demand curve. Cournot pointed out that for A to be a point of maximum revenue, OC must thus be equal to CB (1838, sec. 25).

Cournot did not introduce technical concepts, such as Marshall's price elasticity of demand, to describe the demand curve, but he regarded it as practically important to know whether revenue rises or declines as the price is lowered, and he also related this to the proportionate changes in price and quantity.[3]

As a trained mathematician, Cournot was, of course, aware that the extreme point as determined by equation 15.3 may be either a maximum

---

3. In 1829, William Whewell (1971, 9f., 21) had defined price flexibility as the ratio of the percentage change in price and the percentage change in quantity.

or a minimum. To identify a maximum he used the negative sign of the second derivative of equation 15.2. Cournot was also aware that the revenue curve may have several maxima (1838, sec. 25).

From a historical point of view, it is worth noting that Cournot made no explicit use of the concept of marginal revenue. He expressed revenue as a function of price, not of quantity. However, all of the substance of marginal revenue is clearly implied in his analysis.

Monopoly

Whereas classical economics had different value theories for competition and monopoly, Cournot envisaged a uniform theory embracing all intermediate shades between perfect monopoly and perfect competition. However, while subsequent theory usually started from perfect competition and introduced monopolistic elements as "imperfections," Cournot started from simple monopoly and worked his way toward perfect competition. This was an excellent program, but it is not fully implemented even today.

For simple monopoly, Adam Smith could only say that the price is the highest that can be got. David Ricardo still could not go beyond explaining that the price depended on scarcity and demand. By determining the exact conditions for the "Cournot point" of maximum profit, Cournot provided the analysis that turned out to be definitive.

His paradigm is a monopolistic producer of mineral water (Cournot 1838, secs. 26, 27). Revenue, as was shown in the preceding section, depends on price according to equation 15.2. Production costs depend directly on the quantity produced and thus indirectly on price according to

$$C = \phi(q) = \phi[F(p)]. \tag{15.5}$$

The monopolist's profit, therefore, is

$$G = R - C = pF(p) - \phi[F(p)]. \tag{15.6}$$

For a profit maximum it is necessary that

$$\frac{dG}{dp} = F(p) + pF'(p) - \phi'(q)F'(p) = 0, \tag{15.7}$$

which Cournot writes as

$$q + [p - \phi'(q)]F'(p) = 0. \tag{15.8}$$

This is the standard condition, in modern economics usually written in the form

$$\frac{q}{F'(p)} + p = p \left[\frac{1}{F'(p)} \frac{q}{p} + 1\right] = p \left[\frac{1}{\epsilon} + 1\right] = \phi'(q). \tag{15.9}$$

The expression on the left of the last equality sign is marginal revenue;

that on the right is marginal cost; and ϵ represents the price elasticity of demand.

Cournot recognizes that marginal cost is itself a function of the quantity produced and that the increasing, constant, or decreasing course of the marginal cost curve may be of crucial importance for the solution of economic problems. He points out that costs can affect price only through $\phi'(q)$; fixed costs, therefore, have no influence on the monopolist's optimal price and quantity, though they influence his profit.

Cournot's next question concerns the effect on price of shifts in marginal cost. Will price rise more or less than cost? This is a problem of comparative statics. To solve it, Cournot extends the optimality condition, equation 15.7, by a parameter expressing the location of the cost curve,

$$\frac{F(p)}{F'(p)} + p = \psi(p) + u, \qquad (15.10)$$

where $\psi(p) = \phi'[F(p)]$ is marginal cost as a function of *price*. Shifts in this equilibrium are determined by taking the total differential of equation 15.10:

$$dp - \frac{F(p)}{[F'(p)]^2} F''(p)dp + dp = \psi'(p)dp + du \qquad (15.11)$$

or

$$\{[2 - \psi'(p)]F'(p) - \frac{F(p)}{F'(p)} F''(p)\}dp = F'(p)du. \qquad (15.12)$$

If the cost function is chosen in such a way that $u=0$ initially, equation 15.10 yields

$$-\frac{F(p)}{F'(p)} = p - \psi(p). \qquad (15.13)$$

The change in monopoly price due to a given shift in cost can thus be written (Cournot 1838, sec. 33)

$$\frac{dp}{du} = \frac{F'(p)}{[2 - \psi'(p)]F'(p) + [p - \psi(p)]F''(p)} > 0. \qquad (15.14)$$

Cournot uses the second-order condition to ascertain that the denominator must be negative. It follows that price shifts in the same direction as costs.

Cournot further determines that the change in price can be either larger or smaller than the underlying shift in cost. In the special case of a linear demand curve (and thus $F''(p)=0$) and constant marginal cost (and thus $\psi'(p)=0$) Cournot's result implies that

$$\frac{dp}{du} = \frac{1}{2} ; \qquad (15.15)$$

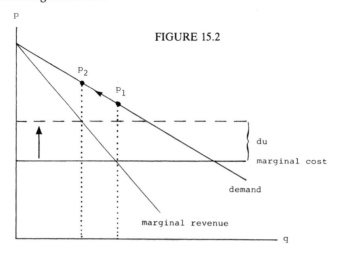

FIGURE 15.2

price rises half as much as cost. This case is depicted, in Marshallian notation, in figure 15.2. It is clear that a given upward shift in the (horizontal) marginal cost curve, since the demand curve has half the slope of the marginal revenue curve, shifts the monopoly price upward by half as much. With Cournot, we are in the middle of a present-day principles course.

Today this sort of analysis is indeed commonplace. One might have thought that, once Cournot had laid the basis, it would become commonplace within ten years. As a matter of fact, it took economic theory, and in particular English-language theory, another ninety years to catch up with Cournot, and, when both Cambridges finally did catch up, this was hailed as a revolution.

Taxation

Cournot raised the further question of how the effects of taxes on particular industries depend on the tax base. He found that lump sum taxes, though influencing the net worth of the entrepreneur, have no influence on his optimal price and output. The loss of net worth, furthermore, is entirely borne by whoever owns the firm at the moment the tax is imposed; his successors will be compensated for the tax by a reduced purchase price for the firm. A tax on profits has similar effects, but Cournot notes the repercussions on the entry of new firms and thus on employment in the industry (1838, sec. 36).

The effects of an excise tax on output are more interesting (Cournot 1838, sec. 38). Cournot notes that such a tax is equivalent to a shift in the demand curve or in the cost curve. The optimum condition, equation 15.10, can thus be rewritten

$$F(p) + [p - \psi(p) - t]F'(p) = 0 \qquad (15.16)$$

where t is the tax per unit of output. The effect of a change in t thus turns out to be the same as the effect of a change in u described by equation 15.14. The same technique is used to determine the effects of sales taxes (sec. 41).

Cournot's discussion of the economic burden of taxes suffers from the lack of the concept of consumer surplus, but he notes correctly that this burden is higher than if the same amount were levied as a tax on the profits of monopolists (1838, sec. 38). In general, Cournot notes, it makes no difference economically whether a tax is paid by the seller or the buyer. There is an interesting exception, however, in that the tax, if it is payable by the producer, is probably paid earlier than if it is paid by the consumer; the earlier the due date, the higher the effective burden.

Duopoly

Cournot takes the first step toward competition by introducing a second supplier (1838, sec. 43). Since the two suppliers produce exactly the same mineral water, the result is homogeneous duopoly. To simplify the analysis, costs are disregarded.

Homogeneity of product implies, evidently, that both duopolists must sell at the same price. As a consequence, each firm is forced to adopt a quantity strategy; it is free to determine its output, but the price will be determined by the market. Market conditions are described by a simple demand curve

$$q = q_1 + q_2 = F(p). \qquad (15.17)$$

The problem for each firm is to determine its optimal quantity.

The crucial feature of the problem is that the optimal output for each supplier depends on the output of the other supplier. Expectations about the competitor's behavior thus become an essential part of price determination. Cournot's assumption is that each firm expects the other firm's output to be independent of the resulting market price and optimizes its own output accordingly. It is evident that this expectation cannot be correct for both firms simultaneously, but in Cournot's model the competitors never find out.

Suppose market demand is described by the downward-sloping curve in figure 15.3, with quantity measured in the conventional way along the horizontal axis. Assuming that the supply of firm 2 is q_2, firm 1 selects its own quantity, q_1, as if the remainder of the demand curve represented the demand for the output of a single monopolist.

Clearly, the optimum q_1^* is a function of q_2; the higher q_2, the smaller q_1^*. This relationship can be expressed by a reaction function $q_1^* = r_1(q_2)$; it is depicted by the r_1 curve in figure 15.4. An analogous reaction curve can

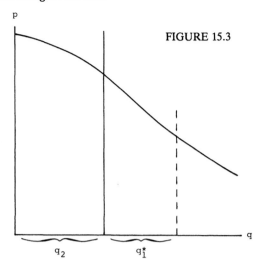

FIGURE 15.3

be constructed for firm 2; it is represented by the r_2 curve in figure 15.4.

At which point will the market be in equilibrium? Clearly at the point, Cournot answers, where each competitor finds his expectations justified by the facts, which means where the reaction curves intersect. It is true that, in fact, each firm's output is not independent of the market price, but at point E the competitors never discover their error.

In figure 15.4, r_2 is drawn less steep than r_1. Could it not be steeper? Cournot answered that this is indeed conceivable, but that the equilibrium

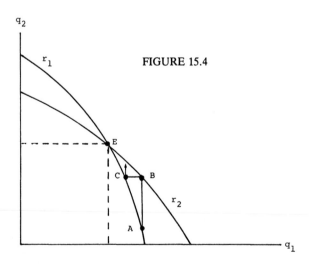

FIGURE 15.4

would be unstable in this case. This observation marks an important point in the history of economic analysis. For the first time a stability requirement was explicitly used to derive properties of a static model. Cournot's reasoning can be explained in terms of figure 15.4 as follows: Suppose the market is initially at A. Firm 1 sees its expectations satisfied, but firm 2 finds that firm 1 supplies less than expected. Firm 2 will then expand its own output, moving the market to B. At B, firm 1 now has reason to contract its output, moving the system to C. As the curves are drawn, these mutual adjustments converge toward E; this is the stable case. If, however, r_2 is steeper than r_1, the sequential adjustments move the system farther and farther away from E; equilibrium will never be reached.

Comparing duopoly profits with those of monopoly, Cournot found that aggregate profits are smaller in the first case. There is thus an incentive for either cartelization or a merger. Why does each duopolist not spontaneously, without a merger, demand the price that promises the highest possible joint profit? The answer is that at this price each duopolist would find it advantageous to increase his supply, which in turn lowers the price, and so on. The underlying point is that, at the monopoly price, the division of demand between the two suppliers is indeterminate.

With his simple model of homogeneous duopoly, Cournot provided the prototype for more than a century of duopoly theory. Wilhelm Launhardt (1885) and Harold Hotelling (1929) extended the analysis to heterogeneous duopoly with differentiated products. Heinrich von Stackelberg (1934) considered the possibility that duopolist A expects duopolist B to react to A's decisions. Finally, after the advent of game theory, Cournot's solution concept was generalized to the so-called Nash equilibrium.

Pure Competition

Starting from duopoly, Cournot imagines that the number of suppliers is gradually increased. Eventually, each supplier will begin to regard the market price as a parameter on which his own output decisions have no appreciable influence (Cournot 1838, sec. 50). In this situation the output of supplier i is just a function of the market price, $q_i = q_i(p)$.

Behind this function, as Cournot makes clear, is the condition that the supplier extends output to the point where marginal cost equals price, which, in turn, presupposes that marginal cost is rising. Once the supply function is known for each firm, market price can be determined by setting aggregate supply equal to market demand,

$$\sum_i q_i(p) = F(p). \tag{15.18}$$

This provides the basis for an analysis of tax incidence in competitive industries.

While this analysis was still confined to partial equilibrium, Cournot finally broadened his perspective to general equilibrium of many markets

(1838, chs. 11, 12). A mathematician, he explained, would conclude that problems of particular industries can be solved completely and rigorously only in the context of the system as a whole (Cournot 1863, 263f.). Such an analysis, however, he regarded as out of reach (1838, sec. 74) and, in the absence of theories of consumption and production, it was, in fact, still out of reach. A large number of equations was thus left for Walras to put on paper.

Place in the History of Economics

The preceding sections are far from exhausting Cournot's contributions to economic analysis. These include an elaborate discussion of the consistency of exchange rates between one or more currencies, which is achieved by arbitrage. They also include a discussion of the gains from trade, though it remained unsatisfactory. There is also a brilliant analysis of the prices of two monopolists supplying intermediate products (such as, say, copper and zinc) that are complementary in the production of a final product (such as brass). The solution is found in close analogy to duopoly, and Cournot shows that integrated monopoly would be preferable to this sort of fragmented monopoly. Though interesting, these contributions did not, however, become building blocks of future economic theory.

Overall, Cournot did not have the broad and deep understanding of the economy of an Adam Smith or Alfred Marshall. He developed the tools of individual optimization, and he applied these tools to the firm, leaving optimization in production to Thünen and optimization with respect to utility to Gossen. Within this field, however, his contribution has not been surpassed by anybody in the history of economics to the present day. In one stroke the theory of the firm was built from scratch. Whereas Smith and Marshall talked around problems, Cournot solved them.

Even more fundamental was the introduction of differential calculus into economics. Inasmuch as marginalist economics can be interpreted as a rewriting of classical theory in terms of calculus, Cournot provided the keynote for a century of economic theory.

The immediate influence of Cournot on the development of economic theory, however, was negligible. His contribution was hardly noticed until it was revived by Jevons and Walras. Unlike the neglect of Thünen and Gossen, this cannot be explained by a cumbersome and idiosyncratic exposition; Cournot's *Researches* are a model of lucidity. The reason is simply that professors of economics did not understand elementary calculus, and the history of economics had to go on for another century before most of them did. All of Cournot's historical influence came through a few outstanding theorists of the following generation such as Walras and Marshall.

Cournot was neither a genius nor a revolutionary. He was an eclectic with first-rate mathematical training and high scientific standards. By applying his training to a field in which, at that moment, calculus promised high rewards, he initiated a long-range evolution in economic science that puts most flamboyant revolutionaries to shame. Though his contribution caused hardly a ripple among his contemporaries, today his standing in the history of economic theory (as distinct from social thought) deserves to be higher than that of John Stuart Mill, even though he wrote the most widely used textbook of his time, and that of Karl Marx, although he caused infinitely more historical commotion.

16

Hermann Heinrich Gossen

He was a man of one idea; but that was an immortal one.
—F. Y. Edgeworth, in Palgrave's *Dictionary of Political Economy*

WITH COURNOT's *Researches* of 1838 and the second volume of Johann Heinrich von Thünen's *Isolated State* of 1850, individual optimization with respect to the profit maximization of firms and production had been given a firm analytical basis. With respect to utility such a basis was still lacking. It is true that value had long been explained by subjective utility and scarcity. Daniel Bernoulli and Jeremy Bentham had postulated a diminishing marginal utility of income, and William Forster Lloyd, extending an old tradition, had established the principle of diminishing marginal utility of individual commodities. However, the key to a fruitful application of these insights to the theory of value was still lacking. This key was provided by Hermann Heinrich Gossen.

Life

Gossen was born in Düren (between Aachen and Cologne) on 7 September 1810. Little is known about his life, partly because the inconspicuous bachelor did not attract attention, partly because most of those who had known him were dead by the time he became famous, and partly also because his literary remains, scant as they must have been, are lost. The principal biographical source is the essay by Léon Walras, published in 1885 and later included in the *Etudes d'économie sociale* (1896). The available facts are admirably surveyed by Georgescu-Roegen, on whose masterly introduction to the English translation of Gossen's book (see Gossen 1854) the following life sketch is mostly based.

Gossen's father was a tax collector under Napoleon and subsequently the Prussian administration; later he managed an estate near Godesberg. Hermann changed high schools several times and finally dropped out, acquiring his diploma through independent study. He nevertheless obtained a good high school education and was said to show ability in elementary mathematics, but his mathematical training never went beyond that level. Since his father insisted on a government career in the tradition of his forebears, his university studies in Bonn and Berlin concentrated on law and government.

In 1834, Gossen entered the civil service as a *Referendar* (junior law clerk) in Cologne. Though he seems to have been a well-mannered young man, the performance of his duties left much to be desired. He simply had no interest in a government career and loved the good things in life. There were complaints and reprimands, and the promotion to the rank of *Regierungsassessor* came rather later than usual. Finally, in 1847, though his superiors seem to hav shown considerable sympathy, he had no choice but to resign.

The transition to a new career was perhaps eased by his father's death, which spared him recriminations about his failure and provided him with the means for a new start. Gossen went to Berlin, where he seems to have sympathized with the liberal revolution, and then returned to Cologne as a partner in a new accident insurance firm. He soon withdrew from the firm but continued to devise grandiose insurance projects.

Living with his two sisters, Gossen now devoted most of his energies to developing the unorthodox ideas he had expressed in his civil service examination papers into his magnum opus. In 1853 an attack of typhoid fever undermined his health, and the disappointment about the fate of his book depressed him. He died from pulmonary tuberculosis on 13 February 1858. He seems to have been an amiable, sincere, and idealistic human being with broad interests (including music and painting). Brought up a Catholic, he developed into an enthusiastic hedonist. He dreamed of reforming the world but lacked the force to conquer it.

Work

The *Entwickelung der Gesetze des menschlichen Verkehrs* was published in 1854 at Gossen's expense by the publisher Vieweg in Brunswick. The preface suggests that the author hoped the book would not only make him the Copernicus of the social universe but also open the door to an academic career. The dream did not come true. Very few copies were sold and the book remained unnoticed for years. Shortly before his death, Gossen withdrew it from circulation and the unsold copies were returned to him. After the author had become posthumously famous, Vieweg's successor, Prager, bought this stock from Gossen's nephew, a professor of mathematics by the name of Hermann Kortum, and put it on the market again with a new title page, as a "second edition," in 1889. There is an Italian translation (1950) by Tullio Bagiotti, and there is now a careful English translation (1983) by Rudolph C. Blitz, nicely divided into chapters. The manuscript of a French translation by Walras was apparently lost.

The first known references to Gossen's book were by Julius Kautz

(1858–60), but they show only that their author did not understand the problems Gossen had solved. Slightly more understanding was shown by F. A. Lange (1875), but again in no more than a footnote. Fortunately, Kautz's reference was seen by Robert Adamson, who was able to get hold of a copy and reported its content to Stanley Jevons. In the preface to the second edition of *The Theory of Political Economy*, Jevons then included a report of more than six pages about Gossen's work with generous tribute to its originality.

Though Gossen's name became famous, his book remains largely unread to this day. Maffeo Pantaleoni (1898) was the only notable economist who based his own work on it. This has inspired many disparaging remarks about the "immaturity" of economic science and the like. The simple fact is that the book, even for a German-speaking economic theorist, is very hard to read. It is true that the reasoning is precise and the material reasonably well organized, but there are no chapter headings, the style is involved, the copious algebra is inelegant, the numerical examples are tedious, and the sermonizing is often disconcerting. Gossen had brilliant thoughts, but he had never learned to communicate them effectively. The following sections represent an effort to make his analysis accessible to a modern economist. Quotations are my translations.

Optimal Allocation of Time

At the level of individual behavior, Gossen's basic theoretical problem concerns optimization with limited resources. Resources are first visualized as time (Gossen 1889, 1f.; 1983, ch. 1) and thus foreshadow an approach recently developed by Gary Becker. The given lifetime, $\bar{E}$, has to be allocated to enjoyable activities $1 \ldots i \ldots m$ in such a way that lifetime enjoyment or, in modern terminology, utility, U, is maximized. In symbols,

$$\max U = \Sigma U_i(e_i), \text{ subject to } \Sigma e_i = \bar{E}, \tag{16.1}$$

where e_i is the time allocated to activity i and U_i is the utility derived from it.

For a given activity, marginal utility, u_i, is assumed to be a declining function of the time spent on it, e_i. In Gossen's words, "the magnitude of a given pleasure decreases continuously if we continue to satisfy this pleasure without interruption until satiety is ultimately reached" (1889, 4f.; 1983, 6). This is the postulate that became known as Gossen's law (Wieser 1889) or, more precisely, Gossen's first law (Lexis, 1895). *In itself*, it was neither new nor profound. W. F. Lloyd had expressed it twenty years earlier just as clearly; it had a long ancestry reaching back to Bentham, the French subjectivists, Bernoulli, and the scholastics; and it is essentially commonplace. To simplify, Gossen assumes the marginal utility curves to be linear, as drawn in figure 16.1. It is important to note that Gossen's

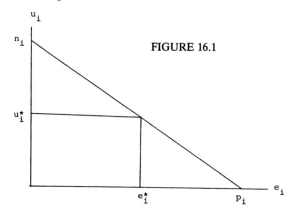

FIGURE 16.1

curves do not describe the decline in the marginal utility of a good as its quantity increases but represent the decline in the utility from the marginal unit of resources as the quantity of resources is increased. This facilitated the analysis in some respects, but it became a crucial handicap in others.

Gossen realized that each of these marginal utility functions must be thought of as being derived by solving a suboptimization problem, inasmuch as time allocated to activity *i* must be spent in the most enjoyable way, probably with interruptions. However, his analysis of this difficult subproblem, though original and suggestive, remained incomplete and unsatisfactory, leaving much to be done by future research on the allocation of time.

Gossen recognized at once that a necessary condition for the optimal allocation of resources is the equality of the marginal utilities in different activities. This is Gossen's second law, which he had printed in boldface: "The magnitude of each single pleasure at the moment when its enjoyment is broken off shall be the same for all pleasures" (1889, 12; 1983, 14). This theorem is Gossen's principal claim to fame. In it he had no forerunners. It was the key that opened the door to a fruitful analytical use of the first law and thus initiated the marginalist era in the theory of value.

The resulting allocation of resources was summarized in a brilliantly constructed graph by the horizontal addition of the marginal utility curves (figure 16.2). The resulting solid line represents the marginal utility of resources, u, as a function of total resources. Its level at the point $E = \bar{E}$, u^*, is the marginal utility of resources in the optimal plan. The resources allocated to each activity, e_i^*, can be simply read off the horizontal distances between the individual marginal utility curves at the level of u^*.

Gossen also succeeds in determining u^* algebraically by starting from a simple tautology,

$$u^* = u^* \frac{\Sigma p_i - \Sigma e_i^*}{\Sigma(p_i - e_i^*)} = \frac{P - \bar{E}}{\Sigma \frac{p_i - e_i^*}{u^*}} = \frac{P - \bar{E}}{\Sigma \frac{p_i}{n_i}}, \tag{16.2}$$

where p_i and n_i are the intercepts in figure 16.1 and P is the sum of the horizontal intercepts. The nontautological step is the last one, where Gossen recognizes that the ratio $(p_i - e_i^*)/u^*$ for each activity corresponds to the slope of the respective marginal utility curve.

Once u^* is known, it is easy to determine total utility as the sum of the triangular areas under the marginal utility curves minus the sum of the triangles with bases $p_i - e_i^*$ and height u^*. These results are derived without the use of calculus. Calculus is used, however, to show that u^* corresponds to the increase in total utility obtainable from a relaxation of the resource constraint, namely to $dU/d\bar{E}$. For the first time, the marginal utility of resources was related to the marginal utility in each particular use; the economic interpretation of Lagrange multipliers seemed to wait just around the corner.

Production

In a second step, the model is extended to include production (Gossen 1889, 34f.; 1983, ch. 2). This is achieved by reinterpreting activities as products and resources as "effort," where total effort can be varied. This requires a transformation of utility curves, each of which now shows the marginal utility resulting from the effort spent on a certain product, taking into account the required amount of effort per unit of product. The time constraint is replaced by a linear function representing the marginal utility of effort. A small amount of effort is assumed to be pleasurable, but beyond

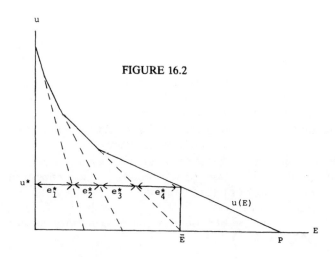

FIGURE 16.2

191

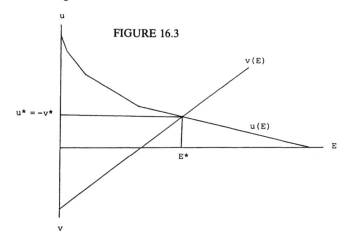

FIGURE 16.3

a certain point diminishing marginal utility changes into growing marginal disutility. As Georgescu-Roegen has noted, an analysis of leisure is lacking. In figure 16.3, the marginal utility of effort, v, is measured downward, positive values thus expressing marginal disutilities. The remainder of the graph corresponds to figure 16.2.

The optimal input of effort, E^*, is characterized by the equality between the utility of the marginal effort spent on each product and the marginal disutility of effort. Total utility is then described by the curved triangle between the two marginal curves. Again Gossen is able to describe the optimal solution algebraically in terms of the intercepts of the individual marginal curves, and he also determines the comparative-static effects on this solution of various changes in the underlying parameters (1889, 48f.; 1983, chs. 4–6).

Exchange

The third stage is reached with the introduction of exchange (Gossen 1889, 80f.; 1983, ch. 7). Gossen begins with the bilateral case. He immediately perceives that there are many different opportunities for mutually beneficial exchange, but his discussion of these possibilities is, understandably, inconclusive. As a necessary condition for optimal exchange, he postulates that the marginal utilities must be equalized between individuals for each product. Though this formulation requires both cardinality and interpersonal comparability of utility, its economic substance, since it can be expressed in terms of marginal rates of substitution, is independent of these assumptions. The concept of a contract curve, however, is not used. The statement that each individual would usually be willing to forgo a portion of what he receives suggests some notion of consumer surplus (Gossen 1889, 89; 1983, chs. 7, 6).

The analysis is then extended to market exchange, where each individual can exchange goods and effort at parametrically given prices, expressed in a common *numéraire* called money. This means that E is again reinterpreted, this time in the sense of expenditure or income. The product curves now relate to marginal utility per dollar spent on a given product, the solid convex line relates to the marginal utility of income, and the rising line expresses the disutility from earning a marginal dollar of income at the going prices. We thus end up with the optimization problem that became the banner of marginalism. Gossen's second law can then be expressed by the condition that "the last atom of money creates the same pleasure in each pleasurable use" (1889, 93f.; 1983, 109).

The solution to this problem determines the individual's market demand and supply for each product and effort. Gossen also shows how the value of intermediate products can sometimes be derived from that of the final goods, thereby foreshadowing Menger's theory of imputation, but he is careful to note that the market mechanism works even where imputation fails (1889, 24f.; 1983, 28f.). If prices are specified at random, aggregate demand and supply will generally differ. Gossen explains how this exerts pressure on prices and factor allocation until all markets are cleared. Prices are thus endogenously determined by general equilibrium. This argument, though concise, is presented in verbal form only. The mathematical formulation of general equilibrium, envisaged by Cournot, had to wait for Walras.

Rent

In the fourth stage, Gossen introduces rent (1889, 102f.; 1983, chs. 8–12). If the profundity of an economist can be gauged by his treatment of rent, he comes out near the top. The worker described by figure 16.3 is assumed to own a specific piece of land. Suppose he is now offered the use of land owned by another individual, at a superior location. This does not affect his utility curves, but for the amount of effort for which the marginal utility of effort is just zero, he can now earn a higher income. At the same time the marginal disutility curve becomes flatter because the same total enjoyment is now spread over a higher income. In figure 16.4 this change is expressed by the dotted line.

In the absence of rent the superior location would, of course, promise higher income. However, moves to superior locations are not free but cost rent. This means that at the new location the individual has to earn a certain amount, $\bar{R}$, before he can even begin to buy commodities. The origin of the marginal disutility curve is thus shifted to the left, as indicated by the broken line.

What is the maximum rent an individual is willing to pay for a superior location? This "warranted rent" is reached at the point where total utility at the superior location, measured by the shaded area, is equal to the total

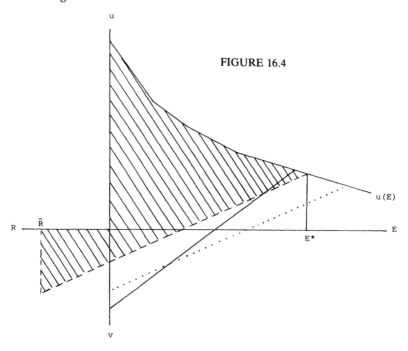

FIGURE 16.4

utility at the original location, described by the solid triangle. Gossen shows algebraically that, with rent at the warranted level, superior locations are associated with higher earned income and higher consumption.

A corresponding experiment can be conducted for a move to an inferior location. In this case the marginal disutility curve is steeper than the solid line, and its origin is shifted to the right, the individual now receiving rent and thus spending more than he earns. Competition in the market for land will see to it that in full equilibrium all rents are at the warranted level.

Though Gossen developed a novel and fruitful way to incorporate rent into a general equilibrium framework, his theory of rent is less rich than Thünen's, published twenty-eight years before. Gossen was no better at reading his predecessors than the later marginalists were at reading Gossen.

Capital and Interest

The fifth step introduces capital and interest (Gossen 1889, 114; 1983, ch. 13). The basic question concerns the highest amount of present utility that could be sacrificed for a piece of land with a given annual rent that continues into the distant future. Gossen finds the answer by discounting the utility of each future rent payment at the appropriate rate of psychological time preference (as we would call it) meant to reflect uncertainty of expectations (1889, 30, 115; 1983, 35, 134). This promising idea is not successfully exploited, however, and the adaptation of the land paradigm to capital goods remains sketchy. Gossen thinks in terms of land and labor, while capital goods are played down (1889, 172; 1983, 194). He also makes an effort to determine the optimal amount of saving by the condition that the highest price the individual is willing to pay for a source of rent should be equal to the market price, but he seems to confuse average and marginal concepts, and the sense of his argument remains obscure.

In an effort to interpret everyday observations in the light of his theory, Gossen offers an elaborate discussion of the effect of price changes on demand and expenditure. This discussion anticipates a lot of later work on demand elasticities, but it is also cumbersome. The reason is that Gossen's analytical engine, while permitting a brilliantly simple determination of the optimal budget at given prices, is ill suited to the analysis of price change. Since Gossen's curves, as was observed above, relate the marginal utility of expenditure to expenditure, they have to be redrawn after each price change. The insights that Marshall's apparatus made so easy to communicate remained virtually incommunicable for Gossen. This may be one of the main reasons why his achievement, though at the highest intellectual level, remained sterile. If he had read Cournot, his fate might have been different.

Nationalization of Land

The second part of Gossen's book is largely devoted to social philosophy and policy. It shows its author as a passionate libertarian. Through free markets, mankind would succeed without effort where all socialist planning must fail, namely in reaching the highest possible happiness. Abhorring all forms of protection, Gossen was in favor of free trade, the protection of property rights, and a liberal education for both sexes. To prevent fluctuations in the value of money, he advocated a metallic currency and the abolition of paper money. That he also asked for restrictions on child labor and government sponsorship of credit unions seems to indicate that he knew externalities and market imperfections when he saw them. Competitive equilibrium was for him much more than an economic theory or an ideology; it was the gospel, revealing the perfection of a benevolent creator. For him the invisible hand was not a didactic metaphor but religion itself. Today this apotheosis of competition, in language closer to a revival meeting than to scientific discourse, strikes one as bizarre.

Major sources of inefficiency, Gossen thought, were distortions in the allocation of land, which prevented land from actually being used by the potentially most efficient user. To correct this defect, he proposed that the government use borrowed money to buy land on the free market and then lease it to the highest bidder (Gossen 1889, 250f.; 1983, ch. 23). Since governments differ from individuals by being immortal, by having a higher credit rating, and by a lower time preference, such a scheme, he argued, would actually improve government wealth, and the initial debt could eventually be repaid out of rising rent income. For a given year the scheme would be viable if the price paid by government for a piece of land, A, did not exceed the sum of the rent, a, and the annual increase in the value of land, capitalized at the market rate of interest, z. This led him to the condition

$$A \leq \frac{a + \frac{z'}{z}a}{z}, \tag{16.3}$$

where z' is the annual rate of rent increase. It is understandable that Walras was attracted to this scheme. It is also evident, however, that Gossen was not a "land socialist"; he was not concerned about "land monopoly" and the "socialization of rent." His objective was the correction of a market imperfection and not the limitation of property rights.

Place in the History of Economics

Werner Sombart's description of Gossen as a "genius idiot" is often quoted. The expression reflects sadly on the style of academic discourse in imperial Germany, but if it is modified to "idiosyncratic genius," it becomes a fitting epitome of Gossen's tragedy. If perhaps he was not quite a genius, he certainly had a brilliant, original, and precise mind, but he failed miserably in communicating his ideas.

Gossen is usually classified as a precursor of the modern theory of value, whereas Jevons, Menger, and Walras are celebrated as the real founders. From the point of view of economic substance this is incorrect. The cornerstone of that theory is Gossen's second law. Once it was in place, the remainder of that theory followed naturally. To have provided it was a considerable intellectual achievement that had eluded the subjectivists for centuries. Even Walras was unable to make use of his father's ideas about utility and scarcity before he had rediscovered Gossen's second law about seventeen years after Gossen's book came out. The real founder was Gossen.

Gossen's fundamental contribution was to move constrained optimization into the center of the theory of value, where it has since remained. With respect to economic content, his was probably the greatest single contribution to this theory in the nineteenth century. He failed, however, to develop the basic principles into a ready-to-use analytical engine. As a consequence, the following generation had to rediscover those principles before they could proceed with their engineering work.

17
William Stanley Jevons

THE FOUNDATIONS of the theory of individual optimization were laid by amateur economists. Johann Heinrich von Thünen was a farmer, Augustin Cournot was a mathematically trained administrator, and Hermann Heinrich Gossen was a failed civil servant. By 1860 there were indeed many university professors offering courses in political economy, but none of them, up to that time, had made a major contribution to what later appeared as the new "research program." Around 1870 this began to change, and by the end of the century most contributions were being made by professors. Economic theory became professionalized. The first professor of political economy to break new ground in the theory of value as derived from individual optimization was William Stanley Jevons.

Life

Jevons was born 1835 in Liverpool and was the ninth of eleven children of a prosperous iron merchant.[1] He had a happy childhood in a cultivated family with many talents, but also with much tragedy. His mother died when he was ten, a brother and a sister became mentally ill, and his father went bankrupt in the aftermath of the 1847 crisis, which left the family impoverished.

As an undergraduate at University College, London, Jevons worked mostly in chemistry and metallurgy but was also interested in social conditions and economic development. At the age of nineteen he left the university, without a degree, to accept the post of assayer at the Sydney mint, which had been opened after the Australian gold discoveries.

His duties left Jevons enough time to do extensive research on meteorology, to publish articles on railroad problems (which led him into capital theory), to study economics, to compile extensive statistics, and to become an excellent amateur photographer. Not only did this young man have a restless and inquisitive mind, but he was also possessed by the overpowering ambition, as he described it to his sister, "to be good, not towards one or a dozen, or a hundred, but towards a nation or the world" (Jevons 1972–81, 2:307). He saw his particular way to be good in the attempt "to define the foundations of our knowledge of man," for the sake of which he declared himself willing to forgo money, fine possessions, present name and position, and even the real pleasures of scientific study (362).

---

1. On Jevons's biography see Jevons 1886; Keynes 1971– , vol. 10, ch. 13; Könekamp 1962; and Jevons 1972–81, with biographical introduction by R. Könekamp.

The Sydney mint was clearly not the place to realize this ambition. After five years in Australia, despite family apprehensions about the loss of a breadwinner, Jevons returned to London to finish his university education. Dionysius Lardner's *Railway Economy* had convinced him that economic analysis required mathematics, but (like Walras) he found mathematics difficult. He was disappointed about his mediocre result in an economics examination and vowed to avenge it by the publication of his own economic theory, which would "reestablish the Science on a sensible basis" (Jevons 1972–81, 2:416). In the end he got a gold medal for the best M.A. candidate in his field. These were intellectually his most creative years, during which he conceived his basic ideas both on marginal utility and on logic.

After an unsuccessful effort to earn a living as a writer, Jevons in 1863 embarked on an academic career with the humble position of a tutor at Owens College, Manchester. He had to overcome a serious fear of lecturing, but he seems to have been an excellent and well-loved teacher. Three years later (1866), after much anguish over his prospects, Jevons was appointed to a professorship in political economy at Owens College. The year after, he married the daughter of the founder and owner of the *Manchester Guardian*. His position in life was now secure. In the following years he wrote the two books that made him, in Lionel Robbins's words, "one of the great Englishmen of the nineteenth century."

In 1876, Jevons accepted a professorship at University College, London. He still was only forty-one, but his health had deteriorated. He had always been subject to periods of nervous exhaustion and depression, which sometimes forced him to interrupt his teaching duties for several months. With Walras, who had similar symptoms, he exchanged letters of mutual commiseration. He seems to have been a reserved introvert, who was happy in the circle of his family and friends but tended to withdraw from the world at large. In 1880 his health forced him to retire, and he intended to devote himself full-time to the writing of the books he had planned. He was drowned bathing in the ocean, probably because of heart failure, in 1882.

Works

In 1862, shortly after getting his M.A. degree, Jevons gave his first papers as an economist. One was on seasonal fluctuations, which he determined by collecting weekly data for several decades and then averaging all first, second, third, etc. weeks (reprinted in Jevons 1884). The other, and historically more important, paper was a "Notice of a General Mathematical Theory of Political Economy." With hindsight one can find in this paper all the basic ingredients of the later *Theory of Political Economy*, but only sketched out in rough outlines and, paradoxically, without any use of mathematics. Its readers must be forgiven for not recognizing the significance of what they read.[2] In fact, to Jevons's bitter disappointment, both papers failed to attract any attention whatsoever. Apparently it was not so easy to be good toward the world.

A pamphlet, *A Serious Fall in the Value of Gold Ascertained and its Social Effects set forth* (published in 1863; also in Jevons 1884) had more success. It addressed a problem vaguely reminiscent of David Ricardo: To what extent were the recent changes in commodity prices caused by the gold discoveries in California and Australia rather than by "real" factors? Jevons solved it by tracing a large number of commodity price indexes and also their (unweighted) averages over two business cycles and showing that they had predominantly a rising trend. This was a pioneering contribution, both methodologically and empirically, to the analysis of index numbers, then in its infancy. Generally acclaimed, it placed Jevons in the ranks of the respected economists of his day.

Nevertheless, Jevons's place in life and the good he had done toward the world were far from satisfying his ambitions. His next effort was a book on a provocative topic of general interest, *The Coal Question*, with the subtitle *An Inquiry Concerning the Progress of the Nation, and the Probable Exhaustion of our Coal-Mines* (Jevons 1865). Its alarming thesis was that the progressive exhaustion of coal would soon become a "limit of growth" for the British economy. Economically, the book was a weak performance and its main thesis turned out to be grievously in error, but it helps to document that leading economists were concerned about exhaustible resources long before the oil crisis of 1974 and the Club of Rome. From Jevons's point of view the important point was that the book brought him instant fame. Within a few months it became a widely debated bestseller, John Stuart Mill mentioned it in the House of Commons, and Gladstone wished to meet its author.

Jevons could now afford to spend the following years elaborating the basic ideas conceived in the early 1860s into full-length treatises. The results were the two books that determine his lasting place in the history of science. On *The Theory of Political Economy*, published in 1871 (Jevons 1957) more will be said in the following sections. With *The Principles of Science— a Treatise on Logic and Scientific Method* (1874), Jevons became one of the founders of modern logic. A decade before the ill-starred *Methodenstreit* between Carl Menger and Gustav Schmoller, Jevons saw clearly that

---

2. The paper (reprinted in Jevons 1957) was supposed to have been read to Section F of the British Association for the Advancement of Science in Cambridge, but, as Howey 1972 reports, nobody except the secretary is known to have heard it. With hindsight, one can even find in the paper of 1862 the basic insight on which Paul Samuelson later built his revealed preference approach, for Jevons wrote, "Our choice of one course out of two or more proves that, in our estimation, this course promises the greatest balance of pleasure" (1957, 304).

the laws of science are not distilled from previously accumulated facts but begin their life with the creative act of inventing a hypothesis. From this, one deduces logical implications, which are tested against observation. If necessary, the hypothesis is modified until its implications agree with experience. Full certainty, however, can never be attained, and probability thus plays a crucial role. Today, Jevons reads like an early Karl Popper. In fact, Ernest Nagel was of the opinion that more recent discussions of this question added substantially little to what Jevons contributed. Where Menger and Schmoller produced acrimonious noise, Jevons provided light.

Jevons published numerous further books and articles, both in the field of economics and in logic. Some of them (like Jevons 1875) were highly successful as textbooks, selling hundreds of thousands of copies overall. They show a fresh and lucid style and wide interests in social problems, but they failed to add fundamental contributions. The primer on political economy, in particular (Jevons 1878), is quite shallow. The comprehensive treatise, which Jevons had planned to be his crowning achievement in economics, remained a disappointing fragment (Jevons 1905).

Only one of these further contributions has a lasting place in the history of economics, albeit with a negative connotation. It is Jevons's effort to explain business cycles by the fluctuations in sun spot activity, which became the paradigm of exogenous business cycle theories (Jevons 1884). The activity of the sun, so Jevons's argument ran, influences the rice harvest in India. Indian incomes, in turn, affect the demand for English exports, which then imposes a cycle on the whole economy. Few took this argument seriously, but it should be noted that no lesser a man than Henry Ludwell Moore was among them. Seven volumes of Jevons's papers and correspondence were edited by R. D. C. Black and R. Könekamp (1972–81).

Utility

Jevons's claim to fame as an economist rests on his *Theory of Political Economy* of 1871. John Stuart Mill had been incautious enough to write that in the theory of value nothing remained to be cleared up, either by him or by any future writer; the theory was complete. Jevons set out to show that this was the exact opposite of the truth. He accomplished this by deriving value from utility. The argument can be summarized in the following propositions.

The starting point is a utilitarian postulate: "to maximize pleasure, is the problem of economics" (Jevons 1957, 37). It is evident, however, that the hedonistic phraseology is inessential. What Jevons means is constrained optimization. Whatever can thus produce pleasure is defined as possessing utility (38). Denoting utility by u and the quantity of a commodity by x, one may regard utility as a function of the quantity consumed:

$$u = u\,(x). \tag{17.1}$$

Jevons also considers negative pleasure, or pain. This is called disutility, and the things that cause it are called discommodities.

The "degree of utility" is defined as the differential coefficient of u with respect to x

$$\phi(x) = \frac{du}{dx} = u'(x). \tag{17.2}$$

For the degree of utility of the last increment in consumption, Jevons uses the term *final degree of utility*. This is what was later called marginal utility. It is "that function upon which the Theory of Economics will be found to turn" (Jevons 1957, 52).

There follows diminishing marginal utility: "We may state as a general law that the degree of utility varies with the quantity of commodity, and ultimately decreases as that quantity increases" (Jevons 1957, 53). This is the "great principle," later called Gossen's first law. Jevons does not claim novelty for it but says that it is implied in the writings of many economists, though seldom distinctly stated (53). (He refers particularly to Richard Jennings, *Natural Elements of Political Economy*, published in 1855.)

If the same commodity can be allocated to different uses (such as barley for food, beer, or cattle feed), then the optimal allocation is such that marginal utility is the same in all uses (Jevons 1957, 60). This postulate is a rudimentary form of Gossen's second law. It is not more than a rudimentary form because it relates only to different uses of the same commodity. The complete form of Gossen's second law would emerge if the postulate were applied to the allocation of money to different uses, but this is not made explicit.

Exchange

Individual utility maximization provides the basis for the theory of exchange. To be explained are the quantities exchanged and the "exchange ratio," the relative price. The relative price, π, is defined as the ratio in which small quantities of two commodities are exchanged against each other:

$$\pi = \frac{p_x}{p_y} = \frac{dy}{dx} \tag{17.3}$$

Note that y is given and x is received, or vice versa.

However, for homogeneous commodities in a well-functioning market, there can be only one price ratio for all exchanges. This is Jevons's law of indifference, according to which "in the same open market, at any one moment, there cannot be two prices for the same kind of article" (1957,

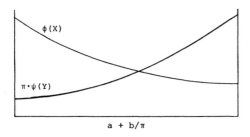

FIGURE 17.1

91). The law of indifference implies that the *total* quantities exchanged by a given trader stand in the same ratio as any small quantities:

$$\frac{y}{x} = \frac{dy}{dx} = \pi. \tag{17.4}$$

This leads up to the proposition that Jevons calls the keystone of the whole theory of exchange, and of the principal problems of economics: *"The ratio of exchange of any two commodities will be the reciprocal of the ratio of the final degrees of utility of the quantities of commodity available for consumption after the exchange is completed"* (1957, 95; Jevons's emphasis). The meaning of this proposition can be explained as follows: Suppose the exchange ratio, π, is given to the individual. The quantities of X and Y available to him, a and b, are also given. If b is expressed in terms of a, total resources are $R = a + b/\pi$. Jevons's graph (97) is similar to figure 17.1. The curve declining from left describes the marginal utility of X. The curve declining from right describes the utility of a marginal unit of X that is exchanged for Y. Optimality requires that $\phi(X) = \pi\psi(Y)$ or $\frac{\phi(X)}{\psi(Y)} = \pi$. This is Jevons's way of formulating Gossen's second law. But

$\pi = \frac{y}{x}$. As a consequence, $\frac{\phi(X)}{\psi(Y)} = \frac{y}{x}$, which is the keystone proposition.

Once it is known how each individual maximizes his utility for a given price, the market price can be determined by the interaction of individuals. Let there be a group of identical individuals represented by A and another group represented by B.

    A has quantity a of corn and no beef;
    B has quantity b of beef and no corn.
The two individuals exchange x of corn for y of beef. After the exchange, therefore,

    A has $a-x$ of corn and y of beef;
    B has x of corn and $b-y$ of beef.
The optimization problem for A (denoted by subscript 1) is

$$\max U_1 = U_{1x}(a-x) + U_{1y}(y), \text{ subject to } x = \pi y. \tag{17.5}$$

This requires

$$dU_1 = - \ \frac{\partial U_{1x}}{\partial x} \ dx + \frac{\partial U_{1y}}{\partial y} \ dy = 0 \tag{17.6}$$

or

$$\frac{\dfrac{\partial U_{1x}}{\partial x}}{\dfrac{\partial U_{1y}}{\partial y}} = \frac{dy}{dx} = \frac{y}{x}. \tag{17.7}$$

On the left there appear marginal utilities, which are functions of the quantities available. Thus, using Jevons's notation introduced above,

$$\frac{\phi_1(a-x)}{\psi_1(y)} = \frac{y}{x}. \tag{17.8}$$

Individual B solves the analogous problem,

$$\max U_2 = U_{2x}(x) + U_{2y}(b-y), \text{ subject to } x = \pi y, \tag{17.9}$$

from which

$$\frac{\phi_2(x)}{\psi_2(b-y)} = \frac{y}{x}. \tag{17.10}$$

The two equations 17.8 and 17.10 suffice to determine x and y and thus $\pi = x/y$. This implies that the ratios of marginal utilities are equalized between individuals. It should be noted that Jevons has nothing to say about isolated exchange between two individuals. This is consistent with the observation in the "Notice" of 1862 (Jevons 1957) that this problem does not have a determinate solution. The solution is made determinate by pure competition together with the law of indifference. There is only one *uniform* price at which supply and demand coincide.

Jevons discusses cases in which the above solution fails. In particular, this may occur for corner solutions and for indivisible commodities. It is interesting to observe that these limitations to the classical (in the mathematical sense) optimization techniques were recognized right from the beginning. On the other hand, the theory is extended to many goods and thus to general equilibrium, but only in a sketchy and discursive way and thus without weakening Léon Walras's claim to originality in this respect. The theory is also extended to labor (by way of disutility, as in Gossen) and to complementary goods.

Capital and Interest

While the main contribution of the *Theory of Political Economy* concerns utility and exchange, another significant contribution concerns capital and interest. Jevons recognized that, in estimating utility, "we are compelled to take account of the uncertainty of all future events" (1957, 35–36). As a consequence, future pleasures and pains have to be *reduced* in proportion as they are uncertain. "If the probability is only one in ten that I shall have a certain day of pleasure, I ought to anticipate the pleasure with one-tenth of the force which would belong to it if certain" (36). Jevons thus postulated time preference, as it would be called today, though not in connection with the rate of interest.

Capital he regarded as a stock of goods waiting to be consumed, either directly (like food) or indirectly (like machines). The essential function of capital is to allow an interval between the input of labor and the final act of consumption. This interval characterizes what Eugen von Böhm-Bawerk later called roundabout methods of production. As Jevons put it, "capital is concerned with time" (1957, 223–4). To measure the interval, Jevons introduced the concept of an "average interval of investment," which anticipates Böhm-Bawerk's average period of production.

Output, Q, is an increasing function of the average interval of investment:

$$Q = F(t) \quad F'(t) > 0. \tag{17.11}$$

This means that "roundaboutness" makes inputs more productive. It is interesting that Jevons expressed this notion in a letter to his sister from Australia long before he had begun to develop his ideas on utility.

The interest rate is equal to the increment in output obtainable from the last increment in time, divided by output.

$$i = \frac{F'(t)}{F(t)}. \tag{17.12}$$

This means that, for a given market rate, the production period is extended to the point where the marginal product of waiting (the expression is not in Jevons) just pays for the interest on the current output, $F'(t) = iF(t)$. Conversely, with a given period of production, the market rate of interest must correspond to the rate of growth of output resulting from waiting. Jevons recognized that optimization does *not* require diminishing marginal returns of waiting, $F''(t) < 0$. Even if $F'(t)$ is a constant, a rise in $F(t)$ would bring $F'(t)/F(t)$ down. In fact, an optimum is compatible even with rising marginal returns, $F''(t) > 0$, if they do not rise "too much."

Jevons, like Böhm-Bawerk, thus describes both of the basic components that Irving Fisher later used in his theory of interest, namely time preference and the productivity of roundabout production. However, again

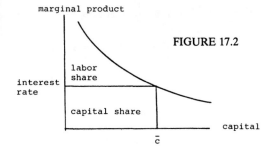

FIGURE 17.2

like Böhm, he fails to see how time preference enters into the determination of interest. This remained for Irving Fisher to explain.

Capital theory leads Jevons to a clear statement of the marginal productivity principle, and he uses a graph that John Bates Clark later made famous (figure 17.2). The quantity of capital per worker is measured horizontally, and the marginal product of capital is measured vertically. For a given amount of capital, $\bar{c}$, total output is thus measured by the area under the curve, capital income by the rectangle, and labor income by the residual triangle. Jevons does not raise the question, however, of whether this principle can be applied simultaneously to each of several factors, and he does not consider the question, later raised by Böhm-Bawerk, of how the rate of interest and the wage rate are simultaneously determined in general equilibrium.

Mathematics

Jevons regarded it as one of his fundamental messages that economic theory is inherently mathematical. As he expressed it in the preface to the second edition, "I contend that all economic writers must be mathematical so far as they are scientific at all, because they treat of economic quantities, and the relations of such quantities, and all quantities and relations of quantities come within the scope of the mathematics" (Jevons 1957, xxi). Jevons and Walras united their forces to gain acceptance of this view.

It is somewhat surprising, therefore, that *The Theory of Political Economy* contains very little mathematics and this does not go beyond the most elementary calculus. Furthermore, the mathematics is rather inelegant and often hard to follow, as Alfred Marshall correctly observed in his review of 1872 (1925, part 2, ch. 1). This is consistent with the fact, noted above, that Jevons found it difficult to learn mathematics. As a mathematician, he was clearly inferior to, say, Cournot or Marshall. Compared to Ricardo, Thünen, or Gossen, he had better mathematical training but probably less innate talent. Thus we see a brilliant scientific mind give a strong impulse to mathematical economics without being an outstanding mathematician himself.

As one of the foremost logicians of his day, Jevons saw no conflict between a mathematical approach to economic theory and empirical research. For him, as for modern economists, mathematics was precisely a means to derive empirical propositions. He collected large bodies of data and tried to develop statistical procedures by which these could be used to test economic hypotheses. His pamphlet on the price of gold is a brilliant piece of research of this modern kind. Like his contemporary Clément Juglar, though with a much stronger analytical orientation, Jevons must thus be regarded as one of the predecessors of modern econometrics.

Place in the History of Economics

Scientific discovery came to Jevons in the form of intuitive revelation. In both economics and logic he was deeply convinced of its validity and importance long before he was able to articulate it in detail.

It must be left to philosophers to pass judgment on Jevons's contribution to logic. In economics, history has vindicated his conviction. Indeed, the interpretation of economic problems as problems of constrained optimization and their solution by techniques of differential calculus became one of the foundation stones of economics.

Jevons was convinced that this contribution was not only valid and important but also novel. In this he was mistaken, because he could have found all the basic elements of the new theory of value in the work, written seventeen years before, of Hermann Heinrich Gossen. However, Gossen's book remained almost completely unnoticed, and it came to Jevons's attention only in 1878 through his friend Robert Adamson. In the second edition of *The Theory of Political Economy*, Jevons acknowledged generously that Gossen had "completely anticipated" him "as regards the general principles and method of the theory of Economics," and he added, "so far as I can gather, his treatment of the fundamental theory is even more general and thorough than what I was able to scheme out" (1957, xxxv).

In contrast to Gossen, Jevons was a successful innovator. It is true that, to his disappointment, the fundamental nature of his contribution was not recognized at once. Only John Elliott Cairnes and Alfred Marshall wrote reviews, both in a negative vein. Cairnes said he did not understand the mathematics but thought it was wrong. Young Marshall, on the other hand, conveyed the impression that he knew more mathematics than Jevons and thought the latter's math was cumbersome and unnecessary (he later revised his judgment on Jevons's economics). In fact, it was largely through his friend Walras that Jevons's fame began to spread. Nevertheless, within a few years, what later was misleadingly called the marginal revolution had succeeded, virtually without bloodshed. In fact, there was no revolution but quiet evolution. The real issue was not whether the new ideas were valid but to what extent the old ones were also still valid.

Yet, precisely by being absorbed into the body of accepted science,

Jevons's theory ceased to provide impulses for further developments, whereas Adam Smith, David Ricardo, Alfred Marshall, Knut Wicksell, Irving Fisher, and John Maynard Keynes continue to stimulate economic thinking, often through their very obscurities.

Jevons left no "school." In the general line of development of English economic doctrine from Ricardo to Marshall, he was an outsider. Raised as a Unitarian, he was an iconoclast with a passionate aversion to "dominant figures" like John Stuart Mill, whose tyranny, as he saw it, he regarded it as his mission to break. While in his clear and lively language he tried to spread understanding even down to elementary school, he made no effort to establish a new dogma. In the history of economics he is one of the few genuine problem solvers.

18

Léon Walras

THE LEITMOTIV of the classical era had been the circular flow of income, the interdependence of economic phenomena. In the marginalist era its place was taken by the principle of individual optimization. This does not mean that the achievements of the classical era were obsolete or forgotten. They still provided the general framework within which individuals and firms were now seen to perform their optimizing calculi. In Johann Heinrich von Thünen, Augustin Cournot, Hermann Heinrich Gossen, and William Stanley Jevons, however, this framework was implicit and sketchy rather than explicit and articulated. The explicit integration of individual optimization into the circular flow system was the achievement of Léon Walras.

Life

Walras was born 1834 in Evreux, France.[1] His father, Auguste Walras, had a disappointing career as a teacher and economic writer who, by championing the notion that the exchange values of commodities reflect the different degrees of their scarcity, became one of the precursors of the theoretical breakthrough that his son helped to achieve. He also expected great things from the use of mathematics in the social sciences. Léon revered his father, and his scientific work can be seen as an effort to live up to his father's expectations.

After finishing high school, Léon applied to the Ecole Polytechnique. It turned out, however, that he did not have the required background in mathematics. He renewed his efforts, but instead of concentrating on ex-

---

1. This biographical sketch is based on the "Notice autobiographique" and other material in Walras 1965, on Jaffé 1983 and on Jaffé 1984. Biographical material can also be found in Boson 1951.

amination requirements, he spent his time exploring the origins of analytic geometry, calculus, and mechanics in the writings of Descartes, Newton, and Lagrange. At this time he also read Cournot. As a consequence, he failed the entrance examination a second time. Thus rejected by the Ecole Polytechnique, he applied to the Ecole des Mines, where he was accepted. Engineering, however, was not to his taste; he soon neglected his courses and devoted his energies to literature, philosophy, history, art, and social sciences. He must have been one of the last economists to become leaders in their field without an academic degree.

Walras decided, as did Jevons at about the same age, to become a writer. He tried his luck with novels, but without success. In 1858, on an evening walk with his father, he experienced what he described as the decisive hour of his life, his conversion to economics. His father, after having forgiven him for dropping his engineering studies, explained to him that two great tasks remained to be accomplished in the nineteenth century, namely the creation of the science of history and the creation of social science, to the second of which, the father said, he had directed his own energies. Whereupon his son promised to abandon literature and to devote his life entirely to the continuation of his father's work. At the age of twenty-four this college dropout had thus conceived his grand design, namely to create a social and economic science comparable to the natural sciences.

Progress at first was frustratingly slow. Walras wrote articles for journals, but they were soon refused. He also worked for a newspaper, but he was not pliable enough to submit to the authority of publishers. Academic life was dominated by a small group of notables, more politicians than scientists, who did not welcome outsiders. Walras could not obtain the necessary permission for a journal of his own. During this difficult period, around 1858, Walras entered into a liaison that was legalized eleven years later. He also adopted his wife's son and later legitimized their daughter. (After the death of his wife, Walras married a second time.) In 1862 Walras gave up and accepted a job with the Chemin de Fer du Nord. A few years later we find him as manager of a bank cooperative, which collapsed in 1868, and then as a bank employee.

Things changed for the better in 1870. In 1860, Walras had participated in an international tax congress in Lausanne. The manuscript he had submitted was awarded only fourth prize, but his oral contribution gained attention, and he was invited to give courses at the Lausanne Academy. Nothing came of it at the time, but when, ten years later, Lausanne established a new chair of political economy in the law faculty, Walras was invited to apply. The search committee consisted of three professors and four regional politicians. Two of the professors were against him because they were suspicious of Walras's socialist leanings. Fortunately, three of the politicians, none of them socialist, were for him, because they regarded scientific promise as more important than ideology. (Does academia need politicians to shield it against politics?) In the end, Walras was appointed, though only for a year at first. He had to borrow the money for the trip to Lausanne.

The 1870s were the most productive period in Walras's life, during which all his principal contributions were worked out. As a social philosopher, he was one of those who wanted to chart a way to welfare and justice by constructing a "scientific" synthesis between liberalism and socialism. As a rationalist, he thought, as did Karl Marx, that his social vision was amenable to scientific proof, which, unlike Marx, he intended to supply by mathematical economics. Spreading the gospel of mathematical economics thus became the burning passion of his life. With a limited gift for mathematics and deficient training, his grand design required a lot of hard work. Only after some mathematical help from his colleague Paul Piccard did he finally learn, in 1872, to incorporate marginal utility into his general equilibrium accounting system. Whereas Marx, the born dilettante, in similar circumstances tried to reinvent the wheel, Walras, the born scientist, toiled to acquire the necessary skills.

As a teacher, Walras was conscientious and respected, but the students in the law faculty had little interest in, or ability for, mathematical economics, and only a handful took his courses. There never was anything that deserved to be called a Lausanne school, for Walras gained all of his followers abroad, mostly in Italy. Teaching in Lausanne left him dissatisfied, and he quarreled with fate because it did not let him teach in a French faculty of philosophy, which would have allowed him to combine philosophy with mathematics. He circulated his writings by sending out free copies at his own expense, for which he spent a large part of the considerable inheritance from his mother (Jaffé 1983, 84f.).

Walras must have been a cantankerous hypochondriac and paranoid who used up much of his energy in the petty struggles of daily life. In 1892, at age fifty-eight, he retired, tired beyond his age, he said, more by the struggle than by his work. After some academic maneuvering he succeeded in having Vilfredo Pareto appointed as his successor.

During the next eighteen years, Walras continued to work incessantly, but there were no further innovative contributions. Honors were not lacking. In 1892, for example, Walras was made an honorary member of the American Economic Association, and his fame was even recognized in what had become his home country, Switzerland. For human beings of his kind, however, honors always manage to be overshadowed by disappointments. It sheds an interesting light on Walras's personality that he applied for the Nobel Peace Prize by submitting a memorandum in which he argued that world peace presupposes free competition, that this requires the abolition of taxes, which in turn can be accomplished by the nationalization of land. One more disappointment; Theodore Roosevelt got the prize.

Walras died in 1910, internationally acclaimed as one of the leading economists of his age.

Works

Walras had planned to publish his work in three volumes on "pure economics," "applied economics," and "social economics," each corresponding to one of the courses he taught in Lausanne. Of these only the first, *Eléments d'économie politique pure; ou, théorie de la richesse sociale* (2 parts, 1874 and 1877), ever came out. Like Marx, Jevons, Menger, Marshall, and Wicksell, Walras found his plan to be beyond his powers.

The first volume received little attention. The exposition is lucid and the mathematics simple, but for the French economists of that time, it was arid reading and largely beyond their comprehension. After his retirement, Walras wrote an abridged version of his *Eléments (Abrégé des éléments d'économie politique pure)*, which was published only in 1938. It provides an excellent introduction into Walrasian economics. For a bird's-eye view in verbal terms, the nonmathematical reader is referred to the introduction to the fourth edition of the *Eléments* (1900).

For the second and third volumes he had planned, Walras later substituted two collections of essays. The *Etudes d'économie sociale* (1896) bears the subtitle *Théorie de la répartition de la richesse sociale,* but there is, in fact, little distribution theory proper. Instead, Walras develops his views about the ideal society, the role of government, private property, and taxation. Land should be nationalized, and land rent should be used in lieu of taxes to finance government expenditures. Government should provide public goods and control natural monopolies. If taxes are levied, they should be on property rather than on income. Everything else should be left to free competition. Walras's reasons for advocating government ownership of land are not entirely economic. He seemed to feel that a scarce natural resource should inherently belong to all, but he also argued, as did Gossen, that privately owned land was unlikely to be used efficiently.

The only significant contribution to economic research in the 1896 volume is a detailed analysis, stimulated by Gossen, of the development of land prices with increasing rent. Of historical interest is the essay on Gossen, originally published in 1885. Walras had heard about him from Jevons. Like Jevons, he generously acknowledged his priority and did his best to spread his fame.[2] Walras, whose linguistic abilities were better than Jevons's, even prepared a French translation of Gossen's difficult book, but it was never published; Georgescu-Roegen reports that the manuscript was lost among the papers of Luigi Einaudi (Gossen 1854; 1983).

The other collection of essays bears the title *Etudes d'économie politique appliquée* (1898). Its subtitle, *Théorie de la production de la richesse*

---

2. It might be added that Walras also helped to make Jevons's work known.

sociale, is even more misleading than that of the earlier volume, because the main (though not the only) topics are money, credit, and banking, first discussed in *Théorie de la monnaie* of 1886. These papers show Walras as an authority on currency problems and an acute commentator on the financial problems of the day. They completely dispel the notion that the father of mathematical equilibrium theory was just a manipulator of abstract equations without a sense for economic reality. Walras proposed a "managed gold standard" (sometimes called a limping standard) under which the government would stabilize the long-term trend of a geometric mean of commodity prices by increasing or decreasing the supply of overvalued silver coins. Bank notes he regarded as potentially destabilizing and therefore dangerous. In a paper on railroads, Walras develops his view that collective goods and natural monopolies have to be exempt from the principle of laissez faire, because competition is bound to fail.

Though many of Walras's significant contributions were first published independently, virtually all of them were eventually incorporated in his *Eléments* and the two collections of *Etudes*.

From Partial Equilibrium to General Equilibrium

Walras begins his theory of exchange, as did Jevons, with the analysis of partial equilibrium for two goods. The economic content of this analysis is the same as that of Marshall's reciprocal demand curves. However, Walras uses ordinary demand curves (with relative prices on the horizontal axis). The quantities supplied in exchange thus have to be expressed by the areas of rectangles. As a consequence, the exposition, which in Marshall's hand became beautifully simple, remains cumbersome. This may help explain why there was to be a Cambridge school, but, in the literal sense of the word, no Lausanne school. It should be noted that Walras, like Marshall, initially explains exchange without reference to utility, introducing utility in a second stage as an analytical underpinning. After much labor, Walras arrives at Gossen's second law concerning the equalization of the utilities of the marginal quantities exchanged against each other. As Jaffé has shown (1983, ch. 16), this proposition had long eluded Walras, which made it impossible to explain price in terms of his father's "scarcity." For Walras, the decline of marginal utilities was a trivial preliminary; the key to analytical progress was their proportionality to prices.

From two goods Walras proceeds to three, and finally to *n*, goods; from partial equilibrium he proceeds to general equilibrium. The explicit analysis of general equilibrium is Walras's great contribution to the history of economics. It is a serious misunderstanding, however, to believe that there was a doctrinal battle line between partial equilibrium, with headquarters in England, and general equilibrium, with headquarters in Lausanne. Walras begins his exposition with partial analysis, and Marshall had more to say about specific market interdependencies than Walras.

In his general equilibrium model Walras considers $1 \ldots i \ldots n$ persons, each of whom comes to the market endowed with given quantities, $\bar{x}_{ij}$, of $1 \ldots j \ldots m$ goods. For person i there is an additive utility function

$$u_i = u_{i1}(x_{i1}) + u_{i2}(x_{i2}) + \ldots + u_{im}(x_{im}), \tag{18.1}$$

where the x_{ij} are the quantities consumed. At commodity prices $p_1 \ldots p_j \ldots p_m$, each consumer plans his purchases and sales in such a way that his utility is maximized, subject to the budget constraint

$$(x_{i1} - \bar{x}_{i1}) + p_2(x_{i2} - \bar{x}_{i2}) + \ldots + p_m(x_{im} - \bar{x}_{im}) = 0. \tag{18.2}$$

The first commodity is arbitrarily chosen as the medium of account or, to use Walras's term, the *numéraire*, whose price is unity by definition. In post-Keynesian debates, this constraint, as if it represented some deep insight, was often called Walras's law. Gossen's second law states that utility maximization requires

$$u'_{i1} = \frac{u'_{i2}}{p_2} = \ldots = \frac{u'_{im}}{p_m}, \tag{18.3}$$

where u'_{ij} is the marginal utility of commodity j.

To determine consumer equilibrium at given market prices, Walras reinvents Gossen's construction in which, for each commodity, the marginal utility of the money spent on it (or received for it) is expressed as a function of the amount spent (or received). The optimum is reached where (1) these marginal utilities are equal, and (2) purchases equal sales.

If prices are experimentally varied, these marginal conditions determine $m-1$ independent market demand functions,

$$x_{ij} - \bar{x}_{ij} = f_{ij}(p_2, \ldots p_3 \ldots p_m), \quad (j = 2 \ldots m) \tag{18.4}$$

while the demand for the first commodity is implied in equation 18.4 together with the budget constraint. A negative market demand is equivalent to market supply.

For each commodity, market demand can be added over individuals to give aggregate market demand. Equilibrium is reached where this is simultaneously zero for all commodities:

$$\sum_i x_{ij} - \sum_i \bar{x}_{ij} = X_j - \bar{X}_j = F_j(p_2, \ldots, p_m) = 0, \quad (j = 2 \ldots m) \tag{18.5}$$

which means that market demand equals market supply for each good. Walras notes that equilibrium for $m-1$ markets automatically establishes equilibrium in the mth market by virtue of the aggregated budget constraints. There are, therefore, $m-1$ independent demand functions to determine $m-1$ prices. The quantities of each commodity bought (or sold) and consumed by each individual are determined simultaneously with prices.

This model was analytically far superior to any notion of general equilibrium available up to that time. It was also superior to the model roughly sketched, sixteen years later, in Marshall's Note XXI (Marshall 1890). Walras realized that the equality of variables and unknowns is no guarantee that a unique solution with nonnegative prices and consumption exists. (Conditions for the existence of an equilibrium are sketched in 1874–77/ 1900, 98.) He also realized that for some goods consumption might be zero and that for such corner solutions the marginal conditions would appear as inequalities. No progress, however, was made in the formal solution of these problems for another half-century.

The *Tâtonnement* Process

The determination of Walrasian equilibrium prices, in principle, requires the solving of a large number of simultaneous (nonlinear) equations. Obviously, there is nobody in the real economy who tries to do this. How, then, could Walras argue that his model was a fruitful idealization of reality? To answer this question, Walras invented his *"tâtonnement"* process. It expresses the idea that the solution to a set of simultaneous equations can be found, starting from arbitrary values, by an iterative process that may be regarded as an idealization of the market adjustments observed in real life.

To implement this idea, Walras specified the adjustment process he had in mind. He recognized that there were two basically different types of mechanisms. In one case, traders would begin to make exchanges at "false" prices. Some sellers would then find no buyers and/or some buyers would find no sellers. These would offer new prices, at which again some trades would be made, and so on. Walras realized that such a process, in general, would not lead to his theoretical equilibrium, because every round of false trading would be equivalent to a change in endowments. He also realized that he could say little about the outcome.

Alternatively, the initial set of prices could be announced by an "auctioneer," who then registers the quantities offered and demanded, as described by equation 18.4. No actual exchanges take place at disequilibrium prices, but whenever the auctioneer notices excess demand, he increases the announced price, and in the case of excess supply, he lowers it. The traders then revise their bids accordingly. This "groping" for equilibrium Walras called the *tâtonnement* process. It would continue until equilibrium was simultaneously reached in all markets. Only then would exchange take place.[3]

In this dynamic process the announced prices react to excess demand or excess supply. This is clearly the plausible assumption to make in this

3. This interpretation of Walras's process is supported by Jaffé (1983, ch. 14).

context. In particular, it would make no sense to assume that the auctioneer calls out quantities to be sold and bought, expecting the traders to report the prices at which they are willing to make these trades.[4]

The question was whether the *tâtonnement* process, if conducted according to this rule, could be relied upon to lead toward equilibrium. This is the question of stability. Walras had learned from Cournot that an equilibrium might be unstable, but he did not provide a conclusive stability analysis for multimarket equilibrium.

Production and the Circular Flow

Walras extended his general equilibrium model to production by visualizing the economy as a circular flow of factors and outputs. Utility-maximizing households sell factor services, consisting of different types of land, labor, and capital goods, to the entrepreneurs, for which they earn, respectively, rent, wages, and interest. The profit-maximizing entrepreneurs transform these factors into products, which they sell to households. Wherever entrepreneurs make profits (beyond the market return on their own land, labor, and capital) they expand production; wherever they incur losses, production is contracted. In equilibrium, therefore, there are neither profits nor losses. Walras thus created the abstraction of the zero-profit entrepreneur under perfect competition.

Walras modeled the transformation of factors into products along the lines of Richard Cantillon, François Quesnay, and David Ricardo, namely by assuming fixed coefficients. The production of one unit of commodity j takes a_{1j} of factor 1, a_{2j} of factor 2, and so on. The production of $\bar{x}_j$ of commodity j would thus require

$$q_{hj} = a_{hj}\bar{x}_j \qquad (h = 1 \ldots k; j = 1 \ldots m) \qquad (18.6)$$

of factor h, where a_{hj} is the input coefficient and $\bar{x}_j$ is the output of good j, now variable. However, Walras regarded fixed coefficients only as a first approximation, and as early as 1877 he also considered variable coefficients (Jaffé 1983, ch. 11). In particular, he wanted to show that the accumulation of capital over and above the growth of population, by lowering the input coefficients for land, could make continuing growth compatible with fixed land. Despite the coaching by his mathematical colleague Hermann Amstein, these efforts were not successful, though. The failure to develop a satisfactory theory of factor substitution effectively prevented Walras from making a significant contribution to the marginal productivity theory of factor prices and distribution.

---

4. In the analysis of production, Walras used another classical assumption, misleadingly called Marshallian, whereby production would expand or contract depending on whether the price exceeds or falls short of the cost of production.

With fixed input coefficients, the equality of prices to factor costs can be written

$$p_j = \pi_1 a_{1j} + \ldots + \pi_h a_{hj} + \ldots + \pi_k a_{kj}, \quad (j = 1 \ldots m) \quad (18.7)$$

where $\pi_1, \ldots \pi_h, \ldots \pi_k$ are the factor prices.

Instead of being endowed with consumer goods, household i is now assumed to be endowed with factors $\bar{q}_{i1}, \bar{q}_{i2}, \ldots \bar{q}_{ik}$. For each factor, aggregate input must equal the aggregate endowment,

$$\sum_j q_{hj} = \sum_i \bar{q}_{ih} . \quad (h = 1 \ldots k) \quad (18.8)$$

Walras takes into account that consumers will not, in general, sell all the factors they are endowed with but use some (say, in the form of a garden, leisure, or a house) in their own household. In the present summary this aspect is disregarded since Walras added nothing new to it. With this simplification the factor income of household i is

$$y_i = \pi_1 \bar{q}_{i1} + \pi_2 \bar{q}_{i2} + \ldots + \pi_k \bar{q}_{ik}. \quad (i = 1 \ldots n) \quad (18.9)$$

For each consumer the demand for good j is now a function of goods prices and income

$$x_{ij} = f_{ij} (p_2 \ldots p_j \ldots p_m; y_i), \quad (i = 1 \ldots n ; j = 2 \ldots m) \quad (18.10)$$

and the value of consumption is constrained by income

$$x_{i1} + \ldots + p_j x_{ij} + \ldots + p_m x_{im} = y_i. \quad (i = 1 \ldots n) \quad (18.11)$$

Finally, aggregate demand equals aggregate supply for each good

$$\sum_i x_{ij} = \sum_i \bar{x}_{ij} , \quad (j = 2 \ldots m) \quad (18.12)$$

but again one of these equilibrium conditions can be derived from the remainder of the system. A check confirms that the system consisting of equations 18.6–18.12 has just as many equations as variables, namely $m + n + mk + k + n(m-1) + n + (m-1)$ equations for m outputs, n incomes, mk factor inputs, k factor prices, nm quantities consumed, and $m-1$ goods prices. Again the solution is supposed to be found by *tâtonnement*.

Investment and Interest

Exchange with production has so far been considered on the assumption that factor supplies are fixed. For land this is realistic, but for labor and capital it is not. For both of these variable factors, Walras essentially uses the classical assumption that their growth depends on the excess of their income over a zero-growth (or "subsistence") level. With respect to labor, Walras contributes nothing new. For capital goods, however, his analysis represents a large step forward (for detailed accounts in Walrasian terms, see Jaffé 1983, chs. 9, 10).

Walras is often described as the incarnation of stationary equilibrium, an example of the alleged neglect of economic growth by neoclassical economists. Nothing could be farther from the truth. Walras visualizes a growing economy with positive investment and saving. A short enough time period is chosen for investment to have no capacity effect. Investment is defined as the value of new capital goods. Suppose a certain collection of capital goods, determined at random, has been produced. The price of each capital good corresponds to the capitalized value of the rental income it provides. The lower the rate of interest, therefore, the higher the amount of investment. This results in a falling curve of investment as a function of the rate of interest.

Saving, on the other hand, is defined as income not consumed. In terms of the concepts introduced in the fourth edition of the *Eléments*, it involves a sacrifice of current consumption for the sake of an infinite stream of future income. In view of the diminishing marginal utility of consumption, the marginal sacrifice increases with increasing saving. The marginal utility of a perpetual income stream, on the other hand, declines with increasing saving. For a given rate of interest, the individual will plan his savings in such a way that the marginal benefit from future income just balances the marginal sacrifice from reducing present consumption. Walras does not enter into the question of why an infinite stream of future income, however small, is not necessarily preferred to any finite sacrifice of present consumption, however large; there is no discussion of time preference.

Saving depends on the rate of interest, because at higher interest rates a dollar of saving yields a larger stream of future income. At low interest rates, a rising interest rate is certain to increase saving, but Walras recognizes that at higher interest rates this may be different, because the savers can afford higher consumption and still provide for their old age.

The growth of capital goods and the rate of interest are determined by the condition that investment must equal saving. Whenever, at the interest rate announced by the auctioneer, investment exceeds saving, the rate is raised, and vice versa.

It has so far been assumed that the quantities of investment goods are arbitrarily given. In general, these quantities will not be consistent with general equilibrium. Equilibrium requires that the market prices of investment goods equal their costs. Whenever the market price exceeds production costs, more capital goods will be produced, and vice versa.[5] If, at the initial quantities of investment goods, capital goods prices deviate

---

5. Walras thus uses what is currently called a q-theory of investment, where q, as defined by Tobin (1971), is the ratio of the market price of capital goods to their production cost.

from cost, the auctioneer would have to increase the quantities of invest-ment goods whose price exceeds cost, while reducing the quantity of capital goods whose price falls short of production costs. This would, of course, require further adjustments in the rate of interest, and probably in other prices, and so on until full equilibrium is reached.

In this way, Walras determined the rate of interest for a growing economy. However, growth was not assumed to be balanced, for popu-lation growth and capacity effects of capital accumulation were not con-sidered. How the rate of interest would be determined in a stationary economy remained unclear.

Money

If all transactions described in the preceding sections could take place simultaneously, there would be no need for inventories. To express the economic function of inventories, Walras had to give his model a time dimension. He imagined time to be divided into periods of, say, a week. Contracts are made at the conclusion of the auction process at the beginning of each week. Each contract carries a specified delivery date sometime during the week, and these dates are assumed to be technically given. Consequently, a store may find that sales are bunched early in the week and new supplies from the manufacturers come in only at the end. To bridge this gap, the store has to keep inventories. These provide a special kind of service for which Walras invented the term *provisioning service*.

The essential point is that Walras treated money like one of these inventories. Since incoming and outgoing payments in the course of a week are generally not synchronized, households and firms can stay solvent only if they use cash balances to bridge the gaps. Once the amounts and dates of receipts and payments are known, each agent can figure out what cash balance he needs at the beginning of the week. This is what Walras called the desired cash balance. For the first time, the demand for money had thus been analytically derived from the time profile of the payments mech-anism.

Walras argued that the demand for cash balances, like that for inven-tories, is a diminishing function of the rate of interest. This is indeed plausible, but it does not strictly follow from the model as long as delivery dates are technologically fixed and known with certainty. To make inven-tories and cash balances really functions of the interest rate, they would have to be derived from an optimization process, either because delivery dates are uncertain or because they are subject to negotiation—at a price. While Walras's theory of the demand for cash balances thus left important problems unsolved, it was not significantly improved upon until Hicks's important "Suggestion for Simplifying the Theory of Money" of 1935 (Hicks 1967, ch. 4).

In this analytical framework Walras was able to show that under a

217

gold standard the quantity theory of money, though not generally valid, is valid on the special assumption that the demand curve for nonmonetary gold is a rectangular hyperbola. The reasoning is as follows. Suppose an exogenous doubling in the quantity of gold results, in fact, in a doubling of all commodity prices. As a consequence, the cash balances held against commodity transactions also double. Furthermore, the doubling of all commodity prices in terms of gold is equivalent to cutting the relative price of gold in half. By assumption, this leads to a doubling in the demand for nonmonetary gold. The cash balance held against transactions in nonmonetary gold, therefore, is doubled also. It follows that the system, if it was in equilibrium before the increase in gold, will be in equilibrium at the doubled prices with the doubled amount of gold. It should be noted that the quantity theory is valid even though the desired cash balance depends on the rate of interest.

Walras also gives a brilliant analysis of bimetallism. On the one hand, he takes issue with those who believe that bimetallism necessarily breaks down because the fixing of the price ratio between gold and silver constitutes a gross violation of the laws of supply and demand. His reasoning is that the variations in the relative proportions of gold money and silver money may be enough to accommodate fluctuations in demand or supply and thus act like a parachute. On the other hand, Walras criticizes the view that a fixed price ratio between gold and silver can always be maintained. He points out that the parachute action of bimetallism finds a limit where either gold money or silver money has disappeared from circulation. The conclusion is that bimetallism is an ingenious and effective technique to dampen price level fluctuations compared to either a gold standard or a silver standard, but only between limits. If Walras's analysis had been remembered at the time of the gold/dollar standard, the collapse of the Bretton Woods system would have been better understood and could perhaps have been prevented.

Welfare

For Walras general equilibrium analysis was in the service of welfare. Its basic purpose was not the demonstration that there were just enough equations to determine the unknowns. It should prove that free competition results in maximum welfare. "Free competition in exchange and production," Walras said in summary, "provides maximum utility of factor services and products on condition that there be only one single exchange ratio for all services and all products for all traders. Free competition for capital formation and credit provides maximum utility for new capital goods on condition that there be only one single rate of interest on capital for all savers." (Walras 1938, 252; my translation.) By later standards, Walras's arguments are lacking in rigor, but his intuition has held up well. Whereas partial and applied welfare analysis followed the lines of Jules Dupuit,

Alfred Marshall, and Arthur Cecil Pigou, Walras thus laid the foundation of general welfare analysis. There is one basic qualification, however. The Walrasian general equilibrium maximizes welfare only once the personal distribution of factor endowments is regarded as given. It has nothing to say about changes in welfare, however measured, that might be obtained by a redistribution of endowments. Walras was well aware of this basic qualification, but he did not pursue its implications.[6] His approach to welfare leads to Pareto optimality rather than to income redistribution.

Place in the History of Economics

To utility theory proper Walras contributed little. The derivation of Gossen's second law was analytically decisive and subjectively original, but it had been anticipated not only by Gossen but also by Jevons (though not by Menger). Walras's pioneering contribution was the incorporation of the new utility theory into an explicit model of general economic equilibrium. In this he had no predecessor.[7]

In constructing his circular flow system, Walras followed the tradition established by Cantillon, Quesnay, and Ricardo. To this extent there is some justification for Morishima's insistence that Walras was a Ricardian (1977, 5f.).[8] Like Jevons, Walras talked like a scientific revolutionary. Much like Marshall, he achieved rather a synthesis of old and new. In particular, in his theory of value both utility and cost (the latter represented by input coefficients) have a role to play.

The main limitation of Walras's system is that, though ostensibly constructed to exhibit the interdependence of economic phenomena, it has little to say on the effect of a change in a specific exogenous variable on a specific endogenous variable. Almost anything seems possible. Paradoxically, partial analysis often has more to say about economic interdependence than general equilibrium theory of the Walrasian type. In the twentieth century most of the valuable insights into comparative statics have been derived from general equilibrium models reduced to a manageable number of significant markets.

Walras's knowledge and understanding of the real economy, despite some brilliant contributions to applied economics such as that on bimetallism, was much more limited than Marshall's. While Marshall's students learned to see complex reality through the trained eye of the economist, Walras's readers learned to abstract from complexities for the sake of

6. This was emphasized by Jaffé (1983, ch. 18).
7. William Jaffé (1983, ch. 3) called Achylle Nicolas Isnard the progenitor of the Walrasian general equilibrium model, but this seems to go too far. What Jaffé attributes to Isnard are trivial identities. Walras's scientific contribution began where Isnard's ended.
8. Unlike Ricardo, however, Walras was not interested in the distribution of income between social classes; Morishima thus goes astray when he likens him to Marx in this respect. Nor is Morishima convincing when he purports to show that Walras was close to Keynes.

economic fundamentals. But whereas Marshall tried to hide his models, Walras deployed his in full detail. As a consequence, Walras, though creating no genuine school, became the founder of a still unbroken tradition of general equilibrium theory, whereas the Cambridge school became analytically sterile.

Joseph Schumpeter called Walras the greatest economic theorist, at least since David Ricardo, and his system of equations the Magna Carta of economic theory (1954, 242). Such literary flourishes should not be taken too seriously, especially coming from Schumpeter, for whom Walras was the incarnation of the type of economic theory Schumpeter himself was unable to produce. In fact, if Walras is measured by the substantive insights he added to economic science, he does not appear in the front rank. However, if he is judged by his contribution to the techniques of economic model building, he is a towering figure. In this sense he may be called the Ricardo of the calculus era.

19
The Viennese School

IN ECONOMICS, as elsewhere, there is much talk about different schools. If schools are meant to be closely knit groups of masters and pupils united by distinctive doctrines, their number and significance in the history of economic science has actually been quite small. Their paradigm, of course, is the physiocrats. The only other indubitable example seems to be the Viennese school, also called the Austrian school. The originator of most of its ideas was Carl Menger, but as a distinct school it was the creation of Eugen von Böhm-Bawerk and Friedrich von Wieser.[1] Some of the most brilliant Viennese theorists, such as Rudolf Auspitz and Richard Lieben, were never accepted into the school and will thus be mentioned elsewhere.

Carl Menger

Carl Menger was born in 1840 in Galicia, which then belonged to the Austrian Empire and is now part of Poland.[2] He studied law in Vienna and Prague and obtained his doctorate from Cracow. After a first job as a financial journalist, he entered the civil service in the press office of the prime minister. This was the one scientifically productive period in his life. He later told Friedrich Wieser that in reporting on market fluctuations he

---

1. Kauder 1965 is a rich mine of historical and bibliographical references about the Viennese school. Leser 1986 contains recent assessments.
2. Most of the factual material in this and the following section is from Friedrich von Hayek's introduction to Menger's collected works (Menger 1934–36). A collection of recent essays on Menger and his followers was edited by J. R. Hicks and W. Weber (1973).

was struck by the discrepancy between the price theory he had been taught and the explanations he heard from practical men of affairs. He decided to devote his energy to a reconstruction of price theory that would overcome this discrepancy. The result was *Grundsätze der Volkswirtschaftslehre* (Principles of Economics), published in 1871. On the title page it is designated as part 1, but the other three parts of the planned treatise never appeared.

The first reception of the book was not encouraging, and Menger's application for a lectureship succeeded only after some difficulties. Soon, however, his reputation grew. He was made professor extraordinary in Vienna (in the Faculty of Law) in 1873 and, in 1876, he was appointed tutor to Crown Prince Rudolph (who later ended his life at Mayerling), whom he accompanied on extensive travels through Europe. In 1879 he obtained a chair of political economy in Vienna. From then on, he led the quiet life of a scholar.

During the decade 1875–84, most of Menger's energies were absorbed by the *Methodenstreit* with Gustav Schmoller. In the following years we find him occupied with monetary problems, both theoretical and applied, and he became the leading Austrian authority on currency questions. He also was appointed to the Austrian Herrenhaus, the upper chamber. His publications came to an end in 1892, except for minor articles. He continued working on an enlarged second edition of his *Principles* and, in 1903, even resigned his chair to have more time for this work, but he could not bring it to a conclusion.[3] He died in 1921, leaving an enormous library, now mostly in Tokyo.

Menger's claim to fame is the *Grundsätze*. His aim, as he explained in the preface, was a general theory of value that would explain all prices, including interest rates, wages, and rents, by the same principle. Economic activities are interpreted as the allocation of scarce means to given ends. Cournot, Gossen, and Jevons had translated this problem into mathematics in the form of constrained optimization. Menger, with his unmathematical turn of mind, rather tried to construct a general philosophy of economic decisions. By purporting to develop what he called a causal analysis, he established a characteristic feature of the Viennese school which had much to do with its early decline.

If a limited number of units of a certain good can be used for different purposes, they will be allocated in such a way that every satisfied need is more important, unit for unit, than every need that remains unsatisfied. The value of this good corresponds to the reduction in satisfaction that the

---

3. The second edition was posthumously published by Menger's son. Overburdened with historical and descriptive material, it is a weak echo of the book that had made its author famous half a century before.

individual would suffer if one unit were lost. Menger thus determined value by what became known as the loss principle; it is evidently of very general applicability.

For each good the value thus determined is assumed to decline as more and more units become available. Though the substance of Gossen's first law is clearly perceived, Menger did not find it necessary to coin a term for the concept of marginal utility. Nor did he make the analytical step from indivisible units of a commodity to infinitesimal variations. Menger imagined his individuals in a "realistic" setting, making one decision at a time, each between "lumpy" alternatives and in an environment full of uncertainty and continual change. As a matter of fact, he was not too far away from the historical school.[4]

The valuation principles apply primarily to consumer goods, which Menger calls goods of first order. They can also be applied, however, to producer goods or "goods of higher order." In fact, the value of the higher-order goods is nothing but the reflected value of the first-order goods into which they are intended to be transformed.

If a consumer good is produced from a bundle of complementary producer goods, it reflects its value on the bundle as a whole. To Wieser this suggested the famous "imputation problem" of how this aggregate value should be divided up between the individual producer goods. Menger himself was not interested in imputation in this sense. He wanted to determine the value of factors one at a time, regardless of any adding-up properties. He determined it again by the loss principle: The value of a unit of the factor is equal to the value of the product that its loss would cause to remain unproduced once the other factors have been optimally reallocated. Together with the variability of factor proportions, which Menger explicitly recognized, this proposition implied a marginal productivity theory of factor valuation. This was probably the most significant of Menger's contributions, though it still did not go beyond Johann Heinrich von Thünen.

The transformation of higher-order goods into first-order goods takes time and is subject to uncertainty. First-order goods that can be directly consumed thus have a somewhat higher value than the higher-order goods from which they are composed. This implies, without naming it, the concept of time preference. On the other hand, a lengthening of the chain of intermediate products usually—though not automatically—offers opportunities for an increase in output. The stock of intermediate products is what Menger, like Jevons, calls capital. It is the essence of capital that it makes inputs more productive by permitting more time-consuming or

---

4. Erich Streissler (1972) argues, therefore, that Menger, his distant predecessor in his economics chair in Vienna, should not even be classed as a marginalist.

roundabout methods. With these notions, Böhm-Bawerk had his research program nicely carved out for him.

A glaring weakness in Menger's theory of value, as Stigler (1941, 146) rightly pointed out, is its failure to explain how the individual allocates his resources to maximize his satisfaction. The principle expressed by Gossen's second law is, at best, hinted at, and there is nothing to take its place. Analytically, Menger was still pre-Gossen.

From value, Menger proceeds to exchange. It is fair to say, however, that in this respect, too, his analysis falls far short of those of Gossen and Jevons. He presents a numerical example in which exchange at a predetermined price just happens to exhaust the opportunities for mutually profitable exchange. He makes no effort to show, however, how this price is determined and how exchange would proceed from different initial exchange ratios. Menger's price theory is similarly limited. Like Cournot he begins with monopoly, but he does not progress beyond the most trivial notions, sometimes mixed with definite error. Unbelievable as it may sound, Menger never developed a theory of price in a fully competitive market nor did he investigate the influence of cost on supply and thus on price.

More fundamentally, Menger lacks the concept of an equilibrium between demand and supply. He catches the market at the fleeting moment when quantities are determined by past production and only the price remains to be determined. While Marshall's short-term fish market would have looked familiar to him, he paid no attention to subsequent adjustments. It may be conjectured that this deficiency has to do with the fact that Menger's economic experience at the time he wrote the *Principles* was limited to financial and commodity markets.

Menger had dedicated his *Principles* to Wilhelm Roscher, and he concluded his preface with a flattering greeting to German economists, to whose debate on "value" he hoped to make a major contribution. His hopes were crudely disappointed. German economics, then dominated by the historical school under the leadership of Gustav Schmoller, had no use for economic theory. Out of this disappointment grew Menger's second book, *Untersuchungen über die Methode der Sozialwissenschaften und der Politischen Oekonomie insbesondere* (Investigations on the Method of the Social Sciences and Particularly of Political Economy, published in 1883) (Menger 1934–36, vol. 2). It provoked a condescending and rankling review from Schmoller himself (Schmoller 1883). Menger replied with a polemic diatribe *Die Irrtümer des Historismus in der deutschen Nationalökonomie* (The Errors of Historicism in German Economics, published in 1884) (Menger 1934–36, vol. 3). This was the culmination of the disastrous *Methodenstreit*.

It should be made clear at once that the controversy was not about marginal utility. In fact, Schmoller, an eclectic, did not hesitate to use the concept in his own *Grundriss der allgemeinen Volkswirtschaftslehre*, giving due credit to Menger. Nor was the controversy about the legitimacy of historical and empirical work in economics. Actually, Menger was a well-read historian himself, and the second edition of the *Principles* was virtually drowned in factual material.

The issue was, ostensibly, the logic and strategy of scientific research. Both adversaries agreed that the ultimate goal was scientific laws. The question was how these were to be discovered. However, neither protagonist was a good logician. As a consequence, the debate did not produce much light. Schmoller took the position that economic laws have to be distilled from a mass of facts, patiently accumulated over decades, and that, for the time being, theoretical work was premature. This position was clearly indefensible. Menger's plea that theory has a role to play side by side with the accumulation of facts deserves sympathy, but the relationship between theory and observation was not correctly perceived, as any perusal of Jevons's book on logic would have shown.

The real historic significance of the *Methodenstreit* should be sought at the level not of epistemology but of academic power politics. Once Schmoller had declared, as Friedrich von Hayek reports in the introduction to Menger's works, "that members of the 'abstract' school were unfit to fill a teaching position in a German university," adherents of the Austrian school had no future in Germany. German economics was cut off from the international development of economic science until it found its way back to the mainstream after World War II.

Historians of economic science usually hold Menger in high esteem. Indeed, with respect to fundamental content, his ideas about value, exchange, and capital were much the same as those of Gossen and Jevons. With Jevons the parallel is particularly striking. These ideas, though anticipated by Gossen, were subjectively original and broke new ground.[5] From the point of view of theoretical analysis, however, Menger was far inferior to both Gossen and Jevons, and even more to Walras. His basic problem was that he failed to use any mathematical or graphical tools.[6] His background was law, and legal thinking is qualitative, not quantitative. It is true that before Adam Smith, in the period of the scholastics and cameralists, economic studies were often associated with law, but in the

---

5. On Pantaleoni's charge of plagiarism, later dropped, see Kauder 1965, 81f.
6. On the basis of the facts that Menger occasionally expressed interest in mathematics, that his library included some contributions to mathematical economics, and that his brother, Anton Menger, was interested in calculus, it was sometimes conjectured that Carl Menger knew more mathematics than his work shows. If one reflects on how men like Jevons and Walras had to struggle to acquire the bare minimum of calculus required for their purposes, it seems highly unlikely that Menger came even close to possessing this minimum without ever showing it.

nineteenth century law faculties were not a fertile breeding ground for economic research.

Thus, when economic theory finally learned to make use of mathematical tools, Menger stood aside. He never made the step from a discontinuous demand curve for indivisible goods to the continuous demand curve, which, though an idealization, is so fruitful in terms of useful results. While Menger was a fresh spring in the theoretical desert of the German-language economics of his day, in the international context his contribution was obsolete before it had been made.

This may well be the ultimate reason why Menger's original work never progressed beyond the first volume of the *Principles*. It is true that he was diverted by the *Methodenstreit*, but, if his mind had really been burning to write volumes 2, 3, and 4, he would not have allowed himself to be diverted. Menger's ideas made sense, and his intuition was brilliant, but his analytical engine was not up to the task, and he was too honest a scientist to escape into academic entrepreneurship.

It seems to have been mainly Böhm-Bawerk who spread the notion of Menger as one of a triumvirate of founders of subjectivism. As a matter of fact, Jevons (who died in 1882) never even knew of Menger's existence, and Walras found out about him only in 1883. Nevertheless, Menger's *Principles* were influential, and its author enjoyed a high international reputation. At a time when Jevons and Walras were inaccessible to most economists and Marshall's *Principles* had not been published, Menger was the torchbearer of the "new economics." This is why Knut Wicksell could say in his obituary in the *Economisk Tidskrift* that since Ricardo's *Principles* there had been no book that exercised such great influence on the development of economics as Menger's *Grundsätze*. Though the building of economics, as it stands today, contains hardly any building blocks created by Menger, he was nevertheless one of its leading architects.

Eugen von Böhm-Bawerk

Menger's fresh approach to economics had early attracted the attention of two young and talented civil servants, Eugen von Böhm-Bawerk and Friedrich von Wieser. Though they had never been his students, they began to elaborate and develop some of his suggestions, thereby forming the core of the Viennese school. Most of their contributions can be traced to ideas expressed by Menger.

Böhm-Bawerk was born 1851, the son of a high government official in Brünn.[7] After studying law and political science, he prepared himself for a civil service career. At the same time he continued to study political economy, particularly with the leaders of the so-called older historical

---

7. For biographical data see Carl Menger's obituary (Menger 1934–36, vol. 3).

school, Wilhelm Roscher, Bruno Hildebrand, and Karl Knies. After obtaining his doctorate at Vienna in 1875, he was attracted into the orbit of Carl Menger. His book on the economics of property rights earned him a lectureship, and he married Baroness von Wieser, the sister of his fellow economist and friend.

Böhm's first professorial post was in Innsbruck. This was his period of scientific productivity. In 1889 he left the university to enter the Ministry of Finance, and in 1895 he became Austrian minister of finance, an office that he held several times with great success. After his resignation in 1904, he was appointed to a chair for political economy in Vienna. From then on, most of his energies went into the obstinate defense of his positions against all comers.

As a great man of the Viennese establishment, Böhm-Bawerk was showered with honors, and a well-known photograph shows him, a little, bespectacled man, in a court uniform covered with crosses, stars, and medals. He died in 1914. Menger said about his star pupil that "as a pugnacious personality and incessantly engaged in polemics, he had indeed many opponents, but he had certainly not a single enemy" (Menger 1934–36, vol. 3).

In his first book, *Rechte und Verhältnisse vom Standpunkte der volkswirtschaftlichen Güterlehre* (1881) (Rights and Relationships as Economic Goods), Böhm-Bawerk applied Menger's subjective valuation approach to property rights. Is a patent, for example, a component of wealth? He answered that it is a component of private wealth but not of social wealth, because its positive value to the inventor is balanced by the negative value it has for those whom it prevents from exploiting the invention.

Böhm-Bawerk's reputation rests on his three-volume work *Kapital und Kapitalzins* (Capital and Interest) (1921). The first part is a critical history of interest theories. It is a mine of information, but Böhm was much better at picking other contributions apart then in entering into their spirit. In the second part he develops his own theory. It is based on Menger, but in the meantime the Austrians had also progressed to competitive supply and demand, incorporating the substance of Gossen's second law, though in terms of (verbal) marginal inequalities rather than of equalities. Menger himself was not happy about the way his pupil had implemented his suggestions on capital. To the systematic exposition of his theory, Böhm added a volume of notes and appendices, in which we see him battling his critics. The book was, academically, a great success, not least because of the controversies it provoked.

Of Böhm-Bawerk's minor works (collected in Böhm-Bawerk 1924–26), the most important is his penetrating critique of Karl Marx's theory of value (Böhm-Bawerk 1949), which draws attention to the "contradiction" between the first volume, where profit is assumed to be proportionate to labor, and the third volume, where it is acknowledged to be proportionate to capital, after all. In the light of subsequent Marx philology, this critique is off the mark, but the final assessment was not: Marx, so Böhm thought, was going to have a permanent place in the history of the social sciences for his enormous influence on the thought and feeling of generations, but socialism would turn away from him, and his economic theory would be revealed as a house of cards.

Böhm-Bawerk's contribution to the theory of capital and interest is best presented under three headings: (1) the reasons for the existence of interest, (2) the period of production, and (3) the interest rate in general equilibrium.

THE EXISTENCE OF INTEREST. The basic question of the theory of interest is why more than one unit of future goods is exchanged for one unit of present goods. Why are present goods more valuable than future goods? Böhm-Bawerk's three reasons became famous. The first reason is the expectation that resources will be less scarce in the future than they are at present. If somebody expects his income to rise, he will usually be willing to pay more than one future dollar for a present dollar. Böhm-Bawerk realized, of course, that this reason might work in reverse because things may be expected to get worse. In this case, however, it would often be possible to store either the cash or the goods. Positive time preference, therefore, was likely to predominate. Böhm-Bawerk's second reason is the systematic underestimation of future wants.[8] Böhm-Bawerk had no doubts that such myopia was a psychological fact, but about its explanation he was less certain. He mostly ascribed it to lack of imagination about future wants, lack of will power, and uncertainty about the future. The third reason is the productivity of more roundabout methods of production. Factor inputs can be made more productive by waiting longer for the output. The growing of trees is an obvious paradigm.

There was not much originality in this list. All three factors had been mentioned by Menger, and all had a long history, which Böhm-Bawerk knew well (though he did not then know John Rae). His exposition nevertheless became the focus of debate, the *locus classicus* for the reasons for a positive rate of interest. This was not so much because Böhm was superior to his predecessors, but rather because he was so dogmatic in his assertions and so obstinate in defending them, even if they were patently wrong. The most famous controversy concerned the third reason.

Böhm-Bawerk's position was strange indeed. In his critical history of interest theory, he had castigated earlier writers mercilessly for erroneously believing that the productivity of capital was enough to explain a positive rate of interest. Now, in his own theory of interest, he went to great lengths

---

8. In modern terminology this myopia is called net (or pure) time preference, and gross time preference is the term for the sum of the first and the second reason.

to explain that the third reason would, in fact, result in a positive rate even in the absence of time preference. To Wicksell, who had asked him about this bewildering discrepancy, Böhm replied that his own theory had not been fully worked out when he criticized the earlier theories (Stigler 1941, 194f.). In the ensuing controversy, Böhm-Bawerk revealed himself as clearly inferior to theorists like Wicksell, Alfred Marshall, and Irving Fisher. In the exchange with Fisher in particular, Böhm's forensic defense of an untenable cause borders on pettifoggery. Others had their "little laughs" (as Marshall wrote to Wicksell) at such displays.

Böhm-Bawerk combined his defensive efforts with the general charge that Fisher's own theory was circular, because it explains the rate of interest in terms of individual behavior while the latter, in turn, depends on the rate of interest. To Fisher's patient explanation that his theory was no more circular than any system of simultaneous equations, Böhm replied that this might perhaps be relevant for a "mathematical" explanation of interest but not for a "causal" explanation as he had tried to give it. From then on, causal analysis was the rallying cry with which the Austrians went into battle against the mathematicians with their "functional" analysis.[9] The historical consequence was that the Austrians fought their own little rearguard actions while the real battles of scientific research were fought elsewhere.

THE PERIOD OF PRODUCTION. Böhm-Bawerk's theory of interest raised the question of how the "roundaboutness" of production could be measured. He answered it by constructing the concept of the average period of production. Suppose a certain output is produced with a total of Q units of input, spread over a number of years. Of this total, q_i units are applied t_i years before output matures, with $\sum_i q_i = Q$. The average period of production is then defined as

$$\tau = \frac{\sum_i (q_i t_i)}{\sum_i q_i}. \tag{19.1}$$

For a given Q, the roundaboutness of production would be higher the farther back in the past the inputs were applied.

The remarkable feature of this measure of capital is the failure to use compound interest. Apparently, in Vienna around the turn of the century, one could still claim to be a leader in the field of interest theory without mastering compound interest. However, though the disregard of compound interest was a serious defect, it had the virtue that the measurement of the capital stock was independent of the rate of interest; it could be regarded

---

9. Mayer 1932 is representative for this dogmatic position.

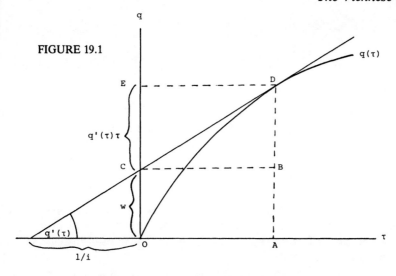

FIGURE 19.1

as a purely technical measurement. It thus made sense to describe output as a function of the capital stock in the same way it can be described as a function of, say, labor. With compound interest, the definition of an aggregate capital stock loses its simplicity. In fact, after much debate, it turned out to be impossible to define it in purely technical terms. Fortunately, it also turned out to be unnecessary.

THE INTEREST RATE IN GENERAL EQUILIBRIUM. The high point of Böhm-Bawerk's theory is the determination of the rate of interest jointly with output, wages, and capital intensity for a given capital stock in a general equilibrium system. In pure logic he used precisely the simultaneous equation approach that he criticized as circular or mathematical when used by Irving Fisher. The only difference is that he expressed himself in terms of tables instead of equations. The tables were later translated into equations and graphs by Knut Wicksell (1954), and the present summary in the main follows his more elegant exposition.

Production per worker, q, is supposed to increase with the average period of production, τ, according to

$$q = q(\tau), \qquad q'(\tau) > 0 \qquad q''(\tau) < 0 \tag{19.2}$$

with a diminishing marginal product of capital, $q'(\tau)$. In figure 19.1 it is represented by the upward-sloping curve. The representative entrepreneur pays the market wage, w, keeping $q-w$ as profits. Each year the entrepreneur starts one of these production processes. To pay wages until the first process is completed, he needs a capital of τw. Capital is thus interpreted as a wage fund of consumer goods. The rate of return, therefore, is

$$i = \frac{q(\tau) - w}{\tau w}. \tag{19.3}$$

The entrepreneur chooses the period of production in such a way that, for parametrically given w, i is a maximum. This optimum is reached where

$$q'(\tau)\tau = q(\tau) - w, \tag{19.4}$$

which, by substituting from equation 19.3, can be expressed as

$$i = \frac{q'(\tau)}{w}. \tag{19.5}$$

The interest rate, defined as the rate of return on capital, is thus made equal to the marginal product of capital as a percentage of the wage rate. In terms of figure 19.1, the representative entrepreneur, with given w, chooses the period of production in such a way that the ray through C is tangent to the output curve.

For the economy as a whole, the wage rate is variable, but the labor force is given. The competitive wage rate must be such that the available stock of capital is just enough to pay the workers during the period of production chosen by the entrepreneurs. If $k = K/L$ is the available stock of capital per worker, this condition can be written

$$w = \frac{k}{\tau}. \tag{19.6}$$

Substituting this into equation 19.4, one obtains as equilibrium condition

$$q'(\tau)\tau^2 = q(\tau)\tau - k. \tag{19.7}$$

In figure 19.1, the left-hand side is expressed by the rectangle $CBDE$, which represents capital income during the production period. On the right-hand side, the first term, expressed by $OADE$, represents total output during the production period. The difference is k, which corresponds to the rectangle $OABC$. The economy is in equilibrium at the point where this rectangle is equal to the available stock of capital per worker.

From the point of view of the history of economics, this analysis is particularly notable for three reasons:

1. It purports to explain the rate of interest without reference to time preference. Böhm's view that time preference is not a crucial ingredient of the theory of interest thus seems to be vindicated.

2. The analysis takes the capital stock as given, a legacy from past saving. This raises the question of how this capital stock itself is determined; specifically, why is the capital stock not so large that the marginal product of capital, and thus the interest rate, are zero? Subsequent developments showed, not surprisingly, that this second point is closely related to the first, inasmuch as time preference or some such

concept can supply the missing element in the explanation of the capital stock and of a positive rate of interest.

3. This was the first time the interest rate, the wage rate, output, and the time profile of production were simultaneously determined in a general equilibrium model. Böhm-Bawerk thereby created the prototype of what came to be known as the Austrian theory of capital.

AROUND the turn of the century, Böhm-Bawerk was one of the most prominent economists internationally. He was the dominating figure of the Austrian school, a successful cabinet minister, and the leading authority on capital and interest.

Not all of this prominence was equally well deserved. Böhm-Bawerk's originality was not great, and his analytical skills were far inferior to those of the leading marginalists of his time. From the point of view of more general audiences, he made up for this weakness by his articulate, elementary, and detailed exposition and also by the dialectic brilliance with which he "annihilated" his opponents, superficial though it was. He must have been a born classroom gladiator. The longer-term consequences for the Austrian school were disastrous. In particular, his denunciation of "functional" theories and thus of mathematics became a curse that condemned his followers to provincialism.

At the same time, through his general equilibrium theory of interest, Böhm-Bawerk laid the basis for most of the important work in this field until far into the 1930s. It is true that the basic concepts were Menger's, but it was Böhm who worked them out into a coherent theory. His model building was primitive, to be sure, but theorists like Irving Fisher and Wicksell, though analytically his superiors, gratefully acknowledged their debt to him.

Friedrich von Wieser

Whereas Menger was the originator of ideas of the Viennese school and Böhm-Bawerk its doctrinarian, Wieser was its principal teacher. For four decades he represented Austrian economics to thousands of students.[10]

Friedrich von Wieser was born in Vienna in 1851, one of nine children of a high civil servant, later ennobled. In high school, where Böhm-Bawerk was his classmate and friend, he obtained an essentially historical education. After acquiring a law degree at the University of Vienna, he embarked on a government career. At about the same time, he and his friend came across Menger's newly published *Principles*. By offering a new perspective on economics, it gave their lives a new direction.

It was 1883, however, before Wieser, with Menger's eventual support,

10. For biography and bibliography see Mayer 1929 and Hayek in Wieser 1929. Streissler 1986, 83–106, provides a sparkling and knowledgeable modern assessment.

obtained a lectureship in Vienna. In the following year he left the government service to become a professor in Prague, first at the associate level. In 1903 he became Menger's successor in Vienna. Though he continued to teach economics, his interests had gradually shifted back to history and sociology. In his intellectual style he was, in fact, closer to the German historical school and the "socialists of the chair" than to, say, Walras or Wicksell. Like many of his contemporaries he adored leadership and power, he was a patriotic nationalist, and he was not free of racial prejudice. His romantic notions about the creative role of the innovative entrepreneur found fertile ground in his pupil Schumpeter. In 1917, Wieser was briefly minister of trade, and in the same year he was appointed to the Austrian Herrenhaus. He retired from his chair in 1922 and died in 1926.

Wieser, though personally aloof, must have been an impressive classroom orator, but his writings are verbose, opaque, and generally ineffective. They nevertheless contain some brilliant insights. His earliest known work in economics is a paper he gave in 1876 in the seminar of Karl Knies, one of the pillars of the historical school. Entitled "The Relationship of Cost to Value" (and first published in Wieser 1929), it is the most concise expression of Wieser's principal contribution, of which his further works are hardly more than an elaboration.

The book *On the Origin and Principal Laws of Economic Value,* published in 1884 (Wieser 1968), had the main virtue of earning Wieser the lectureship in Vienna. For the first time, Jevons's terms *final degree of utility* and *terminal utility* were translated as "Grenznutzen," which was later retranslated as "marginal utility" (Wieser 1968, 128). For the derivation of factor values from product values, Wieser coined the term *Zurechnung.* The imputation problem, thus conceptualized, was destined to haunt the Viennese school for half a century.

The second book, *Natural Value* (Wieser 1889), earned its author the professorship in Prague. It is Wieser's most ambitious scientific undertaking. After that, most of his economic writings concerned applied problems of Austrian currency and finance or were of an expository nature. A selection was edited posthumously by Hayek (Wieser 1929). Successive efforts to extend the Austrian perspective to the value of money produced much turgid prose but no major contributions.[11] Wieser's most comprehensive treatise, *Theory of the Social Economy,* first published in 1914, shows what sort of lectures were given by the man who, with Böhm-Bawerk's death in the same year, had become the leading light of the Austrian school. Though his pupil Hayek praised it as the greatest synthetic achievement of all contemporary economic theory (Wieser 1929, xvii), it

---

11. Wieser believed that the value of fiat money today can be explained only on the basis of its value yesterday, and so on, back to commodity money (1929, 211). This notion, erroneous as it is, became the backbone of Ludwig von Mises's theory of money (1912).

does not compare to Alfred Marshall, Knut Wicksell, or even Gustav Cassel.

Wieser's claim to fame is the assimilation of cost into the theory of subjective value that had emerged from the work of Gossen, Jevons, and Menger. In interpreting cost as forgone utility, Wieser followed Menger's lead. To subjective utility he added technology as the other basic determinant of value. In many cases he was content to represent technology by fixed input coefficients. In other contexts, however, he allowed for factor substitution and for a choice between different methods of producing the same good. With given technology, the cost of one product could be expressed in terms of the alternative product (or products) that could have been produced in its stead from the same factors. This was the concept that D. I. Green (1894) later named opportunity cost. If Wieser had had more expository talent, he could have illustrated it by a production possibility curve, but this was left for Irving Fisher to do.

Menger had always tried "realistically" to catch individual economic decisions from a fleeting chain of transitory phenomena. Wieser went beyond Menger by introducing the notion of economic equilibrium. This important step was disguised by the use of a quite different terminology and by the Austrian polemics against the "equilibrist schools" of economics, but with respect to substance, Wieser's words left no doubt. The introduction of equilibrium resulted in a synthesis of classical and subjectivist theories of value. If two goods can be produced in varying proportions from the same factors, their relative values generally depend both on their utilities and on the technology. Both blades of the Marshallian scissors are in place. In the special case of fixed input coefficients, Wieser fully recognized that relative values would depend solely on these coefficients, marginal utilities adjusting passively through changes in output. By thus building a bridge from Menger and Jevons to Mill and Ricardo, Wieser was neoclassical in the same sense as Marshall.

Though in equilibrium relative prices would correspond to relative costs, Wieser insisted (rightly) that cost is never a valid explanation of value. His demonstration of this proposition led to the concept that economic theory later called efficiency. If cost were a valid explanation of value, it would explain value even if inputs are used inefficiently. In fact, Wieser argued, wasted factors are not reflected in the value of their products. The cost that turns out to equal the value of a product, he concluded, is nothing but the least utility that must be sacrificed in order to obtain it. Cost is always a reflection of utility.

Equilibrium and efficiency became the keys to Wieser's theory of imputation. He visualized an ideal communist state in which given resources are allocated efficiently by an omniscient and benevolent planner (Wieser 1889, and already in 1876 [Wieser 1929]). The values of factors and products in such an economy are called natural values. What natural values will the planner assign to factors? If factors are valued according to

Menger's loss principle, their aggregate value might exceed the value of their products. Wieser pointed out that this was due to the disequilibrium character of Menger's cases. In full equilibrium, the value of the factors would equal the value of their products. The imputation problem concerned the principles by which the value of the product could thus be divided between the contributing factors without excess or deficit.

One aspect of Wieser's problem can be visualized by assuming that a given quantity of a single factor can be used to produce different useful products, each with a fixed input coefficient (1929, appendix). The maximization of utility requires that the ratio between the marginal utility of a product and its input coefficient be the same for all products. Wieser perceives that this common ratio is the marginal value to be imputed to the factor. It measures the loss in utility if the factor endowment is reduced by one unit. Though using no mathematics whatsoever, and working his way through a cumbersome casuistry of numerical examples, he thus arrives at a basic understanding of the economic interpretation of Lagrange multipliers and shadow prices. Whenever a good would be worth less than the required factor inputs, it will not be produced, and whenever it is worth more, the factor allocation is not yet efficient.

To the modern reader it is clear that Wieser was vaguely groping for the concept of duality. His primal problem was the optimization of output quantities in the light of their utilities. His dual problem was the assignment of shadow prices to the given resources, and he realized that these prices would, in some sense, have to be as low as possible. In an efficient economy, the aggregate value of outputs would just equal the aggregate value of inputs, whereas an excess of input costs over output values would indicate inefficiency. Though it takes little imagination today to read this "vision" into Wieser's argument, his techniques were dismally inadequate to the task. As a consequence, the vision, brilliant as it was, remained analytically sterile.[12]

In particular, Wieser's efforts to use these notions to solve the imputation problem were grossly deficient. His argument can be summarized as follows: It may realistically be assumed that the number of products, n, exceeds the number of factors, m. Assume further that input coefficients are technologically fixed. Under these assumptions, the value of each of the n outputs is a linear function of the known quantities of m inputs each multiplied by its unknown shadow price. Any subset of m equations can thus be solved for the m shadow prices.

This imputation theory was sometimes criticized for the wrong reasons. Thus it was argued that a market economy does not require a derivation of factor *values* from goods values; a theory of factor *prices* is enough. This objection is beside the point inasmuch as Wieser's theory is explicitly

12. It may be conjectured, however, that Wieser's vision helped prepare the ground for the portentous work on duality that was initiated in Vienna in the 1930s.

intended for a centrally planned economy and thereby raises fundamental questions potentially important also for a market economy. It was also argued that it is arbitrary to disregard the remaining $n-m$ equations, that the whole system has more equations than unknowns and is, therefore, generally inconsistent. This objection is invalid because, in the optimal solution, the remaining $n-m$ equations are automatically consistent with the selected m equations. The real weakness of Wieser's solution is not that it is incorrect but that it does not explain what it should: In order to compute the shadow prices of factors, one has to know the marginal values of the products and thus the optimal program, but once this is known, the shadow prices of factors are no longer needed. The relevant problem would have been the calculation of the efficiency prices of factors without first knowing the optimal program, but Wieser made no effort to solve it.

Despite this weakness, Wieser's vision suggested further steps. At one level these led directly to the marginal productivity approach to distribution. If a given output is to be efficiently produced from substitutable factors, so Wieser shows, the price of each factor must equal its marginal product evaluated at the value of the product (1968, 177f.). In stating this proposition, Wieser is not detained by problems of product exhaustion and properties of linear-homogeneous functions; efficiency would require the proposition to be true regardless of the form of the production function. Any excess of the product over the payments to variable factors would be efficiently imputed to the fixed factors as rent.

At another level, Wieser's vision led him to a comparison between his ideal economy, an actual socialist economy, and a market economy. He argued that a socialist economy would have to value scarce factors on the basis of their marginal products. Efficient planning would thus have to be based on natural values. A market economy, on the other hand, would in many respects certainly differ from the ideal, not only because of temporary disturbances but also because of monopoly and other market imperfections. Nevertheless, market prices would have a tendency to gravitate toward the natural values. With these arguments, Wieser gave new life to the old debate, to which Cantillon had made an early contribution, about the analogies between efficient markets and efficient planning.

Overall, Wieser was an armchair philosopher rather than a problem solver. He early had some profound ideas about the efficiency of an economic system, but he lacked the analytical talent to make them fruitful.[13] Without mathematical training, he could never establish contact with contemporary theory outside Austria. Together with Marshall, he nevertheless

---

13. In *Natural Value* (1889, 27f.), Wieser came close to articulating the concept of consumer surplus. The point is that he managed to miss it. In the same year, Auspitz and Lieben published an extensive analysis based on this very concept. The differences in analytical power between the ins and outs of the Viennese school are clear indeed.

personifies the integration of the subjectivism of Menger and Jevons with the classical tradition. Even in Vienna there was no revolution.

IN THE EARLY years of the twentieth century, the Viennese school was at the peak of its international renown. After Böhm-Bawerk's death, the school sank rapidly into provincial obscurity. Its pillars were replaced by theoretical nonentities. Joseph Schumpeter and Ludwig von Mises, though not the strongest of theorists, would certainly have been better, but both were passed over. This was often attributed to all sorts of academic politics, prejudice, and intrigues. As so often, these may indeed have played a role. There was, however, a more fundamental cause. The scientific productivity of the Austrian school, not very high even at its peak, had been declining for decades. The school had not produced an analytical apparatus that could serve as an engine of further research. Under the second-generation leadership of Wieser and Böhm-Bawerk, precisely because it was strong, it had lost touch with mainstream economics and had tried to preserve its identity by academic inbreeding. By the time the leaders of the second generation had to be replaced, Vienna had no body of third-generation economists with high analytical standards and keen scientific judgments to make the right decisions. Wieser could, in fact, hand-pick his successor, but Hans Mayer was a bad choice.

Nevertheless, the intellectual ferment of post–World War I Vienna still produced a number of outstanding economists of the fourth generation, among them Friedrich Hayek, Gottfried Haberler, Oskar Morgenstern, and Fritz Machlup. However, the university was no longer the center of their activities, and they were soon dispersed by political events. In the diaspora, after they had ceased to be a school, Austrian economists contributed more to economic science than the Viennese school ever did.[14]

20
Alfred Marshall

TOWARD THE END of the nineteenth century, political economy became rapidly professionalized and, in particular, professorialized. The number of major contributions from outside academia dwindled apace. The professors, however, still lectured and wrote largely for audiences without academic training. The graduate school, where present professors teach future professors, had only just been invented (the first was Johns Hopkins

14. A detailed account of Austrian economists in the interwar period is given by Earlene Craver (1986). The survival of Austrian ideas in modern economics is surveyed in Kirzner 1987.

University, founded in 1873). There was no place yet for "economists' economists," and the economist's public was still the proverbial "intelligent layman." The problem for economists was to translate the results of their research, sometimes based on highly specialized training and quite abstract analysis, into language readily understood by their Victorian public. The personification of this phase of economics was Alfred Marshall.

Life

Marshall was born in Bermondsey, a London suburb, in 1842.[1] His father was then a clerk of the Bank of England, impecunious but educated, with Victorian notions about the supremacy of men over women, and he was, it seems, an unlovable family tyrant. His mother was of humble origins, a butcher's daughter, but charming and greatly beloved (Coase 1984).

Alfred went to good schools. Somewhat like John Stuart Mill, he was relentlessly pushed by his father and was, accordingly, a pale bookworm with few friends. His father's plans for his studies emphasized the classics and Hebrew, but Alfred was more attracted to mathematics (partly perhaps because his father did not understand it). He declined a scholarship to Oxford that would have led to the ministry and, with the aid of a loan from a benevolent uncle, went to Cambridge to study mathematics. In 1865 he obtained a B.A., with the second-best performance. Marshall thus had better tools than "mathematical" economists such as Thünen, Gossen, Jevons, and Walras, though he made less explicit use of them.

Elected to a fellowship, Marshall first planned to go into molecular physics. Gradually, however, he was shifting to philosophy, metaphysics, and ethics. His wife later described how he spent his vacations wandering in the Alps, alpenstock in hand and a volume of Kant in his rucksack. This development was associated with a religious crisis from which he emerged an agnostic, though his missionary zeal and his propensity to preach never left him. While his intellectual interest pulled him toward psychology, Marshall finally decided he could do the most good as a political economist.

It appears that Marshall did not have a rare talent in any particular direction but had a rare combination of talents in different directions. John Maynard Keynes, in his brilliant memoir of his teacher, has argued convincingly (and perhaps not without introspection) that it is precisely this combination that makes a master economist. "He must be a mathematician, historian, statesman, philosopher—in some degree. He must understand symbols and speak in words. . . . He must study the present in the light

1. The following life sketch is based on the biographical essays by Keynes (1982), Cannan (1982), and Whitaker (1982) and on Whitaker's introduction to Marshall 1975, vol. 1, part 1.

of the past for the purposes of the future. No part of man's nature or his institutions must lie entirely outside his regard" (1971– , 10:173f.). It seems Marshall had everything to become the "compleat economist."

The fellowship years in Cambridge were intellectually the decisive period in Marshall's life. By interpreting, correcting, and modifying Adam Smith, David Ricardo, and, above all, John Stuart Mill in the light of his mathematics, by making good use of Cournot and von Thünen, and, later, by absorbing Jevons, Marshall gradually achieved a "neoclassical" synthesis in terms of demand and supply. At the same time, he was already embarked on his lifelong compulsive, and almost tragic, quest for economic "reality," which led him as far as the west coast of the United States. By 1877, though he had published little, he was regarded in Cambridge as the preeminent economist. His early writings were collected by Whitaker (Marshall 1975).

In 1877, Marshall married Mary Paley, a fellow economist and former student, who seems to have put her life completely at the service of her demanding husband. Though she collaborated in his work and also was a lecturer, Marshall was firmly opposed to the granting of Cambridge degrees to women. The couple had no children.

Since fellowships still were only for bachelors, Marshall accepted a post as principal of the newly founded University College in Bristol, where he also taught economics. Soon after, he became seriously ill, and, though he eventually recovered, his health remained a lifelong concern, not without neurotic undertones. Like Karl Marx, he seems to have suffered from the constant fear that his work did not measure up to expectations, and he put the blame on teaching and administrative duties.[2]

In 1885, after a short period in Oxford, Marshall returned to Cambridge as professor of political economy. By that time, though he still had published nothing of importance, he was the almost undisputed leader of British economics (Whitaker 1982, 107). His main purpose for the remainder of his life was the publication and gradual improvement of his "great book," the *Principles of Economics*. He also devoted much energy to statements and testimony to royal commissions (much of it collected in Marshall 1926). His classes were small, and his formal teaching consisted of about forty-five lectures per year, supplemented by "office hours" at home. The lectures are reported to have been completely unsystematic; even students like Keynes were unable to bring home coherent notes. Once the *Principles* were out, they were supposed to provide the systematic exposition. To this was added the famous "oral tradition." Marshall saw his task not in transmitting information, but in teaching students to think. He accomplished it apparently with overwhelming success, for at the time

---

2. As noted in chap. 18, inability to complete major works was endemic among Marshall's contemporaries.

of his death, his pupils populated the British chairs of economics almost entirely.

Marshall retired in 1908 to have, as he said, more time to write his books. However, like old Carl Menger, he found it increasingly difficult to complete his manuscripts, and some of the latest publications actually represented some of his earliest work. He was a frail little man, "querulous and dyspeptic," as he described himself. Edwin Cannan has said that a "tragic air" was so marked in his portrait that he could not suffer it on his own wall; it always seemed to say "If they would *only* let me alone, I could get on with my book" (1982, 69f.). He died in 1924.

Works

Marshall published only one book of historical importance. This is the *Principles of Economics*. When it came out in 1890, it was designated as volume 1, but the second volume was never written. Though the term *economics*, instead of *political economy,* had been used before (for example, by Henry Dunning Macleod), Marshall's *Principles* established it as the dominant terminology. The book resembles the *Wealth of Nations* inasmuch as its analytical structure is embedded in, and often hidden by, a mass of facts, thoughts, and opinions on economic life, history, and institutions. Also, like Adam Smith, Marshall did not write for the professional specialist but wanted his book to reach the general reader. It was meant as a comprehensive treatise, purporting to present the whole of economic science between two covers.

It was consistent with this purpose that the exposition was entirely in verbal terms. The graphs, relatively few in number, are relegated to footnotes and appendixes, and mathematics appears only in appended notes. Thus Marshall's mathematical background was successfully camouflaged. At the same time there is a lot of sermonizing on ethics, values, and social problems; Marshall, his wife has said, was a good preacher. There are also, in keeping with the social Darwinism of the time, many biological analogies of firms with the organisms competing for survival, and Herbert Spencer's influence is acknowledged in the preface. At the same time, Marshall's emphasis on historical evolution puts him close to the historical school, and Hegel's philosophy of history is mentioned as the other principal influence on his views.

The book was an instant success.[3] It fitted the needs of late Victorian Britain to perfection. Though it underwent considerable revision in subsequent editions, the basic content was not changed.

Marshall used to say that all the main ideas of the *Principles* were

---

3. Because it promised to be successful, Macmillan actually used it, despite Marshall's mild misgivings, as the spearhead of the publisher's campaign for resale price maintenance in the book trade.

fixed in his head about twenty years before they were published and, in particular, when Jevons's *Theory of Political Economy* appeared. This was probably an exaggeration. In particular, there is no indication that before 1871 he ever worked in terms of utility. It is true, however, that Marshall had written two essays, one on foreign and one on domestic values, around the middle of the 1870s. Important parts of them were privately printed (since no other duplicating technique existed at that time) by Henry Sidgwick and circulated among friends. They show some of the basic concepts fully developed. However, these essays were published only in 1930. The book *The Economics of Industry,* which Marshall published together with his wife in 1879 (Marshall and Marshall 1881), gives an early but elementary indication of his thinking. The *Elements of Economics of Industry* (1892) was an effort to abridge the *Principles* for beginners, but for this purpose Marshall's style, in contrast to Jevons's, was too ponderous.

Late in life, Marshall finally managed to organize many of the results of his earlier labors in two volumes, *Industry and Trade* (1919) and *Money, Credit, and Commerce* (1923). Though they were successful, it has been said that they were obsolete before they came out. In his last book, in particular, Marshall published some of his earliest results, achieved almost fifty years before. What could have broken new ground had now become stale.

As a consequence of Marshall's reticent publication habits and the paucity of his references to other people's work, it is almost impossible to assign priorities. The important point is that, through both his teaching and his *Principles,* he dominated British economics for forty years.

From General Equilibrium to Partial Equilibrium

The leitmotiv of Marshall's work was the analysis of individual and interrelated markets. This makes him the founder of modern partial equilibrium analysis. It should be made clear at the outset, however, that Marshall did not see a doctrinal conflict between partial equilibrium and general equilibrium. Though his relationship with Walras was cool, he visualized his own work clearly in terms of a general equilibrium system.

This comes out most explicitly in the famous Note XXI in the mathematical appendix to the *Principles.* It considers an economic system with n goods and m factors where each factor is used for only one output. For each good, there is a demand function relating the quantity demanded to its own price. In equilibrium, the price of each good is equal to the sum of its factor costs, where for each factor the input per unit of output is multiplied by the factor price. While the demand for each factor, with fixed input coefficients, is proportionate to commodity output, factor supplies depend on factor prices. Marshall uses this general equilibrium system to show that he has $2(n+m)$ equations to determine $(n+m)$ prices and $(n+m)$

quantities. He also shows that the equality of equations and unknowns is preserved if the initial model is generalized by allowing the same factor to be used in several products, if there are joint products originating from the same process, and if different processes may yield the same product.

This is a very imperfect general equilibrium system, to be sure. In particular, it purports to determine money prices in a moneyless economy, and the role of budget constraints is not made clear. Despite these deficiencies, this general equilibrium system is historically important because Marshall said in a letter written in 1908 to John Bates Clark that his "whole life has been and will be given to presenting in realistic form as much as I can of my Note XXI" (Marshall 1925, 417). He also has described how he began his study of economics by expressing Ricardo and Mill in the form of equations and checking if he had enough equations to determine the unknowns—sometimes with a negative result. He never tired of emphasizing that economics is a field not of unidirectional causal chains but of mutual interdependence. In particular, he insisted that marginal utilities do not determine price, nor vice versa, because both are determined simultaneously.

The important point is that Marshall, though starting from a general equilibrium framework, did not bother to work this out in detail, as Walras did, but rather used the beam of partial analysis to shed concentrated light on different areas of the economic system.

Reciprocal Demand Curves

Classical value theory was pervaded by the dichotomy between goods with a fixed supply, such as land, old masters, or rare coins, and goods with a variable supply, such as corn or cloth. In the first case, quantity was fixed and the price depended only on demand; the supply curve, to use later terminology, would be vertical. In the second case, once rent was eliminated by the subterfuge of the rentless margin of cultivation, the price was determined by costs of production; the supply curve would be horizontal and demand determined only the quantity produced. Marshall saw his main contribution in generalizing the classical theory of value by filling in the gap between the two limiting cases. In contrast to Jevons and Walras, he regarded this not as a revolution but as a gradual evolution.

His first analytical contribution to this program (though published only in Marshall 1923 and, more fully, in Marshall 1930) was the invention of the reciprocal demand curves. John Stuart Mill had pointed out that comparative cost, in general, could determine only an upper and a lower limit for the international exchange ratio but not the ratio itself. He succeeded in showing that the missing element was provided by demand. This was indeed a case where price was determined jointly by cost and demand.

Whereas Mill's demonstration was based on clumsy numerical ex-

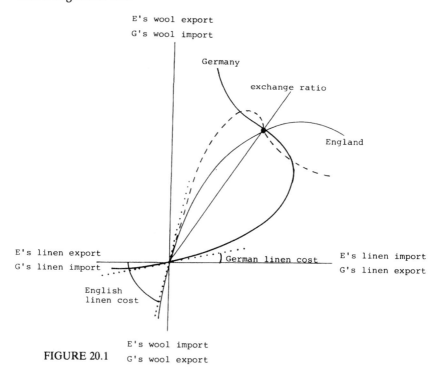

E's wool export
G's wool import

Germany

exchange ratio

England

E's linen export
G's linen import

German linen cost

E's linen import
G's linen export

English
linen cost

FIGURE 20.1

E's wool import
G's wool export

amples, Marshall invented an elegant and powerful graphical apparatus (see figure 20.1). Linen and wool are measured, respectively, on the horizontal and vertical axis. Any ray through the origin expresses a relative price of linen in terms of wool. The dotted lines denote, respectively, the relative costs of linen in terms of wool in the two countries; that this line is flatter for Germany than for England reflects the assumption that the first country has its comparative advantage in linen and the second in wool. Ricardo's theory of comparative cost could only say that the international exchange ratio would be somewhere between these lines.

Marshall now determined the exact location of the exchange ratio by the intersection of two curves. The English curve shows how much linen England would demand at any given exchange ratio; this would implicitly determine the amount of wool it was willing to give up. Marshall showed that a declining price of linen would certainly raise England's demand, but the supply of wool might either rise or fall. The corresponding curve for Germany shows how much linen Germany is willing to give up for any amount of wool. The equilibrium exchange ratio is reached where the curves intersect; English demand for linen is then equal to German supply and German demand for wool is equal to English supply. Marshall also pointed out that there might be multiple equilibria, as illustrated by the broken curve for England, that these would be partly stable and partly unstable, and that only the stable equilibria could endure.[4]

Though this apparatus was originally constructed for international trade, it could clearly be applied to barter in general. It was, in fact, the first graphical apparatus for the equilibrium of demand and supply between two (representative) individuals in pure exchange. It is particularly notable that this apparatus made no use of utility. Individual behavior was described in terms of the quantities demanded and supplied. The underlying utility calculus remained latent. It was Francis Ysidro Edgeworth who, a decade later, used Jevons's utility theory to derive Marshall's reciprocal demand curves.

The Marshallian Cross

To implement his general plan, Marshall needed an analytical apparatus in which demand and supply were not joined together like Siamese twins. He found it in the Marshallian cross of a demand curve and a supply curve for the same commodity, each in terms of money. Though both of these curves had been used before, particularly by Cournot, it was Marshall who made them the fundamental idea of microeconomic analysis. From now on, a novice could hope to pass almost any examination by babbling, "supply and demand."

Demand largely depended on utility (or satisfaction), and supply depended on the cost of production. In general, both sides would jointly determine the price. To dispute whether value is governed by utility or by cost of production, therefore, would be no more reasonable than to dispute whether it is the upper or the under blade of a pair of scissors that cuts a piece of paper (Marshall 1890, bk. 5, ch .3, §7). That cost cannot explain everything was clearly demonstrated by John Stuart Mill's theory of international values. That utility cannot explain everything is shown by the fact that even Jevons and Menger had to use technical relationships between inputs and outputs.

The Marshallian cross was made useful for welfare analysis through the concepts of consumer and producer surplus. While the term was of Marshall's invention, the concept was not. It had long been pointed out that each party is likely to gain from an exchange. Jules Dupuit had measured the gain by the amount of money a trader would have been willing to pay rather than go without the exchange, and he had applied the concept to public investment projects. Dupuit's contribution found little attention, however, and it remained for Marshall to establish the familiar triangles in the key position they have since held in applied and partial welfare analysis.

4. In this context, Marshall initiated the arrowhead technique for the diagrammatic analysis of stability problems.

Elasticity of Demand

For Marshall it was an established fact that demand curves slope downward. Rising demand curves he regarded as a paradox, which he attributed to Robert Giffen, though diligent searches by Stigler and others failed to discover a source in Giffen's voluminous writings.

Marshall's main contribution on the demand side was the invention of the elasticity concept. By making the description of the curve independent of the choice of units, this became of crucial importance for the development of empirical and applied demand analysis. Dating, according to Mary Paley Marshall (1947, 28), from 1882, it was one of the latest of Marshall's conceptual inventions.

Marshall made another contribution to demand analysis by recognizing the significance of the marginal utility of income (or, as Marshall expressed it, of money). He saw that a decline in the price of a given commodity not only shifts demand between commodities but also results in an increase in real income and thus a decline in its marginal utility. Together with Vilfredo Pareto, he thereby prepared the ground for the later separation of a substitution effect and an income effect (in the terminology of Hicks and Allen) by Slutsky. As a practical matter, however, Marshall did not attach much importance to this qualification. He was usually content to proceed on the assumption that the marginal utility of income was practically constant.[5]

Period Analysis of Supply

The gap between the limiting cases of vertical and horizontal supply curves was essentially filled by Marshall's period analysis of supply. It became the hallmark of Marshallian economics.

Marshall used a competitive fish market as his paradigm. In the shortest period, from day to day, the supply of fish depends mainly on the weather and the good or bad fortune of the fishermen. Whatever is caught has to be sold on the same day, regardless of price. The supply curve, therefore, is vertical, and demand is made equal to supply by adjustments in price.

Over an intermediate period, the supply of fish will react positively to its price, because, with a persistently higher price, more fishing boats will be active, and the fishermen will work longer hours. However, the period will still be too short for an expansion of the fleet.

In the long run, both labor and capital investment in the fisheries can be expanded, often at more or less constant cost. As long as depletion of

5. This does not mean that the Marshallian demand curve was supposed to be "income-compensated," as Friedman has argued (1953, 47–99). It rather means that the error involved in using an ordinary (uncompensated) demand curve was considered to be too small to matter, at least for commodities with a small budget share.

the fishing grounds is no problem, the supply curve may thus be close to horizontal. In this case it may be said that price depends on cost of production. *"As a general rule,"* Marshall concludes, "the shorter the period which we are considering, the greater must be the share of our attention which is given to the influence of demand on value; and the longer the period, the more important will be the influence of cost of production on value" (1890, bk. 5, ch. 3, §7; Marshall's emphasis). In brief, whereas the short run is dominated by utility, the long run is dominated by cost. The profits earned by the fishermen before supply is fully adjusted were interpreted by Marshall as temporary rents on their fixed investments. These quasi-rents thus emerged as still another convenient concept.

In this model, the expansion of supply toward its long-run equilibrium level is called forth by a temporary excess of the market price of fish over the production costs for the current supply. For intermediate and long periods, Marshall thus makes use of the classical quantity adjustment, whose driving force is the deviation of the market price from the "normal" price. Its dynamic properties are quite different from the so-called Walrasian mechanism, in which the auctioneer raises the price to eliminate excess demand. It should be clear, however, that the so-called Walrasian and the so-called Marshallian adjustment mechanisms describe not rival but rather complementary hypotheses for successive phases of the adjustment process. In fact, when Walras discusses the same longer-run problem as Marshall, he uses the same adjustment process (Walras 1938, 210, 229).[6]

The Falling Supply Curve and Externalities

Marshall was far from assuming that the long-run supply curve is necessarily horizontal. In agriculture, in view of diminishing returns, it was clearly rising, he thought, but in manufacturing it might often be declining, an increase in output resulting in lower costs or increasing returns to scale through improved organization (1890, bk. 4, ch. 13, §2).

Increasing returns presented Marshall with a problem. He had learned from Cournot that for firms faced with a given market price for their product, marginal cost must be rising. With falling marginal cost, there would be no finite optimum of output. How could he reconcile his notion of falling marginal cost in manufacturing with a finite firm size?

One solution would have been the replacement of pure competition by imperfect or monopolistic competition, with the size of the firm being limited by the decline of the demand curve for its product. This was not Marshall's solution, and it had to wait until after Marshall's death.

Marshall used another expedient, namely a dynamic argument about the rise and decline of firms. The full exploitation of scale economies, so

6. The historical error involved in the distinction between a "Walrasian" and a "Marshallian" adjustment process was pointed out by Samuelson (1947, 264).

he argued, takes time, often many decades. During this time, those who created the economies will usually cede their places to less successful entrepreneurs. As a consequence, the source of scale economies is lost again. In the pure theory of the firm, this is a doubtful argument, because it fails to produce the upturn in marginal costs required for a finite optimum. It foreshadows, however, later findings in empirical research on firm growth to the effect that existing firms tend to become more concentrated forever, while overall concentration is held in check by the birth and death of firms.

Marshall's main defense, however, was the distinction between internal and external economies. Internal economies are those accruing to the individual firm; external economies are due to the expansion of the respective industry in a particular location, regardless of the size of the individual firm. Inasmuch as Marshall let the industry be described by what he called the representative firm, external economies would accrue to the representative firm but not to any individual firm taken in isolation. For each size of the industry, measured perhaps by the number of firms, the individual firm would have rising marginal costs and thus a finite optimum, but with an increasing size of the industry, the individual marginal cost curves would shift downward.

Marshall never produced a satisfactory analysis of increasing returns, and this may have been a reason for his reluctance to publish his early work, as Whitaker conjectured. Though he is the founding father of the modern theory of the firm, he never produced the mathematical or graphical analysis that would have been necessary to put it on a firm basis. Of lasting value, however, was the concept of external economies, which became one of the cornerstones of welfare economics.

Place in the History of Economics

Marshall's place in the economic pantheon must be determined by his *Principles*. These were called by Stigler (1982, 223) the second-greatest work in the history of economics. Indeed, if greatness is measured by the mass of economic truth—analytical, historical, institutional, political, moral, industrial, commercial, and philosophical—packed between its covers, the *Principles* is second only to the *Wealth of Nations*. Marshall was the Adam Smith of his age.

The *Wealth of Nations* also comes to mind if greatness is to be judged by the dominance a book exerts over its field. Marshall wrote the *Principles* in a way that should minimize criticism by polishing away provocative edges and trying to do justice to all sides of an argument. Even members of the historical school should have no complaint. For the late Victorian age he succeeded admirably. His *Principles* dominated the teaching of economics for more than thirty years, and at the time of their author's death, British universities were completely Marshallian.

Joseph Schumpeter has described this situation as classical in the same sense in which the *Wealth of Nations* and John Stuart Mill's *Principles* are supposed to represent "classical situations" in the history of economics. This doctrinal analogy to the (equally hypothetical) Kondratieff cycle may be superficially helpful in providing the historiographer with a pleasing architecture. I believe, however, it does violence to history. Marshall cannot be said to have achieved agreement after a long period of struggle and controversy. From his perspective no new synthesis was called for because there had been no revolution. His economics evolved from John Stuart Mill without a break, and when Marshall reviewed Jevons's *Theory*, the outlines of his own contribution had already been sketched out. Successful textbooks can be written by gifted eclectics at almost any time. It was the fate of British economics to produce two such talents about forty years apart. As a consequence, it was dominated for three-quarters of a century by just two books.

In the end, British economics was all the worse for it. It is true that Marshall attracted some brilliant minds into economics, Arthur Cecil Pigou and John Maynard Keynes foremost among them. It is also true that the Cambridge school of economics, which Marshall founded, still enjoyed a position of great eminence in the 1920s and 1930s. However, Marshall's view that "it is all in Adam Smith" inspired the view that it is all in the *Principles;* it only remained to apply it. Even more importantly, since the master regarded theoretical analysis as a skeleton to be hidden in the closet, his principal followers lacked both the technical equipment and the intellectual motivation for theoretical model building. As a consequence, few of the analytical innovations of the model-building era originated in Cambridge. Leadership had passed elsewhere.

21
Knut Wicksell

MARXISTS have often denounced the body of "neoclassical" theory that emerged toward the end of the nineteenth century as being an ideology in defense of capitalism. This is psychologically understandable. Marginalist theory turned out to be superior analytically to the theory of Karl Marx, and Marxians, on average, are no better losers than other people. As a matter of historical fact, the accusation is unfounded. Marginalist economists ranged over the whole spectrum of social, political, and ideological views. In the case of John Bates Clark, there is some truth in the charge. Léon Walras was a land socialist. Vilfredo Pareto was full of aristocratic contempt for business. The Viennese were pillars of the (tottering) Hapsburg empire. Eugen Slutsky became a Soviet dignitary. Irving Fisher went from rags to riches and back to rags. The man who became the embodiment of "neoclassical" economics was the most passionately radical of them all, namely Knut Wicksell.

Life

Wicksell was born 1851 in Stockholm.[1] His father was a grocer, neither rich nor poor. His mother died young, and Knut grew up in the family of relatives. His talent was recognized early, he obtained a good high school education, and he went to Uppsala to study mathematics, but also Latin, literature, history, and philosophy.

As a university student, Wicksell passed through a spiritual crisis; deeply religious before, he became an atheist who wanted to improve the lot of mankind by rational means. He wrote poetry and also a play that had several performances. At the same time he suffered from depression, and his energy was weakened by self-doubt. He became a perennial student who was thirty-four years old before he obtained his license degree in mathematics.

During this difficult period he came across a book on neo-Malthusianism that made him a social radical. The condition of the working classes, he concluded, could only be improved by birth control. A lecture he gave on "the most important cause of social misery and its remedy, with special reference to drunkenness" produced a scandal. Overnight, Wicksell became famous, or perhaps, rather, notorious. From then on he was a virtually full-time lecturer on vice, prostitution, free love, birth control, women's rights, and similar provocative topics. Though he was at least as radical as any socialist, he was forever separated from the socialists by his Malthusian conviction that social reform would be ineffective without birth control.

Social reform forced Wicksell to acquaint himself with economics. He read the classical and modern economists, and he obtained a private scholarship for extensive studies in England, France, Germany, and Austria.

In 1889, Wicksell took a wife, but his moral principles, as he saw them, forbade him to have the union legally sanctioned. His family and his friends were shocked, of course, but the marriage, if it may be so called, was happy. The couple had two sons, and Wicksell's wife became, so to speak, his business manager, trying to keep the household afloat. Wicksell earned his income as a journalist, but his antimilitarist views combined with his advocacy of closer ties with Russia led to personal isolation.

At the age of thirty-eight, Wicksell seemed to have accomplished nothing. This was when he took up economics in earnest, mostly supported

---

1. This life sketch is based on the biography by Gardlund (1958) and Lindahl's introductory essay to Wicksell 1958.

by a private foundation. The 1890s were scientifically his most productive years. He passed his license examinations in economics and, shortly after, obtained a *doctor philosophiae* degree. It turned out, however, that the doctorate still did not open the door to an academic career. Wicksell had obtained his degrees in the Faculty of Philosophy, but economics belonged to the Faculty of Law, and neither faculty was willing to condone a blurring of academic demarcation lines. There was only one remedy—Wicksell had to study law, which took him just one and a half years. Now the door was open. In 1899, at the age of forty-eight, Wicksell finally became a lecturer in political economy and fiscal law in Uppsala. Two years later he was appointed to a professorship in Lund, where Gustav Cassel had been his rival for the post. The appointment of the dangerous radical created a public sensation—a concert was interrupted with the announcement.

The newly won security did not weaken Wicksell's radicalism, and he loved to provoke. Some rather tasteless remarks about the seduction of Mary by the Holy Ghost actually earned him a conviction for blasphemy, and he proudly spent two months in jail. Gradually, however, his publications on monetary theory made him more respectable, and by the time of World War I, Wicksell had become a recognized expert and adviser on monetary matters. After his retirement in 1916, the Wicksells lived outside Stockholm, in a small country house built with the help of their friends. This was the most peaceful and carefree period of his life. On a trip to London, financed by the Swedish Central Bank, he met young John Maynard Keynes, who seems to have treated him condescendingly, not realizing what he could have learned from him. The younger Swedish economists, however, gathered around him, thus forming the group that later became known as the Stockholm school. When Wicksell died in 1926, his funeral procession, with numerous banners (mostly red), resembled that of a statesman.

Works

Wicksell's first book on economic theory, published in 1893, was *Ueber Wert, Kapital und Rente nach den neueren nationalökonomischen Theorien* (On Value, Capital, and Rent in Recent Economic Theory; see Wicksell 1954). It provides an innovative and elegant synthesis of Walrasian general equilibrium theory with Austrian capital theory. The mathematical treatment got a cool reception, however, and Wicksell reported in a letter that the book was rejected as a doctoral dissertation. From the point of view of economic analysis, it was to remain Wicksell's best performance; it alone would put its author in the first rank of the economists of his day.

The second book, *Finanztheoretische Untersuchungen, nebst Darstellung und Kritik des Steuerwesens Schwedens* (1896) (Investigations in Financial Theory Including a Description and Critique of the Swedish Tax System), was intended to establish Wicksell's competence in public finance.

The first part on tax incidence also served as his doctoral dissertation. The partial equilibrium analysis falls short of Cournot and Dupuit, but the general equilibrium analysis breaks new ground. Like Ricardo's *Principles* it uses a highly aggregative model to determine the economic effects of taxation. It may be interpreted as a comparative-static application of the 1893 model to the problems of taxation.

In the second part, Wicksell develops the dual principle that each fiscal decision should (1) include both government expenditures and taxes, and (2) require near unanimity. From this point of view, it is the basic function of the parliamentary log-rolling process to combine benefits and burdens in such a way that an overwhelming majority can expect a net benefit. Before Pareto optimality had yet been invented as a general welfare concept, Wicksell, in substance, proposed it as a fundamental fiscal criterion. Though recognition came only long after his death, he thereby became one of the founders of modern fiscal theory and of the theory of political choice. He was careful, however, to exempt redistributive measures of social policy.

Wicksell's third book, *Interest and Prices* (1936), published in 1898, contributed the most to his international fame, partly because it discusses a topic of general interest in a provocative and innovative way, partly because its very lack of precision gave rise to so much discussion. Indeed, from an analytical point of view, it is the weakest of Wicksell's books. It is symptomatic that the argument, though coming from one of the foremost mathematical economists of the time, is presented in purely verbal terms, and it is not clear to the present day what exactly the words are supposed to mean. From the efforts to clarify Wicksell there emerged the Stockholm school of macrodynamics.

What we have of Wicksell's *Lectures* (1934–35), published in Swedish in 1901–6, is but the first part of a comprehensive treatise that was never completed. It is a shining example of the synthesis of old and new ideas, of microeconomics and macroeconomics, that could be achieved around the turn of the century. The *Lectures* are, much more than Marshall's *Principles,* the paradigm of marginalist economics at its best. It is perhaps the only book of that period that a good teacher could still use as an intermediate text today. Though the exposition is, for the most part, elementary, its lucidity and precision reveal the underlying analytical structure. While Marshall used words to camouflage his mathematics, Wicksell used the underlying mathematics to give clarity to his words. If Keynes had learnt his economics from Wicksell, the world might have been spared the "Keynesian revolution." Authoritative assessments of Wicksell's work may be found in Uhr 1951 and 1960, Frisch 1952, and Wicksell 1978.

Marginal Productivity Theory of Distribution

Wicksell's first important contribution concerned the marginal productivity theory of distribution. In substance, the fundamental principle had been fully developed by Johann Heinrich von Thünen. Stigler (1941), who mentions Thünen only in passing, thus conveys a misleading impression when he describes the last quarter of the nineteenth century as the formative period. By 1890 the principle had been widely used; it was in the air. To Wicksell, as Stigler rightly points out (Stigler 1941, 293), economic theory owes the first complete mathematical formulation of the marginal productivity theory of distribution (Wicksell 1954, 146–53).

Wicksell began by expressing the general principle in terms of a new concept, namely the production function with continuously variable factors:[2] "If the total output of production is interpreted as a real (continuous) function of the cooperating factors, . . . then efficiency clearly requires that each factor be used to such an extent that the loss of a small portion of it reduces the resulting output by just so much as the share of output going to that portion." In other words, the marginal product of each factor is made equal to its price (in real terms). The argument is then translated into mathematics in the form of the optimum condition "that the output shares of the various productive factors must be proportional to the partial derivatives of the said function with respect to the factor in question as a variable" (my translation from 1893 ed. [see Wicksell 1954], xiif.). Wicksell was justly proud of this elegant generalization of the marginal productivity principle, which he recognized as the true solution to the problem.

Wicksell went far beyond a mere condition for cost minimization by an individual producer. What he achieved was a general equilibrium theory of distribution that could dispense with Walras's fixed coefficients. To develop this theory, Wicksell used Eugen von Böhm-Bawerk's general equilibrium model, generalized by including land alongside labor and capital.[3] This was the first time the representative firm was modeled mathematically as choosing its factor combination so as to maximize profit for given factor prices, while factor prices were, in turn, determined to clear the factor markets. Stigler has shown admirably how in Wicksell's theory, since it is based on a linear-homogeneous production function, the three factor shares actually exhaust the product (Stigler 1941, 289f.). Wicksell did not seem aware, however, that exhaustion could be a problem. It became one only in the following year through Wicksteed's famous paper, discussed in the following section.

---

2. The earliest mathematical statement of marginal products in terms of the partial derivatives of a production function quoted by Stigler (1941, 321f.) was by Arthur Berry in 1890 (a summary of Berry's paper is reprinted in Baumol and Goldfeld 1968, ch. 29).
3. This means that capital is not treated symmetrically with land and labor but is a wage-plus-rent fund from which the other factors are paid during the production process.

Solving the Exhaustion Problem

The question was whether wages, rent, and interest, if each factor is paid according to its marginal product, exhaust the total product. John Bates Clark, who had independently discovered the marginal productivity principle, asserted that they do (1890, 1891). For the benefit of innumerable undergraduates, he also invented the suggestive pair of diagrams in which labor and capital each appear as receiving alternatively their marginal product or the residual (Clark 1899, ch. 13). His main argument was that any nonfactor income would tend to be washed away by competition. While this was plausible, it fell short of a proof.

A proof was supplied by Philip H. Wicksteed (1844–1927). He was a minister at a London Unitarian church. His broad interests led him, on the one hand, to Dante and the Middle Ages and, on the other hand, to economics. He was a highly successful university extension lecturer, but it is reported that he never quite understood why he had larger audiences on Dante than on economics. (After a day's hard work people probably find it more inspiring to contemplate the unlimited possibilities of the human spirit than the dismal limitations of economic means.) Over the years his theology became increasingly unorthodox until he finally retired from the ministry and earned a living as lecturer and writer.

As an economist, Wicksteed was a Jevonian. His *Alphabet of Economic Science* of 1888 (Wicksteed 1955) is remembered mainly because it introduced the term *marginal* into the language of economics. The "Essay on the Co-ordination of the Laws of Distribution" of 1894 (1932) provided the first rigorous solution to the exhaustion problem. Wicksteed's mathematics was cumbersome, but in substance, as A. W. Flux pointed out in his review, it amounted to an application of Euler's theorem on linear-homogeneous functions. The theorem says that if a function

$$y = f(x_1, x_2 \ldots x_n) \tag{21.1}$$

is homogeneous of degree one, then

$$y = f_1 x_1 + f_2 x_2 + \ldots + f_n x_n, \tag{21.2}$$

where f_i is the partial derivative with respect to x_i.

Wicksteed's brilliant contribution was not well received by the leading mathematical economists. Francis Ysidro Edgeworth objected that the world is not linear-homogeneous; Pareto (with Walras's fixed coefficients in mind) argued that production functions might not be smooth enough to have partial derivatives; and Walras fell back on Clark's zero-profit argument. Under the onslaught of criticism, Wicksteed, in the first volume of his *Common Sense of Political Economy* of 1910 (1933), withdrew his argument. In fact, however, the criticism was beside the point. The real problem was how zero-profit competition could be reconciled with the

´rising marginal cost curves that are necessary for a determinate firm size. This problem was solved by Wicksell in 1902 (1958, 121f.; restated in *Lectures*, vol. 1). He distinguished between the individual firm and the industry. Suppose individual firms have rising marginal costs and a U-shaped average cost curve. Suppose further that they are all identical. Perfect competition will thus see to it that all firms produce at the point of minimum average cost. But *at this point,* the average cost curve is horizontal, and marginal cost equals average cost. It follows that the factor shares behave *as if* the production functions were linear-homogeneous, which implies exhaustion of the product.

At the industry level, under perfect competition, output expands or contracts through the entry or exit of identical firms, each of which produces at the minimum cost point. As a consequence, the marginal cost curve for the industry is horizontal, even though it is rising for each firm. From nonhomogeneous production functions for the individual firms, one obtains a linear-homogeneous production function for the competitive industry.[4] This demonstration, which had eluded his contemporaries despite strenuous efforts, was probably Wicksell's most brilliant analytical achievement. It supplies the basic justification for the use of linear-homogeneous production functions at the aggregative level and reconciles perfect competition with determinate firm sizes.

The Capital Paradigm

Böhm-Bawerk in his capital theory had visualized labor inputs as being applied over a period of time, and in *Value, Capital, and Rent,* Wicksell had followed his example. In general, however, Böhm-Bawerk's average period of production (or any other single number) is not an adequate representation of the time profile of inputs. In his *Lectures,* therefore, Wicksell based his basic analysis on the point-input/point-output case, in which all inputs are applied at the beginning of the period and all output accrues at the end.[5] His paradigm is wine that improves by aging, but forestry could have served as well. At the same time the capital stock ceased to be a wage fund and became a stock of immature products. This led to a very instructive model, now, in contrast to that of Böhm-Bawerk, in terms of compound interest.

Wicksell realized clearly that the value of a given inventory of wine depends on the rate of interest. (Uhr [1951] later called the influence of the rate of interest on the value of given capital goods the Wicksell effect.) As a consequence, the value of the aggregate capital stock cannot be treated

---

4. Wicksell specified the Cobb-Douglas production function $q = a^{\alpha}b^{1-\alpha}$ as an example in his marginal productivity paper of 1900 (1958). He had used the same function in his *Finanztheoretische Untersuchungen* (Wicksell 1896, part 1, ch. 4, app.).

5. Wicksell subsequently considered more complicated cases, including, in a famous appendix, Gustav Åkerman's problem of capital goods of different durability.

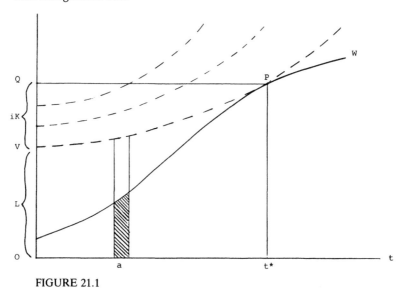

FIGURE 21.1

as if it were a physical quantity. In fact, there is, in general, no way to express the aggregate quantity of heterogeneous capital goods in a single number.

Suppose the market value of the grape juice, turning into wine of increasing quality, as a function of aging time is represented by the W curve in figure 21.1. The wine will be sold when its present value has reached a maximum. Future market values of equal present value are connected by the broken "isovalue" curves. For a given rate of interest they rise exponentially. The optimal selling time, t^*, is reached at the point P, where the W curve is tangent to an isovalue curve. At this point, the marginal product as a percentage of the market value is equal to the rate of interest.

Suppose the winery maintains a steady operation, in which each year new grape juice comes in and mature wine is sold. What is the value of the immature wine of different vintages stored in its cellars? If this inventory were marketed today, vintage a would have a price represented by the shaded bar. The value of the entire inventory would thus be represented by the area under the W curve. This, however, is not the true value of the inventory; it if were, the inventory could just as well be marketed at once. The inventory is held because the value of each vintage can be increased by not selling it at once, the present value of the future mature wine being higher than the market value of the present immature wine. The capital value of the inventory, therefore, is represented by the area under the isovalue curve through P. Interest on this capital is expressed by iK, the difference between the market value of mature wine and its present value at time zero. If perfect competition has washed away all profits, this present value, represented by L, will be paid to land and labor at harvest time.

All this relates to the representative firm, for which capital is variable and the interest rate is given. In the market as a whole, the capital stock is given and the interest rate is to be determined. The interest rate will rise if the demand for capital exceeds the available stock, and vice versa. With this elegant model, side-stepping any problems of capital measurement, Wicksell had constructed a highly efficient engine for the comparative-static analysis of factor prices and distributive shares. However, as Wicksell was well aware, the analysis was not complete, inasmuch as the capital stock was treated as given. To explain its size, one would have to supplement what was later called the missing equation, which, in one way or another, would presumably bring in time preference.

The Cumulative Process

Wicksell's most famous contribution is his theory of the cumulative process. He describes it as an extension, and perhaps even an alternative, to the quantity theory of money. This is not quite accurate. The quantity theory explains the level of prices for the case of an exogenous money supply with endogenous adjustment of interest rates. If this were what Wicksell had wanted to explain, he too would have used the quantity theory. He could not use it because he wanted to explain something different, namely the rate of change of prices for the case of an endogenous money supply with exogenous interest rates.

To make his basic model as simple as possible, he visualized a closed economy with inconvertible bank notes, in which banks set a lending rate and supply all money demanded at that rate. In such an "ideal" banking system, as Wicksell called it, each bank's liquidity loss is another bank's gain. If all banks move in step, therefore, there is no limit to monetary expansion or contraction.

Under these conditions, the banks can set the market rate of interest, i, at any level they wish. However, it is Wicksell's main point that there is only one rate, called the normal rate, r, that keeps prices stable. This normal rate is tightly related to the real return on capital goods, which Wicksell calls the natural rate. The two are not identical, though, because one applies to bank loans and the other to real capital goods, which have different risks. According to Wicksell's hypothesis the course of prices is governed by the difference $i - r$.

Wicksell's approach has a highly classical ancestry. Malthus explained the rate of population growth by the difference between the actual wage and the zero-growth wage. Ricardo explained capital accumulation by the difference between the actual profit rate and the zero-saving profit rate. Even the application to money was anticipated by Henry Thornton, though

Wicksell did not know this in 1898.[6] Moreover, this tradition continued unbroken throughout the nineteenth century. That bank rates may have a controlling influence on monetary expansion and contraction was an idea not easily forgotten in the age of bank panics. Wicksell thus achieved a new breakthrough along a classical path of analysis.

Wicksell presents his argument in the form of a rudimentary circular flow model with annual production periods. Firms borrow from banks at the market rate to pay for the factor services they buy from households. The households use this income to buy last year's output from the firms, and the firms deposit the money in the banks. This leads to the question of how this circular flow is affected by improved profit expectations of entrepreneurs. The discussion is entirely verbal and more intuitive than rigorous. The following summary (simplified from Niehans 1965) tries to condense the basic argument to the most compact form, though at the cost of introducing a mathematical formulation Wicksell did not use.

Resources are assumed to be fully employed; Wicksell's model concerns inflation and not business fluctuations. With constant real income, the rate of inflation equals the rate of expansion of nominal income,

$$\frac{\dot{p}}{p} = \frac{\dot{Y}}{Y}, \tag{21.3}$$

where dotted variables denote time derivatives.

For the future development of macroeconomics, the most significant feature of Wicksell's model is the division of total income into consumption and investment, which formalizes the long-familiar notion that these components might have different determinants:

$$Y = C + I. \tag{21.4}$$

The economy does not grow. In equilibrium, therefore, saving is zero. However, households spend their income with a lag (which later, in honor of Dennis Robertson, was christened the Robertson lag). As a consequence, the latest increase in income cannot be spent in the same period. This can be expressed by writing

$$C = Y - \dot{Y}. \tag{21.5}$$

It implies that the current increment in income is continuously saved. Since these savings are not desired by the households but imposed by the lagged adjustment, they were often called forced saving.[7]

---

6. This genealogy is traced in Hayek 1931a, but Hayek understates the continued presence of these ideas throughout the nineteenth century.

7. On the classical ancestry of this concept see Hayek 1932.

Investment by firms, as a proportion of income, is assumed to depend on the difference between the market rate and the normal rate of interest,

$$\frac{I}{Y} = F(i-r), \tag{21.6}$$

with $F(0) = 0$ and $F'(\ ) < 0$. If the market rate equals the normal rate, firms in a stationary economy are satisfied with their existing capital stock and thus plan no investment. If the market rate declines below this level, the prices of existing capital goods rise above their production costs, making the production of additional capital goods profitable. Wicksell thus uses basically the same investment theory as Walras.

Substituting equations 21.5, 21.4, and 21.6 into equation 21.3, one obtains

$$\frac{\dot{p}}{p} = \frac{Y-C}{Y} = \frac{I}{Y} = F(i-r). \tag{21.7}$$

This means that the rate of inflation must be such that the forced saving it elicits is continuously equal to the investment resulting from the interest differential.

Wicksell's main results follow immediately. At any level of the normal rate, there is only one level of the market rate that keeps prices stable. As long as the market rate stands below the normal rate, prices will continue to rise, and vice versa, until the difference is eliminated. Once it is eliminated, prices will remain at their highest (or lowest) level; the present price level thus appears as the legacy of past interest policies.

The crucial point is that with respect to the banks' lending rate, the economy is unstable. However, a constant market rate would not, in general, suffice to keep prices stable, because the natural rate is subject to constant fluctuations due to, for example, inventions, discoveries, or changes in expectations. This helps to explain why market rates that are high relative to their trend are often associated with rising prices; the real returns on capital may be still higher.

It is consistent with Wicksell's approach that money does not explicitly appear in this summary formulation. Since banks are assumed to use interest rates as their policy variable, the money supply adjusts passively to whatever households and firms demand in each phase of the process. Inflationary expectations, though they might easily be introduced, play no role in the basic process.

Wicksell did not argue that a cumulative process, once set off, would in fact continue forever. He recognized that, in reality, banking systems are not "ideal." Once banks have to worry about their liquidity and a loss of reserves, this would force them, sooner or later, to raise the market rate, thus bringing the process to a halt. Another stabilizer, mentioned by

Cassel, is the capacity effect of investment. As the new capital goods are added to the capital stock, the marginal productivity of capital gradually declines until the normal rate has reached the level of the market rate. Wicksell felt, though, that this might take a very long time indeed.

Wicksell refused to regard his cumulative process as a theory of the business cycle. Business cycles, he thought, were caused by "real" disturbances (such as innovations); monetary policy might possibly dampen them, but it did not produce them (Wicksell, 1953). At the level of economic substance, the cumulative process showed that the use of interest rates as a policy instrument might make the economy unstable; with the disappearance of the gold standard, this insight assumed fundamental importance. At the level of analytical techniques, the cumulative process is the first instance of an explicit (though sketchy) macrodynamic model based on the interaction of saving and investment.

Place in the History of Economics

To Wicksell notoriety came early, but fame came late. He was fifty when he finally became a professor, and he was near retirement when he became internationally prominent.

In retrospect, Wicksell appears as the personification of "neoclassical" economics. It is difficult to give this term any specific meaning, and it would have been better if it had never been invented. By and large, however, it seems to stand for the body of analysis into which Ricardian economics was transformed by the introduction of explicit optimizing techniques based on differentiable utility and production functions. Wicksell's *Lectures* are the representative statement of this body of analysis in verbal, nonmathematical terms.

Wicksell's most important analytical contributions to neoclassical economics were the completion of the marginal productivity approach to factor prices, the incorporation of capital as waiting time into this approach, and the outline of a macrodynamic model of money, interest, and prices.

Wicksell was an original theorist, but he was also an eclectic in the sense that he developed his own contributions out of the existing body of knowledge. His view of scientific progress was not one of "creative destruction" but rather one of a tree on which new branches grow out of the old trunk. It is the view of the true scholar. This is probably why Wicksell spoke with such contempt of the "Hegelian darkness" and "conceit" of Karl Marx (Wicksell 1954, 17). Indeed, marginalist economics sealed the scientific fate of Marxism; however, this was due not to ideological bias but simply to its manifest superiority. Even radicals would henceforth do best to use marginalist economics.

Yet Wicksell was not a school builder, not only because he arrived late on the academic scene but also because this was not his nature. Although he never taught in Stockholm, the progressive elaboration of his macroeconomic ideas by men such as Gunnar Myrdal, Bertil Ohlin, and Erik Lindahl later became the leitmotiv of the Stockholm school.

22
Vilfredo Pareto

As ECONOMICS, toward the end of the nineteenth century, became more professionalized, it also became gradually more specialized. Adam Smith's field of professional competence embraced the whole field of moral philosophy, including law, ethics, literature, history, and economics. John Stuart Mill was philosopher, logician, and political scientist more than an economist. William Stanley Jevons was not only a leading economist but also a leading logician. Then things changed. Léon Walras, Carl Menger, Eugen von Böhm-Bawerk, Knut Wichsell, and Alfred Marshall claimed to be nothing but economists. In the twentieth century, few of the leading economic theorists made major contributions in other fields except statistics. (John von Neumann is, of course, as shining exception.) In this evolution toward economic specialism, Vilfredo Pareto was the last polyhistor.

Life

Pareto was born in 1848 in Paris.[1] His father was an Italian marchese from near Genoa, who, as a follower of Mazzini, was in opposition to the House of Savoy and thus forced to live in exile. He was a civil engineer with a broad education and many-sided interests. Pareto's mother was French.

When Vilfredo (baptized Fritz Wilfried) was six, his father was amnestied, and the family returned to Italy. Vilfredo received a classical education but also learned mathematics. Like Francis Ysidro Edgeworth, he later felt equally at home in Greek literature and in calculus. He studied engineering in Turin, obtaining his doctorate with a dissertation on—what else could it be?—the elastic equilibrium of solid bodies.

Pareto first worked as a railroad engineer in Rome, then as a deputy director and later as director general of the Italian Ironworks in Florence. In 1882 he ran for parliament in Pistoia but was badly beaten. Intellectual superiority, he learnt, was not necessarily a political asset. In 1889, Pareto married Countess Dina Bakunin, apparently no relation of the princely revolutionary. Consistent with his Malthusian convictions, the couple had no children. In the following year, after financial reverses, Pareto was

1. The material for this life sketch is mostly from Bousquet 1928 and 1960, Busino 1987, Cirillo 1979, Eisermann 1987, and the article on Pareto by M. Allais in the *International Encyclopedia of the Social Sciences* (1968).

forced to resign his post. He retired to Fiesole, continuing for sometime as a consultant.

In his spare time and during hours of insomnia, Pareto had acquired an extensive knowledge of political economy and sociology. He also wrote numerous articles on political and social topics, mostly against the government. He was a passionate libertarian and freetrader, not out of sympathy for the capitalist entrepreneurs but out of aristocratic contempt for bourgeois democracy. He shared the view of Adam Smith that governments mostly exploit the public in favor of the strongest interests. The nobility (to which he belonged), the socialists, the clergy, democracy, and the masses were treated with equal disdain. At the same time, he was an ardent antimilitarist, a radical, and an atheist. These views did not endear this social misfit, as Cirillo (1979) has called him, to the government. A public lecture in Milan was interrupted by the police, and permission for a course on mathematical economics in Rome was denied.

At the age of forty-two, Pareto was frustrated; he did not seem to be getting anywhere and thought of emigrating. This was when he met Maffeo Pantaleoni, then Italy's most eminent economic theorist, and read his *Principles of Pure Economics*. This caused him to reread Walras, whose metaphysics had earlier repelled him, and he now discovered in Walras what he called the true gold of general equilibrium. He decided to devote his life entirely to science. The stage was set for the second act in Pareto's professional life.

Walras retired in 1892. Pantaleoni, in order to prevent this chair from falling into the hands of the "old school," proposed Pareto as his successor. But Pareto had hardly any scientific publications to his credit, he had never held an academic post, and the Lausanne authorities, understandably, hesitated. Finally the director of education and a law professor traveled to Fiesole to interview the candidate. He seemed acceptable, and Pareto was appointed in 1893, at first, like Walras before him, on a temporary basis.

Pareto seems to have been a successful teacher; he reported that he had more than fifty students in his class as compared with Walras's six. However, he regarded teaching (like a wife and children) as a drag on research. He also complained that the Lausanne library would buy only two or three economics books each year, provided they were not too expensive.

In 1898 the death of a rich uncle made Pareto a millionaire (in gold francs). Soon after, the marchesa, with thirty suitcases and the young cook, ran off to Russia. The marriage broke up, but Pareto had no legal means of obtaining a divorce. He soon retired to the tax haven of Céligny, near Geneva, where he led the life of a private scholar. At first he traveled to Lausanne for his classes, but in 1907 he finally resigned his chair. For some time he lived in splendor, with a retinue of servants. Later he became a misanthropic recluse, dwelling in disorder in his "Villa Angora" with up to twenty angora cats and a pretty French woman, Jeanne Regis, thirty-one years his junior. They had a daughter, never legitimized. Pareto had an immense erudition and a brilliant mind, but he was hypersensitive to criticism, intolerant of what he regarded as stupidity, and arrogant. There were few people he liked, and not even Walras was among them.

In Pareto's interests, sociology gradually pushed economics into the background. Though he was now internationally famous, mainly as a sociologist, Pareto withdrew more and more from the world. His political views changed. The former radical became a conservative, who regarded parliamentary democracy as decadent. The fascists falsely claimed him as one of their prophets, and Mussolini nominated him to the Senate, but Pareto never did anything in his support (Bucolo 1980). He was no longer politically active, and he still opposed military power. By that time he had lost most of his fortune in bad investments. When Fiume (with its Hungarian laws), after its "liberation" by D'Annunzio, briefly became an Italian Reno, Pareto finally obtained a divorce and married his consort. He died two months later, in 1923, at the age of seventy-five, his productivity long gone.

Works

Pareto was a compulsive writer, and his *Complete Works* are scheduled to fill thirty volumes (Pareto 1964–   ). His fame, however, rests on four books.

Pareto's early papers in economics began to appear in the *Giornale degli Economisti* in 1892. His first major work, based on his Lausanne lectures, was the *Cours d'économie politique,* which came out in two volumes in 1896 and 1897. Of the 755 pages, only the 75 pages of the first chapter are on economic theory. The chapter is essentially an excellent nontechnical introduction into Walrasian economics. It explains why Pareto had more students than Walras. Scientifically, the high point of the book is the chapter on income distribution in volume 2, where Pareto's law is presented in detail. The remainder of the book is remarkable mainly as a display of stupendous erudition reaching from antiquity to current affairs. What it has to say about the structure of society in general is more interesting than its economics.

Pareto's place in the history of economics is mainly determined by the *Manuel d'économie politique.* The Italian edition appeared in 1906, but for the famous appendix one has to go to the French edition of 1909. The exposition follows Marshall's precepts: In chapters 3–5 the theoretical structure is presented in verbal and graphical terms, and the mathematics is relegated to the appendix. To characterize the appendix, Pareto is best compared to the early Paul Samuelson: It was the *Foundations of Economic Analysis* for the beginning of the century. It should be noted, however, that in the *Manuel* pure economics is again presented within a broad social framework. After the *Manuel,* Pareto produced little original economics, though the essay "Economie mathématique" of 1911 (1964–   , vol. 8) (which is completely different from the German essay with a similar title of 1902) restates his approach in the most general terms.

Pareto's two books on economics have a counterpart in two treatises on sociology. In *Les systèmes socialistes,* first published in 1902–3 (Pareto 1964–   , vol. 5), socialist ideas and experiments from antiquity to the present are surveyed with the same impartial contempt with which Pareto treated all human affairs. The book shows an impressive breadth of knowledge, sparkling allusions, and acute criticism, but it is badly organized, rambling, and sometimes almost incoherent. The chapters on Johann Heinrich von Thünen and Karl Marx, for example, are far from conveying a clear picture of those authors' contributions. Of particular importance is the introduction, because it presents a concise early statement of the views for which Pareto later became famous as a sociologist.

The two volumes of the *Trattato di Sociologia generale* of 1916 (French trans. 1964–   , vol. 12), their title notwithstanding, are anything but a systematic sociological treatise. The title of the four-volume English translation, *The Mind and Society,* is more descriptive. At least to the nonsociologist, this work appears like the collected reflections of a brilliant cynic, often profound and sometimes chaotic, about the interactions between ideas, ideologies, and power. Though Pareto was anti-Marx, there is a considerable resemblance between the two. In its obituary, the socialist daily *Avanti,* as Bousquet (1928, 23) reports, could thus call Pareto the "bourgeois Karl Marx."

Pareto's Law of Income Distribution

The distribution of income was the central topic of Ricardian economics. It was interpreted in the sense of distribution between factors such as land, labor, and capital, which, in turn, determined the distribution between social classes such as landlords, workers, and entrepreneurs. The classical problem was the class distribution of income.

In the course of the nineteenth century, it became gradually clear that factor shares are not tightly related to social classes. The classical theory of distributive shares was transformed into the modern theory of factor prices. What emerged as the important social problem was the personal distribution of income, regardless of the type of factor it is derived from. The difference between the rich and the poor was seen to be more important, after all, than the difference between incomes from rent, wages, and interest.

Pareto's law of income distribution, first announced in 1895 and fully described in the *Cours* (1896), was a decisive step in this development. It was based on an extensive collection of income data from many countries. These data seemed to suggest, as one went up the income scale, that for every increase in income by 1 percent, the number of households receiving at least that income declined by about 1.5 percent. In logarithmic form, this observation is expressed by the formula

$$\log N = \log A - \alpha \log x, \tag{22.1}$$

where x = income; N = number of households with *at least* x of income; A = parameter expressing population size (number of households having income of at least $x = 1$); and α = the decisive parameter, about 1.5. This implies $dN/N = -1.5(dx/x)$, which was expressed verbally in the preceding sentence. Graphically, if the logarithm of the number of households at or above a given income is plotted against the logarithm of income, the resulting curve is close to a straight line, with about the same slope under widely different circumstances.

Pareto had recognized from the beginning that in this simple form the fit was far from perfect, particularly at the lower end of the income scale. He therefore tried several refinements, though without complete success. In the big debate about the "social question," his law played about the same role as Malthus's population law a century before: any social policies, it seemed to say, were bound to be ineffective in reducing poverty or the inequality of incomes as long as α could not be significantly modified.

Pareto felt strongly that such an empirical regularity was too extraordinary to be accidental. However, he did not offer an explanation; in contrast to the Malthusian principle, there was no theory behind it. Announced at a time when statisticians were increasingly interested in empirical distributions of this kind, Pareto's law gave a strong impulse to statistical and theoretical work on the personal distribution of income. In the course of time, other distributions (such as the log-normal distribution) seemed to be more easily explained in terms of causal factors, both stochastic and deterministic. Today, the view that economists should hunt for "great constants," though endorsed by Joseph Schumpeter (1949) and held by people like Nicholas Kaldor, is mostly regarded as naïve. Nevertheless, Pareto's law is still important as marking the beginning of modern research on the personal distribution of income.

Ordinal Utility

Every action of a man is the necessary product of his character and the motive that has arisen. If these are given, it follows inevitably.
—Arthur Schopenhauer, *On the Freedom of the Will*

Throughout the nineteenth century economists talked about utility as if it could be measured in a cardinal sense. It was evident that the units and the origin of the utility scale were arbitrary, but discussions of utility implied that it made sense to say, "There is a bigger difference in utility between an apple and a pear than between an orange and a plum." As it turned out, few substantive conclusions were really based on this notion; economic analysis proceeded, by and large, as if its validity did not matter.

Pareto now stated explicitly that, in fact, it does not matter. It is enough if utilities themselves can be ranked; it is not necessary to rank their differences. A purely ordinal measure of utility is enough for the purposes of price theory. All one needs is the shape of Edgeworth's indifference curves and the direction in which they increase; the utility levels they represent can be chosen arbitrarily. "The individual may disappear," Pareto said, "provided he leaves us that photograph of his tastes" (1909, 170). Earlier in the nineteenth century, Arthur Schopenhauer had written the sentence that stands at the head of this section. The similarity to Pareto's phrase is striking. It suggests that, in substance, Pareto's terse utility theory is close to the ponderous arguments by which Schopenhauer reconciled scientific determinism with freedom of the will.

As Pareto described it in the *Manuel,* utility indexes are determined by assigning numbers to commodity bundles in such a way that (1) indifferent bundles have the same numbers, and (2) if one of two bundles is preferred to the other, it has the higher number.[2] Once such numbers have been assigned, they may be transformed in an infinite variety of ways as long as their ranking is preserved. As Pareto described it (1909, 541f.), if $U = f(x_1 \ldots x_n)$ expresses the original ranking, one may derive from this utility function other functions

$$V = F(U), \tag{22.2}$$

whose specification is completely arbitrary provided $F'(U) > 0$. Marginal utility, even in the sterilized form of Pareto's marginal "ophelimity," was unnecessary; the ratios of marginal utilities were all that mattered.[3]

This was not really a revolutionary insight. Throughout the nineteenth century utility theory had gradually moved away from philosophical utilitarianism. The ordinal approach had been developed in all essential aspects by Irving Fisher more than a decade before the *Manuel.* Pareto's contribution consisted of its elaboration and elegant exposition. His lucid analysis finally cut the umbilical cord to cardinal utility. It is interesting to note, however, that even Pareto, like Fisher before him, thought it expositionally convenient to express himself verbally in terms of cardinal utility (Pareto 1909, 265f.).

2. In addition, Pareto had decided, even before he wrote the *Cours,* that it was better to replace the term *utility* by a word without any connotations whatsoever. Being a classical scholar, he invented ophelimity, precisely because to most people it meant nothing.
3. Pareto was fully aware that with three and more commodities the integration of their marginal rates of substitution may conceivably pose a problem.

Pareto Optimality

Early general equilibrium theorists wanted to show, above all, in what sense and in what circumstances free competition maximizes total welfare. However, if differences in utility cannot even be compared for the same individual, they can certainly not be compared between individuals. As a consequence, it is clearly impossible to say, for example, whether the farmers gain more welfare from a protective tariff than the consumers lose. The criterion of total welfare makes no sense.

Pareto, although in the Cours (1896–97, 2:47f.) he still admitted certain interpersonal comparisons, replaced total welfare by a much less demanding criterion. Welfare rises, he proposed to say, if some people gain and nobody loses. Welfare declines if some people lose and nobody gains. In the case of a hung jury, if some gain and some lose, there is no verdict (1909, 617f.). This criterion was later called Pareto superiority.

It is evidently desirable to exhaust all possible Pareto superior moves and thus to reach a state in which nobody can gain without somebody losing. Such a state came to be called Pareto optimal. Clearly, there are many such states, and there is no objective way to discriminate between them. In order to illustrate his concept, Pareto could have used the contract curve, invented by Edgeworth twenty-five years earlier, but he did not. Instead he invented the graph that was later called the Edgeworth box (Pareto 1909, 191, 355), though Edgeworth had never used it.

The concept of Pareto optimality was the scalpel by which problems of efficiency could be neatly separated from problems of equity. It thus became the foundation on which the edifice of the new welfare economics was erected in the 1930s. To the economic substance of welfare economics Pareto had little to contribute, but he raised the interesting question of how the ministry of production in a collectivist economy should plan production so as to reach Pareto optimality (1896–97, 2:90f.; 1909, 362f.). His reply was that in the absence of fixed costs, the planners could do no better than simulate free competition. In the presence of fixed costs, however, free competition would fail to secure a Pareto optimum, because in this case firms cannot sell at marginal cost and still cover total cost. Central planning, on the other hand, by using suitable taxes or price discrimination, may still be able to reach such an optimum (Pareto 1909, 363f., 622f.). This was not a new insight, Wilhelm Launhardt having published it long before, but only Hotelling (1938) would push this analysis further.

Comparative Statics of Demand

Walras had determined household demand for given prices and endowments by solving a mathematical problem of constrained optimization. He did not provide a mathematical analysis of the changes in demand that would be caused by changing prices. This step into comparative statics was taken by Pareto. For the first time, the slope of the demand curve was derived from the characteristics of the utility function. As Stigler (1965, 135) has pointed out, Pareto had been the first to show rigorously, in 1892, that diminishing marginal utility, in the case of independent utilities, implies a falling demand curve. In the *Cours* (Pareto 1896–97, 2:338) he conjectured that interdependent utilities might result in cases of rising demand curves. The *Manuel* (Pareto 1909, 579) provided the first mathematical analysis of the laws of demand for *n* goods.

Reducing the exposition to two goods, the Walrasian optimality conditions can be written as

$$\frac{U_x}{p_x} = m, \tag{22.3}$$

$$\frac{U_y}{p_y} = m, \tag{22.4}$$

$$p_x(x - x_0) + p_y(y - y_0) = 0, \tag{22.5}$$

where U_x, U_y = partial derivatives of the utility function $U = U(x, y)$; p_x, p_y = commodity prices; m = marginal utility of money (or income); x, y = quantities consumed; and x_0, y_0 = quantities in the endowment. Equations 22.3, 22.4, and 22.5 determine x, y, and m for given p_x and p_y.

Since Pareto's problem concerned the displacement of the equilibrium for a given change in p_x, he took the total differentials (treating p_y as constant):

$$U_{xx}\,dx + U_{xy}\,dy - p_x\,dm = m\,dp_x \tag{22.6}$$

$$U_{xy}\,dx + U_{yy}\,dy - p_y\,dm = 0 \tag{22.7}$$

$$-p_x\,dx - p_y\,dy \qquad = (x - x_0)\,dp_x. \tag{22.8}$$

The slope of the demand curve is determined by solving for dx in terms of dp_x. Pareto wrote this solution (1909, 581, eq. 75) in terms of determinants formed from the coefficients on the left-hand side. Concepts like the Hessian determinant

$$\begin{vmatrix} U_{xx} & U_{xy} \\ U_{xy} & U_{yy} \end{vmatrix}$$

thus made their first appearance on the stage of economic theory. In the notation used here, the solution reads

$$\frac{dx}{dp_x} = -\frac{(U_{yy}p_x - U_{xy}p_y)(x - x_0) - mp_y^2}{p_y^2 U_{xx} - 2p_x p_y\,U_{xy} + p_x^2 U_{yy}}. \tag{22.9}$$

U_{xx} and U_{yy} are clearly negative in view of diminishing marginal utility, but U_{xy} may have either sign. With convex indifference curves the denominator is negative, but the sign of the numerator remains ambiguous. Pareto concluded that for independent commodities, which means with $U_{xy}=0$, dx/dp_x is indeed negative for goods bought by the household (so that $x-x_0 > 0$). With interdependent commodities and $U_{xy} < 0$, however, the demand curve might well be rising. To Pareto it was not intuitively clear what the sign of dx/dp_x depended on. It remained for his far-away pupil, Eugen Slutsky, to carry the analysis farther.

Place in the History of Economics

Pareto was, first of all, a social philosopher with articulate opinions about virtually everything. Since sociology, at least in Pareto's time, seems to have consisted largely in the scholarly discussion of other people's views, this made him a great international success.

Though Pareto, like many other marginalists, had an astonishing command of facts, both historical and contemporaneous, he did not offer new insights into the working of the real economy. What he had to say on things such as money, interest, and business cycles was mediocre. Pareto's law on income distribution is the one shining exception.

In economic theory, Walras was much more original, creating from scratch the whole apparatus that Pareto then improved. Pareto's main contribution is the application of professional mathematics to the most basic problems of human choice, resource allocation and exchange. In this field, his contribution is one of the greatest ever made, setting the standard for decades.

This contribution was accessible only to few. Its absorption into mainstream economics took thirty years. Pareto the economist had indeed a number of followers, mainly in Italy. Schumpeter (1949, 153) seems to go too far, however, when he talks about a "school in the full sense of the word." Whatever semblance of a school there might have been, it was in any case not a Lausanne school, since Pareto had left Lausanne by that time and was no longer teaching regularly. His later successors in Walras's chair (after his immediate successor Pasquale Boninsegni) deserted the banner of mathematical economics, declaring that Walras's greatness as a social thinker was marred only by his mistaken use of mathematics.

23
Irving Fisher

In 1870 the United States still had no universities in the modern sense of the word. Graduates from American colleges had to go to Europe for their professional training, and many went to Germany. In economics there was a large, growing, and interesting literature, but still no contribution of the first order. John Bates Clark was the first American economist to acquire an international reputation. The first, however, to become one of the great economists was Irving Fisher. With his work on prices, capital, and interest, he still belongs to the marginalist era. His contributions to monetary macroeconomics, however, stand at the threshold of the era of economic models.

Life

Fisher was born in 1867 the son of a Protestant clergyman in Saugerties, New York.[1] He obtained a good high school education, but his father's death, when Irving was seventeen, confronted the family with a difficult situation. Nevertheless, Irving was sent to Yale. To make this possible, the family moved to New Haven, Connecticut; the mother worked for a dressmaker, the younger brother helped as a delivery boy, and Irving tutored. He also competed for prizes, and scholastic excellence became an important source of income. He was outstanding in mathematics, but he was also good in English, campus rhetorics, and rowing. After graduating first in his class, he stayed on at Yale for graduate work.

Gradually his interests shifted from pure mathematics to economics; while he saw the mathematician as isolated in his abstract thoughts, the economist, he thought, could be an active member of society. Accordingly, his dissertation of 1892 consisted in *Mathematical Investigations in the Theory of Value and Prices* (Fisher 1925). It was immediately acclaimed by the leading mathematical economists of the day. With one stroke, Irving Fisher had become one of them.

The promising young economist married the daughter of a wealthy industrialist. It was a happy marriage. One of the wedding presents from the bride's father was a year-long trip to Europe. It gave Fisher an opportunity to meet many prominent economists, and a little mountain lake in the Swiss Alps became to him what the legendary apple was supposed to be for Newton, namely the source of scientific inspiration: was not the stream like income, while the water in the lake was the capital stock? It was to take Fisher many years to transform this sudden vision into theory.

Another wedding present was a large house that Fisher's father-in-law had built for the couple in New Haven. Fisher began to teach economics at Yale. By 1898 he was a full professor. He seems to have been an excellent undergraduate teacher; however, he later trained few doctoral students but devoted his energy more to the public arena.

At about the time he became a professor, Fisher contracted tuberculosis of the lung. It seemed to be a virtually hopeless case, but after a long illness he recovered completely, though it was six years before he had fully regained his strength. This experience reinforced Fisher's early preoccupation with health, illness, and death. Unlike Walras, Jevons, and Marshall, he was not a hypochondriac, but he became a lifelong crusader for

---

1. This life sketch is based on I. N. Fisher 1956 and Miller 1967.

cornflakes, unrefined sugar, dark bread, vitamins, better mastication, and the like. He also founded a "Life Extension Institute" to popularize periodic physical examinations. He seemed to believe that every fad must be presumed beneficial until proven harmful. Among Yale students he was more ridiculed for his health lectures than admired for his economics.

Fisher was also an inventor. His inventions were not in high technology like those of Edison or Marconi, but rather of the better mousetrap type, including an improvement for rowboats, an oxygen tent for tuberculosis patients, an improvement in piano mechanics, a folding chair for sports events, a map projection, a sundial, and a thermostatic hospital bed. Only one of them was commercially successful, namely a visible card index system, patented in 1913. To exploit it, Fisher founded a firm, which eventually merged with a competitor, and out of this union emerged Remington Rand. During the 1920s, as Remington shares soared, Fisher, speculating heavily, became a multimillionaire.

As a speculator, Fisher displayed the same enthusiasm as in everything else. In the crash of 1929, Remington shares lost about half of their value, but Fisher regarded stocks as all the better bargains now and borrowed as much as he could to buy more. Shortly after, Remington shares were practically worthless; Fisher had to be supported by his family, and the big house was eventually sold to Yale University. Nevertheless, he still put every penny he could lay his hands on into new ventures, which made him an easy prey to fraud.

In the first half of his life, Fisher was primarily a theorist. However, at the age of thirty-seven he wrote to his wife that he wanted to be a *great* man (Fisher's emphasis) and that he wanted to be great by gaining "practically useful knowledge." This ambition made Fisher a crusader for good causes.

His earliest and most persistent crusade was for "stable money." He believed that fluctuations in the purchasing power of money were at the root of most macroeconomic problems, and that these could be eliminated by an appropriately managed currency. The idea of a "compensated dollar," in turn, led him to the problem of the appropriate construction of index numbers and thus into statistics. He was convinced that the progress of economic science required the combination of economic theory, mathematics, and statistics. As early as 1912, Fisher tried to organize a society for the advancement of this program, but the effort failed. A meeting with Ragnar Frisch and Charles F. Roos in New Haven in 1928 was more successful. Its result was the foundation of the Econometric Society in 1930, with Fisher as its first president.

Fisher also championed a large number of other causes, among them the League of Nations, calendar reform, spelling reform, Esperanto, environmental protection, public hygiene, and prohibition. To further their goals, he wrote about twenty books and gave innumerable lectures. He became indeed one of the famous Americans of the interwar period, who tried to gain politicians, presidents, and even Mussolini for his proposals. The catastrophe of his personal finances never weakened the conviction with which he gave advice on public finance. He died of cancer in 1947.

Works

Irving Fisher was a prolific writer, publishing dozens of books, sometimes at a rate of one a year.[2] Many are on noneconomic topics, such as the effect of diet on endurance, how to lengthen human life, eugenics, rules for healthful living, prohibition, and world peace. Others are indeed on economic topics but are more in the nature of popular tracts on booms and depressions, the stock market, and how to stabilize the value of the dollar. They are not devoid of interest. One of them, for example, coined the term *money illusion* for the failure to perceive that the dollar, or any other unit of money, expands or shrinks in value, or, in other words, for the belief that "a dollar is a dollar" (Fisher 1928). Another book advocated 100 percent reserves on bank deposits to stabilize the money supply (Fisher 1935). By and large, however, these tracts contributed little of lasting scientific value.

Fisher's fundamental contributions to economic science are found in three books, namely (1) the *Mathematical Investigations in the Theory of Value and Prices* (1925), (2) *The Rate of Interest* of 1907, which in the second edition, largely rewritten, became *The Theory of Interest* of 1930, and (3) *The Purchasing Power of Money* of 1911.

Around the major books are grouped some other publications that, though of minor weight, nevertheless made significant contributions. In the essay "Appreciation and Interest" (1896), Fisher took up the two topics that were to become the main themes of his scientific work. In *The Nature of Capital and Income* (Fisher 1906) the vision from the Swiss Alps had finally matured into a theoretical analysis of the accounting relationship between the flow of income and the stock of capital. In opposition to the view that regards capital as primary and its services as secondary, Fisher put the expected service flows in the primary position, and capital is just their present value. In his terminology, income consists of the actual service flows and does not include saving. In this respect, economic science did not follow his lead but generally preferred to define income as the flow of services that *could* be consumed without impairing capital. From his terminology Fisher (1937, 1942) derived the postulate that only consumption should be taxed, which made him, in effect, a champion of the expenditure tax.

---

2. For a bibliography see I. N. Fisher 1961. An excellent survey is the article by M. Allais on Irving Fisher in the *International Encyclopedia of the Social Sciences* (1968).

In the 1920s, Fisher's reputation was mainly based on his work on the quantity theory of money and his crusade for a stable managed currency. In *Stabilizing the Dollar* (Fisher 1920) he developed his "plan to stabilize the general price level without fixing individual prices" by appropriate changes in the gold content of the dollar. In *The Making of Index Numbers* (Fisher 1922), he proposed a number of criteria for a successful price index formula, the geometric mean of the Laspeyres and the Paasche index winning the highest marks as the "ideal index." It was later shown by Ragnar Frisch, however, that no formula can simultaneously pass all of Fisher's tests (see Samuelson 1966–86, vol. 3, ch. 184), and these tests were not systematically derived from the purpose of index numbers.

Fisher returned to microeconomics by suggesting a method for measuring the marginal utility of income (1927). Elaborating hints thrown out in the dissertation (Fisher 1925, 87), the method is based on the notion that all tastes are alike and that there exist some goods with independent utilities. The idea can be summarized by making the following assumptions: (1) there are 3 individuals, A, B, and C, with identical utility functions but different incomes; (2) there are two goods, x and y, whose utility depends only on their own quantity; (3) individuals A and B are confronted, say in country one, with the relative price $\pi_1 = p_{x1}/p_{y1}$, while C is observed say in country 2, in another price situation $\pi_2 = p_{x2}/p_{y2}$; (4) C is carefully selected in such a way that he consumes the same amount of x as A and the same amount of y as B.

Elementary utility theory tells us that the marginal utilities of income, μ_A, μ_B, and μ_C, are equal to the marginal utility of a commodity divided by its price,

$$\mu_A = \frac{U'(x_A)}{p_{x1}} \ , \ \mu_B = \frac{V'(y_B)}{p_{y1}} \ , \ \mu_C = \frac{U'(x_C)}{p_{x2}} = \frac{V'(y_C)}{p_{y2}} \ , \quad (23.1)$$

where $U'(x_A)$ is the marginal utility of x consumed by A, $V'(y_B)$ is the marginal utility of y consumed by B, and so on. The assumptions stipulate that $x_A = x_C$ and $y_B = y_C$. As a consequence of equal tastes and independent utilities, therefore, $U'(x_A) = U'(x_C)$ and $V'(y_B) = V'(y_C)$. It follows that

$$\frac{\mu_B}{\mu_A} = \frac{p_{x1}}{p_{y1}} \frac{V'(y_B)}{U'(x_A)} = \frac{p_{x1}}{p_{y1}} \frac{V'(y_C)}{U'(x_C)} = \frac{p_{x1}}{p_{y1}} \frac{p_{y2}}{p_{x2}} = \frac{\pi_1}{\pi_2}. \quad (23.2)$$

The ratio between the marginal utilities of income for A and B in country one can thus be read off the difference in relative prices in the two countries. This is certainly an ingenious idea, but in view of the stringency of the underlying assumptions, it is not surprising that, except for stimulating Ragnar Frisch, it did not look attractive to econometricians.

Interdependent Goods

In the introduction to his *Mathematical Investigations*, Fisher mentions not only William Stanley Jevons but also Rudolf Auspitz and Richard Lieben as the writers who influenced him most. Even if the *Researches on the Theory of Price* of Auspitz and Lieben had been read by nobody else, its formative influence on Fisher would make it one of the influential contributions to marginalist theory. When Fisher worked out his analysis, he did not yet know Walras and Edgeworth. As a consequence, he was subjectively original in certain respects in which he was actually anticipated by others. In particular, he provided the first explicit general equilibrium system in the English-language literature (not counting Marshall's rudimentary Note XXI). The present section focuses on what Fisher added to the existing literature.

Fisher, like Vilfredo Pareto after him, found it expositionally convenient to treat utility as if it were cardinal, measurable in units which he called "utils." At the same time, he may have been the first to make clear that this is not an essential assumption. All that matters, he pointed out, is the shape of the indifference curves and the direction in which utility increases. The numbering of the indifference curves is immaterial. Fisher was also the first to base utility theory on what later was called the preference axiom, according to which the individual can decide whether commodity bundle A is preferred to bundle B, whether B is preferred to A, or whether the two are indifferent. The credit for having developed the ordinal theory of utility thus belongs to Fisher. Pareto, more than a decade later, elaborated what Fisher had expressed in a few terse paragraphs.

The main contribution of the *Mathematical Investigations* is the careful analysis of goods that are interdependent in either consumption or production (or both). On the utility side, Fisher constructed indifference curves, as Edgeworth had done before him, for the general nonadditive utility function $U = U(x,y)$. Marginal utilities thus became first-order partial derivatives. Though Fisher, unlike Edgeworth, did not write second-order derivatives, his verbal explanation is equivalent to the statement that Gossen's first law relates to the negative sign of the direct second-order partial derivatives. Fisher's main attention is directed to the cross relations between interdependent goods. Edgeworth had been inclined to assume that the cross second-order partial derivatives of the utility function are inherently positive, which clearly precludes further analysis. Fisher now made it clear that an increase in the quantity of good A can either raise or lower the marginal utility of good B. In the first case, Fisher called the goods "completing," and in modern terminology they would be called complements. In the second case, Fisher called the goods "competing," and today they would be called substitutes.

Fisher also offered another criterion to distinguish between complements and substitutes, namely the curvature of the indifference curves. In the case of close substitutes, he argued, the curves would be almost straight lines. A small change in relative price would thus produce a large shift in relative quantities. In the case of complements, on the other hand, the indifference curves would be sharply bent, perhaps almost angular, and even a large change in relative price would produce only a small change in relative quantities.

Fisher presents the two criteria as if they were substantially equivalent. Had he written them out in terms of partial derivatives, he would probably have found out that they are very different. Both criteria can occasionally still be found in the literature, but both were soon found wanting. In particular, the signs of the second-order partial derivatives have meaning only for cardinal utility. The curvature of the indifference curves, on the other hand, cannot express the case in which a decline in the price of *A*, at a given utility level, raises the demand for *B*, which is a clear case of complementarity. The work of Eugen Slutsky later provided the analytical basis for the modern distinction between substitutes and complements in terms of the income-compensated cross price effects. It was Irving Fisher, however, who first drew attention to two types of interdependent goods in the theory of utility.

The indifference curves were confronted by Fisher with what he called an income line. It represents the combination of goods that can be bought with a given amount of money. For the first time there appears the familiar graph of the convex indifference curves intersected by the budget line, and for the first time a shift in the budget is seen to produce different reactions in "superior" and "inferior" goods.

On the production side, Fisher introduces the concept of production indifference curves or, in current terminology, production frontiers, connecting alternative output combinations that can be produced with the same inputs.[3] The individual, maximizing his sales proceeds for given inputs, will select the point at which the slope of this production frontier equals the price ratio. Fisher, in 1892, thus possessed all the elements of a general equilibrium system for interdependent goods. It is characteristic of the way his inventive mind worked that he also constructed an intricate hydraulic machine by which this system could be visualized.

Interest Parity and Expectations

In *Appreciation and Interest*, Fisher introduces the fundamental difference between expected and unexpected changes in the value of money. Expected changes are linked to interest rates through arbitrage. This link is based on the fact that the total yield on an asset consists of the interest

---

3. Haberler later used these production frontiers to generalize the theory of comparative cost (1930).

return and the expected capital gain. Arbitrage, therefore, will see to it that the difference in interest between two assets is exactly matched by the expected change in their relative price. This leads to the interest parity formula

$$\frac{1+j}{1+i} = 1+a, \tag{23.3}$$

where j and i, respectively, are the interest rates on assets 2 and 1, and a is the expected appreciation of asset 1 relative to asset 2. It is misleading, therefore, to speak of *the* rate of interest. In fact, each asset has its own interest rate depending on the expected future course of its price.

Fisher concludes that expected changes in the purchasing power of money have no real effects on trade because they are neutralized by interest adjustments. In particular, they do not give rise to booms and depressions. This is consistent with the observation that a growing scarcity of gold, contrary to widespread expectations, did not result in high interest rates; in fact, since it led to falling prices, it tended to result in low interest rates. Fisher also observed that the adjustment of interest rates to price changes is incomplete, particularly in the short run. He concluded that changes in the purchasing power of money are often unexpected in the short run. Expectations adapt to experience, but with a lag. With this idea, Fisher became the pioneer of the statistical analysis of distributed lags, more fully elaborated later in the *Theory of Interest* (1930, 416f.).

His particular conjecture was that borrowers, since they are firms, tend to have better foresight than lenders, which are mostly households. As a consequence, the transition to inflation stimulates investment and trade, and the transition to deflation is depressive. If lenders had better foresight than borrowers, Fisher argued, an outburst of inflation would be depressive.

Today, Fisher's empirical work on inflation and interest rates looks, of course, primitive, and business fluctuations are not generally attributed to systematic differences in expectations formation between firms and households. However, his analysis of the relationship between inflation, interest rates, and expectations broke ground for a field of research that has lost nothing of its fertility ninety years later; it still looks strikingly modern.

The Rate of Interest

The general nature of Fisher's interest theory is well described by the complete title of its final version *The Theory of Interest as Determined by Impatience to Spend Income and Opportunity to Invest It.* Fisher dedicated his book to the memory of John Rae and Eugen von Böhm-Bawerk. This is an apt dedication. Rae had correctly described the interplay of time preference and production possibilities, but he had overlooked what Böhm-

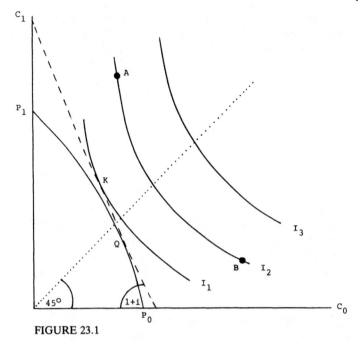

FIGURE 23.1

Bawerk later called the first factor, namely the relationship between present and future income, and his analytical equipment was primitive. Böhm-Bawerk had correctly, but crudely, described each of the three factors that determine the rate of interest, but he was inferior to Rae inasmuch as his general equilibrium model, suprisingly, made no use of time preference but instead assumed a given capital stock. Fisher completed the analysis by expressing the interplay of the three factors in terms of a modern general equilibrium framework. Eighty years later, his solution may still be called definitive.

In the two-period case, time preference can be described by the shape of indifference curves for present consumption, C_0, and future consumption, C_1, as drawn in figure 23.1. The slope of these curves, reflecting the marginal rate of intertemporal substitution, measures the (gross) rate of time preference. It shows at what rate the individual is willing to trade future consumption for present consumption. This rate depends on two sets of circumstances. In part, it depends on the available amounts of present and future goods. Clearly, if future income is expected to be much higher than present income (as at point A), the individual will be willing to give up a larger quantity of C_1 for a given increment in C_0 than if future income is expected to be relatively low (as at point B). This is Böhm-Bawerk's first factor.

In addition, there may be a "pure" or "net" time preference. It is graphically illustrated by the fact that along the dotted 45° line, with equal amounts of present and future goods, the individual still gives up more than one unit of C_1 for an additional unit of C_0. More generally it is reflected in the fact that the indifference curves are asymmetrical with respect to the 45° line. A larger quantity today and a smaller quantity tomorrow is preferred to the smaller quantity today and the larger tomorrow.

The other blade of the scissors is the production frontier, now interpreted in an intertemporal sense. Suppose Robinson Crusoe has corn from the present harvest in the amount P_0. He can eat it all, but then he will have no seed corn and thus no harvest next year. If he did not consume anything, keeping all for seed, he would have a much larger harvest, P_1, next year, but in the meantime he would have nothing to eat. The opportunity frontier P_0–P_1 connects the intermediate possibilities between these extremes. Diminishing returns tend to make the curve concave, but usually the marginal bushel of seed corn will more than just reproduce itself. This is Fisher's reformulation of Böhm-Bawerk's superior productivity of roundabout methods of production.

If Robinson Crusoe were isolated, he would choose the point at which the production frontier is tangent to an indifference curve. The common slope of the two curves would then be the rate of interest. This formulation makes clear what Rae already seems to have known, namely that Crusoe, to make a wise decision, does not need to measure the capital stock. The marginal rate of transformation of present corn into future corn (or present labor into future labor, and so on) is enough. To be sure, once the decision is made, the value of the capital stock can always be calculated by discounting future goods at the rate of interest, but capitalist production does not require a measurement of a physical capital stock or of a period of production. In this respect, Fisher in 1907 was at the level of Robert Solow in 1963, and the intervening discussions about the perplexities of capital measurement were obsolete before they had started.

In a market economy each Robinson Crusoe would come to the credit market on the neighboring island with his own indifference curves and production frontier. If the Walrasian auctioneer announced interest rate i, the individual of figure 23.1 would decide to produce at Q and to consume at K, lending the difference. His optimal investment plan would be independent of his subjective time preference, and it would be based on the maximization of the present value of future net returns. Other individuals might turn out to be borrowers. The announced interest rate would then have to be raised or lowered until aggregate lending equals aggregate borrowing. By extending the analysis to many periods, Fisher thus arrives at a Walrasian general equilibrium model of a multiperiod economy that explains the course of consumption, production, investment, credit, and interest in the course of time.

In pure logic it is easy, as Fisher shows, to construct situations in which the rate of interest is zero or even negative, but the asymmetry of both the indifference curves and the production frontiers will almost invariably give rise to a positive rate of interest even under stationary conditions. Joseph Schumpeter, too, had thus been made obsolete even before his famous thesis about the zero rate of interest had seen the light of day.

The Quantity Theory of Money

The *Purchasing Power of Money* contains little that is really novel, but it became the authoritative modern restatement of the classical tradition about the quantity theory of money. As a basis for his theory of the price level, Fisher constructed an accounting framework, called the equation of exchange. A very similar equation had earlier been used by Simon Newcomb (1886, 326f.), to whom Fisher referred. Its ancestry is traced to the eighteenth century in Marget (1938, 10f.). The equation is derived by writing the aggregate value of annual expenditure, E, in two different ways, namely (1) as the product of the quantity of money, M, and the value of expenditure per unit of money, $V = E/M$; and (2) as the product of a price index number, P, and the value of expenditure deflated by that index number, $T = E/P$. The equation of exchange can then be written $MV = PT$, where V is the velocity of circulation of money and T is the real volume of trade. In addition, Fisher distinguishes between coins and bank notes, each with their own velocity. Too much significance has often been read into the fact that Fisher wrote his equation in terms of velocity, whereas the Marshallians used the cash ratio $k = 1/V$; in substance, the two are clearly equivalent. It is slightly more relevant that Fisher wrote his equation in terms of transactions, whereas others, including the Marshallians, preferred to write it in terms of income; but since money, in equilibrium, affects neither magnitude, the difference is one of convenience rather than of principle.

Fisher emphasized that the equation of exchange has no causal content. Causal content is injected by two propositions:
1. The velocity of circulation is independent of the quantity of money.
2. The volume of trade is, except during transition periods, independent of the quantity of money.

As a consequence, any change in the quantity of money must be reflected in a proportionate change in the price level. Fisher recognized explicitly that V and T are not constant. In fact, he was emphatic in describing their historical variability. The quantity theory, therefore, does not relate to the proportionality of money and prices in the course of time. It rather relates to the *partial* effect of money on prices, to which the parallel effects of coincidental changes in V and/or T would have to be added.

Fisher derived the quantity theory for a gold standard world. At the same time, his brilliant analysis of the money supply both for monometallic and bimetallic currencies drew attention to the fact that the supply of commodity money cannot be exogenously varied, being determined endogenously by the gold content of the coins, the demand for nonmonetary gold, and production conditions in gold mining. It is not possible, therefore, to vary the money supply without also varying production conditions in gold mining and/or consumption of nonmonetary gold, which are "real" factors affecting T and possibly V. This potential source of error, already analyzed by Walras, was recognized by Fisher, but he regarded it as too small statistically to be significant. With a fiat money, this qualification loses its force anyhow.

The quantity theory was meant to apply in the long run only. The short-run deviations, again in the classical tradition, were regarded by Fisher as the principal source of booms and depressions. These deviations were supposed to occur, as was explained above in "Interest Parity and Expectations," mainly because interest rates, in view of the lagged adjustment of expectations, are less flexible than prices. An expansion of the money supply thus tends to result in an expansion of credit and in an investment boom, and a contraction of the money supply, because interest rates do not decline rapidly enough, produces depression. This is in striking contrast to the Keynesian and post-Keynesian view that business fluctuations are essentially due to the rigidity of prices and wages.

Place in the History of Economics

Fisher's contributions, almost incredibly, span the whole period between Jevons and Samuelson. In his *Mathematical Investigations* he provided the key concepts for the general equilibrium analysis of interdependent goods before Wicksell and Pareto had even begun to publish on economic theory. His analysis of interest, inflation, and expectations became the starting point for all modern work on expectations, both theoretical and empirical. His interest theory not only brought half a century of discussion to a successful conclusion, but it also foreshadowed, as Samuelson has observed, Hicks's intertemporal general equilibrium model and contained all the analytical elements of Meade's international trade "butterfly." Fisher's reformulation of the quantity theory of money, finally, has successfully survived seventy-five years of monetary debate without a need for major revision; its analytical content is accepted today by economists of all persuasions, and in the present world of fiat money it is actually more relevant than it was in Fisher's gold standard world.

Unlike Gossen, Jevons, Walras, Pareto, or Schumpeter, Irving Fisher was not an economic philosopher trying to conceptualize the scientific laws of social action. After beginning with the solution of purely intellectual problems, his ambition soon turned to practical, and practicable, improvements; at times he seemed closer to a peddler of patent medicines than to a scientist. If Fisher had resisted the temptation to strive for "practically useful knowledge," he might perhaps have been a Ricardo, Walras, or Samuelson. On the other hand, it was precisely this quest for useful knowledge that helped him to shape his contributions in the form of finished analytical building blocks that could readily be incorporated into the structure of economic theory.

Schumpeter predicted that Irving Fisher would stand in history as the United States' greatest scientific economist. Decades later, this prediction looks valid, provided it is restricted to the period before World War II. Others may occasionally have had more profound or more stimulating ideas, but if achievement is measured in terms of classic contributions to modern economics, Fisher ranks first.

24

Exchange and Prices

As a part of their wide-ranging work on economic theory, most of the authors considered in the preceding chapters made major contributions to the theory of exchange and price. Important additional contributions, more narrowly focused on exchange and price, are reviewed in the present chapter.

There is a widespread notion that marginalism concentrated its attention on pure competition until the 1930s brought the "imperfect competition revolution." Historical reality was different. It is true that Johann Heinrich von Thünen, Hermann Heinrich Gossen, Stanley Jevons, and Léon Walras, though recognizing market imperfections, found it convenient to focus on competitive equilibrium with parametric prices. Others, however, such as Augustin Cournot and Carl Menger, regarded imperfect markets as the general case, from which they worked their way toward the limit of competitive equilibrium. Alfred Marshall, in this respect, was closer to Menger than to Walras. As a matter of fact, between 1880 and 1930 the bulk of contributions to the analysis of prices and exchange concerned imperfect competition. Early in this period, Francis Ysidro Edgeworth and Wilhelm Launhardt made brilliant contributions to the theory of oligopoly. At the end of the period, Edward Chamberlin and Joan Robinson, far from initiating a new era, finally (and belatedly) caught up with Cournot. In between, Rudolf Auspitz and Richard Lieben provided a comprehensive analysis of demand and supply, and Eugen Slutsky later laid the foundation for the modern theory of demand.

Francis Ysidro Edgeworth

Among Victorian economists, Edgeworth was the great eccentric. Where others searched for rules, he found exceptions. Where others strove to be definitive, he was happy to remain tentative. Where others wrote for the "intelligent layman," he discouraged even the experts with his expository idiosyncrasies. And yet he made some of the most fundamental contributions to the understanding of exchange.

Francis Ysidro Edgeworth was born in the country house of Edgeworthtown, Ireland, in 1845.[1] His father was the descendant of an old English family, originally from what is now the London suburb of Edgeware, that had settled in Ireland under Elizabeth I. His mother was a beautiful Spanish refugee, whom his father had met in the British Museum and married three weeks later. The father died before the boy, his fifth and last son, was two years old. Francis grew up in a family with many literary connections and accomplishments. Taught by private tutors, he acquired an extensive classical education, learning Greek, Latin, French, German, Spanish, and Italian.

At the age of seventeen, Edgeworth entered Trinity College, Dublin, where he excelled in the classics. In 1867 he went to Oxford, where he graduated two years later in the humanities (the degree was awarded in 1873). He first embarked, halfheartedly, on a career as a barrister, but at the same time he began an autodidactic study of mathematics, taught Greek and philosophy, and became interested in ethics. In 1880 he finally obtained a regular post as a lecturer on logic in King's College, London.

Shortly before, around 1879, Jevons had aroused Edgeworth's interest in economics and also directed him to Marshall. The two became the revered father figures in his professional life. From economics, Edgeworth branched out into statistics. By 1888 his numerous publications had earned him a professorship at King's College, and in 1891 he was appointed Drummond Professor of Political Economy at All Souls College, Oxford. From 1891 to his death he was editor, joint editor (with Keynes) or chairman of the editorial board of the *Economic Journal*. He retired from his chair in 1922 and he died in 1926.

Edgeworth never married; the obligations of a household would have appeared to him too heavy a burden. He was a kind, unassuming, unworldly, and hard-working scholar with a good sense of humor. He had a brilliant, independent, and original mind, but he was also diffident and loved to defer to authority.

Edgeworth published three slender books. *New and Old Methods of Ethics* (1877) applied differential calculus, including some of the first Lagrange multipliers in economics, to the utilitarian problem of allocating given resources to individuals in such a way that the sum of individual pleasures is maximized. Based on Weber, Fechner, and others, marginal pleasure is assumed to be diminishing, and the interpersonal additivity of

---

1. For his biography the reader is referred to Keynes 1971– , vol. 10, Stigler 1978, Creedy 1986 and, particularly, Newman 1987.

utilities is taken for granted.[2] *Mathematical Psychics* (1881), Edgeworth's main contribution to economics, marks the transition from ethics to exchange. *Metretike, or the Method of Measuring Probability and Utility* (1887) seems to be passed over in silence even by Edgeworth's most ardent admirers.

The major part of Edgeworth's publications consists of numerous articles in journals and in Palgrave's *Dictionary of Political Economy*. In the later 1880s most of his energies seem to have been devoted to probability and statistics. They made him one of the leaders in that field.[3] Of particular interest to economists were the extensive contributions on index numbers and the "mathematical theory of banking" of 1888. In the latter paper an inventory model, the first of its kind, is used to explain a bank's demand for reserves in terms of stochastic deposit losses. With his proposition that "probability is the foundation of banking," Edgeworth had planted the tree of modern banking theory, but more than seventy years elapsed before it began to bear fruit.

Edgeworth's more important papers on economics, including many reviews, were later collected in three volumes (1925).[4] One of the principal subjects is monopoly and price discrimination. Edgeworth showed, among many other things, that in the case of interdependent supply and demand, a tax on a monopolized article might conceivably lower the prices of both goods, but it remained for Harold Hotelling to elucidate the paradox. In the analysis of oligopoly, Edgeworth emphasized the indeterminacy of price as long as the oligopolists' expectations about their mutual reactions are not specified. The proposed modification of Cournot's duopoly model, however, mainly serves to illustrate why Edgeworth's tortuous, if ingenious, reasoning yielded so few definitive contributions. In surveying international trade theory, he paid particular attention to the optimal tariffs resulting from the exploitation of monopoly power. Edgeworth was far from being a defender of laissez faire. He was interested in taxation and market indeterminacy precisely because they seemed to assign an important role to authorities acting in the name of utilitarian principles.

Overall, these economic papers display an extensive mastery of the literature in several languages, they are replete with brilliant and original insights, and they often undertake to provide mathematical proofs where others were content with plausible arguments. The analytical substance of the papers, however, became gradually less weighty. They often read like tentative ruminations on other people's writings. Promising ideas are sel-

2. For a loving review see Newman 1987.
3. For a detailed account and assessment of Edgeworth's statistical work see Stigler 1978.
4. A short survey is provided in Creedy 1986.

dom pursued to definitive conclusions. Their style, with its mixture of mathematics and poetry, has a unique charm, but it makes reading difficult and the meaning often obscure.

Edgeworth's main claim to fame as an economic theorist is his theory of exchange, developed on forty pages of *Mathematical Psychics*. The general intention of the treatise is expressed in its subtitle, *An Essay on the Application of Mathematics to the Moral Sciences*. In particular, Edgeworth wanted to demonstrate that mathematical reasoning can be fruitfully applied to utility even though there are no numerical data corresponding to the mathematical symbols. In fact, this proposition was neither new nor highly controversial. Edgeworth's contribution consisted in the specific pieces of analysis he developed to prove his point.

Two important contributions concerned utility. Edgeworth was the first to express an individual's utility as a joint function of the quantities of all goods consumed, which for two goods reduces to $U = U(x,y)$. He actually expressed utility as a function of the quantity of x bought and the quantity of y sold. In diagrammatic terms this means that he took the endowment point E in figure 24.1 as the origin of his quantity axes. However, once the endowment is specified, the transformation to the utility functions of Irving Fisher and Vilfredo Pareto is straightforward.[5] Edgeworth was also the first to represent preferences by contour lines, for which he introduced the term *indifference curves*. It is true that he regarded utility as cardinally measurable, but his theory of exchange remains valid for purely ordinal utility. By an irony of intellectual history, the ardent utilitarian thus became the pathfinder of ordinalism.

Edgeworth assumed indifference curves to be convex to the origin. For their convexity he already derived the condition that later became familiar in the form

$$U_y^2 U_{xx} - 2U_x U_y U_{xy} + U_x^2 U_{yy} < 0,$$

where U_i and U_{ij} are, respectively, the first-order and second-order partial derivatives of the utility function. He assumed not only that U_{xx} and U_{yy}, in view of diminishing marginal utility, are negative, but also (though with some diffidence) that U_{xy} is inherently positive. As a consequence, indifference curves appeared as unambiguously convex. The lack of a closer analysis of U_{xy} not only precluded a more rigorous analysis of convexity but also prevented Edgeworth from exploring the relationships between substitutes and complements. A few years later, this analytical gap was filled by Auspitz and Lieben and by Irving Fisher.

Edgeworth made his most fundamental and original contribution in the analysis of exchange. He followed Marshall's example of juxtaposing

---

5. That the marginal utility of a good may vary with the quantity of other goods had already been made clear in Edgeworth's first book (1877).

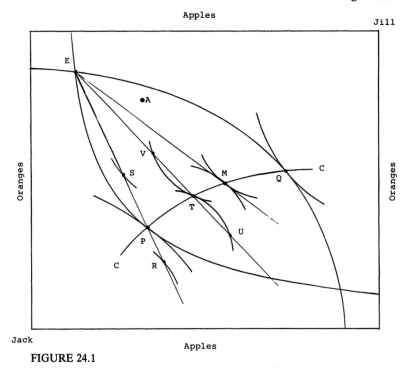

FIGURE 24.1

the offer curves for two representative traders (say, Jack and Jill) for two goods (say, apples and oranges) with inverted axes. He went beyond Marshall by going back to individual preferences. For the first time, market exchange was thus explicitly derived from indifference curves (in Walras the same derivation is, of course, implicit). The resulting apparatus was, in substance, the so-called Edgeworth box, but it had to wait for Pareto to be given the familiar boxlike shape. The following exposition will be based on the box diagram, though Edgeworth used only a segment of it.

In figure 24.1, Jack's and Jill's indifference curves have their origins in, respectively, the southwest and the northeast corner. The dimensions of the box represent the available totals of apples and oranges, and the endowment point *E* indicates the allocation before trade. Every other point describes a potential contract. At *A*, for example, Jack obtains apples from Jill in the amount of the horizontal distance between *A* and *E* by giving up oranges in the amount of the vertical distance.

As a fundamental concept, Edgeworth introduced the contract curve, defined as the set of all those allocations of goods to individuals that cannot be improved for any individual without making it worse for at least one other individual. These are the allocations that were later called Pareto optimal, but the concept was created by Edgeworth. In the Edgeworth box, the contract curve connects all those points in which the indifference curves of the two individuals are tangent to each other. In figure 24.1 it is represented by the *CC* curve.

Edgeworth pointed out that a free bargaining process will always lead to some point on the contract curve; at any other point, both parties could be made better off by renegotiation. He also pointed out that, for each trader, this point must be at least as good as the no-trade point *E*. No contracts will thus be concluded outside the lens-shaped area enclosed by the two indifference curves through *E*. Given *E*, contracts are thus restricted to the portion on the contract curve between *P* and *Q*. Edgeworth called it the available portion, and in the era of game theory, it became known as the core.[6]

The question is at which point in the core the negotiating process will finally settle. It was well known in Edgeworth's time that exchange between single traders is, to some extent, indeterminate, whereas exchange between numerous buyers and sellers in a competitive market is determinate. Walras had visualized this market equilibrium to be established through *tâtonnement* by an imaginary auctioneer announcing successive sets of prices until the market clears. Edgeworth, following Cournot's lead, proposed to begin with bilateral monopoly and work his way toward perfect competition. This was his famous "recontracting" process.

Suppose the market initially consists of just one Jack and one Jill. The outcome, as was explained above, will then be indeterminate between *P* and *Q*. Edgeworth now introduces another pair of traders, identical with the first. In this case a contract at *P* cannot be final, because one of the Jills could offer the two Jacks the trade represented by *R*, which would leave each of the two Jacks with the quantities represented by the midpoint *S*. All three would be better off than at *P*, and the other Jill would be left in the cold at *E*. Edgeworth points out that the Jacks' indifference curve at *S* has the same slope as Jill's indifference curve at *R*. If it were otherwise, the three could find a Pareto superior allocation, to use the later term, among themselves.

Of course, the excluded Jill would not accept her fate lying down but would offer the Jacks a still better trade than *S* by underbidding her competitor. This recontracting process can be repeated until point *T* on the contract curve is reached. One of the Jills would still be ready to trade quantities as high as *U*, by which each Jack would obtain *V*, but the result would be no better, for either party, than *T*. With two traders on each side, the recontracting process, beginning in the southwest portion of the core, would thus stop at *T*. If the initial contract had instead been at *Q*,

---

6. The term *core* was first used in 1953 by Gillies and Shapley. The relationship to Edgeworth's work was later established by Martin Shubik (see Shubik 1982, 175, 379).

a similar recontracting process would have shifted it to the southwest, one of the Jacks constantly underbidding the other.

With just two pairs of traders, there will still be a margin of indeterminacy along the contract curve. But suppose a third pair is added. This gives scope for further underbidding by two Jills (or Jacks) against one, which would narrow the margin. More generally, the market may be assumed to consist of two groups of traders, each including an arbitrary number of identical individuals. For a relative price selected at random, the quantities offered and demanded by one group generally exceed the quantities demanded and offered by the other. Within the group with the larger quantities, a subgroup can then form a coalition in such a way that the other group obtains exactly what it wants while all members of the coalition satisfy their own desires. Equality of demand and supply will thus be achieved by excluding some agents from trade. The excluded members then have an incentive to salvage a part of their trading gains by offering the other side more attractive terms. At these revised terms another round of recontracting will take place, and so on, until the whole potential for profitable coalitions is exhausted.

With numerous traders this process will lead to point M, representing perfect competition. At this point, the quantities offered and demanded by each group coincide. It is not possible, therefore, to satisfy one group by excluding some members of the other group. Edgeworth's recontracting process thus leads to the same market equilibrium as Walras's *tâtonnement*, but the imaginary auctioneer is replaced by an imaginary game of continuous reversal of alliances.

It would not do justice to Edgeworth's contribution, however, to regard it just as an alternative rationalization of perfect competition. His primary interest was not in the limiting case of perfect competition but in the indeterminacy of imperfect competition, in monopoly, oligopoly, coalitions, cooperation, and arbitration. This is entirely consistent with his utilitarian point of view. Precisely because the "economic calculus" of individual optimization does not fully determine the outcome, a "utilitarian calculus" is needed to "split the difference" so as to maximize social utility. The whole second part of *Mathematical Psychics*, therefore, is devoted, in an economic application of his earlier principles, to this utilitarian calculus. Whoever had absorbed Edgeworth's message of 1881 needed no imperfect competition revolution in 1933.

Early in the twentieth century, Edgeworth was not only one of the eminent statisticians but also one of the eminent economists of his time. The success of his contributions was very unequal, however. Utility functions, indifference curves, and contract curves became firmly embedded in the masonry of economic theory. The theory of recontracting, on the other hand, found virtually no response until it was revived in the context of modern game theory and general equilibrium analysis. Not even Edgeworth's heroes, Jevons and Marshall, understood what he was driving at, as their reviews showed. One reason for this neglect was certainly that after the first sketch of 1881, Edgeworth made no further effort to develop his theory. In addition, his approach required concepts that were far ahead of contemporary economics and mathematics. Still another reason is the resistance of these concepts to aggregation. Even in what is called microeconomics, economists are seldom interested in individual decisions, but rather in aggregates such as industries and social groups. Walras's *tâtonnement* approach was well suited to this aggregative orientation, but Edgeworth's recontracting approach was not. A century after *Mathematical Psychics*, Edgeworth's theory of exchange still has not fully realized its potential as seen by its admirers.

Rudolf Auspitz and Richard Lieben

At the time when Menger squandered his energies in the *Methodenstreit*, there were in Vienna two cousins who succeeded where Menger had failed, namely in providing the theory of price with an analytical apparatus. Though never members of the Austrian school, they made the only Austrian contribution to mathematical economics and one of the outstanding contributions in the last two decades of the nineteenth century.

Rudolf Auspitz, born in 1837 in Vienna, grew up in a well-educated Jewish family and studied mathematics and physics, but without acquiring a degree.[7] At the age of twenty-six, apparently with some reluctance, he became a businessman and founded one of the first sugar refineries of the Austrian Empire. As a lifelong opponent of cartels, he was said to have donated the extra profits he obtained from the sugar cartel to the employees' pension fund. A successful liberal politician, Auspitz was a member of the Moravian diet 1871–1900 and of the Austrian lower chamber 1873–90 and 1892–1905, where he acquired a reputation and influence as a financial expert. He seems to have been a man of quiet energy and balanced judgment, untiring but of frail health. In some respects his life reminds one of David Ricardo's. He died in Vienna in 1906.

Richard Lieben was also born in Vienna, in 1842. After studying mathematics and engineering sciences, he became a banker and a respected member of the Viennese business community. In 1892 he advocated the adoption of a gold standard. He married late and had no children. He seems to have been of scholarly and artistic tastes, more contemplative than active. He died in Vienna in 1919. As a correspondent for the *Economic Journal*, he provided a lucid summary of his and his cousin's views on consumer's rent (1894).

7. For biographical material the reader is referred to Weinberger 1931 and 1935 and Winter 1927.

Auspitz's first wife was Lieben's sister, but their marriage was dissolved after twenty years because of the wife's insanity, whereupon Auspitz married his children's governess. The two cousins were also linked as partners in the family bank, Lieben and Company, which after their death became Auspitz, Lieben and Company. For economists they are most closely linked by the fact that all of their significant work was done jointly. Nothing seems to be known about their relative contributions, but a few independent papers by Lieben suggest that he was more than a junior partner.

The reputation of Auspitz and Lieben is based on one book, entitled (in translation) *Researches on the Theory of Price* (1889). When it came out after ten years of work, it was the most comprehensive partial equilibrium analysis of price ever published, based on an ingenious geometrical apparatus.[8] The preface shows that the authors knew and understood most of the leading mathematical economists, including Thünen, Cournot, Gossen, Jevons, Walras, and Launhardt, but they did not know Marshall's privately printed paper of 1879, nor is Edgeworth mentioned.

The subject of the analysis is the exchange of one good against money, usually on the explicit assumption of a constant marginal utility of money. It is based on two fundamental concepts. Aggregate satisfaction is defined as the maximum amount of money buyers are willing to pay for a given quantity of the good rather than go without. If the quantity is denoted X, it can be expressed as a function $U = f(X)$ with $f'(X) \gtreqqless 0$ and $f''(X) < 0$. In figure 24.2 it is represented by the solid curve that first rises to a maximum and then declines. In Marshallian terms aggregate satisfaction corresponds to the area below the demand curve. In terms of Edgeworth's apparatus, the curve of aggregate satisfaction corresponds to the indifference curve through the endowment point. Aggregate cost, on the other hand, is the minimum amount for which producers are willing to supply a given quantity rather than close down. It is expressed in a cost function $C = F(X)$ with $F'(X) > 0$ and $F''(X) > 0$, represented in figure 24.2 by a solid curve with increasing slope.

For any given price, consumers maximize their net satisfaction by buying the quantity for which the derivative of aggregate satisfaction is equal to the price, $p = f'(X)$. Their outlay, called demand, is then given by $D = Xf'(X)$. The corresponding demand curve is depicted as a bow-shaped broken curve. Profit-maximizing suppliers similarly extend production to the point where the derivative of cost equals the market price, $p = F'(X)$. Their aggregate revenue, called supply, is $S = XF'(X)$, and the supply curve is the rising broken curve in figure 24.2. What Auspitz and Lieben call demand and supply curves are, in Marshallian terminology, offer curves

8. The fundamental first chapter, providing the basic tools, was preprinted in 1887 to establish the authors' priority relative to Böhm-Bawerk.

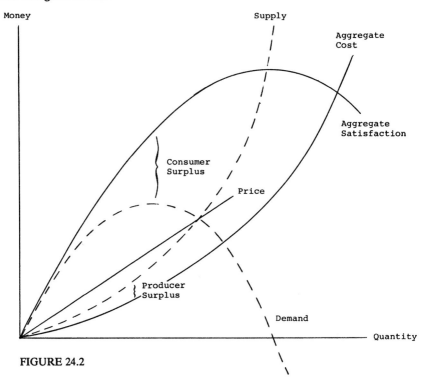

FIGURE 24.2

for one good against money. Under pure competition, market price is such that demand equals supply; the two broken curves intersect, and $f'(X) = F'(X)$.

Consumer and producer benefits (later called surpluses) can be directly read off the graph; this is the principal virtue of this apparatus. Consumer surplus is simply the excess of aggregate satisfaction over outlay, $f(X) - Xf'(X)$, measured by the vertical distance between the two consumer curves. Producer surplus, on the other hand, is the excess of aggregate revenue over aggregate cost, $XF'(X) - F(X)$, represented by the vertical distance between the two producer curves. Total social benefit is expressed by the vertical distance between the aggregate satisfaction curve and the aggregate cost curve, $f(X) - F(X)$. It reaches its maximum where $f'(X) = F'(X)$, which is the same condition as for market equilibrium. Pure competition maximizes social benefit.

The same apparatus is used for monopoly. The profit-seeking monopolist maximizes the vertical distance between the demand curve and the aggregate cost curve. As a consequence, the quantity will fall short of the optimum, and so does social benefit. As Auspitz and Lieben express it, "the exploitation of monopoly imposes on the consumers a disadvantage, which necessarily exceeds the advantages of the monopolist, because at the same time the social advantage declines from its maximum" (1889, 363, my translation). The monopolist clearly equalizes marginal revenue and marginal cost, though the terms are not used (405). The authors show carefully how the underlying curves for individuals can be aggregated to give market curves. Demand is classified on the basis of whether total outlay is rising, roughly constant, or declining as quantity increases. No concept resembling elasticity is used, however, nor is there an explicit theory of consumer preferences or of production.

Over more than five hundred pages, this apparatus is applied to a wide range of microeconomic problems and cases, including interrelated markets, substitutes and complements, indivisibilities, disutility, technical progress, inventories, speculation, security markets, foreign exchange, forward markets, options, and cartels. Among many notable pieces of analysis, one finds the argument that speculation is socially beneficial if it is profitable and also a derivation of long-run curves as envelopes of short-run curves which was not surpassed until Roy Harrod and Jacob Viner. An important final chapter extends the monopoly analysis to excise taxes and international trade, including a brilliant discussion of optimal tariffs (which, though Auspitz and Lieben did not recommend such tariffs, disturbed freetrader Pareto; see *Giornale Degli Economisti* 1892). Four appendixes present the main argument in terms of univariate differential calculus, concluding with an extension to general equilibrium. In contrast to Launhardt, who, as an engineer, loved to compute numerical results for special functional forms, Auspitz and Lieben emphasize the logic of the problem.

Auspitz and Lieben, though highly regarded by their peers such as Edgeworth, Pareto, and Fisher, never got the credit they deserved. In their local environment, in view of the Austrian school's intolerance for mathematics, they were academic outcasts. This is illustrated by Menger's critical review (*Wiener Zeitung*, 8 March 1889, quoted in Weinberger 1931) and by Auspitz's exchange with Eugen von Böhm-Bawerk of 1894, which also shows Auspitz's clear analytical superiority. More importantly, Auspitz and Lieben, cut off from direct scholarly intercourse, were prisoners of their idiosyncrasy and never developed the knack for felicitous terminology and expository devices that in economics is so important for academic success. Most importantly, it also turned out that for partial analysis Cournot's price/quantity diagram, the Marshallian cross, is often more illuminating than the reciprocal demand curves. Nevertheless, Auspitz and Lieben were not without influence, for Irving Fisher, in the preface to his *Mathematical Investigations*, mentions the *Untersuchungen* and Jevons's *Theory of Political Economy* as the two books that influenced him most. This is no mean link to the mainstream of economic theory.

Despite their gentle, scholarly personalities, Auspitz and Lieben also managed to stir up a controversy with Walras (Walras 1965). Already in 1887, Launhardt had warned Walras of the "plagiarism" of those "insolent Jewish pirates." The preface to the *Untersuchungen*, while revealing Launhardt's diatribes as entirely unfounded, added a more substantive irritant by arguing that (1) Walras's simultaneous demand curves were not correctly constructed inasmuch as the curve for one good presupposes a given price for the other; and (2) there cannot be multiple equilibria. This criticism stung Walras all the more since Edgeworth, in his presidential address to section F of the British Association in 1889, described Auspitz and Lieben as more accurate than Walras (an unwarranted observation, deleted in *Papers Relating to Political Economy*). Walras tried to mobilize Pareto and Bortkiewicz in his defense (without success) and began to polemize against those who "make bad theory in mathematical language." His own reply, however, (reprinted in the fourth edition of *Eléments*) missed the essential point and only added to the confusion. Knut Wicksell, as usual, got things right (1954). Auspitz and Lieben had overlooked the fact that Walras's curves, in effect, related to the demand and supply of one good in terms of the other, and the impossibility of multiple equilibria depended on the constancy of the marginal utility of money. After Auspitz's death, Lieben (1908) graciously acknowledged their error (to which Walras, ungraciously, replied that the point was not important after all).

Wilhelm Launhardt

At the time when original economic research was largely still done by amateurs, Germany was the country of origin of some of the most fundamental contributions to the theory of individual optimization. Johann Heinrich von Thünen and Hermann Heinrich Gossen join Augustin Cournot and Jules Dupuit in making early marginalism a French and German preserve. In the second half of the marginalist era, when economic theory became professionalized, this was different. In fact, in the last three decades of the nineteenth century, there was only one significant German contribution to economic theory. Its author was Carl Friedrich Wilhelm Launhardt. In the economic analysis of transportation and location, his contribution was not surpassed until the 1930s. In the theory of prices his work ranks with that of Auspitz and Lieben as the leading German-language achievement of the nineteenth century, far surpassing anything the Viennese school produced in this field. Nevertheless, Launhardt's work, available only in German and some of it hard to find, still has not received the recognition it deserves.

Launhardt was born in 1832 in Hannover. Like Dupuit, he began his professional life as a civil engineer, working for the public road administration. In 1869 he joined the faculty of the Hannover Polytechnic Institute as a professor for roads, railways, and bridges. This was the beginning of a distinguished academic career in the course of which he served as the director of the institute and, when it became the Technische Hochschule Hannover, as its first rector. He was made a member of the Königliche Akademie des Bauwesens and of the Prussian Herrenhaus. Dresden gave him an honorary degree for his contributions to the technology and economics of transportation. He died in Hannover in 1918.

Practical problems of highway planning led Launhardt to the progressively more general analysis of efficient transportation networks, later systematized in *Theorie des Trassirens* (Theory of Network Planning, 1887–88). The contributions to economics are found in part 1, entitled *Commercial Network Planning* and originally published in 1872. It begins with a discussion of investment criteria. From a social point of view, networks should be planned in such a way that the sum of operating and capital costs is a minimum. Private capitalists, however, try to maximize the internal rate of return on their capital. Under perfect competition the two criteria would coincide, since the internal rate of return, if duly maximized, would equal the market rate of interest. In reality, however, since the railroad industry is inherently noncompetitive, rates of return can be pushed above market rates of interest by keeping railroad investment below the social optimum. This was one of Launhardt's basic arguments for government ownership of railroads. For his own analysis he uses, of course, the social criterion.

Using geometry and calculus, Launhardt derived rules, depending on freight costs and volumes, for the optimal direction and density of highways connecting given market centers. Applying his analysis of network nodes to the location of plants, he produced the first substantial theory of industrial location (Launhardt 1882). In this basic contribution he determines the efficient location of a plant with given sources of supplies and given sales outlets by minimizing transportation costs. The optimum is found by an ingenious geometrical construction that became known as the pole principle, later amplified by Tord Palander. It is given a mechanical interpretation as the center of gravity of forces, representing freight rates, acting at the different input and output locations. The analysis is far superior to that in Alfred Weber's later book on the location of industries, in which Launhardt is not mentioned and whose only claim to attention is the appendix by Georg Pick.

Launhardt's main claim to a prominent place in the history of economic analysis is his slender treatise *Mathematische Begründung der Volkswirtschaftslehre* (Mathematical Foundations of Economics) of 1885. It was written in the light of Walras's *Mathematische Theorie der Preisbestimmung der wirtschaftlichen Güter* (1881) and the second edition of Jevons's *Theory of Political Economy*. At the same time, it is clearly pre-Marshall and pre-Edgeworth (though *Mathematical Psychics* had appeared in 1881). Two other books by Walras, sent by the author, arrived too late to be of use, nor was Launhardt acquainted with Cournot at that time. He reports that the copy he finally obtained from a library had apparently never been read, and Gossen could nowhere be found (because virtually no copies had been sold). Launhardt shows what a competent engineer with an economic turn of mind and a little calculus could do in economics a hundred years ago (and also what he could not do). Launhardt's addiction to special functional forms, particularly quadratic utility functions, often results in spurious precision, limited generality, and reduced lucidity, but the basic contributions are sound, important, and original.

In his theory of exchange (1885, part 1), Launhardt rightly criticizes Walras for believing (if taken literally) that there is no way for a trader to improve his position relative to free competition at uniform prices. His counterexamples relate to monopoly and price discrimination and lead him to the idea of an optimal tariff. Though valid in principle, this analysis falls short of Edgeworth's. The discussion of the total gain from trade and its distribution, whose shortcomings were pointed out by Wicksell, was soon obsolete because of its dependence on the interpersonal additivity of utility.

In his discussion of distributive shares, Launhardt recognizes the backward-bending supply curve of labor and the effect of property incomes on labor supply and thus on wages. He also recognizes that the interoccupational mobility of labor tends to equalize relative wage rates with both the ratios of the marginal products of labor and (to the extent an individual can choose between occupations) the ratio of its marginal disutilities. For profits, Launhardt's "basic equation" expresses, substantially, the familiar optimality condition that the profit margin, as a percentage of price, is the inverse of the elasticity of demand (though this concept is not used, of course). It is clearly explained that the entrepreneur, in setting his price, considers only marginal costs, while prices are equalized to the average costs of the marginal firm by exit and entry. The profits of intramarginal firms are correctly interpreted as rents, and the same principle is used to explain wage differentials.

Launhardt's theory of interest is Jevonian in spirit. Though brief and somewhat sketchy, it anticipates all the basic elements of Fisher's theory. In many respects, Launhardt achieves more in twenty pages than Böhm-Bawerk in about five hundred. In modern terminology, the rate of interest is explained by the interplay between a psychological preference for present consumption, modified by variations in expected income, and the marginal productivity of capital (Launhardt 1885, ch. 24). Saving is interpreted as a sacrifice of current consumption for the sake of an infinite stream of additions to future consumption. It is shown mathematically that with a rising rate of interest, given the rate of time preference, saving first rises to a maximum and then declines, because at high interest rates small savings are enough to buy a lot of future income. According to the "basic principle of accumulation," the present value of the future marginal utility of income is made equal to the current marginal utility of income. In the course of time, optimal saving, if initially positive, will decline until a steady state is reached (ch. 15). Investments will be made up to the point where the marginal saving in operating costs is equal to the rate of interest.

The subject of part 3, the most original of the book, is the relationship between location and price. Launhardt starts out by determining production and prices of a single seller supplying an unlimited market of uniform density. Delivered prices are seen to rise toward the periphery in the shape of a hollow cone, later known as the Launhardt funnel (1885, ch. 27). If sellers of differentiated products compete in a uniformly populated plain, their market areas are shown to be polygons whose sides, depending on circumstances, are pieces of ellipses, hyperbolas, or straight lines. In this context there emerges what Palander later called the Launhardt-Hotelling solution for heterogeneous duopoly. It is Launhardt's most brilliant contribution.

Suppose a stretch of highway, Q miles long, requires one unit of gravel per mile. There are two suppliers, A and B, one at each end. A supplies q_1 units at a constant unit cost of k_1 and with transportation costs of t_1 per unit-mile. He decides on his profit-maximizing producer price, p_1, on the assumption that his rival's price, p_2, is given. The same applies, with exchanged subscripts, for B. Cournot's model of the two mineral springs is thus modified to allow for (spatial) product differentiation.

Each firm knows that it can sell more at a lower price. The watershed between the two markets is at the point where the delivered prices are equal,

$$p_1 + t_1 q_1 = p_2 + t_2 q_2, \tag{24.1}$$

with $q_1 + q_2 = Q$. A can thus determine his own quantity in terms of both prices as

$$q_1 = \frac{p_2 - p_1 + t_2 Q}{t_1 + t_2}. \tag{24.2}$$

While q_1 is seen to be negatively related to p_1, it is positively related to p_2.

A's profit is equal to the profit margin multiplied by quantity, namely

$$\pi_1 = (p_1 - k_1) \frac{p_2 - p_1 + t_2 Q}{t_1 + t_2}. \tag{24.3}$$

The dependence of A's profit on both prices is depicted in figure 24.3 by the isoprofit curve I_1. A higher p_2 is always profitable for A, but an increase in his own price will first raise profits and then reduce them. Other isoprofit curves could be drawn for other profit levels.

For given p_2, A maximizes his profit at the price

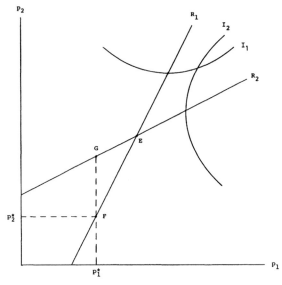

FIGURE 24.3

$$p_1 = \frac{1}{2}(k_1 + p_2 + t_2 Q). \tag{24.4}$$

The optimal level of p_1 associated with different values of p_2 is represented in figure 24.3 by the reaction line R_1. It connects all points at which A's isoprofit curves are horizontal. The same calculus, with sides reversed, is applied by B. It results in isoprofit curves illustrated by I_2 and a reaction line R_2.

If, at the moment, B's price is at, say, P_2^*, A will choose P_1^*. At F, however, B finds that he can raise his profit by moving to G, and so on. The only point at which neither duopolist finds it advantageous to change his price is E. This is the Launhardt-Hotelling duopoly solution. It is the exact counterpart for heterogeneous duopoly to Cournot's solution for homogeneous duopoly.[9] It anticipated in all essentials the solution that helped to make Hotelling famous forty-four years later (Hotelling 1929). Wilhelm Launhardt's duopoly theory, however, was completely forgotten for half a century; neither Harold Hotelling nor even Heinrich von Stackelberg was aware of it.

9. In Launhardt's solution each duopolist considers his rival as the price leader while he himself acts as a satellite. Clearly, one must be wrong, but at E both have reason to believe that they are right. Asymmetric duopoly with a leader and a satellite was later analyzed by Heinrich von Stackelberg (1934).

The same type of analysis that Launhardt developed for homogeneous products in different locations is then applied to differentiated products in the same location, resulting in ring-shaped market areas depending on transportation costs (Launhardt 1885, ch. 29). From the market areas of given suppliers, Launhardt shifts his attention to the supplying areas of given markets, which brings rent to the foreground. His description of the product rings surrounding a single market city in an unlimited plain (Launhardt 1885, ch. 30) adds nothing to Thünen. The analysis is then extended to a number of markets, each with its limited supplying area. If identical cities are located in a pattern of regular triangles, the supplying areas are, of course, hexagonal. While this foreshadows August Lösch's later work, Launhardt's triangular pattern is based on intuition and not on explicit optimality conditions. Launhardt, shows, however, how the mutual limitation of adjoining supplying areas raises rent and product prices (1885, ch. 31).

Launhardt's contribution to the theory of railway rates is mainly found in chapter 32. He establishes the principle that the maximization of social welfare requires—in modern terminology—marginal cost pricing. But this, in turn, requires competition, while profit maximization by monopolistic railway firms implies that rates exceed marginal cost. In particular, if a railroad transports homogeneous goods from a uniform plain to a market center, the monopoly price is calculated to exceed marginal cost by 50 percent (because, in modern terminology, freight volume reacts to the freight rate with an elasticity of -2, and ton-miles thus react with an elasticity of -3). As a consequence, the freight volume is suboptimal. By perfect discrimination according to "what the traffic will bear" over each distance, both railroad profits and general welfare can be increased compared to simple monopoly. This, however, is only a second-best solution. For Launhardt, the efficiency of marginal cost pricing is another basic argument for government ownership.

Launhardt's monetary theory is far inferior to his microeconomics. Its centerpiece is the rejection of the quantity theory of money. In part, this is based, in the tradition of Nassau Senior and the banking school, on the argument that under a gold standard an increase in the quantity of paper money just leads to a (external and/or internal) gold drain, while commodity prices remain tied to international prices or, in a closed economy, the gold price. To this extent Launhardt is on firm ground. He went much farther, however. In the theory of relative prices, he had assumed that the marginal utility of money is constant. When first introduced, this was an innocuous simplification, but in the theory of money it became the source of fatal confusion, for it induced Launhardt to treat money incomes, which he chose as the proximate determinant of absolute prices, as if they were "real" variables, independent of the money supply. After that, one is hardly surprised to read that higher interest rates result in higher prices and that gold discoveries have no influence on prices. The basic argument is found in *Mathematische Begründung* (1885); elaborations in later publications add historical illustrations and applications.

Eugen Slutsky

Irving Fisher had visualized a consumer's optimization problem in the form of convex indifference curves intersected by a budget line. With a change in price, the budget line would rotate around one of its end points; the points of its tangency with the indifference curves would then trace out the reaction of demand to price. Pareto had succeeded in expressing the effect of price on demand mathematically in terms of the parameters of the utility function. He showed that for independent goods the effect must be negative, resulting in a falling demand curve. For interdependent goods, however, this was not certain. Apparently, an increase in price might raise demand.

The comparative statics of the consumer budget was also investigated mathematically by William E. Johnson (1858–1931). He was a Cambridge mathematician who, rather late in life, became a distinguished logician. R. B. Braithwaite said of Johnson's students that they "were infected with his exacting subordination of originality to clarity and truth" (*Dictionary of National Biography*, 1931). Johnson's paper "The Pure Theory of Utility Curves" (1913) was subjectively a remarkable achievement. Its objective contribution was much impaired because Johnson did not seem to know Fisher and Pareto but quoted only Edgeworth. As a consequence, the paper did not contain much that was really new. Johnson recognized, as had Edgeworth before him, that for a utility function, $U = U(x, y)$, convexity of the indifference curves requires

$$- U_y^2 U_{xx} + 2 U_x U_y U_{xy} - U_x^2 U_{yy} > 0,$$

where U_i and U_{ij} are, respectively, the first and second partial derivatives. He also recognized that this condition does not rule out rising demand curves and falling Engel curves, but this is about as far as he got, and others had been there before.[10]

In the comparative statics of consumer demand, it was Eugen Slutsky who took the decisive step beyond Pareto. In comparison to Johnson's, his contribution shines all the more brightly. Slutsky was born in 1880, the son of a Russian schoolteacher.[11] He went to the University of Kiev to

10. Johnson's graphs depicting the influence of price and income changes on demand look as if they were taken from a modern microeconomics text, but they were already used, somewhat less elegantly drawn, by Irving Fisher (1925). Johnson's most interesting result related to the theory of production. The ratio of average cost to marginal cost, he found, is equal to the elasticity of output with respect to a uniform change in the scale of all factor inputs.
11. The biographical data are from the article on Slutsky by A. A. Konüs in the *International Encyclopedia of the Social Sciences* (1968) and from Allen 1950.

study mathematics but was expelled and conscripted into the army because of participation in a student revolt. He was soon able to return to the university, but in 1902 he was expelled a second time and excluded from study in any Russian university. He went abroad to study engineering at the Munich Institute of Technology. After the revolution of 1905 he returned to Russia, and he obtained a law degree in Kiev in 1911, with a gold medal.

Teaching law to engineering students, Slutsky became interested in political economy. This led to the famous paper of 1915 on the consumer's budget, which he submitted to the *Giornale Degli Economisti* (Slutsky 1952). In 1918 he obtained a degree in political economy from the University of Moscow. At the same time he became a professor at the Kiev Institute of Commerce, where he had taught before.

In 1926, Slutsky joined the Institute for Business Cycle Research in Moscow, and from 1931 to 1934 he worked in the Central Institute of Meteorology. While the director of the Moscow Business Cycle Institute, Nicolai Kondratieff, another Russian economist of international reputation, became a victim of Stalin's purges, Slutsky emerged as a dignitary of the academic establishment. In 1934 he was awarded an honorary doctorate in mathematics by the Moscow State University and he was a member of the Mathematical Institute of the Academy of Sciences of the Soviet Union until his death in 1948.

In the second half of his life, Slutsky did little work in economics proper but made a major contribution to mathematical statistics and the theory of probability. In particular, he was one of the originators of the theory of stochastic processes. Best known is his paper "The Summation of Random Causes as the Source of Cyclic Processes" (Slutsky 1937), originally published in 1927. It shows that seemingly periodic fluctuations in time series are not necessarily due to periodic causes but may be a statistical artifact resulting from taking moving sums or averages of random quantities.

In the theory of price, Slutsky's contribution is the partitioning of the effect of price on demand into what later became known as a substitution effect and an income effect. This permitted him to clear up the apparent paradox of a rising demand curve. As in the case of most such paradoxes, the gain in analytical insight far exceeded the significance of the paradox itself, which is negligible.

Much of the mathematical complexity of Slutsky's analysis is due to the large number of goods in a consumer budget. For just two goods, Slutsky's argument can be explained in terms of the simple model that was used above to describe Pareto's analysis of the comparative statics of demand. It should be kept in mind, however, that aspects that seem trivial for two goods may become intricate for n goods.

Pareto, as was shown above (ch. 22, "Comparative Statics of Demand") derived the effect of price p_x on demand x by solving equations 22.6, 22.7, and 22.8, here renumbered,

$$U_{xx}dx + U_{xy}dy - p_xdm = mdp_x \qquad (24.5)$$

$$U_{xy}dx + U_{yy}dy - p_ydm = 0 \qquad (24.6)$$

$$-p_xdx - p_ydy = (x-x_0)dp_x \qquad (24.7)$$

The result (corresponding to Slutsky 1952, 39, eq. 43) can be rewritten

$$\frac{dx}{dp_x} = \frac{mp_y^2 - (U_{yy}p_x - U_{xy}p_y)(x-x_0)}{p_y^2U_{xx} - 2p_xp_yU_{xy} + p_x^2U_{yy}}, \qquad (24.8)$$

where U_{ij} is a second partial derivative of the utility function, $m = U_x/p_x = U_y/p_y$ is the marginal utility of income, and x-x_0 is the quantity the consumer buys beyond his endowment. This may be called the gross price effect. For $U_{xy} = 0$ its sign would be clearly negative, because U_{xx} and U_{yy} are negative from diminishing marginal utility. For $U_{xy} < 0$, however, the sign remained unclear.

Slutsky now visualized an experiment in which the individual, when p_x rises, receives a gift of a certain amount of, say, x_0. As a result, equation 24.7 now reads

$$-p_xdx - p_ydy = (x-x_0)dp_x - p_xdx_0. \qquad (24.7a)$$

The gift is calibrated in such a way that the individual is precisely compensated for the loss in purchasing power. This requires $p_xdx_0 = (x-x_0)dp_x$. If the price of bread rises from \$3 to \$4 on 60 units, the consumer receives a gift of 15 units of bread. The right side of equation 24.7a thus becomes zero.

Equations 24.5, 24.6, and 24.7a can again be solved for the effect of p_x on x, but this is now a net or compensated price effect, later called the substitution effect. It is

$$\frac{dx^*}{dp_x} = \frac{mp_y^2}{p_y^2U_{xx} - 2p_xp_yU_{xy} + p_x^2U_{yy}} = \frac{mp_y^2}{\Delta} < 0. \qquad (24.9)$$

It follows from the convexity of the indifference curve that $\Delta < 0$ (though Slutsky's argument is different). One thus obtains the proposition that the compensated price effect on demand is unambiguously negative. This is the "Slutsky inequality" (1952, 41).

Slutsky also conducts another experiment, in which prices remain constant while the consumer receives additional income in the form of a gift of x_0. In this case $dp_x = 0$, but equation 24.7 now reads

$$-p_xdx - p_ydy = -p_xdx_0. \qquad (24.7b)$$

Writing $p_x dx_0 = dE$ for the change in expenditure, the effect on the demand for x can be determined as

$$\frac{dx}{p_x dx_0} = \frac{dx}{dE} = \frac{U_{yy} p_x - U_{xy} p_y}{\Delta} \gtrless 0. \tag{24.10}$$

The second component of the gross price effect thus turns out to be

$$-\frac{dx}{dE}(x - x_0). \tag{24.11}$$

This is intuitively plausible, because $x - x_0$ is the real income the consumer loses if p_x rises by \$1, and dx/dE indicates how a \$1 change in real income affects demand. This was later called the income effect of a price change.

Slutsky thus exhibited the total effect of price on demand as the sum of two parts, namely

$$\frac{dx}{dp_x} = \frac{dx^*}{dp_x} - (x - x_0)\frac{dx}{dE}. \tag{24.12}$$

This is often called the Slutsky equation (1952, 40, eq. 46). For goods we call superior (and Slutsky called relatively indispensable) one can be certain that an increase in price reduces demand because both terms are negative. For strongly inferior goods, however, (which Slutsky called relatively dispensable) it is logically conceivable that the total effect is positive. This is Marshall's "Giffen case," which nobody has ever observed (or traced to Giffen) yet.

Slutsky's decomposition of price effects is interesting not only from the point of view of price theory but also for empirical work. Suppose dx/dp_x and dx/dE have been econometrically estimated from budget data. Slutsky's inequality then tells us that the estimates should satisfy the condition

$$\frac{dx}{dp_x} + (x - x_0)\frac{dx}{dE} < 0. \tag{24.13}$$

This has been extensively used in econometric budget analysis, either as a test or as a constraint.

Cross price effects, Slutsky further showed, can be partitioned in an analogous way. In the compensated sense, the effect of p_x on y can be determined from equations 24.5, 24.6, and 24.7a as

$$\frac{dy^*}{dp_x} = \frac{m p_x p_y}{\Delta}. \tag{24.14}$$

The net effect of p_y on x can be similarly determined as

$$\frac{dx^*}{dp_y} = \frac{mp_xp_y}{\Delta}.$$ (24.15)

It thus turns out that the compensated cross price effects are pairwise equal. This remarkable result has been called the Slutsky symmetry condition for cross price effects (1952, 43). This condition, too, can be used in econometric work.

Slutsky's compensated cross price effects have become basic for the distinction between substitutes and complements. If this distinction is based on the gross effects, the relationship may be asymmetrical; coffee may be a gross substitute for milk, even though milk is a gross complement of coffee. If the distinction is based on the net effects, it is necessarily symmetrical; if coffee is a net substitute for milk, then milk is a net substitute for coffee. Asymmetry is due to the income effects.

Edward Chamberlin

Alfred Marshall had left the waters of value theory thoroughly muddied; he hinted at everything and was precise about nothing. Arthur Cecil Pigou, unable to clear up the confusion, became its victim. It took price theory about two decades to clear away the analytical debris. The malaise was given a voice by John H. Clapham in a famous article "Of Empty Economic Boxes" (1922), by which he meant Marshall's taxonomy of increasing, constant, and diminishing returns. Though effective as a challenge, the article was actually quite weak; Clapham was a great historian but no theorist. The responses by Pigou and Dennis Robertson were not much better.

A positive contribution was made by Piero Sraffa (1926). Marshall's problem was that a determinate firm size under pure competition requires diminishing returns, whereas his knowledge of industry told him that increasing returns are frequent. The "trick" with which he reconciled the two propositions was the appeal to externalities. Sraffa instead took the bull by the horns by acknowledging that most firms are facing falling demand curves, which means that they are monopolists. "It is necessary," he argued, "to abandon the path of free competition and turn in the opposite direction, namely, towards monopoly." The size of the firm is then limited by what Adam Smith called the size of the market, even though it may enjoy increasing returns.

This approach was fully articulated, without knowledge of Sraffa's paper, by Edward H. Chamberlin. He was born in La Couner in the state of Washington in 1899, the son of a minister. After his father's early death, the family moved to Iowa City, where the mother worked to put her two sons through high school and college. Chamberlin graduated from the University of Iowa, obtained an M.A. from the University of Michigan, and then went to Harvard for his Ph.D. The dissertation, which he submitted in April 1927, became essentially his magnum opus. Its success earned him an appointment at Harvard, where to the end of his days he led the charmed and cultivated life of a distinguished professor. His contribution to economics was recognized by a number of honorary degrees. A stroke in 1961 led to progressive paralysis, and Chamberlin died in 1967.

Chamberlin was indeed a man of one book, the *Theory of Monopolistic Competition* (1962), published in 1933. It is based on the notion that all-pervasive product differentiation makes the typical firm a monopolist for its own products. While the concept of monopolistic competition belonged to the tradition of Marshall and Pigou, the subtitle, *A Reorientation of the Theory of Value*, staked out Chamberlin's claim. Subsequent editions were expanded by additional chapters and papers. Further contributions to the same topic were later collected under the title *Towards a More General Theory of Value* (Chamberlin 1957). In his last years monopoly also led Chamberlin into labor economics. It is sad to observe, however, that no substantial further contributions were added to the dissertation. Instead of attacking new problems, Chamberlin used up his energy (and the patience of his contemporaries) by defending the exaggerated claim expressed in his subtitle. In fact, few economists received so much recognition for a contribution essentially limited to two simple curves. Assessments can be found in Kuenne 1967 and Robinson 1971.

One aspect of Chamberlin's contribution consisted in an improvement in the theory of monopoly. The firm was presented as maximizing profits by letting the marginal cost curve intersect what Chamberlin called the marginal revenue curve. He was right in not regarding this as a great contribution, because in substance it did not go beyond Marshall. In fact, it still fell short of Cournot.[12] It was nevertheless an influential contribution, bringing undergraduate teaching one step closer to the frontier of knowledge that had been established almost a century before. From now on blackboards would be covered with marginal cost curves intersecting U-shaped average cost curves in their minimum and marginal revenue curves derived from demand curves. Chamberlin also noted that a monopolist would pay factors not the price but the marginal revenue of their marginal product, and he described this discovery as one of the "truly revolutionary features of the new analysis" (1957, 7).

Another aspect of monopolistic competition concerned groups of sellers of competing products, for which Chamberlin reinvented the term *oligopoly*. In contrast to Cournot he emphasized product differentiation, but, in the same year in which his oligopoly chapter was originally published (Chamberlin 1929), Hotelling had analyzed differentiated oligopoly much

---

12. Erich Schneider's *Pure Theory of Monopolistic Market Structures* (1932) offers a splendid example of what a competent mathematician and brilliant expositor could then accomplish by essentially elaborating Cournot.

more deeply, and in any case, Launhardt (1885) had done the same two generations earlier. Chamberlin's specific contribution was the case of oligopoly combined with free entry, where the demand curve for each seller has become tangent to his average cost curve, as illustrated in figure 24.4 by point Q.

Chamberlin's analysis of this case was unnecessarily restricted by the assumption of identical demand and cost curves, which is implausible for differentiated products. The two main results, however, are independent of this assumption. First, long-run profits depend not on the slope of the demand curve but on the limitations to entry; under monopoly, as reflected in a falling demand curve, profits are neither inherently higher nor inherently lower than under the horizontal demand curves of pure competition. Second, with falling demand curves, even if profits are zero, output is too small to reduce average costs to their minimum. To have drawn attention to the two essential aspects of competition, namely the slopes of demand curves and freedom (or restriction) of entry, is Chamberlin's main claim to a place in the history of economic science.

A third aspect of Chamberlin's "reorientation" was his emphasis on product variation and advertising as policy variables under monopolistic competition. In this respect, however, his discussion remained essentially descriptive. In the analysis of selling costs, in particular, his powers did not extend to the joint optimization of price and advertising expenses. It must be remembered that this was the time of Ragnar Frisch, Harold Hotelling, Heinrich von Stackelberg, and John von Neumann.

Joseph Schumpeter described the *Theory of Monopolistic Competition* as "one of the most successful books in theoretical economics that the period since 1918 has produced" (1954, 1151). In 1963 the American Economic Association (Chamberlin 1964) held a special session to commemorate its thirtieth anniversary, at which the monopolistic competition revolution was celebrated as the microeconomic counterpart to the Keynesian revolution in macroeconomics. The question is how academic success was related to scientific achievement. On the positive side, the fruitfulness of Chamberlin's concepts was borne out by the strong impulse they gave to the field that became known as industrial organization. Critics, led by Stigler (1949) and centered in Chicago, took a negative view. However, their polemics sounded strident, their methodological excursions into the logics of unrealistic assumptions were not convincing, and Chamberlin's specific contributions were not put in doubt. It is nevertheless true that these contributions, though influential, were very thin. Chamberlin, contrary to his claims, was far from achieving a reorientation of the theory of value. There was a step forward, but no revolution. His service to science consisted not in achieving a breakthrough but in bringing up the rear at the right time. Generals have been decorated for less.

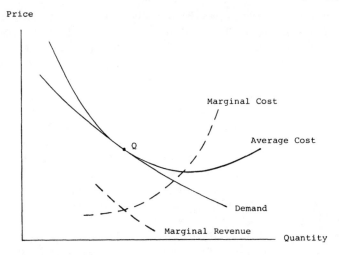

FIGURE 24.4

Joan Robinson

At the time when Chamberlin discovered monopolistic competition in Cambridge, Massachusetts, it was independently discovered in Cambridge, England, by Joan Robinson. As in other cases, the coincidence suggests that economic theory, like research in other fields, has its own endogenous dynamics.

Joan Robinson was born Joan Violet Maurice in 1903.[13] Both her father and her grandfather were major generals in the British army. Of her grandfather, the *Dictionary of National Biography* mentions his "intense hatred of any kind of injustice, or unfairness, and the readiness to sacrifice his personal interests to a cause in which he believed." Her father was cashiered because, after the German spring offensive of 1918, he had publicly accused Lloyd George of deceiving Parliament and the country about the strength of Haig's forces; he thereafter became a respected educator. His children had a family tradition to live up to.

Joan Maurice studied economics at Girton College, Cambridge, from which she graduated with second-class honors in 1925. In the following year she married Austin Robinson, who also became a noted Cambridge economist. They had two daughters, and after a few years in India, they

13. Biographical data are from the *Dictionary of National Biography* and from G.C. Harcourt's article on Robinson in the *International Encyclopedia of the Social Sciences* (1979). A survey of Robinson's work was provided by Gram and Walsh (1983).

returned to Cambridge. In 1931, Joan Robinson became a faculty assistant lecturer, in 1937, university lecturer, and in 1949, reader. She was sixty-two years old when, in 1965, she was finally appointed professor of economics. After her retirement in 1971 she continued to be highly active, speaking to large audiences all over the world and keeping up a stream of publications. She died in 1983.

Robinson was known for her dedication to students and to the cause of whomever she regarded as oppressed and exploited. A strict vegetarian, she led a spartan life, wearing sandals even in winter and sleeping in an unheated, open hut surrounded by birds and squirrels. Her uncritical admiration of Stalin and of China and North Korea was often hard to understand even for her friends. She was intelligent, articulate, and fearless, but also opinionated, arrogant, and vituperative. If in the second half of her life she did not make economics much better, she certainly made it livelier.

As an economist, Robinson followed in the tradition of Marshall and Pigou. Her first book, *Economics of Imperfect Competition* of 1933 (Robinson 1969), was meant not as a revolution but as a further evolution of this tradition. Following Sraffa's (1926) suggestions, she proposed to treat monopoly as the general case with perfect competition as a special case. The analytical apparatus is virtually identical to Chamberlin's, which is not surprising since all essential elements had been available for years, crying out to be put together. In comprehensiveness and lucidity, however, Robinson's treatment is superior to Chamberlin's. Though she later disparaged it as "scholastic" and "orthodox," it became the classic exposition of the theory of the firm for decades; no other work of hers achieved the same quality.

In 1931, Joan Robinson belonged to the little "circus" that helped John Maynard Keynes to make the transition from *A Treatise on Money* to the *General Theory*. She became an ardent left-wing Keynesian of the first hour. Her *Introduction to the Theory of Employment* (Robinson 1937a) was one of the first expositions of Keynesian doctrine, and the *Essays in the Theory of Employment* (Robinson 1937b) contained original contributions to it, including an early extension to an open economy.[14] She considered the disequilibrium character of the Keynesian theory as its essential aspect, and she thought that John R. Hicks denatured it by expressing it as an equilibrium theory.

But Keynes, Robinson soon realized, was not going to revolutionize capitalism. In 1940, encouraged by Michal Kalecki, she began to read Karl Marx. As *An Essay on Marxian Economics* (Robinson 1942) shows, she was not impressed by the labor theory of value, which she regarded as

---

14. However, the condition for a normal effect of a devaluation on the trade balance, though it became known as the Robinson-Metzler condition, was already stated by Bickerdike, though in inverse form, in 1920.

wrong-headed and irrelevant, but she found inspiration in the two-sector model of economic growth. Above all, she was captivated by Marx as an ideologue. She began to see all economics, including her own, as propaganda (Robinson 1951–80, 2:3f.). She was willing to admit that mathematicians or bird watchers could be motivated by the intrinsic interest of their subject, but nobody would go into economics, she thought, except for political reasons. This notion became the leitmotiv of her later life and perhaps its fundamental flaw.

Like Harrod, Robinson conceived the plan of extending the short-run Keynesian system to the long run, thus developing it into a theory of economic growth. The fruit of this effort, strongly influenced by Sraffa's interpretation of Ricardo, was *The Accumulation of Capital* (Robinson 1956). From the point of view of its pretensions it is her magnum opus; from the point of view of scientific achievement it was a failure. In the absence of mathematical training, her analytical abilities, despite her intellectual brilliance, were simply not up to the task. The theory of economic growth passed her by.[15] From then on, her criticism of what she described as neo-neoclassical theory became increasingly strident and ideological.[16]

In more limited fields, however, Joan Robinson was still able to make theoretical contributions. In a controversial article, "The Production Function and the Theory of Capital" (1954), she drew attention to a paradox that became famous. First noted by Ruth Cohen (1951–80, 4:145), it was further explained in *The Accumulation of Capital* (Robinson 1956, 109f.).[17] Sraffa must have been aware of it long before he discussed it in print (1960, 81f.). The paradox consists in the possibility that lower interest rates, though normally encouraging more capital-intensive methods of production, may conceivably have the opposite result. It attracted some of the best brains, including Paul Samuelson and Robert Solow in Cambridge, Massachusetts, and Luigi Pasinetti and Pierangelo Garegnani in Cambridge, England.

In her *Essays in the Theory of Economic Growth* (1962a), essentially an unsuccessful effort to clear up the confusion left by her preceding book, Robinson hit upon another interesting proposition. She showed that an economy in balanced growth maximizes per capita consumption by consuming all wages and saving all profits. She also showed that in this case

15. The comparison with Solow's "Contribution to the Theory of Economic Growth" (1956), published in the same year, is striking.
16. There is an interesting parallel. A few years earlier, Hayek had also suffered scientific defeat in capital theory from which he escaped into ideology, though in the opposite direction.
17. The paradox is also mentioned by D. G. Champernowne in the same issue of the *Review of Economic Studies*. On Ruth Cohen's original idea see Harry G. Johnson's note in Johnson and Johnson 1978, ch. 12.

the rate of interest is equal to the rate of growth. The proposition, discovered almost simultaneously by about half a dozen economists, was later called the golden rule of capital accumulation (see ch. 33 below). Robinson's numerous articles, essays, and lectures are collected in the five volumes of the *Collected Economic Papers* (Robinson 1951–80).

From these voluminous writings two specific contributions to price theory stand out, namely the theory of the firm and, reaching far into the model-building era, the capital paradox. Joan Robinson's theory of the firm is essentially Cournot's theory of monopoly supplemented by Marshall's demand elasticity and the newly invented marginal revenue curve. Of Cournot's ancestry Robinson seemed unaware. She does not mention his name, and his teaching was transmitted to her through Marshall. The origin of the marginal revenue concept is traced to T. O. Yntema (1928), to discussions with Cambridge colleagues, and to Harrod (Robinson 1969, xiv), but this was a contribution to the exposition of Cournot's theory rather than to its substance.

To the lucid and textbooklike exposition of the statics of the firm Joan Robinson added a detailed analysis of comparative statics. It contains a reference to the rigidity of price that may result from a kink in the demand curve (Robinson 1969, 81). The discussion of different market conditions includes the "Chamberlin" case of monopoly with free entry, leading to the famous tangency solution (92f.). Like Chamberlin, Robinson notes that a monopolist equates wages not to the marginal product of labor but to its marginal revenue product (which she calls marginal productivity) (ch. 20). She goes much beyond Chamberlin, however, in applying the theory to a firm's monopsony in the labor market and the resulting "exploitation" of labor. A corresponding analysis of the monopoly power of trade unions is lacking.

The most original contribution of the *Economics of Imperfect Competition* is the analysis of monopolistic price discrimination. The phenomenon had been extensively discussed before World War I, often in relation to railroad rates, and leading theorists such as Edgeworth and Pigou had made important contributions. Almost incredibly, however, the most basic proposition was missed (see, for example, Edgeworth 1925, 1:172f.; 2:426), and it was left to Robinson to state it. According to this proposition, a monopolist who can segment the market for his product into two submarkets will maximize his profit by differentiating the excess of price over marginal cost in inverse proportion to the two price elasticities. In algebraic terms,

$$\frac{(p_1 - c)/p_1}{(p_2 - c)/p_2} = \frac{\epsilon_2}{\epsilon_1}, \tag{24.16}$$

where p_1 and p_2 denote prices, ϵ_1 and ϵ_2 the price elasticities of demand,

and c the marginal cost. Robinson presents most of this analysis in terms of her graphical apparatus, which is then used as a basis for her classic discussion of the effects of price discrimination.

The capital paradox is more difficult to explain in simple terms. Suppose a given output is produced with uniform labor only. There are two methods of production. According to the labor-saving method A, 9 units of labor are applied 1 period before the output is sold. According to the labor-intensive method B, the same output requires 11 units of labor, of which 10 are applied immediately before the output is sold and one unit is applied 3 periods earlier. The question is which method has lower production costs.

The answer depends, as Ricardo had explained so well, on the rate of interest. Wage costs in the preceding period have to be multiplied by the capitalization factor $r = 1 + i$, where i is the interest rate. With a wage rate of $w = 1$, the costs of method A, therefore, are $C_A = 9r$. Under method B, the bulk of labor costs requires no capitalization, but one unit is capitalized for three periods. Total cost, therefore, is $C_B = 10 + r^3$. The relevant possibilities are best illustrated by a numerical example. For computational ease one may assume that the periods are several years long, so that r ranges from 1 to, say, 3. The resulting production costs for methods A and B can be tabulated as follows:

r	1	1.45	1.5	2	3
C_A	9*	13.05*	13.5	18*	27*
C_B	11	13.05*	13.375*	18*	37

The asterisks denote the minimum costs.

The left-hand side of the table shows the familiar results. Low interest rates favor labor-saving methods. As the interest rate is increased, this advantage gradually declines. At the switch point $r = 1.45$, the choice of technology switches to the labor-intensive method B. On the right-hand side of the table, however, there appears the paradox. As the capitalization factor rises toward 2, the advantage of the labor-intensive technology declines again. At $r = 2$, there is another switch point beyond which the labor-saving method A again becomes efficient. This is the phenomenon that became known as reswitching. Joan Robinson always made clear that reswitching, in itself, has no particular interest. The substantive point is that higher interest rates can favor labor-saving methods of production (Robinson 1951–80, 4: 75). This possibility became known as the capital paradox. This is a plausible terminology inasmuch as labor-saving methods are capital-intensive. It should be noted, however, that the explanation of the paradox does not require any measurement of aggregate capital. If desired, capital costs can easily be calculated from the above table.

In Cambridge, England, it was at first thought that this paradox was a fatal blow to the accepted theory of production and distribution (Robinson 1951–80, 5:21). In Cambridge, Massachusetts, on the other hand, there were efforts to prove that the paradox, though conceivable for individual processes, can be ruled out for the economy as a whole (Levhari 1965). As the dust settled, it became clear that both of these positions were untenable.[18] The capital paradox cannot be ruled out even for the economy as a whole, and it is perfectly compatible with the received theory of production. Reswitching, however, can occur only with discrete technologies, where the producer is forced to jump from one method to another. With smooth substitution between inputs, two different interest rates never lead to the choice of exactly the same method of production.

On closer analysis, the capital paradox turned out to be one of the strange consequences of complementarity (Hatta 1976). In the above example method B requires two complementary inputs, namely instantaneous labor and distant labor. Both together can be substituted for method A with its intermediate labor. At very high rates, method B is disqualified by the high capitalization of its distant input. At very low rates, it is disqualified by the high cost of its instantaneous input. In between, there is a range in which method A is disqualified by the high cost of its intermediate inputs. More generally, if near labor and distant labor are complements, whereas intermediate labor is a substitute for both, then the capital paradox may result even from perfectly "neoclassical" production functions.

Joan Robinson had thus discovered that otherwise well-behaved production functions can produce unexpected results. This discovery belongs to the same general class of curiosities as the Giffen paradox of a rising demand curve and Edgeworth's taxation paradox, analyzed by Hotelling. Like the Giffen paradox, the capital paradox has never yet been empirically observed, but in contrast to the Giffen case, there are no strong reasons to regard it as unlikely. Its main value is as a useful test case for the understanding of intertemporal cost minimization, and the initial controversy led to valuable new insights, though perhaps of a secondary order of importance.

With *The Economics of Imperfect Competition* Robinson, together with Chamberlin, made a major contribution to price theory. Though in the shade of Cournot and thus not of the highest originality, it might have been worthy of a Nobel Prize. Like all her valid contributions, it was very much in the mainstream or, as she called it, the neoclassical tradition. She fervently tried to cut herself loose from this tradition, hoping to make progress along a track that led from Ricardo to Marx and farther on to

---

18. Samuelson (1966–86, vol. 3, ch. 148) provides a good introduction to the problem. The same symposium contains other important contributions to the debate.

Sraffa. However, though this led to considerable academic commotion, major results failed to materialize. A disequilibrium theory of economic growth in historical time is indeed a great goal, but so far it is out of reach. Science, like politics, is the art of the possible, and impossible dreams lead to frustration.

III
The Era of Economic Models
(since about 1930)

25
The Leitmotiv of the Model-Building Era

IN THE EARLY 1920s the progress of economic theory seemed to have slowed almost to a standstill. Hardly any original contributions were made between 1920 and 1925. The academic establishment was dominated by historicism, institutionalism, and pragmatism. The collection of facts had precedence over the construction of theories. Yet within twenty years economists saw their own science in a completely different light. The star of Léon Walras rose and that of Gustav Schmoller sank below the horizon.

In mathematics the late nineteenth century had brought a revival of axiomatic methods. In physics, empiricism was giving way to axiomatic systems. In the introduction to his *Principles of Mechanics* of 1894, the physicist Heinrich Hertz described the method of science in the following words:

> We make for ourselves internal images or symbols of the external objects, and we make them in such a way that the consequences of the images that are necessary in thought are always images of the consequences of the depicted objects that are necessary in nature. . . . Once we have succeeded in deriving from accumulated previous experience images with the required property, we can quickly develop from them, *as if from models*, the consequences that in the external world will occur only over an extended period or as a result of our own intervention. (Hertz 1894, 1f.; my translation and emphasis)

The era had begun in which scientists interpreted their activity as model building.

It took about thirty years before this self-interpretation of science conquered economics. John R. Hicks talked about models in 1937 in his famous formalization of John Maynard Keynes. In the same year, Erik Lundberg presented his dynamic analysis in the form of model sequences. In his correspondence with Roy Harrod of 1938, Keynes described economics, with his inimitable power of expression, as "a science of thinking in terms of models joined to the art of choosing models which are relevant to the contemporary world" (Keynes 1971– , 14:296). A little later, Joseph Schumpeter (1939) claimed to have constructed a "model of capitalist evolution." If the use of words were a guide, the model-building era in economic theory would seem to have begun in the late 1930s.

Actual model building, of course, had no such beginning. In one form or another, economic thought had made use of Hertz's images or symbols as long as we have knowledge of it (Aristotle's hapless exchange theory offers an early example). Richard Cantillon and François Quesnay constructed explicit models of the circular flow, David Ricardo used models to prove theorems, Karl Marx struggled with models, and the core of marginalism consisted of optimization models. Irving Fisher had referred to the importance of models in mathematics and physics as early as 1892 (1925, 107f.), and he actually built hydraulic machines as models of the economic system. Nevertheless, up to the 1920s, much of economic theory could not be easily quantified or expressed in symbols that lent themselves to logical manipulation. Alfred Marshall wasted much energy disguising his use of models. Knut Wicksell, though a mathematician, expressed his inflation theory in a form that made its precise content a puzzle even to his disciples. Arthur Cecil Pigou (in his youth), Joseph Schumpeter, and John Maynard Keynes still presented their reasoning with hardly a graph or symbol. They had, to use Schumpeter's term, a vision of a theory, but it was sadly lacking in clarity and rigor. Even Irving Fisher, despite his mathematical investigations of value and interest and his many suggestions for macroeconomic models, limited his formal macroeconomic analysis to the equation of exchange.

After World War I the complexion of economics began to change. The generation born around the turn of the century established different analytical requirements. Many of its members had an extensive training in mathematics, statistics, and physics and looked at the economic world with the eyes of scientists. In the late 1920s, Frank Ramsey produced classic examples of economic models. In the early 1930s, Ragnar Frisch and Michal Kalecki were the first to condense business cycle theory to mathematical models. Within hardly more than a decade, mathematical models seemed to be the primary output of economic science. Economic theory was now seen as a "sequence of models" (Koopmans 1957, 142). To talk of a model-building revolution would be completely misleading, though. No bells rang in a new era, and *model* seemed no more than a new name for an old thing. Nevertheless, if the leading contributions of the early 1950s are compared to those of the late 1920s the contrast could hardly be more striking.

In contrast to the calculus models of marginalism, the principal purpose of these modern models was not to introduce concepts but to prove theorems. Linear programming was developed to make optimal solutions computable. The indefinite number of agents in a Walrasian model with their unspecified interaction was replaced by limited sets of key variables related by a definite structure. The theory of general equilibrium was given a macroeconomic orientation. It was no longer enough to demonstrate that everything depends on everything else; it had to be shown how it depends. The purest incarnation of this theorem-seeking style of model building was Paul Samuelson.

There is no question that this development was, overall, a decisive advance. There is also no question that model building, like the circular flow of the classical era and the optimization calculus of marginalism, is here to stay. Half a century later an observer might perhaps be forgiven for also feeling that this advance was increasingly bought at the expense of vision. To use Keynes's phrase, the "art of choosing models which are relevant to the contemporary world" was not keeping pace with the "science of thinking in terms of models." The 1980s were, in fact, a time of theoretical fermentation. Rapid progress in mathematical techniques struggled with a sense of frustration. Later historians may perhaps discern the time around 1980 as the end of one era and the beginning of a new one.

Hertz, observing a virtually unchanging physical universe, had good reason to hope that experience would lead to the discovery of empirically reliable models. It is not surprising that many economists of the model-building era shared this hope. Arguments can be settled in economics, so they felt, in the same way as in the natural sciences, namely by appeal to observation. National accounting systems were constructed to provide a statistical basis. The effort to develop techniques by which economic theories can be statistically tested led to econometrics. It became fashionable to scorn theories that were not "meaningful" in the sense of having refutable implications. Economists began to talk the language of Karl Popper. Huge amounts of data were fed into ever larger computers to grind out a deluge of parameter estimates. This, too, was a definite advance. It is sobering to observe, however, that after forty years of effort hardly any economic arguments had been settled by econometric methods. Perhaps it will later be realized that these methods were not yet well suited for the analysis of the ever changing complexities of human history. "Relevance" still remained an art, and some of the leading theorists continued to be uninterested in econometric work.

As in earlier eras, historical events and economic conditions provided powerful external motives for economic research. The Great Depression made unemployment and economic stabilization the most important research problem, attracting brilliant young minds into economics. The war effort and postwar reconversion and recovery stimulated work on planning and optimization, one outgrowth of which was operations research. Postwar prosperity and development directed the minds of many economists to long-run economic growth. The cycle of inflation and stagflation beginning in the early 1960s made monetary policy the focus of debate and controversy. The limits to growth imposed by exhaustible resources, accentuated by successive oil crises, provided economics with a new agenda. Poverty and discrimination were powerful concerns. And yet, despite the libraries written on these burning issues, it seems fair to say that the mainstream of economic theory flowed forth, more or less, as if it were kept in motion by its own internal dynamics. The contributions described in the following chapters, though their authors were often motivated by strong social concerns, would probably have been quite similar under very different historical circumstances.

With respect to political ideologies, the economics of the model-building era was just as pluralistic as ever before. In Europe many of the leading economists were social democrats with a passion for planning. In the United States the young generation was attracted to "liberal" social reform. Welfare theorists tended to advocate government intervention to correct market failures. Others remained faithful to the laissez-faire ideas in the European tradition, and not a few were ardent conservatives. Significant contributions continued to be made by economists from communist countries and radicals on the Left. Proposals, postulates, and programs were as diverse as their protagonists. At this political level there was consensus on hardly anything. Nevertheless, all these economists, however different their ideological views, would continue to make contributions to the same mainstream of economic theory. They were united by a common scientific method, no matter how their doctrines might differ.

In their historical self-interpretation, the economists of the model-building era, in conformity with their unhistorical turn of mind, were inclined toward mythology. In his *General Theory*, Keynes had used the familiar dialectic tactics of representing the economics of his rivals as "classical orthodoxy." His phenomenal success caused others to use the same tactics. They were mostly those who had never been, or were no longer, able to contribute to mainstream economics. In due course the mainstream economics of the model-building era, after Samuelson had proclaimed the "neoclassical synthesis," acquired the label *neoclassical* that had earlier been coined for Marshall. This was an unfortunate case of mislabeling for at least two reasons. First, the mainstream economics of the postwar period, just like marginalism, was not a revival of classical economics, or anything else. Second, it is virtually impossible to identify any particular doctrines that distinguish modern mainstream economics from alternative bodies of doctrines that might be labeled nonclassical. As in earlier eras, mainstream economics voraciously absorbed whatever seemed to be scientifically promising.

During the classical and marginalist eras, economics, despite the work of Irving Fisher and other notable American contributions, had largely been a European science. In the course of the model-building era, the center of research activity shifted to the United States. In large part this was due to the emigration of outstanding economists, first from Soviet Russia and later, in much larger numbers, from Nazi Germany and the countries it had subjugated. At the same time, American economics began to attract, for the first time in its history, many of the brightest intellects who would earlier have gone into other fields. A third important factor was the emergence of the American graduate school as the modern incarnation of the classical idea of universities. The owl of Athene, after passing from the Platonic academy to the medieval university and farther on to Germany, Oxford, and Cambridge, had found its modern resting place in the American graduate school.

This shift in the center of gravity was associated with an enormous increase in the intensity of research. Classical economists had written for the general public. The marginalists mainly wrote for untrained undergraduate students. The leading economists in the model-building era, thanks to the growth in their numbers, could afford to write for their peers. Whereas earlier generations had communicated through books, often ponderous and verbose, the model builders (though with some exceptions) communicated mostly through highly condensed journal articles. Journals multiplied, and their editors and referees became the arbiters of what was worthy of a chance to become part of mainstream economics.

Histories of economic doctrines often convey the notion that the past was an age of a few giants, shaking the world with their deeds, and the present is an age of pygmies engaged in agitated babble. This is another aspect of historical mythology. In fact, Richard Cantillon, François Quesnay, David Ricardo, and John Stuart Mill devoted only a small fraction of their lifetimes to economic research. William Stanley Jevons, Carl Menger, and Léon Walras, though professors, did little original research in economics after their initial (and fundamental) contributions. Many of the leading model builders, on the other hand, left many volumes of original research papers, written over a lifetime, and some of these papers are no less notable for their intellectual achievement than entire volumes of an earlier era.

The change in the training, status, and activity of economists seemed to be reflected in their personal lives. The great economists of the marginalist era were, by and large, an unhappy bunch of people. In the lives of Augustin Cournot, Hermann Gossen, Karl Marx, Stanley Jevons, Carl Menger, Léon Walras, Alfred Marshall, Vilfredo Pareto, and Knut Wicksell there was much disappointment, frustration, neurosis, and depression. Their training was usually inadequate for the problems they set out to solve, their main works remained mostly unfinished, and their controversies were often acrimonious and their private lives troubled. In the model-building era this was quite different. The leading economists, considered as a group, generally gave (and give) the impression of being reasonably happy people, well trained for their research, satisfied with their careers, enjoying academic discourse, and well able to cope with their personal problems. Their works did not remain unfinished torsos. As economic science matured, it offered its leading practitioners happier lives. They were still innovators, but, where the marginalists had been pioneers on a hostile frontier, they were venture capitalists in comfortable surroundings.

26
Welfare

THE MARGINALIST ERA had ended with the demise of cardinal utility. Interpersonal addition and comparison of utilities were no longer part of mainstream economics. This does not mean that the normative spirit of utilitarianism was dead; it means only that its range had narrowed. Problems of equity, though still evoking deep feelings and aspirations, were now seen to be outside the purview of economic theory. Problems of efficiency, however, were still a legitimate area of theoretical endeavor. Once an economy was in a state of Pareto optimality somewhere on Edgeworth's contract curve, economic science had little to say about further improvements. It still had much to say, however, on the reasons why an economy might not be on its contract curve and on the ways and means to reach it. These questions became the central problem of welfare economics in the model-building era.

As a matter of fact, normative concerns were no less alive in the model-building era than they were at the time of Léon Walras, John Stuart Mill, or Adam Smith. Most of the leading economists, in one form or another, sought to contribute to economic welfare, and these contributions will play a prominent role throughout the third part of this book. The present chapter is devoted to contributions that are more narrowly focused on what became known as welfare economics.

Arthur Cecil Pigou

At the time when marginalism transformed itself into model building, the foundations of modern welfare economics were laid by Arthur Cecil Pigou. He was born in 1877, the son of an army officer.[1] From Harrow, public school for the elite, he went to Cambridge to study history and literature. Under Alfred Marshall's influence, his interests gradually shifted toward the "moral sciences," which then included political economy. His mathematics was acquired later in life. An essay, "Robert Browning as a Religious Teacher," though winning a prize, failed to win him a fellowship. He succeeded, however, with another prize-winning essay on the changes of relative prices in agriculture, thus becoming a fellow of King's College for the rest of his life.

In 1904, Pigou was made a lecturer in the newly established economics program, and four years later, just thirty-one years old, he succeeded Marshall in the chair of political economy. A faithful pupil of the master,

---

1. The biographical note is based on Johnson 1960 and Austin Robinson's essay on Pigou in the *International Encyclopedia of the Social Sciences* (1968).

he transmitted the famous "oral tradition" of Marshallian economics to later generations. "It's all in Marshall"—waiting to be explicated and applied—was his famous dictum.

During the war his conscience did not permit him to bear arms, but he volunteered as an ambulance driver at various fronts. The experience seems to have changed his personality. The outgoing and sociable young man developed into a withdrawn, shy, and eccentric recluse. The ardent mountain climber began to suffer from heart disease. Unable to talk shop with his colleagues, he communicated with the academic world through his books. He never married and, although a kind man, became almost a misogynist.

In the interwar period Pigou was still the only professor of economics at Cambridge. He, the "prof," represented the establishment. When John Maynard Keynes undertook to assert his ascendancy as an economic theorist, it was, naturally, mainly at Pigou's expense. In the *General Theory*, Pigou was polemically described as the incarnation of "classical" orthodoxy. Though deeply hurt, he reacted with dignity and fairness. After the dust had settled, it became clear that Pigou was a much broader and deeper economist, and that Keynes was less revolutionary, than Keynes had made it appear. Pigou retired in 1943, succeeded by Dennis Robertson. He died in 1959.

Pigou was a prolific writer, publishing nearly thirty books. While many economists, including Marshall, in the course of their lives moved from pure theory and mathematics toward more applied economics, Pigou developed in the opposite direction. His first books were on industrial peace and on import duties. In *Wealth and Welfare* (Pigou 1912) the question of how judicious government intervention can increase welfare was generalized. In 1920, under the new title, *The Economics of Welfare* (1960), and greatly elaborated, this became Pigou's major work. It determines his place in the history of economics.

Concern with welfare led Pigou on the one hand to *A Study in Public Finance* (1951), on the other hand to his books *Industrial Fluctuations* (1927) and *The Theory of Unemployment* (1933). These show that the neoclassical views on unemployment were much richer in economic content and less dogmatic than the anemic representations in the post-Keynesian textbooks would make one believe. In substance, for the short run, Pigou's analysis of 1933 was not much different from that of Keynes in 1936, but Pigou was unable to reduce it to a tractable model, and he refused to truncate his analysis after the short run.

With *The Economics of Stationary States* (1935), Pigou moved toward abstract theory and formal model building. His later publications were largely (though not exclusively) responses to the Keynesian challenge. He is particularly remembered for stressing the equilibrating effect of falling prices on aggregate demand through the rise in real cash balances (Pigou

1943, 349f.). The question of whether this should be called the Pigou or the Haberler effect seems moot, because this effect was, as a matter of fact, fully explained by Keynes himself (1936, ch. 19). Looking back, it is easy to see that truth was more on the side of Pigou than on that of Keynes. If economists were ranked by the mass of "net truth" they commit to paper—that is, by the excess of truth over falsehood—Pigou would come out close to Marshall. His weaknesses were that he had little talent for innovative theory and that his writing, though clear, was dull and ineffective.

Pigou's major contribution to political economy was the creation of welfare economics as a branch of economic science. From this point of view, the central issue was not the choice between alternative economic "systems" but the improvement of the existing economy through government intervention and reform. Pigou, like so many utilitarians before him, was deeply convinced that this required greater equality of incomes, but such convictions clearly go beyond scientific analysis. His scientific contribution concerned not equity but efficiency.

Pigou's basic criterion for the optimal allocation of resources is the equality of their marginal net products in all different uses. Whenever this condition is violated, welfare can be raised by a suitable reallocation. In this connection Pigou noted three problems, which he could not solve, and which, despite strong efforts, have not been completely solved to the present day.

1. Marginal equalities, even if the second-order conditions are satisfied, identify only local optima. In general, there may be other local optima that are even better. Points that are locally suboptimal may thus be superior to a particular local optimum. This raised the problem of finding ways and means to identify global optima, which became the central topic of welfare theory after World War II.

2. If the reallocation of resources is itself costly, a certain allocation, though it fails to equalize marginal products, may still be best relative to the initial allocation and the existing adjustment costs. This raised the problem of the precise meaning of efficiency in the presence of adjustment or transactions costs, which gave modern welfare theory a particularly hard time.

3. If marginal products are unequal for more than two pairs of resource uses, it is not clear that the reduction of just one divergence increases welfare. If freight rates exceed marginal cost by a large margin for rail transport and by a smaller margin on the road, it may well be that marginal cost pricing for road transport alone reduces welfare. Any single equality condition is valid only if all others are satisfied. This raised what James Meade later called the problem of the second-best: If all conditions cannot be satisfied, how can we be sure to achieve at least an improvement?

One important reason for inequalities in marginal social products is, of course, monopoly. Though Pigou discussed this topic extensively, he had nothing new to say; he still had not caught up with Cournot. It may be noted, however, that the term *monopolistic competition* already appears in *Wealth and Welfare* and the term *imperfect competition* in the *Economics of Welfare*. The niche for Robinson and Chamberlin was carved out. Other reasons for the inequality of marginal social products, Pigou noted, are imperfect information, indivisibilities in production or consumption, and market fluctuations.

The key to Pigou's specific contribution is the distinction between private and social marginal products. If the two coincide, so he argues, the free play of self-interest (in the absence of monopoly) tends to bring about an efficient allocation of resources. The invisible hand can do its work. In reality, however, private and social net products often diverge. Pigou's treatise is a veritable compendium of possible cases of such market failures, including congestion, pollution, resource exhaustion, information, and inventions. They have been the daily bread of welfare economics ever since. From Pigou's perspective, they are potential justifications for government intervention. Neoclassical economics has often been indicted as an ideological defense of free enterprise. The example of Pigou is enough to make this charge look ridiculous. With such neoclassicals, who needs a Galbraith?

The most important source of divergencies between private and social marginal values are external costs and benefits. The terms had been introduced by Marshall in his hapless efforts to reconcile rising supply curves for individual firms with falling supply curves for the industry. Pigou now used the concept in a much wider sense, namely for those costs or benefits that accrue to society but not to those who cause them. Improvements or damages by a tenant on rented land, smoke, and irrigation provide obvious examples. Activities with external benefits would tend to be undersupplied compared with the social optimum, while activities with external costs would be oversupplied. In principle, Pigou regarded this as an invitation to the government to close the gap between social and private marginal products with bounties or taxes. The externalities must, in later jargon, be internalized. Government regulation might achieve the same purpose.

At this point, unfortunately, Pigou committed a serious error, inherited from Marshall, that haunted welfare economics for decades. He realized that the expansion of an industry could raise the prices of its factors of production, say, land. He was right in pointing out that this factor price increase is not reflected in the supply curves of individual small firms. It followed that there was indeed a discrepancy between the marginal cost curve of the industry, taken as a whole, and the added supply curves of the individual firms. Pigou's error was in concluding that the output of such industries tended to be excessive and should be reduced by taxation.

The error in *Wealth and Welfare* was quickly spotted by Allyn Young

(1913), and Frank H. Knight (1924) later diagnosed it as a confusion about the nature of rent, but Pigou was slow in correcting it. The issue was settled only by Jacob Viner (1931) with his distinction between pecuniary and technological externalities.[2]

Pecuniary externalities work through the market. Since they are duly reflected in the price system, they create no particular welfare problems. In fact, they are essential for an efficient allocation. To this category belong Pigou's factor price increases. Technological externalities, on the other hand, act directly on production and consumption. They express the fact than an individual's utility may depend not only on his own consumption but also on other people's production and consumption and that a firm's production may depend on other firms' activities. These technological externalities create problems precisely because they are not reflected in market prices. Thus air pollution is an externality problem because the polluter does not have to buy clean air at a high price while selling the polluted air at a low price.

Coase (1960) later pointed out that Pigou had created an exaggerated impression of the need for corrective government measures. His argument may be summarized in three points.

1. If A imposes an external cost on B, the cause is not simply the behavior of A but the joint behavior of A and B. If the humming of A's transformer station disturbs the sleep of some Bs who are used to sleeping with open windows, the damage is caused jointly by A's maintaining the station and by the Bs' insistence on sleeping with open windows.

2. Suppressing the externality may not be an efficient solution. If the Bs keep their windows shut, the social cost may be smaller than if A is prevented from maintaining the transformer. Property rights should be defined in such a way that they contribute to an efficient solution.

3. In principle, private contracts between the interested parties are enough to achieve an efficient solution. Either A can pay the Bs for tolerating the noise or the Bs can pay A for removing the transformer. This proposition became known as the Coase theorem. It is evident, however, that the potential participants in such a contract are often too numerous and dispersed to be easily organized, that negotiations may be costly, that the participants may have strong incentives to misstate their interests, and that the problem of equity remains unsolved.

Pigou appeared to write from the point of view of general equilibrium welfare economics. From this point of view, his analysis is patently unsat-

---

2. In the process, Viner committed a celebrated, though inconsequential, error of his own by instructing his draftsman to draw the declining envelope to a series of U-shaped cost curves through their respective minimum points.

isfactory; progress beyond Vilfredo Pareto and Enrico Barone had to wait for the revival of general equilibrium analysis in the 1930s. Pigou's actual contribution was in the field of partial equilibrium welfare analysis, in the identification of specific sources of market failure. This contribution, though not flawless, is fundamental for applied welfare economics to the present day. With the growing urgency of the problems of the environment, congestion, information, and exhaustible resources, it appears more relevant than ever before.

Frank Ramsey

In Pigou's welfare analysis, the theoretical models were still camouflaged in Marshallian prose. The step to explicit mathematical models was made by Frank Plumpton Ramsey. He was born 1903 in Cambridge, where his father was president of Magdalene College. After a public school education at Winchester, he spent the remainder of his short life at Cambridge, where he became, successively, a scholar of Trinity College, a fellow of King's College, and a university lecturer in mathematics. Though teaching mathematics, he had the mind of a philosopher. His intellectual environment was Russell and Whitehead's *Principia Mathematica*, and at the age of nineteen he translated Wittgenstein's *Tractatus Logico-Philosophicus* from the original German. His death in 1930 at the age of twenty-seven was said by the editor of his papers to have deprived Cambridge of one of its intellectual glories and contemporary philosophy of one of its profoundest thinkers. Had he lived, he might have become a John von Neumann (who was born in the same year). A biographical essay was written by his friend Keynes (1971–　, vol. 10, ch. 29), and three outstanding articles on his life and contributions by Peter Newman, David Newbery, and William Baumol can be found in the *New Palgrave*.

The general title *Foundations*, under which Ramsey's *Essays in Philosophy, Logic, Mathematics and Economics* were recently republished (1978), aptly describes their spirit. Among the philosophical contributions, the essay "Truth and Probability" (of 1926) is of particular interest to economists inasmuch as it lays foundations for a theory of decision making under uncertainty based on subjective probabilities. Only two essays, however, belong to economic science proper, each solving a difficult problem of welfare theory.

In "A Mathematical Theory of Saving" (1928), Ramsey determines the optimal path of capital accumulation along which a fixed population should approach a stationary state of maximum welfare or "bliss." Output is assumed to depend on the capital stock.[3] It can be either consumed or saved. In the first case it provides direct utility; in the second case, through the increase in the capital stock, it provides future utility. If much

---

3. Ramsey also includes labor and its disutility, but these are disregarded here.

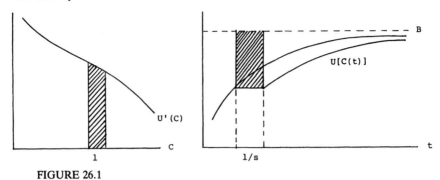

FIGURE 26.1

is saved, bliss is reached more rapidly, but the present utility loss is large; if little is saved, present utility is high, but bliss will be approached more slowly.[4] Capital accumulation is optimal, Ramsey shows, if the marginal utility of consumption declines at a rate equal to the rate of interest. This is plausible. At the margin, the gain in interest from additional savings should be just balanced by the decline in the marginal utility of income due to the increased output. Further analysis leads to the rule that "the rate of saving multiplied by the marginal utility of money should always be equal to the amount by which the total net rate of enjoyment of utility falls short of the maximum possible rate of enjoyment" (Ramsey 1978, 542).

To derive this rule, Ramsey used the calculus of variations. Keynes pointed out to him, however, that it can be made intuitive in the following way. Suppose the representative individual consumes £1 instead of saving it for another year. The gain is the marginal utility of consumption, $U'(C)$. In the left-hand panel of figure 26.1, it is represented by the shaded column of width $\Delta C = 1$ under the marginal utility curve at the current level of consumption. The loss arises from the postponement of the whole future schedule of consumption by the time interval $1/s$, where s is the current amount of saving; the amount s is now saved in $1 + (1/s)$ years instead of in one year. The path of utility corresponding to the optimal path is graphed in the right-hand panel of figure 26.1; it gradually approaches the stationary bliss level B. A reduction in saving by £1 shifts this curve to the right by $1/s$. The loss in utility is represented by the shaded column whose area is $(1/s)\,[B-U(C)]$. If the consumption path is optimal, this marginal loss must equal the marginal gain, $U'(C)$; the two shaded areas must be equal. It follows that

---

4. It should be noted that time preference, though considered later in the essay, plays no role in the basic analysis.

$$sU'(C) = B - U(C), \qquad (26.1)$$

which is the rule stated above.

Ramsey's paper is justly celebrated as the first explicit determination of the optimal path of capital accumulation toward the classical stationary state. Keynes called it not only "terribly difficult reading for an economist" but also "one of the most remarkable contributions to mathematical economics ever made." Nevertheless, however admirable the intellectual achievement, Ramsey's saving rule never became part of mainstream economics. By the end of the 1950s, when the theory of growth and capital accumulation had finally caught up with Ramsey's technique, the approach to stagnation no longer seemed to be the right thing to optimize.[5]

The fate of Ramsey's other paper in welfare economics, "A Contribution to the Theory of Taxation" (1927), was different. Pigou had suggested to Ramsey the following problem: Suppose the government requires a certain amount of revenue. This can be obtained by various types of taxes, for example, on individual commodities, wages, land, and the like. In general, they will impose on the economy a welfare loss due to the distortion of the price system. How should the taxes be levied to minimize this loss?

Ramsey's solution is again a brilliant piece of mathematical economics. Simplified to its bare outlines, it can be summarized as follows: Consider a single market with a linear demand curve of slope $dq/dp = \alpha$ and constant marginal cost c (figure 26.2). If the price equals marginal cost, the quantity sold is $\bar{q}$. If a surcharge t is added to marginal cost, the quantity sold, q, is reduced by $\bar{q} - q = \alpha t$. Tax revenue, graphically represented by the "Tax" rectangle, is $T = tq = \dfrac{q}{\alpha}(\bar{q} - q)$. The deadweight welfare loss, represented by the "Loss" triangle is $L = \dfrac{1}{2} t(\bar{q} - q) = \dfrac{1}{2\alpha}(\bar{q} - q)^2$. With a progressive increase in the tax rate, the revenue first rises to a maximum and then declines, while the loss increases monotonically with the square of the tax rate.

From the point of view of welfare optimization, the ratio between the marginal tax revenue and the marginal welfare loss, dT/dL, plays a crucial role. By taking differentials, this marginal benefit/loss ratio can be calculated as

$$\frac{dT}{dL} = \frac{(\bar{q} - q) - q}{-(\bar{q} - q)} = \frac{q}{\bar{q} - q} - 1. \qquad (26.2)$$

Denoting the price elasticity of demand by $\epsilon = \alpha(p/q)$, this can also be written as

5. Ramsey's approach was, however, used by Meade (1955a).

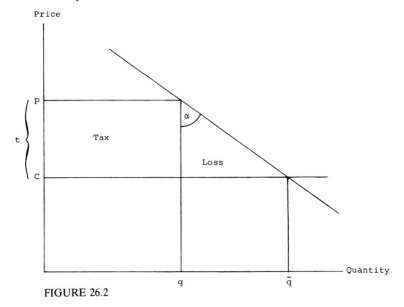

FIGURE 26.2

$$\frac{dT}{dL} = \frac{q}{\alpha t} - 1 = \frac{p}{\alpha(p/q)t} - 1 = \frac{p}{\epsilon t} - 1. \tag{26.3}$$

Suppose there are two such markets with independent demands, generally with different price elasticities and marginal costs. The problem is to determine tax rates t_1 and t_2 in such a way that the aggregate welfare loss is minimized for a given amount of aggregate revenue. Its solution evidently requires that the marginal benefit/loss ratio be the same in both markets; otherwise it would always be possible to reduce the loss by raising the tax in one market while lowering it in the other.

In algebraic terms the solution requires that

$$\frac{q_1}{\bar{q}_1 - q_1} = \frac{q_2}{\bar{q}_2 - q_2}, \tag{26.4}$$

which means that the proportional reduction in sales is the same in both markets. This is what became known as the Ramsey rule of optimal taxation. Alternatively, it can be written as

$$\frac{t_2/p_2}{t_1/p_1} = \frac{\epsilon_1}{\epsilon_2}, \tag{26.5}$$

which says that the taxes as a proportion of the respective prices must be inversely proportional to the price elasticities of demand. If there are more than two markets, these conditions must be satisfied for every pair of them.

326

Though the Ramsey rule was here derived for linear demand curves, constant marginal costs, independent demands, and a loss concept based on the consumer surplus, Ramsey showed that it remains valid in a much wider class of cases. Its basic message is that the maximization of welfare in the presence of a government budget constraint requires deviations of prices from marginal costs depending on demand elasticities. Where demand is highly sensitive to price, price should be close to marginal cost; where demand is less sensitive, the deviation should be larger.

The Ramsey rule is remarkably similar to the rule for optimal price differentiation of a profit-seeking monopolist. It had long been argued that railroad and public utility rates should be differentiated according to "what the traffic will bear." More precisely, profits would be maximized if prices exceeded marginal cost by percentages that are inversely proportional to the demand elasticities:

$$\frac{(p_2 - c_2)/p_2}{(p_1 - c_1)/p_1} = \frac{\epsilon_1}{\epsilon_2}. \tag{26.6}$$

It thus turns out that the rate structure (if not the rate level) of a benevolent public utility might not be much different, after all, from that resulting from monopolistic exploitation.

If there are any commodities with completely inelastic demands, Ramsey pointed out, they should bear the whole tax burden. This is the special case later envisaged by the marginal cost pricing rule: If lump sum taxes are available, all commodities or services should be sold at marginal cost. The Ramsey rule thus made the debate about the Hotelling rule obsolete before it had even started. The trouble was that the participants in that debate did not know this.

It cannot be said that Ramsey's contribution was ignored. As Baumol and Bradford (1970) have reported, it was extensively summarized by Pigou in 1928, it was discussed by Ursula Hicks in 1947, further developed by Boiteux in 1951 and generalized by Samuelson around the same time. The curious fact is that despite the attention it got from leading economists, the general significance of the Ramsey rule for both taxation and pricing policies was not recognized until Baumol and Bradford, forty-three years after Ramsey, published their restatement with the proposed subtitle "The Mystery of the Mislaid Maxim." In the meantime it has indeed become part of mainstream economics.

Abba Lerner

Pigou's substantive contributions to welfare theory related to particular markets. It was left to Abba Lerner to unite the Marshallian tradition to the general equilibrium tradition of Barone and Pareto. Abba Petachya Lerner was born in Bessarabia, Russia, in 1903. His family moved to England when he was a child, and he grew up in London's East End. In his youth he was a cap maker, a teacher in a Hebrew school, a rabbinical student, and a small businessman. A restless preoccupation with all sorts of social and socialist ideas and ideologies drove him to economics, and at the age of twenty-six, so far largely self-taught, he entered the London School of Economics. In every respect except intelligence, the contrast with Frank Ramsey could not have been greater.

Lerner was a brilliant student. Within a few years he had published a number of important articles and became one of the founders and managing editors of the *Review of Economic Studies*. In 1934–35 he went on a fellowship to Cambridge, where he became one of the first enthusiastic missionaries of Keynesianism, representing its socialist wing.

In 1937, after teaching for several terms at the London School of Economics, Lerner moved to the United States, where he held a large number of usually short-term teaching posts at Columbia, Johns Hopkins, the University of Kansas, the New School for Social Research, Roosevelt University, Michigan State, Queens College of the City University of New York, the University of California at Berkeley, and Florida State. In 1943 the London School of Economics awarded him a Ph.D. (the dissertation was a draft of *Economics of Control*), and he was fifty-six years old when he first obtained a permanent appointment in a graduate school. He died in Tallahassee, Florida, in 1982.

Lerner was an individualistic intellectual with a radical and nonconformist life style and unconventional ideas. He dreamed of a democratic market socialism based on welfare theory. In 1938 he traveled in an old car all the way to Mexico City in the futile hope of convincing Leon Trotsky that revolution should be based on marginalism—a true "marginal revolution." He was always full of schemes and proposals, which others usually found unworkable, if not abstruse. He was one of the last economists intelligent enough to make significant theoretical contributions without using explicit mathematics. He was also a talented artist whose moving wire sculptures were intuitive mathematics in the same sense as his economics.

Lerner's numerous contributions to economic theory (representative collections are Lerner 1953 and 1983) can be roughly divided into three groups. To the first group belongs his work on international trade, microeconomic theory, and welfare economics, written mostly before 1944. It culminated in *The Economics of Control* (1944), Lerner's masterpiece. Beginning in 1936, expositions and elaborations of Keynesian economics form a second group. In his later years, it was inflation that absorbed most of Lerner's attention. He typified the view of many Keynesians that full employment may involve inflation, that it is more important than price stability, and that it may be reconciled with stable prices by an incomes policy, particularly wage controls. Lerner felt strongly, however, that such controls could be successful only if the flexibility of relative wages was preserved. The Keynesian did not disavow the marginalist. It is fair to say that this later work, though often provocative and always articulate, did not attain the significance and theoretical quality of his early work on welfare.

Lerner's welfare analysis was guided by the question of how an omnipotent, but democratic, government can increase the welfare of its citizens. One way, for Lerner, was the equalization of incomes, but again, as in the case of Pigou, it was clear that this proposition owed more to his egalitarian convictions than to economic analysis. The other way to increase welfare was by improving, for each distribution of incomes, the allocation of resources. This is where Lerner made his contribution.

His basic criterion for an improvement in resource allocation was that some people be made better off without anybody being worse off. The allocation was optimal if such improvements could no longer be found. With this criterion, Lerner had virtually rediscovered Pareto optimality, apparently without knowing Pareto, and introduced the concept into the English-language literature.

Lerner's original contribution is the first comprehensive statement of the conditions for a Pareto optimal allocation of resources. Each individual aspect had been discussed before; Lerner was the first to describe the system as a whole. This system consists of three sets of conditions. The conditions of the first set govern the allocation of given quantities of consumer goods to individuals. They say that for each pair of goods, X and Y, all individuals must be willing to exchange one additional unit of X for the same quantity of Y. In technical terms, the marginal rates of substitution for any two goods must be the same for all individuals. As long as this condition is not satisfied, it is possible to make some people happier without making anybody less happy by simply reallocating goods among them. If Anna is willing to give up three nuts for an apple while Jim is willing to give up an apple for one nut, both can gain by exchanging an apple for two nuts. This condition, as such, was far from new, of course. It was the main content of Edgeworth's contract curve, which Pareto later expressed in the graphical apparatus that became known as the Edgeworth box.

The conditions of the second set govern the allocation of resources to the production of different consumer goods. Suppose, for the moment, there is only one scarce resource, called labor. It can be used to produce different combinations of consumer goods. For just two commodities, these combinations can be plotted in a production possibility (or transformation) curve (Lerner 1983, 59–69) of the sort used earlier by Fisher (1925) and Haberler (1930). Its slope at any given point indicates in what marginal ratio one good can be transformed into the other by shifting labor from one industry to the other. It is evident that this marginal rate of transformation corresponds to the ratio between the marginal labor costs of the two commodities.

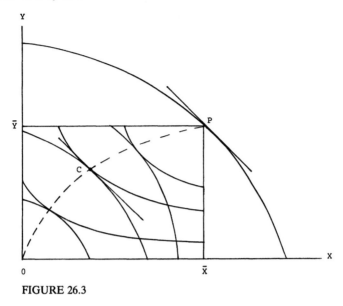

FIGURE 26.3

To be optimal, so the second set of conditions state, resources must be allocated to commodities in such a way that the marginal rate of transformation in production equals the marginal rate of substitution in consumption. If it is possible to produce four units of nuts by reducing apple production by one unit, while consumers need just two units of nuts to be compensated for one unit of apples, the present allocation can clearly be improved upon and thus cannot be optimal.

The interplay between the two sets of conditions was later illustrated in a graph like figure 26.3 (Bator 1957). The concave downward-sloping curve is the production possibility curve for X and Y. At point P, outputs are $\bar{X}$ and $\bar{Y}$. These outputs have to be allocated between Anna and Jim. The corresponding Edgeworth box is represented by the rectangle. Allocations satisfying the first condition are represented by the broken contract curve. The second optimality condition requires that the slope of the transformation curve at P equal the slope of the indifference curves along the contract curve, which is the case at consumption point C. For different locations of P there would be different Edgeworth boxes and different consumption points.

In fact, there is more than one factor of production, and the typical production process consists in the combination of many factors. This is where the third set of conditions comes in. It states that the allocation of factors to industries is not optimal unless the marginal rate at which factor A can be substituted against factor B is the same in all industries. If in wheat production, without changing output, 800 units of additional labor

330

make up for a reduction of acreage by 600 units, while in corn production an extension of the acreage by 600 units, through less intensive cultivation, would produce the same output with a saving of 1,000 units of labor, then more could be produced of both commodities by switching some acreage from wheat to corn.

This condition was illustrated by Lerner in 1933, possibly for the first time, in an Edgeworth box for production (1953, 70). The dimensions of the box in figure 26.4 represent the available quantities of factors *A* and *B*. If they are used in producing *X*, the possible outputs are indicated by the downward-convex isoquants with origin at *0*. If they are used in producing *Y*, the corresponding isoquants are drawn with origin at *Q*. (An isoquant is also drawn, without using the term, in another essay of 1933 [1953, 147]. Erich Schneider, in his compact statement of the production theory of that time, attributes the term to Ragnar Frisch [Schneider 1934, 4].) Efficiency requires that the output of *Y* be maximized for any output of *X*, which means that the respective isoquants are tangent to each other. This condition is satisfied along the broken efficiency curve, the production counterpart to the contract curve. The relationship of these conditions to the others is straightforward, the efficient combinations of *X* and *Y* along the efficiency curve simply providing the data from which the production possibility curve is constructed.

Lerner regarded these abstract conditions as a basis for policy prescriptions. In particular, he sought to devise rules by which a socialist government could hope to improve economic welfare. A direct planning approach, he was convinced, was hopeless. In this context he quoted Trotsky (Lerner 1944, 62): "If there existed the universal mind that projected

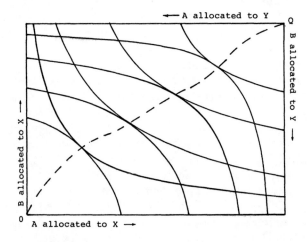

FIGURE 26.4

itself into the scientific fancy of Laplace . . . such a mind, of course, could *a priori* draw up a faultless and an exhaustive economic plan. . . . In truth, the bureaucracy often conceives that just such a mind is at its disposal; that is why it so easily frees itself from the control of the market and of Soviet democracy."

However, the socialist government could solve the planning problems, so Lerner argued, by using the price mechanism and instructing its production managers to follow rather simple rules. The first set of conditions could be implemented by confronting all individuals with the same market prices, thus avoiding any sort of price discrimination and preferential prices, however "social" they might seem. The third set of conditions could be realized by confronting managers with uniform factor prices and instructing them to minimize their production costs. The second set of conditions, finally, requires that prices be equal to marginal costs; it can be implemented by instructing managers to expand output whenever the market price exceeds marginal cost, and vice versa.

Once distribution was taken care of, so the socialist Lerner showed, a socialist planner could do no better than perfect competition. Rational economic control must have the objective of eliminating those deviations from perfect competition that free enterprise, as Adam Smith had argued so untiringly, would inevitably call forth. This was not a new argument. Richard Cantillon had made it two hundred years earlier, and Enrico Barone had made it the subject of his famous 1908 paper on the ministry of production in a collectivist state (Barone 1935). Lerner's analysis nevertheless represented a significant advance. In particular, Barone's analysis had omitted any explicit consideration of the three sets of optimality conditions. He made the plausible argument that for any conceivable deviation from perfect competition the winners would not win enough to compensate the losers, but it was not conclusive. That rational socialist planners would behave like Walrasian auctioneers was assumed, not demonstrated. The main analytical contribution, therefore, is Lerner's.

Is it not sufficient, as was often argued, that prices are just proportional to marginal costs, perhaps exceeding them by an equal percentage? Lerner answered that it was not, mainly because factors, particularly labor, are not only used in production but are also directly consumed, as labor is consumed in the form of leisure. A "wedge" between prices and marginal costs, even if it is proportionally equal for all commodities, thus distorts the allocation of factors between production and own consumption. Lerner won this debate; proportionality is not, in general, enough.

Lerner's optimality criteria, first published in 1934, initiated a wave of further contributions in rapid succession. Abram Burk (1938) (who later changed his name back to Bergson), continuing the Barone tradition, stated the problem as one of maximizing a social welfare function. Oscar Lange, long interested in the theory of socialist planning, derived the conditions in compact mathematical form (Lange 1942b). Nicholas Kaldor (1939) and John R. Hicks (1981–83, vol. 1, ch. 2) proposed to relax the stringent Pareto criterion. Instead of requiring that nobody be actually worse off, they suggested it was good enough if the winner had the means to compensate the losers. The winners should win more than the losers lose. This sort of reasoning indeed underlies much of the cost-benefit analysis for specific projects, but it is clear that an unambiguous improvement, free of all interpersonal comparisons of utility, requires actual, and not merely potential, compensation.

Lerner's *Economics of Control* of 1944 went far beyond the three sets of optimality criteria by including full employment as one of the basic welfare criteria. This led him to the concept of functional finance. By this he meant that fiscal policies should be guided not by conventional principles of sound finance but by their economic functions. Domestic government debt, he argued, does not impoverish an economy, because it only indicates a transfer from the taxpayers to the bondholders. Taxing and spending, borrowing and lending, and buying and selling were regarded as the six fiscal instruments of the government. They are related by the government budget constraint, in which money creation appears as the balancing item. These were not fundamentally new insights, nor were they always stated with the appropriate qualifications, but "functional finance" became the rallying cry of the fiscal activists on the Keynesian Left.

Harold Hotelling

At the time when Lerner distilled abstract efficiency criteria from general equilibrium analysis, Harold Hotelling found solutions to particular pricing problems. Born in 1895 in Fulda, Minnesota, Hotelling grew up in Seattle, Washington. After high school he worked for a small weekly newspaper and then went to the University of Washington to study journalism. An early (unpublished) paper concerned the influence of newspapers on elections. His interests were increasingly attracted to the mathematical side of such problems, and in 1921 he concluded two years of graduate work at the University of Washington with an M.S. in mathematics. For his doctoral work he went to Princeton, where he was awarded a Ph.D. in mathematics in 1924. Hotelling had married in 1920, and the advent of two children was accompanied by papers on birth rates and the duration of pregnancies. His first wife died in 1932, and two years later he entered into a second marriage, from which he had five sons.

After a few years at the Stanford Food Research Unit, Hotelling became an associate professor of mathematics at Stanford University. In 1931 he went as a professor of economics to Columbia University, where he remained until 1946. His reputation both in mathematical statistics and in mathematical economics grew rapidly. He was president of the Econometric Society and of the Institute of Mathematical Statistics and later the holder of several honorary degrees. He did much to find positions for displaced European scientists. One of them was Abraham Wald, for whom Hotelling obtained a professorship at Columbia. Hotelling was an enthusiastic teacher, who attracted many young mathematicians to statistics. Among those he attracted to economics was Kenneth Arrow. In 1946, Hotelling moved as professor of mathematical statistics to the University of North Carolina at Chapel Hill, where he founded the Department of Statistics. He retired in 1966 and died in 1973.

Hotelling's main interest was in applied mathematics. He had a gift for developing "pure theories" for applied problems. A perfectionist, he would often delay the publication of his work, and some of it was never published. In economics, in particular, the number of his major publications was quite limited, but each of them made a significant contribution.

Hotelling's first major paper in economics concerned product differentiation. Sraffa (1926) had suggested that each seller may be surrounded by an area in which he enjoys a spatial monopoly. In his article "Stability in Competition" (1929), Hotelling succeeded in giving this suggestion analytical precision. He started out from Cournot's duopoly case but replaced the assumption of identical products by the assumption of spatially differentiated products. As a consequence, demand would no longer switch completely from one seller to the other with the smallest difference in price but would rather shift continuously depending on the price differential. As his paradigm, Hotelling used two sellers located at different points along a street or railroad, so that the demand for each would depend on both prices and transportation costs. Each seller then calculates his profit-maximizing price on the assumption that his competitor's price is given. A stable market equilibrium is established at the prices that are simultaneously optimal for each competitor.

This analysis represented a significant contribution to the theory of monopolistic competition, several years before the alleged imperfect competition revolution had taken place. However, unknown to Hotelling, it had been almost completely anticipated by Launhardt (1885). Though influential and subjectively brilliant, this paper, therefore, cannot be regarded as Hotelling's claim to fame.

There is one extension with which Hotelling went beyond Launhardt's analysis. If the competitors are free to choose their locations, he argued, they would find it profitable to locate close to each other, somewhere near the midpoint of the road. This led to the conjecture, illustrated by Hotelling with many examples from apple cider to party platforms, that oligopolists tend to offer similar products. Whereas it became very popular and will always be associated with Hotelling's name, it was a suggestive idea rather than a piece of analysis and was later shown to be false (d'Aspremont et al. 1979). Hotelling provided no theory of the steady-state distribution of sellers.

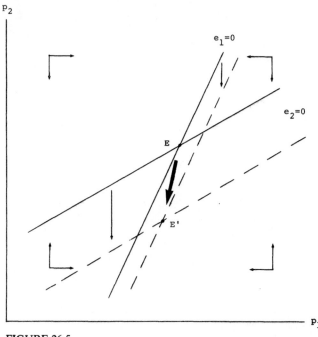

FIGURE 26.5

Hotelling also made a contribution to competitive prices (1932). Edgeworth (1925, 1:132, 143ff., 2:401) had discovered that a tax on a monopolized article may result in a decline in its price to the consumer. Hotelling succeeded in showing that this paradox may occur even in competitive markets if two goods are substitutes in both consumption and production. An excise tax on wheat may result in a decline in the consumer prices of both wheat and rye.

This possibility is illustrated in figure 26.5. The line for $e_1 = 0$ indicates for which combinations of a wheat price, p_1, and a rye price, p_2, the wheat market is in equilibrium, excess demand being zero. The rye market is in equilibrium along the line for $e_2 = 0$. Simultaneous equilibrium for both markets is reached at the intersection E. If the rye curve is flatter than the wheat curve, as drawn, the equilibrium is stable.

An excise tax on wheat shifts both curves downward, as indicated by the broken lines. If the parameters of the demand and supply functions are such that this shift is larger for the rye curve, the new equilibrium E' is characterized by lower prices for both goods. Hotelling investigated mathematically under what conditions this would happen.

Today this analysis looks like a routine exercise in comparative statics; it is hardly a fundamental contribution. It reminds one, however, that half

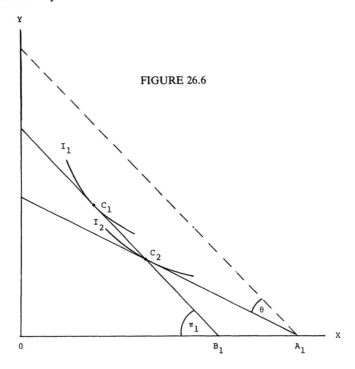

FIGURE 26.6

a century after Walras, simple relationships between two markets remained largely unexplored. It may be easier to write down an abstract general equilibrium system for *n* markets than to determine the specific properties of just two. This was essentially Marshall's position vis-à-vis Walras, but Marshall did not provide the rigorous two-market analysis either. It must also be recognized that Hotelling's paper made contributions to the techniques of mathematical economics, particularly of the theory of the firm, quite distinct from Edgeworth's curiosity.

Hotelling is best known for his welfare argument against excise taxes and for marginal cost pricing (1938). The underlying idea is very old, going back at least to Pierre de Boisguilbert, but Hotelling added analytical precision. He assumed, as a first approximation, that marginal costs are constant. His reasoning was mathematical, but for two goods it can be expressed in a diagram. In figure 26.6 the production possibilities for *X* and *Y* are represented by the broken straight line. Government consumption is assumed to consist of a certain amount of *Y* (to subject it to optimization would require additional dimensions). The private consumption possibilities, therefore, fall short of the production possibilities, as indicated by the solid line through C_1. Since at C_1 the consumption possibility curve is tangent to the social indifference curve I_1, this is the optimal point. The distance $0A_1$ represents national income, A_1B_1 is the income tax necessary to finance government consumption, and $0B_1$ is disposable income, all measured in terms of X.

Suppose now the income tax is replaced by an excise tax on Y. Disposable income is thereby raised to A_1, but for each unit of X the consumer obtains a smaller amount of Y than before. His new budget line is represented by the solid ray from A_1. The yield of the excise tax equals the yield of the former income tax at the point C_2 where the new budget line intersects the old line through C_1. The tax rate, represented by the angle θ, must be calculated in such a way that this intersection point is also the point the consumers want to choose, which means that at C_2 the budget line is tangent to an indifference curve.

Hotelling's argument is based on the observation that the new optimum, C_2, is necessarily on the old budget line. But C_1 is the optimal point on the old budget line. It follows that the excise tax optimum (in the absence of externalities, as Hotelling noted) is inferior to the income tax optimum. The excise tax, by distorting prices away from marginal costs, imposes a deadweight loss on the economy. Though Hotelling had assumed constant marginal costs, it soon became clear that the main result still holds for concave production possibility curves and thus for rising marginal costs (Little 1951).

From the point of view of general equilibrium welfare theory, Hotelling's paper added little to Lerner's analysis. It was far more effective in the context of partial welfare analysis as an argument for marginal cost pricing of public or regulated enterprises. Following in the footsteps of Jules Dupuit, Hotelling argued that the maximization of social benefits requires that such enterprises sell their goods or services at marginal cost. In many cases, particularly with falling marginal cost curves, the firm would then suffer a loss; average costs would not be covered.[6] Such losses should be financed by nondistorting taxes. For Hotelling this was an argument for large-scale nationalization.

As a general proposition, the marginal cost pricing rule was soon revealed to be deficient. It was pointed out that government financing of deficits, however accomplished, would have distorting effects of its own. It was also argued that it would impose a political burden of a different nature that would have to be set against the purely economic gain, if any.[7] It will further have to be kept in mind that marginal cost pricing for a

6. Hotelling seemed to share the widespread notion that the relevant marginal costs, say, for a railroad, can be determined by the experiment of transporting one additional passenger or ton. Since these are virtually nil, transportation should be practically free. This naïve view of marginal cost determination has done much to discredit the marginal cost pricing rule.

7. Ramsey's rule for the minimization of the deadweight burden of deviations from marginal cost pricing was discussed in the section above on Frank Ramsey.

particular commodity cannot be relied upon to increase welfare unless all other goods are sold at marginal cost, too. This problem is further discussed in the following section. Most fundamentally, increasing returns, including fixed set-up costs, would still create efficiency problems even if all goods were sold at marginal cost. Though thus deficient as a general pricing principle, Hotelling's rule retains its value as a guide to cost-benefit analysis in specific cases, and it effectively demolished average cost pricing. In this sense it made a significant contribution to the analysis of regulated prices.[8]

From the vantage point of the 1980s, Hotelling's most important contribution to economic science was his paper "The Economics of Exhaustible Resources" (1931). It was far from being the first attack on this problem. William Stanley Jevons had become famous for his book on the coal question, and the brilliant papers by L. C. Gray (1913, 1914) showed that even before World War I the theory of exhaustible resources had reached a level that would still have been respectable fifty years later. Economic science did not wait for the oil crisis of 1974 to concern itself with exhaustible resources.

In particular, Gray provided what may have been the first analysis of the optimal rate of exploitation of a coal mine. If coal were inexhaustible, he explained, mines would operate at the point where marginal production costs equal the market price. With a fixed total supply, however, production will be limited, if interest is disregarded, to the point of minimum average cost, since this would promise the highest aggregate profit. In the presence of interest, annual net returns have to be discounted before they are added over time. Maximization of the present value of future returns requires that the annual net returns increase at the market rate of interest. This, in turn, is achieved by operating the mine progressively less intensively, thus lowering marginal costs.

Gray's analysis, though remarkable for its economic insight, was limited by the lack of an explicit optimizing calculus and by the failure to consider the rate of change in the value of unexploited resources as a component of the owner's net return. This gap was closed by Hotelling, who thereby initiated the modern theory of exhaustible resources.

Hotelling introduced his analysis by describing a dilemma that has lost nothing of its relevance fifty years later. On the one hand, he said, the progressive disappearance of minerals, forests, and other exhaustible assets has led to demands for their conservation; from this point of view resources are too cheap and thus too rapidly exploited. On the other hand, there is a belief that "monopolies and combinations" have restricted output to extort high prices; from this point of view resources are too expensive, and

---

8. For a classic survey of the marginal cost pricing controversies, see Ruggles 1949 and 1950.

they are not exploited rapidly enough. A resolution of this dilemma, Hotelling pointed out, requires economic analysis.

The basic problem concerns the efficient allocation of a limited stock of commodities over time. The fundamental difference from normal production is that the total supply is fixed. Monopolistic practices do not change it; all they do is change the distribution of consumption over time. Higher prices today have a necessary counterpart in lower prices in the future, and vice versa. To focus on this basic problem, Hotelling abstracted from extraction and marketing costs, concentrating on the net price received by the producer. He also abstracted from the ability of many resources, such as fish and forests, to renew themselves and concentrated on nonrenewable resources such as coal or oil.

If the exploitation of such resources is left to competitive markets, Hotelling observed, it will be governed by a basic rule. According to this rule, the price must, under correct foresight, increase at a rate equal to the market rate of interest (after one allows for possible differences in risk). Arbitrage between oil deposits and other assets will see to it that both have the same yield.

To determine the competitive exploitation path, one also needs to know the demand for oil. It can be described by a demand curve. Suppose, for simplicity, that there is a finite price high enough to reduce demand to zero. Precisely when this price is reached, supplies must be exhausted. If they are not exhausted, the balance cannot be sold; if they are exhausted before, some oil was sold inefficiently cheap. Reckoning backward from the exhaustion price, p_T, one can determine prices for each preceding year by successively subtracting the interest rate. For each price, the demand curve, drawn in figure 26.7 as a solid line, provides the corresponding quantity. On a logarithmic scale, the price, p, declines in equal steps as one approaches the present time.

Beginning at the exhaustion time T, annual consumption can be added to give cumulative consumption over the last two years, the last three years, and so on. This cumulative total, drawn as a broken curve, cannot exceed the available supply, $\bar{q}$. The moment when this limit is reached is the present time. If, as in the graph, the limit is reached at $t = T - 6$, competitive exploitation will satisfy demand at gradually rising prices for 6 more years.

The next step in Hotelling's argument is the demonstration that the competitive rule actually maximizes the social value of the exhaustible resource. In principle, the invisible hand acts also over time. To prove his point, Hotelling determines what consumers would be willing to pay for the oil each year. Aggregate social value is then measured by the present value of these annual utilities, capitalized at the market rate of interest. This means, in Hotelling's view, that the need for regulatory measures is

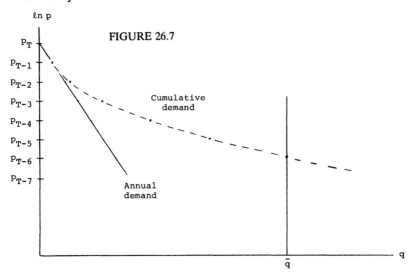

FIGURE 26.7

not inherent in competition itself. It does not mean, however, that regulatory measures are not needed at all, because reality may deviate in many respects from the competitive ideal.

If the exhaustible resource is monopolized, its exploitation will indeed deviate from the competitive ideal. The owner still values the available supplies at an opportunity cost that rises at the market rate of interest, but profit maximization now sees to it that this opportunity cost is equalized, not to the market price, but to the marginal revenue of the monopolist. As a consequence, less is produced at a higher price in the early stages, leaving more at a lower price for later. The general effect of monopoly is to retard exploitation. While this may be welcomed by conservationists, Hotelling shows that it nevertheless reduces the social benefit from the exhaustible resource.

Hotelling uses this general framework to investigate the modifications introduced by diminishing returns, and he also analyzes the effect of severance taxes and depletion allowances. Much of this analysis is based on the application of the calculus of variations to particular numerical examples, but the results, though not general, are nevertheless highly suggestive.

When it appeared, Hotelling's paper on exhaustible resources attracted little attention. In fact, it was hardly noticed for more than forty years until its central problem was moved into the public spotlight by the oil crisis. It is now recognized as a pioneering contribution to the welfare analysis of exhaustible resources.

James Meade

Lerner and Hotelling were concerned with finding criteria for the best allocation of resources. In reality, however, complete efficiency will hardly ever be attainable. This raises the problem, already suggested by Pigou, of finding a second-best solution attainable under given circumstances. It became the primary focus of the work of James E. Meade. Born in 1907, Meade studied at Malvern College and Oriel College, Oxford, where his interests gradually shifted from classics to economics, and he did a year of graduate work in philosophy, politics, and economics in Trinity College, Cambridge.[9] In Cambridge he belonged to the little "circus" that discussed Keynes's ideas then in the process of becoming the *General Theory*. One of the earliest Keynesians, he remained a Keynesian throughout his life. After a few years as fellow and lecturer in Hertford College, Oxford, he left academic life to work for the Economic Section of the League of Nations in Geneva, where he edited the *World Economic Survey*.

During the years of World War II and in the early postwar period, Meade worked for the British government. On Keynes's recommendation he was appointed to the Economic Section of the Cabinet Office, ultimately as its director. He was mainly concerned with planning and public enterprises, and he collaborated with Richard Stone in developing national income accounts. In recognition of his distinguished government service he was knighted in 1947.

In the same year, Meade joined the faculty of the London School of Economics as professor of commerce with special reference to international trade. This was scientifically his most productive period. In 1957 he moved to Cambridge as professor of political economy. After his early retirement from teaching in 1969, he stayed on in Cambridge as a fellow of Christ's College until 1974. During the Cambridge period he also chaired important government committees on the economies of Mauritius and on tax reform. In 1977 he was awarded the Nobel Prize in economic science jointly with Bertil Ohlin.

Meade belongs to the utilitarian tradition of British economics. The price system is regarded as crucial for the efficient allocation of resources. Its numerous failures, however, require rational government intervention. In particular, full employment can be maintained only by appropriate monetary and fiscal policies. In addition, an egalitarian interpretation of justice leads to the demand for strong redistributive measures. Overall, despite the vast differences in origins and life styles, Meade's economic philosophy was not very different from Lerner's. Harry G. Johnson called it the "price-

9. The biographical data are mostly from the article on Meade by Corden and Atkinson in the *International Encyclopedia of the Social Sciences* (1979) and from Johnson 1978.

system socialism of the 1930s vintage." Meade's strong interest in Malthusian problems and eugenics was a natural outgrowth of this utilitarian philosophy.

Like Pigou, Meade communicated with the world mainly through his books. These are characterized by original points of view, balanced judgment, and lucid reasoning, but also by a cumbersome exposition, idiosyncratic mathematics, and an almost unreadable style. Except for some graphical devices, Meade was never able to construct new analytical engines that other researchers were directly able to use, and he does not tell his readers where the exposition of other people's work ends and his own contribution begins.

Planning and the Price Mechanism (1948) developed Meade's "liberal-socialist solution." In *A Geometry of International Trade* (1952), the "international trade butterfly" made its first appearance as an expository device to depict the international equilibrium for two countries and two commodities. *The Theory of International Economic Policy* is Meade's main contribution to economic science. The first volume, *The Balance of Payments* (1951), is important as an extension of the Keynesian model to the open economy. Like Jan Tinbergen at about the same time, Meade distinguishes between weapons and targets of economic policies. The targets are internal balance, meaning full employment, and external balance, meaning balance of payments equilibrium. The weapons are fiscal and monetary policies and also wage adjustments and devaluation. Though full of excellent economics, the book is virtually unreadable. It was left for Robert Mundell (1962) to provide for the turgid prose of his former teacher the same service Hicks had provided for the glittering prose of Keynes, namely a translation into an elegant and manageable model.

The second volume, *Trade and Welfare* (Meade 1955a), is concerned with the allocative aspects of international economic policy under full employment. In earlier monographs, *Problems of Economic Union* (1953) and *The Theory of Customs Unions* (1955b), Meade had extended Viner's (1950) analysis of customs unions in terms of trade creation and trade diversion. *Trade and Welfare* became the classic treatment of the subject, though again in a style that is hard to appreciate for a present-day economist.

The little book with the somewhat presumptuous title *A Neo-Classical Theory of Economic Growth* (Meade 1962a) is notable for the proposition that consumption along a path of balanced growth is maximized if annual savings equal the share of profits in national income. This optimizing condition, however, is not related by Meade to the golden rule in terms of interest and growth rates.

While a planned treatise about the domestic economy remained unwritten, Meade, again in the Mill-Marshall tradition, published four volumes of *Principles of Political Economy* (1965–76). They synthesized his ideas on *The Stationary Economy, The Growing Economy, The Controlled Economy,* and *The Just Economy* in terms accessible to undergraduate students. *The Intelligent Radical's Guide to Economic Policy* (Meade 1975) was intended as a programmatic manifesto of market socialism in an inflationary economy with "indicative planning." In later years, Meade's thinking, like Lerner's, was increasingly preoccupied with stagflation, that bane of Keynesian epigones. He thought that powerful trade unions produce cost inflation. As a countermeasure he advocated wage norms, but he was never able to explain how these could be effective against powerful unions under the free bargaining that he regarded as essential.

The most clearly identifiable of Meade's contributions to economic science is the second-best approach to welfare problems. Both the approach and the term were suggested by J. M. Fleming's (1951) paper, "On Making the Best of Balance of Payments Restrictions on Imports." This was a somewhat inelegant study of limited scope. Meade recognized the potential significance of Fleming's method and, with generous acknowledgement, developed it into a general framework for the analysis of welfare problems.

This approach had two main aspects, one negative and destructive, the other positive and constructive. On the negative side, Meade pointed out that general equilibrium welfare economics does not provide practical guidelines for economic policy, because each of the marginal conditions holds only if all other marginal conditions are satisfied. This was not a new insight, to be sure, and Pigou (though his name does not appear in the index of Meade's book) had formulated it in very explicit terms. It remained for Meade, however, to make its pervasive significance clear.

He distinguished between a utopian and a second-best welfare criterion. Under the utopian criterion a policy is judged on the assumption that all other policies are optimal. According to the second-best criterion, a policy is judged optimal if it represents the best that can be done under the given circumstances. The distinction is important because a policy that would raise welfare under the utopian criterion may well reduce it under the second-best criterion. "If there are a number of existing divergences between marginal values and costs, then the reduction of one of these divergences—the others all remaining unchanged—will not necessarily lead to an increase in economic welfare, but may very well reduce it" (Meade 1955a, 102). It would be a serious mistake, therefore, to take the equalization of marginal values and costs as a guide for piecemeal policy applications.

This negative aspect of the second-best approach was subsequently made mathematically precise by Richard Lipsey and Kelvin Lancaster in their *General Theory of the Second Best* (1956). If a constrained maximum problem, so they showed, is subject to an additional constraint on one of the marginal conditions, the remaining marginal conditions cease to hold. It was characteristic for the spirit of the times that the translation of the economic insight into mathematics, though not particularly difficult, received more attention in contemporary theory than the insight itself.

Meade's second-best approach, however, also had a positive side, for it was an invitation to search for constructive second-best criteria. The problem is that such criteria cannot be expected to have the form of general rules; everything depends on the circumstances of the case. Despite this fundamental pragmatism, Meade, again in the Pigovian tradition, offers some plausible presumptions. One of them says that the reduction of a particular distortion, all others remaining the same, is likely to be beneficial if there are no distortions on close substitutes. In addition, if there are such substitutes, welfare can probably be raised by reducing the divergencies on all of them in about the same proportion. Furthermore, the overall effect is likely to be positive if the elimination of distortions begins with the largest divergencies, particularly if they are successively reduced to the level of the next largest. These presumptions were later made mathematically rigorous in Tatsuo Hatta's "Theory of Piecemeal Policy Recommendations" (1977). Meade concluded that attempts to remove barriers to international trade should be as general in scope as possible and should concentrate particularly on the reduction of the highest barriers (1955a, 566).

Meade also developed a general methodology for the cost-benefit analysis of policy measures. Inspired by Fleming, it essentially consists in an application of the consumer (and/or producer) surplus approach to marginal changes. In the absence of distortions, the *marginal* consumer surplus is zero everywhere. In the presence of import duties (or other distortions) it is equal to the duty. Import duties are a wedge between the value of a commodity in the exporting country and its value in the importing country, and this wedge reflects the increase in the value of the marginal unit when it crosses the border. The marginal effects of a policy measure on welfare can thus be determined as the sum of its effects on the quantities traded, each evaluated at the rate of duty. This method was applied to a wide range of international policies, including bilateral trade, factor movements, and multilateral problems of discrimination and customs unions. Its most concise exposition can be found in section 17 of the mathematical supplement.

This constructive approach to second-best problems had been pioneered by Frank Ramsey, whose rule the results of section 17, though reached in a different way, in fact resemble. In Meade's hands the rule developed into a comprehensive and fundamental welfare analysis of economic policies. In subsequent years this provided the basis for outstanding further contributions to the theory of protection such as those by Harry G. Johnson (1971), Richard Lipsey (1970) and W. M. Corden (1971). In particular, these contributions elaborated Meade's insight (which can already be found in the earlier literature) that tariffs on imported raw materials may have, in part, the opposite effect from those on consumer goods; what mattered for protection, therefore, was their net effect. The result was the modern theory of effective protection. Going beyond trade, the second-best perspective became basic for modern cost-benefit analysis in general. Meade demonstrated that it is not the end of applied welfare economics but rather its beginning.

27
John Maynard Keynes

IN GENERAL, the influence of social, political, and even economic developments on the history of economic theory is weak and unspecific. To "explain" David Ricardo, Johann Heinrich von Thünen, Augustin Cournot, Hermann Heinrich Gossen, Stanley Jevons, and Léon Walras in terms of economic determinants is not a promising undertaking. There are exceptions, though. World history of the 1930s was, directly or indirectly, largely shaped by the Great Depression. Among its legacies was the conviction that mass unemployment is one of the great problems of mankind. It provided the historical background for the phenomenon that was John Maynard Keynes.

Life

Keynes was born in 1883 in Cambridge, England.[1] His father, John Neville Keynes, was a university administrator who, despite a successful book on the method of political economy, never made it to a professorship. His paternal grandfather had prospered as a brush maker and florist, and in his mother's family there were many clergymen. Maynard's genealogical researches later revealed that the Keyneses had earlier belonged to the aristocracy and that one of his forebears was a Norman knight who had fought at Hastings. Maynard Keynes always managed to end up at the top.

The boy grew up as the oldest of three children in comfortable circumstances. He was a precocious but sickly child whose ambitions were early directed to intellectual excellence. A strong performance in mathematics earned him admission to Eton, a school of the elite. There he was a star pupil who not only won prizes with surprising ease but also made friends.

From Eton, Keynes went to King's College, Cambridge. His main field was mathematics, but his heart was more in philosophy, history, and

---

1. The phenomenon of Keynes has given rise to an enormous flow of biographical material. Harrod's early biography (Harrod 1951) was a masterpiece, but Skidelsky 1983–88 and Hession 1984 now offer much additional material. The essays in Milo Keynes 1975, Patinkin and Leith 1977, and Crabtree and Thirlwall 1980 shed light on particular aspects of Keynes's life.

literature—a parallel to Marshall. The exclusive clubs and debating societies to which he belonged determined his circle of friends for the rest of his life. They satisfied his Victorian need for high-sounding ideas and ethical justifications but also tended to accentuate a certain snobbish arrogance and a contempt for those who were intellectually his inferiors. His urge to prove himself superior was seemingly insatiable. Keynes could charm and dazzle, but he was often rude and bruising. The circle at King's was also strongly homosexual. Homosexual relationships, both deep and crude, played an important role in the first part of Keynes's adult life.

After the successful conclusion of his undergraduate work, Keynes remained in Cambridge for another year to prepare for the civil service examination. This included economics. Keynes thus read Marshall, Jevons, Cournot, and Edgeworth and impressed Marshall by his work. Ironically, his worst grades were in economics and mathematics, but overall he was second out of 104 candidates. The fruit of this success was a junior clerkship at the India Office. He remained there for two years. Out of his experience grew his first book, *Indian Currency and Finance* (Keynes 1971– , vol. 1).

The civil service provided Keynes with a good understanding of government, with financial expertise, and with valuable connections. It also left him ample time to work on a fellowship dissertation on probability theory. The first application was not successful, but in 1909, Keynes was awarded a fellowship at King's College. He resigned his post to return to Cambridge as a lecturer in economics, which he had to learn largely through teaching. Keynes was never a professor, but up to the war his teaching load was relatively heavy (though still light by present standards). His seminar, called the Political Economy Club and fashioned after the student clubs, became famous.[2] His main interest was in money and finance. In economic theory, both his interest and his knowledge always remained limited. In any case, he was a faithful Marshallian, quantity theorist, and freetrader. In 1911 young Keynes became editor of the *Economic Journal,* which he remained, for a time jointly with Edgeworth, with outstanding success until 1945.

Keynes always retained a foothold in London. He was one of a group of young intellectuals and artists that became known as the Bloomsbury Group. They were elitist bohemians, proud of what they regarded as their avant-garde values, with much talent, arrogance, and neurosis. While trying his hand at journalism and publishing *Indian Currency and Finance,* Keynes labored on making his dissertation into a book. The *Treatise on Probability* finally appeared in 1921 (Keynes 1971– , vol. 8).

During World War I, Keynes joined the Treasury, where his influence

---

2. Even Keynes, like so many other teachers, had to use compulsion to ensure student participation: he made students draw lots to determine who had to speak and in what order.

rose rapidly. At one time he applied for exemption from military service as a conscientious objector, but the tribunal saw no reason to consider his moral arguments, confused as they were, because the government had already given him an exemption in view of the importance of his work for the war effort. As a Treasury representative, Keynes participated in the Paris Peace Conference, where he could observe all the leading figures at first hand. The result was *The Economic Consequences of the Peace* (Keynes 1971– , vol. 2), a devastating critique of the peace treaty and a brilliant piece of writing. It made its author world famous overnight. He was now the most influential financial journalist, an opinion leader governments had to reckon with. The *Essays in Persuasion* (Keynes 1971– , vol. 9) show him as a Cassandra against the dangers of deflation, but he also acquired a reputation for often changing his mind.

The 1920s saw Keynes as a financier. Around 1920 he began to speculate in foreign exchange and commodities, transacting most of his business in the late morning from his bed. His first speculations failed, and he had to be rescued by a friend, but later Keynes gained a comfortable fortune. It enabled him to become a patron of the arts and a collector of rare books and manuscripts. Keynes also managed the finances of his college with much success, he became director of two insurance companies, and he managed an investment trust. His aggressive portfolio policies were successful in the 1920s, but they led to considerable losses in the 1930s, and Keynes later became more conservative.

In his late thirties, Keynes began to be attracted by a member of the opposite sex. She was Lydia Lopokova, prima ballerina of the Diaghilev ballet.[3] They were married in 1925 after she had obtained a divorce from her first husband. It was a happy marriage. His wife gave up her career, and Keynes became a producer of ballets and later the founder and owner of the Cambridge Art Theatre.

In the 1930s, Keynes made his entry into the history of economics. As an economic scientist he was a late bloomer. At the beginning of the decade, he hardly rated even a footnote in future histories of economic thought. At its conclusion, his contribution was seen by many as being comparable to that of Adam Smith. He was celebrated as the leading economic theorist of his age and as the man who revolutionized capitalism. How this came about will be told in the following section. In 1937, Keynes suffered a severe heart attack, and his wife became the dedicated protector of his fragile health.

The 1940s, finally, saw Keynes as the great financial authority and adviser of his government, which, in 1942, made him Baron Keynes of

3. A friend of hers was another Diaghilev ballerina, Olga Koklova, who was then Mrs. Picasso, and both were guests at a party Keynes gave for Picasso and Derain. There are sketches of Lydia Lopokova by Picasso.

Tilton (where he had a farm). He also was one of the principal architects of the gold/exchange standard system devised at Bretton Woods in 1944, but the result was closer to the U.S. views than to his own. There were now hardly any peaks he had not reached. He succumbed to another heart attack in 1946.

Principal Economic Works

Keynes's arduous ascent to scientific fame is marked by three books. *A Tract on Monetary Reform* (Keynes 1971– , vol. 4), which grew out of articles in the *Manchester Guardian Commercial,* shows him in full mastery of the intricacies of monetary policy and international finance. It develops sensible and progressive ideas, but without being revolutionary or even particularly innovative. Irving Fisher had said similar things twelve years earlier. The basic evils are inflation and deflation; capitalism needs a stable standard of value. True, money is neutral, but only in the long run, and "in the long run we are all dead" (65). In the short run inflation and deflation have serious consequences. Price fluctuations are explained by the traditional Cambridge version of the quantity theory, which Keynes calls fundamental (61). Efforts to stabilize the price of gold or foreign exchange rates are not compatible with price stability. The gold standard is a "barbarous relic" (138), and the future belongs to managed fiat currencies. Long-run stability of prices can be combined with a dampening of short-run exchange rate fluctuations by central bank operations in gold and forward exchange markets.

With the *Tract* Keynes had conquered the City. With the *Treatise on Money* (Keynes 1971– , vols. 5, 6) he set out to conquer academia. He undertook to discover "the dynamical laws governing the passage of a monetary system from one position of equilibrium to another" (5:xvii). The instability of the price system is still the central problem, but it is now explained, Wicksellian fashion, in terms of differences between investment and saving, which differences are said to equal profits. If profits are positive, prices rise, and vice versa. Prices are flexible, and the dynamic process is driven, in the traditional way, by discrepancies between prices and costs. The quantity theory of money is extended, but not invalidated.

This theoretical framework is used as a basis for a detailed analysis of monetary policy in all its ramifications. Though this contains a wealth of valuable economics, it is basically flawed by the deficiencies of the underlying theory. Keynes's effort to explain a dynamic process by accounting identities (called fundamental equations) was doomed from the beginning. As a contribution to monetary theory, the *Treatise* was a failure. Keynes still had not made his mark in economic science. He realized this before the book was even published and called it in the preface "a collection of material rather than a finished work." He thought now that he could do it "better and much shorter" if he were to start over again (Keynes 1971– , 5:xvii–xviii).

Start over again he did, spurred on by the dissatisfaction with the *Treatise,* by the deepening world depression, and by the critical comments of a seminar of young Cambridge economists, called the circus. The result was the *General Theory of Employment, Interest and Money* (1936). Price fluctuations had now disappeared from center stage. Their place was taken by fluctuations in output and employment. Saving and investment were now defined to be equal at all times, but output had to fluctuate to make them so. Employment could not rise much above full employment, but it could easily fall far below. On average, therefore, employment was likely to be unsatisfactory. This was diagnosed as a fundamental defect of capitalist economies. Its correction, Keynes concluded, required an active stabilization policy based on a new social philosophy.

This time the exposition was almost entirely verbal; no more fundamental equations. There was one graph, suggested by Roy Harrod, and a few scattered formulas. Keynes, the man of the persuasive word, had now become decidedly antimathematical. Nevertheless, the argument was more coherent than in the *Treatise,* and Hicks (1981–83, vol. 2, ch. 8) soon succeeded in expressing it in graphs and equations. It was embedded in polemic attacks on "classical orthodoxy," supposedly personified in many of his former friends and colleagues, particularly Pigou. The quantity theory and Say's law of markets were displayed as the villains from whose tyranny economics had to be liberated. This time, academia was indeed conquered. Keynes, at fifty-three, had finally won his place in the pantheon of economics. At the same time, he had bequeathed to the profession an entirely distorted picture of the classical tradition.

Wage Rigidity

The basic assumption of Keynesian economics is the rigidity of money wages. True, it is introduced in the *General Theory* only as a provisional simplification, and Keynes, particularly in chapter 19, has much to say about the consequences of wage changes, but to the extent that Keynes erected a coherent analytical structure, this is based on the assumption of given money wages. Without it, there could be no involuntary unemployment.

The notion that unemployment was basically due to the imperfect flexibility of wages was, of course, far from new. In fact, it was one of the traditional features of what Keynes, unhistorically, called classical economics. However, mainstream economics tended to regard wage rigidity, and thus unemployment, as an adjustment problem, albeit possibly a serious one, to be handled by dynamic analysis. Stationary equilibrium would be characterized by complete wage adjustment and thus full employment.

It was left for Keynes to use rigid wages as the basis of a purely static theory, thus generating the concept of equilibrium unemployment.

Once money wages are assumed to be invariant, it is analytically convenient to use them (in the place of, say, commodity prices) as the general deflator. This is precisely what Keynes did, thus expressing all real variables, in Ricardian fashion, in wage units.

Effective Demand

Income and output, in the Keynesian system, are governed by the principle of effective demand. In equilibrium, the principle says, aggregate demand must equal aggregate supply at prices that cover costs. This principle, again, was deeply embedded in the tradition of mainstream economics as exemplified by, say, Adam Smith, David Ricardo, Léon Walras, and Alfred Marshall. However, in mainstream economics wage adjustments saw to it that equality of supply and demand would take place at a point of full employment. Keynes departed from this approach by constructing, through his fixed-wage assumption, a case in which equality of demand and supply was compatible with unemployment.

Deviating from the unfortunate terminology of the *Treatise,* Keynes now defined his concepts in such a way that any (hypothetical) excess demand would imply an equal (hypothetical) excess of investment over saving. The principle of effective demand could thus be translated into an equivalent principle of saving and investment.

Aggregate supply was supposed to depend on employment and the stock of capital goods in the conventional way. While employment was variable, capital was regarded as given by the history of investment. It remained for Harrod (1952, ch. 13) to consider the capacity effect of investment and thus to set the Keynesian economy in motion. Firms are assumed to expand production to the point where the marginal product of labor is equal to the real wage rate. Given money wages, this fixes the price level compatible with any amount of employment.

Following Léon Walras, Knut Wicksell and other "classical" economists, Keynes divided aggregate demand into consumption and investment, thus making use of the old insight that macroeconomic fluctuations have much to do with the characteristic differences in the behavior of these components.

For what he christened the propensity to consume, Keynes postulated that it rises with increasing income, but by (absolutely) less than income. This postulate later called forth extensive empirical research, making the consumption function the most thoroughly researched of all behavior functions.

The inducement to invest was seen to depend on the addition to the capital stock that, with given expectations, is necessary to bring the marginal efficiency of capital down to the level of the rate of interest. What

Keynes called the marginal efficiency of capital was the same concept as Fisher's marginal rate of return over cost, the marginal internal rate of return.

There is, in Keynes's system, no automatic mechanism assuring that, at any arbitrary level of income, the demand for investment would just make up for the amount of income people did not wish to consume. For a given rate of interest, there was likely to be only one amount of total output at which the principle of effective demand was satisfied. Keynes believed that the absence of such a mechanism constituted his crucial departure from "classical" economics, a denial of Say's law. This was not, in fact, true. Even in pre-Keynesian general equilibrium theory, output is perfectly determinate. For each wage rate, there is only one output at which investment matches saving. The relevant point is that in pre-Keynesian theory, flexible wages see to it that equilibrium output is at the full-employment level, whereas in Keynesian theory they are prevented from performing this job.

The Multiplier

Once equilibrium output is determined, there is the question of how it would be affected by an exogenous shift in investment demand. It was answered by a multiplier which, in the simplest possible case, is the reciprocal of the marginal propensity to save and thus, normally, greater than one. One million dollars' worth of additional investment would result in several million dollars' worth of additional income.

This was not a new idea. It had long been recognized that public works in a certain amount might, with unused capacity, expand employment by more than this amount.[4] In fact, it may be suspected that this is one of those commonsensical notions that have accompanied humanity through much of its civilized history. The question was how the additional employment could be estimated. To answer it, Nicholas Johannsen developed his multiplying principle in various papers, mostly in German, beginning in 1903. He also applied the principle, much as did Keynes, to effective demand.[5] The concept was reinvented by Richard F. Kahn (1931), a leading member of the circus. He interpreted his employment multiplier as the sum of an infinite convergent series of successive increments. Keynes applied the concept to the effect of investment changes on income. At the same time, he recast Kahn's dynamic multiplier in the equivalent form of a comparative-static multiplier. In this form, it became the ancestor of an innumerable family of similar multipliers, each relating the change in one

4. The argument was used, for example, by the Saint-Simoniens at the time of Napoleon III in support of government expenditures in connection with the rebuilding of Paris.
5. There is a reference to Johannsen's English paper (1908) in the *Treatise* (1971– , 6:90), but, strangely, not in the *General Theory*. Extensive excerpts from Johannsen's articles can be found in Bombach et al. 1983.

particular endogenous variable to the underlying change in a particular exogenous variable. François Quesnay's vision had been implemented. Comparative macrostatics was born.

Liquidity Preference

In the preceding sections the rate of interest was regarded as given. To explain it, Keynes had to look beyond the output market to asset markets. Faced with the choice between bonds and money, he chose to focus on money. He seems to have believed that this choice was of momentous importance. In fact, as later became clear, he was mistaken, because the demand for the omitted asset can always be derived from the remainder of the system. The real question concerned not the asset to focus on but the behavior assumptions to be made.

Keynes regarded the demand for real cash balances, called liquidity preference, as depending positively on real income and negatively on the rate of interest. The first influence primarily reflected transactions and precautionary motives, whereas the second mainly reflected speculative considerations concerning future capital gains or losses on bonds. The lower the present rate of interest, the larger, ceteris paribus, would be a future rise, the larger the expected capital loss on securities, and the higher, therefore, the preference for liquid cash balances. As an extreme, though unlikely, possibility, Keynes envisaged the case in which even the smallest decline in interest rates would produce a sizable switch into cash balances, which would make the demand curve for cash balances virtually horizontal. This limiting case became popular among Keynesians as the liquidity trap. Keynes thought, correctly, that these speculative motives were relevant mainly for interest-bearing time deposits, whereas non-interest-bearing demand deposits would mainly be held for transactions and precautionary purposes. Though historically influential, Keynes's analysis of the demand for money went hardly beyond the Cambridge tradition. It offered less than Hicks (1981–83, vol. 2, ch. 5) had offered the year before, and further progress had to wait for James Tobin.

In the special case of interest-insensitive investment, equilibrium output was independent of liquidity preference. The latter became a sideshow, determining nothing but the rate of interest. In the special case of the liquidity trap, liquidity preference sufficed to determine the rate of interest. The latter could then be used to help determine output. In general, demand and supply of output interacted with the demand and supply of money to determine jointly both output and the rate of interest. Though Keynes was quite clear about the fact of this interaction, he was not able to give it a lucid analytical expression. The IS/LM diagram remained to be invented by Hicks.

The Futility of Wage Reductions

With money wage rates above their critical level, the Keynesian economy suffers from unemployment. This will persist as long as wages remain fixed. Keynes realized that this state cannot last forever. Sooner or later money wages have to give way. In a purely static context, Keynes agreed this would indeed eliminate unemployment. The required decline in real wages could conceivably be achieved through a reduction in money wages. His most fundamental reason for this conclusion is that lower wages result in higher real cash balances and thus in lower interest rates and higher output. Since this became known as the Pigou effect and was regarded as a crucial objection to Keynes, it is worth noting that it was fully described by Keynes himself.

It was also Keynes's emphatic view, however, that this static argument did not decide the issue. His reasons had to do with the dynamics of expectations. *Lower* wages cannot be achieved overnight but require a prolonged period of *falling* wages. Once such wage deflation sets in, entrepreneurs will begin to expect lower prices and wages in the future and thus curtail their current investments even further. Output and employment, therefore, would contract rather than expand, at least for some time. Things would get much worse before they could get better. Such a deflationary collapse could be avoided if the additional real balances were created through an expansion of the money supply instead of through wage reductions.

It has often been claimed that this dynamic argument signals Keynes's crucial departure from classical economics. If this were so, he would have been under a scientific obligation to support his argument, plausible as it is, by an explicitly dynamic analysis. Around 1936, with the work of Ragnar Frisch, Michal Kalecki, Jan Tinbergen, and others, many elements of such an analysis were available; economic dynamics made rapid progress. With the mathematical tools at Keynes's disposal, a decisive contribution was not out of reach. In fact, Keynes was content with suggestive observations about expectations and psychology. If his vision was perhaps dynamic, he could not implement it. The body of his theory remained entirely static. Actually, far from pushing macroeconomic theory forward to dynamics, he pulled it back to statics.

Stabilization Policy

On business cycles, Keynes offered suggestions but no theory. He shared the widespread view that industrialized economies, though not violently unstable, were subject to marked fluctuations in investment demand and thus in output and employment. Relatively brief periods of boom and prosperity, he thought, would be separated by prolonged depressions. Inventions, discoveries, and population growth were unlikely in the future to provide the stimulus to investment they had provided in the past. There was a prospect of secular stagnation. It was the task of government stabilization policies to counteract depression and to raise average employment.

In the 1920s there had been high hopes that the business cycle could be eliminated by an enlightened monetary policy using open-market operations. Keynes argued that the effectiveness of monetary policy was likely to be disappointing, either because the money supply, caught in the liquidity trap, had little impact on the rate of interest or because the rate of interest, in view of a rapid decline in the marginal efficiency of capital, had little influence on investment demand, or for both reasons.

This left the major role to fiscal policy. Through the multiplier, government expenditures, even for unproductive pyramid building, could raise national income and employment. Similarly, an appropriate tax/transfer system could stimulate aggregate demand both for consumer and investment goods. Keynes did not push this argument beyond broad suggestions, but he provided the framework for what Abba Lerner later elaborated as "functional finance."

The "Keynesian Revolution"

Keynes claimed to have demonstrated, contrary to the doctrines of orthodox economics, that an economy can be trapped in an underemployment equilibrium. A genius of persuasion, he convinced many contemporaries, particularly among the younger professors and advanced students, that this claim was valid. This was the rallying cry of the "Keynesian revolution" (Klein 1947).

As a matter of fact, Keynes had proved nothing of the sort. He probably knew that his claim was exaggerated, for he wrote to Harrod, "I *want*, so to speak, to raise a dust; because it is only out of the controversy that will arise that what I am saying will get understood" (Keynes 1971– , 13:548; Keynes's emphasis). To quote H. G. Wells, "To get maximum attention, it's hard to beat a good, big mistake."

What Keynes was able to demonstrate was far more modest. He showed that money wages, held rigid above their equilibrium level, result in unemployment. This proposition was neither new nor startling. In fact, it was in the mainstream of the traditional theory of unemployment. This is well illustrated by Pigou's *Theory of Unemployment* (1933). Pigou, like the later Keynes, divided output into consumption and investment, using wage goods as deflator. Consumption is taken to depend on income, whereas investment depends on interest rates, expectations, innovations, and the like. Employment depends on aggregate demand. With a high elasticity of labor supply, a contraction of demand would result in a large decline in employment, but a small decline in wage rates (and vice versa). Pigou conjectured that wage adjustments are likely to be relatively slow.

Clearly, if wages were kept above their market-clearing level, there would be "involuntary unemployment." While Pigou is dull and arid where Keynes is brilliant, in economic substance the difference between the self-proclaimed revolutionary and the alleged archorthodox seems minor.

What, then, was the Keynesian revolution all about? Its core was the emergence of a new model by which the short-run consequences of rigid wages became amenable to simple static analysis. This model was not entirely novel. Its outlines could clearly be discerned in pre-Keynesian literature (as, for example, in Pigou). Nor was the model fully articulated in the *General Theory* and left much confusion to be cleared up.[6] Still, the static Keynesian model became an important addition to mainstream economics, the centerpiece of what became known as macroeconomics. What had taken its place in pre-Keynesian economics, namely the quantity theory for the long-run effect of money on prices and the dynamic business cycle theory for short-run fluctuations, dropped into the background.

Fifty years later, it may be hard to understand why this addition to macrostatics looked revolutionary. One reason was, certainly, that Keynes went out of his way to present it as such, using distorted effigies of predecessors and contemporaries as straw men to knock over. Another reason was, probably, that Keynes understood better than most economists what sort of social philosophy people were looking for in the turmoil of the Great Depression. Still another contributing factor may have been the generally low standard of economic theory in the post-Marshallian period.

Place in the History of Economics

Since Adam Smith economics has had no genius of persuasion like Keynes. Like Smith, Keynes seemed not only to lay new foundations for his science but also to effect a change in the way people thought about social policy and, thereby, in their everyday life.[7]

There is a difference, though. The influence of Adam Smith, both in science and policy, turned out to be permanent, if this word can be used in human affairs. Keynes's influence, never uncontested, may be said to have reached its high-water mark about twenty-five years after the *General Theory,* at about the time when J. F. Kennedy became president of the United States. Thereafter it waned. At the level of ideological isms, Keynesianism was put on the defensive by monetarism. With the better understanding of the limitations of Keynesian analysis, the evolution of mainstream economics gradually absorbed what had appeared as revolutionary.

Keynes's contribution to macrostatics remained. For short-run pur-

6. Keynes realized this, but his plan to present the further revisions of his thoughts in still another book fell victim to the heart attack of 1937.
7. Critical assessments of Keynes's work are collected in Wood 1983.

poses, his model of output determination with fixed wages turned out to be of wide and continued applicability. It has become an important building block of the structure of economic theory. It also gave an important impulse to econometric work and formed the foundation of innumerable macro-econometric models.

By and large, mainstream economics, fifty years after the *General Theory,* is probably not much different from what it would have been if Keynes had not insisted on becoming a famous theorist. Far from providing a general theory, Keynes, in fact, complemented the special case of per-fectly flexible wages by the special case of perfectly rigid wages. The general problem of the dynamic adjustment process, left unsolved by the *Treatise,* remained for others to explore.

Keynes added a solid and useful brick to the building of economic theory. A brilliant writer, he offered this brick packed in a glittering gift-wrap, sparkling with hints, allusions, suggestions, and quotable *obiter dicta.* Half a century later, the *General Theory* still glitters, but economic science has learned to distinguish the wrapping from the brick.

The question has often been raised whether statics with fixed wages could really have been all Keynes had in mind. The question led to an enthusiastic and still continuing debate about "what Keynes really meant." Could it have been dynamics, imperfect competition, multiple budget con-straints, non-market-clearing prices, corner solutions, multiple equilibria or transactions costs? Even though such conjectures may be suggested by passages in the *General Theory,* none of these elements was analytically worked out. For a competent scientist, endowed with Keynes's command over words, fifty years should be long enough for him to have made himself understood.

All in all, Keynes was a superb writer, both financial and otherwise (as his *Essays in Biography* [1971– , vol. 10] show). He was also a foun-tainhead of provocative ideas and an outstanding general economist. How-ever, as an economic theorist, he was not of the very highest order, nor did he have the dedication to scholarship to bother about what he regarded as analytical trifles. Although neither a David Ricardo, a Léon Walras, an Irving Fisher, nor a Paul Samuelson, he found the perfect response to the intellectual needs and aspirations of a generation of economists.

28
John Hicks

LÉON WALRAS had been the first to construct a general equilibrium system based on individual optimization of each agent, and Vilfredo Pareto had shown that this did not require cardinal measurement of utility. Up to the beginning of the 1930s, however, these developments had hardly an echo in the English-language literature. It was John Hicks who linked up the Marshallian tradition with the Walrasian heritage and thus became the founder of modern general equilibrium theory.

Life

John Richard Hicks was born into a baptist family in Warwick, England, in 1904.[1] A good high school education earned him a scholarship to Balliol College, Oxford. He mainly studied mathematics but finally graduated (in 1926) in a new program of philosophy, politics, and economics. His training in economics had been scant, but he began to learn more as a lecturer at the London School of Economics. Though he was considered to be an applied labor economist, Hugh Dalton, later chancellor of the exchequer, referred him to Pareto, which also brought him into contact with Walras, Marshall, Edgeworth, Cassel, Wicksell, and Böhm-Bawerk. From a visiting appointment in South Africa, he returned with the conclusion that trade unions are not simply benevolent associations for self-help but also monopolistic organizations for the defense of privileges, to be understood in terms of monopoly theory. In 1929, Hicks joined the group around Lionel Robbins, which included Abba Lerner, Nicholas Kaldor, Roy Allen and, later, Friedrich von Hayek.

In 1935, Hicks accepted a fellowship at Cambridge. In the same year he married Ursula Webb, also a member of the Robbins group, who became a distinguished public finance economist. This was scientifically the most productive period in Hicks's life. Though John Maynard Keynes became a dominating influence on his later thinking, neither the Keynesians nor their opponents ever regarded him as one of theirs; while becoming a friend of Keynes he retained the friendship of Pigou and Robertson.

In 1938, Hicks was appointed to the Stanley Jevons Professorship at Manchester, where he remained until 1946. Following a few years as a fellow of Nuffield College, Oxford, he then became Drummond Professor of Political Economy in Oxford. After his retirement in 1965 he still remained active at All Souls College. Hicks was knighted in 1964, and in 1972 he shared with Kenneth Arrow the Nobel Prize in economics in recognition of their work on general equilibrium and welfare.

Hicks was a lecturer with far-ranging erudition but unimpressive delivery. He also became known as an enthusiastic gardener and a believer in cold baths and physical exercise who rode his bicycle to the university. He had no love for econometrics, and he professed none for economic

---

1. Autobiographical notes can be found in Hicks 1981–83, vol. 3, ch. 31, and other essays in that collection.

theory for its own sake. Theory, he said, should be the servant of applied economics. Nevertheless, all his major contributions consisted of theoretical concepts, and none provided substantive new insights into the actual working of the economy. He died in 1989.

Works

Hicks authored and coauthored more than two dozen books and numerous essays, virtually all on economic subjects.[2] His major contributions to economic science, however, are found in three books and about half a dozen articles.

In his first book, *The Theory of Wages* (1932), Hicks developed what was later regarded as the prototype of the "neoclassical" theory of wages. It is all the more interesting to note that the mathematical analysis of distribution in terms of a linear-homogenous production function is confined to six pages in the appendix and that most of the book is devoted to the deviations of the labor market from pure competition in a realistic institutional setting. Actual "neoclassicism" was indeed very different from what later mythology made it out to be. The main theoretical contribution was the elasticity of substitution.[3]

The elasticity of substitution led Hicks to price theory. In the paper "A Reconsideration of the Theory of Value" of 1934 (Hicks 1981–83, vol. 1), written jointly with Roy G. D. Allen, he reinvented Eugen Slutsky's decomposition of the total effect of price on demand into (in later terminology) a substitution effect and an income effect. The article also marks the breakthrough of Paretian (and Fisherian) ordinalism in Anglo-Saxon utility theory. Once Hicks and Allen had become aware of Slutsky's work, they readily acknowledged his priority (Allen 1936). Indeed, though their article was historically influential, in substance it contained little that was not available in the literature eighteen years earlier.

Under the influence of the Great Depression, conscious of the shortcomings of his macroeconomic wage theory, Hicks turned to money. "A Suggestion for Simplifying the Theory of Money" of 1935 (Hicks 1981–83, vol. 2) became one of the great papers on monetary theory by providing an analysis of the demand for money that was in most respects (except on speculative balances) superior to that in Keynes's *General Theory*. Cash balances, rather than interest-bearing assets, would be held over short periods, for which the interest return on bonds does not compensate for the transactions costs of buying and selling them. Cash would also

---

2. Important essays were collected in three volumes (Hicks 1981–83). A bibliography is appended to volume 3.
3. What Hicks had to say about the exhaustion of the product by the sum of the factor shares was good economics, but it did not go beyond Wicksell twenty-five years earlier.

be held if the expected return on bonds did not compensate their holder for the added risk. This analysis, clearly foreshadowing the mean variance approach to portfolio selection, was surpassed only by James Tobin in 1958.[4]

As a macroeconomist, Hicks was gradually attracted into the orbit of Keynes. The article of 1937 "Mr. Keynes and the Classics" (Hicks 1981–83, vol. 2) succeeded admirably (and to Keynes's own satisfaction) in reducing the core of Keynes's theory to two simultaneous equations represented by the now familiar pair of IS/LM curves. This did much to make Keynes analytically tractable, but it also contributed to the distortion of views about his difference from his opponents. In particular, it overemphasized the significance of an interest-inelastic demand for money for pre-Keynesian theory and of the liquidity trap for Keynes. The essential differences, if any, are not expressed by the shapes of these curves.

Even before Hicks had seen the *General Theory,* he had begun working on *Value and Capital* (1939). It became his peak achievement, his main claim to fame. In the field of pure theory it was probably the most influential book of the first half of the twentieth century. To some extent this was due to the new pieces of analysis it contained, explained lucidly enough to be readily incorporated into existing theory. To an even larger extent the book's extraordinary influence was due to the timely synthesis it offered. The general equilibrium of Walras, Pareto's ordinal utility, and Slutsky's analysis of comparative-static effects were all integrated with post-Wicksellian dynamics, Keynesian macrostatics, and a capital theory along the lines of Böhm-Bawerk.[5] By combining all these elements in a unified theoretical apparatus, *Value and Capital* provided the springboard from which the brilliant theorists of the next generation would jump off.

From value it was natural for Hicks to move to welfare. His principal contribution is again not an innovation but the rehabilitation of the consumer surplus as introduced by Jules Dupuit and developed by Alfred Marshall. Hicks's papers (1981–83, vol. 1, part 2) succeeded in establishing

---

4. Hicks had nothing new to say about the transactions demand for money relative to goods and services, in the absence of interest-bearing assets. In fact, he did not even see the theoretical problems it posed, which were the most difficult of them all.

5. It was soon observed that Hicks's verbal definition of the substitution effect differed from that used by Slutsky and by Hicks himself in their mathematical analyses. Whereas the first provides the consumer with just enough income to remain on the same indifference curve, the second provides him with just enough income to buy at the new prices the same bundle of goods he bought at the old prices. Mosak (1942) conjectured that the difference, relative to the substitution effect itself, tends to vanish as the underlying price change approaches zero. He also reproduced a proof of the conjecture supplied by Abraham Wald.

the consumer surplus as the central concept in the welfare analysis of particular projects.

Following Kaldor (1939), Hicks also argued that such projects should be regarded as increasing social welfare whenever the beneficiaries gain enough to compensate the losers, even if such compensation is not actually paid. By this criterion, if valid, welfare economics could clearly pass judgment on many measures on which it has to be silent in the light of the old criterion of Pareto optimality. With some fanfare, Hicks thus proclaimed a new welfare economics. It was soon pointed out, however, that the compensation may be calculated in different ways, possibly with contradictory results.[6] More fundamentally, the Kaldor-Hicks criterion implies some sort of interpersonal comparability of utilities. If this is excluded, welfare economics is again reduced to Pareto's criterion. In pure theory, therefore, the new welfare economics was short-lived. In applied economics, however, the Kaldor-Hicks criterion continues to dominate the field.

During World War II and the early postwar years, Hicks, together with his wife, worked mostly on practical problems of public finance, including those of former British colonies. He also found time to write *The Social Framework* (Hicks 1942), a widely used and widely translated introduction to economics from a macroeconomic point of view. *A Contribution to the Theory of the Trade Cycle* (Hicks 1950) was once more a major piece of original work. Ragnar Frisch had explained business cycles by random shocks hitting a system that reacts with dampened oscillations. Hicks now explained them by the explosive interaction of a multiplier and an accelerator, alternately pushing the system against a full-employment ceiling and an autonomous-investment floor, each moving upward in the course of economic growth. Mathematically this meant introducing nonlinear difference equations with different regimes for different phases of the cycle. Empirical research, however, tended to follow Frisch rather than Hicks.

Gradually, perhaps under the influence of his applied work, Hicks's outlook on economic science changed. He was no longer creating theory but discussing it. Where he had been the insider looking out, he became

6. Tibor Scitovsky (1941), in particular, pointed out that the Kaldor-Hicks criterion may possibly justify both a move from situation A to situation B and a move from B to A. For pure exchange this apparent paradox is most easily explained in terms of an Edgeworth box. In the accompanying figure the indifference curves of John and Ivan are, respectively, J_1, J_2 (with origin in the lower left) and I_1, I_2 (with origin in the upper right). In a transition from A to B, John could compensate Ivan by a transfer equal to the distance $B - B'$ and still be better off than at A. In a transition from B to A, Ivan could compensate John by a transfer equal to the distance $A - A'$ and still be better off than at B.

the outsider looking in. His favorite subject became his own past work, which he was forever explaining, criticizing, defending, repudiating, amending, and editing.[7] His fertile and inquisitive mind continued to produce books and essays on value, capital, growth, dynamics, money, history, causality, and current affairs, full of wisdom and valuable insights, but there were no further fundamental contributions to economic theory.

Production

In addition to his brilliant syntheses, as was pointed out above, Hicks provided economic theory with innovations of his own. They are mainly found in the fields of production, aggregation, stability, and intertemporal processes. In the theory of production, Hicks's main original contributions relate to the elasticity of factor substitution, the classification of inventions, and the discovery of regressive factors.

ELASTICITY OF SUBSTITUTION. In a theory of wages, one of the central problems concerns the reaction of the demand for labor to a change in wages. It was clear to Hicks that one of its significant determinants must surely be the degree of substitutability between labor and capital (and/or other factors). In graphical terms this can be expressed by the curvature of an isoquant. If the isoquants are nearly linear, the substitutability is high; if they are sharply bent, it is low. Assuming a linear-homogenous production function, the curvature can be expressed in terms of the reaction of the marginal product of one factor to an increase in the quantity of the other as measured by the cross second-order partial derivative of the production function. This measure has the inconvenience, however, that it depends on the units of measurement. To make it independent of the choice of units, Hicks followed Marshall's example of transforming it into an elasticity. The result was the elasticity of substitution.

The elasticity of substitution is the percentage reaction of the factor input ratio, for a given output, to a given percentage change in the factor price ratio. If a and b are the quantities of the factors while p_a and p_b are their prices, the elasticity of substitution can be written as

$$\sigma = \frac{d(a/b)(b/a)}{d(p_b/p_a)(p_a/p_b)}.$$ (28.1)

In terms of figure 28.1, σ measures the influence of a change in the relative factor price p_b/p_a on the factor proportion a/b along the same isoquant.

---

7. That in 1978 he could rank Walras and Pareto "much below" Menger (1981–83, 3: 128) is a measure of the eventual shift in his standards.

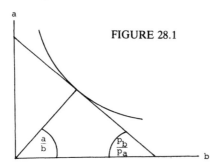

FIGURE 28.1

The new concept turned out to be widely useful. It was particularly illuminating in the analysis of factor shares. Suppose the distribution of income between labor and capital is described by the ratio of their incomes,

$$\rho = \frac{p_a a}{p_b b}. \qquad (28.2)$$

The relative change in distribution can then be expressed by

$$d\rho/\rho = d(a/b)(b/a) - d(p_b/p_a)(p_a/p_b), \qquad (28.3)$$

and the change in distribution due to a change in relative factor prices is seen to depend on the elasticity of substitution,

$$\frac{d\rho/\rho}{d(p_b/p_a)(p_a/p_b)} = \sigma - 1. \qquad (28.4)$$

An elasticity of substitution of unity thus turns out to be the watershed at which an increase in the relative price of one factor begins to raise the share of the other factor (and to reduce its own share).

One of the fruitful developments initiated, with some delay, by Hicks's concept was the search for particular production functions that would permit a meaningful analysis of the elasticity of substitution and distribution. The Cobb-Douglas function of the form $q = a^\alpha b^\beta$ clearly does not serve the purpose because it implies an elasticity of substitution of unity. Decades later, in 1961, Kenneth Arrow and Robert Solow (Arrow 1983–85, vol. 5, ch. 3) constructed the constant-elasticity-of-substitution (CES) production function to combine constant returns to scale with constant, but possibly nonunitary, substitution elasticities.

The most fruitful development, however, concerned the pure theory of value, and it was immediately initiated by Hicks himself. It occurred to him (as it occurred to others, such as Hayek) that the indifference curves of consumers could be analyzed in the same way as the isoquants of pro-

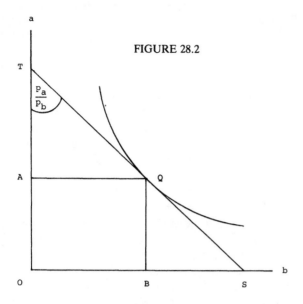

FIGURE 28.2

ducers. In fact, Joan Robinson (1969, 256) had independently constructed the same concept to describe demand. Just as the substitutability between factors along a given isoquant was one of several determinants of the reaction of labor demand to wages, so the substitutability between goods along a given indifference curve should be one of several determinants of the reaction of demand to price. The result of this conjecture was Hicks's rediscovery, in collaboration with Allen, of the Slutsky decomposition. They succeeded in showing that the price elasticity of demand can be written as the sum of two components, namely the elasticity of substitution along the same indifference curve (weighted by one minus the budget share) and the income elasticity of demand (weighted by the budget share).

This was only a halfway house, though. In *Value and Capital* the elasticity of substitution is mentioned only in a footnote, and the decomposition is presented, as in Slutsky, in terms of the effect of an absolute price on an absolute quantity.

THE CLASSIFICATION OF INVENTIONS. A second contribution of *The Theory of Wages* to mainstream economics concerns the classification of technical progress and its effect on factor shares. Consider an economy with given endowments of labor, *OA*, and capital, *OB* (see figure 28.2). Its output can be read off the isoquant through *Q*, while the relative price of labor, p_a/p_b, is expressed by the slope of the tangent at *Q*, namely *QA/ AT*. The ratio of wage income to capital income is

$$\rho = \frac{p_a a}{p_b b} = \frac{QA}{AT} \frac{OA}{QA} = \frac{OA}{AT}. \tag{28.5}$$

With given factor inputs, the labor share simply varies hand in hand with the relative price of labor.

Technical progress, in this framework, means that the isoquants shift to the southwest; the same output can now be produced with less input. If the new isoquant through Q, which had been somewhere to the northeast before, has the same shape as the old isoquant through Q, distribution will remain unchanged, factor incomes increasing in equal proportion. This is what Hicks calls neutral technical progress. If the new isoquant through Q is flatter than the old one, distribution changes in favor of labor; the marginal product of labor rises relative to that of capital. Such an invention is classified by Hicks as capital-saving, because at unchanged factor prices producers would be induced to employ less capital (but more labor). If, on the other hand, the isoquant through Q is now steeper than before, distribution changes in favor of capital. Since the marginal product of labor rises in a lesser proportion than the marginal product of capital, firms have an incentive, at constant factor prices, to employ less labor and more capital. Inventions of this sort are thus classified as labor-saving.

This was a confusing nomenclature, to be sure. It would have been more natural to call an invention labor-saving if the replacement of a given amount of capital, for the same output, now required less additional labor than before, which means that the isoquant in figure 28.2 becomes flatter (and vice versa). Aside from terminology, it later became clear that the appropriate definition of the neutrality of technical progress depends on the context in which the concept is used. Different types of growth models, for example, would require different definitions of neutrality. As a consequence, Hicks's classification provoked perhaps more controversy than any other of his conceptual innovations, but in the process it became the point of departure of far-reaching developments, both empirical and theoretical.

REGRESSIVE FACTORS. Pigou had observed in a footnote (1960, 223) that an increase in output, since it may initiate a shift to large-scale methods of production, may reduce the demand for certain factors. Hicks pointed out in *Value and Capital* that this case was the exact counterpart in production theory to inferior goods in consumption theory; he proposed to call such factors regressive.

Regressivity of factors, just like the inferiority of goods, turned out to have some interesting implications. Most obviously, if the demand for a product rises, the demand for a regressive factor declines. Less obviously, if the price of a regressive factor rises, the marginal cost curve of the product may shift downward (though total costs rise). Finally, if the price

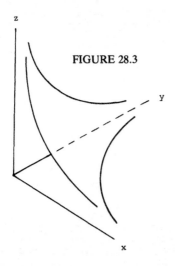

FIGURE 28.3

of a regressive factor rises, the supply of the product may rise, and its price, therefore, may decline.[8]

Composite Goods

In economic reality, there are innumerable different goods. Economic models are usually confined to but a few, and graphical representations are often limited to two. The aggregation of variables is one of the economist's most inevitable expedients. To Hicks economic science owes a fundamental theorem on aggregation. (An earlier contribution is Leontief 1977, ch. 12.) Mathematically proved in the appendix to *Value and Capital*, it says that "a collection of physical things can always be treated as if they were divisible into units of a single commodity so long as their relative prices can be assumed to be unchanged, in the particular problem in hand" (Hicks 1939, 33). In other words, "if the prices of a group of goods change in the same proportion, that group of goods behaves just as if it were a single commodity" (313).

The meaning of this theorem is best explained in graphical terms. The convex surface in figure 28.3 is an indifference surface for 3 goods, x, y, and z. Imagine that cross-sections are made at successive values of x. The resulting curves are then projected on a plane with y and z on the axes as shown in figure 28.4. What in figure 28.3 was an indifference surface is thus transformed into a family of "indifference curves," all of which relate to the same utility level, but each for a different value of x. Suppose now the relative price of y and z is exogenously given and constant as expressed

8. Another analogy, though seemingly obvious, fails to be valid: Even for strongly regressive factors there is no Giffen paradox.

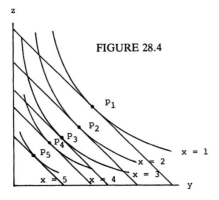

FIGURE 28.4

by the common slope of the downward-sloping straight lines. Their tangency with the "indifference curves" determines the combinations of y and z that are demanded at any level of x.[9]

The values of these combinations, expressed in units of y, are measured by the intercepts of the tangent lines along the y axis. They can be taken as measures of the composite good (y, z).[10] This measure is used in figure 28.5 to construct an indifference curve in just two dimensions. The further analysis can then be conducted as if it related to only two goods, namely x and the composite good (y, z). Whenever disaggregated information is needed, it can be obtained in a two-stage procedure. First use figure 28.5

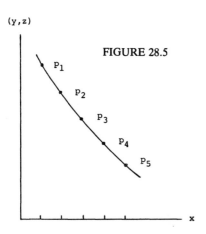

FIGURE 28.5

9. It should be noted that the proportion of y and x will generally vary. Hicks's theorem does not relate to the trivial case of unchanged bundles of goods.

10. The intercepts along the z axis or any fixed-weight average of them would have served just as well.

to solve the problem in terms of the aggregative model, then use figure 28.4 to determine y and z individually.

The composite goods theorem is important primarily because it helps to give the macroeconomist a good conscience. For many purposes, for example, it would be perfectly legitimate to reduce labor of different skills to "common labor." In some cases, however, the theorem is important precisely because it gives the macroeconomist a bad conscience. The most important of these cases concerns capital goods of different longevity. The macroeconomist, in explaining the rate of interest, would often like to aggregate them to a composite capital good. However, any decline in the market rate of interest implies an increase in the price of long-lived capital goods relative to short-lived capital goods. As a consequence, the basic requirement of the composite goods theorem is not satisfied; different capital goods cannot be meaningfully aggregated in physical terms if the interest rate is variable.

Comparative Statics and Stability

Walras had constructed a comprehensive system of general equilibrium, but he had virtually nothing to say about the effects of given changes in the underlying conditions. A comparative statics was lacking. Marshall had much to say about comparative statics, but it was not based on an explicit general equilibrium system. It remained for Hicks to initiate the comparative-static analysis of a general equilibrium system.

The problem may be illustrated, though at the cost of some oversimplification, in terms of just two markets, say for wheat (commodity 1) and rye (commodity 2). For each commodity, excess demand can be expressed as a function, here assumed to be linear, of both prices. In equilibrium both excess demands must be zero:

$$E_1 = a_{11} p_1 + a_{12} p_2 + \alpha_1 = 0 \tag{28.6}$$

$$E_2 = a_{21} p_1 + a_{22} p_2 + \alpha_2 = 0 \tag{28.7}$$

The two equations determine the two equilibrium prices. The question is how shifts in, say, α_1 affect p_1 and p_2.

After taking differentials, the two equations can be solved to give

$$\frac{dp_1}{d\alpha_1} = -\frac{a_{22}}{a_{11} a_{22} - a_{12} a_{21}}, \quad \frac{dp_2}{d\alpha_1} = \frac{a_{21}}{a_{11} a_{22} - a_{12} a_{21}}. \tag{28.8}$$

Once the parameters a_{ij} have been empirically estimated, the effect of $d\alpha_1$ on dp_1 and dp_2 can thus be calculated. In general, however, the parameter values are unknown. In fact, even their sign is often ambiguous. Can anything be said about the sign of $dp_1/d\alpha_1$ and $dp_2/d\alpha_1$ in the absence of parameter estimates? Can the possibility be excluded that an increase in α_1 actually lowers p_1?

Hicks gave a positive answer to these questions. Its source was stability analysis. Comparative statics makes sense only in a stable system. An unstable system, after a change in conditions, would not gravitate toward the new equilibrium but move away from it, thus being useless for comparative-static prediction. In principle, this was not a new insight. For single markets it had been extensively exploited by Marshall and later also for aggregate demand in Keynesian models. Hicks, in *Value and Capital*, was the first to exploit this insight for a systematic analysis of multiple markets.

Hicks proposed two stability criteria. He called a system imperfectly stable if excess demand for a commodity is reduced by an increase in its price, provided each of the other prices adjusts instantaneously to maintain continuous equilibrium in its own market. The implications of this test in the wheat and rye example can be found by letting $E_2 = d\alpha_1 = d\alpha_2 = 0$ and calculating

$$\frac{dE_1}{dp_1} = \frac{a_{11}a_{22} - a_{12}a_{21}}{a_{22}} < 0. \tag{28.9}$$

Imperfect stability requires that this expression be negative. It follows from equation 28.8 that $dp_1/d\alpha_1 > 0$. In an imperfectly stable system, an increase in demand raises the price, regardless of empirical parameters.

The sign of $dp_2/d\alpha_1$ is still unclear, though. In addition, this simple stability test may not be stringent enough. Not all markets adjust instantaneously, and in the meantime the system might still "explode." Hicks thus postulated a more demanding criterion for what he called perfect stability. It requires that excess demand be reduced by an increase in price even if any subset of other prices is unable to adjust at all, thus failing to eliminate excess demand in their respective markets. In the two-market example this means that $dp_2 = d\alpha_1 = d\alpha_2 = 0$ and $dE_2 \neq 0$. What remains is very simple, namely

$$\frac{dE_1}{dp_1} = a_{11} < 0. \tag{28.10}$$

An analogous condition

$$\frac{dE_2}{dp_2} = a_{22} < 0. \tag{28.11}$$

can be derived for the rye market. These conditions must be added to those for imperfect stability. In conjunction with equation 28.9, condition 28.11 implies $a_{11}a_{22} - a_{12}a_{21} > 0$; the direct price effects must dominate the cross effects, whatever the latter's signs may be. Without any appeal to a priori knowledge about parameters, it is thus possible to conclude that an increase in demand (1) raises the price of the same commodity and (2) increases the price of a gross substitute ($a_{21} > 0$) and lowers the price of a gross complement ($a_{21}<0$). The two-market example was chosen precisely because it makes this conclusion trivial and thus intuitively plausible. Hick's main analytical contribution is the extension to any number of markets. It initiated modern stability analysis.

Paul Samuelson (1947) later showed that Hicks's stability criteria are defective. Their main shortcoming is that they are based on intuition rather than on an explicit dynamic analysis. When such an analysis is used, they turn out to be, in general, neither necessary nor sufficient for stability. Hicks's intuition was nevertheless brilliant. Lloyd Metzler (1973, ch. 20) showed that Hicks's perfect stability is necessary and sufficient for dynamic stability if all goods are gross substitutes. He also showed that perfect stability is necessary (but not sufficient) for dynamic stability if the latter is required to hold for all adjustment speeds of the individual markets. This is often enough for comparative statics. Robert Mundell could thus call Hicks's stability analysis one of the most successful failures of economic theory.

Period Dynamics and the Term Structure

Whereas the first part of *Value and Capital* is about the statics of Walrasian equilibrium, the second part concerns dynamics. There are no dynamic models in the tradition of Frisch, Kalecki, and Tinbergen, though. In Frisch's terminology the analysis remains static, but Hicks found an ingenious way to capture evolutionary processes with static techniques. He imagined time to be divided into periods, the Hicksian weeks. All business is transacted on Mondays; during the remainder of the week the markets are closed.

On a given Monday all households and firms come to the market with their products, factors, and assets. From past experience they have derived expectations about the prices likely to rule in the present and all future weeks. In the light of these expectations they have formed their plans. For the present Monday, a temporary equilibrium is established in the way envisaged by Walras. Though all markets clear (including those for future delivery), previous expectations are not necessarily fulfilled, and plans may have to be modified. On the second Monday, agents will come to the market with different products, factors, assets, expectations, and plans. A new temporary equilibrium is established, and so on. Economic change is thus represented by a chain of temporary equilibria. One of the crucial links between periods consists of expectations. Again Hicks introduces a new elasticity, namely the elasticity of expected future prices with respect to changes in the current price. An elasticity of zero means that expected prices are not affected by current price changes. In the case of an elasticity of unity, current price changes are regarded as permanent. If the elasticity of expectations is low, the economy tends to be stable, if it is high, the economy threatens to become unstable. Hicks was later very conscious of the limitations of his expectations theory, but at least it helped to make the problem clear.

This conception permitted Hicks to consider macrodynamic problems in terms of general equilibrium. The idea turned out to be very fruitful. Knut Wicksell, in his cumulative process, had envisaged a macrodynamic model, but he had failed to make it explicit. His Swedish followers, such as Bertil Ohlin, Gunnar Myrdal, and Erik Lindahl, in their efforts to find out what Wicksell "actually meant," tried to provide macrodynamics with a suitable accounting framework. For each period they distinguished between planned magnitudes, which Myrdal (1933) called *ex ante*, and realized magnitudes, which he called *ex post*. The main contribution of this conception was to clear up the confusion about the equality of saving and investment, which turned out to be not merely an accounting identity *ex post*, but an equilibrium condition *ex ante*. In general, however, the Swedes were unable to construct an effective and intellectually lucid analytical engine. By combining Swedish period analysis with Walrasian equilibrium, Hicks succeeded where they had failed.

One of the special problems to which Hicks applied his multiperiod model was the term structure of interest rates. The question is how the interest rates for loans of different maturities, say, from one day to thirty years, are related among each other. Fisher (1930, 70) had answered it by the proposition that the long rate is essentially an average of the corresponding short rates. Hicks supplemented Fisher's brief statement by a detailed analysis.

Suppose time is divided into weeks and the loan market is open at the beginning of each period. On any market day, loan contracts can be made both "spot" (to be executed at once) and "forward" (to be executed in a specified future week). Loans can be made for any number of weeks, but all interest rates are quoted per week, so that a two-week loan carries twice the stated rate. The interest rate on a weekly spot loan may be denoted by i_1, the rate on a weekly forward loan beginning in the second week by i_2, and so on. These weekly short-term rates are to be compared with the rates for spot loans, made today, for maturities of 1, 2, 3, . . . weeks. They will be denoted by I_1, I_2, I_3, and so on.

According to Hicks's argument, arbitrage will see to it that it makes no difference whether credit for n weeks is provided by one n-week spot loan or a 1-week spot loan combined with $n-1$ forward loans for successive weeks. In symbols this means that

$$(1+I_n)^n = (1+i_1)(1+i_2) \ldots (1+i_n). \tag{28.12}$$

What appears on the left is the terminal value of an n-week loan of \$1 if compound interest at a weekly rate of I_n is paid at the end. The expression on the right is the corresponding value of a succession of one-week loans contracted for in today's spot and forward markets, with each loan financing the cumulative interest on the preceding loans. Whenever the two sides differ, arbitrageurs will find unexploited profits until the reaction of interest rates to their transactions has restored equality. As a result, the long-term rate, as measured by $(1 + I_n)$, gravitates toward the geometric mean of the short-term rates, as measured by $(1 + i_1)$, and so on. If compound interest, as a first approximation, is disregarded, the long-term rate is simply the arithmetic mean of the relevant short-term rates,

$$I_n = \frac{1}{n}(i_1 + i_2 + \ldots + i_n).$$ (28.13)

It follows that, for given disturbances, the short-term rates tend to fluctuate more violently than the long-term rate.

Hicks made it perfectly clear that this was not meant to be a complete explanation of the term structure but only an important element of it. In particular, risk and transactions costs would have to be brought in. Hicks also made it clear that the forward rates for a given week are not necessarily equal to the spot rates expected for that week. Nevertheless, his expectations hypothesis, as it is often called,[11] became the basis for all future research in this field.

Place in the History of Economics

The influence of Hicks's early work, and particularly of *Value and Capital*, was not only powerful but virtually instantaneous. Indeed, hardly a famous economist saw his work accepted so generally and promptly. Of his later writings, though they were received with respect and interest, none had much impact. In his early work, Hicks posed problems that, as he would later point out, were perhaps not always very profound but whose solutions were within reach (usually his own). This was the secret of its success. The problems he posed in his later work were perhaps deeper and more pertinent, but their solution transcended his (and his contemporaries') powers. This was the main reason for the late work's lack of success.[12]

Overall, Hicks will probably appear in the history of economics as the greatest British theorist of the century. On the one hand, this reflects the fact that post-Marshallian England was no longer in the forefront of economic theory. On the other hand, it means that Hicks was a much better theorist than Keynes. Whereas Keynes's power of the pen created the impression of a glorious revolution, Hicks's power of analysis created modern general equilibrium analysis.

---

11. In honor of Friedrich Lutz's important contribution to its development (Lutz 1940), it is often called the Hicks-Lutz hypothesis.

12. The problem of the "traverse" of a heterogeneous capital stock from one growth equilibrium to another is a case in point. It had defeated Hayek (1941) and Joan Robinson (1956), and it now defeated Hicks (1965, 1973).

29

The Planners

FOR THE GENERATION of economists who began their scientific lives around 1930, one of the big issues became planning, pro or con. A number of factors contributed to pushing this issue into center stage. The Great Depression was widely regarded as proving the failure of laissez faire. Welfare economics had demonstrated that the shortcomings of the invisible hand of competition left much for the visible hand of planners to do. The planning ideologies of Marxism and fascism influenced even intellectuals of democratic convictions. In the thinking of men such as Werner Sombart and Joseph Schumpeter, the revolutionary collapse of capitalism predicted by Karl Marx was supplanted by a peaceful "march into socialism" associated with progressively more rational planning. The progress of administrative techniques, greatly stimulated by experiences during World War II and later by the electronic computer, seemed to make such planning increasingly possible. The tradition of benevolent utilitarianism was revived in rationalist dreams of solving the problems of mankind by enlightened planning, possibly on a global scale.

This was the intellectual environment in which, together with many others, Ragnar Frisch, Jan Tinbergen, and Wassily Leontief made their contributions to economics. They believed that the future belonged to planning, perhaps to socialism. However, being outstanding scientists, they never succumbed to the Marxian delusion that alternative policies require an alternative science. This enabled them, each in a different way, to make pioneering contributions to mainstream economics. All three began their research in the area of business cycles and econometrics, whence they moved to policy planning and economic development. Eventually they all had to recognize that the harsh realities were more resistant to their planning ideas than they had hoped, but their analytical contributions proved to be of lasting value.

Ragnar Frisch

Ragnar Frisch was born in 1895 in Oslo, where his father was a jeweler. After high school, planning to follow in his father's footsteps, he acquired a goldsmith's diploma. At the same time he went to the University of Oslo to study economics. He does not seem to have learned very much, though, and the deficiencies of his early training in economics were never fully corrected.[1]

---

1. His innovative article on rent (Frisch 1932b), with its hints of what later was called activity analysis, shows the limitations that were imposed on his accomplishments, despite

Upon graduation, Frisch finally decided in favor of an academic career. Newly married,[2] he spent the next years in France, England, the United States, and Italy, training himself in mathematics and statistics. He obtained a doctorate in mathematical statistics from Oslo in 1926; two years later he became a lecturer, and in 1931, after a visit to Yale, the University of Norway offered him a professorship that had been newly created to keep him in Oslo. He occupied this chair until his retirement in 1965, and he also directed the University Institute of Economics.

Right from the beginning, Frisch's great program was the quantification of economics, its transformation into a science like the natural sciences. A compulsive inventor of neologisms, he christened the new field econometrics. What before had been interdisciplinary research at the intersection of economics, mathematics, and statistics thus became a new discipline.[3] In 1930, Frisch was one of the founders of the Econometric Society. Two years later, he became the first editor of its journal, *Econometrica*, a position in which he continued with great success for twenty-one years.

Ideologically, Frisch was a social democrat with a deep distrust of the invisible hand and the profit motive. Under the influence of the Great Depression, his interest began to shift toward planning, for which purpose he helped to develop a system of national income accounts. During World War II he was for some time interned in a concentration camp. In the postwar period he emerged as a prophet of planning, first at the national level, later at the international level and for developing countries. He also served as adviser to the governments of Egypt and India. Indeed, Frisch talked about planning as if it were the only way to salvation, almost a religion. That his hobby was beekeeping may be symbolic of his vision of society. With growing disappointment about the world's response to his message, his outlook became increasingly radical.

In 1969, Frisch received, jointly with Tinbergen, the first Nobel Prize in economics. It was awarded mainly for his work on macrodynamics, but also for his contributions to quantitative methods and planning models. He died in 1973.

Frisch's fertile mind was incessantly working on his research problems. The results flowed forth in an enormous stream of manuscripts. However, only a fraction reached the stage of a working paper, and an even smaller fraction was ever published.[4] In fact, Frisch published only two full-grown

---

his superb analytical ability, by the lack of a broader understanding of economic theory (including Thünen).

2. After the death of his wife in 1952, Frisch married a second time.

3. This illustrates the basic reason why interdisciplinary research tends to be inherently ephemeral: if it is productive, it becomes a new discipline, and if it remains unproductive, it disappears.

4. A bibliography, excluding only the last three to four years, can be found in *De Economist* 118 (2), 1970. For assessments of Frisch's contributions see Arrow 1960, Johansen 1969, and Edvardsen 1970.

books, namely *Theory of Production* (1965) and *Maxima and Minima* (1966). Both were based on his lectures, and when these were first given, decades earlier, they probably included important original contributions, but much more detailed research would be necessary to identify them in the eventual books. Frisch's powerful influence came entirely from his lectures, working papers, articles, and pamphlets. While early publications show him as a master of lucid and forceful exposition, he later cared less and less for scientific communication, and his writing became sometimes idiosyncratic.

Frisch's first contribution to economics was an axiomatic treatment of utility, probably the first of its kind. He used it to derive a method for measuring the marginal utility of income (Frisch 1957, 1932a). Like Irving Fisher's method, published around the same time, it was based on the existence of some "want-independent" goods whose utility depends only on their own quantity. It clearly implies cardinal measurability of utility, for which it was widely criticized. However, Frisch's belief in the measurability assumption remained unshaken; decades later he still used it to compute demand elasticities as a part of a multisectoral planning model (1959). He regarded it as the task of the true scientist to accomplish the impossible, and he needed measurable utility as an intellectual underpinning for his egalitarian convictions. From utility theory it was natural for Frisch to proceed to the theory of index numbers, which work culminated in a celebrated survey (1936a). It cannot be said, however, that Frisch's contribution to value theory left a clear imprint in present-day economics.

At the same time, Frisch's extensive statistical work led him to a problem that became central for the new discipline of econometrics. Later called the identification problem, it was nontechnically described in a famous paper by Elmer Working (1927) and clearly stated in Frisch's critique of Leontief's efforts to estimate demand curves (Frisch 1933a). The problem is that observations on prices and quantities are usually generated by joint shifts in a demand curve and a supply curve. As a consequence, it is difficult to identify the separate parts played by each curve individually. Generalizing the problem, Frisch also developed techniques to separate the variables that should be included in a multiple regression from those that, in view of multicollinearity, should be excluded (1934a). These pioneering contributions stimulated much further work by others, by which most of them were rapidly made obsolete. In post–World War II econometrics, Frisch was no longer a leading contributor.

Frisch's enduring contributions to economic science concerned dynamics. Just before World War I, Henry Ludwell Moore (1914) had interpreted economic cycles as superimposed sine curves resulting from exogenous cycles in crop yields and ultimately in rainfall. There was yet no endogenous dynamic mechanism. In the 1920s, economists had, so to speak, discovered differential and difference equations. Frisch used these tools to make mainstream economics dynamic. One contribution, though a minor one, was the clarification of terminology. Frisch (1936b) proposed to use the terms *static* and *dynamic* to characterize not the stationery or changing state of nature but the theory used to describe it. A relation should be called static if all variables refer to the same time; it should be called dynamic if it includes variables relating to different points in time or periods. A theory should be classified as dynamic if it contains at least one dynamic relation. This terminology has been generally accepted.

Another minor contribution was the introduction of explicit dynamics into oligopoly theory (Frisch 1933b). In the theories of Augustin Cournot, Wilhelm Launhardt, and Harold Hotelling, each oligopolist (falsely) assumes that his opponent does not react to his actions. Frisch now introduced the "conjectural variation," with which each oligopolist expects his opponent to react. He thus built a bridge from the static oligopoly theory of the past to the dynamic game theory approaches of the future.

Frisch's major contribution was the creation of a macrodynamic theory of business cycles (1933c).[5] In a discussion with John Maurice Clark about the latter's acceleration principle (Clark 1917), Frisch had been able to show that this principle, taken in isolation, is insufficient to explain turning points of the cycle (Frisch 1931). At least it was necessary also to include the replacement demand for investment goods. More generally, a complete explanation requires a fully determined model with several behavior relations. Frisch shares with Michal Kalecki the fame of having constructed the first such model.[6]

Kalecki's "Macrodynamic Theory of Business Cycles" (1935), inspired by Tinbergen's shipbuilding model, consists of a system of mixed difference and differential equations. Whereas workers do not save, capitalists have a certain propensity to consume their profit income; what is not consumed is invested. This results in a sort of multiplier mechanism, and the capitalists find that the more they spend, the more they earn. Current investment is negatively related, through the profit rate, to the capital stock, and there is also a gestation lag. The interaction of consumption and investment results in a path for the economy that can be either monotonic or oscillatory and either dampened or explosive. Kalecki took it as a fact that actual business cycles are neither dampened nor explosive and restricted his fur-

5. The terms *microdynamics* and *macrodynamics* were, it seems, invented by Frisch. The (perhaps obvious) generalization to micro and macroeconomics appears to be of later date.

6. Both papers were originally published in 1933, Kalecki's in Polish, and both were presented at the same meeting of the Econometric Society in October 1933.

ther analysis to the borderline case of constant amplitude. Inserting plausible parameter values, he obtained a cycle of about ten years. Kalecki later prided himself on having anticipated Keynes. In fact, he far exceeded Keynes not only in economic substance but also in analytical rigor and in lucidity of exposition.

Frisch's basic model is similar to Kalecki's, but its further elaboration turned out to be more fruitful.[7] The core consists of four behavior relations. The demand for money, w, depends positively on contemporaneous expenditures for consumption, x, and investment, z:

$$w_t = rx_t + sz_t. \tag{29.1}$$

The change in consumption demand depends negatively on the demand for cash balances,

$$\dot{x}_t = c - \lambda w_t. \tag{29.2}$$

This assumption, which was widely criticized, is intended to capture Frisch's notion that money plays an evil role in the causation of depression. New orders for investment goods, y, depend positively both on the change in consumption (through an accelerator) and on its level (through replacement demand),

$$y_t = \mu \dot{x}_t + mx_t. \tag{29.3}$$

To explain current investment expenditures, Frisch uses a hypothesis proposed by Albert Aftalion, a French professor from Bulgaria (1913). It relates to the lag, often long, between the planning of a new piece of capital equipment and its first use in production. In view of these delivery (or gestation) lags, the investment expenditures in a given period depend on the investment orders in a series of earlier periods. More specifically, the change in investment expenditures is assumed to be proportionate to the difference between current new orders and current completions,

$$\dot{z}_t = \frac{1}{\epsilon}(y_t - y_{t-\epsilon}). \tag{29.4}$$

The gestation period, ϵ, indicates over how many periods a given amount of investment orders is spread out. Its reciprocal, therefore, is the fraction of the total project that is carried out in one period. It turns out that ϵ is of crucial significance for the dynamic process.

This dynamic system, like Kalecki's, allowed for a wide variety of paths. With plausible parameters, Frisch identified three superimposed

---

7. Andvig 1981 provides an excellent survey of Frisch's business cycle research.

cycles, all heavily dampened, with periods of, respectively, 8.57, 3.50, and 2.20 years. Even a quite simple dynamic model was thus shown to be capable of generating rather complicated and irregular-looking fluctuations. In particular, turning points required no special explanation but resulted simply from the initial situation and the built-in laws of motion.

However, Frisch's conception of business cycles, unlike Kalecki's, went beyond the core mechanism. The fluctuations described by the dynamic model were classified by Frisch as propagation problems. If left to themselves, they would soon die out. They are kept alive by exogenous disturbances or shocks to which the system is constantly exposed. These shocks represent the impulse problems. Kalecki's highly artificial assumption of constant amplitudes can thus be dispensed with. In a metaphor suggested earlier by Knut Wicksell, the economy thus appears as a rocking horse that responds to exogenous pushes with dampened endogenous swings.

Frisch distinguished two classes of impulses. Some are simply stochastic. In this connection, he referred to Eugen Slutsky (1937) and G. U. Yule, who had investigated the cyclical processes that might result from random causes. It should be noted, however, that they did not specify a deterministic propagation mechanism. It was Frisch's view that the empirical cycles may well be the result of random shocks acting on a system with a deterministic response. Irma and Frank Adelman (1959) later derived support for this view from their investigation of the Klein-Goldberger model of the U.S. economy.

The other source of impulses, for Frisch, are technological and entrepreneurial innovations. In the spirit of Schumpeter, he visualized a virtually continuous flow of inventions that a dynamic control mechanism transforms into intermittent breakthroughs of innovations. This analytical suggestion, however, is not further pursued. Nor did Frisch, perhaps under the influence of the identification problem, proceed to the empirical implementation of his macro model, and thus he left the lead in this field to Tinbergen. As a matter of fact, by the time World War II broke out, Frisch had pretty much left positive economics, the explanation of what happens, for normative economics, the determination of what should happen.

In the postwar period, Frisch's energies were almost entirely absorbed by planning. The paper "Circulation Planning" (1934b) is an early contribution. Depressions are attributed to the fact that purchases in a money economy are limited by past sales; what later was called disequilibrium economics makes an early appearance. The money economy should therefore be replaced by a multilateral barter system based on warrants; Robert Owen and the ill-fated National Equitable Labor Exchange of 1832 come to mind. A similar system was later proposed by Frisch for international trade.

These early notions gradually developed into an elaborate planning system, based on input-output accounts and linear programming and with a detailed investment sector. Frisch's particular research effort went into the improvement of computing algorithms and the practical specification of the social preference functions that planning was supposed to maximize (Frisch 1976; Johansen 1974). He believed that democracy should decide on the ends, for which the planners should then find the means. He never understood that democracy essentially limits its decisions to the means and leaves individuals free to pursue their own ends. This widely scattered work again testifies to the fertility and ingenuity of Frisch's mind, and its author probably ranked it above his earlier work. Fundamental contributions to economic science, however, failed to materialize, and Frisch's technocratic rhetoric is hardly less shallow than much free enterprise oratory.

Overall, Ragnar Frisch was the leading econometrician of the 1930s, and he made a decisive contribution to macrodynamic theory, which rendered Keynes's static theory technically obsolete before it was even published. For a decade, Frisch carried the torch of quantitative economics. However, when Frisch the econometrician became dominated by Frisch the crusader of planning, fundamental contributions became rare. The frontier of scientific research, even on planning and programming, left him in the rear. Perhaps the unpublished manuscripts still contain hidden treasures.

Jan Tinbergen

The scientific career of Ragnar Frisch had a close counterpart, with a lag of several years, in that of Jan Tinbergen. Tinbergen was born in the Hague in 1903.[8] His father was a language teacher who seems to have insisted that complicated ideas be expressed in simple language. His five children were all intellectually gifted; one of Jan's brothers shared the Nobel Prize in biology in 1973, and another became a professor of zoology.

Tinbergen studied physics at the University of Leyden. Gradually his interests shifted to economics, and his dissertation was on minimum problems in physics and economics. In fact, Tinbergen had become a mathematical statistician. He learned to attack economic problems in the spirit of a social engineer who, without undue concern for analytical foundations, tries to solve practical problems by feeding a large amount of facts into a pragmatically constructed model. He early developed a strong concern for peace, justice, and the welfare of humanity. He became an active member of the Social Democratic Labor party and a conscientious objector.

After leaving the university, Tinbergen joined a new unit for business cycle research at the Central Bureau of Statistics, whose leading spirit he

8. For a biographical note see Bos 1984, and for an assessment of Tinbergen's contribution, see Hansen 1969.

remained until 1945. At the same time he was part-time professor at the Netherlands School of Economics in Rotterdam, and for two years he worked as a League of Nations expert in Geneva. These were scientifically his most productive years; by 1939 he had given business cycle research a new direction.

In 1945, Tinbergen became director of the Central Planning Bureau of the Dutch government. During this period he made his important contributions to the methodology of policy planning. He resigned in 1955 to devote his energies to the problems of developing countries. After a visiting professorship at Harvard, he became professor of development planning at the Netherlands School of Economics (which is now Erasmus University). In 1969 he shared with Ragnar Frisch the first Nobel Prize in economics. It was awarded for the development and application of "dynamic models for the analysis of economic processes." Tinbergen is described as a kind man with simple habits and an optimistic conviction that the condition of man can be improved by reason and good will.

Tinbergen was a prolific writer whose contributions are widely scattered over numerous articles, pamphlets, and small books. The *Selected Papers* (Tinbergen 1959) bring together a small number of important and influential essays.

In a first stage, during the 1930s, Tinbergen's research concentrated on business cycles. His model of shipbuilding cycles was important as the first economic application of mixed difference-differential equations (Tinbergen 1959). From the multiple correlation of individual time series (1935), he proceeded to the construction of a dynamic macroeconometric model of the Dutch economy consisting of twenty-two equations (1937). As a League of Nations expert, he was assigned the task of testing the various theories of the business cycle surveyed by Gottfried Haberler. He did not actually do this, but instead he produced the first treatise on macroeconometric model building (Tinbergen 1939). A synthesis of Tinbergen's business cycle research is provided in *The Dynamics of Business Cycles*, written with J. J. Polak and first published in Dutch in 1942 (Tinbergen and Polak 1950). It shows impressively what non-Keynesian approaches had achieved by the time of World War II. Finally extending his perspective to the long run, Tinbergen, in a remarkable paper of 1942, constructed the first "neoclassical" model of (unbalanced) economic growth based on a Cobb-Douglas production function.

By modern standards, Tinbergen's League of Nations study looks primitive. However, it laid the foundation for the building of large-scale models of economic fluctuations. The first part is devoted to an explanation of the multiple regression approach. For several countries and periods, each of three investment series (namely an overall investment indicator, residential construction, and investment in railroad rolling stock) is regressed on several determinants (such as profits, capital goods prices, interest rates, profit margins, the rate of price change, and production growth). Regression coefficients are used to measure the influence of each explanatory variable, and the quality of the "explanation" is judged in the light of a priori information on signs, correlation coefficients, serial correlation of residuals, and standard errors of regression coefficients. Tinbergen was fully aware of the limitations of his method, and he was careful to put the word "explanation" always between quotation marks.

The method is used in the second part to explain the business cycle in the United States from 1919 to 1932. Each endogenous variable of the model is explained in terms of a number of past and present values of exogenous variables and also lagged values of endogenous variables. All estimates are based on the technique of single equation least squares.

Whereas Keynes's *General Theory* was static, Tinbergen's model was dynamic. It may be regarded as an empirical implementation of Frisch's analytical framework, in which disturbances, working through the exogenous variables, act on a system with certain inherent dynamic properties. Tinbergen undertakes to disentangle these properties by starting with corporate profits and successively substituting for the lagged endogenous variables from other equations. In the end, profits appear in "reduced form" as a function of only their own lagged values and exogenous disturbances. Abstracting from stock speculation and hoarding, Tinbergen finds a heavily dampened cycle with a period of 4.8 years. Fluctuations in stock prices, if large enough, threaten to make the system temporarily explosive, but the bubble will soon burst. The cycle is also accentuated by hoarding. The effects of changes in economic policies are described by dynamic multipliers. In contrast to R. F. Kahn's employment multiplier of 1931, these are the sum not simply of a convergent geometric series but of a fluctuating series.

Tinbergen's effort received a mixed reception; it was ten years ahead of its time. Keynes wrote a long, condescending, and scathing review of volume 1 in the *Economic Journal,* belaboring statistical problems and ignoring the pioneering achievement. It is worth keeping in mind that Tinbergen's model owes hardly anything to the *General Theory*. For all we know, econometric model building would have taken its course even if Keynes had never written. One feature of Tinbergen's model of which later Keynesian models made no use was the prominent role it assigned to stock speculation.

A second stage in Tinbergen's work was marked by his contributions to the theory of economic policy. Policy debates are usually characterized by apparent conflicts between targets. Full employment, for example, seems to be incompatible with price stability and balance of payments equilibrium. In journalistic jargon, such conflicts were often called magic triangles (or higher-order polygons). To have clarified the logic of such target conflicts is Tinbergen's second major contribution to mainstream economics. He thereby laid the foundation for the modern theory of macroeconomic policy with many targets and instruments. The conceptual framework, suggested in unpublished papers by Frisch, is outlined in the pamphlet *On the Theory of Economic Policy* (Tinbergen 1952), further elaborated in *Centralization and Decentralization in Economic Policy* (1954), and fully developed, with many applications, in *Economic Policy: Principles and Design* (1956).

Tinbergen distinguishes three classes of variables. Targets (denoted by the vector $y = y_1 \ldots y_t \ldots y_T$) are the variables that the policy maker cares about; income, employment, and inflation are examples. Instrument variables ($z = z_1 \ldots z_p \ldots z_P$) describe the available policies, such as government expenditures, the money supply, or tax rates. Variables that are neither targets nor instruments are classified as irrelevant, and they will here be called neutral ($x = x_1 \ldots x_n \ldots x_N$). Between the variables there are a number of relations,

$$F_e(x,y,z) = 0, \qquad e = 1 \ldots E, \tag{29.5}$$

describing the structure of the economy. Consider, for example, the following Keynesian model (with a fixed price level $\bar{p}$):

$$Y = C + I + G \tag{29.6}$$

$$C = C_Y Y + C_i \, i \tag{29.7}$$

$$I = I_Y Y + I_i \, i \tag{29.8}$$

$$M/\bar{p} = L_Y Y + L_i \, i \tag{29.9}$$

Output, Y, and investment, I, may be regarded as targets; government expenditures, G, and the money supply, M, represent the policy instruments; and the interest rate, i, is classified as neutral.

There are two ways of using such a model. In the usual analytical (or predictive) applications, specific values are assigned to the instruments. The model is then solved for the values of the targets. If the model has as many equations as it has targets and neutral variables ($T + N = E$), there is (with certain qualifications) a determinate solution for the targets. If the number of the target and neutral variables exceeds that of the equations ($T + N > E$), the model does not suffice to predict the target values resulting from given instruments. If, finally, the number of target and neutral variables falls short of the number of equations ($T + N < E$), the model is inconsistent, no set of target values satisfying, in general, the postulated relationships.

In policy applications the perspective is reversed. Specific values are now assigned to the targets, and the model is solved for the required settings of the policy instruments. There are again three cases. If the model has as many equations as it has instrument and neutral variables ($P + N = E$), there

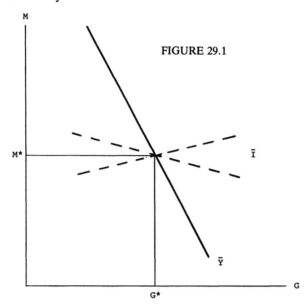

FIGURE 29.1

is (again with qualifications) a determinate solution for the instruments. If there are more policy and neutral variables than equations $(P+N>E)$, the specified targets can be reached by various combinations of the instruments, which may facilitate the policy maker's job. In the reverse case $(P+N<E)$ it is generally impossible to reach all targets with the available instruments.

Even for policy applications, however, the system must be analytically determinate; otherwise given policies have unpredictable results. This adds the requirement $T+N=E$. In combination with $P+N\geq E$, this implies the condition $P\geq T$. For the targets to be simultaneously attainable, there must be at least as many policy instruments as there are targets. This is Tinbergen's basic condition for the avoidance of policy dilemmas in the case of exogenously fixed targets. If it is satisfied, the polygon loses its magic.

In the above example this condition is satisfied. Its analytical application is usually illustrated in the Hicksian IS/LM diagram. Its policy application can be illustrated in a diagram along whose axes are measured the policy variables (figure 29.1). The solid income target line connects all those combinations of M and G that result in target income $\bar{Y}$; it will generally be falling. The broken investment target line connects all those instrument settings that keep investment at its target value, $\bar{I}$; it may be rising or falling. The intersection of the target lines indicates the levels of the money supply, M^*, and fiscal expenditures, G^*, that are required to attain both targets. The relative effectiveness of monetary and fiscal policy in influencing income can be measured by the slope of the $\bar{Y}$ line. The slope of the $\bar{I}$ line expresses their relative effectiveness in influencing investment.

So far, variables and equations were just counted. In principle, for given targets, the required values of the policy instruments may range between minus and plus infinity. Tinbergen recognized that policy instruments in reality are often subject to boundary conditions. Some, such as the money supply, cannot be negative. Others, such as tax rates, can perhaps be changed only by limited amounts for political reasons. If the system hits such a boundary, it effectively loses an instrument. As a consequence, the targets may become unattainable.

Tinbergen also recognized, as did Frisch, that the targets are usually not immutably fixed but more or less flexible. For the sake of higher employment, a society would perhaps be willing to tolerate a moderate amount of inflation. This idea is formalized by expressing social utility, as perceived by the policy maker, as a function of the target values,

$$W = W(y_1 \ldots y_t \ldots y_T). \tag{29.10}$$

Policy instruments have to be chosen in such a way that this function is maximized, subject to the structural equations of the model. Such a problem will, as a rule, have a determinate solution regardless of the relationship between the numbers of targets and instruments. It is generally unproductive to agonize over policy dilemmas. Wise policy makers rather consider how much closer they can get to one target by compromising another.

In many cases different instruments are controlled by different policy makers, generally with different social utility functions. This poses the problem of the relative advantages of centralized and decentralized policy making. Tinbergen analyzed it in close analogy to the theory of oligopoly, where each seller maximizes profits for given expectations about the behavior of the other sellers. This aspect opened a rich mine of problems, down to differential games, with high analytical demands but so far with little practical relevance.

In the third stage of his work, Tinbergen moved to development planning. He worked untiringly on ways and means to reduce the income differences between rich and poor countries, devising planning techniques, quantitative models for educational and regional planning, and advising international organizations and the governments of many developing countries, particularly in Asia. The published results are scattered over numerous smaller writings, many written for planning bureaucrats the world over and for popular readerships. Though voluminous and cumulatively influential, they made no major contributions to economic science. Overviews of Tinbergen's philosophy of global planning can be found in his report for the Twentieth Century Fund (1962) and in *Lessons from the Past* (1963).

It may have been disillusionment with the response to his development planning efforts that later caused Tinbergen to shift his attention, in a fourth stage of his work, to the personal distribution of income and economic inequality in industrial economies. His approach was first outlined in a paper, "On the Theory of Income Distribution" (in Tinbergen, 1959), and the main results are collected in *Income Distribution: Analysis and Policies* (1975).

At that time, research in this field was dominated by stochastic approaches. They interpret life as a lottery in which individuals repeatedly draw random numbers. The observed distribution of income is regarded as the result of this stochastic process. In contrast, Tinbergen made himself the protagonist of a deterministic approach based on microeconomic theory.

Each person is considered as coming to the market with a given endowment of abilities, which can be transformed into certain streams of productive services. That person also has subjective preferences for work, income, leisure, risk, and different occupations. For each individual, the actual supply of services will depend on prospective remuneration. The services are demanded by firms in the light of technology and market conditions. Wage rates and employment, and thus earned incomes, depend on the interaction between demand and supply for services. High incomes go to those whose services are in short supply but high demand; poor are those whose services are abundantly supplied but not in high demand. This approach is used as a basis for extensive empirical work.

It was Tinbergen's tentative conclusion that the continuation of the trend toward more equality in industrial societies depends mainly on a race between improvements in education, which reduce inequality, and technological progress, which (by raising the demand for high skills) tends to increase it. It was clear to Tinbergen that a complete explanation of the personal distribution of income would combine both stochastic and deterministic elements, but he saw his contribution in the economic analysis of supply and demand.

To sum up, Tinbergen became world famous mostly as a missionary of planning, particularly development planning. His lasting contribution to economic science, however, was in other areas. As an econometrician, his claim to fame is the development of the first empirical model of business fluctuations. It turned out to be a decisive breakthrough, with Lawrence Klein's *Economic Fluctuations in the United States, 1921–1941* (1950) as the next milestone. Another major contribution was Tinbergen's theory of economic policy. It was, like the macrodynamic model, inspired by Ragnar Frisch's work, and James Meade had presented similar ideas at about the same time, though much less lucidly. However, Tinbergen's development of these ideas was an original contribution that became the point of departure for extensive work by others. Tinbergen's work on income inequality, finally, shows that deep concern with social justice may find no better analytical tools than those provided by modern mainstream economics.

Wassily Leontief

Wassily Leontief was born in Saint Petersburg in 1906, the son of a university professor.[9] He was admitted to the University of Leningrad at the age of fifteen, but his independent socialist views seem to have brought him into conflict with the Bolsheviks. He went to Berlin, where he obtained a doctorate in 1928. He first worked as a research assistant at the World Trade Institute in Kiel and then as an economic adviser to the Chinese government in Nanking. In 1931, Wesley Mitchell persuaded him to move to the United States as a research associate at the National Bureau of Economic Research.

Soon afterward, Leontief became an economics instructor at Harvard, where he rose through the ranks to a professorship in 1946. From 1953 to his resignation in 1975 he was Henry Lee Professor of Economics, and he also directed the Harvard Economic Research Project from its inception in 1946 until its termination in 1972. After his retirement from Harvard, he became a professor of economics at New York University. He was awarded the Nobel Prize in economics in 1973.

Leontief, with his ebullient personality, combines intellectual brilliance with a gift for provocative formulations and a talent for scientific entrepreneurship. He also had the stamina to devote most of his life to the development of a single research tool, and he had the satisfaction of seeing it applied all over the world. Though well trained in mathematics, he always remained an economist at heart. He used theory, mathematics, and statistics to obtain practical economic results. He despised analytical elegance for its own sake. "Elegance is for the tailor," he was heard to say.[10] What matters in his political opinions is the technocratic conviction that what he regarded as the next stage in the development of capitalism would require comprehensive national planning, not in the sense of a socialist economy but as a framework for decentralized decisions.

Leontief published his first paper at the age of nineteen.[11] Originally written in Russian, it was a short critical review of the social accounts for the Soviet Union used by the Central Statistical Administration (Leontief 1977, 2:3f.). Leontief points out that the Soviet accounts differ from the U.S. and British censuses by attempting to give a general picture of the entire structure of the economy in the form of a *tableau économique*. The

9. The biographical data on Leontief's early life are from Cave 1981.
10. He once said it in German in the presence of Erich Schneider, whose name means "tailor."
11. A sympathetic evaluation of his contributions can be found in Dorfman 1973.

TABLE 29.1

Input-Supplying Industry	Output-Receiving Industry			Total Output
	1	2	3	
1		x_{21}	x_{31}	x_1
2	x_{12}		x_{32}	x_2
3	x_{13}	x_{23}		x_3
Total input	x_1	x_2	x_3	Σx_i

concepts of input-output are unmistakably recognizable, though only in vague outline. Leontief probably did not realize at the time that he had intoned the leitmotiv of his life's work.

In the following years, Leontief published papers on industrial concentration, statistical supply and demand curves, international trade theory in terms of indifference and transformation curves, index numbers, and cobweb dynamics. At the National Bureau he also began to work out the basic concepts for input-output analysis. The statistical work took several years, but the first input-output tables could be presented in 1936. They were described in the opening sentence "as an attempt to construct . . . a Tableau Economique of the United States for the year 1919" (Leontief 1936, 105).

THE INPUT-OUTPUT TABLE. Richard Cantillon and François Quesnay had envisaged a national accounting system recording all commodity flows between different sectors of the economy. The national income accounts that gradually emerged from Adam Smith's basic concepts had a different orientation. They concentrated on the flows of final goods to income recipients, particularly households, whereas interindustry flows of intermediate goods were netted out as double counting. With his input-output accounts, Leontief returned to the concept of Cantillon and Quesnay.

The table that Leontief presented in 1936 distinguished ten sectors, including foreign trade and households. It consisted essentially in a square ten by ten array of numbers of the sort illustrated for just three industries in table 29.1. At the column heads appear the industries as receivers of output. At the row heads appear the same industries as suppliers of inputs. Row entries thus record the dollar value of a given industry's sales to each other industry. Column entries reveal the dollar value of an industry's purchases from each of the other sectors. Leontief initially left the main diagonal empty; things such as agricultural products used in agriculture and household services used in households were omitted. (In later publications subscripts are written in reverse order.)

If the sales equaled purchases for each sector, the row totals would equal the respective column totals. This would be the case for a completely stationary economy. In reality, sales may differ from purchases, the difference being reflected in the accumulation or decumulation of financial assets. Though Leontief paid careful attention to such differences, they are disregarded in the present exposition.

THE LEONTIEF PRODUCTION FUNCTION. Five years later, Leontief was able to go beyond these statistical tables. The results were published in *The Structure of American Economy* (Leontief 1941) with data for 1919 and 1929. Suppose each entry in a given column is divided by the column total, as described in table 29.2. The resulting coefficients show what proportion of an industry's costs is paid to each of the other industries. For each column they evidently add up to unity, but horizontal addition does not make sense any more.

These coefficients are essentially dimensionless numbers. Leontief managed to give them a dimension, however, by a particular choice of units. Suppose a unit of agricultural output is defined as that bundle of wheat, corn, eggs, or the like, in their normal composition, that costs 1 monetary unit (say \$1 or \$1 million). In this case all prices are automatically normalized at unity, and the entries in the input-output accounts can be interpreted as quantities. The coefficients then say, for example, how many units of output of the metal industry are used to produce one unit of agricultural products. The value ratios are thus transformed into technological input coefficients. Leontief's fundamental assumption is that these coefficients, though certainly variable in the course of economic development, can be treated as constants in applying the model.

With this assumption, Leontief returned to the fixed coefficient technology that had dominated production theory—though with exceptions—from Richard Cantillon to Léon Walras. Each unit of output is assumed to require a specified amount of each input; substitution and scale econ-

TABLE 29.2

Input-Supplying Industry	Output-Receiving Industry		
	1	2	3
1		$\dfrac{x_{21}}{x_2} = a_{21}$	$\dfrac{x_{31}}{x_3} = a_{31}$
2	$\dfrac{x_{12}}{x_1} = a_{12}$		$\dfrac{x_{32}}{x_3} = a_{32}$
3	$\dfrac{x_{13}}{x_1} = a_{13}$	$\dfrac{x_{23}}{x_2} = a_{23}$	

omies are excluded. Leontief did not use this assumption because he thought that factor substitution and diminishing returns did not exist. He used it because nonlinear general equilibrium systems presented insurmountable computational difficulties (and to some extent they still do), and he wanted a system that could be computationally implemented. Experience would have to show how much of the economic baby was thrown out with the nonlinear bathwater.

THE CLOSED LEONTIEF MODEL. Leontief first investigated an economic system in which all outputs also appear as inputs. This is called a closed system, regardless of whether it relates to an open or a closed economy. There are no primary factors of production and no final outputs. The theoretical analysis of such systems had been initiated by John von Neumann (1937) a few years earlier.

Once the array of technical coefficients is known, it can be used in two basic ways. By adding the entries horizontally, one can use it to determine the structure of the economy. Each entry in table 29.1, as table 29.2 shows, can be represented as the product of the respective coefficient and the output of the corresponding industry. Industry outputs are thus related by the following equations:

$$x_1 - a_{21} x_2 - a_{31} x_3 = 0 \tag{29.11}$$

$$-a_{12} x_1 + x_2 - a_{32} x_3 = 0 \tag{29.12}$$

$$-a_{13} x_1 - a_{23} x_2 + x_3 = 0 \tag{29.13}$$

There are as many equations as unknowns, but the system is homogeneous: if one set of x's satisfies the equations, any multiple will satisfy them, too. This means that the system determines not the levels of outputs but only their proportions. This is related to the fact that the technical coefficients, since they add vertically to unity, are not independent. If they are known for all but one product, those for the last product can be computed. With this qualification the model determines the structure of the x's and thus of the economy.

By adding entries vertically, one can use the array of technical coefficients to determine the structure of prices. In equilibrium each industry just covers its cost. This means that the sum of the inputs per unit of output, each multiplied by its price, must equal the output price. This leads to three equations in three prices, namely

$$p_1 - a_{12} p_2 - a_{13} p_3 = 0, \tag{29.14}$$

$$-a_{21} p_1 + p_2 - a_{23} p_3 = 0, \tag{29.15}$$

$$-a_{31} p_1 - a_{32} p_2 + p_3 = 0. \tag{29.16}$$

Again the system is homogeneous; it clearly cannot determine absolute money prices, but it determines relative prices. The corresponding dependence among the technological coefficients has already been noted.

With the two interpretations, Leontief provided an early illustration of duality; in its simplicity it is a particularly striking one. The same set of technical coefficients provides two sets of answers. With quantity weights and added horizontally, the coefficients determine the structure of outputs. With price weights and added vertically, they determine the structure of prices.

The results so far described are not exciting, though, because the structure of industry had to be known to construct the table in the first place, and prices were normalized at unity by the choice of units. Leontief's real questions concerned the effects of given changes in the coefficients on output and prices. His model is built for comparative statics. In particular, he used it to determine the effects of productivity gains on prices and industrial structure, and he also investigated the repercussions of investment and saving. Shifts in consumer demand could similarly be analyzed by considering changes in the input coefficients of households.

THE OPEN LEONTIEF MODEL There are many interesting questions, however, that a closed Leontief model cannot answer. For example, it cannot determine the capacity of the various industries and the size of the labor force that would be required to produce a specified bill of final outputs for consumption, investment, government, and foreign trade. Starting in 1944, stimulated by the problems of war and reconversion to peace, Leontief thus began using an open system. The results for 1939 were presented in the second edition of *The Structure of American Economy* (Leontief 1951).

The input-output table of an open system is derived from the closed system of table 29.1 by classifying one column (or more) as final output and one row (or more) as primary input. As a simple illustration, we may assume that industry 3 comprises households, that their purchases represent final demand, and that their sales represent the primary factor inputs for which they receive wages or, more generally, the value added by industries. One thus obtains the arrangement of table 29.3. Input coefficients can then be derived in the same way as before.

This system can be used to determine the output levels required for any vector of final demand. In the present example there are two equations, namely

$$x_1 - a_{21}x_2 = c_1, \tag{29.17}$$
$$-a_{12}x_1 + \quad x_2 = c_2. \tag{29.18}$$

Together they determine x_1 and x_2 for any prescribed bundle of c_1 and c_2. Once these are known, the labor coefficients for the primary inputs in the bottom row, which may again be labeled a_{13} and a_{23}, determine the associated employment levels.

TABLE 29.3

Input-Supplying Industry	Output-Receiving Industry		Final Demand	Total Output
	1	2		
1		x_{21}	c_1	x_1
2	x_{12}		c_2	x_2
Primary input	L_1	L_2		

The results of these computations can be exhibited in a table of coefficients that looks superficially like table 29.2 but has actually a quite different content. The input coefficients of table 29.2 measured the *direct* per unit requirements of a given industry for the outputs of other industries. The new table, in contrast, contains the sums of all *direct and indirect* requirements per unit of final demand. For example, if a_{21} in table 29.2 is the direct coal input per unit of steel without regard to the additional requirements of the coal industry, and so on, the corresponding coefficient A_{21} would measure the required expansion of coal output per unit of additional steel exports after allowing for all repercussions in the entire structure of industry. It is precisely for the sake of the differences between the two sets of coefficients that the whole input-output analysis is undertaken. While the a's are the data, the A's are the results. Mathematically, the matrix of the a's has to be inverted to obtain that of the A's.

Again there is a dual. If the wage rate is denoted by w, the price equations now state that

$$p_1 - a_{12} p_2 - a_{13} w = 0, \tag{29.19}$$

$$-a_{21} p_1 + p_2 - a_{23} w = 0, \tag{29.20}$$

which determines relative prices and the real wage. The system is constructed in such a way that aggregate wage incomes will just suffice to buy the final output. It should be noted, however, that changes in final output have no influence on prices. With Leontief's linear technology prices are determined by unit costs alone; demand affects only the composition of output.

Leontief used the open model, with great effect, to predict the repercussions of changes in final demand, including those in foreign trade, on output and employment in U.S. industries. The reliability of such predictions would seem to depend strongly on the homogeneity of the industries. For iron making it is plausible to assume that input proportions depend largely on technology. For "industries not elsewhere specified" this does not sound convincing. Leontief's initial study for ten industries was thus followed by larger and larger tables as rapidly as computer technology permitted. When Leontief began, computations for ten industries, he notes, would have taken a person two years. When he got to the computing stage, this time had already been considerably reduced, and with the later electronic computers matrix inversion eventually ceased to be an effective constraint.

THOUGH the two volumes of Leontief's essays (1977) testify to the range of his interests, his major work remained essentially focused on input-output. Most of these contributions are collected in two volumes published in 1953 and 1966. Some of them concern applications of U.S. data to particular problems such as manpower, foreign trade, wage policy, or disarmament.[12] Others extend input-output analysis to economic development, interregional relationships, environmental economics, and natural resources. The United Nations finally financed a project in which Leontief and his collaborators used input-output to derive grandiose projections for the world economy to the end of the century (Leontief et al. 1977).

Of particular theoretical importance was Leontief's effort to add a dynamic dimension to his system. Static input-output analysis relates flows of goods and services. Dynamic input-output analysis adds stocks of capital goods. An increase in the output of shoes is now shown to require not only additional flows of leather and labor but also an addition to the stock of machines and buildings. In contrast to the current flows, these additions to capital goods are temporary; once the stock is built up, the additional demand (except for replacement) disappears. This is what makes the problem dynamic and thus opens the way for an analysis of growth. One problem in this dynamic analysis is clearly the asymmetry between expansion and contraction; by felling trees one can build houses, but if there is an excess of houses, they cannot be turned back into trees. Overall, the usefulness of the dynamic system remained limited.

Leontief's early work attracted little attention, but once input-output analysis was fully developed, it was a great and immediate success. Within a few years, numerous staffs collected and processed data in more than fifty countries; large conferences were held to exchange experiences; input-output became a status symbol for any developing country, and after Stalin's death it also became acceptable in the Soviet Union. While Cournot, Thünen, and Walras wrote for future generations, Leontief, like Adam Smith and Keynes, wrote for his contemporaries.

This success had diverse sources. In the early 1940s linear systems became the wave of the future. At a time when von Neumann's models

---

12. Leontief found that U.S. exports, surprisingly, embody less capital and more labor than the domestic substitutes for imports. On international trade theory, this "Leontief paradox" had the impact of a bombshell. Nothing stimulates research like an apparent paradox.

were not yet understood and economists were still laboring on the solutions to the simplest programming problems, Leontief provided the first ready-to-use linear model of an economy, prepared to devour and digest vast amounts of data. The development of input-output also coincided with the advent of the digital computer. The progress in computer technology thus permitted the inversion of ever larger Leontief matrices. In addition, input-output rode the crest of the postwar planning wave. Planning bureaucracies at all levels, international, national, regional, and local, in developed and developing countries, found in input-output a framework that was conceptually simple, relatively robust in handling, and versatile in its applications.[13]

In the course of the 1970s, however, scientific activity in this field began to stagnate. What had been a flood of publications dwindled in the 1980s to a trickle. In part this was simply a sign that the methodology was now fully matured, ready for routine use. In part, however, it reflected the fact that the explicit optimizing techniques of activity analysis had made input-output theoretically obsolete. Input-output was, so to speak, a sturdy propeller plane and the future belonged to the jet. At the academic level input-output had never inspired many budding geniuses; they preferred existence proofs, theorems, and rational expectations.

Overall, Leontief did not enrich mainstream economics with deep new insights, but he provided it with a practically usable and robust tool for empirical planning. This is both less and more than what other distinguished economists achieved.

30
John von Neumann

MATHEMATICAL geniuses have sometimes applied their minds to economic problems. Before the twentieth century, however, the results used to fall far short of their contributions to mathematics or physics. What Copernicus and Newton had to say on currency and coinage was competent, to be sure, but not highly original. Daniel Bernoulli made a brilliant contribution to decision making under uncertainty, but he failed to explore the wider implications of declining marginal utility. Economic problems, it seems, had not been articulated in a form that fired the imagination of creative mathematicians. During the marginalist era this began to change. Mathematical amateurs such as Johann Heinrich von Thünen, Hermann Heinrich Gossen, Stanley Jevons, and Léon Walras joined forces with

---

13. In the United States federal support for input-output tended to wax and wane with the planning enthusiasm of successive administrations.

trained mathematicians such as Augustin Cournot, Alfred Marshall, Vilfredo Pareto, Knut Wicksell, and Irving Fisher in making basic economic theory amenable to mathematical analysis. In the second quarter of the twentieth century, it happened for the first time that a mathematical genius made fundamental contributions to economic theory. He was John von Neumann.

Life

Von Neumann was born in Budapest, then part of the Austro-Hungarian monarchy, in 1903.[1] He was the oldest of three sons of a wealthy banker of Jewish origin who had been ennobled. Johann was first educated privately and then entered the *Gymnasium*, where his unusual abilities were soon recognized. He was excused from mathematics classes and received private tutoring from mathematics professors. By the end of high school, he was regarded as a professional mathematician and had published, jointly with one of his tutors, his first paper. Though registering and taking examinations as a student of mathematics at the University of Budapest, he actually went to Zürich to study chemistry at the Federal Institute of Technology, where he met some of the outstanding mathematicians of the day. From Budapest he obtained a doctorate in mathematics and from Zürich a diploma in chemical engineering.

From 1927 to 1930 von Neumann was a lecturer (*Privatdozent*) in mathematics in Berlin and Hamburg. His publications in set theory, algebra, and quantum theory had already made him world famous; he had become recognized as one of the geniuses of the mathematical world. However, it seemed to him that in Germany too many lecturers were aspiring to one of too few chairs, and he also had dark forebodings about the political future. Thus, after visiting Princeton in 1930, he accepted Princeton's offer of a professorship in 1931. Two years later, he gave up this post to join the newly founded Institute for Advanced Study, also at Princeton, as its youngest permanent faculty member.

In 1930, von Neumann had married Marietta Kovesi, also a Hungarian. Their daughter, now Marina von Neumann Whitman, later became a distinguished American economist. The young professor, well paid and from an affluent family, maintained a spacious house in Princeton, where he entertained many guests and gave frequent parties, though he would sometimes slip away to his mathematics. He knew about half a dozen languages (including Latin and Greek), and he had an amazing knowledge of history, a keen interest in politics, and a good sense of humor. At the same time he seems to have had a certain aloofness in his human relations. His marriage was unhappy and ended in divorce. In 1938, during a summer

1. The following biographical note is based on Ulam 1958 and 1976.

visit to Budapest, von Neumann married Klara Dan, who later became one of the first computer programmers. Their house continued to be the gathering place of scientists.[2]

In Princeton early in 1939, von Neumann met Oskar Morgenstern (1902–77). Morgenstern had been born in Germany, the son of a small businessman and one of the illegitimate daughters of Frederick III of Germany. He grew up in Vienna and became a professor at the University of Vienna and director of the Austrian Institute of Business Cycle Research. After Hitler's annexation of Austria, he was dismissed as "politically unbearable," whereupon he accepted a post at Princeton. He and von Neumann became close friends, and his efforts to write an expository paper on the theory of games seems to have persuaded von Neumann, step by step, that his early mathematical paper on game theory was worth expanding into a fundamental treatise on economic behavior. Their collaboration is described in Morgenstern 1976.

By the time the war broke out, von Neumann had become one of the most illustrious American scientists. In the course of the years, he was showered with honorary doctorates, academy memberships, prizes, medals, and other distinctions. He also became a member of important committees and advisory groups, did important defense work, and later served as chairman of the Intercontinental Ballistics Missiles Committee. The responsibility of scientists was a heavy burden on his conscience, and he strongly defended Robert Oppenheimer, but he had made up his mind that the United States could not dispense with nuclear weapons. At the end of 1954 he thus accepted a presidential appointment to the Atomic Energy Commission. He took leave of absence from Princeton and moved to Washington, D.C. Soon after, his health deteriorated; cancer was detected, and John von Neumann died in Washington after a long illness in 1957.

Works

Von Neumann was a prolific writer, publishing (or coauthoring) five books and six volumes of collected papers (von Neumann, 1961–63). For an economist with little knowledge of modern mathematics, it is perhaps most appropriate to describe the range of his mind by listing the titles of these volumes: *Logic, Theory of Sets and Quantum Mechanics*; *Operators, Ergodic Theory and Almost Periodic Functions in a Group*; *Rings of Operators*; *Continuous Geometry and Other Topics*; *Design of Computers, Theory of Automata and Numerical Analysis*; and *Theory of Games, Astrophysics, Hydrodynamics and Meteorology*.

Von Neumann believed that mathematics is constantly rejuvenated by

2. Klara von Neumann collected things in the shape of elephants, and figure 4 on page 64 of the *Theory of Games* was drawn to amuse her.

receiving new problems from the empirical sciences. A passage from a lecture "The Mathematician" is worth quoting in full. "As a mathematical discipline travels far from its empirical source . . . it is beset by very grave dangers. It becomes more and more purely aestheticizing, more and more purely *l'art pour l'art*. . . . Whenever this stage is reached, the only remedy seems to me to be the rejuvenating return to the source: the reinjection of more or less directly empirical ideas" (1961–63, vol. 1, no. 1, p. 9).

One source of von Neumann's empirical inspiration, besides physics, computers, and others, was economics. As mathematics had been inspiring to creative economists, so economics began to be inspiring to creative mathematicians. From then onward, the mathematical fringe of economics would blend imperceptibly into mathematical research. At the same time, the danger of aesthetical inbreeding, which von Neumann saw for mathematics in general, would also begin to threaten mathematical economics.

In the 1928 paper "Zur Theorie der Gesellschaftsspiele," the relationship to economics was only hinted at in a footnote. In the paper "Ueber ein ökonomisches Gleichungssystem und eine Verallgemeinerung des Brouwerschen Fixpunktsatzes," published in 1937, economics had moved to center stage. In the *Theory of Games and Economic Behavior*, first published in 1944 (1947), von Neumann and Morgenstern's work had grown to a massive treatise replete with references not only to specific games but also to a wide range of social and economic phenomena. The preface states that the theory had been developed by one of the authors since 1928, and it is clear which of the authors this was.[3] Without the other author, however, the book would probably not have been written, at least not as a book on economic behavior. John von Neumann was the inventor and Oskar Morgenstern the innovating entrepreneur, and both are necessary, so Joseph Schumpeter assures us, for successful innovations. After the *Theory of Games*, von Neumann published several further papers on game theory and gave an important further impulse to duality theory, but these were contributions of a limited and more technical nature. His main interest, besides his extensive advisory responsibilities, had shifted to problems related to computers.

The Theory of Games

The theory of games is essentially a theory of small groups. Crops depend on rainfall, but rainfall does not depend on crops. Similarly, the quantity of wheat that an individual farmer sells depends on the market price, but the market price does not (significantly) depend on his sales. In

---

3. As his specific contributions, aside from general collaboration, Morgenstern mentioned the example of Sherlock Holmes and Professor Moriarty and the discovery of a paper by Jean Ville giving a more elementary proof of the minimax theorem, based on convexity (Morgenstern 1976, 806, 811).

many economic contexts, particularly if they relate to whole economies or large markets, it is quite legitimate, therefore, to treat the environment as if it were independent of the decision in question. In other contexts, however, the reactions of the environment are an essential part of the decision problem. This is particularly true if the number of economic agents is small, as in oligopoly and bilateral monopoly. In such cases, all agents have to take into account how the other agents will react to their behavior.

An important contribution to the analysis of such problems had been made by Augustin Cournot (1838) and extended by Wilhelm Launhardt (1885). The first fundamental attack on small group problems, however, was made by von Neumann in his extraordinary early paper "Zur Theorie der Gesellschaftsspiele" (1928) (On the Theory of Games of Strategy). It required tools that were not available in classical mathematics.[4]

In contrast to mere games of chance, the games von Neumann had in mind are characterized by the fact that the profits or losses of a player depend, besides perhaps on chance, on the moves of the other players. As a consequence, the postulate that each player tries to achieve the best possible result loses its clear meaning. Von Neumann tried to determine what *best possible* could mean in such a case. Though the paper was addressed to mathematicians, he indicated in a footnote that the economic implications of the problem were clear to him: he wanted to determine the behavior of a *homo oeconomicus* in a reactive situation.

Von Neumann began with the analytical description of a game, consisting in an exact specification of the sequence of the players' conceivable moves, the chance elements that may intervene, and the information each player has at each step. It is clear that only the simplest games can be described in this, as it was later called, extensive form. For more complicated games and most real-life situations, the number of possible sequences rapidly becomes staggeringly large; the game tree, as the graph of the extensive form was called, has an enormous mass of branches.

Once the game is thus described, each player can, in principle, calculate his gains or losses for each conceivable sequence of moves. This provides the basis for his choice of a strategy, by which is meant the set of rules that control his moves at each moment. For each alternative strategy, the outcome will depend on the strategies chosen by the other players. Von Neumann called this simplified description the normal form of the game, and later it was also called the strategic form.

In the light of the joint outcomes, each player will have to choose his optimal strategy. The nature of this problem may be illustrated by a numerical example of a game in which each of two players, A and B, can choose between two strategies (table 30.1). The game is supposed to be,

---

4. The classic introduction into the problems discussed in this section and in "Cardinal Utility," later in this chapter, is Luce and Raiffa 1957.

TABLE 30.1

Strategies of A	Strategies of B		Row minimum
	b_1	b_2	
a_1	-2	1	-2
a_2	-1	2	-1
Column maximum	-1	2	

in later terminology, zero sum, which expresses the fundamental assumption that the profits of A and B add to zero. The entries in the table thus represent both the gains of A and the losses of B. A chooses his strategy in such a way that the outcome is maximized, whereas B will try to minimize it. This duality of a maximum problem intertwined with a minimum problem became the theme for four decades of research, unfolding its implications in ever richer variations. In economics the maximum typically related to the value of output and the minimum to the cost of inputs. Thus parlor games, surprisingly, became mathematical paradigms for economic equilibrium.

How will A decide? If he chooses a_1, the least he can obtain is -2; if he chooses a_2, he assures himself of at least -1. Maximizing this row minimum he chooses a_2. On the basis of similar reasoning, B will minimize the column maximum by choosing b_1. Each player is supposed to be ignorant of the other player's strategy when he makes his choice, but in the case of table 30.1, it makes no difference if he can divine his opponent's thoughts. B will choose b_1, no matter what A does, and vice versa. Mathematically, this feature can be attributed to the fact that table 30.1 has what von Neumann called a saddle point, which means that the maximum of the row minima equals the minimum of the column maxima. If such a saddle point exists, the choice of strategies presents no further problem.

In many cases, fortunately for the development of economic theory, there is no saddle point. Table 30.2 illustrates this case. Strategy a_2 still assures A of a higher minimum than a_1, and b_1 still assures B of a lower maximum than b_2, but A's maximum row minimum is now lower than B's minimum column maximum. In this case penetration of each other's thoughts becomes important. Once A realizes that B chooses b_1, he has good reason to change his decision to a_1, which in turn causes B to switch to b_2, and so forth.

Von Neumann nevertheless succeeds in guaranteeing a saddle point by means of what he calls a trick. The trick, earlier used by E. Borel,[5]

---

5. Borel's contribution is described in von Neumann 1953.

TABLE 30.2

Strategies of A	Strategies of B		Row minimum
	b_1	b_2	
a_1	1	-1	-1
a_2	0	2	0
Column maximum	1	2	

consists in admitting what came to be called mixed strategies. If a player loses by being found out, it may be best for him to select his strategy at random, say, by picking the strategy number out of an urn in which each number is represented in a certain proportion. Instead of the strategy itself, his decision now selects the proportions of the strategy numbers in the urn, that is, their probabilities. Each player chooses his probabilities in such a way that the expected value of his profits is maximized. Von Neumann shows that the optimal mixed strategy is never worse than the best pure strategy and often better. What is more important, for mixed strategies there is always a saddle point. This proposition is von Neumann's celebrated minimax theorem.

In its mathematical structure, the minimax theorem for zero-sum games later turned out to be similar to duality in linear programming.[6] This can perhaps be made intuitively plausible by pointing out that player A maximizes a weighted sum of the values of his pure strategies with his probabilities as weights, while player B minimizes a weighted sum of the values of his own strategies with his probabilities as weights. In 1928, von Neumann was not aware of such reinterpretations of his model. However, his early paper on games provided him with the concepts for his 1937 paper on general equilibrium. In a working paper, written in 1947, he applied these concepts to maximum problems in linear models (von Neumann 1961–63, 6:89–95). Though the paper was only published in the collected works, the editor could say in his prefatory note that it had an important influence on the early theoretical development of linear programming and played a great role in initiating the theory of duality.

In economic life the choice of strategies is often not a two-person game. Already in the 1928 paper, von Neumann extended the analysis to three persons, which led him to a theory of coalitions. On the basis of the

6. The similarity of the two problems was noted in the *Theory of Games* (von Neumann and Morgenstern 1947, 154) as a subject for further clarification.

strategic form of the game, each possible group of players is assumed to calculate the potential gains that it could obtain by forming a coalition. The result is the cooperative form of the game. These extensions were further elaborated in the *Theory of Games*, where coalitions are among the principal topics. In addition, economic life is usually not a zero-sum game, and it is one of the oldest insights of economic science that all players may gain or at least some may gain more than the others lose. Von Neumann and Morgenstern thus proceeded to non-zero-sum games. The *Theory of Games* also introduced economists to the theory of convex sets (ch. 16) and provided a (relatively) elementary proof of the minimax theorem in terms of this theory (ch. 17). It thereby inaugurated in mathematical economics the era of set theory and topology.

Though von Neumann's 1928 paper had received little attention, the *Theory of Games*, to the surprise of its authors, was an immediate success and became the point of departure for a rapidly growing literature of increasing complexity. A new mathematical discipline was born with important applications to statistics, operations research, political science, biology, computer science, and military decisions. There was also, once again, much talk about a revolution in economics. Indeed, the title of the treatise promised a theory of economic behavior, and it seemed that oligopoly, bilateral monopoly, bargaining, and coalitions might now become amenable to a more insightful analysis. It is true that references to game theory solutions soon began to appear, even in elementary textbooks, often accompanied by little numerical illustrations like table 30.1. The "zero-sum game" and A.W. Tucker's (non-zero) "prisoner's dilemma" became part of daily jargon. The substantial economic insights, however, remained sparse. The hoped-for revolution did not materialize.

The main reason for this—to an economist—disappointing development is the enormous complexity of most real-life small group situations if interpreted as a game. Almost anything is possible, and general theorems, applicable to a wide range of situations, are hard to find. It seems that economists, when they concentrated most of their attention on problems of large groups, displayed sound intuition.[7] In such circumstances the most useful aspect of the game theory approach is often the impulse it provides for a more explicit and complete description of the decision problem than would otherwise have been available. This may still change, and in the light of possible future breakthroughs the *Theory of Games* may yet be seen as the foundation of a new theory of economic behavior.

7. The link between game theory and Walrasian equilibrium was established by J. F. Nash (1950). In twenty-eight lines, with hardly any formulas, he was able to prove that an *n*-person game, in which each player chooses the optimal strategy given the strategies of the other players, has a solution. The paper may well be the second most famous page in the history of economic theory after Quesnay's *Tableau Economique*.

The Existence of Growth Equilibrium

From Princeton, von Neumann visited in Vienna the mathematical seminar of Karl Menger (son of the economist), later professor of mathematics at Notre Dame and at the Illinois Institute of Technology. The Viennese school of economics had declined, but in that seminar von Neumann found economists and mathematicians thinking along the same lines he had followed in his 1928 paper.[8]

One point of departure for the Menger group was Friedrich von Wieser's theory of imputation. It was supposed to explain how factor values are derived from product values. In competitive equilibrium, so Wieser argued, the value of the product equals its cost of production, consisting of the required quantities of factors valued at the respective factor values. With fixed technical coefficients, the value of each product could thus be expressed as a linear function of factor values. Wieser's notion was that these equations could be simultaneously solved to give the factor values in terms of the product values. The trouble was that, except for special cases, he seemed to have either too many equations or not enough. Of course, Wieser's formulation of the imputation problem was highly imperfect in the first place. It nevertheless induced the group around Karl Menger to discuss the logic of economic equation systems.

The other point of departure was the Walrasian general equilibrium system in the stripped-down version of Gustav Cassel. Hans Neisser (1932), Friedrich Zeuthen (1933) and, in a different sense, also Heinrich von Stackelberg (1933) had noted that the counting of variables and equations does not assure a solution with nonnegative prices and that the system itself ought to determine which prices, if any, are zero, which would make the respective commodities free goods. Karl Schlesinger, a Viennese banker and talented amateur theorist, discussed this problem in Menger's seminar, indicating important elements of the solution. He had asked Abraham Wald, a brilliant young mathematician from Roumania, to tutor him in mathematics. In three papers, the last of which (1936) was intended as a nontechnical introduction, Wald came up with the first rigorous proof of the existence of an economic equilibrium. Modern existence analysis was born. The economics of Wald's model, however, was not satisfactory, and the mathematics remained opaque.[9] It was von Neumann who provided the decisive contribution. First presented in Princeton in 1932, it found its

8. The early history of existence analysis has been lovingly traced by Roy Weintraub (1983), to whom the following account is much in debt.

9. Schlesinger, after having helped many Jewish scientists to emigrate, committed suicide when Hitler annexed Austria. Wald, who had worked as a statistician in the institute that Morgenstern directed, escaped to the United States, where he had a distinguished career in mathematical statistics as the founder of sequential decision analysis. He died with his wife in an airplane crash in India in 1950.

final form in the paper of 1937, which Menger published in the last volume of his seminar papers.

Von Neumann considered an economy in balanced growth, in which all inputs and outputs grow at the same constant rate g. Relative prices, therefore, are constant, and so are returns to scale. This is essentially Cassel's growth model, but g is not predetermined, say, by population growth, but determined by the model itself.

Technology is represented by production processes. A given process is characterized by the inputs it requires and the outputs it produces if operated at unit level. Substitution possibilities between inputs and outputs are modeled by specifying alternative processes. The outputs become available one period after the inputs have been applied. Processes of longer duration are broken down into successive one-period processes in which capital goods and inventories appear both as outputs and inputs. The system is closed in the sense that all outputs in one period become productive inputs in the following period. As with Richard Cantillon, François Quesnay, and Robert Malthus, consumer goods are simply inputs in the production of labor. There is no primary input, such as land, that is provided by nature in a fixed quantity.

Though von Neumann's analysis is valid for any number of goods and processes, its basic idea will be illustrated here for two goods, wheat, x_1, and labor, x_2, and two processes, used at levels X_1 and X_2. The input of good i in process j, if operated at unit level, is denoted by a_{ij}. The output of good i in process j is denoted by b_{ij}.

For each commodity, the aggregate output resulting from all processes must at least equal the input required to operate the same processes over the next period at a scale expanded at the general rate of growth. This means that

$$b_{11}X_1 + b_{12}X_2 \geq (1+g)(a_{11}X_1 + a_{12}X_2) \qquad (30.1)$$

$$b_{21}X_1 + b_{22}X_2 \geq (1+g)(a_{21}X_1 + a_{22}X_2). \qquad (30.2)$$

If these conditions are violated, the growth process cannot be maintained, supply falling short of demand. If the conditions hold with a $>$ sign, supply exceeds demand. The growth process can be maintained, but the respective commodity j becomes a free good whose price p_j is zero. If the equality sign applies, j is an economic good with a positive price.

In a market economy the allocation of resources to processes is governed not by overall supply and demand requirements but by profits and losses. The unit costs of a process are obtained by multiplying inputs by their market prices. Since production takes time, costs also include interest at rate r. Sales proceeds, on the other hand, are obtained by valuing outputs at market prices. If the comparison of costs and proceeds shows a profit, the process will be expanded, which will cause a change in prices. Profits, therefore, are not compatible with steady growth. Losses, in principle, are compatible with steady growth, but the unprofitable processes will be shut down. To be continuously operated at a positive level, a process, therefore, must just break even. This requirement can be written

$$(1+r)(a_{11}p_1 + a_{21}p_2) \geq b_{11}p_1 + b_{21}p_2 \tag{30.3}$$

$$(1+r)(a_{12}p_1 + a_{22}p_2) \geq b_{12}p_1 + b_{22}p_2, \tag{30.4}$$

with the proviso that the level of a process is zero if this condition holds with a $>$.

The question is whether process levels, prices, a growth rate, and an interest rate can be found that satisfy these requirements. This is the fundamental existence problem. Von Neumann's solution is based on the idea that the overall problem can be divided into two interrelated subproblems—the two players of a game at once come to mind. In the primal problem the growth rate is maximized subject to the supply requirement. In the dual problem the interest is minimized subject to the profitability requirement. If the maximal growth rate is equal to the minimal interest rate, then a solution exists and can, in principle, be computed. Von Neumann was able to show that under his assumptions this is always the case. An equilibrium is proved to exist.

What does growth maximization imply? Supposed a diligent planner tries to structure the economy in such a way that growth is maximized. If he chooses an excessively high growth rate, the supply requirement for some commodities will be violated. By gradually lowering g, he will arrive at the highest growth rate at which the supply requirement is satisfied for all commodities. For at least one commodity, the supply requirement will then be satisfied with an equality sign; there will be at least one economic good.

What is, in intuitive terms, the meaning of the minimization of interest? Inefficient use of a resource is, in a sense, equivalent to a reduction in the quantity available and thus increases its scarcity and thereby its price. The more efficiently it is used, the lower its price. In von Neumann's model, the resource is capital. Its efficient use is thus accomplished by the minimization of interest. If r is assigned an excessively low level, some processes are bound to be profitable; the profitability requirement is violated. If r is gradually raised, fewer and fewer processes will remain profitable. At some point, r will be just high enough to make profits disappear in all processes. The profitability requirement then holds as an equality for at least one process. At this point, r is at its minimum.

At first sight the primal and the dual problem look quite different. Von Neumann showed that they are closely interrelated. In fact, the maximal growth rate is equal to the minimal interest rate. The economy may be visualized in the shape of a saddle: the highest point between the stirrups coincides with the lowest point between pommel and cantle.

To show that maximal g is equal to minimal r, we write the supply requirements as equalities with excess supplies of commodities, u_1 and u_2, appearing on the right-hand side.[10] At the same time we write both equations in value terms by multiplying quantities with the respective commodity prices:

$$[b_{11} - (1+g)a_{11}]p_1 X_1 + [b_{12} - (1+g)a_{12}]p_1 X_2 = p_1 u_1 \tag{30.5}$$

$$[b_{21} - (1+g)a_{21}]p_2 X_1 + [b_{22} - (1+g)a_{22}]p_2 X_2 = p_2 u_2. \tag{30.6}$$

The profitability requirements are similarly written as equations for the losses per unit of the two processes, v_1 and v_2, again expressed in value terms:

$$[(1+r)a_{11} - b_{11}]p_1 X_1 + [(1+r)a_{21} - b_{21}]p_2 X_1 = v_1 X_1 \tag{30.7}$$

$$[(1+r)a_{12} - b_{12}]p_1 X_2 + [(1+r)a_{22} - b_{22}]p_2 X_2 = v_2 X_2. \tag{30.8}$$

Since all equations are now in value terms, they can be added. It turns out that many terms on the left-hand side cancel. What is left is the following equation:

$$(r - g)[a_{11}p_1 X_1 + a_{12}p_1 X_2 + a_{21}p_2 X_1 + a_{22}p_2 X_2]$$
$$= p_1 u_1 + p_2 u_2 + v_1 X_1 + v_2 X_2. \tag{30.9}$$

All terms on the right are zero, because a commodity with excess supply ($u_i > 0$) has price zero ($p_i = 0$) and a process with a loss ($v_i > 0$) will not be operated ($X_i = 0$). On the left, the square bracket is not zero, provided at least one process is operated ($X_i > 0$) and at least one good is not free ($p_j > 0$). It follows that r must equal g; the maximal rate of growth is equal to the minimal rate of interest.

The square bracket represents the aggregate production outlays of the economy. Multiplied by r it measures the capital cost for investing these outlays for one year. On the other hand, outlays bear fruit at the rate g. In equilibrium, so the saddle point theorem tells us, the productivity of capital is equal to its cost.

Von Neumann's paper on general equilibrium, though only ten pages long, has been called the most important article in mathematical economics. Never has one fundamental idea had so many fruitful ramifications. These go in very different directions.

For the first time, the existence of equilibrium was proved for an economically meaningful model. With respect to its inequality features, this model was more complex than the Walrasian system, but in other respects it was much simpler. In particular, it did not include optimizing

10. The following exposition is based on Brems 1986.

consumers and diminishing returns. There was little further work along these lines until around 1950, when Kenneth Arrow and Gerard Debreu took up the problem.

At the level of the theory of value and allocation, von Neumann showed that, as Dorfmann, Samuelson, and Solow expressed it, "hidden in every competitive general-equilibrium system is a maximum problem for value of output and a minimum problem for factor returns" (1958, 370). The bookkeeping identity of national product and national income, already noted by Adam Smith, reflects the working of the invisible hand in the dual role of output maximizer and factor price minimizer. Von Neumann was careful to note, however, that in reality the invisible hand cannot be expected to work to perfection.

From the point of view of what later became known as operations research, von Neumann had constructed the first (nonlinear) programming problem, in both its primal and dual aspects. These aspects were further developed in the late 1940s by the scientists at the Cowles Commission, including Dantzig and Koopmans. Whereas optimizing models based on calculus could, at best, establish local conditions for an optimum, von Neumann made it possible to construct the optimum, so to speak, from scratch.

The paper also made a substantive contribution to the theory of economic growth by revealing for the first time an intimate relationship between the growth rate of an economy and its rate of interest. Von Neumann showed that Cassel's model could be in balanced growth at different growth rates. Only one of these rates was efficient, however, namely the maximal growth rate, and this was equal to the (minimal) rate of interest. In a stationary state, with $g = 0$, the rate of interest would be zero.[11] At the time von Neumann wrote his paper, growth was a neglected topic in economics, and further development took place only in the late 1950s.

From the point of view of mathematical tools, von Neumann's paper had demonstrated the fruitfulness, and for some problems indeed the necessity, of topology for economic analysis. Calculus, which had been not only the workhorse but the pride of mathematical economists, gradually came to be regarded as the poor man's mathematics. If in a future century, so Morgenstern reported von Neumann as saying, when people unearth books such as Hicks's *Value and Capital*, they will believe it was written around the time of Newton, so primitive is its mathematics (Morgenstern 1976, 810). Within a few decades there was a veritable topology revolution in economics, and economics began to attract some of the best mathe-

---

11. Schumpeter had argued that interest was a dynamic phenomenon in the sense that it would disappear in full equilibrium. Brems (1986, 313) thought that von Neumann had vindicated Schumpeter. This is not so, however. In Schumpeterian terms, the von Neumann model is purely static; there are no innovations and structural changes. The von Neumann model confirmed, therefore, that a positive interest rate may appear in a static model.

matical brains. Von Neumann's (reported) contempt, however, was not fully justified, and a stream of major contributions to economics continued to be based on more pedestrian mathematics.

Cardinal Utility

Until Pareto economists used to describe utility as if it were measurable cardinally in about the same way as, in everyday usage, temperature.[12] The origin of the scale was perhaps as arbitrary as the choice between the freezing point of water and that of alcohol, and the units were perhaps as arbitrary as the choice between Celsius and Fahrenheit degrees. However, the utilities that the same individual derives from different goods could be meaningfully added, and it made sense to say that the difference in utility between an apple and a banana is larger than between a banana and a cherry.[13]

However, most economists used the cardinality of utility only for expository purposes and they refrained from making statements for which cardinality was essential. This was particularly clear in the case of Fisher. Pareto then made the final step by discarding any pretense of cardinality, describing utility (or what he called *ophélimité*) as a purely ordinal concept. Utilities could be compared, but utility differences could not; the above statement about apples, bananas, and cherries was declared devoid of substantive content. As a consequence, diminishing marginal utility lost its meaning and was replaced by the diminishing marginal rate of substitution. It turned out that the entire structure of value theory nevertheless remained intact. Cardinality was neither obtainable nor necessary.

This whole development concerned utility under full certainty. Economic theorists had much to say about uncertainty, but they had not yet found a way to incorporate it explicitly into their analytical framework. The moment somebody tried, namely the mathematician Daniel Bernoulli, cardinality began to play a crucial role. The same thing happened almost two centuries later in the theory of games of von Neumann and Morgenstern.

Bernoulli had based his solution of the Saint Petersburg paradox on the assumption of a particular utility function. Von Neumann and Morgenstern went the other way by showing that an individual's gambling behavior can be used to derive a cardinal utility function. Their approach is described in chapter 3 of the *Theory of Games*, and the axiomatic treatment of utility is set out in an appendix, added in the second edition. Though it is important for many problems of decision making under un-

---

12. It should be noted that the present discussion does not touch upon interpersonal comparisons of utility.

13. The same Viennese environment that generated the existence debate also inspired a contribution to utility theory. In a remarkable paper, Franz Alt (1936) derived cardinal utility from a set of seven axioms including the comparability of utility differences.

certainty, in the context of their theory of games it is more an important digression than an essential component.

Suppose an individual prefers an apple to a banana and a banana to a cherry. This ranking can be symbolically expressed as

$$A > B > C, \tag{30.10}$$

but so far no numbers are involved. This individual is now presented with a choice between B and a lottery ticket promising A with probability α and C with probability $(1-\alpha)$. If $\alpha=1$, the lottery ticket will certainly be preferred; if $\alpha=0$, the banana will be chosen. Somewhere in between there must be a probability at which the individual is just indifferent between the banana and the lottery ticket. Suppose this happens at $\alpha=2/3$. This probability can then be used to determine the location of the banana on the utility scale between the apple and the cherry.

This is best illustrated numerically. The apple and the cherry can be assigned utility numbers that are arbitrary except that the apple has the higher number. This implicitly fixes the origin and the units of the utility scale. Suppose $U_A=9$ and $U_C=3$. In this case the utility of the banana can be interpreted as $U_B=(2/3)9+(1/3)3=7$. By confronting the individual with more and more choices of this sort, any goods or bundles of goods can be located on the scale defined by the arbitrary values for U_A and U_B. It is clear that the resulting set of numbers is not unique; different sets are obtained for different choices of U_A and U_B. The essential point for cardinal measurement is that all of these sets are linear transformations of each other. For ordinal measurement, the transformation is unique only up to a monotonic (which means rank-preserving) transformation. However, the cardinal utilities derived in this way have meaning only in the context of risk; under full certainty, contrary to what Morgenstern expected, ordinal utility continued to rule the field.

Von Neumann and Morgenstern use these utilities, which have here been illustrated for consumer goods, only for the dollar amount of income or wealth. What they construct is a utility function for money income. The result of their logical analysis can be expressed by saying that, if certain axioms are accepted, it is possible to assign utility numbers to sums of money in such a way that the individual chooses the action with the highest expected value of utilities. The Bernoulli hypothesis was legitimized.

Such an axiomatic system cannot be directly subjected to empirical tests. It has to prove itself useful in interpreting empirical observations. In the case of the von Neumann–Morgenstern utility function, certain observations created obvious difficulties. One of them is the popularity of gambling. It is a problem because the expected values of most gambles are negative, and on the basis of the Bernoulli hypothesis they will be accepted only if the utility gain from gaining \$100 is regarded as much larger than the utility loss from losing \$100, which means that the marginal utility of money must be rising. This line of reasoning was further developed by Milton Friedman and Leonard Savage (1948).

A related problem is that the theory leaves no room for the pleasure or pain of risk itself. What appears as risk aversion is rationalized as an implication of the diminishing marginal utility of income. The cobbler of the fable who recovered his happiness once he had lost his worldly riches, and thus the worry about losing them, appears just as an irrational fool. Von Neumann and Morgenstern clearly indicated that they regarded this as a weakness of their theory rather than of the cobbler, to be corrected by future, and more difficult, research (1947, 629f.).

The central problem concerns the nature of the postulated probabilities. Von Neumann and Morgenstern are content to interpret them as objective frequencies (1947, 19). This is open to the objection that human decisions often do not seem to be guided by such frequencies. To the extent that each decision is in some sense unique, even the meaning of such frequencies is unclear. Von Neumann and Morgenstern suggest, therefore, that the probabilities, interpreted as subjective judgments, could be axiomatized together with utility.

Such an approach had already been proposed, unknown to von Neumann, by Frank Ramsey in 1926. A different variant, based on Bruno de Finetti's subjective interpretation of probabilities, was subsequently developed by Savage (1954). Suppose an individual is given the choice between two lottery tickets relating to a football game between the Arrows and the Bears. Ticket A pays $100 if the Arrows win and nothing if they lose; ticket B pays $100 if the Bears win and nothing if they lose. If the individual then chooses ticket A, he is interpreted as assigning a higher probability to the Arrows' winning. Probabilities are inferred from choice. By confronting the same individual with more and more such choices, one can, in theory, determine his subjective probabilities for all relevant events, scaled to be positive numbers between zero and one adding to unity over all conceivable events. These numbers can then be inserted into the von Neumann–Morgenstern utility theory. The joint axiomatization essentially means that, under plausible conditions, it is possible to find numbers that look like probabilities and other numbers that serve as utilities in such a way that decisions look as if they were guided by the Bernoulli principle.

This clearly falls far short of a demonstration that the Bernoulli principle either is used or should be used. The extensive experimental research that has been conducted in this field seems to indicate that the principle is widely violated, that people often have motives inconsistent with the maximization of expected utility, and that they do not consistently conform to any specific hypothesis that the researcher may have put forth.

Nevertheless, the Bernoulli hypothesis, for the time being, remained victorious in the sense that among the rivaling hypotheses about decision making under uncertainty, it is the only one that became part of mainstream economics. The main reason is that von Neumann and Morgenstern gave it a solid logical foundation, that it made the whole body of theoretical statistics applicable to economic decisions, and that it permitted a fruitful analysis of important economic phenomena such as security markets and insurance. Von Neumann and Morgenstern gave the mathematicians a good conscience.

31

Tjalling Koopmans

FOR MATHEMATICAL economics the early post–World War II years were a period of unusual creativity. Econometrics developed the first body of classic methods for multiequation models. The pioneering efforts of John von Neumann and Wassily Leontief in the use of linear production models matured to linear programming and activity analysis. New mathematical tools opened new perspectives on welfare, efficiency, and resource allocation. Many people contributed to this creative outburst, but none of them, taken individually, contributed more than Tjalling Koopmans.

Life

Tjalling Charles Koopmans was born near Hilversum, Netherlands, in 1910. He grew up in a family of the educated middle class; his father was a school principal, one of his brothers became a minister, and the other an engineer. Koopmans studied physics and mathematics at the University of Utrecht, obtaining an M.A. degree in 1933. His first two publications, both in German, are mathematical investigations in theoretical physics. His graduate work in Leiden, however, was in mathematical statistics, and his Ph.D. dissertation of 1936 was already in the discipline that was then becoming known as econometrics. In the same year Koopmans married, in due course becoming the father of three children.

During the following two years, Koopmans taught at the Netherlands School of Economics in Rotterdam. There he was the colleague of Jan Tinbergen, to whose early scientific development from physics to economics his own career offers a striking parallel. In 1938, like Tinbergen a little earlier, Koopmans went to work for the League of Nations in Geneva, where he studied tanker freight rates and shipbuilding cycles.

In 1940, Koopmans emigrated with his family to the United States. He first was a research associate at Princeton and also taught at the business school of New York University. For a time he then worked for the Penn Mutual Life Insurance Company in Philadelphia. From 1942 to 1944, as statistician of the Combined Shipping Adjustment Board, he did the work on wartime transportation planning that led him to linear programming.

In 1944, Jacob Marschak and Trygve Haavelmo brought him to the Cowles Commission for Research in Economics in Chicago. Two years later he was appointed associate professor at the University of Chicago, and in 1948 he became professor and research director of the Cowles Commission.

In 1955 the entire Cowles group moved to Yale, where Koopmans was professor of economics, and later was Alfred Cowles Professor of Economics, until his retirement in 1981. From 1961 to 1967 he was also director of the Cowles Foundation. In 1975 he won the Nobel Memorial Prize in economics, jointly with Leonid V. Kantorovich, "for their contributions to the theory of optimum allocation of resources." He died in 1985.[1]

Koopmans was a quiet, unpretentious, and kind man who spoke with the deliberate firmness of one who is able to substantiate his every word. One may conjecture that his political views were, in European terminology, those of a social democrat, but he did not permit political views to color his research, except perhaps in the choice of topics that he found interesting. He never succumbed to the temptation, endemic among economists, to found an ism, to proclaim a revolution, or to publicize imaginative visions of things before he could also supply the required analysis. Nor did Koopmans write for newspapers, become active in consulting, offer development and other policy advice, or engage in scientific entrepreneurship. He had broad interests, and he loved music, but to the outside world he did not want to appear as anything but a scientist and professor.

Works

Of the works that made Koopmans famous, only one is a full-length book written by him alone. This is the admirable *Three Essays on the State of Economic Science* (Koopmans 1957). Modestly, the book does not claim to offer major new results, but rather gives "one man's explanations of some recent developments in economic theory, his comments and perplexities about the character and basis of economic knowledge" (vii). The book is a magnificent example of Koopmans's ability to explain difficult abstract concepts, without the slightest adornment, in simple and perfectly lucid language. The first essay, in particular, has introduced thousands of economists to the analysis of economic problems in terms of linear spaces, set theory, and convexity. Koopmans's other major works were published in journals and collective volumes. Most of them, except for some late essays, are collected in the *Scientific Papers of Tjalling Koopmans* (Koopmans 1970). They all relate to basic theoretical concepts, making fundamental contributions to econometric methods, linear programming, and

---

1. The paucity of biographical material is probably a reflection of Koopmans's reticent personality. The above sketch is based on the preface to Koopmans 1970. For assessments of Koopmans's work see Malinvaud 1972 and Werin and Jungenfelt 1976.

activity analysis. The nature of these contributions will be described in the following sections.

One of the fundamental problems in activity analysis concerns the efficiency of resource allocation. A natural extension of this problem led Koopmans to the allocation of resources over time. The basic intertemporal analysis was provided by Edmond Malinvaud (1953). It demonstrated, among other things, that capital theory does not need the concept of an aggregated capital stock; marginal rates of substitution between commodities at different points of time are all the theorist needs. Koopmans's contributions in this field concerned the further extension of intertemporal allocation to economic growth. In particular, he extended Ramsey's analysis to a growing population by determining the optimal path along which an economy, starting from an arbitrary situation, could reach the golden rule path of the highest possible per capita consumption (Koopmans 1970, 485f.). He also tried to axiomatize time preference, and he discussed the baffling question of how the future welfare of a larger population should be weighed against the present welfare of a smaller population. As this work inevitably involved the intertemporal allocation of natural resources, Koopmans became a leading authority on the theory of exhaustible resources. These contributions were important in synthesizing earlier work, in clarifying concepts, and in articulating issues, but they failed to produce further building blocks for economic theory.

Koopmans hardly ever expressed himself on substantive economic questions such as employment, inflation, income distribution, monopoly, regulation, development, or exchange rates. An early essay on the dynamics of inflation (Koopmans 1970, 50f.) suggests that this was indeed not his strong side. He was reluctant to venture into fields in which his scientific standards did not seem to be fully applicable. Perhaps this testifies not only to his intellectual self-discipline but also to certain limitations of his view of science as applied to economics.

Econometrics

The first field to which Koopmans made a fundamental contribution was econometrics. This may be an appropriate place for a short note on the early history of this new discipline. Economists had long used mathematics and/or statistics, and Joseph Schumpeter thus described men such as William Petty, Richard Cantillon, and François Quesnay as econometricians. The distinctive program of modern econometrics, however, became the unification of economic theory, mathematics, and statistics in an integrated methodology of quantitative economics.

As early as 1912, Irving Fisher envisaged a society in support of this program, but it did not materialize. He revived his plan in 1926–27, after a disappointing experience with one of his papers: An economic journal accepted only the economic part, a statistical journal wanted the economics and higher mathematics deleted, and a mathematical journal was not interested in the economics and statistics. What so far had been regarded as interdisciplinary research, so Fisher decided, had to be transformed into its own discipline. In Europe, Ragnar Frisch was thinking along the same lines, and he also named the new discipline econometrics.[2]

In the 1930s the main efforts of the new discipline were devoted to the estimation of single economic relations by linear regressions. The demand studies of Henry Schultz (1938) in microeconomics and the multiple regressions of Jan Tinbergen (1939) in macroeconomics are representative of this stage. This method, however, was better suited for experimental sciences than for economics. If one wants to estimate the effect of fertilizer on crop yield, one would probably conduct an experiment in which the amount of fertilizer is varied while all other conditions are held constant as far as possible. In economics, such controlled experiments are rarely possible. The economist is thus forced to work with historical data whose interrelated variations are the joint effect of several (and possibly infinitely many) determinants. As a consequence, single equation regressions may result in biased estimates.

This problem was the subject of Ragnar Frisch's early contributions to econometric methods. A satisfactory solution, however, could be found only by considering each economic relation explicitly as a part of a set of simultaneous equations. Thus a demand function, to use a particularly simple example, would have to be considered as a component of a system consisting of a demand function and a supply function. This required a new methodology for statistical inference. The early partial solutions of Philip Wright, Jan Tinbergen, and Ragnar Frisch were described by Carl Christ (1985). The goal was finally reached by the joint effort of at least a dozen eminent scientists, of whom Abraham Wald and Trygve Haavelmo (Haavelmo 1944) were perhaps particularly influential.

Much of this work was conducted at the Cowles Commission for Research in Economics, then located in Chicago. It had been founded by Alfred Cowles III, an investment banker, who also financed the new journal, *Econometrica*. He had been Fisher's student at Yale and himself published excellent investigations on the reliability of stock market forecasts (with largely negative results). By 1945 the Cowles Commission had become the Mecca of quantitative economics.

This leads back to Koopmans because he became the research director of the Cowles Commission and also made a major contribution to its work. His dissertation, *Linear Regression Analysis of Economic Time Series* (Koopmans 1937), was still concerned with the single equation case, but its main subject is the problems arising from the possibility that there are, in fact, other relations between the variables. Koopmans made a decisive

2. The word had been used before, but for a different purpose (Frisch 1936c).

step beyond Frisch by firmly basing his solution on R. A. Fisher's sampling theory.

Koopmans's next publication, *Tanker Freight Rates and Tankship Building* (1939), was mainly a study in applied economics in the tradition of Tinbergen (whose data Koopmans had already used in his dissertation). It led to the general conclusion, however, that economic problems must typically be described by a set of simultaneous equations. To develop econometric methods for simultaneous equation models became one of Koopmans's main research topics for the next fourteen years.

The crowning achievement of this work was the famous Cowles Commission Monograph no. 10, *Statistical Inference in Dynamic Economic Models* (Koopmans 1950).[3] A subsequent collection of essays, *Studies in Econometric Method* (Hood and Koopmans 1953), provided a more widely accessible exposition of the "Cowles Commission approach," to which Koopmans again made some of the principal contributions. The Cowles Commission approach had now been established as the first classic methodology of econometrics. With its further developments, it dominated the field for twenty-five years until it was challenged by rational expectations and vector autoregressions.

In the construction of econometric models, Koopmans distinguished between problems of identification, problems of estimation, and problems of computation. While estimation and computation do not belong to the history of economic theory, the identification of economic relations indeed concerns the fundamental links between economics and statistics. It is here that Koopmans, together with others, made his most important contribution.

The nature of this contribution can best be explained by again using demand and supply functions as paradigms. Suppose there are two observations each on the price and the quantity of a commodity. In all three panels of figure 31.1 they are represented by the same pair of dots. In his famous paper of 1927, Elmer J. Working had pointed out that such observations, even if they are numerous, permit no inference about the slope of the demand curve. By drawing a line connecting the two points, one would indeed obtain a valid approximation to the demand curve, *D*, if only the supply curve, *S*, had shifted between the two observations (left-hand panel). This is a special case, however. If demand had shifted while supply remained unchanged, the line through the two points would, in fact, be a (declining) supply curve (center panel). In general, both demand and supply will have shifted (right-hand panel). In this case the connecting line represents neither the demand nor the supply curve but rather, in a sense, a mixture of both. To say more, one would have to know how much each of the two curves has shifted.

---

3. From a historical point of view, it is worth noting that the volume is based on a conference held at the beginning of 1945.

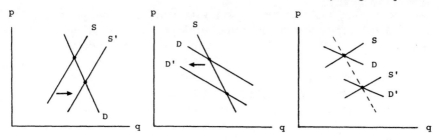

FIGURE 31.1

Working's argument concerned a model with only two simultaneous equations. Most econometric models would consist of a much larger number of equations. The basic question, however, remains the same: how can an individual economic relation be identified on the basis of observations generated jointly by all relations? This was called the identification problem.

The solution, so Koopmans and his collaborators showed, was to be found not in statistics but in economics. The model has to be constructed in such a way that not all explanatory variables appear in every equation. In the case of demand and supply curves, for example, the demand function could be extended to include income as a determinant, while the supply function is extended to include rainfall. In terms of the right-hand panel, these additional variables then provide information about the shifts in each of the curves. In general, it turned out to be a necessary condition for the identification of a given equation that the number of variables that do not appear in it be at least as large as the number of equations minus one. However, this condition is not sufficient; for conditions that are both necessary and sufficient, the reader must be referred to Koopmans (or the other econometric literature).

What is the significance of the identification problem? The answer depends on the purpose of model building. If the model is used for predictive purposes with an unchanged structure of the economy, identification is unimportant. Simple extrapolation is enough. However, if the model is used to predict the effect of changes in the economic structure, identification becomes essential. Without it, the effects of given changes in policy cannot be traced. The prominence that the Cowles Commission group attributed to identifiability thus reflects their view that econometrics should be able to help in economic decision making.

His econometric work had led Koopmans to develop articulate views about the general methodology of economic science. They were pointedly expressed in the 1947 paper "Measurement without Theory" (1970, 112f.), a critique of the business cycle research of the National Bureau of Economic

Research.[4] The ensuing controversy with Rutledge Vining became the classic twentieth-century reenactment of the *Methodenstreit* between Carl Menger and Gustav Schmoller. Koopmans was effective in demolishing the notion that it is possible to "let the facts speak for themselves," that the collection of facts has to precede the formulation of hypotheses, and that economic theory has no role to play in the collection of facts and the formulation of hypotheses. It remained an open question, however, how the economic scientist finds hypotheses worthy of being tested and whether intuitive empirical work may not lead to the discovery of promising hypotheses.

Linear Programming

The second main area of Koopmans's contributions is linear programming. Optimization by individuals and firms had been at the center of economic research for a century. It had usually been regarded as enough, however, to know the general conditions for an optimal solution, often in terms of the marginal equalities of differential calculus. The new problem was to make the optimum numerically computable. Its solution required, at least in a first stage, a limitation to linear models. What was to be maximized, therefore, was a linear objective function of certain variables that are subject to a number of linear restrictions, generally in the form of inequalities.

Kantorovich had solved such a problem, considered from a management point of view, in 1939, but this brilliant work was not known in the West at the time.[5] Frank Hitchcock (1941) solved the problem for the case in which a product has to be distributed from several sources to numerous localities with the lowest possible transportation costs. The solution was made relatively simple in this case by the fact that the restrictions appear as equalities. Koopmans, who did not know Hitchcock's work, was led to the same type of problem by his wartime work on shipping. The main results were available in 1942, but the memorandum "Exchange Ratios between Cargoes on Various Routes," in which they are described, strictly for practical application, was published only in the *Scientific Papers* (Koopmans 1970, 77–86). An excellent nontechnical exposition was given in 1947 in the paper "Optimum Utilization of the Transportation System" (184–93).

Around the same time, in response to problems of the U.S. Air Force and partially stimulated by Koopmans, George B. Dantzig had provided a general formulation of the linear programming problem and the Simplex algorithm for its solution. Koopmans's particular contribution (though this, too, had been anticipated by Kantorovich) was the early insight into the

4. Koopmans later provided a more systematic expositon of his methodological views in the second of the *Three Essays* (1957).

5. Kantorovich's contribution to economics is described in Johansen 1976. A concise summary is given in Koopmans's Nobel Lecture (Koopmans 1977).

TABLE 31.1

	Deficit Port (j)			
Surplus Port (i)	1	2	3	Surplus
1	c_{11}	c_{12}	c_{13}	a_1
2	c_{21}	c_{22}	c_{23}	a_2
Deficit	b_1	b_2	b_3	$\Sigma a_i = \Sigma b_j$

economic significance of what became known as shadow prices. A full presentation of this linear programming work was given by Koopmans, together with Stanley Reiter, in "A Model of Transportation" (in Koopmans 1951).

The nature of Koopmans's contribution can be explained in terms of a simple example. Suppose there are 2 ports where the incoming freight exceeds the outgoing freight so that there is a tonnage surplus expressed by a_i ($i = 1, 2$). There are also 3 deficit ports, where the incoming freight falls short of the outgoing freight, so that there is a tonnage deficit b_j ($j = 1$, 2, 3). Overall, the deficits equal the surpluses, but empty cargo ships, assumed to be of identical type, have to be dispatched from surplus ports to deficit ports. This can be done in many ways, and each voyage of an empty freighter imposes a certain cost. The problem is to assign vessels from surplus ports to deficit ports in such a way that the total cost is a minimum.

Table 31.1 describes the data in symbolic terms with c_{ij} representing the cost of sending an empty vessel from surplus port i to deficit port j. If the number of freighters sent from i to j is denoted by x_{ij}, the problem is to minimize total cost

$$C = \sum_i \sum_j c_{ij} x_{ij}, \tag{31.1}$$

subject to the restrictions

$$\sum_j x_{ij} = a_i, \tag{31.2}$$

$$\sum_i x_{ij} = b_j, \tag{31.3}$$

There are as many restrictions as there are ports, but since surpluses and deficits add to the same number, one of them depends on the others. In the present example, therefore, the number of independent restrictions is four.

The further exposition is simplified by using the proposition that the number of positive cargo flows in the optimal solution does not exceed the

TABLE 31.2

	Deficit Port			
Surplus Port	1	2	3	Surplus
1	1	3	2	50
2	3	7	5	70
Deficit	60	20	40	120

number of independent restrictions (Koopmans 1951, 241, n. 11; more explicitly Dantzig, in Koopmans 1951, ch. 23). In table 31.1, at least two cells will thus remain empty. Koopmans showed that the empty cells can be selected by an iterative process of marginal trial and error based on the principle of comparative advantage. Once no further marginal improvement can be found, so Koopmans's first theorem (1970, 188) asserts, then no possible rearrangement of the program, no matter how large, will offer an improvement. Marginal improvements indeed lead to the absolute optimum.

The nature of the search procedure can be illustrated numerically. Suppose the symbols in table 31.1 are replaced by the numbers in table 31.2. The shipping agency first happens to try the program

	1	2	3	
1	50	0	0	50
2	10	20	40	70
	60	20	40	120

In a first iteration this is compared with the alternative program

	1	2	3	
1	30	20	0	50
2	30	0	40	70
	60	20	40	120

The difference is that 20 units from surplus port 1 are now rerouted to deficit port 2 instead of deficit port 1, while the resulting deficit in port 1 is covered by vessels from surplus port 2. Is this an improvement? The answer could be found by calculating and comparing total costs in the two cases. The point is that this is not necessary. A look at table 31.2 is enough.

It shows that the rerouting of a vessel from surplus port 1 to deficit port 2 instead of deficit port 1 causes additional costs of 2. The rerouting of a vessel from surplus port 2 to deficit port 1 instead of deficit port 2 reduces costs by 4. Since there is, therefore, a net reduction in cost, the alternative is preferable to the original solution. This search procedure is continued with other alternatives until no further improvements are found, which will happen after a finite number of steps. At this point, according to the first theorem, the overall optimum will be reached. This is the basic idea that Dantzig developed into the Simplex algorithm.

In a second step, Koopmans considered the marginal cost of an additional cargo flow between any two ports. It is determined by comparing the optimal solutions for two shipping programs differing by one loaded vessel on one particular route. The marginal cost consists of two parts, namely the direct marginal cost of the loaded vessel and the indirect marginal cost arising from the necessity of rearranging the optimal program for empty vessels.[6] The direct marginal cost can simply be taken from management data as before. For the indirect marginal costs, Koopmans found a representation with far-reaching implications for economic theory. To a ship in a given port he assigned a number that he called its potential and was later called a shadow price. He also showed how the potentials are derived from the optimal program and the cost figures in tables 31.1 and 31.2. According to Koopmans's second theorem, these potentials have the property that their difference between any two ports equals the indirect marginal cost on that route. Just like Kantorovich before him, Koopmans recommended these shadow prices as useful planning instruments.

This led Koopmans to the final question: Could not the optimal shipping program be achieved by just letting ship owners maximize their profits (or minimize their losses) in a competitive freight market? The suggested answer was yes; there are indeed prices, derivable from the above shadow prices, that would induce profit-seeking shipowners to realize the optimal program, and these prices have the properties of competitive market prices.

Efficient Production

By describing an optimal shipping program in terms of certain shadow prices, Koopmans had, in fact, already moved beyond linear programming proper. Whereas linear programming seeks the solution that maximizes a specific objective function, Koopmans was primarily interested in the set of solutions that are efficient regardless of the choice of the objective function. Leaving questions of individual preferences and distribution aside, he limited his field to efficiency in production.

---

6. The former are, of course, positive, but the latter may be positive or negative.

Up to that time such problems had been handled in terms of production and transformation functions (or production frontiers). A production function indicates the *highest* amount of output that can be obtained from given factor inputs. A production frontier says what amount of a certain product can, *in the maximum*, be produced from given factors for given amounts of the other products. As this wording makes clear, each of these functions is already the result of an optimizing operation, but this operation is not explicitly analyzed. Koopmans wanted to provide a fundamental infrastructure to production theory by making these operations explicit.

He achieved this by interpreting technology as a set of blueprints for certain activities. Each activity is characterized, as in von Neumann's model of 1937, by a vector of fixed inputs and outputs. By operating this activity at different levels, all inputs and outputs are varied in the same proportion. This seems to be in sharp contrast to the smooth substitutability in the production and transformation functions. Koopmans was careful in explaining, however, that the smooth curves of the calculus approach can be approximated to any desired degree by specifying different activities for the same types of inputs and outputs. The result of this approach was (linear) activity analysis.[7]

In terms of this approach, the efficiency of production is defined by the fact that with given resources it is impossible to increase one final output without reducing another. Clearly, such productive efficiency is desirable whatever people's preferences, whatever their views on social justice and whatever the economic system.

This conceptualization of efficiency led Koopmans to a new, and highly fruitful, interpretation of prices. A primal problem in terms of quantities had already been associated by von Neumann with a dual problem in terms of prices. His model, however, was not suitable as a framework for welfare economics because it did not treat consumption as a final output. Koopmans now succeeded in applying the same sort of reasoning to problems of efficiency in terms of final output.

Suppose a production program is efficient. In this case, Koopmans showed, each input and output can be assigned an efficiency price in such a way that, nonrigorously stated,

1. no activity has a positive profitability;
2. any activity appearing in the efficient program just breaks even; and
3. any inefficient activity would show a loss.

Furthermore, final outputs have positive prices, intermediate goods may have negative prices if they consist of waste, and primary factors are free if they are not fully used. These are the prices Enrico Barone's Ministry

---

7. The basic contribution is included in Koopmans 1951. An excellent nontechnical introduction is the paper "Efficient Allocation of Resources" in Koopmans 1970, and a careful exposition is provided in Koopmans 1957.

of Production should use. Though the determination of these efficiency prices has nothing to do with the existence of markets, with demand and supply, the remarkable fact is that their properties are very similar to those of the prices in Léon Walras's general equilibrium system.

Koopmans also proved the converse proposition: whenever a system of prices with the above properties can be found, the corresponding production program is efficient.[8] In addition it turns out that the ratio of two efficiency prices equals the marginal rates of substitution between the respective commodities.

Overall, both Kantorovich's and Koopmans's analyses showed that the concept of prices is built deeply into the notion of efficiency, regardless of the existence of markets. This helps to explain why major contributions to the modern theory of prices have come from economists over the whole spectrum of ideologies, from fervent libertarianism to socialism. However, Koopmans's welfare analysis was still limited to production and to linear activities. It took Kenneth Arrow and Gerard Debreu a few more years to generalize it in both respects.

Place in the History of Economics

Koopmans, even more than Tinbergen, was a gift of physics to economics. He brought to economics not only the mathematical training of a physicist but also his perception of scientific research. At the stage that economics had reached just before World War II, these ingredients turned out to be extremely fruitful. On the other hand, Koopmans had never been systematically trained as an economist. This may help to explain why he concentrated his attention on a relatively narrow range of fundamental conceptual problems. His uncompromising devotion to the solution of these problems gave a strong impulse to rigorous theoretical analysis.

It is difficult to identify in Koopmans's work individual discoveries that belong to him alone. In most cases the scientific achievement was the cumulative result of a number of contributions by different people, often working in close contact. This became more and more typical for economics as a whole, as it had become in other sciences. Koopmans's self-effacing scholarship strongly encouraged this development.

Koopmans's claim to fame is based on his being a leading spirit in several scientific advances of great importance, above all in econometrics and linear activity analysis, but also in capital and growth theory. These advances provided the indispensable basis for the large-scale econometric models of the 1950s and 1960s, they made linear models useful for the

---

8. Koopmans and Beckmann reported, however, that they could not find prices that lead to the optimal assignment of plants to locations once interplant transportation costs are allowed for (Koopmans 1970, 258–81). The existence of efficiency prices, it appears, cannot be taken for granted.

solution of practical planning problems, and they provided new insights into welfare and the price system.

Koopmans's work was hardly ever controversial (the debate with Vining is an exception). This was not because it was not interesting but because Koopmans did not speak before he could prove that he was right. Indeed, most of Koopmans's contributions were rapidly absorbed into the mainstream of research. Perhaps paradoxically, this impeded rather than aided the spreading of his fame beyond the inner circle of economic theorists. The fame of economists thrives on controversy, which puts a premium on immature work.

Of course, the spreading of Koopmans's fame was also impeded by the abstract and highly demanding character of his research. He was an economist's economist par excellence. Among professional economists, however, nobody was perhaps more universally respected and admired. His gift for lucid exposition and synthesis also made his name a household word for every graduate student. Even more impressive than the results of Koopmans's research was, for his contemporaries, his uncompromising adherence to exacting scientific standards. It may have had an even more profound influence on the history of economics than the important building blocks that Koopmans contributed.

32
Paul Samuelson

The mental features discoursed of as the analytical . . . are always to their possessors, when inordinately possessed, a source of the liveliest enjoyment.
—Edgar Allan Poe, *The Murders in the Rue Morgue*

IT IS AN ENTERTAINING parlor game to find human beings who most perfectly personify the spirit of an era. Classical economics, broadening scholastic price theory to the concept of a circular flow of income, was incarnated in Adam Smith. A century later, the distinctive features of marginalism, including its limitations, became flesh in Léon Walras. The model-building era, finally, was most completely embodied in Paul Anthony Samuelson—no theorist has created more models that others found economically interesting and inspiring.

Life

Samuelson was born in 1915 in the steel town of Gary, Indiana.[1] His father prospered during the war but later saw his fortune diminished by bad investments. The parents imbued their son not only with liberal views,

---

1. Most of the material for this biographical note is from the autobiographical essays

in the American sense, but also with an irrepressible urge to exercise his intellectual superiority. Paul loved school and was consistently the star pupil, graduating from Hyde Park High School in Chicago at the age of sixteen.

As an undergraduate at the University of Chicago, Samuelson was first attracted to sociology, but what he learned from teachers like Jacob Viner, Frank Knight, Henry Schultz, Henry Simons, and Paul Douglas made him decide to choose economics. Upon graduation in 1935, he was awarded a prestigious national fellowship as one of the eight most promising economics graduates.

For his graduate work Samuelson went to Harvard, attracted, as he said, by its ivy. The Harvard economics faculty then included Frank Taussig, Joseph Schumpeter, Gottfried Haberler, young Wassily Leontief, Edward Chamberlin, and later Alvin Hansen. What was perhaps even more important, Samuelson found himself in an outstanding group of graduate students. This was perhaps the first time that many of the very best young brains were attracted into economics.

With the same ease with which he absorbed economics, Samuelson made himself an excellent mathematician and physicist with a special gift for deriving interdisciplinary inspiration from the common mathematical structure of problems in the economic and natural sciences. His first paper was published before he was twenty-two. From then on, writing papers was the joy of his life. The *Wunderkind* published eleven of them while still a graduate student. When John Maynard Keynes's *General Theory* came out in 1936, Samuelson was puzzled at first, but with the appearance of the mathematical formulations he gradually convinced himself of its importance. The classical economist from Chicago became a Keynesian.

At the age of twenty-three, Samuelson married an economics graduate of Radcliffe College. He later recorded that his wife used to do the driving so he could let his mind create the next paper. Six children arrived in the course of the years, including triplets. In 1981, after his wife had died of cancer, Samuelson married a second time.

Samuelson made a name at Harvard not only for his brilliance but also as a brash young man, who never let his teachers forget their limitations. In 1940, when his junior fellowship had run out, Harvard offered to keep him on as an instructor. The Massachusetts Institute of Technology, however, offered him an assistant professorship in its newly established graduate program in economics. The Harvard department voted to match this offer, but no action was taken in view of the sizable opposition. Harvard's decision to let the minority rule thus led to the departure of the most outstanding economist it had ever produced and to the rapid rise of

---

and references in Samuelson 1966–86. Other important sources are Lindbeck 1970, Feiwel 1982, Breit and Ransom 1982, and Brown and Solow 1983.

the Economics Department in the neighboring MIT. Academic decorum may have its price.

At MIT, Samuelson rapidly became the glory, the pillar, and the heart of the Economics Department. He was made an associate professor in 1944 and professor in 1949. In 1947 the American Economic Association awarded him the first John Bates Clark Medal for the economist under forty "who has made the most distinguished contribution to the main body of economic thought and knowledge." In fact, Samuelson was already one of the leading theorists of any age. The many honors he subsequently received were topped in 1970 by the award of the Nobel Prize.

In the post-World War II period, Samuelson served as adviser to many government agencies. He was appointed by John F. Kennedy, when he was president elect, to head a task force to draw up recommendations for economic policy, but he declined the chairmanship of the Council of Economic Advisers.

For many years, like Milton Friedman, Samuelson wrote regular columns for *Newsweek*. They show him as a Keynesian liberal, but market oriented, essentially middle-of-the-road, and pragmatic. Whereas Friedman was always highly (and perhaps overly) articulate about the point he wanted to make, Samuelson tended to see two sides to every argument. To Friedman's forensic dialectics Samuelson, of all people, opposed "economics from the heart," as he called it, not without a touch of cant (Samuelson 1983). As a matter of fact, Samuelson found it more difficult to make up his mind about policies than about models, and stagflation confronted him with the same intellectual dilemma as other Keynesians. He was a leader of theorists and not of policy makers.

The success of his textbook made Samuelson a wealthy man, a multimillionaire. The professor also became an investor and financier, the general equilibrium theorist branched out into portfolio analysis. His irreverence, however, survived success. As his friend James Tobin put it, Samuelson never sacrificed brashness to maturity; his egotism remained so boyishly unabashed as to be engaging. His example may have been partially responsible for the healthy lack of academic decorum that is so characteristic of postwar economics in the United States. The undergraduate mannerisms are only a surface, though. As matter of fact, Samuelson is known as a highly responsible academic statesman, a loyal colleague, and a helpful friend. He gives fair, and even generous, credit to the contributions of others, including lesser lights, and he is conscientious and gracious in clearing up past errors and ambiguities.

Biographers love to search for influences on a famous person's work. In Samuelson's case, textbook writing and portfolio analysis had obvious, if only partial, economic motives. For most of his work, however, it is difficult to find economic, social, ideological, or philosophical motives or influences outside the current state of science. While he loves to relate his theoretical arguments to policy questions as an expository device, his only major motive seems to be the solution of intellectual problems. The choice of these problems, furthermore, is typically determined by their solvability rather than by their urgency. His work is a prime exhibit for those who believe that the progress of science is mainly driven by its own endogenous dynamics and not by external influences.

Works

Economists who see themselves in the mirror of Karl Popper learn to describe the object of their labors as refutable hypotheses. Those who borrow their jargon from Thomas Kuhn imagine themselves inventing persuasive paradigms (whatever these might be). In the wake of Imre Lakatos, the mark of greatness was seen to be an ambitious research "programme" (of which the spelling seems to be a distinctive part). Samuelson's claim to fame, like that of most other great economists, fits none of these categories. In particular, there is no indication that he ever had a long-range research program. He constructed models that promised interesting theorems, and he did it as the spirit moved him. This is reflected in the character of his scientific works.

These include three books. The first was *Foundations of Economic Analysis*. Though published only in 1947, it was accepted as a dissertation in 1941, and a considerable part was written as early as 1937. The title was meant to be exactly as ambitious as it sounds, and the book's impact on the profession has largely justified it. Displaying a mastery of calculus, differential and difference equations that was stupendous at the time (but soon became standard under its influence), the book restated, clarified, and developed the intuitive reasoning of John Hicks's *Value and Capital* in the lucid language of mathematics. For the first time in a book in English on economic principles, the mathematics, instead of being relegated to an appendix, provided the skeleton of the argument. Among the many fundamental ideas the book put forth, none was perhaps more pregnant than the insight that Lagrange multipliers have an economic interpretation as prices, later to be called shadow prices. Fifty years after it was written, the *Foundations* (together with *Value and Capital*) is still one of the most inspiring classics of general equilibrium economics.

Samuelson's second book was *Economics: An Introductory Analysis*. First published in 1948, it soon became the most successful textbook ever published in any field. Over forty years it appeared in twelve editions, sold more than ten million copies and was translated into numerous other languages (including Russian, with heavy censorship). No other book has contributed so much to the emergence of a universal body of economic knowledge that is considered standard wherever teaching and learning are free. There are several reasons for this success. No other comprehensive introduction was written by one of the world's foremost modern theorists

(Hicks's *Social Framework* covering only a fraction of the ground). This theorist, furthermore, is a superb expositor who knows how to weave theory, discussion, facts, and history into an exciting tale. Above all, the content over the years did not remain static but was continually adapted to the evolution of science, experience, and history, making the last edition a different book from the first. In 1888, John Stuart Mill's *Principles* was obsolete; in 1988, Samuelson's *Economics* was still fresh.[2]

Samuelson's third book, written jointly with Robert Dorfman and Robert Solow, was *Linear Programming and Economic Analysis* (1958). It was primarily a superb expository synthesis of linear economics but also included at least one important original development, to be mentioned below.

Samuelson's principal contributions are found in his papers. He is the Picasso of economics, creating his work in an abundant stream, usually at a rapid pace and apparently for the joy of it. The five volumes of *Collected Scientific Papers* (Samuelson 1966–86) contain 388 essays, published over fifty years, with over 4,600 pages of text. The topics cover the whole range of economic theory, including general equilibrium, optimization, duality, linear economics, utility, welfare, index numbers, dynamics, capital, growth, trade, macroeconomics, population, public finance, money (though this is a relatively neglected subject), social accounting, portfolio analysis, risk, rational expectations, and the history of economics. Some specific contributions are reviewed in the following sections. A few other notable papers are briefly mentioned here.

An early paper on the consumption function stands out as Samuelson's only (feeble) foray into econometrics. The multiplier-accelerator model was influential as an instructive example of Keynesian macrodynamics, but analytically it stayed well within the frontiers reached by Ragnar Frisch and Michal Kalecki years before. A three-page paper, written with C. C. Holt, shows that in 1946 a graphical depiction of the elasticity of demand was still deemed worthy of publication in the *Journal of Political Economy*. The papers on social welfare made decisive contributions to a field that was already degenerating into empty formalism. A joint article with Robert Solow demonstrated that capital theory does not require the concept of capital as a homogeneous factor of production. It provided a solution to the problem of the changing structure of heterogeneous capital goods that had defeated the analytical powers of Friedrich von Hayek, Joan Robinson, and John Hicks. In another joint paper, Samuelson and Solow recommended the Phillips curve as a basic tool of macroeconomic policy making,

---

2. This does not mean the book does not have its weaknesses. For example, in the opinion of one teacher who has used the text for over thirty years, Samuelson's discussion of monetary policy tends to lag many years behind the state of the art. In later editions the analytical frills also tend to blur the main lines of the argument.

but in the end, the Phillips curve turned out to be a Greek gift to political economy.

Samuelson was also one of the principal protagonists in the famous controversy on capital theory between the two Cambridges. His contributions show him as graciously correcting an initial error and then explaining the alleged paradox of reswitching in terms that could be understood outside Sraffa's circle, thus synthesizing it into mainstream economics. In the process there emerged the concept of the factor-price frontier, whose substance had already been used by Samuelson in an earlier paper on Marx. The frontier indicates the highest profit rate an economy can reach for any given level of wages.[3] Finally, the numerous papers on the history of economics show Samuelson as one of the foremost modern interpreters of past economic theory from François Quesnay, Adam Smith, David Ricardo, Johann Heinrich von Thünen, and Karl Marx down to the twentieth century.

Some of these papers were rapidly written, and others resulted from arduous efforts (with the first not always inferior to the second). Though there was no research program, many problems occupied Samuelson's mind for years, if not decades, and gave rise to a sequence of contributions. Never in the history of economics (and rarely in the history of any science) has one scholar produced such a voluminous stream of outstanding research over half a century.

Revealed Preference

What we do just reveals to us what we are.
—Arthur Schopenhauer, *On the Freedom of the Will*

Samuelson's first major contribution, published when he was twenty-two, concerned the theory of consumer demand (1966–86, vol. 1, ch. 1). Vilfredo Pareto had purged value theory of cardinal utility. Eugen Slutsky, extending the work of his master, had shown that the theory of ordinal utility implies a set of interesting propositions about the partial effects of prices on demand, net of income effects. With the work of John Hicks and R. G. D. Allen, ordinal utility had finally conquered English-language economics.

Young Samuelson thought that the repudiation of utility was still incomplete, though. After all, utility functions were still being written. He proposed to purge the theory of consumer demand of the last vestiges of utility. The result was, in his later terminology of 1948, the revealed preference approach to consumer choice. It purported to develop the whole theory of demand from simple observations about consumer behavior.

The basic postulate was, again in later terminology, the weak axiom

---

3. Samuelson's contributions to capital theory are concisely surveyed by Solow in Brown and Solow 1983.

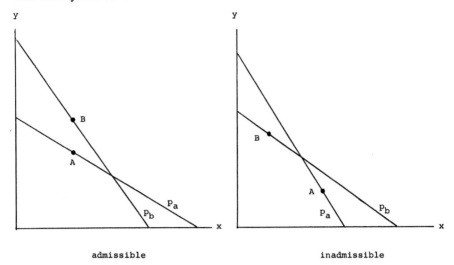

admissible   inadmissible

FIGURE 32.1

of revealed preference. Its meaning can be explained by confronting a consumer with two sets of prices, p_a and p_b. Suppose in situation p_a, with given income, she buys commodity bundle A, and in situation p_b she buys a different bundle, B. Can the observer infer whether A is preferred to B or vice versa? Possibly, Samuelson answers. If at prices p_b the consumer, with unchanged income, could still buy A, but does not, she reveals by her action that B is preferred to A. Could it not happen, though, that by the same sort of observation A is revealed to be preferred to B inasmuch as in situation p_a she could buy B but does not? This is excluded by the weak axiom, which says that such a contradiction does not occur.

The axiom can be expressed symbolically by denoting the value of bundle A at prices p_a by p_aA, and so on. It then says that if

$$p_bA \leq p_bB,\qquad(32.1)$$

then it will not be observed that

$$p_aB \leq p_aA,\qquad(32.2)$$

and thus it must be true that

$$p_aB > p_aA.\qquad(32.3)$$

For two goods, x and y, this is illustrated in figure 32.1. The left-hand panel represents the admissible case. When the consumer bought B at prices p_b, her budget constraint was the solid line through B. Since point A was well inside this budget constraint, the consumer must have preferred B to A. At the same time, when in situation p_a she bought A, the bundle

B was outside the solid budget constraint p_a, so that the consumer was not free to reveal her preference. There is no contradiction. The inadmissible case is illustrated by the right-hand panel of figure 32.1. In situation p_a the consumer had enough income to buy bundle B instead of A, thus revealing a preference for A. In situation p_b, on the other hand, she had enough income to buy A, but did not, thus revealing a preference for B. The weak axiom declares that this case does not occur. It essentially postulates that the consumer does not change her mind about preferences.

At first, Samuelson combined this axiom with two others, but he soon discovered that these are redundant. The weak axiom, he showed, was enough to demonstrate that marginal rates of substitution are declining and that a fall in price, after correcting for income effects, produces an increase in demand. Almost the whole theory of demand could be derived from this single axiom. The exception was Slutsky's symmetry condition for the net cross price effects.

Like many significant innovations, revealed preference had hardly any impact for years. The *Foundations* of 1947 was needed to focus interest on the subject, but thereafter the discussion between the best logicians in the economics profession remained active for three decades. It is not possible here to identify individual contributions. A brief reference to important developments must suffice.[4] Their main thrust was, paradoxically, to restore utility functions to their former place by the stepwise demonstration that they are implied in revealed preference.

For two goods it was soon perceived (and elaborated by Samuelson [1966–86, vol. 1, ch. 9]) that revealed preference is enough to construct the equivalent of a set of indifference curves. The extension to more than two goods was achieved, after some unsuccessful efforts, by the addition of Hendrick Houthakker's strong axiom of revealed preference (discussed in Samuelson 1966–86, vol. 1, ch. 10). It says, in effect, that if bundle A is revealed to be preferred to B and B to C, then C is never revealed to be preferred to A. Once this postulate was added, the equivalent of indifference surfaces could be constructed for any number of commodities. In addition, Slutsky's symmetry proposition could also be shown to be implied. Conversely, it could later be demonstrated that the Slutsky conditions, taken together, also imply the existence of a utility function. Though Samuelson originally set out to purge economic theory of the last vestiges of utility, the important developments he initiated ultimately had the main effect of giving the users of ordinal utility functions a clear conscience. When Samuelson wrote his paper, the concept of utilty was at the center of theoretical debates. Thirty years later, its further refinements had become an esoteric field for the mathematical specialist.

---

4. For excellent surveys of these developments, the reader is referred to Houthakker 1983 and Chipman 1982.

Factor Price Equalization

One of Samuelson's best-known theorems asserts that under certain restrictive assumptions the international exchange of goods results in the international equalization of factor remunerations. The theorem was inspired by the work of Bertil Ohlin. In his "Interregional and International Trade" of 1933, Ohlin had extended international trade theory to factor prices. It had always been recognized that factor prices are equalized by migration. However, the international trade theory of David Ricardo, John Stuart Mill, and Alfred Marshall provided no reason to believe that remunerations would be equalized even for immobile factors. Surely in the absence of migration, it was felt, international wage differences could persist forever.

Bertil Ohlin, extending earlier work by Eli Heckscher, challenged this tradition by showing that trade would tend to reduce the inequality of remunerations even for immobile factors. If trade between two countries is opened, so his argument runs, each will tend to export those products that make intensive use of those factors with which that country is relatively abundantly endowed. This implies that the demand rises for those factors that in the absence of trade would be relatively cheap. For the relatively expensive factors, on the other hand, demand tends to fall. As a consequence, the original gap in factor remunerations is partially closed. Commodity trade can thus serve as a partial substitute for factor movements. This is what Samuelson called the Heckscher-Ohlin theorem. As a matter of fact, Heckscher (whose pertinent work was not available in English before 1949) had argued, though not proved, that factor price equalization would be complete.

The first to demonstrate complete factor price equalization was Abba Lerner. In 1933 he wrote a brilliant seminar paper that Samuelson, once he had discovered it, called "a masterly, definitive treatment of the question, difficulties and all" (1966–86, 2:869). Unfortunately the paper (which also contained the first Edgeworth production box), seemingly forgotten by its author but later remembered by Lionel Robbins, remained unpublished until 1952 (Lerner 1953, 67–84).

Samuelson's earliest contribution in this field was his important joint article with Wolfgang F. Stolper (Samuelson 1966–86, vol. 2, ch. 66) in which it was shown that free trade definitely lowers the real remuneration of the relatively scarce factor. At this point, Samuelson still accepted Ohlin's argument that factor price equalization can only be partial (and he even accepted the fallacious explanation that complete equalization would eliminate all comparative advantages and thus trade). Seven years later, Samuelson had found an interesting special case in which factor price equalization is complete (ch. 67).

The case is characterized by four basic assumptions. First, the number of factors equals the number of products. The following exposition will be restricted to two countries, two commodities (called cloth and wine) and two factors (called labor and capital). The second assumption is that all four production functions exhibit constant returns to scale. As a consequence, the marginal product of each factor depends only on the factor proportions (or intensities) and thus remains unchanged if both factors are augmented in the same proportion. Third, both countries have the same production functions for each good. Equal factor intensities thus imply equal marginal products. Fourth, the international differences in factor endowments are not large enough to cause any country to specialize in one product only. The statement of these assumptions indicates that Samuelson's theorem is essentially an ingenious exercise in linear-homogeneous production functions. The argument can be developed in four steps.

The first step consists in the simple statement that international trade, in the absence of transport costs and tariffs, equalizes the relative price of the two goods between the two countries. There is, therefore, a common international price ratio

$$p_{cloth}/p_{wine} = \pi. \tag{32.4}$$

Second, in view of the linear-homogeneity of the production functions, it is true in each country that the marginal product of labor in the clothing industry depends on nothing but the capital/labor ratio in this industry,

$$MPLC = f(k_c). \tag{32.5}$$

Similar relationships hold for the marginal product of labor in wine production,

$$MPLW = g(k_w), \tag{32.6}$$

and the marginal products of capital in the two industries,

$$MPKC = h(k_c), \tag{32.7}$$

$$MPKW = i(k_w). \tag{32.8}$$

The decisive step is the third. Factor mobility within each country sees to it that the marginal product of labor has the same market value in both industries. This can be expressed by stating that the ratio of the marginal products of labor is the reciprocal of the commodity price ratio,

$$\pi = \frac{p_c}{p_w} = \frac{MPLW}{MPLC} = \frac{g(k_w)}{f(k_c)}. \tag{32.9}$$

The same is true for capital,

$$\pi = \frac{p_c}{p_w} = \frac{MPKW}{MPKC} = \frac{i(k_w)}{h(k_c)}. \tag{32.10}$$

Once π is known, these two equations can be solved to determine the factor intensities k_w and k_c. (This is where the equal number of factors and products is important.) The same can be done for the other country. Since both countries have the same production functions, their factor intensities in each industry must be the same, regardless of factor endowments.

The fourth step, finally, leads from factor intensities to factor prices. With identical factor intensities, each factor has the same marginal product in both countries. Since factor prices, in real terms, correspond to marginal products, they are also equalized internationally, Q.E.D. Commodity movements, in this case, are indeed a perfect substitute for factor movements; wage differentials, even with immobile labor, cannot survive free trade.

The fact that Samuelson's theorem was based on highly restrictive assumptions immediately led to an extensive debate about possible generalizations. What can be said, for example, in the case of many factors and products, of unequal numbers of factors and products, of complete specialization in some products, of nonhomogeneous production functions, and of unequal production functions? This discussion, in which Samuelson was one of the main participants, cannot be traced here. By and large it tended to confirm Ohlin's intuition about partial equalization; full equalization is indeed a special case. It would be entirely erroneous to conclude from this that Samuelson's theorem has not made a significant contribution after all. This contribution, however, must be sought at a more general level.

First, Samuelson's paper lifted international trade theory to a higher plane of analytical rigor; views were supplanted by theorems. Second, the method of embedding an analytical problem in a general equilibrium model reduced to a few key variables became a standard approach in a wide area of economics; microeconomics and macroeconomics were reunited. Third, Samuelson demonstrated how results can be sharpened by focusing on well-chosen special cases. Fourth, the discovery that to a given set of commodity prices there corresponds a certain set of factor prices was of far-reaching significance for general economic theory. This "mapping" proposition was perhaps the deepest message of the factor price equalization theorem.

The Transfer Problem

The ability to combine micro and macroeconomics also permitted Samuelson to clear up a question that had been confused for two centuries. David Hume had argued as if a transfer of gold from England to Portugal would result in an increase in Portuguese prices relative to English prices. At the same time he had already pointed out that in the absence of trade impediemtns and transportation costs, such price differentials could not actually occur. Others had argued, therefore, that the essential price differential was not between English and Portugese prices but between the prices of English exports (or Portugese imports) and English imports (or Portugese exports). This shifted the discussion to the terms of trade. The main issue was whether, besides prices, there were other factors at work, such as relative incomes.[5]

German reparations after World War I caused this discussion to flare up again. Keynes, consistent with his strictures on the peace treaty, argued that, in additon to the primary burden of the reparations, Germany would have to bear a secondary burden arising from a deterioration of its terms of trade. Ohlin replied that this was by no means certain and that Germany's terms of trade might actually improve. A correct analysis was provided by Arthur Cecil Pigou in 1932. It showed that, from a general point of view, Ohlin was right. Again it was Samuelson who put the analysis on a rigorous basis (1966–86, vol. 2, chs. 74, 75).

His conclusion was that changes in the terms of trade, if any, may go in either direction and that this direction depends on the reaction of demand to income and not to prices. This conclusion can be made intuitive as follows. Suppose England pays a subsidy to Portugal. The effect on the terms of trade depends on the relative shift in demand between cloth and wine. If prices were unchanged (and excluding the case of inferior goods), Portugal's demand would rise for both goods, and England's demand would be reduced. The question is in what proportions the increases and reductions are distributed between the two goods. But this, in turn, depends exclusively on the marginal propensities to spend additonal income, respectively, on cloth and wine.

Samuelson supported this intuitive argument by a graphical demonstration in terms of an Edgeworth box (figure 32.2). Suppose England and Portugal are engaged in pure exchange without production. If their endowments with wine and cloth are described by point A, exchange will bring them to point A' on the contract curve. The terms of trade are reflected in the slope of the line $A-A'$. Suppose further that England makes Portugal a gift consisting of a certain quantity of cloth.[6] This will shift the endowment point horizontally to the left—say, to B. The corresponding exchange point is B'. The question is whether the new price line $B-B'$ is steeper or flatter than $A-A'$. The answer is that either result is possible.

In his long, two-part article, Samuelson modified his assumptions in many directions, also introducing production, tariffs and transportation costs. This revived the long and still inconclusive debate about the question of whether there are valid reasons to believe that the terms of trade are more likely to shift in one direction than in the other.[7] In this case, the significance of Samuelson's contribution was at the level more of economic

5. The discussion is admirably surveyed in Viner 1937, ch. 6.
6. The conclusion remains the same if the gift consists of wine or a mixture of both commodities.
7. Samuelson 1966–86, vol. 3, ch. 163, is a contribution to this debate.

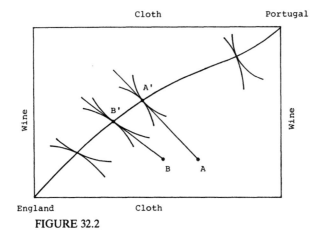

FIGURE 32.2

substance than of analytical method. It provided the crucial basis for an improved theory of Hume's specie flow mechanism, of the relationship between trade flows and the terms of trade, and of international capital flows.

The Correspondence Principle

That a price is determined as an equilibrium of demand and supply is not, in itself, a valuable insight. What one would like to know is the change in price resulting from a given shift in demand or supply. The interesting questions concern comparative statics. Quantitative answers usually require empirical estimates of parameters. Qualitative answers, however, with respect to the mere direction of the change, can sometimes be obtained from economic theory alone.

In his *Foundations*, Samuelson distinguished two sources of such "meaningful propositions." One source is the assumption that individuals and firms usually try to maximize (or minimize) something. This source of enlightenment was systematically exploited during the marginalist era, and the *Foundations* is the capstone, the crowning achievement, of this effort. The other source is the fact that comparative statics makes sense only in a stable system. A shift in the equilibrium price clearly has no predictive power unless the price actually tends to gravitate toward its equilibrium. This is where the correspondence principle comes in.

Hicks had already made wide use of the second source of meaningful propositions. His analysis suffered, however, because it was based more on intuition than on rigorous analysis. Samuelson, soon after the publication of *Value and Capital* (Hicks 1939), began to supply the rigor (Samuelson 1966–86, vol. 1, ch. 38). Rigorous stability analysis, he pointed out, requires an explicit dynamic system. There is, therefore, an intimate re-

432

lationship or correspondence between comparative statics and dynamics (Samuelson 1966–86, vol. 1, ch. 40). This was Samuelson's principle, whose name he had borrowed from Niels Bohr.

Its nature can be illustrated here only with the simplest possible example. Suppose a demand function is

$$q = ap + a_0, \tag{32.11}$$

and the corresponding supply curve is

$$Q = Ap + A_0, \tag{32.12}$$

with the equilibrium condition $q = Q$. Optimizing individuals, the first source of meaningful propositions reveals, will usually (though not necessarily) have a negative a, but they may well have a negative A, too. As a consequence, it seems uncertain whether an increase in demand, expressed by a shift in a_0, leads to a rise in price. This is where dynamics may help. Suppose the adjustment in price under the pressure of excess demand is expressed by

$$\dot{p} = \lambda[(ap + a_0) - (Ap + A_0)], \tag{32.13}$$

where λ measures the (positive) adjustment speed. At the equilibrium price $\bar{p}$ this is zero:

$$0 = \lambda[(a\bar{p} + a_0) - (A\bar{p} + A_0)]. \tag{32.14}$$

Subtracting equation 32.14 from equation 32.13, one obtains the price adjustment as a function of the deviation of the actual price from its equilibrium value:

$$\dot{p} = \lambda[a(p - \bar{p}) - A(p - \bar{p})] = \lambda(a - A)(p - \bar{p}). \tag{32.15}$$

Stability clearly requires $(a - A) < 0$; whenever the current price is above its equilibrium value, it must decline, and vice versa. Assuming the demand curve is falling, the equilibrium may be stable even with a falling supply curve, but then its slope must be closer to the vertical than that of the demand curve. It follows that an increase in demand is certain to raise the price, but it may conceivably reduce the quantity supplied.

From such homely examples, both micro and macroeconomic, Samuelson proceeded to the most rigorous dynamic analysis economics had yet seen. It turned out that the Hicksian conditions were, in general, neither sufficient nor necessary for stability. More important was that modern stability analysis had been launched. The application of the correspondence principle is often handicapped by the fact that the relevant dynamic system is not known. For the practitioner of macro and microeconomics, the principle became nevertheless one of the standard sources of qualitative information.

Nonsubstitution

Classical economics, from Richard Cantillon to Karl Marx, usually argued that in competitive markets relative prices are determined by costs; demand determined the quantities produced but was allowed no influence on prices. A first breach in the classical fortress had been made by the analytical guns of John Stuart Mill. Marginalism brought the great reversal. Marshall regarded demand as one of the two blades of the price-determining scissors, and the Austrians tended to give the impression that cost, being itself demand-determined, was not an independent force at all.

In Leontief's input-output models, with their fixed coefficients, this turned out to be different. If there is only one primary input—say, labor—relative prices depend only on the input coefficients, regardless of the composition of final demand. Was this a vindication of the classical notion? An inveterate marginalist might have been tempted to reject this conclusion. He was conditioned to argue that, in reality, input coefficients are not fixed, that inputs can be substituted more or less smoothly, and that different demand conditions would make different input combinations efficient. As a consequence, he would conclude, production costs and relative prices remain dependent on demand.

Samuelson's famous nonsubstitution theorem showed that such a marginalist argument would be invalid.[8] With constant returns, only one among the many input combinations can ever be efficient, regardless of the final demand. In the production function depicted in figure 32.3, the factors x and y can be substituted along smooth isoquants, but only one point on each isoquant has a chance of being selected by cost-minimizing producers. As a consequence, the smooth isoquants might just as well be replaced by fixed coefficients. Substitution, though possible, does not take place. The classical cost theory of value thus remains valid even for substitutable factors; the scissors have only one blade.

The reasoning behind this conclusion can be roughly explained in terms of a simple example. Suppose there is a given quantity of one primary factor, called labor, and two processes with final outputs x_1 and x_2. Each process uses as inputs some of the primary factor and some of each output with smooth substitutability and constant returns to scale. In figure 32.4, quantitites of the two goods are measured along the positive axes if they are outputs and along the negative axes if they are inputs. Consider first a case in which all labor is allocated to industy 1. This industry can then increase x_1 by using up more x_2, but, in view of fixed labor, with a dimin-

8. The original paper (Samuelson 1966–86, vol. 1, ch. 36) is four pages long; an intuitive exposition is given in Dorfman, Samuelson, and Solow 1958. Alternative proofs were simultaneously provided by Georgescu-Roegen, Koopmans, and Arrow.

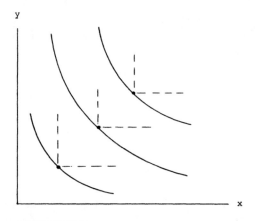

FIGURE 32.3

ishing marginal product. This is expressed by the product curve X_1 in the southeast quadrant. A similar experiment can be conducted by allocating all labor to industry 2 and results in product curve X_2 in the northwest quadrant.

The two production curves depict extreme cases. In fact, labor can be allocated to the two industries in any proportion. In view of constant returns, the resulting combinations of net outputs are found along straight lines connecting two points on the product curves. For example, one may select P_1 on the X_1 curve and P_2 on the X_2 curve. The obtainable output combinations are then found along the broken line connecting the two points. If, say, one-half of labor is allocated to each of the industries, the resulting net outputs are halfway between P_1 and P_2 as indicated by R.

Production methods P_1 and P_2 are clearly inefficient, however. Efficiency requires that a maximum of x_2 is obtained for any specified amount of x_1. This is achieved by combining Q_1 and Q_2, resulting in the solidly drawn production possibility frontier for the net outputs. The essential point of Samuelson's nonsubstitution theorem is the observation that the production possibility frontier is a straight line in this case. In whatever proportion x_1 and x_2 are demanded, the marginal rate of transformation between them remains the same, and so does their relative price. Their relative price can thus be determined without considering demand.

The inveterate marginalist is not quite beaten yet, however. The nonsubstitution theorem, as Samuelson was the first to point out, depends crucially on the assumption that there is only a single primary factor such as labor or land. As soon as there are two or more primary factors (such as land and labor, or land, labor, and impatience, or different types of labor) the nonsubstitution theorem ceases to be valid. The same is true in

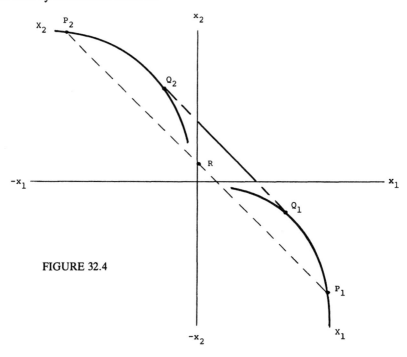

FIGURE 32.4

the presence of joint products. The production possibility frontier for final outputs is then no longer a straight line, and demand affects relative costs and prices. In general, therefore, Marshall's scissors are still an appropriate metaphor, but Samuelson had provided an important link between modern general equilibrium analysis and classical (and Marxian) economics.

Public Goods

In 1954, Samuelson aimed his beam of rigorous analysis at fiscal expenditures. The resulting three-page paper became the point of departure for the modern theory of public goods (Samuelson 1966–86, vol. 2, ch. 92).[9] Private goods and public (or collective) goods are distinguished as polar cases. If a private good is consumed by one individual, no utility (or disutility) accrues to others. Public goods, however, are jointly consumed by all, and the utility accruing to one individual does not reduce the utility of others. Church bells are an example.[10] For private goods, efficiency requires that all individuals pay the same prices, and these prices must be equal both to the marginal amounts individuals are willing to pay and to

9. Musgrave (1983, 141–56) places this paper in the historical context.
10. Samuelson makes clear that the private or public character of the goods does not depend on whether they are supplied by the private or the public sector of the economy.

marginal costs. It had long been recognized that this condition cannot be applied to public goods, but what is the corresponding condition for public goods? For the theory of public finance, the answer to this question is clearly of fundamental importance.

As in other cases, Samuelson answered the question by constructing a highly aggregative general equilibrium model. The resulting efficiency condition says that for public goods (1) the marginal amounts different individuals are willing to pay for an additional unit must be added over individuals, and (2) the supply must be such that this sum is equal to the marginal cost. Suppose, for example, the question is whether a firehouse should be equipped with 1, 2 . . . *n* fire trucks. To answer it, it should be ascertained what marginal amount each citizen is willing to pay for the first truck, the second, and so on. The amounts should be added "vertically," for each number of fire trucks, for all citizens, and the plans for the firehouse should then be expanded to the point where the collective marginal willingness to pay ceases to exceed the marginal cost of the expansion.

These conditions clearly imply that different individuals, in view of their unequal willingness to pay, generally pay different prices. Whereas private goods have the same price for individually different quantities, public goods provide to all individuals the same quantity, but at different prices. Another implication is that there is no market mechanism to provide for an efficient allocation of resources to public goods. In particular, individuals have no incentive to contribute the highest amount they would be willing to pay because, as long as others pay, they get the full benefit free.

In economic substance these conclusions were not new, and Samuelson already mentioned earlier contributions from Richard Musgrave back to Knut Wicksell. What was new was the lucid and rigorous derivation of these results from a beautifully simplified model. This was a seminal contribution, initiating rapid further developments.[11] One main line of development concerned the policy-making mechanisms that might be used to improve the efficiency of budgetary decisions, so far with inconclusive results. The other main development started from the observation that instances of pure public goods are hard to find; in most cases a given supply cannot satisfy an unlimited number of consumers. Though Samuelson's polar cases may be analytically convenient, they turned out to make application difficult. In a more general case, consumption by individual A was recognized as having some external effect on the utility of B. The theory of public goods thus became integrated into the more general theory of externalities with its numerous extensions and applications.

---

11. Samuelson's own further contributions can be found in 1966–86, vol. 2, part 12; and vol. 3, part 12.

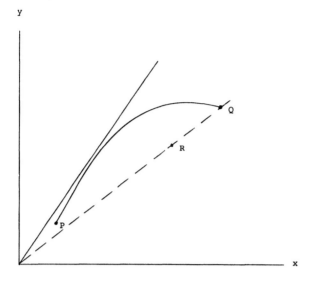

FIGURE 32.5

The Turnpike

In Solow's growth model the balanced growth rate of the economy is determined by the exogenous rate of population growth. The only normative question concerns the level of per capita consumption. Twenty years earlier, John von Neumann had already constructed a growth model in which per capita consumption is fixed while the rate of population growth is determined by the model. In this model the normative question concerns the rate of growth. Such an economy may achieve balanced growth with different internal structures. Each internal structure, however, is generally characterized by a different growth rate, and one of them promises the highest attainable growth rate. The balanced growth path with the maximal growth rate was later called the von Neumann path.

It is not clear that the von Neumann path is better than any other path, because people (or the planners) may not like the proportions in which the goods are produced. There may be too many steelworks and not enough dwellings, and so forth. This is where Samuelson's turnpike theorem comes in. Whatever composition of goods one would like to achieve at the end of the planning period, one obtains the most of all goods if the growth path of the economy is close to the von Neumann path for most of the time.

The meaning of this argument is illustrated for a two-good economy in figure 32.5. Suppose the economy ultimately prefers to have x and y in the proportion indicated by the broken ray. Along the solid von Neumann ray, growth would be more rapid, but the composition of goods less desirable. In this case the economy, now at P, will reach, at a given time, the outermost possible point Q on the broken ray by moving along the curved path. This means that industry structure is first changed in an undesirable direction for the sake of more rapid growth. If it had immediately been changed to the broken ray, the economy would find itself only at a point such as R after the same time. Metaphorically, the fastest route to the given destination is not the shortest; one saves time by making a detour to the turnpike.

Samuelson conjectured the existence of a "turnpike" as early as 1949 (1966–86, 1:489). The theorem appeared in print in the volume he wrote with Dorfman and Solow. He also added a "sketch of a proof," but this was not yet watertight. Among mathematical growth theorists the idea called forth a burst of energy. Various sorts of turnpike theorems were proved, several by Samuelson himself. For a time there was hope that they might become important instruments in development planning, perhaps providing a justification for a temporary expansion of heavy industry at the expense of consumer goods and the like. The turnpike became proverbial.

Those hopes were not fulfilled, though. This was due not only to problems of practical implementation but also to analytical limitations. In its original form the turnpike theorem does not balance the gain in efficiency at the end of the planning period against the temporary loss from an undesirable structure. Furthermore, if a new plan is made when the economy is at Q, it will again result in a turnpike path, and the resulting zigzag would certainly be inefficient. For an infinite planning horizon the theorem gives no guidance at all; if the turnpike requires an expansion of heavy industry, the correction might be postponed indefinitely, as sometimes seems to be the case in the Soviet Union. From this point of view, explicit utility maximization offers a more straightforward approach. The resulting optimal growth, however, may again include temporary detours, as Samuelson showed in later papers (1966–86, vol. 3, part 3). The concept of a turnpike seems to be a durable addition to economic theory.

Overlapping Generations

In the early post–World War II period, the attention of economists became focused on the fact that saving is largely an effort to provide for old age. Samuelson had already used this notion in 1939. Franco Modigliani and Milton Friedman later based their econometric theories of saving and consumption on it. In 1947, Maurice Allais constructed an aggregative general equilibrium model in which society, at any given time, consists of an active generation and a retired generation (1947). He used it primarily to determine the comparative-static effects of alternative government policies. This work, buried in a long and economically unrewarding appendix to a difficult treatise in French, remained unnoticed in the English-speaking world. In fact, it was hardly noticed by Allais's French pupils. It remained for Samuelson to make the life cycle concept fruitful for general equilibrium analysis (1966–86, vol. 1, ch. 21).

Samuelson was not interested in comparative-static exercises. He went straight to the heart of the fundamental welfare problem. This stands out most sharply in the case of just two generations. Suppose there are no storable goods or assets, so that individuals cannot provide for old age by putting goods into a freezer. For society as a whole it is then evidently efficient if the active generation feeds the retired generation. The efficient rate of interest, Samuelson shows, would reflect the rate of population growth, being zero in a stationary society but positive for a growing population. In this "biological" theory of interest the effects of population growth thus turn out to be similar to those of time preference and the productivity of capital goods in Irving Fisher's theory. There is a fundamental problem, though, inasmuch as there is nothing that the retired can offer to the active population in return for supporting them. When today's retired had earnings, today's active population was not born. As a consequence, there is no market mechanism to guide society to the efficient solution.

This may seem to be different for three generations, with the young and middle-aged working, and the old in retirement. In this case the middle-aged can make a transfer to the young in exchange for a return transfer when the middle-aged have become old and the young have become middle-aged. Efficiency would require that both the young and the middle-aged save to maintain the retired, and (unless population shrinks) this never involves a negative interest rate.

Samuelson shows, however, that such an intertemporal bargain can never result in positive savings of the young and middle-aged to maintain the retired. It can only result in large savings by the middle-aged subsidizing both riotous living by the young and the necessities of life for the old. The market can only achieve such a tilting of consumption patterns by a negative interest rate, inducing the young to overspend at the price of future sacrifices. In a free market, therefore, an efficient intergenerational allocation of resources is impossible.

Efficiency can be achieved in two ways. In one case the working generation is compelled by law or custom to support the retired; the state undertakes to correct the failure of the free market. The same purpose may be served, so Samuelson argues, by the use of money as a store of value. In this case the young and the middle-aged accumulate cash balances to finance their retirement. Money may thus serve as a social contrivance to make the market economy more efficient.

Samuelson's extension of general equilibrium analysis to intergenerational resource allocation became the basis of a large and fruitful literature on the interactions between institutional arrangements and the distribution of income and wealth. In addition, it provided a surprising stimulus in an area for which it was not really intended, namely monetary theory. It is evident that in Samuelson's model, "money" is meant not to be interpreted literally as a means of payment but just as a paradigm for any storable asset (such as shares, land, houses, or whiskey). Some monetary theorists, however, interpreted it literally as an explanation of the demand for cash balances. In one sense, this was actually quite fruitful. Monetary theory was in need of a model of constant stationary motion, and overlapping generations provided such a model. In another sense, however, this was a blind alley, because cash balances are usually not an efficient means to provide for old age, and their circulation is governed by quite different types of stationary motion. The economic motion that is relevant for the demand for money is not that of population dynamics.

Randomness of Speculative Prices

In the interwar period it was widely believed that the past behavior of stock prices permits profitable inferences about future price changes. In the post–World War II period, the growing volume of empirical stock market research, including that of Alfred Cowles of Cowles Commission fame, cast doubt on this notion. To all intents and purposes it seemed as if successive price changes in speculative markets were essentially random. In this case the observation of past trends would give no profitable clue about the future. By 1965 financial statisticians had developed and tested a variety of stochastic models that might account for the observed facts. What was lacking was a theory connecting descriptive statistics with analytical economics.

Such a theory was published by Samuelson in 1965 under the title "Proof that Properly Anticipated Prices Fluctuate Randomly" (1966–86, vol. 3, ch. 198).[12] The intuitive wisdom behind this theory is commonplace and had long been familiar: if reasons are known for a speculative price to rise, it will already have risen; that knowledge, therefore, offers the speculator no profit opportunities. Samuelson replaced this intuition by analysis.

His model relates to a commodity market, say, for wheat. The spot price plays the role of the market fundamentals. Influenced by all sorts of things such as weather, crop yields, plantings, incomes, and tastes, there is no reason why it should fluctuate randomly. The main point is that the fluctuations in speculative futures prices should nevertheless be random. In particular, Samuelson showed that next period's futures price differences

12. Essentially the same approach was developed around the same time by Benoit Mandelbrot (1966).

are uncorrelated with price differences in the preceding periods. It follows from this "martingale" property that the expected value of the speculator's capital gain is zero.

Of course, futures prices depend on spot prices. Samuelson develops this relationship backward in time. When a futures contract falls due, its price (abstracting from commissions) equals the spot price, which is certain. A month earlier, the spot price at due date is uncertain, but traders, on the basis of past experience, are assumed to know its probability distribution. In a competitive market, the futures price will then settle at the mathematically expected level of next month's spot price. The same applies to earlier periods back to the present moment. This is Samuelson's axiom about price formation.

From his fairly general probability distribution and the pricing axiom, Samuelson derives his basic theorem. It says that the sequence of futures prices for a given maturity from now to the terminal date exhibits no upward or downward drift anywhere, regardless of expected fluctuations in spot prices. No effort to analyze the past behavior of futures prices promises any profit. The current futures prices embody all that needs to be known. Intuitive wisdom is vindicated.

Samuelson was very careful not to make exaggerated claims for his theorem. "It does not prove," he wrote, "that actual competitive markets work well. It does not say that speculation is a good thing or that randomness of price changes would be a good thing. It does not prove that anyone who makes money in speculation is *ipso facto* deserving of the gain or even that he has accomplished something good for society or for anyone but himself" (1966–86, 3:789). Indeed, Samuelson confessed that he oscillated over the years between regarding the theorem as trivially obvious and almost trivially vacuous and regarding it as remarkably sweeping (786). He consoled himself with the thought that this was perhaps characteristic of basic results.

Indeed the result turned out to be basic, providing the foundation for the theory of efficient markets as developed by Eugene Fama and others and for the theory of rational expectations as developed from John Muth's seminal concept by Robert Lucas, Thomas Sargent, and others. Though these developments were very fruitful, they are still subject to the reservation with which Samuelson concluded his paper. He left open the questions, he said, of where the postulated probability distributions came from, whose expectations they are supposed to describe, and in what sense they might possibly be optimized. Why is there just one set of "rational" expectations?

Place in the History of Economics

Samuelson is often described as the embodiment of "neoclassical" or even "neo-neoclassical" economics. As a characterization of distinctive doctrines, these terms are devoid of content. Samuelson, the eclectic, cannot be identified with any particular set of doctrines, views, or concepts in opposition to other such sets. As a pragmatist, he has shown himself willing to consider anything that promises fruitful results.

To be meaningful, those terms must be taken in the sense of "standard," "state of the art," or "mainstream" economics, whatever its substantive content may be in any given period. Classical economics is the perennial dream or myth of valid economics reduced to its essentials. In this sense, Samuelson was indeed the incarnation of the classical tradition in the middle third of the twentieth century. He personifies not only the unbroken continuity of this tradition since the early eighteenth century but also its pluralistic openness to new developments, its power to integrate conflicting views, and its relative (and sometimes hard-won) independence from particular ideologies.

Samuelson did not open up large new fields of economic research, such as econometrics, input-output analysis, or linear programming. His work concerned the central core of economic theory, and his special strength was the discovery of the essential unity in the analytical structure of different theories. Historically, he represents the stage in which general equilibrium analysis, as founded by Walras and revived by Hicks, finally became the master technique for the solution of a broad range of problems. The rigorous formalization of general equilibrium analysis he left to others. He was seeking not existence proofs but economically interesting theorems (which he loved to call fundamental, often with good reason).

From this point of view, Samuelson thought, 1935 was a golden time to enter economics. Theory had been in decadence after Marshall. The imperfect competition pseudo revolution had still stopped short of Augustin Cournot. Thus the terrain, in Samuelson's metaphor, "was strewn with beautiful theorems begging to be picked up and arranged in unified order" (1966–86, 4:886). Samuelson picked them up in large numbers, thereby giving the single most powerful impulse to the upsurge of economic theory after 1940. He also had a knack for selecting problems whose solution was well within reach. As a consequence, most of his results were promptly absorbed into the mainstream, though hidden pearls may still be discovered by future historians.[13]

Through this work, Samuelson became the greatest teacher that economics ever had. His courses may not always have been painstakingly prepared, but, by the example of his untiring and uncompromising research, by his inspiring results, and by his introductory text, he lifted economic science globally to a higher plane. Smith, Ricardo, and Marshall each had left economic theory in decay; Samuelson initiated a golden period. Whereas others had perhaps directed their mistaken efforts to the

13. It may console lesser mortals, however, that even some of Samuelson's best papers were at first rejected by editors and referees.

establishment of so-called schools or isms, Samuelson was one of the few who built a real school, namely the Economics Department of MIT.

It is significant to observe that the leading economist of his generation chose to remain entirely noneconometric. Samuelson believes that economic theory has to prove itself before historical reality, but he does not believe that the existing methods of econometrics are able to capture this reality. He is too much historian to be econometrician. Inasmuch as professional economists in the last quarter-century have devoted a large part of their energies to econometric measurement and testing, they did not follow Samuelson's lead. Samuelson's view may still be vindicated, though.

The history of science sometimes creates the impression that the past was an age of giants and the present is an age of dwarfs. Samuelson helps to dispel this mythological delusion. He displayed the synthetic ability of an Adam Smith, but combined with a superior and more innovative analytical power. Whereas Ricardo was an untrained amateur who gave to economics no more than ten years, Samuelson is a most highly trained scientist who is now in his sixth decade of productive research. Whereas Marshall, never fulfilling his early promise, camouflaged his analytical apparatus until he himself had lost it from sight, Samuelson presented his tools in broad daylight, for everyone to judge and use. Keynes became famous for his persuasive vision of things, which Samuelson lacks, but as a theorist, Keynes was neither strong nor very original. The revolution he seemed to have produced is thus likely to have less lasting effect than the evolution initiated by Samuelson. Judged by their scientific achievement, the dead are not necessarily greater than the living.

33
Economic Growth

It takes all the running you can do, to keep in the same place.
—Lewis Carroll, *Through the Looking Glass*

LONG-TERM GROWTH has been one of the central preoccupations of political economy for centuries. The mercantilists regarded it as crucial for the rise and fall of political power. Adam Smith made it the subject of the *Wealth of Nations*. The "canonical" model of classical economics showed how the limitation of natural resources gradually retards the growth of factor supplies unless technical progress intervenes. Karl Marx argued that the relentless progress of the productive forces eventually leads to the collapse of the capitalist system. The theorists of the Marshallian age, living in the time of historicism, were conditioned to regard the economy as an evolutionary process.

Despite this perennial interest in growth, formal economic theory in the era of individual optimization remained essentially confined to stationary equilibrium. The historical perspective and empirical observations led to tentative visions of the growth process but not to explicit growth theories. In the era of model building this began to change. Growth economics was gradually transformed from vision to analysis, losing in the process most of its historical content. In the present chapter, the stages of this transformation will be described by four outstanding contributions, namely those of Joseph Schumpeter, Roy Harrod, Robert Solow, and the so-called golden rule of capital accumulation.

Joseph Schumpeter

Joseph Alois Schumpeter represents the stage of vision without theory. He was born in Moravia (now part of Czechoslovakia) in 1883, the son of a textile manufacturer.[1] After his father's early death his mother married a lieutenant general of the Austro-Hungarian army, thirty-three years her senior. From then on, Schumpeter grew up in Vienna on the fringe of an aristocracy with which he could never compete in terms of high birth and wealth. This, together with his mother's unlimited devotion, seems to have had a decisive influence on his insatiable need for success. He later used to say that he had three goals in life, namely to be Austria's greatest lover, Europe's greatest horseman, and the world's greatest economist, but that he failed to reach the second.

At the high school of the aristocratic elite, the *Theresianum*, Schumpeter received a good education in the humanities, but with little mathematics or science, a deficiency that he was never able to correct. As a law student at the University of Vienna, he also took courses in economics. He thus heard Friedrich von Wieser and Eugen von Böhm-Bawerk and did work in statistics. Out of Böhm-Bawerk's seminar grew Schumpeter's lifelong interest in the Marxian question about the development of capitalism. At the same time, Schumpeter acquired an extensive knowledge of economic literature in several languages, which he became fond of parading in innumerable footnotes.

After obtaining his doctorate of law in 1906, Schumpeter went to Cairo to practice law and to manage, among other things, the finances of an Egyptian princess. On the side he finished his first book, which helped him to a lectureship in Vienna in 1909. In the same year he became a professor at Czernowitz (which is now in the Soviet Union), where he had two highly productive years. He loved to shock his colleagues by coming to faculty meetings in riding boots and by wearing evening dress for dinner at home,

---

1. This biographical sketch is based on the obituaries by Arthur Smithies and Gottfried Haberler, and other papers in the volumes edited by Harris (1951), Frisch (1981), and Seidl (1984). I am greatly indebted to Wolfgang F. Stolper for significant biographical details.

thus giving the impression of being frivolous and affected. It was as if he were trying to create the role of the young genius in a stage play.

In 1911, only twenty-eight years old, Schumpeter was appointed to a chair at Graz. The faculty would have preferred a less colorful colleague, but Böhm-Bawerk is reported to have helped to get the appointment for Schumpeter. Students at first boycotted his classes but then seem to have accepted him.

Schumpeter's reputation now grew rapidly. By the time World War I broke out, he was internationally famous; he was just thirty-one years old when Columbia University gave him an honorary degree. At home, however, he was embroiled in controversy, his weak performance in the theory of interest had turned Böhm-Bawerk from a supporter into an opponent, and he failed to get a chair at Vienna.

There was also failure of another sort. One of the consequences of a trip to England had been Schumpeter's marriage to the daughter of a church dignitary. It ended in disaster. When the war broke out, Mrs. Schumpeter, who then happened to be in England, refused to return to Vienna, and the two were divorced in 1920.

During World War I, Schumpeter was pro-British, anti-German, and in favor of a separate peace for Austria. After the collapse of the monarchy, though he had earlier played up to the conservatives, he joined his socialist friends Rudolf Hilferding and Emil Lederer in working for the German Socialization Commission, which, under the leadership of Karl Kautsky, made the coal industry its first target. Schumpeter thus came to be regarded as a socialist. This he was not, but his reputation with the Austrian socialists, who were Marxists, was nevertheless high enough for Hilferding to propose him to Otto Bauer as minister of finance in 1919. He was no success—perhaps nobody could have been. Without political support, the measures he proposed (a capital levy and foreign borrowing to stop inflation) failed, and his phrase that "a crown remains a crown" made him unpopular with those who suffered as a result of inflation. A nationalization scandal, though it was not his fault, led to his resignation after only seven months in office.

Shortly afterward, Schumpeter tried his hand as a banker and became president of a small but reputable private bank. At the same time he seems to have engaged in speculative activities. Schumpeter lost his shirt and incurred large debts, which it took him many years to repay out of his journalist's income and academic salary. He also had to resign from the bank.

In 1924, Schumpeter married the daughter of his mother's janitor, twenty-one years his junior, whose education the Schumpeters are said to have financed. It was a classic Pygmalion story and a great romantic love. The young wife died two years later in childbirth, and Schumpeter's mother died in the same year. There was much tragedy in Schumpeter's relationships with women. He was deeply attached to those who offered him motherly protection or childlike affection, but he also boasted to be a Don Juan.

In 1925, after a visiting appointment in Japan, Schumpeter reentered academic life as a professor at Bonn. He became one of the most enthusiastic sponsors of the Econometric Society, though he was never able to do econometric research of his own. In 1932, Schumpeter moved to Harvard, and in 1937 he married the economic historian Elizabeth Boody, who became his protector.

During World War II, Schumpeter was isolated and depressed. Hating Roosevelt and the New Deal, with sympathy for the people (but not the governments) of Germany and Japan and with dark forebodings about Soviet Russia, he had no influence, and nobody cared for his advice. He was a tireless worker, though, forever working on ambitious projects, none of which was completed. He died in 1950 from a stroke.

Schumpeter's first book, *Das Wesen und der Hauptinhalt der theoretischen Nationalökonomie* (1908) (The Nature and Main Content of Theoretical Economics), shows its author as a persuasive, but eclectic, expositor and defender of general equilibrium theory. Even German historians could acclaim it as a masterwork (though some criticized it severely). There were no substantive contributions, though.

In *Theorie der wirtschaftlichen Entwicklung* (1912) (Theory of Economic Development), Schumpeter tried to set the economy in motion. The motor was innovative entrepreneurship. The entrepreneur, imposing his innovations on a recalcitrant environment by "creative destruction," becomes the romantic hero of the play. This was not particularly novel. Karl Marx, in his hate-love for the capitalists, had assigned the entrepreneurs about the same role. Inventions appeared as the driving force of development, as the saviors from stagnation, throughout nineteenth-century economics. Alfred Marshall (1925, ch. 17) had even compared the entrepreneurs to medieval knights. Schumpeter's teacher Wieser and the Austrians in general, as Streissler (1981, 60–83) has stressed, were used to assign the entrepreneur a crucial function. The vision, to use Schumpeter's term, was all there.

What was missing was the transformation of this vision into economic theory. Walras confined himself to statics not because he believed the world was really stationary but because he knew how to select problems he could solve. Schumpeter could not construct the missing theory of innovation either. How could a second-best theorist succeed where the best feared to tread? Over the years, however, Schumpeter's conjectures about entrepreneurial innovation, vague as they were, stimulated a growing number of studies about entrepreneurial history and the role of research and development in economic growth. That Schumpeter was only a second-best theorist became clear from his treatment of interest. He argued that in the stationary state the rate of interest would be zero, that the source of interest was entrepreneurial innovation in an environment of imperfect competition, and that the level of interest rates depends largely on credit creation by banks. Though each of these points is arguable, Schumpeter's analysis was weak.[2]

Two years later, Schumpeter published his third treatise in six years. Entitled "Epochen der Dogmen- und Methodengeschichte" (1914) (Economic Doctrine and Method, a Historical Sketch), it was a brief history of economic doctrines written for a multivolume handbook. It may be described as a tourist guide to the literature for the trained economist. The leitmotiv is the prevalent body of ideas about scientific method while the substantive results of economic research are left in the background. Numerous names are briefly mentioned—Schumpeter would later call such a name-dropping exercise a review of the troops. The reader is dazzled by the superior manner in which the scientific rank of so many writers is judged, as if young Schumpeter had really had the time not only to read but also to digest their works. Surprisingly, economic theory since 1870, with the exception of Böhm-Bawerk, is treated only perfunctorily; the reader is not told what marginalism was all about.

Schumpeter is often quoted for the view that scientific creativity ends at thirty. What he wrote after that age was, in fact, a successive elaboration of his early works. More than twenty-five years went by before he published another major book, namely the two volumes of *Business Cycles: A Theoretical, Historical and Statistical Analysis of the Capitalist Process* (Schumpeter 1939). It was mainly an implementation, based on a mass of descriptive material, of the theoretical framework he had outlined in 1912. The main thesis may be summarized as follows: Inventions and discoveries take place irregularly but continuously. Their transformation into entrepreneurial innovations, however, occurs in distinct waves. The reason is that the economic, social, and institutional environment is resistant to change. A breakthrough can occur, therefore, only after a considerable reservoir of new ideas has accumulated. Once a few entrepreneurs have broken through, success is easier for others. The reservoir is quickly emptied in a wave of innovation. The environment, though changed, again resists further change, and a new breakthrough cannot occur before the innovative pressure in the reservoir has again risen to the critical point. It is clear that this is basically the Marxian mechanism of social dynamics, but transferred from class struggles to business cycles.

Innovation, in Schumpeter's view, is the main motor of investment. The bunching of innovation thus results in fluctuations in investment, financed by bank credit, and thereby in business cycles. But there are waves

2. For a critical analysis see Haberler 1951, 72–78, and Samuelson 1981, 1–27.

of different magnitude and duration, superimposed on one another. Long waves, resulting from fundamental innovations, follow one another about every half-century, producing the so-called Kondratieff cycles.[3] Intermediate waves last between six and eleven years; these are the Juglar cycles.[4] Minor waves, the Kitchin or "American" cycles, break about every forty months. Schumpeter also admits the possibility of still other cycles. Economic history is their sum. The view that there are different cycles was not original; in fact, there was intensive research about them in the interwar period, one of its leaders being Arthur Spiethoff, Schumpeter's colleague in Bonn. It was Schumpeter's ambition to construct from these pieces a comprehensive interpretation of the capitalist system.

Criticism did not deal kindly with this undertaking (Kuznets 1940 is an example). It was pointed out that any sequence of random numbers can be approximated by a series of superimposed sine curves. As a consequence, a plausible historical fit of Schumpeter's model did not mean much. It was also pointed out that the existence of different dynamic mechanisms had not been demonstrated. Furthermore, Schumpeter used neither the dynamic models nor the econometric techniques that had become available by that time. Today, the three-cycle scheme seems to survive only in the sheltered habitat of outdated textbooks. Modern business cycle research has rather been based on the rocking chair idea of Knut Wicksell and Ragnar Frisch, according to which random disturbances act on an economic system whose dynamic properties tend to produce oscillating reactions.

Capitalism, Socialism, and Democracy (1942) was the last book Schumpeter finished. It was also the most widely read and most controversial. It develops the thesis that capitalism will come to an end, that socialism is inevitable, and that it may turn out to be compatible with democracy. Schumpeter reaffirmed the prophecy of an inevitable "march into socialism" in a lecture a few days before his death (1950). He was far from

3. Nikolai Kondratieff, born in 1892, was, after the Bolshevik revolution, the founder and director of the Moscow Institute for Business Cycle Research. Inspired by suggestions in the earlier Marxist literature, he found statistical evidence for long swings in economic activity in price and production series. The first results were published in 1922 and elaborated in 1925 (Kondratieff 1984). He was arrested in 1930 and last heard of in 1931.

4. Clément Juglar (1819–1905), originally a practising physician, had been led to business conditions by his research on birth and death rates. Using data for three countries over three centuries, he identified a cycle of six to ten years as a concomitant of economic growth. In thoroughly modern fashion he interpreted it as an endogenous fluctuation, the cause of recession being prosperity (and the cause of prosperity, recession). Saving, investment, and bank credit creation were assigned important roles. Awarded first prize in a competition in 1860, Juglar's main work (1889) was first published in 1862. Empirical business cycle research had been firmly established five years before Marx published the first volume of *Capital*. Juglar seems to have been not only a pillar of French statistics but also a friend of the arts, a devout Catholic, and a dedicated scientist.

predicting a catastrophic collapse. Capitalism would rather be gradually transformed by its own success, largely because innovation could now be achieved, even without entrepreneurs, by bureaucratic routine.

Though not a Marxist, Schumpeter belonged to the numerous bourgeois economists who had let themselves be convinced by Karl Marx that capitalism was a distinct economic system with its own inherent dynamics. The future course of this system, therefore, could be scientifically predicted once its properties were understood. Again, Schumpeter's predictions about the gradual transformation of capitalism were not very original, for Werner Sombart had made his fame with similar ideas in the 1920s (before he embraced Nazism).

Schumpeter's tract is full of brilliant observations and conjectures. In particular, some recent commentators (such as Frey [1981]) have found in his characterization of democratic government as being based on "a competitive struggle for the people's vote" (Schumpeter 1942, 269) all the main ingredients of the modern theory of public choice. Nobody will deny, moreover, that the economic and social system is subject to continual change. However, in divining the trends of future history, Schumpeter fared no better than many brilliant journalists such as, say, Walter Lippman. If he could have observed the world toward the end of the twentieth century, it is unlikely that he would still describe those trends as a march into socialism.

Over many years, Schumpeter had worked on what was intended to become his magnum opus, the *History of Economic Analysis* (1954). At his death it remained unfinished, but the manuscript was edited and published by his wife. Even in this form it is an overwhelming work. The sketch of 1914 had grown into a monumental tapestry, full of significant—and mostly accurate—details, but also with a grandiose, if baroque, architecture. The three-four beat of Hegelian dialectics that Schumpeter had transferred from the Marxian class struggle to business cycles is now imposed on the history of economics: scientific revolutions are supposed to merge into "classical situations," which, after a while, set the stage for a new revolution. The display of erudition, though somewhat theatrical, is stupendous.

Certainly, the book would have been even better with fewer names dropped, less classroom sermonizing, fewer digressions, less literary flourish, and fewer rankings of performances. Instead, one would have preferred more succinct accounts of actual research results of the sort Jacob Viner, George Stigler, or William Jaffé so admirably provided. The Hegelian periodization, furthermore, distorts rather than enlightens the inherent dynamics of economic research. Nevertheless, as a historian of economic thought from antiquity to the present day in the context of general social and intellectual developments, Schumpeter has no equal.

In the history of economics Schumpeter is a tragic figure. He came to economics with the most burning ambition. If Gossen saw himself as the Copernicus of the social universe and Jevons wanted "to be good towards the world," Schumpeter wanted to excel as the world's greatest economist. By using innovation to transform a general equilibrium model into a theory of social dynamics, he tried to outdo both Marx and Walras.[5]

In a way he came close to reaching his goal. He was regarded as one of the leading economists at the age of thirty-one, and he still was when he died. Today, thirty-nine years after his death, he is called great, a genius, or a giant as routinely as Hera was called cow-eyed. He seems to have made a deep and lasting impression on many who knew him personally.

Nevertheless, he knew he had failed. Beyond suggestive interpretations of history, economics now required models of economic growth, and such models Schumpeter could not provide. He used to distinguish between the vision of an economic theory and its implementation by economic analysis (1954, 41). It was Schumpeter's tragedy that he could provide only vision. For original scientific analysis he had neither the gift nor the training. He was, as Samuelson (1981, 1–27) said, the patron of economic theory, the collector, the connoisseur, the critic, but he could not do it himself. He extolled theory to the historians, history to the econometricians, and econometrics to the theorists. He was a Samuel Johnson of economics, neither a Shakespeare nor a Balzac. Schumpeter knew this, at least after his defeat about the rate of interest. This helps to explain his reluctance to talk about his own theories, which would otherwise be surprising in a man not conspicuous for his modesty.

Yet, what was weakness in Schumpeter the theorist was strength in Schumpeter the historian of doctrines. With his enormous knowledge, his ability to understand other people's theories, and his untiring energy, he was, overall, the greatest historian economic science has ever had. As a historian of his science, he posthumously achieved the success that was denied to him as an original theorist during his lifetime.

Roy Harrod

In the same year, 1939, in which Schumpeter published his *Business Cycles*, Roy Harrod initiated the modern theory of economic growth. The basic concepts he used were not new. Gustav Cassel, an incarnation of "neoclassical" economics, had articulated the concept of an economy in balanced growth, with unchanging structure, in which all components grow at the same rate as population (1921). Though growth may, of course, be accelerated by technical progress, Cassel (disregarding the scarcity of natural resources) shows clearly that it can proceed even with unchanged technology. Schumpeter's innovations, it seems, are not indispensable for

5. See the preface to the Japanese translation of *Theorie der wirtschaftlichen Entwicklung* (in Schumpeter 1951, 158f.).

growth after all. It was Cassel's main point that balanced growth, since more and more populous generations have to be equipped with capital goods, requires saving, and that capital accumulation may continue forever without turning into stagnation. This was close to the Marxian concept of "reproduction on an extended scale" (which equally abstracted from natural resources).

By the early 1930s business cycle research had matured to the stage of the elaborate dynamic models of Ragnar Frisch and Michal Kalecki. Of particular importance to growth theory was Erik Lundberg's *Studies in the Theory of Economic Expansion* (1937). While mainly focusing on short-term fluctuations, Lundberg, as a by-product, also gave mathematical precision to Cassel's balanced growth model. In particular, he pointed out that all components of such an economy must grow at a constant exponential rate and that this common growth rate equals the ratio between the savings rate and the capital/output ratio (185). This was the core of what later was called the Harrod-Domar model. A model of the same type had been used even earlier by Edward Theiss (1935), a Hungarian then in Oslo, in a study of economic fluctuations.

Under the influence of John Maynard Keynes's *General Theory*, however, the attention of economic theorists was diverted away from the dynamics of growth to the statics of unemployment. It was Harrod who reunited Keynesian macroeconomics with the classical tradition of growth economics. Whereas Schumpeter had to be content with a preanalytical vision of economic development, Harrod provided the analytical starting point for an integrated theory of economic growth and cycles.

Roy Harrod was born in Norfolk, England, in 1900, the only child of a highly educated and talented family.[6] Instead of children's books he was given Shakespeare and Shelley to read. The father saw his fortune disappear in a copper mine, but the boy won a scholarship that enabled him to go to Westminster School. He lost his father, then a clerk, when he was eighteen, but he remained closely attached to his mother to the end of her long life, either seeing her or writing to her daily.

From Westminster, Harrod went to New College, Oxford. After graduating in philosophy and history, he began as a lecturer in modern history and economics. Soon after he was made a fellow of Christ Church, which he remained until 1967. Spending a term at Cambridge, he became a close friend of Keynes, then already a celebrity, who stimulated his interest in economics. Back in Oxford, he went to old Edgeworth to learn economic theory.

Harrod's first original contribution to economics was the reinvention, ninety years after Cournot, of the marginal revenue concept, though under a different name (Harrod 1952, ch. 3). Keynes, as the editor of the *Eco-*

6. The following biographical note is based on Phelps Brown 1980.

nomic Journal, first rejected the note, which caused Harrod to suffer a nervous breakdown. When the note was finally published in 1930, he had lost any possible claim to priority, dubious as it would have been in the first place. In the following year, almost simultaneously with Jacob Viner, Harrod represented the long-run average cost curve as the envelope of short-run cost curves (Harrod 1952, ch. 4). He was in close contact with Keynes when the latter worked on the *General Theory* and Harrod was given credit for the only diagram in the book (Keynes 1936, 180). The two slender books that Harrod published in the 1930s, namely *International Economics* (1933) and *The Trade Cycle* (1936), staked out the area of his principal economic interest. Business cycles were already explained in a Keynesian spirit by the interaction of the acceleration principle with the multiplier, but without an explicit model. This interaction also led Harrod beyond Keynes to the problem of economic growth. This is where he made his fundamental contribution, first outlined in 1939 in the "Essay in Dynamic Theory" (Harrod 1952, ch. 13) and later elaborated in *Towards a Dynamic Economics* (1948). His important papers are collected in a volume of essays (Harrod 1952).

After Keynes's death, his brother entrusted Harrod with the writing of his life. The result was an outstanding biography, a work of both art and scholarship (Harrod 1951). All this time, Harrod had still remained a philosopher at heart. His *Foundations of Inductive Logic* of 1956 he regarded as his greatest work, but he failed to persuade the logicians. Though his mathematical skills were limited, he was an effective writer with a prodigious output of books, articles, and journalistic writings. Further contributions to economic theory failed to materialize, though.

Harrod was, in fact, never a pure theorist but an applied economist with a strong policy orientation along Keynesian lines. Politically active, he began as an ardent Liberal but later leaned first toward Labour and then to the Conservatives. During the early war years he served on Churchill's personal staff but discovered that his influence was more limited than he had hoped. Thereafter he occupied himself with plans for the postwar international order. In recognition of his public service he was knighted in 1959. To his disappointment, Oxford never offered him a professorship; he remained a reader until his retirement. After his marriage in 1938, he and his wife maintained a hospitable home and raised two sons. Harrod died in 1978.

When Harrod wrote down his growth model, he was not aware of Lundberg's work. His natural habitat was Keynesian macroeconomics. He started from the observation, already foreshadowed in *The Trade Cycle* (Harrod 1936, 102), that a state with positive saving cannot be stationary, positive saving involving investment, which, in turn , expands the productive capacity of the economy. He suggested that it may be possible to analyze a growing economy by essentially static techniques by simply expressing all magnitudes in per capita terms. The structure of such an economy would then depend on the rate of population growth.

In particular, Harrod visualized an economy producing real output, X, with both captial, K, and labor, L. The increment in capital goods is investment, $\Delta K = I$, which is equal to saving, S. The rate of output growth can thus be written

$$g = \frac{\Delta X}{X} = \frac{\Delta K/X}{\Delta K/\Delta X} = \frac{S/X}{I/\Delta X} = \frac{s}{a}, \qquad (33.1)$$

where s is the average propensity to save and a is the accelerator relating investment to the increment of output. If capital grows at the same rate as output, the accelerator can also be interpreted as the average capital/output ratio, $a = \Delta K/\Delta X = K/X$. As it stands, equation 33.1 is a mere accounting identity. Its economic fruitfulness, like that of the equation of exchange, must depend on the economic relationships that can be discovered to hold between the various terms. Harrod had no doubts about the fruitfulness of his framework. He said he knew of no alternative formulation, in the world of modern economic theory, of any dynamic principle of comparable generality (Harrod 1948, 80).

Harrod was not the only economist thinking along these lines. During the war, Evsey Domar, born in 1914 in Lodz (then in Russia, now in Poland) and with a doctorate from Harvard, had considered government debt in the context of a growing economy (1957, ch. 2). This had led him to the conclusion that the burden of the debt resulting from a government deficit of a given fraction of national income is inversely proportional to the rate of economic growth. With his attention thus turned to growth, Domar then applied his tools to employment problems. Without being aware of Harrod's 1939 paper, and before Harrod's book, he developed essentially the same fundamental equation. His conclusion was that continuous full employment requires a rate of economic growth equal to the product of the propensity to save and the productivity of investment (which is the inverse of the capital/output ratio). He took his motto from Lewis Carroll: "It takes all the running you can do, to keep in the same place." Domar subsequently applied the same perspective to foreign investment and accelerated depreciation, but as a professor at MIT he gradually left the field of growth theory to become an authority on the Soviet economy. The growth model with a fixed capital/output ratio is commonly called the Harrod-Domar model, but it might just as well be called the Cassel-Lundberg-Harrod-Domar model.

Harrod's equation can be interpreted simply as determining the savings required to achieve a certain growth rate depending on the capital/output ratio. In this sense, it became the starting point of a large literature on development planning and macroeconomic policy making. An increase in the propensity to save and in the average productivity of capital appeared as the crucial prerequisites of more rapid growth.[7] From the point of view of economic theory, this interpretation is relatively trivial, though. What Harrod had in mind was the problem of stability and business cycles. He raised it at two levels.

At one level, the problem concerned the capacity utilization of capital goods. In this context, Harrod interpreted a as the required capital per unit of output in economic equilibrium. The accounting ratio was elevated to a behavior relation. Harrod regarded a, at a given moment, as essentially fixed. This may be regarded as an implication of a technology with fixed input coefficients. Harrod preferred another interpretation, under which the capital intensity of production, though technologically variable, is prevented from changing by the inflexibility of interest rates.

With a interpreted as the required capital/output ratio, the corresponding growth rate became "that over-all rate of advance which, if executed, will leave entrepreneurs in a state of mind in which they are prepared to carry on a similar advance" (Harrod 1948, 82). Harrod called this the warranted rate of growth. His main point was that this growth path is unstable. If actual growth is above warranted growth, existing capital goods are below required capital goods; orders will be increased, and growth will be further stimulated. If, on the other hand, growth is too slow, the capital stock will appear as underutilized, and growth will be further retarded. Thus, Harrod argued, "centrifugal forces are at work, causing the system to depart further and further from the required line of advance" (86). In an often used phrase, the growth path seemed to be a knife edge. With better mastery of the analytical techniques of his day, Harrod could have represented this argument as an unstable accelerator-multiplier model, but he was content with intuitive reasoning.

At another level, Harrod's stability problem related to the full employment of labor. His knife is double-edged. With given rates of population growth and of technological progress, continued full employment results in a certain rate of output growth, which Harrod calls the natural rate. It clearly has no direct relationship to the warranted rate, but it sets a limit that actual growth cannot exceed for prolonged periods. If the warranted rate falls short of the natural rate, so Harrod argues, there is no reason why the economy should not enjoy boom conditions most of the time, though perhaps of an inflationary character. However, if the warranted rate exceeds the natural rate, actual growth must fall short of warranted growth for most of the time. As a consequence, depressions will be long and severe whereas booms will be short-lived. Harrod never tried to develop these suggestions into a complete theory of the business cycle but left this task to John Hicks (Hicks 1950). His contribution essentially con-

7. That the propensity to save may, in turn, depend on the distribution of income between wages and profits was emphasized by Kaldor (1957).

sisted in providing a view of economic growth in which a fixed capital/output ratio created the danger of frequent and prolonged depressions. The economic system seemed inherently flawed.

Robert Solow

A few years later it seemed that the conclusions from the Harrod-Domar model might appear overly pessimistic. Growth theory was given a new dimension. This reorientation was mainly due to a classic paper by Robert Solow.

Solow was born in Brooklyn, New York, in 1924. Having graduated from Harvard in 1947, he obtained his Ph.D., also from Harvard, in 1951. The dissertation was on random processes as a cause of the inequality of incomes, and income distribution remained one of his lifelong concerns. In 1950, Solow joined the faculty of the Massachusetts Institute of Technology as an assistant professor of statistics. Four years later he was made an associate professor, in 1957 he became a professor of economics, and in 1977 he was appointed an Institute Professor.

Besides being brilliant and innovative in his research, Solow has always been an enthusiastic and dedicated teacher, inspiring not only a great number of future scientists but also large classes of undergraduates. With Paul Samuelson he developed a close friendship and collaboration. Under the Kennedy administration he worked as a senior economist on the staff of the Council of Economic Advisers, and under President Johnson he served on the Commission on Income Maintenance Programs. For five years in the late 1970s he was a director of the Federal Reserve Bank of Boston. Over the years, he received many honors, including the John Bates Clark Medal of the American Economic Association, a number of honorary degrees, and finally, in 1987, a Nobel Prize.

Solow's field was (and is) macroeconomics. Not a builder of large econometric models, he rather used Samuelson's approach of reducing problems to a few key relationships amenable to microeconomic reasoning. Like other eminent economists of his generation, he published no book-length works; his fame rests on a number of exceptional papers.

After early work on multipliers and linear models, Solow became attracted by problems of economic growth. Together with Samuelson (1953), he showed that a closed von Neumann system with constant returns to scale and substitutable factors has a unique structure and a unique and stable growth rate. "A Contribution to the Theory of Economic Growth" (Solow 1956) made the step to an open system with exogenous population growth.

Solow observed that the knife-edge property of the Harrod-Domar model, its propensity to alternate between unemployment and overemployment, may be due to the assumed rigidity of the capital/output ratio rather than to inherent flaws of the economic system. If factors cannot be used except in fixed proportions, it is hardly surprising that some cannot be efficiently employed. Solow thus proposed to allow for the substitutability of factors. He continued to assume that labor grows at a constant rate, n, and that capital accumulation is a constant fraction of income, $\dot{K} = sY$. The fixed capital/output ratio, however, was replaced by a linear-homogeneous production function, $Y = F(K, L)$, allowing for substitution between capital and labor for the same output.[8]

Solow was not the first to use such a growth model. As early as 1942, Jan Tinbergen used a Cobb-Douglas production function as the backbone of an elaborate analysis of growth processes (Tinbergen 1942). He attracted no attention, however. In part, this was certainly due to the publication of his paper in German in a German journal during the war. To this must be added the fact that Tinbergen, though developing a new methodology, got bogged down in a cumbersome mathematical taxonomy. Furthermore, his main subject was not balanced growth but various types of unbalanced growth. It was James Tobin (1971–75, vol. 1, ch. 8) who first generalized the Harrod-Domar model by allowing for factor substitution. At the same time he added the demand for real cash balances, which is satisfied either by money paid out as transfer payments or by deflation. The path of economic growth thus became dependent, in part, on monetary factors.

Solow proceeded by defining capital intensity as $k = K/L$. Output can thus be expressed as

$$Y = LF(k,1) = Lf(k). \tag{33.2}$$

The change in k can then be written

$$\frac{\dot{k}}{k} = \frac{\dot{K}}{K} - \frac{\dot{L}}{L} = \frac{sY}{K} - n = s\frac{L}{K}f(k) - n, \tag{33.3}$$

or

$$\dot{k} = sf(k) - nk. \tag{33.4}$$

This is Solow's "fundamental equation" (1956, 69). In words: The change in capital intensity in the course of time is what is left over from per capita saving after the additional workers have been equipped with capital goods. If $sf(k) = nk$, the capital intensity remains unchanged; the economy grows without changing its structure. This is the path of balanced growth.

The stability of this path is best examined in terms of the graph that Solow invented for this purpose (figure 33.1). The ray nk indicates how

8. Shortly after Solow, Trevor Swan (1956) also presented essentially the same model. His exposition of the "unclassical" case of constant returns was less elegant, and thus less effective, than Solow's, but his treatment of the "classical" case of diminishing returns is particularly illuminating.

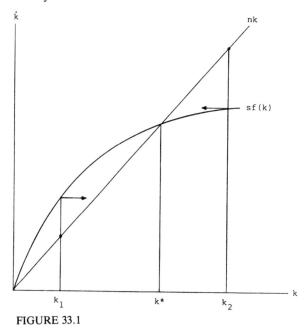

FIGURE 33.1

much the average worker has to save at each capital intensity to equip his children with capital goods. The curve *sf(k)* shows how much he actually saves from the income accruing at each capital intensity. The change in capital intensity is measured by the vertical distance between the two curves. If the economy is originally at k_1, this change is positive; the economy thus moves to the right toward higher k's. If the economy is initially at a point such as k_2, the change is negative; the economy moves to the left. From both sides, the economy will converge toward k^*, which denotes the balanced growth path. This growth path, therefore, is stable; there is generally no knife edge.

In Solow's model the rate of balanced growth is entirely independent of savings. The propensity to save determines the capital intensity of production and thus real income, but the growth rate depends only on population and technology. All those policy prescriptions that, based on Harrod-Domar models, were meant to accelerate long-term growth were now revealed to provide only temporary impulses. However, whether these impulses would last for only a few years or for decades remained in doubt.

Solow also extended and modified his basic model by considering alternative production functions (including that of Harrod and Domar), the course of factor prices, technological change, an endogenous labor supply, a variable savings rate, and taxation. Overall, his paper became the most seminal piece of analysis in the theory of growth ever written. It also contributed to doctrinal mythology by labeling production functions with substitutable factors as neoclassical, though, in fact, Walras wrote his most important work in terms of fixed coefficients. This was unfortunate, because a brilliant theoretical contribution thus became misinterpreted as the banner of a particular school of economics. The production function became the bone of contention between the Keynesian Left and the Keynesian Right.

Solow's paper initiated a rapid expansion of growth theory in various directions, to which Solow himself was one of the principal contributors. The observation that different savings rates result in growth paths with different per capita output led to the question of how one might choose between them and thus to the problem of optimal growth. It will be considered in the following section.

Another extension concerned scarce natural resources. In the 1956 model (as in Marx) all factors can grow, and returns are constant. In this respect it was unclassical in spirit, far removed from the diminishing returns of Malthus and Ricardo. However, a production function with diminishing returns is enough to reconcile it with the classical tradition. In combination with endogenous population growth (depending on the wage rate) and endogenous saving (depending on the rate of interest), growth theory thus became a modern version of the "canonical classical model" (Samuelson 1966–86, vol. 5, ch. 340).[9] In due course, the one-sector model was also extended to two sectors (Uzawa 1961–63), thus connecting modern growth theory to the Marxian tradition of reproduction on an extended scale.

The introduction of technical change raised the further question of the extent to which the historical increase in per capita income is due to, respectively, capital accumulation and technological progress. Moses Abramovitz (1956) and Solow (1957) concluded from their empirical analyses that by far the major part must be attributed to technical progress, whereas the contribution of capital accumulation is small. The classical notion, reemphasized by Schumpeter, of the crucial role of technical change thus received powerful support.

It soon appeared, however, that the contribution of capital goods might be underestimated. Technical progress, it was argued early by Nicholas Kaldor and others, is largely embodied in capital equipment. Its exploitation thus requires new equipment while existing equipment continues to apply old technologies. To allow for this factor, Solow developed models in which capital goods of different vintages embody different technologies (1960).

Solow's early empirical work on economic growth was based on Cobb-Douglas production functions. It naturally led to experimentation with other classes of functions that would be less restrictive, allowing for changes

9. An early effort in this direction was Niehans 1963.

in factor shares. The result, published with Arrow, Chenery, and Minhas in 1961, was the constant-elasticity-of-substitution (CES) production function (Arrow 1983–85, vol. 5, ch. 3).

Though diminishing returns take account of the nonaugmentability of natural resources (such as land), they still do not allow for their depletion (as in the case of oil). With the limits to growth moving to the foreground, Solow's attention became focused on the consequences of depletion for economic growth. Developing a theme of Harold Hotelling, he determined criteria for the optimal rate of depletion of an exhaustible resource (Solow 1974a). He also considered the intergenerational equity of resource depletion in the light of John Rawls's principle that the poorest generation, present or future, should be made as well off as possible. This is shown to permit a gradual drawing down of natural resources by early generations accompanied by the accumulation of reproducible capital goods (Solow 1974b).

Though his work on economic growth made Solow an incarnation of "neoclassical" economics, he nevertheless remained a Keynesian macro-economist. Jointly with Samuelson, he had recommended the Phillips curve as a basic tool of macroeconomic policy making (Samuelson 1966–86, vol. 2, ch. 102). Together with Alan Blinder (1973) he later considered the long-run dynamics of monetary and fiscal policy in a Keynesian model with a government budget constraint. The process is driven by the continuous changes in the supply of money and/or bonds resulting from the financing of budget deficits. The conclusion is that open market purchases may be contractionary and that in a stable economy bond-financed expenditures have stronger long-run effects on output than money-financed expenditures. These propositions, paradoxical as they appeared, were provocative rather than definitive, but the paper added a new aspect to the post-Keynesian debate.

Besides being a ground-breaking researcher, Solow is a brilliant expositor with a talent for combining lucid synthesis with novel insights. The volume *Linear Programming and Economic Analysis*, written jointly with Dorfman and Samuelson (1958), became a classic introduction into a new and difficult field. The lectures *Capital Theory and the Rate of Return* (Solow 1963) argue forcefully that economic theory, as Malinvaud had shown earlier (Malinvaud 1953), does not need a factor of production called capital. *Growth Theory* (Solow 1970) is a synthetic exposition of the subject as it appeared a dozen years after the 1956 paper.

The Golden Rule

Subject chapters in this book carry personal names as section headings. The present section is the only exception. The reason is that substantially the same proposition was discovered independently by half a dozen writers at about the same time without clear priority. It was a conspicuous case of multiple discovery.

This multiplicity was not a coincidence. Solow had shown that an economy can follow a balanced growth path if its capital intensity is appropriately adjusted to its savings rate. The more that is saved, the higher is the capital intensity in balanced growth and the higher is per capita output. This raised the further question of whether higher per capita output is always preferable. Growth theory seemed to cry out for an answer, and such an answer was not very difficult to find. It is hardly surprising, therefore, that the same answer occurred to several growth theorists within a few years after Solow's paper. That it still took several years suggests that the proper conceptualization of the problem was perhaps more difficult than it appears after the fact. Hindsight helps.

The first to publish the answer seems to have been Edmund Phelps, then a young associate professor at Yale. Remembering that "one should do to others as he would have others do to him," he expressed it as a golden rule of capital accumulation. By this he meant that each generation should invest on behalf of future generations that share of income that it would have wished past generations to invest on its behalf (Phelps 1961, 642). This required, it turned out, that the rate of interest equal the rate of economic growth. This condition became the standard form of the golden rule.

Even before Phelps's "fable for growthmen" was published, essentially the same rule had occurred to others. Jacques Desrousseaux is credited by Maurice Allais with having used it in 1959, and he developed it further in a paper published in 1961. Trevor Swan presented it in 1960 at a conference of the International Economic Association (Swan 1964). James Meade added a variant to the second edition of *A Neo-Classical Theory of Economic Growth* (1962a). Carl Christian von Weizsäcker made it the analytical centerpiece of his dissertation, which he finished in the summer of 1961 (1962). Shortly after Phelps's paper, Maurice Allais made the golden rule a part of his Bowley-Walras Lecture of 1961 (1962). In the following year it appeared in the contributions of Joan Robinson (1962b), David Champernowne (1962) and James Meade (1962b) to a symposium in the *Review of Economic Studies*.

To derive the golden rule, Phelps assumed that the economy is constrained to follow a path of balanced growth with a growth rate determined by population (and perhaps technology). Suppose at a certain moment some benevolent goddess promises to equip this economy with any capital stock, however large, that it desires, on condition that the capital/labor ratio thus achieved must be maintained forever out of the economy's own savings. What capital stock should the economy pray for? If the capital stock is large, per capita output will be high, but most of it will have to be saved, leaving little for consumption. If the capital stock is low, almost the whole income is available for consumption, but income itself will be low. In between there must be a capital stock for which per capita consumption is a maximum. If initial capital is free, this seems to be a plausible objective to aim at. The criterion for maximal consumption, as pointed out by Solow (1962), is intuitive. An increment in the per capita capital stock by dk increases output by $f'(k)dk$, where the symbols relate to the model of the preceding section. At the same time, the savings required to maintain the capital stock increase by ndk. An increase in k is advantageous, therefore, as long as $f'(k) > n$, and maximum consumption is reached where $f'(k) = n$. The marginal product of capital must equal the rate of economic growth.

The result is simple to derive more formally from explicit optimization. In balanced growth, Solow's fundamental equation requires that $nk = sf(k)$. Per capita consumption is output not saved, namely

$$c = f(k) - sf(k) = f(k) - nk. \tag{33.5}$$

This is maximized for

$$\frac{dc}{dk} = f'(k) - n = 0, \tag{33.6}$$

or

$$f'(k) = n, \tag{33.7}$$

which is the form in which the condition was derived by Weizsäcker (1962).

The effect of more rapid growth on consumption can be determined by taking the derivative of equation 33.5 with respect to n and substituting from equation 33.7, namely

$$\frac{dc}{dn} = [f'(k) - n]\frac{dk}{dn} - k = -k < 0. \tag{33.8}$$

More rapid growth, since it imposes higher savings, is thus associated with lower steady-state consumption. The sacrifice in consumption, furthermore, is in direct proportion to the capital intensity of production.

The optimization calculus is illustrated in figure 33.2, derived from figure 33.1 by adding the curve for per capita output, $f(k)$. What is to be maximized is the vertical distance between this curve and required capital accumulation, nk. It is maximized where $f(k)$ has the same slope as nk, namely n. The savings rate, s, then has to be chosen in such a way that $sf(k)$ intersects the nk curve at the optimal capital intensity $\bar{k}$.

Basically, the golden rule, once the growth rate is given, relates just to the production function and thus to technology. Any other aspect of the economy is inessential. By introducing additional assumptions, however, the rule can be related to other aspects of the economy. With com-

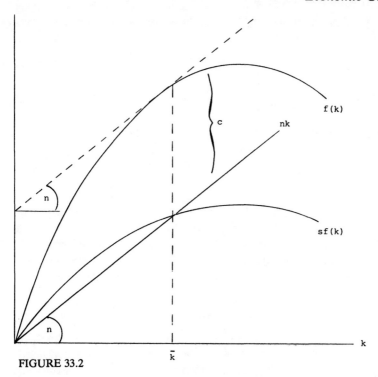

FIGURE 33.2

petitive factor markets, the marginal product of capital equals the rate of interest. The golden rule then says that consumption along a balanced growth path is maximized if the rate of interest is equal to the rate of growth,

$$i = n. \tag{33.9}$$

In this standard form the proposition appeared in Deṣrousseaux 1961, Weizsäcker 1962, Robinson 1962b, Champernowne 1962, and Allais 1962, but not in Phelps 1961. Rapidly growing economies would thus be characterized by high interest rates. A stationary economy, on the other hand, would maximize its consumption by maintaining its capital stock at the satiation level, thereby keeping the rate of interest at zero. On the surface this seems to vindicate Schumpeter's notion that interest is essentially a dynamic phenomenon. In fact, Schumpeter's view was quite different. He argued that interest was due to technological innovation. With constant technology, therefore, it should vanish, regardless of the rate of population growth. Far from supporting Schumpeter, the golden rule contradicts him by showing that in a growing economy the rate of interest is positive even in the absence of innovation, in permanent equilibrium.

By expanding equation 33.7 and substituting for Solow's fundamental equation, one obtains

$$f'(k)\frac{k}{f(k)} = \frac{nk}{f(k)} = \frac{sf(k)}{f(k)} = s. \qquad (33.10)$$

The golden rule thus implies, as pointed out in Phelps 1961 and Meade 1962b, that the savings rate is equal to the elasticity of output with respect to the capital stock. If capital is paid its marginal product, this is equivalent to the proposition that the savings rate must equal the profit rate. This is the variant used by Swan, Phelps, Meade, and Robinson. All profits, and nothing but profits, must be saved. It is clear, however, that a law whereby all profits must be saved would not be enough to put an economy on the maximum consumption path, because it does nothing to guarantee that the economy initially has the right capital stock.

In a two-factor model with constant returns to scale, wages, w, are the residual left of output after capital has been paid its marginal product. By the use of the golden rule in equation 33.5, they can thus be written as

$$w = f(k) - f'(k)k = f(k) - nk = c. \qquad (33.11)$$

Along the maximum consumption path, all wages are consumed. In general, equations 33.9 and 33.10 say nothing about the division of saving and consumption and of profits and wages between different classes of society. The same people may earn both wages and profits, and individual savings do not have to correspond to individual capital incomes. In the special case of a two-class Kaldorian society, in which workers receive only wages and capitalists receive only profits, the golden rule implies that the workers do not save and the capitalists do not consume.

The golden rule captured the imagination of economists because, on the surface, it seems to offer a straightforward criterion for the evaluation of economic performance. This was accomplished at the price of radical simplifications. Their nature can best be appreciated by posing the problem of optimal capital accumulation in a more general form. Frank Ramsey (1928) had been the first to use the calculus of variations to determine an optimal savings path. The key was the proper weighing of future consumption against present consumption. Ramsey's model, however, was restricted to a constant population with a fixed satiation level of consumption. The specification of the corresponding problem for a growing population with unlimited needs turned out to be difficult and had not been accomplished by 1961 (as shown by Tinbergen [1960] and Chakravarty [1962]). It is clear, however, that the optimal path, starting with an arbitrary initial capital stock, generally involves a variation of savings over time. In this situation, the assumption of a free gift of initial capital goods combined with the restriction to balanced growth, by obviating the need to weigh present against future consumption, provided the radical simplification that opened the door to tangible results.[10]

As a matter of fact, the golden rule provided little practical guidance. In real life there are no bountiful goddesses bringing gifts of capital goods. If the inherited capital stock is below the golden rule stock, it will first have to be increased by savings in excess of golden rule savings. In the reverse case the economy can first afford extra consumption. In both cases optimization requires a weighing of present against future consumption. That Phelps originally presented the golden rule as a spoof of "growthmen" indicates clearly that he realized its limitations from the beginning.

Despite its limitations as a policy rule, the golden rule was a significant contribution. It was significant mainly in drawing attention to a new type of relationship between interest rates and growth. In classical growth models with scarce land, the tendency of profits to fall would lead to stagnation by stifling the incentive to save. In the forest paradigm of capital theory, interest corresponds to the rate at which trees grow. In John von Neumann's general equilibrium model (1937), the equality of the growth rate and the interest rate results from the dual problems of maximizing the former and minimizing the latter in a model with variable growth and without any optimizing of consumption. In the Solow model, constructed very differently, the same equality turned out to be a condition for maximal permanent consumption for a given growth rate. Whichever way they are looked at, interest and growth seem to hang together as if by magic. Since interest *is* a form of growth, this should perhaps not be surprising after all.

THE GOLDEN RULE marked a climax in the development of growth theory. This was not because it was an intellectual achievement of an exceptionally high order but because it was the last theorem on economic growth that made a contribution to mainstream economics. Schumpeter's entrepreneurial innovation, Harrod's knife edge, Solow's self-regulating engine of growth, Phelps's golden rule, all seemed to convey significant insights about real economies. The same had been true of the von Neumann path and Samuelson's turnpike, however abstract the underlying reasoning. After the golden rule, growth theory became the preserve of mathematical specialists with little apparent output for those interested in substantive economic insights. Analysis had finally chased away vision.

10. Samuelson's turnpike theorem may be interpreted as another effort to derive growth rules without comparing present and future satisfactions.

34

Monetary Macroeconomics: Neoclassical Synthesis

THE 1950s and 1960s were the period of what Paul Samuelson proclaimed as the neoclassical synthesis in macroeconomics. Its program, only vaguely perceived at the beginning, was to derive the great macroeconomic functions of the Keynesian system for consumption, investment, and liquidity preference from the optimizing behavior of households and firms. At the end of this period, a superficial observer could gain the impression that Keynesianism had been absorbed by the classical tradition virtually without a scar.

Lloyd Metzler

The first major contribution to the neoclassical synthesis came from Lloyd A. Metzler. He observed a renaissance of classical doctrines, and he undertook to integrate them with the Keynesian elements. In particular, he initiated an effort to consider money in the context of total wealth, both financial and otherwise.

Metzler, born in Lost Springs, Kansas, in 1913, went from the University of Kansas to Harvard in 1937 for his graduate work.[1] His outstanding ability was soon recognized, and it was later said of him that never had such brilliance and gentleness been combined in the same individual. After receiving his Ph.D. in 1942, Metzler managed to combine government jobs in Washington, D.C., with theoretical research, and from 1944 to 1946 he belonged to the research staff of the board of governors of the Federal Reserve System. In 1947, after a year at Yale, he went to Chicago, where he succeeded Jacob Viner in the field of international trade and also taught economic theory. An inspiring teacher, he seems to have had the gift of imparting self-confidence to his students. Around 1950, Metzler was one of the half-dozen most brilliant and promising American theorists. After a highly productive period of little more than ten years he was struck by a brain tumor. An operation in 1952 saved his life, he still wrote some papers that most economists would be proud of, and he continued to teach, but his creativity was gone. He died in 1980.

Metzler's contributions to economics are contained in his collected papers (1973). In the present context, all but one of them can be only sketchily described. By introducing the lag of output behind sales into an accelerator-multiplier model of the business cycle, Metzler provided the basis for subsequent work on inventory fluctuations. In international trade

---

1. The biographical note is mostly based on the introduction to Horwich and Samuelson 1974.

theory, he solved classical problems in the context of a Keynesian system with fixed national prices. His analysis of multipliers for interdependent economies, published in 1942 (Metzler 1973, ch. 10), is greatly superior, both in its lucidity and by including stability, to Fritz Machlup's treatment of the same problem a year later (Machlup 1943). In reconsidering the transfer problem (1973, ch. 2), Metzler found that the resulting trade surplus of the paying country, provided both countries are stable in isolation, is smaller than the transfer. His influential survey on international trade theory (ch. 1) made C. F. Bickerdike's condition for a positive effect of devaluation on the trade balance (often called the Robinson-Metzler condition) widely known. Together with Svend Laursen he introduced the effect of the terms of trade on aggregate demand into balance of payments theory (ch. 11). The result was an international transmission of disturbances even under floating exchange rates. More specifically, expansion at home would probably be accompanied by contraction abroad. Though this kind of inverse transmission does not seem to be empirically significant, the terms of trade effect is, in principle, important.

Another group of papers concerns the stability of multiple markets. In particular, Metzler confirmed Samuelson's result that Hicks's static stability conditions are neither sufficient nor necessary for true dynamic stability. He also showed, however, that perfect stability in the sense of Hicks is necessary for true stability if it is required to hold for any configuration of adjustment speeds. Furthermore, Hicks's conditons are identical to the true conditions if all commodities are gross substitutes. These results provided an important bridge between statics and dynamics.

Metzler's most influential paper was "Wealth, Saving, and the Rate of Interest" of 1951 (1973, ch. 12). The key features of the argument may be summarized, with some simplification, as follows.[2] The model relates to a full-employment economy with flexible prices. Saving and investment depend on the rate of interest in the usual way, and saving also depends negatively on wealth. Wealth consists of securities, representing capital goods, and real cash balances. For given capital goods the equalization of saving and investment (or of aggregate supply and demand) thus requires that a higher interest rate be associated with higher real balances. The points at which this condition, relating to aggregate wealth, is satisfied lie along the rising *WW* curve in figure 34.1 There is another condition, represented by the liquidity preference schedule *LL*, relating to the composition of wealth. The higher the interest rate, the lower the proportion of assets that people want to hold in the form of cash balances. Once capital goods are given, the *LL* curve has a negative slope. The intersection of the curves determines the macroeconomic equilibrium.

What happens in figure 34.1 if the money supply is increased through

2. A more detailed assessment of Metzler's contribution is given in Niehans 1978.

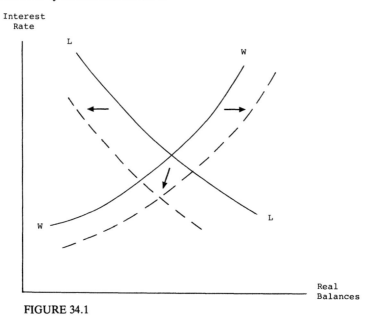

FIGURE 34.1

transfers, at unchanged holdings of capital goods? The answer is, "Nothing at all." The only effect takes place behind the scenes: nominal cash balances increase, and prices thus rise in proportion to keep real balances constant. The quantity theory is valid, and money is neutral.

This is different if the money is created by central bank purchases of securities, representing capital goods. In this case the private sector is left with a reduced quantity of capital goods. The *WW* curve shifts to the right, since the aggregate wealth gap at any rate of interest has to be closed by an increase in real balances. The liquidity schedule, on the other hand, shifts to the left, since invariant proportions of the two assets at any given interest rate now require lower cash balances. As a result of these shifts, the interest rate declines. The same change in the quantity of money thus has a different effect depending on how it is brought about.

At a distance of several decades, it is difficult to understand how such a simple piece of analysis could be so influential. Not all of the influence was beneficial, though. Two lines of argument, in particular, turned out to be misleading rather than enlightening.

The first related to the interpretation of doctrinal history. Metzler described the classical theory of interest as maintaining that a change in the quantity of money, however accomplished, can *never* influence the rate of interest. The Keynesian theory, on the other hand, was described as asserting that a change in the money supply, however accomplished, *always*

468

influences the rate of interest. Metzler's own model was interpreted as intermediary between these poles inasmuch as a change in the money supply does or does not affect the interest rate depending upon how it is brought about. This was a faulty reconstruction of doctrinal history, because hardly a classical economist would have denied that a government purchase of capital goods with new money can influence the rate of interest, and Keynes would certainly have agreed that a replacement of one-dollar bills with ten-dollar bills would leave interest rates unchanged.[3]

The paper was also misleading in attributing a crucial significance to aggregate wealth as a determinant of economic behavior. This was misleading because (1) wealth effects are, in fact, neither necessary nor sufficient for real effects of money; and (2) wealth effects were treated as static phenomena, whereas in fact, as Archibald and Lipsey (1958) later showed, they are transitory adjustment phenomena. As a consequence, the protracted debate about wealth and real balance effects produced considerably more noise than light; Metzler's formulation impeded progress rather than accelerating it.

Metzler's real contribution must be sought at other levels. One of them concerns the methodology of macroeconomic theory. By first constructing an elegant and lucid model and then deriving its comparative statics and dynamics in verbal, graphical, and mathematical terms, Metzler provided an analytical masterpiece that set a standard for post-Keynesian macroeconomics.

The paper had its most important influence, however, through the question it raised: Do the effects of money on the economy depend only on its quantity or also on the way it is created? Metzler's answer was that the method of money creation indeed makes a difference. Money distributed through transfers or temporary deficits leaves the equilibrium interest rate unchanged, whereas open market operations produce a lasting change. This conclusion was perhaps less innovative than Metzler believed, for it was already deeply embedded in the tradition of monetary theory. The important point is that subsequent analysis has generally confirmed it. The precise nature and the size of the differences between alternative methods of money creation became the bone of contention in a protracted controversy. Keynesians, following Metzler, tended to regard the differences as relatively large and persistent. Monetarists, on the other hand, following Friedman, tended to describe them as relatively small. Both sides found it difficult, however, to specify what the word *relatively* was supposed to mean. Metzler's question thus became the leitmotiv for three decades of macroeconomic research.

---

3. In fact, Metzler noted himself (1973, 314, n. 7) that even in the 1920s Pigou's views on interest rates were not, in Metzler's terminology, purely classical.

Franco Modigliani

With respect to consumption, the decisive contribution to the neo-classical synthesis came from Franco Modigliani. He was born in 1918, the son of a distinguished Roman pediatrician of Jewish ancestry.[4] A happy youth in comfortable circumstances was overshadowed by the early death of his father and the rise of fascism. At the age of seventeen, Modigliani entered the University of Rome to study law, but a first prize in an essay contest on price controls awakened his interest in economics. When the racial law went into effect in 1939, Modigliani prepared to leave Italy. He married and obtained his law degree, and the couple left Europe for the United States on the day the German-Soviet pact was signed.

At the New School of Social Research in New York, Modigliani took up the study of economics, in which he was much encouraged by Jacob Marschak. He earned his living as a bookseller and later by college teaching. After obtaining his Ph.D. in 1944, he became chief statistician of the Institute of World Affairs. A political economy fellowship of the University of Chicago enabled him to join the Cowles Commission, then in its most productive period. From 1949 to 1961, Modigliani successively held professorships at the University of Illinois, the Carnegie Institute of Technology, and Northwestern University. In 1962 he accepted an appointment as professor of economics and finance at MIT.

Like most outstanding teachers, Modigliani trained many successful scientists but founded no school. He may be regarded as the embodiment of empirical macroeconomics in the third quarter of this century. He is a Keynesian inasmuch as he built his macroeconomics from Keynesian building blocks, always remained deeply convinced of the possibility and necessity of short-term stabilization policies, and was analytically unprepared for the inflationary consequences of these policies in the 1960s.[5]

Modigliani was never a dogmatic crusader, though, but an open-minded pragmatist. Nobody could accuse him of underestimating the significance of monetary policy for economic fluctuations, and he was perfectly willing to concede that monetary policy may well make things worse rather than better. It would be hard, moreover, to infer his social and political concerns from his scholarly publications. As in so many cases, his scientific contribution is entirely independent of these concerns and actually even of his Keynesian background. In 1985 this contribution was recognized by the award of a Nobel Prize.

Like many leading American economists of his generation, Modigliani was no book writer. The three volumes of his *Collected Papers* (1980)

---

4. A biographical introduction can be found in Modigliani 1986.
5. His address as president of the American Economic Association (Modigliani 1980, vol. 1, ch. 1) offers a summary of his views.

contain all of his principal published contributions.[6] Many are coauthored with collaborators, often graduate students, which reflects the changing style of academic economics. One contribution, however, is not adequately represented by the collected papers, namely Modigliani's work as a builder of macroeconometric models. As one of the chief architects of the so-called MPS (MIT, University of Pennsylvania, Social Science Research Council) model in the second half of the 1960s, he stands at the peak of the post-Keynesian development of large-scale macromodels with detailed monetary sectors.

Modigliani recognized early that the persistent unemployment in the Keynesian model is primarily due to the rigidity of wages (1980, vol. 1, ch. 2). This insight opened the way for a reconciliation of Keynes with the pre-Keynesian tradition. Modigliani regarded it as his particular task to improve the empirical implementation of Keynesian models by deriving the behavior of economic aggregates from the optimizing behavior of economic agents.

Among Modigliani's many-sided contributions, three, in particular, have entered the mainstream of economics. One concerns the term structure of interest rates. It had long been recognized that in a well-working financial market the long-term rate over a given period, after due allowance for risk differentials, should be the average of the expected short-term rates over successive subperiods. It had usually been assumed that risk increases with the time to maturity. Modigliani and his collaborator, Richard Sutch, realized that this was not necessarily correct (Modigliani 1980, vol. 1, chs. 9, 10). If an investor needs cash in three months, a three-month Treasury bill is indeed riskless while a ten-year bond is risky. However, if he plans to liquidate his asset after ten years, the ten-year bond is riskless while a succession of three-month Treasury bills would entail considerable risk. Risk premiums were thus seen to depend on the preferred timing of cash flows, which Modigliani and Sutch called the preferred habitat of investors. According to the preferred habitat theory of the term structure, it was quite possible, in principle, that shifts in supply between different maturities would result in a shift in the required risk premiums and thus a twist in the term structure.

In fact, Modigliani and Sutch had developed their approach precisely to investigate such a twist. At the beginning of 1961, the incoming Kennedy administration had tried to raise short-term rates relative to long-term rates in the hope of stopping the capital outflow without monetary restraint. The basic question this should have raised concerned the influence of interest rates on international capital flows, but the nature of this problem was not perceived at that time. Modigliani and Sutch addressed the related question of whether a shift in the supply of securities from long maturities to short

6. For a detailed survey see Kouri 1986.

maturities can produce an appreciable twist in the term structure. Their empirical analysis in the light of the preferred habitat approach led to the result that it could not. "Operation Twist" was, by and large, ineffective. The enthusiasm for such operations, including those through the foreign exchange market, was considerably dampened by this result.

Another contribution to mainstream economics was the Modigliani-Miller theorem (Modigliani 1980, vol. 3, chs. 1–3), whose coauthor was Merton Miller, who then took Modigliani's money course at the Carnegie Institute of Technology. The theorem relates to the market value of a firm, including both equity and debt, in a perfect capital market in which everybody can borrow or lend at the market rate of interest. In such a market, individual investors can provide themselves with any proportion of equity and debt, regardless of a firm's financial structure, by borrowing or lending. Since they can thus "undo" the corporate financial structure, the latter is irrelevant for the value of the firm, which depends only on the income stream generated by the firm's assets. The theorem says, in summary, "that the value of a firm should not be affected by the share of debt in its financial structure or by what will be done with the returns—paid out as dividends or reinvested (profitably)" (1:xiii). Modigliani regarded these propositions, under the stated assumptions, as quite evident. Nevertheless, they provoked a vigorous discussion that changed the character of the literature on corporate finance. Within the stated assumptions, the theorem survived, but under real world conditions, with their market imperfections, bankruptcies, and taxes, the financial structure of corporations may be far from irrelevant.

Modigliani's most fundamental contribution was the life cycle hypothesis of consumption (or saving), suggested to him by Margaret Reid. He developed it jointly with Richard Brumberg, a graduate student who died soon after, and the results were published in 1954 (Modigliani 1980, vol. 2, chs. 3, 4). Early Keynesian consumption functions, relating current consumption to current income, resulted in a large underprediction of postwar consumption. Various ad hoc corrections had been proposed; James Duesenberry had emphasized relative income, and Modigliani himself had drawn attention to cyclical factors (ch. 1). Modigliani and Brumberg now undertook to derive consumption (or saving) explicitly from intertemporal optimization in the theoretical framework of Irving Fisher.

The individual is assumed to maximize the utility both of consumption over his remaining life span and of bequests. He is constrained by the sequence of his future incomes and by the conditions, represented by interest rates, at which he can shift his income from one period to another by borrowing or lending. The main implication was that consumption in a given year does not directly depend on income in the same year, but on the present value of expected lifetime income. Over the whole remaining life, and disregarding the bequest motive, the marginal propensity to consume would be equal to the average propensity and identical for all households, namely one. Household saving would appear whenever current income exceeded planned consumption, to be used up in other periods with the opposite conditions.

From their optimizing model, Modigliani and Brumberg derived a consumption function that makes current consumption depend on current income, expected average income, and initial assets. The influence of current income was essentially reduced to its contribution to average income. In its empirical application this consumption function succeeded in providing a unified and persuasive explanation for observed regularities in saving behavior, such as the short-run variability and the long-run stability of the saving ratio, the decline of the saving ratio at given incomes in a developing economy, the rise and decline of family income through life, and the association of the saving rate with economic growth and the age structure of the population. (Modigliani provides a retrospective overview in 1980, vol. 2, ch. 2.) It became the prototype of macroeconomic behavior functions derived from individual optimization.

James Tobin

The extension of the neoclassical synthesis program to money and financial assets was mainly the work of James Tobin. He was born in the university town of Champaign, Illinois, in 1918.[7] His father was a journalist whom his son described as a political liberal, a learned man, and a voracious reader. His mother was a social worker whom the Depression recalled to her career. James was an excellent student who loved to argue and was early attracted to journalism. Fascinated by politics as a teenager, he became an ardent New Dealer.

A Conant Prize Fellowship enabled Tobin to go to Harvard. In his sophomore year, in connection with his first economics course, his graduate student tutor made him read John Maynard Keynes's *General Theory*. The experience shaped the course of his life; he became a crusader against "orthodoxy" before he had quite mastered demand and supply. Once he had mastered it, however, it became clear to him (just as it became clear to Modigliani) that Keynes should not have claimed that unemployment could persist even in full equilibrium. This became the topic of his senior honors thesis (Tobin 1971–75, vol. 1, ch. 1).

After graduation in 1939, Tobin stayed on at Harvard for graduate work, obtaining an M.A. in 1940. In the following spring, he left the university for a job in Washington, D.C., with the Office of Price Administration and Civilian Supply. His later papers on rationing (Tobin 1971–

---

7. The biographical material is from the autobiographical essay in Breit and Spencer 1986 and from Tobin's introductory remarks to his *Essays in Economics* (1971–75, 1982). For a bibliography see *Scandinavian Journal of Economics*, 1982.

75, vol. 2, chs. 39–41) were the scientific fruit of this experience. In 1942 he entered the navy, where he served as a line officer on a destroyer until Christmas 1945.[8]

In 1946, Tobin returned to Harvard as a junior fellow to write his dissertation on the determinants of household consumption and saving. His faculty adviser, Joseph Schumpeter, is unlikely to have contributed much to his econometrics, but Tobin admired him as one of the truly great social scientists of the century. He also had great admiration for Alvin Hansen, under whose leadership Harvard had become, as Tobin later called it, the beachhead for the Keynesian invasion of the New World. In the same year he married, in due course becoming the father of four children. He obtained his Ph.D. in 1947. A visit to Richard Stone's Department of Applied Economics in Cambridge, England, and later another visit to George Katona's Michigan Survey Research Center provided new impulses to his econometric consumption research.

In 1950, Tobin accepted the offer of an associate professorship at Yale. He became a professor in 1955 and also research director of the Cowles Foundation after its move from Chicago. Since 1957 he has been Sterling Professor of Economics at Yale. From a purely scientific point of view, the 1950s were probably his most productive years.

After the presidential election of 1960, Kennedy made Tobin a member of the transition task force on the domestic economy, chaired by Paul Samuelson. In 1961, Tobin became, together with Walter Heller and Kermit Gordon, a member of the Council of Economic Advisers, whose staff included Robert Solow, Kenneth Arrow, and Arthur Okun. The twenty months of his membership in the famous "Heller Council" mark the high tide of Keynesianism in U.S. economic policy. Its manifesto is the 1962 *Annual Report of the Council of Economic Advisers*, of which Tobin always was proud. Those were the golden times when monetary and fiscal expansion made growth accelerate while inflation was still dormant.

After his return from the seats of power, Tobin resumed his research, but a growing proportion of his energy was now devoted to the apology of Keynesianism and its defense against Friedman's critique. As the temporary growth effects subsided and the permanent inflation effects began to dominate, short-term stimulation became increasingly difficult to advocate. Like other Keynesians, Tobin recommended productivity-geared wage guidelines as a solution to what he regarded as the dilemma, and he remained convinced that a little inflation could buy considerable employment gains.

Tobin's concern about full employment had always been accompanied by a strong concern about equality and poverty (1982, vol. 3, chs. 20–25).

---

8. Herman Wouk, who had been with Tobin at training school, let him appear as Midshipman Tobit in *The Caine Mutiny*.

In this spirit he had become one of the main proponents of the so-called negative income tax as a way to redistribute income without suppressing incentives. In the election campaign of 1972, he designed such a plan for George McGovern, but the large sums that inevitably go to the nonpoor repelled people more than the preservation of incentives attracted them.

Tobin did not write books. His contribution to economics is to be found in the three volumes of his *Essays in Economics* (1971–75, 1982). Articles for a more general audience were collected under the title *National Economic Policy* (Tobin 1966).

Tobin's early work was mainly on consumption. He took up the problem of why the early consumption functions derived from cyclical experience gave bad predictions if applied to long-run growth, without, however, providing an answer (Tobin 1971–75, vol. 2, ch. 30). He later concluded that the life cycle hypothesis can account for the order of magnitude of the U.S. capital stock (ch. 32). His contribution to econometric techniques is a method of regression analysis for cases in which the dependent variable has a concentration of observations at zero. An example is the demand for an article that many consumers do not buy at all. Since the method is a hybrid of probit analysis and multiple regression, Arthur Goldberger christened it Tobit analysis (Tobin 1971–75, vol. 2, ch. 44). Later in his life, Tobin, together with William Nordhaus, proposed that national income accounting be extended to a comprehensive measurement of economic welfare (Tobin 1982, vol. 3, ch. 17). To increase the national autonomy in monetary policy in the face of a high mobility of international capital flows, he also proposed a tax on foreign exchange transactions (ch. 20).

The core of Tobin's contribution, however, concerns the domestic financial system. He later described it as his research program to improve the theoretical foundations of macroeconomic models, to fit them into neoclassical economics, and to clarify the roles of monetary and fiscal policies.

Tobin's initial motivation was indeed Keynesian. He had convinced himself early that the sensitivity of the demand for money to interest rates is crucial for the Keynesian position, whereas the quantity theory, he believed, was based on the assumption of a constant velocity (Tobin 1971–75, vol. 1, ch. 3). He thus set out to explain exactly why cash balances depend on interest rates. The outlines of an explanation had been provided, even before the *General Theory*, by John Hicks (1981–83, vol. 2, ch. 5); Tobin gave it greater analytical precision.

For transactions balances he relied on transactions costs on security purchases (Tobin 1971–75, vol. 1, ch. 14). His analysis covered largely the same ground as William Baumol's (1952) four years earlier. It went beyond Baumol's paper by including both fixed and variable transactions costs but fell short of it by not explicitly deriving the square root formula or, for

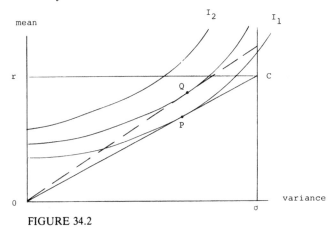

FIGURE 34.2

that matter, any demand function for money. Even the square root formula would hardly have been a major contribution since it had been suggested to William Baumol by Thomas Whitin, who had found it in the inventory literature of the mid-1920s (Whitin 1952). Hardly ever has an older and simpler device been more successful in monetary theory. Tobin never tried to provide an analysis of the demand for money in an exchange economy without interest-bearing assets. The pure theory of money was neglected in the Keynesian era.

Tobin's most influential contribution was the classic paper "Liquidity Preference as Behavior towards Risk" of 1958 (1971–75, vol. 1, ch. 15). The first part is a definitive treatment, at least in the Keynesian framework, of speculative balances. The second, and more important, part explains precautionary balances in terms of the yield and risk of securities. Harry Markowitz (1952) had earlier begun to develop a theory of portfolio selection, in which the mean value of returns is regarded as desirable and the variance of returns as undesirable. An efficient portfolio would thus minimize variance for any level of mean return. The investor could then choose among efficient portfolios in the light of his preferences. Whereas Markowitz developed this approach for portfolio selection, Tobin applied it to the demand for money.[9]

Individuals are assumed to have indifference curves in terms of mean and variance. If they are risk averse, these curves, as drawn in figure 34.2, will be rising and often with an increasing slope. If individuals, in fact, maximize the expected utility of their wealth, their preferences cannot always be reduced to such indifference curves, but Tobin showed that this

9. The main argument was already used in a 1955 paper (Tobin 1971–75, vol. 1, ch. 8).

476

is possible for quadratic utility functions and also for normal distributions.[10]

Suppose the portfolio consists of cash balances, which are interest free and riskless, and a certain security, which promises a yield (consisting of interest and capital gain) of r, but with a standard deviation of σ. All the investor has to choose is the respective proportions of his portfolio. If the whole portfolio consists of securities, the individual finds himself at C; if he holds no securities he will be at O; and with a diversified portfolio he can reach any point along the solid opportunity locus. In the light of his risk preference, the individual of figure 34.2 chooses point P, which means he holds roughly ⅓ of his assets in the form of cash balances and ⅔ in the form of securities.

If the interest rate rises at unchanged risk, the budget line rotates upward as indicated by the broken line. As the graph is drawn, this results in a decline in cash balances, the new optimum Q being on the right of P. It is conceivable, however, that cash balances decline, and Tobin points out that the ambiguity results from the familiar interplay of an income effect and a substitution effect.

Extending the analysis to several risky assets, Tobin showed that the proportions among the risky assets are independent of the cash proportion. Optimization can thus proceed in two stages, of which the first determines the optimal composition of the security portfolio and the second determines the relative proportions of cash and securities. This became known as the separation theorem, destined to play a central role in portfolio theory.

In pure theory, the mean variance approach may not be the most satisfactory way of incorporating risk into portfolio analysis, but it turned out to be widely useful. In monetary theory, in particular, it gave the interest elasticity of liquidity preference a firm basis. In strict analysis, however, its application to cash balances requires that there be no assets that are both interest bearing and riskless. If such assets exist—for example, in the form of time deposits—nobody, according to Tobin's theory, would ever hold cash balances. To explain their presence, one would have to look to their services as a medium of exchange, which Tobin disregarded.

The mean variance approach explains how an individual optimizes the composition of his asset portfolio. In the next step, Tobin and his collaborators, particularly William Brainard, applied the approach to the interaction of individuals in the market for assets. The result was a general equilibrium model of the financial system; the Walrasian perspective was extended to financial markets (Tobin 1971–75, vol. 1, ch. 18).

Twenty years later this extension looked commonplace, but when it was achieved, it was an innovation. Since the early 1920s the theory of the

---

10. Tobin falsely assumed that this was also possible for other two-parameter distributions, but he duly pointed out that quadratic utility functions eventually lead to negative marginal utilities.

money supply had been dominated by Phillips's (1920) money multipliers. They postulated fixed ratios between a bank's reserves and its demand deposits. Similar fixed ratios were attributed to the private sector. It was then a matter of simple algebra to express the money supply to the private sector as a multiple of the "high-powered money" or "monetary base" created by the central bank. One limitation of this approach was its concentration on the money supply at the expense of other assets and liabilities. This could be corrected, though, by calculating more multipliers. A more fundamental shortcoming was the assumption of fixed coefficients, analogous to the fixed technological coefficients in early production theory, which masked the influence of interest rates and other market conditions. The innovation was to replace the fixed coefficients by an optimizing calculus and the Phillips multipliers by the comparative statics of a general equilibrium system.

This approach had a long ancestry. Immediately before Tobin, John Gurley and Edward Shaw (1960) proposed to consider money in the context of what they called a theory of finance. Though their plea was suggestive and influential, their analytics was inadequate. Much earlier, Francis Ysidro Edgeworth (1888) had outlined an optimizing approach to banking theory based on stochastic reserve losses. In classical economics, Henry Thornton was the great protagonist of a general equilibrium view of money and financial markets. What emerged as the "new view" or Yale approach may thus be interpreted as a return, on a higher analytical level, to the classical tradition after the multiplier interlude.

Tobin never constructed an explicit optimizing model for banks and other financial intermediaries, but he used the asset demand and supply functions that would presumably result from such a model to develop an aggregative general equilibrium system for the financial sector (1971–75, vol. 1, chs. 13, 16–18, 20, 21; 1971–75, vol. 1, ch. 18 and 1982, vol. 3, ch. 1 are useful as expositions). Though this system was most influential as a framework of analysis, compatible with any logically coherent views, it also led Tobin to important substantive insights.

One of them concerned the macroeconomic effects of public debt. David Ricardo had argued that an increase in government debt, since it is matched by an increase in the present value of future tax liabilities, does not make the private sector wealthier. Nevertheless he did not regard debt and tax liabilities as economically equivalent. Tobin pointed out that one reason for this nonequivalence was the fact that public debt changes the *composition* of private wealth, making it, at unchanged present value, more liquid. In a sense, the government acts as a financial intermediary (Tobin 1971–75, vol. 1, ch. 5, also p. 2).

Another point concerned banks. Multiplier theory had assigned them a special role among financial intermediaries inasmuch as they could create money. This was then used as a justification for special legislation. Tobin argued that what appeared as a special role was due to imperfections in the markets for bank deposits and reserves, which in turn were largely caused by special legislation. The special role was the consequence of the legal restrictions and not their cause (Tobin 1971–75, vol. 1, ch. 16). In perfect credit markets the whole multiplier approach would lose its basis, as banks could borrow and lend any amount of funds at current interest rates.

A third specific contribution was the emphasis on the market price of investment goods relative to their replacement cost as the main link between monetary and fiscal policies and the demand for real capital goods (Tobin 1971–75, vol. 1, chs. 20, 18; 1982, vol. 3. chs. 1, 4). This relative price was soon given the name Tobin's q. Its value could differ from unity for extended periods because the planning and building of investments takes time. During this time it could be used to measure the incentives for the expansion or contraction of capital goods. The concept as such was not new; Walras had used it, and its ancestry leads back to classical economics. It had long been forgotten, however, and Tobin, together with Brainard, may be said to have led investment theory back to the classical tradition.

The last point to be mentioned related to the expansionary effect of open market purchases. Tobin pointed out that this effect is essentially due to the fact that the interest on central bank reserves is exogenously fixed, often at zero, whereas security yields can fluctuate. If security yields were exogenously fixed while interest rates on central bank deposits are market-determined, then open market purchases would have a contractionary effect (Tobin 1971–75, vol. 1, ch. 18). Tobin might have added, of course, that it is usually money that has a fixed interest rate (at zero) because it serves as a means of payment.

The third stage of Tobin's program was the extension of asset equilibrium to a growing economy. As early as 1955 (Tobin 1971–75, vol. 1, ch. 8) he used for this purpose a macroeconomic production function with smooth substitution between capital and labor. What emerged was later called the neoclassical growth model, though Tinbergen had used it long before. It differed from the growth models of Harrod and Domar by the flexibility with which the capital intensity could adjust to different propensities to save. The knife edge became a smooth hill.

In successive papers, Tobin elaborated the role of money in such a model (1971–75, vol. 1, chs. 8–10; 1982, vol. 3, ch. 9). The capital intensity of production, and thus per capita output, would depend not only on savings but also on the division of wealth between such capital goods and real cash balances. The latter, in turn, was influenced by the real yield on cash balances, measured by the rate of inflation. By a higher rate of monetary expansion, since it produces higher inflation and thus a lower demand for real balances, government policy can thus raise real output. This was far from being a complete welfare analysis of monetary expansion, to be sure, but it was one of various components of such an analysis. Inflation, even if it proceeds at a constant rate and is generally expected, has real effects, at least as long as no explicit interest is paid on cash balances.

Tobin became prominent as one of the intellectual defenders of the Keynesian faith. His strong political and social views inevitably involved him in controversy, and his moral indignation was easily aroused. It is important to note, therefore, that the results of his monetary research program are entirely independent of his Keynesian beliefs. They provided an analytical framework that can be used to advantage by economists of any political and doctrinal persuasion. In particular, his devastating satire of Kaldor's distribution theory (Tobin 1971–75, vol. 1, ch. 7) shows him as a convinced general equilibrium theorist.

Tobin was never interested in abstract mathematical theory devoid of operational implications. The best economists, he felt, have taken their subjects from the world around them. Arrow's contingent claims approach to general asset equilibrium may be theoretically more elegant, but Tobin's general equilibrium approach to monetary theory is eminently serviceable. While one is the thoroughbred, the other is the workhorse. In the field of monetary macroeconomics, Tobin made the leading contribution of the 1950s and 1960s. Its importance was acknowledged by the award of the John Bates Clark Medal in 1955, by numerous honorary degrees, and in 1981 by a Nobel Prize.

IN ONE RESPECT, the American Keynesians left the neoclassical synthesis incomplete. Their blind spot was secular inflation. Its basic monetary cause had dropped out of sight, and it was commonly attributed to "structural" factors, "inconsistent claims" or "cost inflation." Satisfactory employment was widely believed to be obtainable at the price of some creeping inflation, and it was assumed that the creep could be held at a low rate forever. Samuelson and Solow (Samuelson 1966–86, vol. 2, ch. 102) recommended the Phillips curve, purporting to express the trade-off between inflation and unemployment (Phillips 1958), as one of the basic macroeconomic policy instruments. The cure of inflation was sought in an incomes policy and not in monetary policy. This is where Friedman's contribution came in.

35
Kenneth Arrow

IN THE SECOND HALF of the twentieth century, the center of gravity in economics shifted from maroeconomics to microeconomics. From about 1920 until around 1950, the dominating problems concerned output and employment. Between 1950 and 1970, resource allocation again moved to center stage. At first, this shift was discernible only in advanced research, but later it became clearly visible in the bulk of scientific literature. No single economist contributed more to this shift than Kenneth J. Arrow.

Arrow did little work on positive economics, that is, on the creation and testing of hypotheses about the actual working of an economy. The invention of a production function with a constant elasticity of substitution (CES), simultaneously with Solow, is one of relatively few contributions of this nature (Arrow 1983–85, vol. 5, ch. 3). Arrow's main field, consistent with his background in mathematical programming, was normative economics. Something is usually optimized, be it an individual decision, the plan of a firm, a public investment project, a social choice, or the allocation of resources in general. Arrow is the modern representative of the great utilitarian tradition from Jeremy Bentham to John Stuart Mill, Alfred Marshall, Arthur Cecil Pigou, and farther on to the welfare economics of the 1930s.

It is characteristic for this tradition that an intellectual with high moral values and human concerns constructs a rational model of an ideal economy, confronts this ideal with the imperfect reality, and seeks ways and means for the state to correct the imperfections. Whether one likes or dislikes this utilitarian ideology is immaterial from the point of view of scientific achievement, just as in the opposite case of a libertarian ideology. What matters is that Arrow's utilitarian motivations led him to important contributions to economic theory.

Life

Kenneth J. Arrow was born in New York in 1921.[1] His parents had both come to the United States with their families as infants. In the 1920s his father's business prospered, and Arrow spent his childhood in a comfortable home with many good books. His intellectual capacity was recognized early; he was a voracious reader with a particular interest in history.

His father lost everything in the Depression, and the Arrows became very poor. It seems that this experience had a profound influence on Kenneth Arrow's social views. Risk and security became dominant concepts in his later work. After high school, he went to the City College of New York, mainly because it was free. His interests led him to mathematics and logics, but employment concerns caused him to add more applied fields such as statistics. At the end of his undergraduate work, he was awarded a medal for the highest grades in his class. In that summer of 1940 he earned money as an actuarial clerk with a small insurance company. The

1. The biographical material is from the introductory notes to Arrow 1983–85, from Breit and Spencer 1986, and from the introduction to Heller, Starr, and Starrett 1986.

concepts of moral hazard and adverse selection, with which he thus became familiar, were to play an important role in his work.

Since the employment prospects in high school teaching, fortunately for economic science, were bleak, Arrow went to Columbia University to study mathematical statistics under Harold Hotelling. But Hotelling's post was in the economics department, and his course in mathematical economics introduced Arrow to economics. John Hicks's *Value and Capital* became for him a challenge to complete and extend this general equilibrium vision of the economic system in its purest form (Arrow 1983–85, 2: 46). He still remained a statistician, however. From Harold Hotelling and Abraham Wald he learned to consider a random variable as a function of the underlying "states of nature." Statistical decision theory led him to the general problem of decision making under uncertainty. He also became acquainted with Wald's earlier papers on the existence of economic equilibrium, but Wald discouraged him from further work along these lines. John von Neumann's 1937 paper he found too far removed from "normal economic reasoning" (58). In 1941, Arrow obtained an M.A. in mathematics, but in economic theory Columbia had left him largely on his own.

The war delayed Arrow's further graduate work for several years. As a weather officer he developed a method to determine the optimal trajectory for airplanes, generalizing the available techniques from flat to spherical surfaces. This became not only his first published paper but also his first contact with recursive optimization, the central concept of his later work on capital and growth.

In 1946, Arrow returned to Columbia, and Hotelling, for doctoral work. In the following year he joined the Cowles Commission at the University of Chicago, which under the directorship of Jacob Marschak was then at the height of its creativity. Arrow was unsure of his vocation and originality, which may have had something to do with an abortive dissertation project inspired by *Value and Capital*. Mindful of job security, he had trained himself on the side as an actuary, and an insurance company offered him a job. Tjalling Koopmans convinced him, however, that "there was no music" in actuarial statistics. Thus Arrow continued his research. He also married a graduate student in economics at Chicago. The association with the newly formed Rand Corporation, which was then a center for mathematical programming and game theory, stimulated his interest in the logic of social choice. The result was *Social Choice and Individual Values* (Arrow 1951), which Columbia accepted as a doctoral dissertation.

In 1949, Arrow became an assistant professor in economics and statistics at Stanford University. In the following year he was already associate professor, and in 1953, at the age of thirty-two, he was appointed to a professorship. In 1957 the American Economic Association honored his brilliant early work with the John Bates Clark Medal. In 1962, when Walter

Heller, Kermit Gordon, and James Tobin were members of the Council of Economic Advisers, Arrow served on its research staff. As a visiting fellow at Churchill College, Cambridge, he began his collaboration with Frank Hahn.

In 1968, Arrow accepted a professorship at Harvard. Jointly with John R. Hicks, he was awarded the Nobel Prize in Economic Science in 1972. In 1979 he returned to Stanford as Joan Kenney Professor of Economics and also professor of operations research. There is virtually no honor available to an American economist that he has not received, yet he is liked for his unpretentiousness, kindness, and accessibility. He is admired for his lightning-fast mind, for the breadth of his interests and erudition, and for his ability to inspire and stimulate research. Though his main scientific contribution has been to the logical foundations of economic analysis, his motivation was the concern of an intellectual liberal for the efficiency of the competitive system, for social justice, and for the resulting role of government.

Works

Many of Arrow's important contributions were in the field of mathematical programming.[2] Of his contributions to economics proper only three were conceived as books. The first was *Social Choice and Individual Values* (Arrow 1951). Though it took, as Arrow reports, many months to write, the main theorems were worked out in about three weeks, and the impossibility theorem made Arrow famous virtually overnight. The second book, written jointly with Frank Hahn, is *General Competitive Analysis* (1971), a comprehensive exposition of the theory of an economy in perfect competition as it emerged from the set theory evolution of the 1950s. The third book, *Public Investment, the Rate of Return, and Optimal Fiscal Policy*, written jointly with Mordecai Kurz (1970), is a formal analysis of optimal public investment in the context of a Solow-type growth model with infinite horizon. The other books Arrow published are either large essays or collections of essays. His work thus exemplifies the decline of books in the transmission of advanced economic research in the course of the post–World War II period.[3]

Arrow's essays are now conveniently available in six volumes of *Collected Papers* (1983–85). They overwhelm not only by their scientific weight but also by their number and diversity. It is clearly impossible to describe them at all adequately. One group of papers, mainly in volume 1, leads from the axioms of social choice to problems of social values and justice.

---

2. Collections of such papers are Arrow, Karlin, and Scarf 1958; and Arrow, Hurwicz, and Uzawa 1958. The contributions that earned Arrow a Nobel Prize are surveyed in Weizsäcker 1972.

3. A bibliography of Arrow's publications can be found in Heller, Starr, and Starrett 1986, vol. 3.

It is the main source about Arrow's moral philosophy, and chapter 3, written in 1952, is an excellent nontechnical introduction into the impossibility theorem. Other papers, mainly in volume 5, are concerned with capital accumulation, production, and growth. The essays on general equilibrium in volume 2 include two introductory surveys, one written for the *International Encyclopedia of the Social Sciences*, the other the Nobel Prize Lecture. Volume 3 on individual choice includes the classic survey "Alternative Approaches to the Theory of Choice in Risk-Taking Situations" from 1951 and a more recent (and more mathematical) exposition of the same theory.

Together with competitive equilibrium, uncertainty indeed became one of the leitmotivs of Arrow's work. Thanks to his knowledge of statistics, he found an elegant way to incorporate risk into general equilibrium. The implications were pursued over a wide area of applied problems including insurance, health, securities, information, inventions, education, discrimination, environmental damage, exhaustible resources, property rights, and organizational structures. Some of these papers were more effective as closely reasoned surveys than as original analyses, but together they virtually created the economics of risk and information as a field of applied microeconomics. The following sections describe in more detail Arrow's major contributions to economics.

Social Choice

In connection with his first abortive dissertation project, Arrow reflected on the decision making of firms with many owners. Suppose a committee has to select one of three investment projects. The decision is by majority vote. In the first vote project B receives a majority over C. In the second vote A receives a majority over B. The chairman then rules that further voting is unnecessary because A is evidently preferred to C, too. In technical terms, he is convinced that social choice, like the choices of reasonable individuals, may safely be assumed to be transitive.

It occurred to Arrow that the chairman might have been wrong. Even in a committee of reasonable individuals, C might still have obtained a majority over A. Majority voting by individuals with transitive preferences may result in social preferences that are intransitive and thus irrational. Such cases can easily be constructed. Suppose the above committee consists of three members. Member X ranks projects in the sequence A, B, C; Y's ranking is B, C, A; and Z's is C, A, B. If everybody votes according to his preferences, the outcomes of the first two votes will be as described above, but the third vote would have revealed a majority for C over A. There would be deadlock. Arrow thought at that time that this paradox was well known, but though it had been mentioned by the Marquis de Condorcet in 1785 and the Australian E. J. Nanson in 1882, it had apparently received no attention until Duncan Black (1948) took up the prob-lem.[4] It became known as the voting paradox.

Arrow asked himself whether there was a way to make social choices that would avoid this paradox. If no further requirements are imposed, this is clearly possible. An example is a dictatorial procedure under which the committee simply decides according to the wishes of its chairman. Arrow thus formulated a series of minimal conditions that a democratic decision procedure should satisfy.[5] First, the decision procedure should be viable whatever the individual rankings might be; a procedure that works only, say, if there are no differences of opinion is clearly not very helpful. Second, if one individual raises the ranking of one alternative while all other rankings remain unchanged, the social ranking of that alternative should not thereby be degraded. The association between individual and social rankings should be positive. Third, if for a set of alternatives every individual has the same ranking, then this is also the social ranking. The social ranking within a set of alternatives is thus independent of "irrelevant" alternatives outside this set. Fourth, the social choice should not be imposed from the outside in the sense that it does not result from the individual rankings. Finally, the social change should not be dictatorial in the sense that it depends on the preferences of only one individual.

These requirements look reasonable enough. Arrow's contribution was the logical proof that no conceivable decision procedure can satisfy all of them and at the same time guarantee the transitivity of social choices for three or more alternatives. This became known as Arrow's impossibil-ity theorem. The proof was a brilliant feat of deductive logic, which be-came the point of departure for a rapidly expanding literature on social choice.

In itself, Arrow's theorem was purely negative. From the point of view of democratic decision making, it was clearly important to examine the rationality of existing decision procedures and possibly construct better ones. Aside from a recent essay on the evaluation of corporate projects (Arrow and Raynaud 1986), Arrow did not participate in this work. His mind became focused on problems of Pareto optimality, where no collective choices have to be made. Beyond the field of social choice, Arrow's analysis was influential in the application of set theory to economic problems. It initiated a period in which set theory rapidly replaced differential calculus as the favorite tool of mathematical economics. In addition, it demon-strated how axiomatic methods, as exemplified by John von Neumann and Oskar Morgenstern, can be used to make social theories rigorous.

4. For a history of the problem see Black 1958.
5. The following summary follows Arrow's nontechnical exposition in his 1952 paper, originally written in French, and published in English as vol. 1, ch. 3, of the *Collected Papers*.

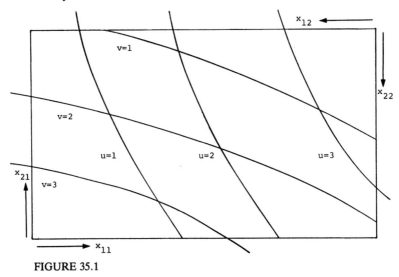

FIGURE 35.1

The Welfare Theorems

Arrow's contribution to welfare theory was directly inspired by the discussion about the criteria for Pareto optimality in the late 1930s and early 1940s. Hotelling had made an important contribution to that debate, and he was Arrow's teacher. The criteria were derived by calculus techniques as first-order conditions for internal maxima. During a debate on rent control, it occurred to Arrow that most people buy only one type of housing, having zero demand for all others. If different types of housing are regarded as different commodities, consumer budgets thus represent corner solutions for which the marginal conditions do not apply.

The problem is illustrated for two individuals and two goods in the Edgeworth box of figure 35.1. The dimensions of the box measure the aggregate supplies, $X_1 = x_{11} + x_{12}$ and $X_2 = x_{21} + x_{22}$. A's preferences are described by the indifference curves $u = 1$, 2, and so on, with origin in the southwest corner. B's preferences, described by $v = 1$, 2, and so on, have their origin in the northeast corner. (Note that A's indifference curves do not end at B's intercepts, and vice versa.) As the indifference curves are drawn, they are nowhere tangent to each other. The contract curve runs along the eastern and southern border of the box, and at the Pareto optimal points the marginal rates of substitution are unequal. This raised the question whether competitive prices still guarantee Pareto optimality in such a case. Calculus clearly did not provide the answer.

At the Rand Corporation, Arrow had become acquainted with the theory of games of von Neumann and Morgenstern and thus with convex sets and separating hyperplanes. In connection with a seminar paper by Paul Samuelson, Arrow realized that the theory of convex sets could provide an answer to the above question. The mathematical concepts that had been so fruitful in the analysis of linear models might also be turned to good use for nonlinear systems. The result was his 1951 paper "An Extension of the Basic Theorems of Classical Welfare Economics" (Arrow 1983–85, vol. 2, ch. 2). The local optimality criteria were replaced by global criteria. The main result was that the optimality properties of competitive prices survive even if the marginal conditions fail. Very similar results were independently derived and published at about the same time by Gerard Debreu (1983, ch. 1).[6]

While Arrow's proofs relate to any number of persons and commodities and also include satiation and negative goods, the main line of the argument can be described in terms of the two by two case with positive utilities for all goods. For a single individual, say, Robinson Crusoe, the optimization problem is depicted in figure 35.2 The left-hand panel illustrates the case of an interior optimum, and the right-hand panel represents the corner solution. The indifference curves are convex downward, whereas the transformation (or production possibility) curve is convex upward. These are the essential convexity properties. Arrow's theorem 1 states that there is a unique optimal point, x^*, on the transformation curve.

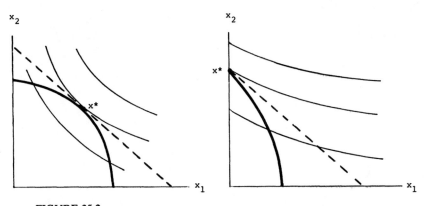

FIGURE 35.2

6. The production possibilities of an economy can be described by a convex transformation frontier in terms of physical quantities. Debreu's problem was to construct from individual utility functions a "required consumption frontier" (the term is not Debreu's) for the whole economy that is similarly in terms of physical quantities. He solved it by determining the minimal quantities of commodities that are required to keep each individual at some prescribed utility level (where minimal means that no quantity can be further reduced without increasing another). If the individual indifference curves are convex, so is the required consumption frontier. The procedure can be repeated for other sets of preassigned utilities. The efficiency of resource utilization can be judged by confronting the two frontiers.

The crucial point is that it is possible to draw a straight line through x^* in such a way that the indifference curve through x^* is wholly on one side and the transformation curve wholly on the other. The line thus "separates" the two curves. Its slope can be interpreted as a relative price. If Robinson as producer is exposed to this price, he maximizes his income by producing commodity bundle x^*. If he is exposed to the same price in his capacity as a consumer, he uses his income to buy commodity bundle x^*, thereby maximizing his utility.

This leads to Arrow's theorem 2. If there are prices, so it states, that in this manner equalize production and consumption, then production is optimal in the sense that it maximizes utility. The counterpart is theorem 3. It says that for any optimal point there is a price system through which it can be reached.

In itself, a price system for Robinson Crusoe is not very interesting. Its interest arises from the fact that an economy made up of many firms and individuals can be reduced to a similar model, as is illustrated in figure 35.3. Suppose, for example, there is one other individual, Friday. Suppose further, the two are actually at a Pareto optimal point. In the left-hand panel of figure 35.3, this point is denoted by X^* on the transformation curve of the island economy, with Robinson consuming bundles x_1^* and Friday x_2^*. Could not Robinson perhaps do better than at X^* without Friday being worse off? Friday not being worse off means that in the right-hand panel he does not move below his indifference curve $\bar{v}$. Robinson thus has to reserve for him (at least) the quantities x_{12} and x_{22} found along this curve. By turning the right-hand panel upside down and placing its

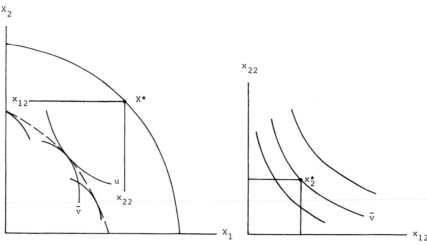

FIGURE 35.3

488

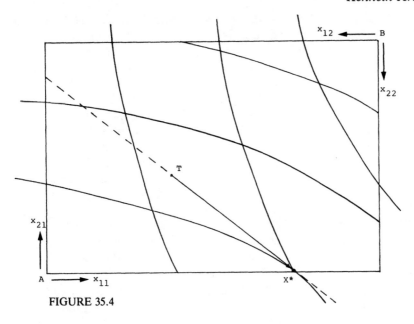

FIGURE 35.4

origin in the left-hand panel on point X^*, one can trace out the bundles left for Robinson. The same can be done for other points along the collective transformation curve. The envelope of these bundles, drawn as a broken line, is the transformation curve for Robinson alone.

With this construction, one possesses for Robinson as part of the economy exactly the same elements that were previously used for Robinson in isolation. A transformation curve can be contrasted with indifference curves. Arrow is able to prove that there is again a price system under which at point X^* Robinson minimizes his expenditures for a given utility level and the value of output is maximized. Exactly the same analysis can be applied to Friday, and it turns out that the relevant price systems are the same for both (theorem 4). This leads to the fundamental welfare theorems 5 and 6. If prices equate supply and demand for all commodities, the allocation is Pareto optimal, and for every Pareto optimal allocation there is a system of prices for which the value of output is a maximum and every individual obtains the highest possible satisfaction out of his income. In the words of Dorfman, Samuelson, and Solow, "Every competitive equilibrium is a Pareto-optimum; and every Pareto-optimum is a competitive equilibrium" (1958, 410).

How Arrow's approach handles corner solutions is finally illustrated in figure 35.4. The transformation curve is replaced by a given endowment of goods as denoted by T. At the relative price indicated by the downward-sloping broken line, individual B finds it optimal to sell commodity 1 and buy commodity 2 as indicated by the solid arrow. For B, the optimum at X^* is indeed a point of tangency; he is not in a corner. A finds it optimal to sell what B buys and vice versa. His trading is constrained, however, by the fact that at X^* he is running out of commodity 2.

Arrow thus accomplished what he set out to do, namely to extend the basic welfare propositions to corner solutions. Together with Debreu and others around the same time, he thereby demonstrated that the theory of convex sets, which had been used with so much success for linear models, was a powerful tool also in the analysis of Walrasian general equilibrium models with their nonlinear production and utility functions.

Arrow-Debreu Equilibrium

By 1950, largely under the influence of the *Theory of Games* (von Neumann and Morgenstern 1947), convexity and duality were very much on the minds of mathematical economists. Nevertheless, the only economic models for which the existence of an equilibrium had been proved were those of Wald and von Neumann, the first for an economically unappealing model, the other for a growth model without final consumption. In *Value and Capital*, though it introduced English-reading theorists to general equilibrium, Hicks never bothered about existence proofs and negative prices. Indeed, he sometimes expressed himself as if he believed that the counting of equations and variables is enough (Hicks 1939, 59). Morgenstern (1941), then learning about these things from von Neumann, chided Hicks mercilessly (and unfairly) for his mathematical complacency.

It remained for Arrow, who admired Hicks, and Debreu (Arrow 1983–85, vol. 2, ch. 4) to prove the existence of a competitive equilibrium for a Walrasian general equilibrium model. J. F. Nash's existence proof for an n-person game, mentioned above in the chapter on von Neumann, showed the way. The result was the 1954 Arrow-Debreu model of general equilibrium, the neatest and most compact model of an economy since Cantillon's *Tableau Economique* in terms of land, and vastly richer and more general.[7]

Gerard Debreu, born in Calais in 1921, studied mathematics and physics. As a lecturer in mathematics, he was inspired to work on problems of economic equilibrium by Maurice Allais. After several years as a research associate at the Centre National de la Recherche Scientifique in Paris and as a Rockefeller Fellow, he joined the Cowles Commission in Chicago in 1950. In 1955 he became an associate professor at Yale, and in 1962, after a year at the Center of Advanced Study in the Behavioral Sciences in

---

7. An existence proof of a somewhat different kind was published earlier in the same year by Lionel McKenzie (1954).

Stanford, he went to the University of California at Berkeley, first as a professor of economics, later also as a professor of mathematics. Though his abstract concepts are accessible only to people with similarly logical minds, he is known as an inspiring teacher and brilliant expositor.

Debreu's dissertation, *Theory of Value* (1959), has the fitting subtitle *An Axiomatic Analysis of Economic Equilibrium*. It became the bible of the new mathematical economics based on topology. Twenty papers are collected in Debreu 1983 with a useful introduction by Werner Hildenbrand. Chapter 19, "Regular Differentiable Economies," reprinted from the *American Economic Review* (1976), conveys an intuitive impression of Debreu's style of work. The importance of this work was recognized by the award of a Nobel Prize in 1983.

The principal results of Debreu's topological approach relate to the existence and optimality of competitive equilibrium. In this field they give the traditional propositions a rigor and aesthetic lucidity never attained before. Hildenbrand compared general equilibrium theory to a gothic cathedral of which Léon Walras and Vilfredo Pareto were the architects and Debreu the master builder. This may indeed be an apt comparison, but besides cathedrals, which are great to admire and worship in, the community of economists also needs factories and machinery, ugly as they might look, to produce new insights. Surely general equilibrium theorists hope that what today is admired as a cathedral will eventually turn out to be an efficient factory.

Arrow and Debreu specified four assumptions under which their existence proof was supposed to hold, namely:

1. Firms transform inputs into outputs according to a technology that yields a convex transformation curve (or surface); increasing returns to scale are excluded.
2. Households supply labor services and consume positive amounts of commodities.
3. Household choices are guided by utility functions with convex indifference curves (or, more generally, surfaces).
4. Households are endowed with a positive amount of every commodity available for trading in the market, and they also possess claims to certain shares of profits.

These assumptions are paraphrased here in a highly simplified and nonrigorous way. An important part of Arrow's and Debreu's work consisted in making them mathematically precise. The first part of assumption 4 is clearly unrealistic. Its purpose can be explained by considering the extreme case of a household endowed with only one commodity. As long as it can be exchanged for other commodities at a positive price, household demand will probably fall short of the endowment and certainly not exceed it. It may turn out, however, that the market price of that commodity is zero. In this case household demand for this free good may jump to any amount, however large. Assumption 4 rules out such discontinuities at zero prices.

For an economic system described by these assumptions, Arrow and Debreu undertook to prove the existence of a competitive equilibrium. This concept was defined by the following conditions, again in a non-mathematical formulation:

1. Firms maximize profits for the given market prices.
2. Households maximize utility for given market prices and profit shares.
3. There are no negative prices.
4. If some commodity is in excess supply, its price is zero.

The mathematical analysis of these assumptions and conditions, with the aid of sophisticated topology, enabled Arrow and Debreu to prove their theorem 1: for any economic system satisfying assumptions 1–4 there is a competitive equilibrium.

Arrow and Debreu, troubled by the lack of realism of assumption 4, proceeded to replace it by a weaker one. It says essentially that each household is endowed with at least one type of productive labor. At the price of adding three further assumptions, they were then able to prove their theorem 2, which states the existence of a competitive equilibrium under these modified assumptions.

From the point of view of economic substance, the existence proofs of the early 1950s were far from revolutionary. They essentially confirmed the intuition of general equilibrium theorists from Walras and Pareto to Hicks and Samuelson. The economic systems they had in mind, more or less precisely, indeed have an equilibrium solution. By merely counting the number of equations and variables (knowing full well that this does not guarantee a solution), they had not missed a really essential point.

From the point of view of analytical rigor, however, those existence papers were indeed revolutionary. In this respect they established entirely new standards, which could be met only by economists with much better mathematical ability and training than before. Up to that time the active use of a little calculus made one a mathematical economist. After that time mathematical economics became the preserve of those with the competence of a professional mathematician. In many respects, this was clearly a big step forward. It came at a price, though. People with the mind and training of a mathematician are somewhat less likely to have a broad interest in social problems, an understanding of historical processes, and innovative economic ideas. As a consequence, the increase in mathematical competence was not associated with a marked acceleration in the progress of economic insight. The new mills could grind the corn more and more finely, but they did not process more grist.

In retrospect the existence problem perhaps does not look quite as important as it appeared in the early 1950s. If for some economic system a solution cannot be proved to exist, this does not imply that a solution cannot, in fact, exist or that the system is inconsistent. It would be unsettling if it were otherwise, because existence proofs are so far available only for rather rarefied models. Even commonplace phenomena such as fixed costs, transfer costs, and money present obstacles that have not yet been completely surmounted. In addition, the new techniques were not well suited to answer one important type of question for which calculus had been particularly useful, namely comparative-static questions about the effects of small changes in economic conditions.

Contingent Claims and Insurance

The theory of general equilibrium as developed from Walras to Hicks assumed that expectations about the future are held with certainty. The same theorists knew perfectly well, of course, that human expectations tend to be more or less uncertain, but they had not found a way to express this manifest fact in their theoretical models. Such a way was shown by Arrow in the form of his contingent claims approach (1983–85, vol. 2, ch. 3).

Imagine that a farmer is uncertain about his harvest yield. This can be reformulated by saying that he is actually quite certain about the yield for a given kind of weather, but he is uncertain about the weather, which is called the state of nature. Besides production, the state of nature may also affect utility in consumption inasmuch as beer, for example, tends to be more highly esteemed in hot weather.

Suppose now there are two subsistence farmers, Robinson and Friday. Imagine, for simplicity, that they know that some disaster will destroy one of the two crops, but they do not know which one. This information can be summarized in an Edgeworth box, but with the crucial modification that both axes relate to the same commodity, say corn, but to different states of nature (see figure 35.5). Quantities of corn if Robinson is struck by disaster are measured horizontally. The corresponding quantities if disaster strikes Friday are measured vertically. Robinson's quantities are measured from the southwest corner and Friday's from the northeast corner. Point Q indicates what harvest each expects under the two states of nature.

At this point the other core component of modern uncertainty economics comes into play, namely the expected utility concept as developed by von Neumann and Morgenstern. It implies, as Arrow showed, that an individual's attitude toward risk can be represented by a set of indifference curves, as illustrated by I_R and I_F. As stated in Arrow's theorem 3, this is true provided the individual is risk averse in the sense that he always prefers a sure thing to a gamble of equal present value. Following Bernoulli and von Neumann-Morgenstern, this is identified with a declining marginal utility of income. If utility as a function of income is $u(y)$, then $u'(y)>0$ and $u''(y)<0$.

In another paper, "The Theory of Risk Aversion" (1983–85, vol. 3, ch. 9), Arrow showed how risk aversion can be measured. Simply to mea-

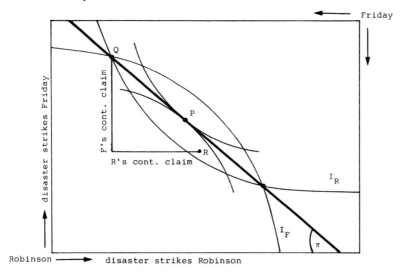

FIGURE 35.5

sure it by $u''(y)$ would not do, because a multiplication of all utilities by the same number should not change risk aversion. Arrow thus defined two measures that satisfy this requirement, namely absolute risk aversion, $-u''(y)/u'(y)$, and relative risk aversion, $-[u''(y)/u'/y)]y$. The latter is the income elasticity of the marginal utility of income. Each of these concepts, useful in different contexts, indicates to what extent the odds have to be better than fair in order to induce an individual to accept a bet of a certain size, measured either as an absolute amount or as a percentage of income.

Though the indifference curves for risky situations look qualitatively similar to ordinary indifference curves, they have a fundamentally different meaning, relating not to commodities but to the preference for different types of gambles. If the crop prospects are somehow reduced in the case of good weather, then Robinson, if he is to feel equally happy as before, has to be compensated by a better prospect in the case of disaster. It follows that the indifference curves are falling. In addition, if the crop prospects under good weather conditions are gradually reduced by equal amounts, compensation requires a progressively larger improvement in the case of disaster. This implies that the indifference curves are convex to the origin.

As the two indifference curves through Q indicate, there are other allocations of risk, such as R, which both Robinson and Friday would prefer. They are found in the lens-shaped area between the curves. The essential point is that every such point can be reached by an exchange of contingent claims. Robinson acquires a claim to Friday's crop in the amount of the horizontal distance between R and Q, contingent on his being struck by disaster. In exchange he offers Friday a claim on Robinson's crop in the amount of the vertical distance between the two points, contingent on Friday's being struck by disaster.

There are certain Pareto optimal points on the graph, such as P, in which no further improvements are simultaneously possible for both parties. If the initial point is Q, if contingent claims are offered at the relative price π, and if Robinson and Friday are each representative of a large group of identical individuals, then perfect competition in the market for contingent claims will result in market equilibrium at P. Perfect competition results in a Pareto optimal allocation of risk. Arrow's theorem 1 says that, by varying the initial point Q, any Pareto optimal allocation of risk bearing can be realized by perfectly competitive markets for contingent commodity claims. Though the present review of this theorem is restricted to two persons, two states, and one commodity, Arrow proved it directly for any number of persons, states, and goods.

The preceding argument required that there be barter markets for contingent claims in which, for example, water in the case of a drought is bartered against an automobile in the case of a collision. In reality there are no such markets. In a money economy their place is taken by contingent money claims, appearing in the form either of insurance or of securities. In automobile insurance, for example, the insured acquires a money claim against the insurance company contingent on his car being damaged in a collision. Common stocks, Arrow pointed out, can be similarly interpreted as money claims on a firm contingent on its profit. For the purpose of his analysis, Arrow defines a security simply as a claim to \$1 contingent on a certain state of nature. He is then able to prove his theorem 2 to the effect that perfect competition in the markets for commodities and such securities achieves an optimal allocation of risk bearing even in the absence of contingent barter markets.

With this conceptualization of contingent claims, Arrow brought financial markets, risk, and insurance within the purview of general equilibrium analysis, thereby providing the key for rapid further developments in these fields.

Health Economics

In about half a dozen papers, Arrow applied his theory of contingent claims and insurance to health economics. It was an impressive demonstration of the theory's fruitfulness. The basic paper, published in 1963, is "Uncertainty and the Welfare Economics of Medical Care" (Arrow 1983–85, vol. 6, ch. 3). Planned as a theoretical survey of health economics, it became the starting point of a new understanding of health economics in the context of uncertainty. Economists had often discussed health problems before. To mention just two examples, Milton Friedman and Simon Kuznets (1945) investigated the effect of entry restrictions on physicians' incomes, and Reuben Kessel (1958) analyzed price discrimination in medicine. Arrow now provided an integrated framework. Its effect was enhanced by the fact that the paper, except for the appendix, was entirely nonmathematical and accessible to noneconomists.

The basic theme is the sources of market failure in the provision of health services. Arrow's ideal is a perfectly competitive market, resulting in a Pareto optimal allocation of resources. This ideal is confronted with the actual condition in the health sector. The discrepancies are regarded as making a prima facie case for policy measures. The Pigou-Lerner tradition of welfare theory is extended to health economics.

Some sources of inefficiencies in the health sector are clearly no different from other industries. For example, contagious diseases create external costs that are similar, in principle, to other externalities, and hospitals may be subject to increasing returns. Arrow identified uncertainty as the source of the specific problems of the health industry. He held "that virtually all the special features of this industry in fact stem from the prevalence of uncertainty" (Arrow 1983–85, vol. 6, ch. 3, p. 21). More exactly, the source was not uncertainty itself but a series of specific difficulties in coping with it. Arrow had shown that under perfect competition uncertainty would be optimally allocated by markets for contingent claims. The problem was, he argued, that in the case of health services these markets are far from working perfectly.

First, Arrow noted, many health risks are not marketable; there are no insurance markets for them. The reason is that the state of nature, on which a given claim should ideally depend, is hard to define, and it is difficult to separate it from the individual's own actions. Most insurance contracts, therefore, make payments not contingent on states of nature but on expenses, and this is something entirely different. As a consequence, Arrow concludes, many health risks are not insured though insurance would be in everybody's interest. One flaw of this argument, not noted by Arrow, is that it disregards transactions and contract costs. If the definition, distinction, and specification of the relevant states of nature is in itself costly, then the nonexistence of many contingent claims markets may be economically justified. Surely the fact that many commodities (say, grades of gasoline) are not produced is not, in itself, a symptom of inefficiency.

A second major source of market failure is moral hazard. Besides depending on the state of nature, health expenses also depend on the behavior and demands of the patient and the physician. To the extent that these expenses are covered by insurance, they become for the patient external costs, with the usual consequence of an inefficiently high demand for health services. Physicians could conceivably exert a certain control, but since they are supposed to be the trustees of their patients' interests, they may, in fact, rather pull in the other direction.

496

A third basic source of market failure is asymmetrical information and the consequent adverse selection of risks. Suppose a patient knows more about his health than the insurance company. At any given level of premiums, the bad risks will then take out more insurance than the good risks. As a consequence, the health costs of the insured will be higher, on average, than those of the whole population. This forces the insurance company to raise the premiums, which drives out more good risks, and so on. As a result, many good risks will remain uninsured. The same phenomenon (though not noted by Arrow) can occur with physicians' liability insurance against malpractice suits; it may actually cause conscientious physicians to close their practices. Arrow shows (and proves mathematically) that the optimal response to the administrative costs of the insurance company is a fixed deductible. The appropriate countermeasure against moral hazard is coinsurance.

Arrow did not make policy prescriptions. He wanted to provide a conceptual basis from which others could continue the work. He succeeded admirably, providing the outline of a new discipline of health economics and, more generally, of an economics of information.

Place in the History of Economics

Those who believe that the history of science is a succession of crises and revolutions may find it difficult to interpret Arrow's role in it. None of his numerous seminal contributions involved a revolutionary break with the past. None of them, to the extent this can be judged by the end of the 1980s, was too far ahead of its time to be immediately recognized as important. There were no giant leaps forward. Arrow's particular genius was for developing fundamental conceptual frameworks just when the time and the state of science were ripe for them.

Nevertheless, Arrow became the embodiment of a new stage in the history of economic theory. For about a century, from Augustin Cournot in 1838 to John Hicks in 1939, the progress of economics was accompanied by the progressive absorption of differential calculus. Von Neumann then demonstrated the scientific potential of set theory and topology. In the hands of Arrow and Debreu these mathematical tools, then already widely used in mathematical programming, conquered economic theory. Graduate students no longer worried about bordered Hessian determinants but about fixed point theorems and convexity. Old economic insights were not thereby proved false, but they could be derived more generally and rigorously, and new insights became possible.

Most of the new insights were inevitably of a somewhat esoteric nature. Few of them filtered down to undergraduate textbooks, and even fewer can be explained to the "intelligent layman." Arrow is not even an economist's economist, but an economist's economist's economist, and Debreu is better described as a mathematician's economist. And yet, their work had a decisive influence on the type of talents that are attracted to graduate work in economics, on the type of economics they are taught, and thus on the shape of economic science in the closing decades of the twentieth century.

36
Monetary Macroeconomics: Policy Rules

THE AMERICAN Keynesians of the neoclassical synthesis tended to regard economic policy as a sequence of discrete measures each of which was historically unique. This was the perspective from which they advocated the Phillips curve as an instrument of monetary policy. However, if similar measures are taken routinely under similar circumstances, they begin to be expected in advance, which in turn will often change their effect. As seemingly noninflationary growth degenerated into stagflation in the course of the 1960s, this aspect, long known but theoretically unexplored, became the focus of macroeconomic attention. The relevant question, it now appeared, was not the effect of individual policy measures but the effect of changes in policy rules.

Milton Friedman

An early champion of rules was Milton Friedman. He was born in Brooklyn, New York, in 1912.[1] His parents had been poor immigrants from Carpatho-Ruthenia. Milton and his three sisters grew up in Rahway, New Jersey, where his parents earned a modest living as merchants. His father died when he was a senior in high school, but a state scholarship permitted him to go to Rutgers College, which then was a small private school. A high school teacher had taught him to love mathematics, and, like Kenneth Arrow about a decade later, he prepared for a career as an insurance actuary. At the same time, economics courses by Arthur F. Burns, later Federal Reserve chairman, and Homer Jones, later research director of the Federal Reserve Bank of Saint Louis, aroused his interest in economics. Eventually he majored in both fields.

Upon graduation in 1932, influenced partly by his teachers and partly by the Depression, Friedman chose a tuition fellowship in economics at Chicago over one in applied mathematics at Brown University. He described Jacob Viner's first-year graduate course in economics as the greatest intellectual experience of his life. One of his classmates was Rose Director, who later became his wife, his lifelong collaborator, and mother of his two children.

---

1. The biographical data are mainly from Breit and Spencer 1986, Butler 1985, and *Current Biography* 1969.

For his second year of graduate work, Friedman received a fellowship from Columbia University. There he learned mathematical statistics from Harold Hotelling, while Wesley C. Mitchell introduced him to institutionalism and empirical business cycle research. In his third year, he returned to Chicago as a research assistant of Henry Schultz.

From 1935 to 1943, Friedman worked in Washington, D.C., and New York as an economist for the National Resources Committee, for the National Bureau of Economic Research, and for the Treasury Department, and he also lectured part-time at Columbia. He then joined the War Research Division of Columbia University for two years of applied statistical work, and in 1945 he became an associate professor at the University of Minnesota. His dissertation had essentially been completed before the war, but a controversial finding about the effect of restrictive practices on physicians' income caused a delay. Columbia finally awarded him a Ph.D. in 1946.

In the same year, Friedman moved to Chicago, where he became a full professor in 1948 and eventually Paul Snowden Russell Distinguished Service Professor. Together with his friend George Stigler, he created and personified the spirit of what came to be called the Chicago school.[2] In 1951 he received the John Bates Clark Medal, and in 1976 he was awarded a Nobel Prize "for his achievements in the fields of consumption analysis, monetary history and theory, and for his demonstration of the complexity of stabilization policy." Since 1977 Friedman has been a senior research fellow in the conservative Hoover Institution, located in Stanford, and upon his retirement from Chicago in 1982, he and his wife moved to San Francisco.

In the second part of his life, Friedman increasingly expanded his audience from the seminar room to the public arena. Popular books established him, together with his wife, as the leading creator of an economic program in the spirit of Adam Smith (Friedman 1962, Friedman and Friedman 1980, 1984). Friedman, with good historical reasons, called this spirit radical liberal. However, since the adjective *liberal* had in the United States been appropriated by the New Dealers, his ideas, though proposing change rather than conservation, were commonly labeled conservative. Barry Goldwater as a presidential candidate and Republican Presidents Nixon, Ford, and Reagan all sought Friedman's advice, and Nixon also made him a member of the President's Commission for an All-Volunteer Army. Regular columns in *Newsweek* from 1966 to 1984 (Friedman 1975, 1983) and a ten-part television series made his name a household word around the world, known probably to more people than that of any economist

---

2. Don Patinkin (1981) has rightly insisted that this distinctive spirit was not part of the older Chicago tradition.

who had ever lived with the exception of Karl Marx. He became an oracle for millions and was execrated by millions.

Since economic policies and ideologies do not belong to the subject matter of this book, the description of Friedman's program must be brief. Its main thrust is the reduction in the power of the state. Rules should take the place of discretionary decisions. In particular, Friedman postulates the abolition of industrial regulation, security and exchange controls, farm price supports, minimum wages, public schools, national parks, compulsory military service, corporate income taxes, progression of income taxes, fractional reserve banking, fixed exchange rates, import duties, the Federal Reserve System, price and rent controls, interest regulation, licensing of physicians, and social security in its present form.

On the other hand, Friedman advocates a vigorous antitrust policy, state support of education by vouchers redeemable at private schools, legalization of marijuana and heroin, indexation of wages, prices, and tax schedules, the maintenance of government control over the money supply, and a proportional income tax. For the relief of the poor he launched the idea of a negative income tax, later taken over by his political opponents. He believes taxes should be reduced even at the risk of large deficits, because such deficits exert pressure for a reduction of government expenditures.

To say that some of these postulates are controversial would be an understatement. If they were not, Friedman would not bother to propose them. Some of them may be considered unwise even by people who generally share his social convictions. However, most of his adversaries agree with his admirers that he appeals to reason and not to passion, that his authority is evidence and not dogma, and that he is effective in making his points. While contentious and divisive, he is cheerful and personally kind. His judgment of persons and political situations may sometimes have failed him, but he always had the courage of his principles.

The subject matter of this section is Friedman's contribution to economic science. His early contributions were in statistics, where he developed an important significance test for ranked data (Friedman 1937). His dissertation, grown out of his collaboration with Simon Kuznets, analyzed the incomes from independent professional practice (Friedman and Kuznets 1945). It already introduces the distinction between permanent and transitory components of income, which became the key to the *Theory of the Consumption Function* (Friedman 1957). Early econometric efforts had related annual consumption to annual income. Kuznets then observed that the average propensity to consume, contrary to John Maynard Keynes's postulate, does not decline with rising income (Kuznets 1952). Friedman now proposed to explain what people regard as their permanent consumption by what they regard as their permanent income. The transitory components were assumed to have no significant relationship with the permanent components or among themselves. This was a brilliant and persuasive piece of econometric detective work, and the concept of permanent income foreshadowed the rational expectations of the following generation. However, Franco Modigliani's life cycle hypothesis had actually accomplished about the same, and in some respects more, three years earlier.

An essay on the "Methodology of Positive Economics" (Friedman 1953) advanced the proposition that it is futile to evaluate the realism of the assumptions on which an economic theory is built. The furious controversy it provoked illustrates the old wisdom that economists should be judged by what they do and not by what they say they do (or ought to do). Friedman was certainly right in insisting that a hypothesis must be tested by its implications. It is also true that a hypothesis is usually valuable precisely because it promises to be valid outside the assumptions from which it was derived. However, whether a hypothesis is a promising candidate for testing still depends, in part, on the perceived realism of its assumptions. The implications of the assumption that the moon consists of green cheese hardly invite testing.

A more tangible contribution was Friedman's effort, together with the statistician Leonard Savage, to derive the implications of the von Neumann–Morgenstern cardinal utility function for risky choices (Friedman and Savage 1948). Von Neumann and Morgenstern had assumed that the marginal utility of income is diminishing, as illustrated in the left-hand panel of figure 36.1. If an individual maximizes expected utility, he will always prefer a sure thing, say income I^* with utility A, to an equal chance of winning either I_1 or I_2 with associated utility B. As a consequence, he will be willing to pay for insurance.

However, some individuals like to gamble, and they are thus willing to pay for lottery tickets. This can be rationalized by assuming that their marginal utilities are increasing, as illustrated in the center panel of figure 36.1. In this case, an equal chance of winning I_1 or I_2 has utility B, which exceeds the utility A of the riskless outcome I^*. Furthermore, some individuals buy both insurance and lottery tickets. In such cases, Friedman and Savage hypothesized, their utility function must be S-shaped, as described in the right-hand panel of figure 36.1, so that, depending on the odds offered, both cases can occur.

In the course of the 1950s, Friedman's research became increasingly focused on money. For the difficult problems of monetary microeconomics he had little interest, though. The advancement of the pure theory of money and financial intermediation he left to others.[3] His field was monetary

---

3. In discussing the "optimum quantity of money" (Friedman 1969, ch. 1), Friedman observed, as did Samuelson, that there tends to be a discrepancy between the private marginal cost of holding real cash balances, which is equal to the rate of interest, and its social marginal

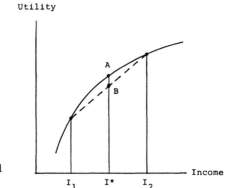

FIGURE 36.1

macroeconomics. In particular, he made himself the champion of the quantity theory of money. For the short term, however, his concept of the quantity theory differed from that of Keynes more in terminology than in substance. Whereas the genuine quantity theory is a long-run theory of the price level, Friedman reinterpreted it as either a quasi-Keynesian theory of the demand for money (Friedman 1969, ch. 2) or a short-run theory of nominal incomes (Gordon 1974). In both respects his theoretical analysis fell short of what had already been achieved by the neoclassical synthesis. Despite repeated efforts, Friedman was never able to articulate the theoretical model that generates his specific conclusions.

Friedman's real contribution concerned the practical operation of monetary policy (most of it is found in Friedman 1948, 1960, and, particularly, 1969). First, he insisted that "money matters" for macroeconomic fluctuations. In this respect, the American Keynesians of the neoclassical synthesis had no disagreement, and the point was less controversial than Friedman made it sound. It is true, however, that the "liquidity trap" Keynesians had all but forgotten about money and a reminder of its power was in order.

Second, Friedman argued that monetary policy affects output and prices with a long and variable lag. Again, this was quite compatible with the neoclassical synthesis, but Friedman's contributions stimulated empirical research in this field and had considerable influence on macroeconometric model building, particularly by Modigliani. However, Friedman's long and variable lags are hard to reconcile with his insistence on the relative constancy and predictability of the velocity of money.

Third, Friedman concluded that, in view of the very imperfect predictability of these lags, discretionary monetary policy can hardly do better

---

cost, which is virtually zero. As a consequence, the level of real balances may be inefficiently low.

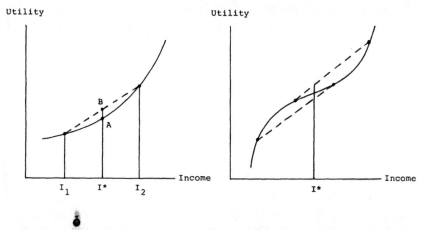

than a fixed rule to expand the money supply by a constant annual percentage, say 4 percent.[4] At this point he indeed parted company with the leading Keynesians who relied on monetary policy as a potentially effective stabilization tool. It was Friedman's deep conviction that misguided monetary policy had done more to destabilize the economy than enlightened monetary policy had ever done to stabilize it. To demonstrate its truth, he and Anna Schwartz wrote their massive *Monetary History of the United States, 1867–1960* (1963), supported by supplementary volumes on monetary statistics (Friedman and Schwartz 1970) and on monetary trends in the United States and the United Kingdom (Friedman and Schwartz 1982). In particular, Friedman argued, the Great Depression was due not to the ineffectiveness of expansionary monetary policies but to the effectiveness of monetary contraction (Friedman and Schwartz 1965).

The fractional reserve banking system, however, is regarded by Friedman as potentially unstable, because changes in risks and expectations can result in cumulative expansions or contractions of money creation by banks. To eliminate this source of instability, Friedman proposed bank reserves in the full amount of demand deposits. In any case, what should grow at a constant rate is not simply the money created by the central bank but the money in the hands of the public. If the commercial banks contract their money supply to the public, the central bank should automatically engage in a compensating expansion of its own money supply.

In retrospect, many of Friedman's contributions on short-run monetary policy appear to be presented in an unnecessarily controversial light. Overall, the range of consensus was quite large. This was not so with respect to secular inflation. According to the quantity theory, long-run inflation is, as Friedman pointedly put it, "always and everywhere a mon-

---

4. It should be noted that such a rule is incompatible with fixed exchange rates; only the collapse of the Bretton Woods system opened the door for Friedman's rule.

etary phenomenon" (Friedman 1970), and it can be ended only by monetary restraint. Though Keynes would never have denied this old truth, the neoclassical synthesis had pushed it into the background. Friedman was far from being the only one to remember it, but he became the vocal leader of those who undertook to restore it to its rightful place at the center of the monetary stage.

His specific contribution related to the Phillips curve (Friedman 1969, ch. 5). He pointed out that this curve relates unemployment not to measured inflation but to unexpected inflation. Once measured inflation has become expected, the employment effect disappears. The long-run Phillips curve, therefore, is a vertical line; there is no lasting trade-off between inflation and employment. When Friedman gave his famous presidential address to the American Economic Association in 1967, this point was not new. Friedman himself had made it before, and Edmund Phelps had published a paper about it (Phelps 1967). In fact, it was familiar to many economists and financial writers who had not been trained in the short-run perspective of Keynes. It was Friedman's contribution to make it again a part of mainstream economics. Twenty years later, history had amply demonstrated that monetary restraint, at the price of temporary recession, can indeed eliminate secular inflation. The quanitity theory tradition was vindicated.

Friedman's message became known as monetarism. He himself did not relish this label, because he did not mean his message to be narrowly confined to money. The creator of the ism was Karl Brunner (1968), who, together with his friend Allan Meltzer, became its leading dogmatist. Both were far from simply following Friedman, though. In fact, they were often his critics, differing from him in both theory and policy prescriptions. Brunner summarized the doctrine he called monetarist in three propositions:

1. The Federal Reserve actions dominate the movement of the monetary base over time.
2. Movements of the monetary base dominate movements of the money supply over the business cycle.
3. Accelerations and decelerations of the money supply are closely followed by accelerations and decelerations in economic activity (Brunner 1968, 24).

By 1980 the money supply targets recommended by monetarists had become part of policy procedures in many central banks. They played a historic role in bringing down inflation, but once this was accomplished they were relegated to a secondary position.

As in most such cases, the creation of an ism, though it helped to propagate ideas, was an impediment to scientific progress rather than an impulse. Imitating Keynes, who had proclaimed himself a revolutionary against classical orthodoxy, the monetarists now proclaimed themselves revolutionaries (or counterrevolutionaries) against Keynesian orthodoxy.

As a matter of fact, by about 1972 it had become very difficult to distinguish between the two camps at the level of scientific analysis. Both agreed that the quantity theory is valid for long-run inflation. Both agreed that money may have powerful effects in the short run. There was also agreement that these effects were different depending on the way money is created, though it was not clear how much different. This implied that fiscal policy also had real effects, though their strength and durability was controversial. If the debate remained nevertheless acrimonious, the reasons must be sought more at the level of power and influence, both academic and political, than at the level of research.

Overall, Friedman's place in economics in the second half of the twentieth century bears some resemblance to that of Adam Smith two centuries before. Inasmuch as economics is an art, he represents it in all its diverse facets. He knows how to use theory as a guide to action, he is as decisive as an army commander, as lucid as a teacher, and as articulate as a lawyer. He has a legislator's understanding of institutions, a statistician's respect for figures, and an econometrician's ability to draw inferences. He derives lessons from the past as a historian does, can talk the language of the small businessman, and has the social vision of a missionary.

Friedman's contribution to economics in its more narrow sense of a science is more difficult to pin down. He was not primarily a scientific innovator, and he was not a great builder of theoretical models. His main contribution was the demonstration that monetary policy is difficult to use for short-term stabilization but of decisive importance for long-term inflation. As a consequence, the focus of the monetary policy discussion shifted from discretionary measures to policy rules. The stage was thus set for a new theoretical challenge.

John Muth

The proposition that fiat money, though neutral in the long run, may have powerful short-run effects is part of the unbroken tradition of macroeconomics. Until 1970 this proposition, though intuitively compelling, had never been rigorously derived from a theoretical model. The literature seemed to suggest that there might be several possible approaches. One of them, developed in the course of the 1970s, turned on the formation of expectations. It was crucially based on the hypothesis that expectations, in a sense to be specified presently, are formed rationally. This hypothesis had been put forth, more than a decade earlier, by John F. Muth. Not only did it provide one of the keys to a rigorous analysis of monetary policy rules, but for a while it even seemed to shatter the virtual consensus about the short-term effects of monetary policy.

Muth was born in Chicago in 1930. Like his older brother he became an economist, but whereas Richard became known for his work on urban problems, John saw economics from the perspective of industrial engineering. After obtaining a B.S. degree from Washington University in Saint Louis, he did his graduate work at the Carnegie Institute of Technology (which is now Carnegie-Mellon University), where Franco Modigliani, Herbert Simon, Abraham Charnes, and William Cooper were his most influential teachers. He was awarded a Ph.D. (in mathematical economics) in 1962. Until 1964 Muth taught at Carnegie-Mellon, then for several years at Michigan State University, and since 1969 he has been professor of production management at Indiana University.

While still in graduate school, Muth published a note on growth theory, but most of his writings are on process analysis and production scheduling. Though active in research, he did not publish very much, being one of the rare modern economists who became famous without following the motto "Publish or perish." His fame he owes essentially to a single paper, "Rational Expectations and the Theory of Price Movements," first presented in 1959 and published in 1961. A related paper, "Optimal Properties of Exponentially Weighted Forecasts," appeared in 1960. A third paper on the same subject, though written in 1960, was published only in 1981. The three essays were reprinted in the two volumes of collected papers on rational expectations edited by Lucas and Sargent (1981, chs. 1, 2, 17). Seldom have fewer pages from a single outburst of creativity had more impact on economic theory.

It had always been recognized by economists that human decisions depend on expectations. The Swedish followers of Knut Wicksell and John Hicks, in particular, had constructed dynamic general equilibrium theories in which the successive short-term equilibria are linked by expectations. For such an approach to yield substantive results, expectations have to be linked to experience. This can be done, say, by extrapolating the expected value of each variable from the past values of the same variable. To use price as an example, in the most trivial case the future price would simply be expected to equal the present price. Under a more general assumption, called the adaptive expectations hypothesis and widely used in the late 1950s, the expected future price appears as a mean of lagged prices with exponentially declining weights. Muth showed that expectations of this type, though perhaps plausible psychologically, generally fail to satisfy a fundamental requirement. To correct this deficiency he developed a new approach.

This approach was based on the central hypothesis that the expectations of decision makers "are essentially the same as the predictions of the relevant economic theory" (Muth 1961, 315). The relevant economic theory embodies the available knowledge about an economic process, imperfect as it may be, and the decision makers, so Muth argued, are best assumed to make use of this knowledge. The theory relevant for the future course of prices, however, includes more than past prices. In fact, it generally includes all aspects of the underlying economic model. Muth's hypothesis, therefore, asserts "that expectations depend specifically on the structure of the entire system" (315). To avoid misunderstandings it should be added that Muth did not assume that all agents have the same expectations, that their predictions are identical to those derived from the relevant theory, or that their forecasts are perfect. He merely assumed, in statistical terms, that expectations "tend to be distributed, for the same information set, about the prediction of the theory" (316).

To explain the meaning of this hypothesis, Muth used the example of an individual market. More specifically, he considered a good that reaches the market one period after production decisions have been made. Such a market would thus be subject to what theorists called cobweb cycles and agricultural economists illustrated by the hog cycle. In the following exposition prices and quantities are measured as deviations from the values they would assume in a stationary state without disturbances.

Let demand for the good in period t depend on the concurrent price,

$$q_t = -\beta p_t \qquad . \qquad (\beta > 0) \tag{36.1}$$

Supply depends on the price expected for the present period and a random disturbance—say, due to the weather. The supply function can thus be written

$$Q_t = \gamma p_t^e + u_t, \qquad (\gamma > 0) \tag{36.2}$$

where u_t is assumed to have an expected value $Eu_t = 0$ and no serial correlation. Market equilibrium requires $q_t = Q_t$ or, substituting from equations 36.1 and 36.2,

$$p_t = -\frac{\gamma}{\beta} p_t^e - \frac{1}{\beta} u_t. \tag{36.3}$$

Since $Eu_t = 0$, the expected value of p_t is

$$Ep_t = -\frac{\gamma}{\beta} p_t^e. \tag{36.4}$$

To complete the model, one has to specify how the expected price is derived from past history. In the simplest case, the price expected for the present period is equal to the actual price in the preceding period,

$$p_t^e = p_t - 1. \tag{36.5}$$

Substituting into equation 36.4, the model, once p_{t-1} is known, thus predicts a price of

$$Ep_t = -\frac{\gamma}{\beta} p_{t-1}. \tag{36.6}$$

A comparison of equations 36.5 and 36.6 shows that this prediction is in striking contrast to the way expectations are assumed to be formed. Whereas producers believe that a high present price will be followed by a high future price, the model builder "knows" that it will, on average, be followed by a low price. If the model is correct, a producer or speculator can earn easy money by applying it. It is hard to understand why producers have not learned from their disappointments long ago. Expectations formed according to equation 36.5 are clearly not rational in the sense of Muth.

How would rational expectations have to be formed? Expectations of firms are rational if they correspond to the predictions of the model, or in symbols

$$p_t^e = Ep_t = -\frac{\gamma}{\beta}p_t^e. \tag{36.7}$$

Abstracting from the fortuitous case $\gamma/\beta = -1$, this requires that $p_t^e = 0$. The rational expectation is that next period's price is the stationary price. If producers use this prediction, the market price will actually fluctuate randomly and unpredictably around the stationary price. Expectations will thus turn out to be justified on average. There are no profit opportunities left to be exploited by producers or speculators who happen to know the model. There is nothing further to be learned from experience.

The essential point is that rational expectations have to be derived from the model as a whole. Psychological considerations about the forecasting behavior of economic agents do not enter into the matter at all. The question can be turned around by inquiring which economic model, if any, would make adaptive expectations rational. To this question Muth devoted much of his energy, showing that the required model would have to include both permanent (or cumulative) and transitory disturbances.

Muth had nothing to say about specific macroeconomic implications of rational expectations for the evaluation of monetary rules. He was clear, however, about their general significance for econometric techniques (Muth 1961, 316). At the time of the Cowles Commission, it was recognized that econometrics is useful for policy evaluation inasmuch as it provides parameter estimates that remain unaffected by the relevant policy measure. So-called reduced form estimates, though sufficient for forecasting with unchanged policies, do not satisfy this requirement. The required parameter estimates are those of individual structural equations, which led to the identification problem. As it turned out, its solution depends on the model as a whole.

Rational expectations, as Muth pointed out, now raised a similar sort of problem at a different level. Policy changes will often affect the relationship between expected and past values of given variables. Empirical estimates of such relationships, therefore, are unlikely to remain invariant under policy changes, and models incorporating such estimates are unreliable for policy evaluation. To correct this deficiency one would again have to look beyond individual behavior equations to derive expectations from the model as a whole. In a few terse lines, Muth thus anticipated what later became known as the Lucas critique. And Muth did not stop with the critique. Of the paper that was belatedly published in 1981, Lucas and Sargent said (1981, xx) that it "points the way to literally all of the estimation techniques for rational expectations models that subsequent researchers have used or proposed."

Muth's role in the history of economics is unusual. Like Herman Heinrich Gossen, he became famous for one idea, he provided the analytical key to developments that, in the jargon of scientific journalism, were described as revolutionary, and he was virtually ignored by his immediate contemporaries. However, whereas Gossen had no influence on those developments, his key results being independently rediscovered by Jevons and Walras, the rational expectations economics of the 1970s and 1980s was a direct outgrowth of Muth's seminal idea. In fact, Muth's contribution is one of the relatively few instances in which there is no indication that the history of economics would have taken about the same course in its absence. It was a novel and ingenious idea, it was not "in the air," and no multiple discovery has yet come to light.[5]

Muth's contribution may also be likened to that of Cournot and Thünen inasmuch as in all three cases a brilliant piece of analysis became an important part of mainstream economic theory, with considerable delay, through the work of others. However, whereas the writings of Cournot and Thünen, for reasons of language, mathematics, and exposition, were inaccessible to most professional economists of their day, Muth's decisive paper appeared, with an exposition of admirable lucidity, in the most prestigious international journal. It is a case of a building block of far-reaching importance being temporarily ignored by the profession because its creator, it seems, was not aggressive and ambitious enough to force it upon his contemporaries. His claim to fame is not thereby diminished.

Robert Lucas

Friedman's views on monetary policy rules were based on observation, judgment, and intuition rather than on rigorous analysis. Muth's work on rational expectations was a piece of rigorous analysis, but it was far removed from the policy discussion. In the course of the 1970s, the two strands became united, making the theory of monetary policy rules the most active segment of economic research. There was talk of a rational expectations revolution. A number of people contributed to this rapid development, but the single most decisive contribution came from Robert E. Lucas, Jr.

Lucas was born in Yakima, Washington, in 1937. His parents' restau-

---

5. Malthus discussed "our rational expectations regarding the future improvement of society" at the end of the fourth edition (1807) of his *Essay on the Principle of Population* (see Malthus 1926), but both classical and marginalist economics, following Smith, stressed the frequent irrationality of expectations.

rant, the Lucas Ice Creamery, went bankrupt soon after. The father found a job as a steamfitter in Seattle and later had his own refrigeration business. Both parents, though from Republican families, had become ardent New Dealers, and the four children learned to argue about social issues (like the efficiency gains from socialism) in endless debates. Lucas studied history at the University of Chicago and even started graduate school in history at the University of California at Berkeley. Soon, however, he felt the need to acquire professional competence in economics, for which he returned to Chicago. His general views about how the economy works were strongly influenced by Milton Friedman; for analytical techniques, Paul Samuelson's *Foundations* became his shining example; and the macroeconomics he learned was mostly Keynesian. His early research interests were, accordingly, along the lines of the neoclassical synthesis, and his Ph.D., awarded in 1964, was based on a dissertation on capital/labor substitution. From 1963 to 1974 Lucas taught at Carnegie-Mellon University in Pittsburgh, where Muth was for a few years his colleague. He then moved to Chicago, where in 1980 he became John Dewey Distinguished Service Professor of Economics.[6]

Lucas has written no books. His most brilliant, influential, but also difficult paper is "Expectations and the Neutrality of Money," published in 1972. (Like other pioneering articles, it had first been rejected by a journal). A response to Phelps's quest for "microfoundations of macroeconomics," it marks the breakthrough of rational expectations into general economic theory. Papers on business cycles are collected in Lucas 1981. Additional important articles on rational expectations by Lucas and others were edited by Lucas and Sargent (1981). Lucas's Jahnsson Lectures (Lucas 1987) provide a relatively nontechnical, though abstract, survey of his approach to business cycles. It should be noted that in 1980, at the time this historical narrative ends, Lucas was just forty-three years old. The contributions reviewed on the following pages may thus fall short of indicating the ultimate scope of his work.

Lucas sees himself as reviving the great tradition of dynamic business cycle research interrupted by the powerful statics of Keynes. His conception of dynamics is quite different, however, from that of Clément Juglar and the model builders of the 1930s who had tried to explain a recession by the preceding upswing, which was in turn explained by the preceding recession, so that the whole oscillatory path was, in principle, determined once the laws of motion and the initial conditions were specified. Lucas's conception also differs from that of Karl Marx and Joseph Schumpeter, who regarded cycles as concomitants of innovation and capitalist development.

---

6. Further biographical material can be found in Klamer 1984 and in the introduction to Lucas 1981. Supplementary information from Robert Lucas is gratefully acknowledged.

Lucas rather envisaged an economy in a stationary state except that it is perpetually hit by random disturbances whose distributions are known and constant. His basic question is how the model of such an economy must be constructed to replicate those broad facts about business fluctuations that Wesley C. Mitchell, following in Juglar's footsteps, had so patiently distilled from innumerable statistical series. In particular, Lucas undertook to develop a macroeconomic model in which random disturbances in the money supply produce cycles in prices, output, and employment.

This program is in the spirit of Walras inasmuch as the economy is always in equilibrium, but this equilibrium is interpreted in a stochastic sense. The program is also in the spirit of Slutsky's stochastic approach to business cycles, though Lucas's cycles are not merely optical illusions but embedded in the structure of the model. It is probably most accurate to regard Lucas as the heir to the Wicksell-Frisch approach, in which stochastic impulses keep an oscillatory propagation mechanism in perpetual motion.

Lucas's business cycle theory contains several specific components. One of them is the so-called Lucas supply function. It first appeared in 1969 in the paper "Real Wages, Employment, and Inflation" authored jointly with Leonard Rapping (Lucas 1981, 19f.) and thus should, as Lucas insists, really be called the Lucas-Rapping supply function. Written from the point of view of the neoclassical synthesis, the paper undertook to provide for employment what Milton Friedman and Franco Modigliani had provided for consumption, James Tobin for money, and Robert Eisner and Dale Jorgenson for investment, namely a microeconomic foundation based on household optimization.

Aggregate output, y_t, is regarded conventionally as a function of labor, m_t, and capital, k_t. The same is true of the real wage rate, w_t, since it is equal to the marginal product of labor. The centerpiece of the supply function is the notion that employment fluctuations are due to the intertemporal substitution of labor. Employment increases if households find it advantageous to work more now and to have more leisure in the future. This substitution is mainly governed by relative wages over time: if real wages are expected to rise, labor supply will be postponed and vice versa. In addition, labor supply depends positively on the rate of price increase (as a proxy for real yields) and past labor supply. By appropriate substitutions, Lucas and Rapping derived the aggregate supply function

$$y_t = F(y_{t-1}, k_t, k_{t-1}, \Delta p_t). \tag{36.8}$$

The important point is that rising inflation calls forth an expansion of output. The Phillips curve is inverted: while it is usually interpreted as explaining inflation in terms of aggregate output or employment, the Lucas-Rapping supply function explains output in terms of inflation. The authors make it clear, however, that this explanation holds only in the short run.[7]

In the history of macroeconomic theory, the Lucas-Rapping supply function marks a return to an earlier tradition. Prior to 1930, output fluctuations were usually regarded as triggered by price changes. For Irving Fisher stable money was the key to stable output, and this was still the perspective of John Maynard Keynes's *Treatise*. During the interwar period, partly under the influence of Wicksell, prices receded into the background. In the *General Theory* they played no essential role, and the same was true in the neoclassical synthesis. Lucas and Rapping again moved prices to center stage.

This is consistent with Lucas's objective to construct what he calls an equilibrium theory of the business cycle. Walrasian agents decide on quantities to be bought and sold in the light of market prices. They do not set prices in the light of quantities bought and sold, though one seems to know from experience that such behavior is widespread. That workers in Lucas's model are supposed to be unemployed because they prefer leisure to income at the current wages has been one of its most controversial features. Sometimes Lucas sounds as if market-clearing prices were for him indeed a matter of faith. This impression is misleading, however. In fact, he makes it clear that the Walrasian assumption is used as a matter of analytical convenience, because other assumptions, though perhaps looking realistic, are too difficult for him (and others) to handle in a general equilibrium framework.

The second ingredient of Lucas's approach to business cycle theory is imperfect information. It was fully articulated in his famous paper of 1972 (Lucas 1981, 66f.). The key idea had been provided by Phelps, who had imagined traders to be scattered over an archipelago of islands with full information only about their own island. Lucas's contribution is the precise analytical implementation of this idea. He began by adapting Samuelson's overlapping generations model to his particular purpose, thus initiating the questionable practice of motivating the use of a medium of exchange by the necessity of providing for old age. The young generation produces, selling a part of its output to the old generation for money. The old generation spends the money it has earned when young plus what it obtains from the government through transfers. These additions to the money supply fluctuate randomly, and their distribution is known.

Exchange takes place in two separate markets, each of which is populated by exactly one-half of the old people and a share of the young that fluctuates randomly, again with a known distribution. The state of the

---

7. Lucas and Rapping still explained expected future wages and prices by the familiar adaptive scheme according to which expectations are adjusted each period by a fraction of the excess of the observed values over those that were earlier expected for the same period. Though aware of Muth's work, they had not yet perceived its potential significance.

economy at a given moment is entirely described by three variables, namely the existing money supply, the current addition to the money supply, and the proportion of the young assigned to the first market. The important point is that within a given trading period there is no communication between the two markets, so that current prices are determined in each market separately in the light of local supply and demand. They are determined jointly with output, employment, and consumption in such a way that the demand for cash balances equals the supply.

The disturbances in this economy have two sources. Some are monetary, arising from the random additions to the money supply. The others are real, caused by the fluctuating proportions of young people in each market. If disturbances are exclusively monetary, so Lucas shows, the current price adjusts proportionally to the monetary change. Money is neutral; employment and consumption remain unchanged. The remarkable—and for Lucas, surprising—fact is that this is true even for unanticipated monetary changes, because prices are a perfect indicator for them in this case. If, on the other hand, the disturbances are exclusively real, they will have real effects, every absolute price change signaling a relative price change. In general, the economy will be disturbed by both monetary and real forces. In this case, the current price does not inform traders with certainty about the sources of the disturbances. As a consequence, monetary disturbances are partly mistaken for real disturbances, thus producing output fluctuations in the same direction.

The third component of Lucas's business cycle theory is rational expectations. Muth's hypothesis had already been used in 1971 in the paper "Investment under Uncertainty," written jointly with Edward Prescott, (Lucas and Sargent 1981, ch. 6), but in the 1972 paper, though it is fully consistent with rational expectations, this hypothesis is implied rather than explicitly emphasized. In the 1973 paper on output-inflation trade-offs (Lucas 1981, 131f), it became the pivot of the analysis.

Suppose output depends on expected price. With adaptive expectations, this can be determined from nothing but the past price history. Specifically, a change in monetary policy will have no influence on the way expectations depend on past prices. It will usually turn out, however, that the path of actual prices is systematically different from the path of expected prices. Under rational expectations, on the other hand, the behavior of expected prices is postulated to be similar to that of actual prices. Actual prices, however, are, in principle, the joint result of all parts of the model. In particular, they will be affected by any change in monetary policy. As a consequence, every policy change must be suspected to influence the way expectations are derived from experience. An econometric model that is quite successful for monetary efforts to fine-tune the economy may cease to be valid with a constant rate of monetary expansion.

This argument led Lucas to a sweeping condemnation of the macroeconometric models of the 1950s and 1960s. While it would be accurate to call it the Muth-Lucas critique, it became known as the Lucas critique (Lucas 1981, 104f.). Its protagonist summarized it in the following syllogism: "Given that the structure of an econometric model consists of optimal decision rules of economic agents, and that optimal decision rules vary systematically with changes in the structure of series relevant to the decision maker, it follows that any changes in policy will systematically alter the structure of econometric models" (126).

For short-term forecasting this critique is not of primary importance; the traditional models might be quite adequate. For the evaluation of alternative policy rules, however, the critique was seen as fundamental; the traditional models were likely to provide invalid results. The prime example was, of course, the Phillips curve. Though producing satisfactory forecasts of the short-run consequences of monetary expansion, it failed miserably in predicting the effects of secular inflation. Adding variables, Lucas pointed out, is no remedy. The only remedy consists in regarding expectations formation as a property not of individual behavior equations but of the model as a whole. To develop econometric techniques immune to the Lucas critique became a vast program of econometric research absorbing much of the best brain power in this field.

The preceding argument is able to explain why random disturbances in the money supply produce parallel changes in prices, output, and employment. Imperfect discrimination between absolute and relative prices makes agents behave as if they suffered from temporary money illusion. One important feature of business cycles was still missing from this account, though, namely the persistence of expansionary and contractive effects over prolonged periods. Economic data tend to be serially correlated. Also missing was the procyclical fluctuation of investment relative to total output, which had been identified as a typical feature of business cycles since the time of Juglar. Lucas provided the missing features in his paper "An Equilibrium Model of the Business Cycle" of 1975 (1981, 179f.). The key was the addition of information lags and of capital goods governed by an accelerator. The door was open to the reactivation of all those dynamic mechanisms, such as Albert Aftalion's gestation lags, which had been the stock-in-trade of business cycle theory in the interwar period. However, every addition to the model also increased the technical difficulty of deriving the rational expectations, and the analytics rapidly became very complex.

Lucas has written little on economic policy. Nevertheless his work, together with that of Thomas Sargent, Neil Wallace (Lucas and Sargent 1981, chs. 10, 11), and others, initiated a vigorous policy debate. This debate was not concerned with the effects of discretionary measures every step of which is historically unique; on these, rational expectations shed no new light. It was rather concerned, in the spirit of Milton Friedman, with rules that are adhered to in an unchanging way. Could one conceive a program whereby the observations available at any given time would automatically trigger a response in, say, the money supply so that average output is raised and/or its fluctuations dampened? Could fine-tuning of the economy be programmed? The answer of rational expectations economics was no. Money has real effects only to the extent that it is at first mistaken for a source of changes in relative prices. Once the money supply is programmed, the program will be fully reflected in people's expectations and thus cease to be misinterpreted. The only remaining effect will be on prices.

Monetary policy, it was concluded, should be used to stabilize the long-term trend of prices; it is ineffective in raising and stabilizing output. Friedman's intuition thus obtained rigorous analytical support. In U.S. graduate schools the advocates of an activist monetary policy were put on the defensive; they had to search for new models to support their intuition. The influence on actual policy making, however, was slight. Central banks continued their efforts to mitigate business fluctuations. From their point of view, it seems, disturbances are not random events with constant and known distributions but a sequence of unique historical events.

The sociology of economic science made it probably inevitable that the rational expectations approach, too, was proclaimed as a new school. Its battle cry, at least in its cruder versions, was the famous policy ineffectiveness proposition according to which money is supposed to have no real effects even in the short run. It purported to distinguish the new school from both Keynesians and monetarists. Lucas and Sargent's articulate criticism of what they called Keynesian macroeconomics (Lucas and Sargent 1981, ch. 16) gave this doctrinal development an added impulse.

The label for the school was new classical macroeconomics. It was intended to convey the notion that the unclassical interlude of Keynesianism was finally over and that the new school was the legitimate heir to the classical tradition. It was a flagrant misnomer for at least three reasons. First, price and wage rigidities, non-market-clearing prices, irrational expectations, and strong real effects of money in the short run have always been important ingredients of the classical tradition in macroeconomics[8]. Second, Keynes, though posing as an iconoclast, was himself part of the classical tradition; a critic of Keynes is not necessarily a classical economist. Third, Lucas at least was far from arguing that money has no real effects in the short run. In fact, his program was precisely to show why money has powerful short-term effects on output and employment.

The true significance of Lucas's work must be sought not at the level of economic ideas or ideologies but at the level of analytical techniques. He recognized the potential of Muth's concept of rational expectations; he shaped it into a useful contribution to mainstream economics with wide

8. This is further elaborated in Niehans 1987.

applications both in theory and in econometrics; and he thereby opened a rich and extensive field for economic research. Model building had finally caught up with still another part of economic vision.

37
Epilogue: The Dynamics of Scientific Progress

THE HISTORY of science is interesting for the light it sheds on the dynamics of scientific progress, on its driving forces, their interactions, and the causes and criteria of success and failure. What this book has to say on this inexhaustible subject is, in substance, contained in the preceding chapters. This epilogue can do no more than recapitulate some of the main contours as they emerge from the historical material.

The Driving Forces

The first task is to identify the main forces that are propelling the progress of economic theory and to evaluate their relative importance.

EXTERNAL CONDITIONS. A first group of forces can be subsumed under the heading of external conditions. Growth and fluctuations of an economy are usually thought to be partly determined by forces exogenous to the economy itself. Similarly, the progress of economic theory may conveniently be thought to result, in part, from historical changes in its political, social, economic, ideological, and intellectual environment. The question is how strong these exogenous forces may have been.

Political events have left clear imprints on economic theory. The physiocrats responded to the desolate state of the French monarchy. The French revolutions from 1789 to 1848 provided Marx with the paradigms from which he abstracted his revolutionary model of history. With the gradual extension of suffrage, economists tended to move from laissez faire to social reform and welfare economics. Overall, however, the influence of political developments on economic theory is remarkable mostly for its weakness. Momentous events such as the Seven Years' War, the American Revolution, the Napoleonic Wars, imperialist expansion, the Civil War and World Wars I and II, considered at the political level, left hardly a trace in economic theory. Conversely, few of the theoretical contributions reviewed in the preceding chapters were associated with specific political developments.

The influence of social conditions is stronger. In constructing his population theory, Malthus was motivated by the pressure on living standards resulting from the decline in mortality without a corresponding decline in fertility. Classical distribution theory associated factor shares with social classes. The dissolution of feudalism directed the attention of economists from factor shares to income inequality. For some of the leading economists (including Wicksell, Tobin, and Arrow) social concerns were the main motive that attracted them to economics. Nevertheless, social change cannot explain more than a small fraction of theoretical developments.

Once the perspective is narrowed to the economy, the influences on economic theory become more specific. The quantity theory of money emerged from early experiences with inconvertible paper money. The catastrophe of John Law demonstrated that the stimulating effect of inflation is only temporary. Banking crises were the background of Thornton's theory of money creation in a three-tiered banking system. Depression motivated the controversy on general gluts, and the recurrent crises of the nineteenth century inspired the notion that cycles are inherent in capitalist growth. It is a truism that the so-called Keynesian revolution can be understood only against the background of the Great Depression. It is equally obvious that the oil shock of 1974 gave a spur to resource economics. Characteristically, however, most of these specific influences are found in applied fields, particularly in monetary macroeconomics. The development of basic theory from circular flow economics to marginalism and farther on to modern general equilibrium models owes hardly anything to economic influences. However, it will be pointed out in the section on historical selection below that historical experience plays an important role in the validation of analytical pieces.

With respect to ideologies, many economists had articulate views. The weights tended to shift with the currents of the times. When the tide of liberalism was rising, a majority of economists extolled the virtues of competition, free enterprise, and free trade. In the age of social reform, many became interventionists and even what the Germans called *Kathedersozialisten,* "socialists of the chair." The New Deal produced a crop of liberal economists (in Roosevelt's sense of the term). Democratic socialism caused economists to turn to planning in market economies.

Marx went so far as to argue that economics as a whole is merely a component of the ideological superstructure erected by the ruling class to defend its dominance. The history of economic theory does not bear him out. First, even economists with passionate convictions have often succeeded (like Wicksell) in making the results of their research independent of their ideology. Second, successive waves of ideologies have all left their enduring sediments in economic theory so that modern mainstream economics cannot be identified with any one of them. Third, even in the same generation important contributions were usually made by economists with widely different views. The bourgeois Viennese and the land socialist Walras, the clergyman Wicksteed and atheist radical Wicksell, the libertarian Pareto and his communist pupil Slutsky—all contributed to late marginalism.

In the course of the history of economics, the importance of ideological factors gradually declined. In Ricardo they are less pronounced than in Adam Smith, in Jevons and Walras they have receded farther into the background, and in the scientific writings of Hicks, Samuelson, and Arrow they are hardly noticeable. Friedman is, of course, a strong counterexample, and there are others. Overall, however, it is easier today to separate economic theory from ideology than it was in earlier periods.

External influences may also arise from developments in other intellectual and scientific fields. Again the results are meager. Bentham and Edgeworth were philosophical utilitarians, but their contributions to utility theory were not different in kind from those of Bernoulli and Pareto, who were not. The progress of mathematics had little influence before von Neumann, simply because economists were still busy catching up on elementary calculus already available at the time of Adam Smith. Developments in physics, medicine, and biology provided economic writers with suggestive metaphors about equilibrium, friction, circular flows, communicating vessels, survival of the fittest, entropy, and the like. The substantive effect on the history of economic theory, however, was negligible. The big exception is computer technology; by changing the fundamental complexion of applied economics, it also affected the types of models economic theorists were looking for.

Overall, the effects of external conditions, though clearly visible, were mostly confined to the short-run details of the growth of economic theory; they added an impulse here and an impediment there. On the direction and speed of the long-run trend of economic theory, they seem to have had no marked and identifiable influence. For the explanation of long-term progress one has to look elsewhere.

RESOURCES. A large part of the growth of economic theory over the last three hundred years is simply the result of the increasing resources devoted to it. In contrast to the natural sciences, equipment still does not play a major role. Increasing amounts were indeed spent on data collection and processing, but the benefits to economic theory were minor. Most of the best theoretical work continues to be done with pencil and paper. It is still the human capital that counts.

The increase in human capital devoted to economic theory has been enormous. Population has increased; from Europe economics has spread to all continents; out of given populations economics seems to attract a rising proportion of scientific talent. This quantitative increase has been associated with a qualitative change. Its hallmark is professionalization. Classical economics was created by one professional, Adam Smith, and many amateurs. Marginalism was initiated by amateurs but completed by professors. The model-building era has seen the rise of graduate schools where senior professionals train junior professionals.

Professionalization was accompanied by an increase in mathematical competence. With the exception of Cournot, the founders of marginalism, though spreading the gospel of mathematical economics, found it difficult to solve even the simplest calculus problems. Late marginalists such as Pareto, Wicksell, and Slutsky had solid mathematical training. After set theory and topology had made their triumphal entry into economics, many of the leading economists might have become productive mathematicians. Among the driving forces of scientific progress in economic theory, the rise in mathematical competence was one of the strongest.

Inevitably, historical literacy and understanding declined. At the time of Hume and Ricardo, the background of political economists was philosophy, history, and the classics. John Stuart Mill's encyclopedic mind still embraced virtually everything outside the sciences. From Marshall to Hicks, the weights were distributed about equally between the humanities and mathematics. After that, following Fisher's example, leading economists began to be distinctly science-oriented. Schumpeter was perhaps the last of the humanists (or does this honor go to Harrod?). It is hard to resist the conclusion that this was associated with a decline in the art of devising potentially relevant economic models. If graduate students with mediocre mathematical talent have to devote all their energy to the acquisition of mathematical skills, they are unlikely to become wise and imaginative observers of history, politics, and social problems. In economic analysis, rigor may thus become the enemy of relevance. At such a point economics may have to rejuvenate itself in the spring of history. Later historians may perhaps perceive that in the last generation of the twentieth century, such a reaction had actually set in.

LOGICAL FLAWS. Science is driven forward mostly by the detection of flaws in existing science. These flaws may be empirical in nature. It is a common notion that progress is initiated by observations that are difficult to reconcile with received doctrine. Some such cases seem to have occurred in economics, too. Menger was led to subjectivism, according to his own story, by the discrepancy between the price theory he had learned and the action he observed on the market floor. The imperfect adjustment of interest rates to price changes caused Fisher to study distributed lags. The disappointing performance of Keynesian consumption functions led Modigliani and Friedman to their modified hypotheses. Overall, however, irreconcilable observations were not a major factor in economic theory. The core of economic theory mostly relates to everyday experiences that were commonplace centuries ago; it is unlikely, therefore, that new observations will challenge it.

The flaws that drive economic analysis forward are predominantly of a logical nature. Some of them concern the lack of precision in existing theory. Adam Smith was surely imprecise when he described a monopoly price as the highest that can be got, and his imprecision left much for

Cournot to do. Ricardo's theory of comparative cost left the terms of trade indeterminate between two limits, which stimulated Mill to his most original contribution. Böhm-Bawerk left the interaction between time preference and capital productivity in confusion, which was cleared up by Fisher. Slutsky derived the precise condition for falling demand curves. Hicks, with his IS/LM model, made the Keynesian theory analytically precise. It was precision that Samuelson added to Ohlin's factor price analysis. In this perennial quest for precision, the use of mathematics clearly brought large rewards.

Inconsistency is another spur to analytical effort. The apparent inconsistency in Hume's exposition of the specie flow mechanism initiated a two-centuries-long debate about the role of price differentials in the transfer process. That some prices in Walras's general equilibrium system might turn out to be negative led to modern existence proofs. Marshall found it difficult to reconcile increasing returns with increasing marginal cost. He found a solution in the concept of external economies, and his successors found it in imperfect competition. Product exhaustion was seen to require constant returns to scale, whereas determinate firm sizes seemed to require diminishing returns. The apparent inconsistency was resolved, after strenuous debate, by Wicksell. In the macroeconomics of the 1930s, the equality of saving and investment was used both as an identity and as an equilibrium condition; it took years of controversy to clear up the apparent contradiction.

A third type of logical flaw is lack of generality. Classical economics had different price theories for competition and monopoly. To construct a general theory embracing both of these polar cases became an important item on the marginalist agenda. Haberler generalized the theory of comparative cost by introducing Fisher's concave transformation curves. Harrod generalized Keynes's theory by adding the capacity effect of investment, and his growth model was in turn generalized by Tobin and Solow by allowing for factor substitution. Where calculus had determined only local optima, topological approaches determined global optima. Decision theory generalized optimization to actions with uncertain outcomes. A large part of the energies of general equilibrium theorists is spent on efforts, possibly futile, to bring their models closer to reality by relaxing their rarefied assumptions.

Still another, though minor, sort of logical impulse comes from seemingly unintelligible paradoxes. The water/diamond paradox, though long solved, was regarded as a challenge to value theory far into the nineteenth century. The paradox that Marshall attributed to Giffen gave rise to the theoretical developments culminating with Slutsky. The paradox that taxes may lower prices led Hotelling to an important contribution on the interdependence of markets. The paradox of saving put in focus the difference between Keynes and Adam Smith. Robinson's Ruth Cohen paradox shed new light on intertemporal substitution and complementarity.

Overall, it is tempting to interpret the history of economic theory as an endogenous dynamic process, driven by the detection of logical flaws, in which the same fundamental economic insights are expressed in models that are progressively more precise, consistent, general, and intelligible. For the basic core of economic theory there is much truth in this interpretation. The fundamental insights that it expresses were part of commonplace experience centuries before economics became a science. Its progress consists largely in understanding better and better what has always been known. Beyond the core, however, much has been added to economics that cannot be explained purely in terms of the elimination of logical flaws.

CREATIVE MINDS. The transformation of external influences and logical flaws into scientific achievements requires creative minds. What sort of mind does it take to make classic contributions to economics?

When one contemplates the personalities of leading theorists, it is striking how many had burning intellectual ambitions. Both Hume and Smith were ambitious men. Malthus worked hard to take the place of his friend Ricardo as the leading economist of his day. Gossen saw himself as the Copernicus of the social universe. Jevons wanted "to be good" to a whole nation or even the world. Fisher decided early to become a great man. Walras, forever hungry for recognition, nominated himself for a Nobel Peace Prize. Both Keynes and Schumpeter found it insufferable not to come out at the top. Samuelson has never tried to hide the enjoyment he derives from his intellectual superiority.

Surely ambition is not enough, though. It must be associated with the gift of seeing interesting problems and the ability to solve them. Thornton, Ricardo, Wicksell, Koopmans, and Tinbergen give the impression of having been motivated more by their problem-solving ability and social responsibility than by ambition. As economic science progressed, it attracted more of the best brains of a generation, which meant that more difficult problems could be solved. So far, however, economics does not seem to have attracted many geniuses such as Newton or Einstein. Cantillon may have been one, though we shall never know. Marx was an ideological genius. Keynes was a genius of persuasion. Von Neumann was a mathematical genius who also changed economic theory. Among those who appear in this book, Samuelson may be the one who is a genius precisely for economic theory.

Classic contributions to economic theory usually require, in Schumpeter's words, both vision and analysis. Vision without analysis, though it may be stimulating, interesting, and provocative, is rather cheap. The literature, particularly at the lower levels of scientific quality, is full of it, and sometimes it is widely acclaimed. The Viennese school declined early because it could not produce the analysis commensurate to its vision. Capital and capitalism seem to have a particular attraction to visionaries with insufficient analytical ability. Marx, Veblen, and Schumpeter, each in his own way, illustrate the tragedies that may result. Joan Robinson, Hayek, and Hicks all found that their analytical abilities were not up to their vision of the dynamic changes in the composition of the capital stock.

On the other hand, analysis without vision, though perhaps arduous and clever, is unrewarding. The progress of economic theory, like that of other sciences, is strewn with innumerable competent papers of this sort. The problem is that at the time of publication it is hard to predict which papers will later turn out to be significant. The process of science, like procreation, seems to be inherently wasteful. As thousands of seeds produce one tree, so thousands of papers produce one classic contribution.

This leads to the question of the extent to which creative minds have shaped the course of economic theory. Was a given contribution really crucial for the direction of this course, or would in its absence a similar contribution have taken its place? Multiple discoveries permit at least a partial answer. The classical theory of rent was independently provided by Anderson, West, and Malthus. Gossen's second law was rediscovered by both Jevons and Walras. An ordinal approach to utility was developed by Fisher before Pareto. Fisher also possessed all the ingredients for a general equilibrium model before he had read Walras. In view of Hotelling, the theory of differentiated duopoly would not look different today if Launhardt had never lived. The Slutsky partition was reproduced by Hicks and Allen. Robinson's imperfect competition and Chamberlin's monopolistic competition were almost perfect substitutes. The marginal revenue concept could have been found in Cournot.

These examples can be multiplied almost at will. The models of Frisch and Kalecki could equally well have provided a starting point for macrodynamics. Factor price equalization was demonstrated by Lerner before Samuelson did so. Friedman's permanent income and Modigliani's life cycle income are roughly equivalent in explaining consumption. Arrow and Debreu approached the efficient allocation of resources along convergent paths. Kantorovich, Hitchcock, and Koopmans made independent starts toward linear programming. The golden rule was discovered almost simultaneously by about seven persons. Speculative prices were shown to be random at about the same time by Samuelson and Mandelbrot.

The frequency of multiple discoveries suggests that the general course of economic theory does not depend much on individual economists, however brilliant and creative. Its main direction seems to be determined by the endogenous dynamics of science and the growth of resources. It is true that without John Muth the rational expectations evolution might not have taken place, but there are not many such cases. Creative minds are indispensable to push economic theory forward along its path, and they can give forceful short-term impulses. Each one of them, taken individually, does not seem to have the power, however, to deflect economic theory much from its long-run path.[1]

Responses

The dynamic process of economic theory cannot be explained solely in terms of some driving forces. Many of its specific characteristics arise from the responses of the science to some specific advance. They account for what Frisch might have called the propagation problems in the history of economic theory.

REINFORCEMENTS. Some of these responses have the nature of reinforcements. An economist may liken them to multiplier effects. A primary contribution calls forth a series of secondary and tertiary contributions, thus raising the total effect far beyond the primary impulse. The strength of the total effect depends, metaphorically speaking, on the propensity to apply new results rather than to "save" them.

In the older history of economic theory, these reinforcement effects are more remarkable for their relative weakness than for their strength. Cantillon inspired Quesnay, but the *Tableau Economique* did not spark further analytical developments. The *Wealth of Nations,* despite its success, was not followed by a burst of analytical activity. Ricardian economics failed to grow much beyond Ricardo, and Marxian economics, except in business cycle research, failed to grow much beyond Marx. Schumpeter is much invoked, but the figure of the innovative entrepreneur is analytically still as vague as he left it in 1912. The oral tradition of Cambridge was slow in advancing beyond Marshall.

In the latter part of the marginalist era, the reinforcement effects became stronger. The contributions of Böhm-Bawerk and Wieser were secondary effects of Menger's *Principles.* Walras ignited the chain reaction of general equilibrium analysis that ended with Slutsky. The seeds of Auspitz and Lieben were quick in bearing fruit in Fisher. Wicksteed's coordination paper led to the solution of the exhaustion problem by Wicksell. The efforts to clarify the *General Theory* lifted short-term macroeconomics to a higher plane. The introduction of capacity effects by Harrod led to a general expansion of growth theory. The Cowles Commission methodology for econometric model building established econometrics as a discipline. Von Neumann's seminal innovations, by attracting other brilliant theorists, blossomed into a whole new approach to optimization and general equi-

---

1. That the preceding paragraphs were written in ignorance of Robert K. Merton's work on multiple discoveries (1961) is perhaps the most fitting tribute to it.

librium within fifteen years. In the chapter on Samuelson it was described how many of his contributions became the starting point of rapid further developments. Clearly, the progressive professionalization of economics and the improvements in academic communication resulted in a strengthening of these multiplier effects.[2]

IMPEDIMENTS. Other responses have the form of impediments to the application and extension of theoretical contributions. They are the counterpart to the gestation lags of economic theory. Just as it may take years before an intended investment expenditure results in additional output, so it may take decades before a new piece of analysis is made use of in published work. Each of the intervals from Ricardo's comparative costs to Mill's reciprocal demand principle, to Marshall's reciprocal demand curves, and finally to Haberler's concave transformation curves lasted decades. Cournot, Thünen, and Dupuit had no influence on further work before the 1870s. No use was made of Marx's two-sector growth model for more than half a century. Edgeworth's theory of exchange had to wait seventy years to be further developed. Pareto had no impact on English theory for about two decades. Frank Ramsey, though never forgotten, did not stimulate further contributions before the advent of growth theory.

As economic theory progressed, these exploitation lags tended to shorten. Within some closely knit groups of specialists they are quite short today. It is remarkable how rapidly econometric techniques and the concepts of linear programming developed in the late 1940s and early 1950s. In fact, some recent papers seem to have had most of their effect before they were even published. In other cases, however, the lags are still amazingly long. Muth's famous paper (1961) lay dormant for a decade before the rational expectations hypothesis was exploited. Hotelling's analysis of exhaustible resources attracted no attention before the oil crises of the 1970s. The continued occurrence of long exploitation lags is one of the reasons why the historian of economic theory finds it difficult to carry the narrative forward to the time of writing.

The length of the exploitation lag depends in part on whether the significance of a contribution is large and evident enough. A new machine supplants an old machine if the expected savings in operating costs exceed the added capital cost. Similarly, a new economic model supplants an old model if its advantages are seen to be great compared to the time and effort it takes to master it. The progress of marginalism was slow because its advantages were not evident to most economists at that time. The

---

2. It would be tempting also to investigate the acceleration effects of theoretical advances on research capacities, the scale effects generated by interactions in close in-groups of specialists, and the synergy effects arising from complementary contributions in different fields. This must be left for more detailed study, though.

progress of linear programming and econometrics was rapid because the rewards seemed to be large and tangible. Small, well-defined improvements in techniques, such as Marshall's price elasticity of demand, spread very rapidly; broad conceptual reorientations, such as the transition to explicit model building, may take much time.

As in other fields, the cost-benefit calculus for new pieces of equipment is based on expectations. These, in turn, are highly dependent on exposition. Adam Smith can hardly be blamed for failing to make use of the *Tableau Economique,* because the physiocrats could never make its meaning clear. Thünen and Gossen are slow and difficult reading. It would have taken a prophet to divine the significance of Jevons's first paper on value theory. Launhardt's algebra and the intricate diagrams of Auspitz and Lieben discourage all but the hardiest souls. Good exposition and writing, on the other hand, often account for much of the success of new work. Fisher and Keynes are impressive, though very different, examples.

The exploitation lag may also be lengthened by the use of techniques that are ahead of their potential users. Cournot, though a master expositor, did not find economists who understood calculus. Von Neumann's early papers had no immediate effect because economists were not ready for set theory and topology. If, since the beginning of the nineteenth century, all economists had been familiar with elementary calculus, the state of economics in 1933 could easily have been reached by 1860.

An often mentioned impediment to scientific innovation is the resistance of established orthodoxy. Thus Jevons attacked the alleged orthodoxy of Ricardo and Mill, and Keynes that of the Marshallians. Robinson enjoyed provoking what she regarded as neo-neoclassical orthodoxy with her self-proclaimed economic heresies.[3] Powerful establishments have indeed sometimes impeded the progress of economic theory. The closing of the German academic market to adherents of Carl Menger by Gustav Schmoller is perhaps the most manifest case. It set back German economics for seventy years, indirectly perhaps to the present day. The centralized Paris establishment excluded the Walrasians from French chairs, and for a century most of the best French contributions came from outside the universities. The Viennese had no use for Auspitz and Lieben or any other "mathematician." Schools, in the sense of intellectual lobbies or power structures, belong to the dark side of academic life.

Overall, however, orthodoxy was not a major impediment. It did not prevent Jevons from obtaining a chair at University College, London, at the age of forty-one and his books from being widely read. Marginalism, though not victorious overnight, steadily won adherents. The Marshallian establishment had treated Keynes very well, and it is difficult to imagine

---

3. English authors seem to be particularly fond of these theological metaphors; perhaps this has to do with the history of Anglicanism.

diffident Pigou as the defender of orthodox dogma. Keynes's problem was not that he was resisted by his environment but that he found it difficult to differentiate himself from it. In Robinson's time, there was actually a high premium on novel and provocative ideas. Journals of every orientation competed for papers. For an orthodox establishment to suppress innovative ideas was virtually impossible. The irrepressible Robinson got a worldwide hearing.

THE REVOLUTIONARY MODEL. In the process of economic growth, the interactions between the driving forces often produce oscillations. In the nineteenth century these were interpreted as *the* business cycle. Current interpretations of the growth of economic theory are dominated by similar notions. There is much talk about revolutions, which are supposed to be separated by periods of broad consensus, thus producing the image of successive cycles.

In part, this notion, together with much loose talk about paradigms, is an echo of Thomas Kuhn's general description of scientific revolutions (Kuhn 1970). For the most part, however, the cyclical model of the history of economics goes back to Schumpeter. He described the cycle of classical economics as beginning with "fresh activity that struggled hopefully with the deadwood; then things settled down and there emerged a typical classical situation. . . . Then followed stagnation" (1954, 380). The marginalist cycle was supposed to begin with "revolutions" followed by "two decades of struggle." There emerged another "classical situation," eventually showing "signs of decay" (754).

Schumpeter's theory of analytical cycles is an obvious analogy to his theory of business cycles, in which bursts of innovations are separated by periods of near equilibrium. The genealogy of this notion leads to Marx, who visualized history as a sequence of revolutions separated by periods of relatively quiet class rule. This philosophy of history was, in turn, the materialist inversion of Hegel's dialectics of the spirit. After the Glorious Revolution the Aristotelian idea of a rotation of different forms of government seems to have merged with the notion that governments revolve like the heavenly bodies in Copernicus's system. It may be left to the intellectual historian to trace this tradition back to the theology of a millennium and the mythology of successive ages of humanity separated by struggles between the gods. Ancient myths survive in ever changing guises.

To return from mythology to historical facts, a revolution is a violent overthrow of a ruler (or ruling group) by those ruled. In contrast to a coup d'état, it comes from below. It is not clear that any upheaval deserving this description has ever occurred in economic theory. Certainly nothing like it took place before 1870. Despite the frequent talk of a marginal revolution, no scientific revolution occurred in the 1870s either (see Blaug 1972). The real breakthroughs were achieved much before 1870, and the important contributions of the 1870s generated quiet evolution rather than a revolution. No heads were rolling and no tyrants were deposed. Even Mill's *Principles* continued to be used as a text for decades.

Nor was there a revolution in the 1930s, despite all talk about a Keynesian revolution. That the *General Theory* amounted to a revolution against Pigovian orthodoxy was a myth engendered mainly by Keynes himself. In fact, Keynes, though creating a highly useful short-term model, belonged firmly to the Marshallian tradition. Consequently, the continuation of that tradition required no subsequent counterrevolution. A quiet synthesis was enough.

The main reason for the absence of revolutions in economic theory is the absence of an overarching power structure. There is no ideological superstructure resisting innovation. At any given time, mainstream economics resembles a chaotic babble rather than a dogmatic system. The comprehensive treatises, that marginalist professors (as well as Karl Marx) loved to plan, used to remain fragments. Marshallian economics hardly created the impression of "the finality of a Greek temple that spreads its perfect lines against a cloudless sky," as Schumpeter rhapsodized (1954, 754). Rather, it was a rambling structure that, though in parts quite habitable, was patently unfinished. In the twentieth century, the increasingly irreverent spirit of the economics profession makes dogmatic systematization look pompous.

Since there are no walls of resistance that have to be breached by pent-up innovation, economic theory does not grow in cycles. Surely there are periods of rapid progress and others of relative stagnation. Little happened between 1776 and 1798. The post-Ricardian era brought stagnation in England, but it was also the era of Thünen, Cournot, Dupuit, and Gossen. The post-Marshallian years around World War I brought another trough in analytical activity, followed by bursts of activity in the 1930s and 1940s. The point is that these irregularities in the flow of analytical innovation cannot be attributed to a cyclical mechanism of intermittent tension and relaxation.

AN EVOLUTIONARY MODEL. Wicksell compared economic fluctuations to the movements of a rocking horse exposed to irregular shocks rather than to cyclical revolutions. Frisch then developed this idea into his impulse/propagation model. In the post–World War II period, this became the dominant approach to business fluctuations. The history of economic theory suggests that this approach may also be applicable to its own development. In contrast to the cycles of the revolutionary model, this leads to an evolutionary conception of the history of science. Its main outlines can be summarized as follows.

The eternal drive for the elimination of logical flaws and the increase in scientific resources result in a persistent growth trend. The history of economic theory has been one of progress. The general direction of this process depends on the existing logical flaws, and thus it may seem, in principle, determinate. However, since it involves a sequence of new solutions to previously unsolved problems, it cannot actually be predicted. The speed with which economic theory moves along this path depends largely on the available resources and the problem-solving ability of economists. External conditions and the creativity of human minds produce impulses that look random and are certainly unpredictable. Reinforcement effects and impediments cause each of these impulses to be followed by inherent dynamic reactions. In contrast to the revolutionary model, however, there are no systematic cycles but only irregular fluctuations.

From this brief summary, an important element is still missing. It has not yet been explained by what criteria the theoretical contributions that are destined to become part of mainstream economics are distinguished from those that are forgotten. This question will be taken up in the following section.

Success and Failure

Fortune indeed rules supreme, covering things with fame or oblivion more by whim than by merit.
—Sallust, quoted by Montaigne, *Essais*

This concluding section concerns the nature of scientific progress in economic theory, the signs and measures of success and failure. The discussion of this vast topic will be limited to three specific aspects, namely (1) the success or failure of individual economists, (2) the criteria by which theoretical contributions are either incorporated into mainstream economics or forgotten, and (3) the cumulative character of the history of economic theory.

MARKS OF GREATNESS. In the prologue, this book was metaphorically described as a pantheon of economic theory. In the subsequent chapters the pantheon was gradually populated. The erection of each monument implied a decision about what makes a contribution classic and an economist great. In a review of these decisions, an effort will now be made to make the answer explicit.

The first requirement is a clear distinction between fame and accomplishment. Fame reflects what people are commonly saying, regardless of whether it is true or false, justified or unjustified. Accomplishments are the good deeds that have actually been done, regardless of whether they have been acclaimed or ignored. Fame is based on a sort of vote (partially recorded in citation indices and the like); it is a mass judgment. Accomplishment has to be evaluated by critics individually, using their own best judgment.

If fame is the criterion, Adam Smith and Karl Marx tower over the pantheon. They were the only economists to appear in the history not only of economics but of mankind. They would be followed by Malthus, Keynes, and possibly Friedman, who helped to form public opinion, stirred public debates, and influenced public policy. Mill, Marshall, and Samuelson became household names through their long-dominating textbooks. After that there is a rapid decline. The fame of Ricardo, Jevons, Walras, Menger, Wicksell, Fisher (despite his popular crusades), Schumpeter, Hicks, and Samuelson (as a theorist) is limited to the group of professional economists. Quesnay, Edgeworth, Ramsey, Hotelling, Koopmans, and Arrow are admired by specialists.

It is clear that fame is not necessarily commensurate with accomplishment as an economic theorist. Smith and Marx were the creators of, respectively, the discipline of economics and a socialist ideology, but they did not add major new building blocks to economic theory. Malthus, Keynes, and Friedman added useful building blocks, but they acquired fame more as controversialists and persuaders than as theorists. In the cases of Malthus and Keynes, just as in that of Marx, part of the fame is actually due to an analytical shortcoming, namely to their suggestive opaqueness. Obscurity is often taken for profundity, and lucidity, by comparison, may seem trite. In the cases of Ricardo, Menger, Böhm-Bawerk, Marshall, Chamberlin, and Robinson, the accomplishments, though substantial, fall more or less short of their fame. Schumpeter is famous, at least with nontheorists, for his vision of capitalism, though he could never produce a piece of original theoretical analysis.

On the other hand, Cantillon, Rae, Thünen, Cournot, Dupuit, and Gossen added contributions of primary importance to modern mainstream economics but are nevertheless regarded as failures by all but a few. None of them had the slightest influence on further developments within twenty years after publication of their main works. Rather than being famous in their own right, they are relegated to the role of precursors of the famous. Launhardt, Auspitz, and Lieben, though appreciated by some of the best of their contemporaries, are virtually forgotten except by a few historians of economics.

Finally, there are the success stories of those who indeed won fame for their brilliant theoretical achievements. Among them are Jevons, Walras, Wicksell, Fisher, Pareto, Hicks, von Neumann, Samuelson, and Arrow. One reason for their success is that they were able to combine vision with analysis. Related to this is their ability to limit themselves to analytical questions they could indeed solve. By and large, successful science takes up problems in the order not of their urgency but of their solvability. To pose great unsolvable problems may lead to fame; to solve small problems is an accomplishment. The fundamental condition for success seems to be the solution of analytical problems that provides the key to rapid further advances. Reinforcement effects are the path to glory.

HISTORICAL SELECTION. Economic theory, as it has evolved over the last three hundred years, consists of pieces of pure logic, often expressible in the form of mathematics. The notion that these pieces, taken together, are supposed to be a representation, an image or a model of economic reality is patently absurd. Economic theory is not the theorist's view of the world. It is not even clear that the progress of science can be expected to bring economic theory closer to reality, whatever that may mean. Nevertheless, most people feel that economic theory should have something to do with economic reality, and most good economists are convinced that it actually does. Many of them are, in fact, proud to regard economics as an empirical science. What then is the link between those pieces of logic we call economic theory and observable reality?

The link is that empirical observation provides the ultimate criterion by which those pieces of analysis we call mainstream economics are selected from the infinite number of conceivable pieces. Empirical observation is the winnow that separates the wheat of classic contributions from the chaff of empty formalism.

Different generations have visualized this winnowing procedure in different ways. The historicists believed that economic laws are distilled from a mass of accumulated facts. Jevons's work on logic should have been enough to dispel this notion, Menger exploded it, and Koopmans restated the criticism in the age of econometrics. Econometrics undertook to develop a methodology by which economic theories could be subjected to empirical testing. Economics seemed to become an empirical science "like any other." Half a century later this could be seen to have been an illusion. Very few economic disputes, as was pointed out in chapter 25, were actually settled by appeal to econometric tests; econometric work produced few propositions that can be regarded as reliably confirmed; and the selection of classic contributions to economic theory is usually not based on econometric testing. In recent years the pendulum has even seemed to swing back toward "measurement without theory" and "letting the facts speak for themselves."

Others were hopeful to find the link between pure theory and observation in some great regularities or great ratios in economic life. In the second half of the nineteenth century, "the" business cycle began to be seen as a pervasive regularity. Kondratieff and others then claimed to have found a long cycle. Leading indicators promised to signal upturns and downturns. Pareto discovered a surprising regularity in the size distribution of income. In the heyday of the Cobb-Douglas production function, factor shares were said to be remarkably constant. P. J. Veerdorn postulated a close relationship between the growth rates of labor productivity and output, and Arthur Okun proclaimed a similar law for short-run changes in employment and output. The Phillips curve purported to establish a trade-off between inflation and employment. However, none of these alleged regularities survived very long. They could not provide the missing link either.

As a matter of fact, this link seems to be of a different kind. History confronts the economist with an ever changing stream of specific problems, each of them in some respects unique. Each of them has to be solved by marshaling the empirical evidence with the aid of a theoretical model, sometimes as vague as an intuitive understanding of the problem. In principle, this model will be as unique as the historical situation it is intended to cover. The work of economists is greatly helped, however, if they possess an inventory of models that have been analyzed before. The inventory typically available at a given moment is what in this book has been called mainstream economics. A new and untested piece of economic logic will be added to the inventory if there is a hope that it will turn out to be useful; otherwise it will be ignored. An old piece of analysis will be retained in the inventory if it has been successfully used in the past; otherwise it will be forgotten.

The decisive tests, in this view, are provided not by correlation coefficients and the like but by historical experience. This is particularly evident in macroeconomics. Since 19 October 1987, at the latest, it has been hard to argue that daily stock price changes reflect nothing but new information. The experience of 1979–83 makes it difficult to maintain that monetary policy has no real effects even in the short run. Cassel's theory of exchange overshooting, as revived by Dornbusch, was restored to the inventory in the aftermath of the collapse of the Bretton Woods system. The stagflation of the late 1960s brought the demise of the Phillips curve.

In other cases, particularly in microeconomics, the process of historical validation is less tangible. It is nevertheless true that theories tend to be successful if they are helpful in understanding specific problems. By this test, to illustrate with a few examples, marginalist optimization, utility theory, linear programming, portfolio theory, the IS/LM-model, and Tinbergen's theory of economic policy have been overwhelmingly successful, as any perusal of economic journals shows. The empirical validation of economic theory results, in general, not from formal economic testing but from a process of historical selection.

THE CUMULATIVE PROCESS. This book is meant to be a history of what is regarded in the last quarter of the twentieth century as mainstream economic theory. It is logically inherent in this conception that this history appears as one of cumulative progress. It would so appear even if the mainstream economics of 1980 were actually inferior to the mainstream economics of 1930, 1880, or 1830. This raises the question of whether the image of a cumulative process is nothing but a mirage, an artifact created by the particular conception of the historiographer, or whether it reflects, at least to a large part, real scientific progress.

If cumulative progress were merely an illusion, the diligent historiographer would be able to find in the earlier literature valuable pieces of analysis that were later forgotten or perhaps never even recognized. The history of economic theory would be a gold mine for contemporary economics. Economic theory would be like a pure art in which the great masters of different ages, perhaps back to earlier millenniums, continue to be a source of inspiration. In actual fact this is not so. The great masters of earlier centuries have virtually ceased to provide inspiration. The neo-Ricardians from Cambridge, England, hoped to wash gold from Ricardo, and the Marxians still mine *Capital*, but little gold seems to be left in those hills for modern theory. It follows that the successive additions to the analytical inventory recorded in the preceding chapters were not matched, to any appreciable extent, by deletions. By and large, the gross additions were net additions.

This corresponds to the observation that few pieces of economic analysis ever really die. It is difficult to find examples of theories that were thought to be useful and persuasive at one time but were later completely discarded as worthless. Fallacies are corrected, ambiguities are cleared up, limitations are removed, but the old idea usually lives on. The specie flow mechanism, the quantity theory, purchasing power parity, monetary macrodynamics, the canonical classical model, comparative advantage, the wage fund, the cost theory of value, and the *Tableau Economique* are some of the innumerable examples.

The same observation applies to the successive leitmotivs of economic theory. The circular flow, the leitmotiv of classical economics, never lost its significance. Economic interdependence is as important today as it ever was. Historians of economics often pictured classical economics as declining after Ricardo. In fact, it was not so much declining as being supplemented by the new approaches of marginalism. By explaining economic optimization by households and firms, marginalism filled extensive gaps left open during the classical era. It did not decline either, and its analytical accomplishments are still the daily bread of economists. During the model-building era economists learned to express their specific problems in terms of general equilibrium models of reduced size, making full use of the optimizing calculus. Again this brought a vast extension of the power of theoretical analysis without a loss of earlier achievements.

The ultimate test of cumulative progress, of course, is practical applicability and usefulness. A considerable part of recent theory has not passed this test yet; it is still an investment for the future. A large part, however, has been in wide use at all levels of policy making. It is true that the application of economic theory will always remain an art, and in art there may not be a cumulative progress. As a consequence, there continue to be dissension, confusion, and failures. There is no reasonable doubt, however, that the progress of economic theory has enabled policy makers to find reasonably workable solutions to innumerable problems that in earlier periods would have remained unsolved or even might have led to disaster.

Finally, one has to recognize that despite a considerable amount of cumulative progress, economic theory is still very imperfect. It is psychologically understandable that mathematicians and natural scientists continue to regard it as scientifically immature. Nevertheless this patronizing attitude, just like the analogous attitude of the economist relative to other social scientists, is unjustified. Economics is more imperfect than some natural sciences, not because it has had less time to mature but because it is more difficult. The universe is much more immutable and less complicated than history, and intelligent people thus found it easier to build theories on the interactions of celestial bodies than on the interactions of human beings. Economic theory indeed continues to be very imperfect, but it represents the best that human minds have yet achieved in explaining parts of history with the means of science.

THE SAME FORCES that have shaped the course of economic theory in the past will probably shape it in the future. Ambitious and creative scientists will make their contributions. Most of them will be forgotten, but some will become classic in the sense of being added to mainstream economics. There will continue to be controversy, and some dissenters will continue to promote alternatives to mainstream economics. To the extent that their contributions are good, they will sooner or later be absorbed by mainstream economics. To the extent they are not absorbed, they are probably not very good. To the tradition of classic contributions there is no alternative, whatever ideological, political, or social predilections individual economists might have.

References

Abramovitz, Moses. 1956. Resource and Output Trends in the United States Since 1870. *American Economic Review Papers and Proceedings* 46(2): 5–23.

Adelman, Irma and Frank L. 1959. The Dynamic Properties of the Klein-Goldberger Model. *Econometrica* 27(4): 596–625.

Aftalion, Albert. 1913. *Les Crises périodiques de surproduction.* 2 vols. Paris: Rivière.

Ahiakpor, James C. W. 1985. Ricardo on Money: The Operational Significance of the Non-Neutrality of Money in the Short Run. *History of Political Economy* 17(1): 17–30.

Åkerman, Gustaf. 1923–24. *Realkapital und Kapitalzins.* 2 parts. Stockholm: Centraltryckeriet.

Allais, Maurice. 1947. *Economie et intérêt.* 2 vols. Paris: Imprimerie Nationale.

———. 1962. The Influence of the Capital-Output Ratio on Real National Income. *Econometrica* 30(4): 700–728.

Allen, R. G. D. 1936. Professor Slutsky's Theory of Consumers' Choice. *Review of Economic Studies* 3(2): 120–29.

———. 1950. The Work of Eugen Slutsky. *Econometrica* 18(3): 209–16.

Alt, Franz. 1936. Ueber die Messbankeit des Nutzens. *Zeitschrift für Nationalökonomie* 7(2): 161–69.

Anderson, James. 1777. *Observations on the Means of Exciting a Spirit of National Industry.* . . . Edinburgh: Cadell & Elliot.

———. 1859. Extract from an Inquiry into the Nature of the Corn Laws with a View to the New Corn-Bill Proposed for Scotland (1777). In *A Select Collection of Scarce and Valuable Tracts,* ed. J. R. McCulloch. London.

Andvig, Jens Christopher. 1981. Ragnar Frisch and Business Cycle Research During the Interwar Years. *History of Political Economy* 13(4): 695–725.

Archibald, G. C., and R. G. Lipsey. 1958. Monetary and Value Theory: A Critique of Lange and Patinkin. *Review of Economic Studies* 26(1): 1–22.

Aristotle. 1921. *Politica.* Trans. B. Jowett, ed. W. D. Ross. Rev. ed. Oxford: Clarendon.

———. 1924? *Nicomachean Ethics.* Trans. F. H. Peters. 14th ed. London: Kegan Paul, Trench, Trubner.

———. 1928. *Topica.* Trans. W. A. Pickard-Cambridge. In *Works,* ed. W. D. Ross, vol. 1. Oxford: Clarendon.

Arrow, Kenneth J. 1951. *Social Choice and Individual Values.* New York: Wiley.

———. 1960. The Work of Ragnar Frisch, Econometrician. *Econometrica* 28(2): 175–92.

———. 1983–85. *Collected Papers.* 6 vols. Cambridge, Mass.: Harvard University Press.

Arrow, Kenneth J., and F. H. Hahn. 1971. *General Competitive Analysis.* San Francisco: Holden-Day.

References

Arrow, Kenneth J., Leonid Hurwicz, and Hirofumi Uzawa. 1958. *Studies in Linear and Non-Linear Programming*. Stanford, Calif.: Stanford University Press.

Arrow, Kenneth J., Samuel Karlin, and Herbert Scarf. 1958. *Studies in the Mathematical Theory of Inventory and Production*. Stanford, Calif.: Stanford University Press.

Arrow, Kenneth J., and Mordecai Kurz. 1970. *Public Investment, the Rate of Return, and Optimal Fiscal Policy*. Baltimore: Johns Hopkins Press.

Arrow, Kenneth J., and Hervé Raynaud. 1986. *Social Choice and Multicriterion Decision-Making*. Cambridge, Mass.: MIT Press.

d'Aspremont, C., J. J. Gabszewicz, and J.-F. Thisse. 1979. On Hotelling's "Stability in Competition." *Econometrica* 47(5): 1145–50.

Aspromourgos, T. 1986. On the Origins of the Term "Neoclassical." *Cambridge Journal of Economics* 10(3): 265–70.

Auspitz, Rudolf. 1894. Der letzte Maasstab des Güterwertes und die mathematische Methode. *Zeitschrift für Volkswirtschaft, Socialpolitik und Verwaltung* 3(4): 489–511.

Auspitz, Rudolf, and Richard Lieben. 1889. *Untersuchungen über die Theorie des Preises*. Leipzig: Duncker & Humblot. *Recherches sur la théorie du prix*, trans. L. Suret. Paris: Giard & Brière, 1914.

Bagehot, Walter. 1880. *Economic Studies*. Ed. R. Holt Hutton. London: Longmans, Green.

Barone, Enrico. 1935. The Ministry of Production in the Collectivist State. In *Collectivist Economic Planning*, ed. F. A. von Hayek, 245–90. London: Routledge.

Bator, Francis M. 1957. The Simple Analytics of Welfare Maximization. *American Economic Review* 47(1): 22–59.

Baumol, William J. 1952. The Transactions Demand for Cash: An Inventory Theoretic Approach. *Quarterly Journal of Economics* 66(4): 545–56.

———. 1974. The Transformation of Values: What Marx "Really" Meant (An Interpretation). *Journal of Economic Literature* 12(1): 51–62.

Baumol, William J., and David F. Bradford. 1970. Optimal Departures from Marginal Cost Pricing. *American Economic Review* 60(3): 265–83.

Baumol, William J., and Stephen M. Goldfeld, eds. 1968. *Precursors in Mathematical Economics: An Anthology*. Series of Reprints of Scarce Works on Political Economy no. 19. London: London School of Economics and Political Science.

Bentham, Jeremy. 1952–54. *Economic Writings*. Ed. W. Stark. 3 vols. London: Allen & Unwin.

Bernoulli, Daniel. 1968. Exposition of a New Theory of Risk Evaluation. In *Precursors in Mathematical Economics: An Anthology*, ed. William J. Baumol and Stephen M. Goldfeld, 15–26. Series of Reprints of Scarce Works on Political Economy no. 19. London: London School of Economics and Political Science.

Bickerdike, C. F. 1920. The Instability of Foreign Exchange. *Economic Journal* 30(117): 118–22.

Black, Duncan. 1948. On the Rationale of Group Decision-Making. *Journal of Political Economy* 56(1): 23–34.

———. 1958. *The Theory of Committees and Elections*. Cambridge: Cambridge University Press.

Blaug, Mark. 1972. Was There a Marginal Revolution? *History of Political Economy* 4(2): 269–80.

———. 1978. *Economic Theory in Retrospect*. 3d ed. Cambridge: Cambridge University Press.

———. 1987. Classical Economics. In *The New Palgrave: A Dictionary of Economics*, ed. John Eatwell, Murray Milgate, and Peter Newman, 1:434–44. London: Macmillan.

Blinder, Alan S., and Robert M. Solow. 1973. Does Fiscal Policy Matter? *Journal of Public Economics* 2(4): 319–37.

Bodin, Jean. 1946. *The Response of Jean Bodin to the Paradoxes of Malestroit and the Paradoxes*. Trans. G. A. Moore. Washington, D.C.: Country Dollar Press.

Böhm-Bawerk, Eugen von. 1881. *Rechte und Verhältnisse vom Standpunkte der volkswirtschaftlichen Güterlehre*. Innsbruck: Wagner.

———. 1921. *Kapital und Kapitalzins* (part 1, 1884; part 2, 1889) 4th ed., 3 vols. Jena: Fischer. *Capital and Interest*, trans. G. D. Huncke and H. F. Sennholz. 3 vols. South Holland, Ill.: Libertarian Press, 1959.

———. 1924–26. *Gesammelte Schriften*. Ed. F. X. Weiss. 2 vols. Vienna: Hölder-Pichler-Tempsky.

———. 1949. *Karl Marx and the Close of His System*. (Zum Abschluss des Marxschen Systems. In *Staatswissenschaftliche Arbeiten: Festgabe für Karl Knies*, ed. O. von Boenigk, 1896.) Ed. P. M. Sweezy. New York: Kelley.

Boisguilbert, Pierre de. 1966. *La Naissance de l'économie politique*. 2 vols. Paris: Institut National d'Etudes Démographiques.

Bombach, G., et al., eds. 1976–84. *Der Keynesianismus*. 5 vols. Berlin: Springer.

Bordo, Michael D. 1983. Some Aspects of the Monetary Economics of Richard Cantillon. *Journal of Monetary Economics* 12(2): 235–58.

Bos, Henk C. 1984. Jan Tinbergen: A Profile. *Journal of Policy Modeling* 6(2): 151–58.

Boson, Marcel. 1951. *Léon Walras, fondateur de la politique économique scientifique*. Paris: Pichon; Lausanne: Rouge.

Botero, Giovanni. 1956. *The Reason of State (Della ragion di stato*, 1589), trans. P. J. and D. P. Waley, and *The Greatness of Cities (Delle cause della grandezza e magnificenza della città*, 1588), trans. R. Peterson. London: Routledge & Kegan Paul.

Boulding, Kenneth E. 1955. The Malthusian Model as a General System. *Social and Economic Studies* 4(3): 195–205.

Bousquet, Georges Henri. 1928. *Vilfredo Pareto, sa vie et son oeuvre*. Paris: Payot.

———. 1960. *Pareto (1848–1923): Le savant et l'homme*. Lausanne: Payot.

Bowley, Marian. 1937. *Nassau Senior and Classical Economics*. London: Allen & Unwin.

Breit, William, and Roger L. Ransom. 1982. *The Academic Scribblers*. Rev. ed. Hinsdale, Ill.: Dryden.

Breit, William, and Roger W. Spencer, eds. 1986. *Lives of the Laureates: Seven Nobel Economists.*. Cambridge, Mass.: MIT Press.

Brems, Hans. 1978. Cantillon versus Marx: The Land Theory and the Labor Theory of Value. *History of Political Economy* 10(4): 669–78.

———. 1986. *Pioneering Economic Theory, 1630–1980: A Mathematical Restatement*. Baltimore: Johns Hopkins University Press.

References

Brown, E. Cary, and Robert M. Solow, eds. 1983. *Paul Samuelson and Modern Economic Theory.* New York: McGraw-Hill.

Brun, Jean, and André Robinet, eds. 1978. *A. Cournot: Etudes pour le centenaire de sa mort (1877–1977).* Paris: Economica.

Brunner, Karl. 1968. The Role of Money and Monetary Policy. *Federal Reserve Bank of St. Louis Review* 50(7): 9–24.

Buckle, Henry Thomas. 1873. *History of Civilization in England.* New ed. 3 vols. London: Longmans, Green.

Bucolo, Placido, ed. 1980. *The Other Pareto.* London: Scolar Press.

Burk (Bergson), Abram. 1938. A Reformulation of Certain Aspects of Welfare Economics. *Quarterly Journal of Economics* 52(2): 310–34.

Busino, G. 1987. Vilfredo Pareto. In *The New Palgrave: A Dictionary of Economics,* ed. John Eatwell, Murray Milgate, and Peter Newman, 3:799–804. London: Macmillan.

Butler, Eamonn. 1985. *Milton Friedman—A Guide to His Economic Thought.* Aldershot, England: Gower.

Campbell, R. H., and A. S. Skinner. 1982. *Adam Smith.* London: Croom Helm.

Cannan, Edwin. 1982. Alfred Marshall, 1842–1924. In *Alfred Marshall: Critical Assessments,* ed. John Cunningham Wood, 1:66–70. London: Croom Helm.

Cantillon, Richard. 1931. *Essai sur la nature du commerce en général* (1755). With English trans. ed. H. Higgs. London: Macmillan.

Cassel, Gustav. 1921. *Theoretische Sozialökonomie.* 2d ed. Leipzig: Winter.

Cave, Martin. 1981. Wassily Leontief: Input-Output and Economic Planning. In *Twelve Contemporary Economists,* ed. J. R. Shackleton and G. Locksley, 160–82. New York: Wiley.

Chakravarty, S. 1962. The Existence of an Optimum Savings Program. *Econometrica* 30(1): 178–87.

Chamberlin, Edward Hastings. 1929. Duopoly: Value Where Sellers Are Few. *Quarterly Journal of Economics* 44(1): 63–100.

———. 1957. *Towards a More General Theory of Value.* New York: Oxford University Press.

———. 1962. *Theory of Monopolistic Competition: A Reorientation of the Theory of Value* (1933). 8th ed. Cambridge, Mass.: Harvard University Press.

Chamberlin, Edward Hastings (subject). 1964. The Theory of Monopolistic Competition after Thirty Years. *American Economic Review Papers and Proceedings* 54(3): 28–57.

Champernowne, D. G. 1962. Some Implications of Golden Age Conditions When Savings Equal Profits. *Review of Economic Studies* 29:235–37.

Chipman, John S. 1965. A Survey of the Theory of International Trade. Part 1, The Classical Theory; part 2, The Neo-Classical Theory. *Econometrica* 33(3): 477–519; 33(4): 685–760.

———. 1979. Mill's "Superstructure": How Well Does It Stand Up? *History of Political Economy* 11(4): 477–500.

———. 1982. Samuelson and Consumption Theory. In *Samuelson and Neoclassical Economics,* ed. George R. Feiwel, 31–71. Boston: Kluwer. Christ, Carl F. 1985.

Christ, Carl F. 1985. Early Progress in Estimating Quantitative Economic Relationships in America. *American Economic Review.* 75(6): 39–52.

Cirillo, Renato. 1979. *The Economics of Vilfredo Pareto.* London: Cass.

References

Clapham, Sir John Harold. 1922. Of Empty Economic Boxes. *Economic Journal* 32(3): 305–14.

Clark, John Bates. 1890. The Law of Wages and Interest. *Annals of the American Academy of Political and Social Science* 1 (July): 43–65.

———. 1891. Distribution as Determined by a Law of Rent. *Quarterly Journal of Economics* 5 (April): 289–318.

———. 1899. *The Distribution of Wealth.* New York: Macmillan.

Clark, John Maurice. 1917. Business Acceleration and the Law of Demand: A Technical Factor in Economic Cycles. *Journal of Political Economy* 25(3): 217–35.

Coase, Ronald H. 1960. The Problem of Social Cost. *Journal of Law and Economics* 3:1–44.

———. 1984. Alfred Marshall's Mother and Father. *History of Political Economy* 16(4): 519–27.

Corden, W. M. 1971. *The Theory of Protection.* Oxford: Oxford University Press.

Cournot, A. A. 1838. *Recherches sur les principes mathématiques de la théorie des richesses.* Paris: Hachette. *Researches into the Mathematical Principles of the Theory of Wealth,* trans. N. T. Bacon. New York: Macmillan, 1897.

———. 1863. *Principes de la théorie des richesses.* Paris: Hachette.

———. 1877. *Revue sommaire des doctrines économiques.* Paris: Hachette.

———. 1913. *Souvenirs (1760–1860).* Ed. E. P. Bottinelli. Paris: Hachette.

———. 1973– . *Oeuvres complètes.* Ed. A. Robinet. 14 vols. Paris: Vrin.

Crabtree, Derek, and A. P. Thirlwall, eds. 1980. *Keynes and the Bloomsbury Group.* London: Macmillan.

Craver, Earlene. 1986. The Emigration of the Austrian Economists. *History of Political Economy* 18(1): 1–32.

Creedy, John. 1986. *Edgeworth and the Development of Neoclassical Economics.* Oxford: Blackwell.

Davanzati, Bernardo. 1965. *Lezione delle monete* (1588). In *Scrittori classici italiani di economia politica,* ed. P. Custodi, parte antica, vol. 2 (1804). Reprint. Rome: Bizzarri.

Debreu, Gerard. 1959. *Theory of Value: An Axiomatic Analysis of Economic Equilibrium.* New Haven, Conn.: Yale University Press.

———. 1983. *Mathematical Economics: Twenty Papers of Gerard Debreu.* Cambridge: Cambridge University Press.

Dempsey, Bernard William. 1943. *Interest and Usury.* Washington, D.C.: American Council on Public Affairs.

De Quincey, Thomas. 1890a. *The Collected Writings.* Ed. D. Masson, vol. 9. Edinburgh: Black. (Including: Dialogues of Three Templars on Political Economy [1824]; Ricardo and Adam Smith [1842]; The Logic of Political Economy [1844]).

———. 1890b. Measure of Value (1823). In *The Uncollected Writings of Thomas De Quincey,* ed. J. Hogg, vol. 1. London: Swann, Sonnenschein.

De Roover, Raymond. 1949. *Gresham on Foreign Exchange.* Cambridge, Mass.: Harvard University Press.

———. 1951. Monopoly Theory Prior to Adam Smith: A Revision. *Quarterly Journal of Economics* 65(4): 492–524.

———. 1955. Scholastic Economics: Survival and Lasting Influence from the Six-

References

teenth Century to Adam Smith. *Quarterly Journal of Economics* 69(2): 161–90.

———. 1958. The Concept of the Just Price: Theory and Economic Policy. *Journal of Economic History* 18(4): 418–34.

———. 1971. *La Pensée économique des Scholastiques: Doctrines et méthodes.* Montreal: Institut d'Etudes Médiévales.

Desrousseaux, Jacques. 1961. Expansion stable et taux d'intérêt optimal. *Annales des Mines*, 829–44.

Dickinson, H. D. 1969. Von Thünen's Economics. *Economic Journal* 79(316): 894–902.

Domar, Evsey D. 1957. *Essays in the Theory of Economic Growth.* New York: Oxford University Press.

Dorfman, Robert. 1973. Wassily Leontief's Contribution to Economics. *Swedish Journal of Economics* 75(4): 430–49.

———. 1986. Comment: P. A. Samuelson, "Thuenen at Two Hundred." *Journal of Economic Literature* 24(4): 1773–76.

Dorfman, Robert, Paul A. Samuelson, and Robert M. Solow. 1958. *Linear Programming and Economic Analysis.* New York: McGraw-Hill.

Dupuit, Jules. 1933. *De l'utilité et sa mesure.* Ed. M. de Bernardi. Turin: Riforma Sociale.

———. 1952. On the Measurement of the Utility of Public Works (De la mesure de l'utilité des travaux publics. *Annales des ponts et chaussées*, 1844). In International Economic Papers no. 2, 83–110. London: Macmillan.

———. 1962. On Tolls and Transport Charges (De l'influence des péages sur l'utilité des voies de communication. *Annales des ponts et chaussées*, 1849). In International Economic Papers no. 11, 7–31. London: Macmillan.

Eagly, Robert V. 1963. Money, Employment and Prices: A Swedish View, 1761. *Quarterly Journal of Economics* 77(4): 626–36.

Eagly, Robert V., ed. 1971. *The Swedish Bullionist Controversy. P. N. Christiernin's "Lectures on the High Price of Foreign Exchange in Sweden" (1761).* Philadelphia: American Philosophical Society.

Edgeworth, Francis Ysidro. 1877. *New and Old Methods of Ethics.* Oxford: Parker.

———. 1881. *Mathematical Psychics: An Essay on the Application of Mathematics to the Moral Sciences.* London: Kegan Paul.

———. 1887. *Metretike, or the Method of Measuring Probability and Utility.* London: Temple.

———. 1888. The Mathematical Theory of Banking. *Journal of the Royal Statistical Society* 51 (March): 113–27.

———. 1925. *Papers Relating to Political Economy.* 3 vols. London: Macmillan.

Edvardsen, Kare. 1970. A Survey of Ragnar Frisch's Contribution to the Science of Economics. *De Economist* 118(2): 174–96.

Einaudi, Luigi. 1952. Einaudi on Galiani. In *The Development of Economic Thought: Great Economists in Perspective*, ed. H. W. Spiegel, 62–82. New York: Wiley.

Eisermann, Gottfried. 1987. *Vilfredo Pareto: Ein Klassiker der Soziologie.* Tübingen: Mohr.

Evans, G. Heberton. 1967. The Law of Demand—The Roles of Gregory King and Charles Davenant. *Quarterly Journal of Economics* 81(3): 483–92.

Fage, Anita. 1952. La Vie et l'oeuvre de Richard Cantillon. In R. Cantillon, *Essai sur la nature du commerce en général*, ed. A. Sauvy et al., xxiii–xli. Paris: Institut National d'Etudes Démographiques.

Feiwel, George R., ed. 1982. *Samuelson and Neoclassical Economics*. Boston: Kluwer.

Fisher, Irving. 1896. *Appreciation and Interest*. New York: Macmillan.

———. 1906. *The Nature of Capital and Income*. New York: Macmillan.

———. 1907. *The Rate of Interest: Its Nature, Determination and Relation to Economic Phenomena*. New York: Macmillan.

———. 1911. *The Purchasing Power of Money: Its Determination and Relation to Credit, Interest, and Crises*. New York: Macmillan.

———. 1920. *Stabilizing the Dollar: A Plan to Stabilize the General Price Level without Fixing Individual Prices*. New York: Macmillan.

———. 1922. *The Making of Index Numbers: A Study of Their Varieties, Tests, and Reliability*. Boston: Houghton Mifflin.

———. 1925. *Mathematical Investigations in the Theory of Value and Prices* (1892). Reprint. New Haven, Conn.: Yale University Press.

———. 1927. *A Statistical Method for Measuring "Marginal Utility" and Testing the Justice of a Progressive Income Tax*. New York: Macmillan.

———. 1928. *The Money Illusion*. New York: Adelphi.

———. 1930. *The Theory of Interest as Determined by Impatience to Spend Income and Opportunity to Invest It*. New York: Macmillan.

———. 1935. *100% Money: Designed to Keep Checking Banks 100% Liquid; to Prevent Inflation and Deflation; Largely to Cure or Prevent Depressions; and to Wipe Out Much of the National Debt*. New York: Adelphi.

———. 1937. Income in Theory and Income Taxation in Practice. *Econometrica* 5(1): 1–55.

Fisher, Irving, with Herbert W. Fisher. 1942. *Constructive Income Taxation: A Proposal for Reform*. New York: Harper.

Fisher, Irving Norton. 1956. *My Father, Irving Fisher*. New York: Comet Press.

———. 1961. *A Bibliography of the Writings of Irving Fisher*. New Haven, Conn.: Yale University Library.

Fleming, J. Marcus. 1951. On Making the Best of Balance of Payments Restrictions on Imports. *Economic Journal* 61(241): 48–71.

Foley, V. 1973. An Origin of the Tableau Economique. *History of Political Economy* 5(1): 121–50.

Fox-Genovese, Elizabeth. 1976. *The Origins of Physiocracy—Economic Revolution and Social Order in Eighteenth-Century France*. Ithaca, N.Y.: Cornell University Press.

Frey, Bruno S. 1981. Schumpeter, Political Economist. In *Schumpeterian Economics*, ed. Helmut Frisch, 126–42. New York: Praeger.

Friedenthal, Richard. 1981. *Karl Marx. Sein Leben und seine Zeit*. Munich: Piper.

Friedman, Milton. 1937. The Use of Ranks to Avoid the Assumption of Normality Implicit in the Analysis of Variance. *Journal of the American Statistical Association* 32(200): 675–701.

———. 1948. A Monetary and Fiscal Framework for Economic Stability. *American Economic Review* 38(3): 245–64.

References

———. 1953. *Essays in Positive Economics*. Chicago: University of Chicago Press.

———. 1957. *A Theory of the Consumption Function*. Princeton, N.J.: Princeton University Press.

———. 1960. *A Program for Monetary Stability*. New York: Fordham University Press.

———. 1962. *Capitalism and Freedom*. Chicago: University of Chicago Press.

———. 1969. *The Optimum Quantity of Money, and Other Essays*. Chicago: Aldine.

———. 1970. *The Counter-Revolution in Monetary Theory*. London: Institute of Economic Affairs.

———. 1975. *An Economist's Protest*. Glen Ridge, N.J.: Norton.

———. 1983. *Bright Promises, Dismal Performance: An Economist's Protest*. New York: Harcourt Brace Jovanovich.

Friedman, Milton and Rose. 1980. *Freedom to Choose: A Personal Statement*. New York: Harcourt Brace Jovanovich.

———. 1984. *Tyranny of the Status Quo*. San Diego: Harcourt Brace Jovanovich.

Friedman, Milton, and Simon Kuznets. 1945. *Income from Independent Professional Practice*. New York: National Bureau of Economic Research.

Friedman, Milton, and L. J. Savage. 1948. The Utility Analysis of Choices Involving Risk. *Journal of Political Economy* 56(4): 279–304.

Friedman, Milton, and Anna J. Schwartz. 1963. *A Monetary History of the United States, 1867–1960*. Princeton, N.J.: Princeton University Press.

———. 1965. *The Great Contraction, 1929–1933*. Princeton, N.J.: Princeton University Press.

———. 1970. *Monetary Statistics of the United States: Estimates, Sources, Methods*. New York: National Bureau of Economic Research.

———. 1982. *Monetary Trends in the United States and the United Kingdom: Their Relation to Income, Prices, and Interest Rates, 1867–1975*. Chicago: University of Chicago Press.

Frisch, Helmut, ed. 1981. *Schumpeterian Economics*. New York: Praeger.

Frisch, Ragnar. 1931. The Interrelation between Capital Production and Consumer-Taking. *Journal of Political Economy* 39(5): 646–54.

———. 1932a. *New Methods of Measuring Marginal Utility*. Tübingen: Mohr.

———. 1932b. Einige Punkte einer Preistheorie mit Boden und Arbeit als Produktionsfaktoren. *Zeitschrift für Nationalökonomie* 3(1): 62–104.

———. 1933a. *Pitfalls in the Statistical Construction of Demand and Supply Curves*. Leipzig: Buske.

———. 1933b. Monopole—polypole—la notion de force dans l'économie. *Nationaløkonomisk Tidsskrift*, April, 241–59. Monopoly—Polypoly—The Concept of Force in the Economy. In International Economic Papers no. 1, 23–36. London: Macmillan, 1951.

———. 1933c. Propagation Problems and Impulse Problems in Dynamic Economics. In *Economic Essays in Honour of Gustav Cassel*, 171–205. London: Allen & Unwin.

———. 1934a. *Statistical Confluence Analysis by Means of Complete Regression Systems*. Oslo: University Economics Institute.

———. 1934b. Circulation Planning: Proposal for a National Organization of a Commodity and Service Exchange. Parts 1, 2. *Econometrica* 2(3): 258–336; 2(4): 422–35.

———. 1936a. Annual Survey of General Economic Theory: The Problem of Index Numbers. *Econometrica* 4(1): 1–38.

———. 1936b. On the Notion of Equilibrium and Disequilibrium. *Review of Economic Studies* 3(2): 100–105.

———. 1936c. Note on the Term "Econometrics." *Econometrica* 4(1): 95.

———. 1939. The Dupuit Taxation Theorem. *Econometrica* 7(2): 145–50.

———. 1952. Frisch on Wicksell. In *The Development of Economic Thought: Great Economists in Perspective*, ed. H. W. Spiegel, 652–99. New York: Wiley.

———. 1957. Sur un problème d'économie politique pure. *Metroeconomica* 9(2): 79–111.

———. 1959. A Complete Scheme for Computing All Direct and Cross Demand Elasticities in a Model with Many Sectors. *Econometrica* 27(2): 177–96.

———. 1965. *Theory of Production*. Dordrecht: Reidel.

———. 1966. *Maxima and Minima: Theory and Economic Applications*. Dordrecht: Reidel.

———. 1976. *Economic Planning Studies: A Collection of Essays*. Ed. F. Long. Dordrecht: Reidel.

Galiani, Ferdinando. 1803. Dialogues sur le commerce des blés (1770). In *Scrittori classici italiani di economia politica*, ed. P. Custodi, parte moderna, vols. 5–6. Milan: Destefanis.

———. 1977. *On Money (Della Moneta*, 1750). Trans. P. R. Toscano. Ann Arbor: University Microfilms International.

Gardlund, Torsten. 1958. *The Life of Knut Wicksell*. Trans. N. Adler. Stockholm: Almqvist & Wiksell.

Glasner, David. 1985. A Reinterpretation of Classical Monetary Theory. *Southern Economic Journal* 52(1): 46–67.

Gordon, Barry. 1975. *Economic Analysis before Adam Smith: Hesiod to Lessius*. New York: Harper & Row.

Gordon, Robert J., ed. 1974. *Milton Friedman's Monetary Framework—A Debate with His Critics*. Chicago: University of Chicago Press.

Gossen, Hermann Heinrich. 1854. *Entwickelung der Gesetze des menschlichen Verkehrs, und der daraus fliessenden Regeln für menschliches Handeln*. Brunswick: Vieweg. (2d ed. Berlin: Prager, 1889.) *Sviluppo delle leggi del commercio umano*, trans. T. Bagiotti. Padua: Cedam, 1950. *The Laws of Human Relations and the Rules of Human Action Derived Therefrom*, trans. R. C. Blitz (with intro. by N. Georgescu-Roegen). Cambridge, Mass.: MIT Press, 1983.

Gram, Harvey, and Vivian Walsh. 1983. Joan Robinson's Economics in Retrospect. *Journal of Economic Literature* 21(2): 518–50.

Grampp, William D. 1974. Malthus and His Contemporaries. *History of Political Economy* 6(3): 278–304.

Gray, Alexander. 1963. *The Development of Economic Doctrine: An Introductory Survey* (1931). New ed. New York: Wiley.

Gray, Lewis Cecil. 1913. The Economic Possibilities of Conservation. *Quarterly Journal of Economics* 27(3): 497–519.

———. 1914. Rent under the Assumption of Exhaustibility. *Quarterly Journal of Economics* 28(3): 466–89.

Green, David I. 1894. Pain-Cost and Opportunity-Cost. *Quarterly Journal of Economics* 8(1): 218–29.

References

Grice-Hutchinson, Marjorie. 1952. *The School of Salamanca: Readings in Spanish Monetary Theory, 1544–1605.* Oxford: Clarendon.

———. 1978. *Early Economic Thought in Spain, 1177–1740.* London: Allen & Unwin.

Groenewegen, Peter D. 1977. *The Economics of A. R. J. Turgot.* The Hague: Nijhoff.

———. 1983. Turgot's Place in the History of Economic Thought: A Bicentenary Estimate. *History of Political Economy* 15(4): 585–616.

Gurley, John G., and Edward S. Shaw. 1960. *Money in a Theory of Finance.* Washington, D.C.: Brookings Institution.

Haavelmo, Trygve. 1944. The Probability Approach in Econometrics. *Econometrica* 12 (suppl.): 1–115.

Haberler, Gottfried. 1930. Die Theorie der komparativen Kosten und ihre Auswertung für die Begründung des Freihandels. *Weltwirtschaftliches Archiv* 32(2): 349–70.

———. 1951. Joseph Alois Schumpeter, 1883–1950. In *Schumpeter, Social Scientist*, ed. Seymour E. Harris, 24–47. Cambridge, Mass.: Harvard University Press.

Hamilton, Earl J. 1936. Prices and Wages at Paris under John Law's System. *Quarterly Journal of Economics* 51(1): 42–70.

Hansen, Bent. 1969. Jan Tinbergen: An Appraisal of His Contributions to Economics. *Swedish Journal of Economics* 71(4): 325–36.

Harris, Seymour E., ed. 1951. *Schumpeter, Social Scientist.* Cambridge, Mass.: Harvard University Press.

Harrod, Roy F. 1933. *International Economics.* London: Nisbet.

———. 1936. *The Trade Cycle: An Essay.* Oxford: Clarendon.

———. 1948. *Towards a Dynamic Economics.* London: Macmillan.

———. 1951. *The Life of John Maynard Keynes.* London: Macmillan.

———. 1952. *Economic Essays.* London: Macmillan.

Hartwick, John M. 1988. Robert Wallace and Malthus and the Ratios. *History of Political Economy* 20(3): 357–79.

Hatta, Tatsuo. 1976. The Paradox in Capital Theory and Complementarity of Inputs. *Review of Economic Studies* 43(133): 127–42.

———. 1977. A Theory of Piecemeal Policy Recommendations. *Review of Economic Studies* 44(136): 1–21.

Hayek, Friedrich A. von. 1931a. *Prices and Production.* New York: Macmillan.

———. 1931b. Richard Cantillon. In R. Cantillon, *Abhandlung über die Natur des Handels im allgemeinen*, trans. H. Hayek, ed. F. A. Hayek, v–lxvi. Jena: Fischer.

———. 1932. A Note on the Development of the Doctrine of "Forced Saving." *Quarterly Journal of Economics* 47(1): 123–33.

———. 1941. *The Pure Theory of Capital.* London: Routledge & Kegan Paul.

Heckscher, Eli F. 1955. *Mercantilism* (1931). Trans. M. Shapiro. Rev. 2d ed., 2 vols. London: Allen & Unwin.

Heller, Walter P., Ross M. Starr, and David A. Starrett, eds. 1986. *Social Choice and Public Decision Making. Essays in Honor of Kenneth J. Arrow.* 3 vols. Cambridge: Cambridge University Press.

Hertz, Heinrich. 1894. *Die Prinzipien der Mechanik, in neuem Zusammenhange dargestellt.* Vol. 3 of *Gesammelte Werke.* Leipzig. Reprint. Darmstadt: Wissenschaftliche Buchgesellschaft, 1963. *The Principles of Mechanics*, trans. D. E. Jones and J. T. Walley. London, 1899.

Hession, Charles H. 1984. *John Maynard Keynes: A Personal Biography of the Man Who Revolutionized Capitalism and the Way We Live*. New York: Macmillan.

Hicks, John R. 1932. *The Theory of Wages*. London: Macmillan.

———. 1939. *Value and Capital: An Inquiry into Some Fundamental Principles of Economic Theory*. Oxford: Clarendon.

———. 1942. *The Social Framework: An Introduction to Economics*. Oxford: Clarendon.

———. 1950. *A Contribution to the Theory of the Trade Cycle*. Oxford: Clarendon.

———. 1965. *Capital and Growth*. New York: Oxford University Press.

———. 1967. *Critical Essays in Monetary Theory*. Oxford: Clarendon.

———. 1973. *Capital and Time: A Neo-Austrian Theory*. Oxford: Clarendon.

———. 1981–83. *Collected Essays on Economic Theory*. 3 vols. Oxford: Blackwell.

Hicks, John R., and Wilhelm Weber, eds. 1973. *Carl Menger and the Austrian School of Economics*. Oxford: Clarendon.

Hitchcock, Frank L. 1941. The Distribution of a Product from Several Sources to Numerous Localities. *Journal of Mathematics and Physics* 20:224–30.

Höffner, Joseph. 1941. *Wirtschaftsethik und Monopole im 15. und 16. Jahrhundert*. Jena: Fischer.

Hollander, Jacob H. 1910. *David Ricardo: A Centenary Estimate*. Johns Hopkins University Studies in Historical and Political Science, series 28, no. 4. Baltimore: Johns Hopkins Press.

Hollander, Samuel. 1973. *The Economics of Adam Smith*. Toronto: University of Toronto Press.

———. 1979. *The Economics of David Ricardo*. Toronto: University of Toronto Press.

———. 1985. *The Economics of John Stuart Mill*. 2 vols. Toronto: University of Toronto Press.

Hone, Joseph. 1944. Richard Cantillon, Economist—Biographical Note. *Economic Journal* 54(1): 96–100.

Hood, W. C., and Tjalling C. Koopmans, eds. 1953. *Studies in Econometric Method*. New York: Wiley.

Horwich, George, and Paul A. Samuelson, eds. 1974. *Trade, Stability, and Macroeconomics. Essays in Honor of Lloyd A. Metzler*. New York: Academic Press.

Hotelling, Harold. 1929. Stability in Competition. *Economic Journal* 39(153): 41–57.

———. 1931. The Economics of Exhaustible Resources. *Journal of Political Economy* 39(2): 137–75.

———. 1932. Edgeworth's Taxation Paradox and the Nature of Demand and Supply Functions. *Journal of Political Economy* 40(5): 577–616.

———. 1938. The General Welfare in Relation to Problems of Taxation and of Railway and Utility Rates. *Econometrica* 6(3): 242–69.

Houthakker, Hendrik S. 1983. On Consumption Theory. In *Paul Samuelson and Modern Economic Theory*, ed. Cary E. Brown and Robert M. Solow, 57–68. New York: McGraw-Hill.

References

Howey, Richard S. 1960. *The Rise of the Marginal Utility School, 1870–1889.* Lawrence: University of Kansas Press.

———. 1972. The Origins of Marginalism. *History of Political Economy* 4(2): 281–302.

Hume, David. 1875. *Essays, Moral, Political, and Literary.* Ed. T. H. Green and T. H. Grose. 2 vols. London: Longmans, Green.

———. 1955. *Writings on Economics.* Ed. E. Rotwein. Madison: University of Wisconsin Press.

International Encyclopedia of the Social Sciences. 1968. Vols. 1–17. New York: Macmillan and Free Press.

International Encyclopedia of the Social Sciences. 1979. Vol. 18, Biographical Suppl. New York: Macmillan and Free Press.

Jaffé, William. 1983. *Essays on Walras.* Ed. D. A. Walker. Cambridge: Cambridge University Press.

———. 1984. The Antecedents and Early Life of Léon Walras, ed. D. A. Walker. *History of Political Economy* 16(1): 1–57.

James, Patricia. 1979. *Population Malthus, His Life and Times.* London: Routledge & Kegan Paul.

James, R. Warren. 1965. *John Rae, Political Economist; An Account of his Life and a Compilation of His Main Writings.* 2 vols. Toronto: University of Toronto Press.

Jevons, William Stanley. 1865. *The Coal Question: An Inquiry Concerning the Progress of the Nation, and the Probable Exhaustion of our Coal-Mines.* London: Macmillan.

———. 1874. *The Principles of Science—A Treatise on Logic and Scientific Method.* London: Macmillan.

———. 1875. *Money and the Mechanism of Exchange.* London: King.

———. 1878. *Primer of Political Economy.* London: Macmillan.

———. 1884. *Investigations in Currency and Finance.* Ed. H. S. Foxwell. London: Macmillan.

———. 1886. *Letters and Journal of W. Stanley Jevons.* Edited by his wife. London: Macmillan.

———. 1905. *The Principles of Economics: A Fragment of a Treatise on the Industrial Mechanism of Society, and Other Papers.* London: Macmillan.

———. 1957. *The Theory of Political Economy* (1871). 5th ed. London: Macmillan.

———. 1972–81. *Papers and Correspondence.* Ed. R. D. Collison Black and R. Könekamp. 7 vols. London: Macmillan.

Johannsen, Nicolas August Ludwig Jacob. 1908. *A Neglected Point in Connection with Crises.* New York: Bankers Publishing Co. (Reprint. New York: Kelley, 1971.)

Johansen, Leif. 1969. Ragnar Frisch's Contribution to Economics. *Swedish Journal of Economics* 71(4): 302–24.

———. 1974. Establishing Preference Functions for Macroeconomic Decision Models: Some Observations on Ragnar Frisch's Contributions. *European Economic Review* 5(1): 41–66.

———. 1976. L. V. Kantorovich's Contribution to Economics. *Scandinavian Journal of Economics* 78(1): 61–80.

Johnson, Elizabeth S. and Harry G. 1978. *The Shadow of Keynes*. Oxford: Blackwell.

Johnson, Harry G. 1960. Arthur Cecil Pigou, 1877–1959. *Canadian Journal of Economics and Political Science* 26(1): 150–55.

———. 1971. *Aspects of the Theory of Tariffs*. London: Allen & Unwin.

———. 1978. James Meade's Contribution to Economics. *Scandinavian Journal of Economics* 80(1): 64–85.

Johnson, William E. 1913. The Pure Theory of Utility Curves. *Economic Journal* 23(92): 483–513.

Juglar, Clément. 1889. *Des crises commerciales et de leur retour périodique en France, en Angleterre et aux Etats-Unis* (1862). 2d ed. Paris: Guillaumin.

Kahn, Richard F. 1931. The Relation of Home Investment to Unemployment. *Economic Journal* 41(162): 173–98.

Kaldor, Nicholas. 1939. Welfare Propositions of Economics and Interpersonal Comparisons of Utility. *Economic Journal* 49(195): 549–52.

———. 1957. A Model of Economic Growth. *Economic Journal* 67(268): 591–624.

Kalecki, Michal. 1935. A Macrodynamic Theory of Business Cycles. *Econometrica* 3(3): 327–44.

Kaplan, Steven Laurence, ed. 1979. *La Bagarre: Galiani's "Lost" Parody*. The Hague: Nijhoff.

Kauder, Emil. 1965. *A History of Marginal Utility Theory*. Princeton, N.J.: Princeton University Press.

Kautz, Julius. 1858–60. *Theorie und Geschichte der National-Oekonomik*. 2 vols. Vienna: Gerold.

Kessel, Reuben A. 1958. Price Discrimination in Medicine. *Journal of Law and Economics* 1:20–53.

Keynes, John Maynard. 1936. *The General Theory of Employment, Interest and Money*. London: Macmillan.

———. 1971– . *The Collected Writings*. 30 vols. London: Macmillan.

———. 1982. Alfred Marshall, 1842–1924. In *Alfred Marshall: Critical Assessments*, ed. John Cunningham Wood, 1:7–65. London: Croom Helm.

Keynes, Milo, ed. 1975. *Essays on John Maynard Keynes*. Cambridge: Cambridge University Press.

Kirzner, Israel M. 1987. Austrian School of Economics. In *The New Palgrave: A Dictionary of Economics*, ed. John Eatwell, Murray Milgate, and Peter Newman, 1:145–51. London: Macmillan.

Klamer, Arjo. 1984. *Conversations with Economists: New Classical Economists and Opponents Speak Out on the Current Controversy in Macroeconomics*. Totowa, N.J.: Rowman & Allenheld.

Klein, Lawrence R. 1947. *The Keynesian Revolution*. New York: Macmillan.

———. 1950. *Economic Fluctuations in the United States, 1921–1941*. New York: Wiley.

Knapp, Georg Friedrich. 1865. *Zur Prüfung der Untersuchungen Thünen's über Lohn und Zinsfuss im isolierten Staate*. Brunswick: Vieweg.

Knight, Frank H. 1924. Some Fallacies in the Interpretation of Social Cost. *Quarterly Journal of Economics* 38(4): 582–606.

Kondratieff, Nikolai. 1984. *The Long Wave Cycle* (1925). Trans. G. Daniels. New York: Richardson & Snyder.

547

References

Könekamp, Rosamond. 1962. William Stanley Jevons (1835–1882): Some Biographical Notes. *Manchester School* 30(3): 251–73.

Koopmans, Tjalling C. 1937. *Linear Regression Analysis of Economic Time Series*. Haarlem: Bohn.

———. 1939. *Tanker Freight Rates and Tankship Building: An Analysis of Cyclical Fluctuations*. Haarlem: Bohn.

———. 1957. *Three Essays on the State of Economic Science*. New York: McGraw-Hill.

———. 1970. *Scientific Papers of Tjalling C. Koopmans*. New York: Springer.

———. 1977. Concepts of Optimality and Their Uses. *American Economic Review* 67(3): 261–74.

Koopmans, Tjalling C., ed. 1950. *Statistical Inference in Dynamic Economic Models*. New York: Wiley.

———. 1951. *Activity Analysis of Production and Allocation. Proceedings of a Conference*. New York: Wiley.

Kouri, Pentti J. K. 1986. Franco Modigliani's Contributions to Economics. *Scandinavian Journal of Economics* 88(2): 311–34.

Kuczynski, Marguerite, and Ronald L. Meek. 1972. *Quesnay's Tableau Economique*. London: Macmillan.

Kuenne, Robert E., ed. 1967. *Monopolistic Competition Theory: Studies in Impact. Essays in Honor of Edward H. Chamberlin*. New York: Wiley.

Kuhn, Thomas S. 1970. *The Structure of Scientific Revolutions*. 2d ed. Chicago: University of Chicago Press.

Kuznets, Simon. 1940. Schumpeter's Business Cycles. *American Economic Review* 30(2): 257–71.

———. 1952. Proportion of Capital Formation to National Product. *American Economic Review Papers and Proceedings* 42(2): 507–26.

La Harpe, Jean de. 1936. *De l'ordre et du hasard: Le Réalisme critique d'Antoine Augustin Cournot*. Neuchâtel: Université de Neuchâtel.

Laistner, M. L. W., trans. 1923. *Greek Economics*. London: Dent.

Lange, F. A. 1875. *Die Arbeiterfrage. Ihre Bedeutung für Gegenwart und Zukunft*. 3d ed. Winterthur: Bleuler-Hausheer.

Lange, Oscar. 1942a. Say's Law: A Restatement and Criticism. In *Studies in Mathematical Economics and Econometrics*, ed. O. Lange, Francis McIntyre, and Theodore Yntema, 49–68. Chicago: University of Chicago Press.

———. 1942b. The Foundations of Welfare Economics. *Econometrica* 10(3/4): 215–28.

Lauderdale, eighth earl of. 1804. *An Inquiry into the Nature and Origin of Public Wealth and into the Means and Causes of its Increase*. Edinburgh: Constable.

Launhardt, Carl Friedrich Wilhelm. 1882. Die Bestimmung des zweckmässigsten Standortes einer gewerblichen Anlage. *Zeitschrift des Vereins deutscher Ingenieure* 26:105–16.

———. 1885. *Mathematische Begründung der Volkswirtschaftslehre*. Leipzig: Engelmann. (Reprint. Aalen: Scientia, 1963.)

———. 1887–88. *Theorie des Trassirens*. 2 parts. Hanover: Schmorl & von Seefeld.

Law, John. 1750. *Money and Trade Considered, with a Proposal for Supplying the Nation with Money* (1705). New ed. Glasgow: Foulis.

———. 1934. *Oeuvres complètes.* Ed. P. Harsin. 3 vols. Paris: Sirey.

Leontief, Wassily W. 1936. Quantitative Input and Output Relations in the Economic System of the United States. *Review of Economics and Statistics* 18(3): 105–25.

———. 1941. *The Structure of American Economy, 1919–1929: An Empirical Application of Equilibrium Analysis.* Cambridge, Mass.: Harvard University Press.

———. 1951. *The Structure of American Economy, 1919–1939.* 2d ed. New York: Oxford University Press.

———. 1966. *Input-Output Economics.* New York: Oxford University Press.

———. 1977. *Essays in Economics.* 2 vols. (Vol. 1: 2d ed.; vol. 2: 1st ed.). White Plains, N.Y.: Sharpe.

Leontief, Wassily, et al. 1953. *Studies in the Structure of the American Economy: Theoretical and Empirical Explorations in Input-Output Analysis.* White Plains, N.Y.: International Arts and Sciences Press.

———. 1977. *The Future of the World Economy. A United Nations Study.* New York: Oxford University Press.

Lerner, Abba P. 1944. *The Economics of Control. Principles of Welfare Economics.* New York: Macmillan.

———. 1953. *Essays in Economic Analysis.* London: Macmillan.

———. 1983. *Selected Economic Writings.* Ed. D. C. Colander. New York: New York University Press.

Leser, Norbert, ed. 1986. *Die Wiener Schule der Nationalökonomie.* Vienna: Böhlau.

Levhari, David. 1965. A Nonsubstitution Theorem and Switching of Techniques. *Quarterly Journal of Economics* 79(1): 98–105.

Levy, S. Leon. 1970. *Nassau W. Senior, 1790–1864, Critical Essayist, Classical Economist, and Adviser of Governments.* New York: Kelley.

Lexis, Wilhelm. 1895. Grenznutzen. *Handwörterbuch der Staatswissenschaften,* Suppl. 1. Jena: Fischer.

Lieben, Richard. 1894. On Consumer's Rent. *Economic Journal* 4(16): 716–19.

———. 1908. Die mehrfachen Schnittpunkte zwischen der Angebots- und der Nachfragekurve. *Zeitschrift für Volkswirtschaft, Sozialpolitik und Verwaltung* 17(5): 607–16.

Lindbeck, Assar. 1970. Paul Anthony Samuelson's Contribution to Economics. *Swedish Journal of Economics* 72(4): 342–54.

Lipsey, Richard G. 1970. *The Theory of Customs Unions: A General Equilibrium Analysis.* London: London School of Economics and Political Science.

Lipsey, Richard G., and Kelvin Lancaster. 1956. The General Theory of Second Best. *Review of Economic Studies* 24(63): 11–32.

Little, I. M. D. 1951. Direct versus Indirect Taxes. *Economic Journal* 61(3): 577–84.

Lloyd, William Forster. 1834. *A Lecture on the Notion of Value, as Distinguishable not only from Utility but also from Value in Exchange.* London: Roake & Varty.

———. 1837. *Two Lectures on the Justice of Poor-Laws and One Lecture on Rent.* London: Roake & Varty.

Longfield, Mountifort. 1971. *The Economic Writings of Mountifort Longfield* (with intro. by R. D. C. Black). New York: Kelley.

References

Lucas, Robert E., Jr. 1981. *Studies in Business Cycle Theory*. Oxford: Blackwell.

———. 1987. *Models of Business Cycles (Yrjö Jahnsson Lectures 1985)*. Oxford: Blackwell.

Lucas, Robert E., Jr., and Thomas J. Sargent, eds. 1981. *Rational Expectations and Econometric Practice*. 2 vols. Minneapolis: University of Minnesota Press.

Luce, R. Duncan, and Howard Raiffa. 1957. *Games and Decisions: Introduction and Critical Survey*. New York: Wiley.

Lundberg, Erik. 1937. *Studies in the Theory of Economic Expansion*. London: King.

Lüthy, Herbert. 1961. *La Banque Protestante en France*. 2 vols. Paris: SEVPEN.

Lutz, Friedrich A. 1940. The Structure of Interest Rates. *Quarterly Journal of Economics* 55(1): 36–63.

Machlup, Fritz. 1943. *International Trade and the National Income Multiplier*. Philadelphia: Blakiston.

Maital, Shlomo. 1972. The Tableau Economique as a Simple Leontief Model: An Amendment. *Quarterly Journal of Economics* 86(3): 504–7.

Malinvaud, Edmond. 1953. Capital Accumulation and Efficient Allocation of Resources. *Econometrica* 21(2): 233–68.

———. 1972. The Scientific Papers of Tjalling C. Koopmans: A Review Article. *Journal of Economic Literature* 10(3): 798–802.

Malthus, Thomas Robert. 1815. *An Inquiry into the Nature and Progress of Rent and the Principles by which it is Regulated*. London: Murray.

———. 1820. *Principles of Political Economy, Considered with a View to their Practical Application*. London: Murray.

———. 1827. *Definitions in Political Economy. . . .* London: Murray.

———. 1926. *An Essay on the Principle of Population, as it Affects the Future Improvement of Society, with Remarks on the Speculations of Mr. Godwin, M. Condorcet, and other Writers* (1798). Reprinted as *First Essay on Population*. London: Macmillan. (2d ed. London: Johnson 1803. 3d ed., 2 vols. London: Johnson 1806. 4th ed., 2 vols. London: Johnson 1807. 5th ed., 3 vols. London: Murray, 1817.)

———. 1970. *The Pamphlets*. Reprints of Economic Classics. New York: Kelley.

Mandelbrot, Benoit. 1966. Forecasts of Future Prices, Unbiased Markets, and "Martingale" Models. *Journal of Business* 39(1/II): 242–55.

Mangoldt, Hans Karl Emil von. 1863. *Grundriss der Volkswirthschaftslehre. Ein Leitfaden für Vorlesungen an Hochschulen und für das Privatstudium*. Stuttgart: Engelhorn.

———. 1962. The Exchange Ratio of Goods (Das Tauschverhältnis der Güter im Allgemeinen. *Grundriss der Volkswirthschaftslehre*, Stuttgart 1863). In *International Economic Papers* no. 11, 32–59. London: Macmillan.

Manz, Peter. 1986. Forestry Economics in the Steady State. The Contribution of J. H. von Thünen. *History of Political Economy* 18(2): 281–90.

Marget, Arthur W. 1938. *The Theory of Prices: A Re-Examination of the Central Problems of Monetary Theory*. Vol. 1. London: King.

Markowitz, Harry. 1952. Portfolio Selection. *Journal of Finance* 7(1): 77–91.

Marshall, Alfred. 1890. *Principles of Economics*. London: Macmillan.

———. 1892. *Elements of Economics of Industry, being the first volume of Elements of Economics*. London: Macmillan.

———. 1919. *Industry and Trade*. London: Macmillan.

———. 1923. *Money, Credit, and Commerce*. London: Macmillan.

———. 1925. *Memorials of Alfred Marshall*. Ed. A. C. Pigou. London: Macmillan.

———. 1926. *Official Papers*. London: Macmillan.

———. 1930. *The Pure Theory of Foreign Trade. The Pure Theory of Domestic Values*. Series of Reprints of Scarce Tracts in Economic and Political Science no. 1. London: London School of Economics and Political Science.

———. 1975. *The Early Economic Writings of Alfred Marshall, 1867–1890*. Ed. J. K. Whitaker. 2 vols. London: Macmillan.

Marshall, Alfred, and Mary Paley Marshall. 1881. *The Economics of Industry* (1879). 2d ed. London: Macmillan.

Marshall, Mary Paley. 1947. *What I Remember*. Cambridge: Cambridge University Press.

Marx, Karl. 1905–10. *Theorien über den Mehrwert*. Ed. K. Kautsky. 3 vols. Stuttgart: Dietz. *Theories of Surplus-Value*, trans. E. Burns. Moscow: Foreign Language Press, 1963.

———. 1911–19. *Das Kapital: Kritik der politischen Oekonomie*. Ed. F. Engels. 3 vols. (Vol. 1 [1867], 7th ed., 1914. Vol. 2 [1885], 5th ed., 1919. Vol. 3 [1894], 3d ed., 1911.) Hamburg: Meissner.

———. 1913. *A Contribution to the Critique of Political Economy*. (*Zur Kritik der politischen Oekonomie*, 1. Heft, 1859.) Trans. N. I. Stone. Chicago: Kerr.

———. 1932. *Der historische Materialismus: Die Frühschriften*. Ed. S. Landshut and J. P. Mayer. 2 vols. Leipzig: Kröner.

———. 1939–41. *Grundrisse der Kritik der politischen Oekonomie (Rohentwurf 1857–58)*. 2 vols. Moscow: Foreign Literature.

———. 1957–62. *Capital*. English trans. 3 vols. Moscow: Foreign Languages Publishing House.

Marx, Karl, and Friedrich Engels. 1956–71. *Werke*. Ed. Institute for Marxism-Leninism. 43 vols. East Berlin: Dietz.

Mayer, Hans. 1929. Friedrich Freiherr von Wieser. In *Neue österreichische Biographie: 1815–1918*, 4:180–98. Vienna: Amalthea.

———. 1932. Der Erkenntniswert der funktionellen Preistheorien. In *Die Wirtschaftstheorie der Gegenwart*, ed. H. Mayer, 2: 147–239. Vienna: Springer.

McCulloch, John Ramsay. 1886. *Principles of Political Economy* (1825). New ed. London: Ward, Lock.

McCulloch, John Ramsay, ed. 1954. *Early English Tracts on Commerce* (1856). Reprint. Cambridge: Cambridge University Press.

McKenzie, Lionel. 1954. On Equilibrium in Graham's Model of World Trade and Other Competitive Systems. *Econometrica* 22(2): 147–61.

Meade, James E. 1948. *Planning and the Price Mechanism: The Liberal-Socialist Solution*. London: Allen & Unwin.

———. 1951. *The Balance of Payments* and *Mathematical Supplement*. Vol. 1 of *The Theory of International Economic Policy*. London: Oxford University Press.

———. 1952. *A Geometry of International Trade*. London: Allen & Unwin.

———. 1953. *Problems of Economic Union*. London: Allen & Unwin.

———. 1955a. *Trade and Welfare* and *Mathematical Supplement*. Vol. 2 of *The Theory of International Economic Policy*. London: Oxford University Press.

———. 1955b. *The Theory of Customs Unions*. Amsterdam: North-Holland.

References

———. 1962a. *A Neo-Classical Theory of Economic Growth*. 2d ed. London: Allen & Unwin.

———. 1962b. The Effect of Savings on Consumption in a State of Steady Growth. *Review of Economic Studies* 29:227–34.

———. 1965–76. *Principles of Political Economy*. 4 vols. London: Allen & Unwin.

———. 1975. *The Intelligent Radical's Guide to Economic Policy: The Mixed Economy*. London: Allen & Unwin.

Meek, Ronald L. 1960. The Interpretation of the "Tableau Economique." *Economica* 27(4): 322–47.

———. 1962. *The Economics of Physiocracy: Essays and Translations*. London: Allen & Unwin.

Meek, Ronald L., ed. 1953. *Marx and Engels on Malthus: Selections from the Writings of Marx and Engels Dealing with the Theories of Thomas Robert Malthus*. London: Lawrence & Wishart.

Mehring, Franz. 1918. *Karl Marx: Geschichte seines Lebens*. Leipzig: Leipziger Buchdruckerei.

Menger, Carl. 1871. *Grundsätze der Volkswirtschaftslehre*. Vienna: Braumüller. (2d ed., largely rewritten. Vienna: Hölder-Pichler-Tempsky, 1923). *Principles of Economics*, trans. J. Dingwall and B. F. Hoselitz; Glencoe, Ill.: Free Press, 1950.

———. 1934–36. *The Collected Works*. Ed. F. A. Hayek. 4 vols. Series of Reprints of Scarce Tracts in Economic and Political Science nos. 17–20. London: London School of Economics and Political Science.

Merton, Robert K. 1961. Singletons and Multiples in Scientific Discovery: A Chapter in the Sociology of Science. *Proceedings of the American Philosophical Society* 105(5): 470–86.

Metzler, Lloyd A. 1973. *Collected Papers*. Cambridge, Mass.: Harvard University Press.

Mill, James. 1808. *Commerce Defended*. 2d ed. London: Fox & Baldwin.

———. 1821. *Elements of Political Economy*. London: Baldwin, Cradock & Joy.

———. 1966. *Selected Economic Writings*. Ed. D. Winch. Chicago: University of Chicago Press.

Mill, John Stuart. 1844. *Essays on Some Unsettled Questions of Political Economy*. London: Parker.

———. 1848. *Principles of Political Economy*. 2 vols. London: Parker.

———. 1963–85. *Collected Works*. 21 vols. Toronto: University of Toronto Press.

Miller, John Perry. 1967. Irving Fisher of Yale. In *Ten Economic Studies in the Tradition of Irving Fisher*, ed. W. Fellner et al., 1–16. New York: Wiley.

Mirabeau, Victor de Riqueti, Marquis de. 1763. *Philosophie rurale ou économie générale et politique de l'agriculture*. Amsterdam and Paris.

Mises, Ludwig von. 1912. *Theorie des Geldes und der Umlaufsmittel*. Munich and Leipzig: Duncker & Humblot.

———. 1949. *Human Action: A Treatise on Economics*. New Haven, Conn.: Yale University Press.

Modigliani, Franco. 1980. *Collected Papers*. Ed. A. Abel. 3 vols. Cambridge, Mass.: MIT Press.

———. 1986. *The Debate over Stabilization Policy*. Cambridge: Cambridge University Press.

Monroe, Arthur Eli. 1951. *Early Economic Thought* (1924). 7th ed. Cambridge, Mass.: Harvard University Press.

Montchrétien, Antoyne de. 1889. *Traicté de l'oeconomie politique* (1615). Ed. T. Funck-Brentano. Paris: Plon, Nourrit.

Moore, Henry Ludwell. 1905. The Personality of Antoine Augustin Cournot. *Quarterly Journal of Economics* 19(3): 370–99.

———. 1914. *Economic Cycles: Their Law and Cause*. New York: Macmillan.

Morgenstern, Oskar. 1941. Professor Hicks on Value and Capital. *Journal of Political Economy* 49(3): 361–93.

———. 1976. The Collaboration between Oskar Morgenstern and John von Neumann on the Theory of Games. *Journal of Economic Literature* 14(3): 805–16.

Morishima, Michio. 1973. *Marx's Economics—A Dual Theory of Value and Growth*. Cambridge: Cambridge University Press.

———. 1977. *Walras' Economics: A Pure Theory of Capital and Money*. Cambridge: Cambridge University Press.

Mosak, Jacob L. 1942. On the Interpretation of the Fundamental Equation of Value Theory. In *Studies in Mathematical Economics and Econometrics*, ed. O. Lange, Francis McIntyre and Theodore Yntema, 69–74. Chicago: University of Chicago Press.

Mossner, Ernest Campbell. 1954. *The Life of David Hume*. Oxford: Clarendon.

Mundell, Robert A. 1962. The Appropriate Use of Monetary and Fiscal Policy for Internal and External Stability. *IMF Staff Papers* 9(1): 70–79.

Murphy, Antoin E. 1986. *Richard Cantillon: Entrepreneur and Economist*. Oxford: Clarendon.

Musgrave, Richard A. 1983. Public Goods. In *Samuelson and Modern Economic Theory*, ed. Cary E. Brown and Robert M. Solow, 141–56. New York: McGraw-Hill.

Muth, John F. 1961. Rational Expectations and the Theory of Price Movements. *Econometrica* 29(3): 315–35.

Myrdal, Gunnar. 1933. Der Gleichgewichtsbegriff als Instrument der geldtheoretischen Analyse. (*Monetary Equilibrium*. London: Hodge, 1939). In *Beiträge zur Geldtheorie*, ed. F. A. Hayek. Vienna: Springer.

Nash, John F. 1950. Equilibrium Points in N-Person Games. *Proceedings of the National Academy of Sciences* (United States) 36:48–49.

Neisser, Hans. 1932. Lohnhöhe und Beschäftigungsgrad im Marktgleichgewicht. *Weltwirtschaftliches Archiv* 36(2): 415–55.

Neumann, John von. 1928. Zur Theorie der Gesellschaftsspiele. *Mathematische Annalen* 100:295–320.

———. 1937. Ueber ein ökonomisches Gleichungssystem und eine Verallgemeinerung des Brouwerschen Fixpunktsatzes. In *Ergebnisse eines mathematischen Kolloquiums, 1935–36*, Heft 8, ed. K. Menger, 73–83. Vienna: Deuticke. A Model of General Economic Equilibrium. Trans. G. Morton. In *Precursors in Mathematical Economics: An Anthology*, ed. William J. Baumol and Stephen M. Goldfeld, 296–306. Series of Reprints of Scarce Works on Political Economy no. 19. London: London School of Economics and Political Science, 1968.

———. 1953. Communication on the Borel Notes. *Econometrica* 21(1): 124–25.

———. 1961–63. *Collected Works*. Ed. A. H. Taub. 6 vols. Oxford: Pergamon.

References

Neumann, John von, and Oskar Morgenstern. 1947. *Theory of Games and Economic Behavior* (1944). 2d ed. Princeton, N.J.: Princeton University Press.

Newcomb, Simon. 1886. *Principles of Political Economy.* New York: Harper.

Newman, Peter. 1987. Francis Ysidro Edgeworth. In *The New Palgrave: A Dictionary of Economics,* ed. John Eatwell, Murray Milgate, and Peter Newman, 2:84–98. London: Macmillan.

Niehans, Jürg. 1963. Economic Growth with Two Endogenous Factors. *Quarterly Journal of Economics* 77(3): 349–71.

———. 1965. Interest Rates, Forced Saving, and Prices in the Long Run. *Review of Economic Studies* 32(4): 327–38.

———. 1969. The Neoclassical Dichotomy as a Controlled Experiment. *Journal of Political Economy* 77(4): 504–11.

———. 1978. Metzler, Wealth, and Macroeconomics: A Review. *Journal of Economic Literature* 16(1): 84–95.

———. 1987. Classical Monetary Theory, New and Old. *Journal of Money, Credit, and Banking* 19(4): 409–24.

Nutzinger, Hans G., and Elmar Wolfstetter, eds. 1974. *Die Marxsche Theorie und ihre Kritik. Eine Textsammlung zur Kritik der Politischen Oekonomie.* 2 vols. Frankfurt: Herder & Herder.

O'Driscoll, G. P., ed. 1979. *Adam Smith and Modern Political Economy.* Ames: Iowa State University Press.

Officer, Lawrence H. 1982a. The Purchasing-Power-Parity Theory of Gerrard de Malynes. *History of Political Economy* 14(2): 256–59.

———. 1982b. *Purchasing Power Parity and Exchange Rates: Theory, Evidence and Relevance.* Greenwich, Conn.: JAI Press.

Olson, Mancur. 1982. *The Rise and Decline of Nations: Economic Growth, Stagflation and Social Rigidities.* New Haven, Conn.: Yale University Press.

Oncken, August. 1886. *Die Maxime Laissez faire et laissez passer, ihr Ursprung, ihr Werden.* Berner Beiträge zur Geschichte der Nationalökonomie no. 2. Bern: Wyss.

———. 1902. *Geschichte der Nationalökonomie, 1. Teil: Die Zeit vor Adam Smith.* Leipzig: Hirschfeld.

Packe, Michael St. John. 1954. *The Life of John Stuart Mill.* London: Secker & Warburg.

Pantaleoni, Maffeo. 1898. *Pure Economics* (Manuale di Economia Pura, 1889). Trans. T. B. Bruce. London: Macmillan.

Pareto, Vilfredo. 1896–97. *Cours d'économie politique.* 2 vols. Lausanne: Rouge. (Vol. 1 of *Oeuvres complètes,* ed. Busino.)

———. 1909. *Manuel d'économie politique* (1906). Trans. A. Bonnet. Paris: Giard & Brière. (Vol. 7 of *Oeuvres complètes,* ed. Busino.) *Manual of Political Economy,* trans. A. S. Schwier. New York: Kelley, 1971.

———. 1964– . *Oeuvres complètes.* Ed. G. Busino. 30 vols. Geneva: Droz.

Patinkin, Don. 1948. Relative Prices, Say's Law, and the Demand for Money. *Econometrica* 16(2): 135–54.

———. 1981. *Essays On and In the Chicago Tradition.* Durham, N.C.: Duke University Press.

Patinkin, Don, and J. Clark Leith, eds. 1977. *Keynes, Cambridge and the General Theory.* London: Macmillan.

Petty, Sir William. 1963–64. *The Economic Writings* (1899). Ed. C. H. Hull. 2 vols. New York: Kelley.

Phelps, Edmund S. 1961. The Golden Rule of Accumulation: A Fable for Growthmen. *American Economic Review* 51(4): 638–43.

———. 1967. Phillips Curves, Expectations of Inflation and Optimal Unemployment over Time. *Economica* 34(135): 254–81.

Phelps Brown, Henry. 1980. Sir Roy Harrod: A Biographical Memoir. *Economic Journal* 90(1): 1–33.

Phillips, Almarin. 1955. The Tableau Economique as a Simple Leontief Model. *Quarterly Journal of Economics* 69(1): 137–44.

Phillips, A. W. 1958. The Relation between Unemployment and the Rate of Change of Money Wage Rates in the United Kingdom, 1861–1957. *Economica* 25 (100): 283–99.

Phillips, C. A. 1920. *Bank Credit*. New York: Macmillan.

Pigou, Arthur Cecil. 1912. *Wealth and Welfare*. London: Macmillan.

———. 1927. *Industrial Fluctuations*. London: Macmillan.

———. 1933. *The Theory of Unemployment*. London: Macmillan.

———. 1935. *The Economics of Stationary States*. London: Macmillan.

———. 1943. The Classical Stationary State. *Economic Journal* 53(212): 343–51.

———. 1951. *A Study in Public Finance* (1928). 3d ed. London: Macmillan.

———. 1960. *The Economics of Welfare*. Reprint of 4th ed. (1932). London: Macmillan.

Pribram, Karl. 1983. *A History of Economic Reasoning*. Baltimore: Johns Hopkins University Press.

Quesnay, François. 1888. *Oeuvres économiques et philosophiques*. Ed. A. Oncken. Frankfurt: Baer; Paris: Peelman.

———. 1894. *Tableau Oeconomique* (1759). Reprint. London: British Economic Association.

Raddatz, Fritz J. 1975. *Karl Marx—Eine politische Biographie*. Hamburg: Hoffmann & Campe.

Rae, John (b. 1796). 1834. *Statement of Some New Principles on the Subject of Political Economy, Exposing the Fallacies of the System of Free Trade, and of Some Other Doctrines Maintained in the "Wealth of Nations."* Boston: Hilliard, Gray.

Rae, John (b. 1845). 1965. *Life of Adam Smith* (1895). Reprint. New York: Kelley.

Ramsey, Frank Plumpton. 1927. A Contribution to the Theory of Taxation. *Economic Journal* 37(145): 47–61.

———. 1928. A Mathematical Theory of Saving. *Economic Journal* 38(152): 543–59.

———. 1978. *Foundations: Essays in Philosophy, Logic, Mathematics and Economics*. Ed. D. H. Mellor. London: Routledge & Kegan Paul.

Recktenwald, Horst Claus. 1976. *Adam Smith—Sein Leben und sein Werk*. Munich: Beck.

Ricardo, David. 1951–55. *The Works and Correspondence of David Ricardo*. Ed. P. Sraffa. 10 vols. Cambridge: Cambridge University Press.

Roberts, Hazel van Dyke. 1935. *Boisguilbert, Economist of the Reign of Louis XIV*. New York: Columbia University Press.

References

Robinson, Joan. 1937a. *Introduction to the Theory of Employment*. London: Macmillan.

———. 1937b. *Essays in the Theory of Employment*. London: Macmillan.

———. 1942. *An Essay on Marxian Economics*. London: Macmillan.

———. 1951–80. *Collected Economic Papers*. 6 vols. Oxford: Blackwell.

———. 1954. The Production Function and the Theory of Capital. *Review of Economic Studies* 21(2): 81–106.

———. 1956. *The Accumulation of Capital*. London: Macmillan.

———. 1962a. *Essays in the Theory of Economic Growth*. London: Macmillan.

———. 1962b. A Neo-Classical Theorem. *Review of Economic Studies* 29:219–26.

———. 1969. *The Economics of Imperfect Competition* (1933). 2d ed. London: Macmillan.

Robinson, Romney. 1971. *Edward H. Chamberlin*. Columbia Essays on Great Economists no. 1. New York: Columbia University Press.

Romano, Richard M. 1977. William Forster Lloyd—A Non-Ricardian? *History of Political Economy* 9(3): 412–41.

Roscher, Wilhelm. 1874. *Geschichte der National-Oekonomik in Deutschland*. Munich: Oldenbourg.

Ruggles, Nancy D. 1949. The Welfare Basis of the Marginal Cost Pricing Principle. *Review of Economic Studies* 17(1): 29–46.

———. 1950. Recent Developments in the Theory of Marginal Cost Pricing. *Review of Economic Studies* 17(2): 107–26.

Salin, Edgar. 1926. Der isolierte Staat 1826–1926. *Zeitschrift für die gesamte Staatswissenschaft* 81(3): 410–31.

Samuelson, Paul A. 1947. *Foundations of Economic Analysis*. Cambridge, Mass.: Harvard University Press.

———. 1948. *Economics: An Introductory Analysis*. New York: McGraw-Hill.

———. 1966–86. *Collected Scientific Papers*. 5 vols. Cambridge, Mass.: MIT Press.

———. 1981. Schumpeter as an Economic Theorist. In *Schumpeterian Economics*, ed. Helmut Frisch, 1–27. New York: Praeger.

———. 1983. *Economics from the Heart: A Samuelson Sampler*. New York: Harcourt Brace Jovanovich.

———. 1986. Yes to Robert Dorfman's Vindication of Thünen's Natural-Wage Derivation. *Journal of Economic Literature* 24(4): 1777–85.

Sauvy, A., ed. 1958. *François Quesnay et la Physiocratie*. 2 vols. Paris: Institut National d'Etudes Démographiques.

Savage, Leonard J. 1954. *The Foundations of Statistics*. New York: Wiley.

Say, Jean-Baptiste. 1803. *Traité d'économie politique, ou simple exposition de la manière dont se forment, se distribuent, et se consomment les richesses*. 2 vols. Paris: Deterville. (4th ed., 2 vols. Paris: Deterville, 1819. 6th ed., 3 vols. Brussels: De Mat & Remy, 1827.

———. 1815. *Catéchisme d'économie politique*. Paris: Crapelet.

———. 1843. *Cours complet d'économie politique pratique*. 6 vols. (1828–29). 2d ed. Brussels: Meline, Cans.

Schlegel, Friedrich. 1967. *Charakteristiken und Kritiken I (1796–1801)*. Ed. H. Eichner. Munich: Schöningh.

Schmoller, Gustav. 1883. Zur Methodologie der Staats- und Sozialwissenschaften.

Jahrbuch für Gesetzgebung, Verwaltung und Volkswirtschaft im deutschen Reiche 7(3): 239–58.

Schneider, Erich. 1932. *Reine Theorie monopolistischer Wirtschaftsformen.* Tübingen: Mohr.

———. 1934. *Theorie der Produktion.* Vienna: Springer.

Schreiber, Edmund. 1913. *Die volkswirtschaftlichen Anschauungen der Scholastik seit Thomas v. Aquin.* Jena: Fischer.

Schultz, Henry. 1938. *The Theory and Measurement of Demand.* Chicago: University of Chicago Press.

Schumacher, H. 1868. *Johann Heinrich von Thünen. Ein Forscherleben.* Rostock: Leopold.

Schumpeter, Joseph Alois. 1908. *Das Wesen und der Hauptinhalt der theoretischen Nationalökonomie.* Leipzig: Duncker & Humblot.

———. 1912. *Theorie der wirtschaftlichen Entwicklung.* Leipzig: Duncker & Humblot.

———. 1914. Epochen der Dogmen- und Methodengeschichte. In *Grundriss der Sozialökonomik,* 1:19–124. Tübingen: Mohr.

———. 1939. *Business Cycles: A Theoretical, Historical and Statistical Analysis of the Capitalist Process.* 2 vols. New York: McGraw-Hill.

———. 1942. *Capitalism, Socialism, and Democracy.* New York: Harper.

———. 1949. Vilfredo Pareto, 1848–1923. *Quarterly Journal of Economics* 63(2): 147–73.

———. 1950. March into Socialism. *American Economic Review Papers and Proceedings* 15(2): 446–56.

———. 1951. *Essays.* Ed. R. V. Clemence. Cambridge, Mass.: Addison-Wesley.

———. 1954. *History of Economic Analysis.* Ed. E. B. Schumpeter. New York: Oxford University Press.

Scitovsky, Tibor. 1941. A Note on Welfare Propositions in Economics. *Review of Economic Studies* 9(1): 77–88.

Seidl, Christian, ed. 1984. *Lectures on Schumpeterian Economics—Schumpeter Centenary Memorial Lectures, Graz 1983.* Berlin: Springer.

Seligman, E. R. A. 1903. On Some Neglected British Economists. Part 1. *Economic Journal* 13 (September): 335–63.

Senior, Nassau William. 1829. *Two Lectures on Population (including Correspondence with T. R. Malthus).* London: Saunders & Otley.

———. 1830. *Three Lectures on the Cost of Obtaining Money.* London: Murray.

———. 1840. *Three Lectures on the Value of Money.* London: Fellowes.

———. 1928. *Industrial Efficiency and Social Economy.* Ed. S. L. Levy. 2 vols. New York: Holt.

———. 1938. *An Outline of the Science of Political Economy* (1836). Library of Economics, vol. 1. London: Bradford & Dickens.

Shackle, G. L. S. 1967. *The Years of High Theory: Invention and Tradition in Economic Thought, 1926–1939.* Cambridge: Cambridge University Press.

Shubik, Martin. 1982. *Game Theory in the Social Sciences: Concepts and Solutions.* Cambridge, Mass.: MIT Press.

Skidelsky, Robert. 1983–1988. *John Maynard Keynes.* Vol. 1, *Hopes Betrayed, 1883–1920*; vol. 2, *The Economist as Prince, 1920–1937.* London: Macmillan.

References

Skinner, A. S., and T. Wilson, eds. 1975. *Essays on Adam Smith*. Oxford: Clarendon.

Slutsky, Eugen. 1937. The Summation of Random Causes as the Source of Cyclic Processes. (Russian original, 1927.) *Econometrica* 5(2): 105–46.

———. 1952. On the Theory of the Budget of the Consumer (Sulla teoria del bilancio del consumatore, 1915). In *Readings in Price Theory*, ed. G. J. Stigler and K. E. Boulding, 27–56. Chicago: Irwin.

Smith, Adam. 1776. *An Inquiry into the Nature and Causes of the Wealth of Nations*. 2 vols. London: Strahan & Cadell.

———. 1976–83. *The Glasgow Edition of the Works and Correspondence of Adam Smith*. 6 vols. Oxford: Clarendon.

Solow, Robert M. 1956. A Contribution to the Theory of Economic Growth. *Quarterly Journal of Economics* 70(1): 65–94.

———. 1957. Technical Change and the Aggregate Production Function. *Review of Economics and Statistics* 39(3): 312–20.

———. 1960. Investment and Technical Progress. In *Mathematical Methods in the Social Sciences*, ed. K. J. Arrow, S. Karlin, and P. Suppes, 89–104. Stanford: Stanford University Press.

———. 1962. Comment. *Review of Economic Studies* 29:255–57.

———. 1963. *Capital Theory and the Rate of Return*. De Vries Lectures. Amsterdam: North-Holland.

———. 1970. *Growth Theory: An Exposition*. New York: Oxford University Press.

———. 1974a. The Economics of Resources or the Resources of Economics. *American Economic Review Papers and Proceedings* 64(2): 1–14.

———. 1974b. Intergenerational Equity and Exhaustible Resources. *Review of Economic Studies, Symposium*, 29–45.

Solow, Robert M., and Paul A. Samuelson. 1953. Balanced Growth under Constant Returns to Scale. *Econometrica* 21(3): 412–24.

Sommerfeld, Erich. 1978. *Die Geldlehre des Nicolaus Copernicus: Texte, Uebersetzungen, Kommentare*. Vaduz: Topos.

Spengler, Joseph J. 1954. Richard Cantillon: First of the Moderns. Parts 1, 2. *Journal of Political Economy* 62(4): 281–95; 62(5): 406–24.

———. 1965. *French Predecessors of Malthus*. New York: Octagon.

Spiegel, Henry William. 1983. *The Growth of Economic Thought*. Rev. ed. Durham, N.C.: Duke University Press.

Sraffa, Piero. 1926. The Laws of Returns under Competitive Conditions. *Economic Journal* 36(144): 535–50.

———. 1960. *Production of Commodities by Means of Commodities: Prelude to a Critique of Economic Theory*. Cambridge: Cambridge University Press.

Stackelberg, Heinrich von. 1933. Zwei kritische Bemerkungen zur Preistheorie Gustav Cassels. *Zeitschrift für Nationalökonomie* 4(4): 456–72.

———. 1934. *Marktform und Gleichgewicht*. Vienna and Berlin: Springer.

Stephen, Leslie. 1950. *The English Utilitarians*, vol. 1. (1900). Series of Reprints of Scarce Works on Political Economy no. 9. London: London School of Economics and Political Science.

Stigler, George J. 1941. *Production and Distribution Theories—The Formative Period*. New York: Macmillan.

————. 1949. Monopolistic Competition in Retrospect. In his *Five Lectures on Economic Problems*, 12–24. London: Longmans, Green.

————. 1965. *Essays in the History of Economics*. Chicago: University of Chicago Press.

————. 1972. The Adoption of the Marginal Utility Theory. *History of Political Economy* 4(2): 571–86.

————. 1982. Marshall's Principles after Guillebaud. In *Alfred Marshall: Critical Assessments*, ed. John Cunningham Wood, 2:223–230. London: Croom Helm.

Stigler, Stephen M. 1978. Francis Ysidro Edgeworth, Statistician. *Journal of the Royal Statistical Society 141(3): 287–322.*

Streissler, Erich. 1972. To What Extent Was the Austrian School Marginalist? *History of Political Economy* 4(2): 426–41.

————. 1981. Schumpeter's Vienna and the Role of Credit in Innovation. In *Schumpeterian Economics*, ed. Helmut Frisch, 60–83. New York: Praeger.

————. 1986. Arma virumque cano. Friedrich von Wieser: The Bard as Economist. In *Die Wiener Schule der Nationalökonomie*, ed. Norbert Leser, 83–106. Vienna: Böhlau.

Swan, Trevor W. 1956. Economic Growth and Capital Accumulation. *Economic Record* 32 (November): 334–61.

————. 1964. Growth Models: Of Golden Ages and Production Functions. In *Economic Development with Special Reference to East Asia, Proceedings of a Conference Held by the International Economic Association*, ed. K. Berrill, 3–18. London: Macmillan.

Teilhac, Ernest. 1927. *L'Oeuvre économique de Jean-Baptiste Say*. Paris: Alcan.

Theiss, Edward. 1935. Dynamics of Saving and Investment. *Econometrica* 3(2): 213–24.

Theocharis, Reghinos D. 1983. *Early Developments in Mathematical Economics*. 2d ed. London: Macmillan.

Thornton, Henry. 1939. *An Enquiry into the Nature and Effects of the Paper Credit of Great Britain* (1802). Ed. F. A. von Hayek. London: Allen & Unwin.

Thünen, Johann Heinrich von. 1842–63. *Der isolierte Staat in Beziehung auf Landwirtschaft und Nationalökonomie*. Rostock: Leopold. (Part 1: *Untersuchungen über den Einfluss, den die Getreidepreise, der Reichtum des Bodens und die Abgaben auf den Ackerbau ausüben* [1826], 2d ed., 1842. *Von Thünen's Isolated State*, ed. P. Hall, trans. C. M. Wartenberg. Oxford: Pergamon Press, 1966. Part 2: *Der naturgemässe Arbeitslohn und dessen Verhältniss zum Zinsfuss und zur Landrente*. 1st section, 1850. Trans. in B. W. Dempsey, *The Frontier Wage*. Chicago: Loyola University Press, 1960. 2d section, 1863. Part 3: *Grundsätze zur Bestimmung der Bodenrente, der vorteilhaftesten Umtriebszeit und des Werts der Holzbestände von verschiedenem Alter für Kieferwaldungen*, 1863.)

————. 1951. *Ausgewählte Texte*. Ed. W. Braeuer. Meisenheim: Hain.

Tinbergen, Jan. 1935. Annual Survey: Suggestions on Quantitative Business Cycle Theory. *Econometrica* 3(3): 241–308.

————. 1937. *An Econometric Approach to Business Cycle Problems*. Paris: Hermann.

————. 1939. *Statistical Testing of Business-Cycle Theories: I. A Method and Its Application to Investment Activity; II. Business Cycles in the United States of America 1919–1932*. Geneva: League of Nations.

References

————. 1942. Zur Theorie der langfristigen Wirtschaftsentwicklung. *Weltwirtschaftliches Archiv* 55(3): 511–47.

————. 1952. *On the Theory of Economic Policy*. Amsterdam: North-Holland.

————. 1954. *Centralization and Decentralization in Economic Policy*. Amsterdam: North-Holland.

————. 1956. *Economic Policy: Principles and Design*. Amsterdam: North-Holland.

————. 1959. *Selected Papers*. Amsterdam: North-Holland.

————. 1960. *Optimum Savings and Utility Maximization over Time*. *Econometrica* 28(2): 481–89.

————. 1962. *Shaping the World Economy: Suggestions for an International Economic Policy*. New York: Twentieth Century Fund.

————. 1963. *Lessons from the Past*. Amsterdam: North-Holland.

————. 1975. *Income Distribution: Analysis and Policies*. Amsterdam: North-Holland.

Tinbergen, Jan, and J. J. Polak. 1950. *The Dynamics of Business Cycles: A Study in Economic Fluctuations*. Chicago: University of Chicago Press.

Tobin, James. 1966. *National Economic Policy—Essays*. New Haven, Conn.: Yale University Press.

————. 1971–75. *Essays in Economics*. Vol. 1, *Macroeconomics*; vol. 2, *Consumption and Econometrics*. Amsterdam: North-Holland.

————. 1982. *Essays in Economics*. Vol. 3, *Theory and Policy*. Cambridge, Mass.: MIT Press.

Torrens, Robert. 1815. *An Essay on the External Corn Trade*. London: Hatchard.

Turgot, Anne Robert Jacques. 1913–23. *Oeuvres de Turgot et documents le concernant*. Ed. G. Schelle. 5 vols. Paris: Alcan.

Uhr, Carl G. 1951. Knut Wicksell—A Centennial Evaluation. *American Economic Review* 41(5): 829–60.

————. 1960. *Economic Doctrines of Knut Wicksell*. Berkeley: University of California Press.

Ulam, Stanislaw M. 1958. John von Neumann, 1903–1957. *Bulletin of the American Mathematical Society* 64(3/2): 1–49.

————. 1976. *Adventures of a Mathematician*. New York: Scribner's.

Uzawa, Hirofumi. 1961–63. On a Two-Sector Model of Economic Growth. Parts 1, 2. *Review of Economic Studies* 29:40–47; 30:105–18.

Viner, Jacob. 1931. Cost Curves and Supply Curves. *Zeitschrift für Nationalökonomie* 3(1): 23–46.

————. 1937. *Studies in the Theory of International Trade*. New York: Harper.

————. 1950. *The Customs Union Issue*. London: Stevens.

Wald, Abraham. 1936. Ueber einige Gleichungssysteme der mathematischen Oekonomie. *Zeitschrift für Nationalökonomie* 7(5): 637–70.

Walras, Léon. 1874–77. *Eléments d'économie politique pure; ou, théorie de la richesse sociale*. Lausanne: Corbaz. (4th ed. Lausanne: Rouge, 1900.) *The Theory of Social Wealth*, trans. of new ed., 1926, by W. Jaffé. Homewood, Ill.: Irwin, 1954.

————. 1881. *Mathematische Theorie der Preisbestimmung der wirtschaftlichen Güter*. Stuttgart: Enke.

————. 1886. *Théorie de la monnaie*. Lausanne: Corbaz.

———. 1896. *Etudes d'économie sociale (Théorie de la répartition de la richesse sociale)*. Lausanne: Rouge; Paris: Pichon.

———. 1898. *Etudes d'économie politique appliquée (Théorie de la production de la richesse sociale)*. Lausanne: Rouge; Paris: Pichon.

———. 1938. *Abrégé des éléments d'économie politique pure*. Paris: Pichon; Lausanne: Rouge.

———. 1965. *Correspondence of Léon Walras and Related Papers*. Ed. W. Jaffé. 3 vols. Amsterdam: North-Holland.

Weatherall, David. 1976. *David Ricardo. A Biography*. The Hague: Nijhoff.

Weinberger, Otto. 1931. Rudolf Auspitz und Richard Lieben. *Zeitschrift für die gesamte Staatswissenschaft* 91(3): 457–92.

———. 1935. Rudolf Auspitz. In *Neue österreichische Biographie 1815–1918*, 8:37–44. Vienna: Amalthea.

Weintraub, E. Roy. 1983. On the Existence of a Competitive Equilibrium: 1930–1954. *Journal of Economic Literature* 21(1): 1–39.

Weizsäcker, Carl Christian von. 1962. *Wachstum, Zins und optimale Investitionsquote*. Basel: Kyklos; Tübingen: Mohr.

———. 1972. Kenneth Arrow's Contribution to Economics. *Swedish Journal of Economics* 74(4): 488–502.

Werin, Lars, and Karl G. Jungenfelt. 1976. Tjalling Koopmans' Contribution to Economics. *Scandinavian Journal of Economics* 78(1): 81–102.

West, Sir Edward. 1903. *The Application of Capital to Land* (1815). Ed. J. H. Hollander. Baltimore: Johns Hopkins Press.

West, E. G. 1976. *Adam Smith: The Man and His Work*. Indianapolis: Liberty.

Whewell, William. 1971. *Mathematical Exposition of Some Doctrines of Political Economy* (1829). Reprints of Economic Classics. New York: Kelley.

Whitaker, J. K. 1982. Alfred Marshall—The Years 1877 to 1885. In *Alfred Marshall: Critical Assessments*, ed. John Cunningham Wood, 1:98–147. London: Croom Helm.

Whitin, Thomas M. 1952. Inventory Control in Theory and Practice. *Quarterly Journal of Economics* 66(4): 502–21.

Wicksell, Knut. 1896. *Finanztheoretische Untersuchungen, nebst Darstellung und Kritik des Steuerwesens Schwedens*. Jena: Fischer. Partial trans. in *Classics in the Theory of Public Finance*, ed. R. A. Musgrave and A. T. Peacock, 72–118. London: Macmillan, 1964.

———. 1934–35. *Lectures on Political Economy* (*Förenläsningar i nationalekonomi*, 1901, 1906). Trans. E. Classen; ed. L. Robbins. 2 vols. London: Routledge & Kegan Paul.

———. 1936. *Interest and Prices* (Geldzins und Güterpreise, 1898). Trans. R. F. Kahn. London: Macmillan.

———. 1953. The Enigma of Business Cycles (Krisernas Gata. *Statsøkonomisk Tidsskrift*, 1907). In International Economic Papers no. 3, 58–74. London: Macmillan.

———. 1954. *Value, Capital, and Rent* (Ueber Wert, Kapital und Rente nach den neueren nationalökonomischen Theorien, 1893). Trans. S. H. Frowein. London: Allen & Unwin.

———. 1958. *Selected Papers on Economic Theory*. Ed. E. Lindahl. Cambridge, Mass.: Harvard University Press.

References

Wicksell, Knut (subject). 1978. The Arne Ryde Symposium on the Theoretical Contributions of Knut Wicksell. *Scandinavian Journal of Economics* 80(2): 127–249.

Wicksteed, Philip H. 1932. *An Essay on the Co-ordination of the Laws of Distribution* (1894). Series of Reprints of Scarce Tracts in Economic and Political Science no. 12. London: London School of Economics and Political Science.

———. 1933. *The Common Sense of Political Economy and Selected Papers and Reviews on Economic Theory* (1910). Ed. L. Robbins. 2 vols. London: Routledge.

———. 1955. *The Alphabet of Economic Science* (1888). Reprint. New York: Kelley & Millman.

Wieser, Friedrich von. 1889. *Der natürliche Werth*. Vienna: Hölder. *Natural Value*, trans. C. A. Malloch, 1893. (Reprint. New York: Kelley & Millman, 1956.)

———. 1914. Theorie der gesellschaftlichen Wirtschaft. In *Grundriss der Sozialökonomik*, 1:125–444. Tübingen: Mohr. *Social Economics*, trans. A. F. Hinrichs. London: Allen & Unwin, 1928.

———. 1929. *Gesammelte Abhandlungen*. Ed. F. A. von Hayek. Tübingen: Mohr.

———. 1968. *Ueber den Ursprung und die Hauptgesetze des wirthschaftlichen Werthes* (1884). Reprint. Frankfurt: Sauer & Avermann.

Winter, Josefine. 1927. *Fünfzig Jahre eines Wiener Hauses*. Vienna: Braumüller.

Wolfstetter, Elmar. 1973. Wert, Mehrwert und Produktionspreis: Eine elementare Darstellung der Marxschen Arbeitswertlehre. In *Jahrbuch für Sozialwissenschaft*, 24:117–44. Göttingen: Vandenhoeck & Ruprecht.

———. 1977. Das Gesetz des tendenziellen Falls der Profitrate in der Marxschen und in der klassischen Wirtschaftstheorie. In *Jahrbuch für Sozialwissenschaft*, 28:270–99. Göttingen: Vandenhoeck & Ruprecht.

Wood, John Cunningham, ed. 1982. *Alfred Marshall: Critical Assessments*. 4 vols. London: Croom Helm.

———. 1983. *John Maynard Keynes: Critical Assessments*. 4 vols. London: Croom Helm.

———. 1985. *David Ricardo: Critical Assessments*. 4 vols. London: Croom Helm.

Working, Elmer J. 1927. What Do Statistical "Demand Curves" Show? *Quarterly Journal of Economics* 41(2): 212–35.

Würgler, Hans. 1957. *Malthus als Kritiker der Klassik. Ein Beitrag zur Geschichte der klassischen Wirtschaftstheorie*. Winterthur: Keller.

Yntema, Theodore O. 1928. The Influence of Dumping on Monopoly Price. *Journal of Political Economy* 36(6): 686–98.

Young, Allyn Abbott. 1913. Review of Pigou's "Wealth and Welfare." *Quarterly Journal of Economics* 27(2): 672–86.

Zeuthen, Friedrich. 1933. Das Prinzip der Knappheit, technische Kombination und ökonomische Qualität. *Zeitschrift für Nationalökonomie* 4(1): 1–24.

Author Index

Subject Index

CPSIA information can be obtained
at www.ICGtesting.com
Printed in the USA
FFOW04n0439050117
30985FF